MAKING A MODERN CENTRAL BANK

Making a Modern Central Bank examines a revolution in monetary and economic policy. This authoritative guide explores how the Bank of England shifted its traditional mechanisms to accommodate a newly internationalized financial and economic system. The Bank's transformation into a modern inflation-targeting independent central bank allowed it to focus on a precisely defined task of monetary management, ensuring price stability. The reframing of the task of central banks, however, left them increasingly vulnerable to financial crisis. Harold James vividly outlines and discusses significant historical developments in UK monetary policy, and his knowledge of modern European history adds rich context to archival research on the Bank of England's internal documents. A worthy continuation of the previous official histories of the Bank of England, this book also reckons with contemporary issues, shedding light on the origins of growing backlash against globalization and the European Union.

Harold James is Professor of History and International Affairs and Claude and Lore Kelly Professor of European Studies at Princeton University.

STUDIES IN MACROECONOMIC HISTORY

The titles in this series investigate themes of interest to economists and economic historians in the rapidly developing field of macroeconomic history. The four areas covered include the application of monetary and finance theory, international economics, and quantitative methods to historical problems; the historical application of growth and development theory and theories of business fluctuations; the history of domestic and international monetary, financial, and other macroeconomic institutions; and the history of international monetary and financial systems. The series amalgamates the former Cambridge University Press series Studies in Monetary and Financial History and Studies in Quantitative Economic History.

Gianni Toniolo (with the assistance of Piet Clement), *Central Bank Cooperation at the Bank for International Settlements, 1930–1973* (2005)

Richard Burdekin and Pierre Siklos, Editors, *Deflation: Current and Historical Perspectives* (2004)

Pierre Siklos, *The Changing Face of Central Banking: Evolutionary Trends since World War II* (2002)

Michael D. Bordo and Roberto Cortés-Conde, Editors, *Transferring Wealth and Power from the Old to the New World: Monetary and Fiscal Institutions in the 17th through the 19th Centuries* (2001)

Howard Bodenhorn, *A History of Banking in Antebellum America: Financial Markets and Economic Development in an Era of Nation-Building* (2000)

Mark Harrison, Editor, *The Economics of World War II: Six Great Powers in International Comparison* (2000)

Angela Redish, *Bimetallism: An Economic and Historical Analysis* (2000)

Elmus Wicker, *Banking Panics of the Gilded Age* (2000)

Michael D. Bordo, *The Gold Standard and Related Regimes: Collected Essays* (1999)

Michele Fratianni and Franco Spinelli, *A Monetary History of Italy* (1997)

Mark Toma, *Competition and Monopoly in the Federal Reserve System, 1914–1951* (1997)

Barry Eichengreen, Editor, *Europe's Postwar Recovery* (1996)

Lawrence H. Officer, *Between the Dollar-Sterling Gold Points: Exchange Rates, Parity and Market Behavior* (1996)

Elmus Wicker, *The Banking Panics of the Great Depression* (1996)

Norio Tamaki, *Japanese Banking: A History, 1859–1959* (1995)

Barry Eichengreen, *Elusive Stability: Essays in the History of International Finance, 1919–1939* (1993)

Michael D. Bordo and Forrest Capie, Editors, *Monetary Regimes in Transition* (1993)

Larry Neal, *The Rise of Financial Capitalism: International Capital Markets in the Age of Reason* (1993)

S. N. Broadberry and N. F. R. Crafts, Editors, *Britain in the International Economy, 1870–1939* (1992)

Aurel Schubert, *The Credit-Anstalt Crisis of 1931* (1992)

Trevor J. O. Dick and John E. Floyd, *Canada and the Gold Standard: Balance of Payments Adjustment under Fixed Exchange Rates, 1871–1913* (1992)

Kenneth Mouré, *Managing the Franc Poincaré: Economic Understanding and Political Constraint in French Monetary Policy, 1928–1936* (1991)

David C. Wheelock, *The Strategy and Consistency of Federal Reserve Monetary Policy, 1924–1933* (1991)

Making a Modern Central Bank

The Bank of England 1979–2003

HAROLD JAMES

Princeton University

CAMBRIDGE
UNIVERSITY PRESS

CAMBRIDGE
UNIVERSITY PRESS

University Printing House, Cambridge CB2 8BS, United Kingdom

One Liberty Plaza, 20th Floor, New York, NY 10006, USA

477 Williamstown Road, Port Melbourne, VIC 3207, Australia

314–321, 3rd Floor, Plot 3, Splendor Forum, Jasola District Centre,
New Delhi – 110025, India

79 Anson Road, #06–04/06, Singapore 079906

Cambridge University Press is part of the University of Cambridge.

It furthers the University's mission by disseminating knowledge in the pursuit of
education, learning, and research at the highest international levels of excellence.

www.cambridge.org
Information on this title: www.cambridge.org/9781108835015
DOI: 10.1017/9781108875189

First published 2020

A catalogue record for this publication is available from the British Library.

Library of Congress Cataloging-in-Publication Data
Names: James, Harold, 1956– author.
Title: Making a modern central bank / Harold James.
Description: New York : Cambridge University Press, 2020. | Series: Studies in macroeco-
nomic history | Includes bibliographical references and index.
Identifiers: LCCN 2020009240 (print) | LCCN 2020009241 (ebook) | ISBN 9781108835015
(hardback) | ISBN 9781108875189 (ebook)
Subjects: LCSH: Bank of England – History. | Banks and banking, Central – Great Britain –
History. | Finance – Great Britain. | Globalization – Economic aspects.
Classification: LCC HG2994 .J296 2020 (print) | LCC HG2994 (ebook) | DDC 332.1/10941–
dc23
LC record available at https://lccn.loc.gov/2020009240
LC ebook record available at https://lccn.loc.gov/2020009241

ISBN 978-1-108-83501-5 Hardback
ISBN 978-1-108-79949-2 Paperback

Ex praeterito praesens prudenter agit, ni futurum actione deturpet
(*Titian*, The Allegory of Prudence, *National Gallery*)

Contents

Figures

Tables

Acknowledgements

I was delighted and greatly honoured to have been asked by the Bank of England to prepare a history to be published by Cambridge University Press that would follow the distinguished works of Sir John Clapham, R.S. Sayers, John Fforde and Forrest Capie. The previous histories had plenty of excitement and turmoil, but except for the first thirty years after 1694, there is no real parallel to the sustained process of modernization and reform that occurred in the twenty years after 1979. This is the story of the institutions and the people who drove through that change. I was invited to write this chronicle of change and progress in 2012, at a moment when independent inflation-targeting central banks seemed all powerful: commentators at that time liked to call them the only grown-ups in the room. That verdict seems to me to be dramatically true of the Bank of England in the very recent history of the United Kingdom. But there was also a dark side to the unleashing of financial markets that went in parallel with the institutional reforms, and that underbelly will also be analysed in the following pages.

John Footman, secretary of the Bank, accompanied the project from beginning to end in a sympathetic and constructive way. Ryland Thomas was an invaluable guide to the Bank's statistical history as well as to the visual presentation of figures. Sarah Millard and Mike Anson, the Bank's archivists, helped me to understand the Bank's voluminous archival holdings, and Margherita Orlando did an absolutely outstanding job in keeping track of references and identifying additional documents, a search that often resembled looking for needles in a haystack. I would also like to record my thanks to their predecessor, Henry Gillett, who first welcomed me to the Bank's historical archive in the 1980s. David Kynaston, the pre-eminent historian of the City of London, who in parallel to my research was working on an overall history of the Bank, which was published in 2017, helped me in numerous agreeable and productive discussions. Sharon Hughes sorted out countless logistical issues associated with working in the Bank.

I benefited from discussions with many former Bank of England officials, as well as with others who interacted with the Bank over the years covered in this volume: William Allen, John Arrowsmith, Ed Balls, Claudio Borio, Gordon Brown, Markus Brunnermeier, Sir Alan Budd, Terry Burns (Baron Burns), Forrest Capie, Tim Congdon, Sir Howard Davies, Sir Angus Deaton, Jacques Delors, Jean-Pierre Landau, Jacques de Larosière, Emilio Galli Zugaro, Charles Goodhart, Charles Grant, Otmar Issing, William Keegan, Anatole Kaletsky, Mervyn King (Baron King of Lothbury), Norman Lamont, Nigel Lawson (Baron Lawson of Blaby), Anthony Loehnis, Rachel Lomax, David Marsh, Sir Peter Middleton, Charles Moore, Alain Naef, Duncan Needham, Michael Oliver, Rupert Pennant-Rea, Brian Quinn, Helmut Schlesinger, John Trundle, Sir Paul Tucker, Sir David Walker, Sushil Wadhwani, Sir Brian Williamson and Geoffrey Wood. I also recall with gratitude inspiring conversations in the past (sometimes quite distant) with some major historical figures who sadly can no longer see this book: Sir Andrew Crockett, Denis Healey, Peter Kenen, Alexandre Lamfalussy, Sir Jeremy Morse, Karl Otto Pöhl, Gordon Richardson (Baron Richardson of Duntisbourne, whom I met as an undergraduate at a dinner in my Cambridge college, Gonville and Caius), Hans Tietmeyer and Sir Alan Walters.

William Allen, Peter Andrews, Graham Hacche, Anthony C. Hotson, Rosa Lastra, Rachel Lomax and Sebastian Mallaby, together with Mike Anson and John Footman, kindly formed a reading group and very helpfully and constructively discussed a draft of the manuscript in March 2019. Michael Bordo, Howard Davies, Lord King, Ed Nelson, Brian Quinn, Pierre Siklos and Sir Paul Tucker also read the entire manuscript and gave me invaluable tips and comments. Of course no one listed here is responsible for any remaining errors or for the interpretations of events presented in the book.

Terry Deal and Robert Yee assisted me greatly in the preparation of the final manuscript. Karen Maloney, Rachel Blaifeder and Chris Harrison at Cambridge University Press were most supportive.

In Princeton, I must also record my gratitude to Marzenna James and to Maximilian, Marie Louise and Montagu, who have put up with their father's attachment to the Bank of England and its history.

Abbreviations

AD	authorized depositories
BBME	British Bank of the Middle East
BCCI	Bank of Credit and Commerce International
BEQB	*Bank of England Quarterly Bulletin*
BIS	Bank for International Settlements, Basel
BNP	Banque Nationale de Paris
BoE	Bank of England (also in some documents B/E)
CBI	Confederation of British Industry
CHAPS	Clearing House Automated Payments System
CI	Certificates of Indebtedness
CMMO	Central Money Market Office
CoG	European Community Committee of Central Bank Governors
DCE	domestic credit expansion
DGC	Deputy Governor's Committee
DM	Deutschemark
DTI	Department of Trade and Industry
EC	European Community
ECB	European Central Bank
ECI	Equity Capital for Industry
ECOFIN	Economic and Financial Committee (of European Commission)
ECU	European Currency Unit
EEC	European Economic Community
EMS	European Monetary System
EMU	(European) Economic and Monetary Union
ERM	Exchange Rate Mechanism

ESCB	European System of Central Banks
Exco	(Bank of England) Executive Committee
FCI	Finance Corporation for Industry
FCO	Foreign and Commonwealth Office
FFI	Finance for Industry, later Investors in Industry or 3i
FPC	(Bank of England) Financial Policy Committee
FSA	Financial Services Authority
FSR	*Financial Stability Review*
G-5	Group of Five
G-7	Group of Seven
G-10	Group of Ten
GDP	gross domestic product
GEMMs	gilt-edged market makers
HADB	Historical Archive of Deutsche Bundesbank
HMG	Her Majesty's Government
HMT	Her Majesty's Treasury
HSBC	Hong Kong and Shanghai Bank Corporation (also in some documents HKSB)
IBEL	interest-bearing eligible liabilities
ICFC	Industrial and Commercial Finance Corporation
IFU	Industrial Finance Unit
IMF	International Monetary Fund
JMB	Johnson Matthey Bankers
LDC	less developed country
LIFFE	London International Financial Futures and Options Exchange
LLR	lender of last resort
LSE	London School of Economics
M	money (for list of various monetary aggregates, see pages 467–471)
MBC	monetary base control
MLR	minimum lending rate
MPC	(Bank of England) Monetary Policy Committee
MTFS	Medium-Term Financial Strategy
NAIRU	non-accelerating inflation rate of unemployment
OECD	Organisation for Economic Co-operation and Development
OMOs	open market operations
PM	prime minister
PRA	Prudential Regulation Authority
PSBR	Public Sector Borrowing Requirement

PSL	private sector liquidity (for list of monetary aggregates, see page 467–471)
RBS	Royal Bank of Scotland
RPI	Retail Price Index
RPIX	Retail Price Index (excluding mortgage interest payments)
RTGS	real-time gross settlement
SBC	Swiss Bank Corporation
SCB	Standard Chartered Bank
SEMBs	stock exchange money brokers
SIB	Securities and Investment Board
SIMEX	Singapore International Monetary Exchange
SRO	self-regulatory organization
SSDS	Supplementary Special Deposit Scheme
SWOT	strengths, weaknesses, opportunities and threats
TARGET	Trans-European Automated Real-time Gross Settlement Express Transfer
TCSC	Treasury and Civil Service Select Committee (UK Parliament)
TML	Trans Manche Link
TNA	The National Archives (UK)
TUC	Trades Union Congress
VAT	value-added tax
Y2K	year 2000

1

Introductory

At the end of the 1970s, the Bank of England was a microcosm of the UK. It was steeped in history, but at the same time deeply confused about its identity and quite inconstant in its performance. Within a quarter of a century, both the country and the Bank changed. The country became modern – with the subsequently widely derided slogan of 'Cool Britannia' – and so did the Bank. By the beginning of the 2000s, the Bank of England exemplified what was then thought to be the best practice of a modern central bank, running a clearly defined rule-based system based around an inflation target. The UK became more dynamic but more questioning and cynical. A country that was being transformed and opened up demanded more explanations of its political leaders. The Bank needed to add open mouth operations to its open market actions.

The changes can be described as an informational revolution, but also as part of a broader process of globalization: there was much more awareness of international activity and of how the UK was affected by what went on beyond its frontiers. Paul Krugman thinks that the Bank of England punches internationally above its weight not because of the strength of the British economy but because of its 'intellectual adventurousness'.[1] At the outset of a previous volume of the Bank of England's history, Richard Sayers started with the remark that the Bank of England in the last generation before 1914 was 'not a central bank according to the mid-twentieth century usage of this term'.[2] He told a story of evolution. In a similar way, the late 1970s Bank of England was far from being a central bank as the late twentieth century understood it. But it became one.

A modern central bank has a much narrower and more limited set of tasks or functions than the often historic institution from which it developed. The objective is the provision of monetary stability, nothing more and nothing less. In order to achieve that goal, it is essential to observe and use policy instruments to respond to macro-economic aggregates, price and wage behaviour and financial activity. The old type of central bank would intervene directly and specifically in all these areas; the modern bank relies on economic agents to respond predictably to monetary signals. The aim of a prudent path is to prevent false inferences and dangerous gambles on an uncertain future. The central bank is a certainty- and confidence-generating institution that lives up to the maxim of Titian's Allegory of Prudence. There was a conceptual break as to how that prudence might be realized. Before, the central banks were promiscuous, dabbling everywhere; after, they were mono-maniacal about their fixation on the new goal. The new central banks also believed that the new simplification of their task made them more clearly and transparently accountable to a larger political process. By the early 2000s, when this account comes to an end, that task looked as if it had been achieved with stunning success, and a hubris of central banks (and of the economics profession) ensued. The financial crisis after 2007–2008 was a nemesis, a demonstration that life, and economics, was more complicated. The creation of the new central bank took place in the late twentieth century as a response to major shocks that did not look as if they could be treated by the vast panoply of the bank's traditional mechanisms. Those shocks are the subject of this volume, and include the inflationary shocks of the 1970s, following from a mixture of government fiscal policy (fiscal dominance in modern parlance), poor management practices in the UK, external shocks (in particular the oil price increases), financial openness and globalization from the 1980s, and the strains arising out of both international and European efforts at exchange rate coordination and control. All these turbulences produced messy and unclear signals, and made it hard to calculate the core concept of modern central banking theory and practice, a clearly articulated reaction function that could be generally understood by every participant in the economic process.

The Bank of England, established by an Act of Parliament of 1694, is an old central bank, second only to the Sveriges Riksbank (Imperial Bank) in its antiquity. The names of those old institutions were quaint: Sweden no longer has an empire; the Bank of England is also the central bank for Scotland, Wales and Northern Ireland. Walter Bagehot, the great editor of the *Economist*, who explained much of the modern theory of central banking in *Lombard Street* (1873), also observed, in *The English Constitution*, published six years earlier, that: 'The most imposing institutions of mankind are the oldest; and yet so changing is the world, so fluctuating are its needs, so apt to lose inward force, though retaining outward strength, are its best instruments, that we must not expect the oldest institutions to be now the most efficient.'[3] The story of the years covered in these pages is a struggle over what efficiency and effectiveness meant. A large part of that struggle involved shedding a strongly entrenched idea about British peculiarity or British exceptionalism and learning from the rest of the world: at first, in the late 1970s and 1980s from US and European debates about monetary targeting, then later in the 1980s from Europe, with the result that an exchange rate anchor was seen as the cornerstone of credibility; and then, in the 1990s, from elsewhere, with an inflation target imported on the basis of New Zealand's pioneering experience. In the 1960s, the economist Fred Hirsch opined that 'while these foreign central banks have had a mixed record in adjusting their economies, they seem to be notably better adjusted themselves, in the psychological sense'.[4] Central bankers communicated in this period much more across national frontiers than they had in the thirty years after the Second World War. In the mid- to late twentieth century, the Bank maintained many institutional arrangements that looked quite exceptional, with no parallels in other central banks. The provision of liquidity to the banking system, for example, which in the US went through an open market trading desk, in Threadneedle Street required a procession of money brokers dressed in top hats. By the twenty-first century, the Bank was obviously a very global institution: for the 2012 London Olympic Games, it set up a map in its cafeteria showing the countries of the world of its employees, with virtually no country unrepresented; and from 2013 its Governor was a no-nonsense Canadian citizen who regularly appeared in the staff cafeteria as well as in the gym. His predecessor, Mervyn King, had liked to interact with Bank economists, and encouraged them to call him 'Mervyn'.

The 1980s and 1990s in fact marked a fundamental change in thinking about central banking all over the world. The new approach was driven by the social and political disruption that followed from high levels of inflation – from what was often termed the 'Great Inflation' of the 1970s, when inflation had soared all over the industrial world, but when the UK rates were higher than in any other industrial country. The practice of the central banks that delivered a better inflation performance – especially Germany and Switzerland – looked like an attractive model for emulation. The practical lesson began to have a theoretical or academic underpinning. An insight into the problem of time-consistent policy demonstrated that an independent central bank could deliver a superior performance as it was not subject to short-term political pressures to give an inflationary boost.[5]

The theoretical result was supported by a large amount of empirical data on the lower inflation achieved by independent central banks.[6] In consequence, the accepted international best practice for central banks meant the ability to determine monetary policy, based on a low inflation target set through a political consensus.

Accounts of how central bank independence affected market decisions rested crucially on how market participants reacted to their perceptions of central bank actions. In consequence, central banks needed to change the way they dealt with their audiences. In the 1990s, Eddie George as Governor appeared on television. He had already been quite effective in this medium as Deputy Governor, when the Bank's media advisers believed that the then Governor would be counterproductive because of his patrician manner. The chief economist (and eventually George's successor) Mervyn King emphasized clear and simple communication, and initiated an expansion of the Bank's publications and communications, most importantly in the presentation at press conferences of the Inflation Report. He argued that the Bank should 'forsake mystique and mumbo jumbo for transparency and openness'.[7] In the aftermath of the financial crisis of 2007–2008, the Bank felt that it needed to go further to draw the full consequences of the information revolution. It was crucial to communicate clearly and effectively with the general public, whose choices and behaviour would ultimately affect output, consumption and price behaviour.[8] The Bank now started to worry about the complexity of language in its reports and in the speeches of its officials, and it now went beyond simply speaking to the 'markets' or the financial community.

From the late 1990s, the Bank of England generally featured high in comparative academic rankings of central bank transparency – along with the even older Sveriges Riksbank and the Reserve Bank of New Zealand. In 1997–1998, in the new legal framework created by the 1998 Bank of England Act, it was the leader: others then emulated and caught up.[9]

At the outset, the Bank – and central banks in general – were secretive and functioned behind multiple veils: of language, of statistics, even of location. Hirsch commented on 'the over-riding concern for appearance and form that hits every visitor who enters the fortress doors of Threadneedle Street, and goes on hitting him the deeper he penetrates into the Bank parlours'.[10] The Bank's seclusion was reflected in the physical architecture. The Bank of England's main building – as elaborately reconstructed in the 1930s – was blocked off from the outside world. The only visible part of the great eighteenth-century bank designed by Sir John Soane that survived was the austere outside wall, intended as a defence against attack by the people, in the aftermath of the Gordon riots. When it was rebuilt in the 1920s and 1930s, the architect Herbert Baker stated that he wished his design to embody 'the three values of efficiency, conservatism, and architectural expression'. He asked the directors of the Bank what their institution stood for and was told: 'Not the amassing of money, but rather that invisible thing, Trust, Confidence, which breeds Credit; it is by these "starres not to be told" that London regained her position as the nerve centre of the world's finance when it might have been lost after the Great War.'[11] By contrast, in the twenty-first century, central banks conceived of themselves in a different way. In 2005, the European Central Bank (ECB) chose a design by Coop Himmelb(l)au that in the view of the ECB Council 'reflected the ECB's values and translated them into architectural language'. The competition brief had specified that the new premises should 'foster interactive communication' and 'promote teamwork'.[12] The design concept was intended to reflect the ECB's 'transparency, communication, efficiency and stability'.[13] Did the Bank of England fully move along in this direction, and could it? There were some architectural adjustments, and as Deputy Governor in the early 2000s David Clementi supervised the knocking down of partition walls and the creation of large open plan offices. Especially after the Global Financial Crisis, all the old objections came back. The Governor appeared, in the words of Labour Chancellor Alistair Darling, like 'some kind of Sun King around whom the court revolves'. Deputy Governor Sir John Gieve suggested that the Bank is 'a monarchy and always has been – sometimes constitutional, other times autocratic': and Darling viewed it as 'an autocratic fiefdom of the Governor, which is anachronistic'.[14]

Communication in particular became the central concern of the new philosophy of central banking. The modern representatives of the Bank of England repeatedly emphasize that they have 'come a long way' from the alleged motto of Montagu Norman: 'never explain, never excuse'.[15] Actually, this is unfair, and represents a distortion of the real history. There is no evidence that Norman ever used this phrase, which is first put into his mouth in a thoroughly unreliable biography by Andrew Boyle.[16] Even in the interwar period, explaining was important. When Norman appointed Henry Clay as his economic adviser in 1935, he told Clay, 'Let me tell you that you are not here to tell us what to do, but to explain to us why we have done it.'[17] On the other hand, it is true that unarticulated feelings and understandings were at the heart of the Bank's practice. As Norman told the Macmillan committee: 'Reasons, Mr Chairman? I have no reasons, I have instincts.'[18]

MONEY AND BANKS

Central banking clearly had to do with money and banks, and the evolution of the Bank went alongside an evolution of monetary theory. In one account, the fundamental function of a central bank was the issue and control of money; in another it was the management of a banking system that generated money through credit. There was a real problem lying behind the lack of statutory clarity. No one really knew precisely what either money or a bank was. But they were clearly linked, and banks provided a way of making money – a dangerous and potentially deadly way, as Adam Smith had pointed out in the famous metaphor of the Daedalian wings, which he introduces in the *Wealth of Nations* (1776) immediately after he describes the founding of the Bank of England:

The gold and silver money which circulates in any country may very properly be compared to a highway, which, while it circulates and carries to market all the grass and corn of the country, produces itself not a single pile of either. The judicious operations of banking, by providing, if I may be allowed so violent a metaphor, a sort of waggon-way through the air, enable the country to convert, as it were, a great part of its highways into good pastures and corn-fields, and thereby to increase very considerably the annual produce of its land and labour. The commerce and industry of the country, however, it must be acknowledged, though they may be somewhat augmented, cannot be altogether so secure when they are thus, as it were, suspended upon the Dædalian wings of paper money as when they travel about upon the solid ground of gold and silver. Over and above the accidents to which they are exposed from the unskillfulness of the conductors of this paper money, they are liable to several others, from which no prudence or skill of those conductors can guard them.[19]

Rival interpretative traditions see the tasks of central banks in contrasting ways. A version that goes back to Walter Bagehot and continues through John Clapham, Ralph Hawtrey and Theodore Gregory to Charles Goodhart sees central banks as designed to produce one fundamental public good, financial stability, through lender of last resort operations.[20] An alternative way of thinking, best encapsulated by Curzio Giannini, is that the basic good was the provision of money and the maintenance of a payments system.[21]

Money. When the 1694 or the 1844 acts were drawn up, there was no doubt in anyone's mind that what was referred to was metallic money. The 1694 act was accompanied by a far-reaching monetary and coinage reform, overseen by Isaac Newton as Master of the Mint, and indeed that step rather than the establishment of the Bank was the initial foundation of British monetary stability. The Great Recoining established a currency that was protected by milling from the abuse of clipping. It was extremely costly, as the Mint bought in low-weight coins at face value; but the expenditure amounted to an investment in credibility. Confidence in the Bank of England was finally established when in the aftermath of the Napoleonic wars, and the abandonment of convertibility in 1797, the equivalence of banknotes and gold was restored in 1817.

But the certainty of the old Bank had been destroyed by the abandonment of the gold standard in September 1931, in the middle of the maelstrom of the Great Depression. A. J. P. Taylor's celebrated *English History 1914–1945* has this event as the turning point, the 'end of an age': 'A few days before, a managed currency had seemed as wicked as family planning. Now, like contraception, it became a commonplace.'[22] It was the departure from gold that made modern monetary policy a possibility. Modern accounts mostly emphasize the new room for monetary autonomy as the reason why Britain's experience of the 1930s was much more positive than the dismal 1920s.

To continue, perhaps impermissibly, Taylor's analogy, the managers were not very proficient with the new techniques, and like contraception, monetary management often failed (but generally over time became more reliable). The ensuing debate is the major subject of this book. It was tense and mostly unproductive. Mervyn King, chief economist (and eventually Governor), later lamented 'the striking fact' that 'as economics have become more and more sophisticated, it has less and less to say about money'.[23]

The story of the Bank's debate about money began with confusion, and ends with inflation targeting. The June 1977 *Quarterly Bulletin* stated: 'It is too soon to make a definitive judgement about the usefulness of monetary targets and how they should be operated.'[24] The Bank's historian Forrest Capie concludes his survey of monetary policy debate at the end of the 1970s with the remark: 'It is not really clear what the Bank's view on monetary control was. There were differences within the Bank and changing positions.'[25] A battle took place over which monetary aggregate best represented the idea of 'money'. Inflation targeting was successful in anchoring inflation expectations, but it also was no complete panacea: it solved one problem, but created a new dilemma. A large monetary and credit expansion might occur without price inflation, but where monetary behaviour was rather reflected directly primarily in asset prices, and where in consequence the development posed a potential threat to financial and, more generally, to economic stability. The discussion of financial stability raises the question of the Bank's attitude to banks.

Banks. The 1946 act gave no help in saying who a banker (or a bank) was. This issue is still unresolved, as one of the consequences of financial regulation is the emergence of banklike activities (shadow banking) outside the regulatory regime. The 1946 act simply stated: 'The expression "banker" means any such person carrying on a banking undertaking as may be declared by order of the Treasury to be a banker for the purposes of this section.' Gordon Richardson liked to resolve the issue by saying that banks were like elephants: you recognized one when you saw it.[26] In practice, banks to the Bank of England meant the merchant banks and clearing banks that had accounts with the Bank. There were other banks, but they only obtained legal clarity through the 1967 Companies Act, which, in Section 123, allowed the Board of Trade to issue a certificate to firms 'bona fide carrying on the business of banking for purposes of the Moneylenders Acts 1900–1927'. After that, there were 'objective criteria' for such banks, including a minimum capital (£250,000) and the provision of current and deposit account services.[27] In 1973–1974, the eruption of the 'secondary banking crisis', when the Bank of England needed to provide some £120 m for rescues of financial institutions, showed that these smaller institutions might indeed pose a systemic risk. The delayed legislative response to the 1973–1974 failures, also driven by the first European Community Banking Directive of 1977, was the 1979 Banking Act. The new legislation introduced a two-tier system of recognized banks and licensed deposit takers. Both were subject to supervision and surveillance by the Bank of England, but the higher-level superior (recognized) banks were inherently trusted – a trust that proved quite problematical over the next years.

The British banking and financial system was in fact highly segmented at the beginning of the period considered here. There were the large clearing banks, which had been grouped in a cartel until 1971, and which had long maintained balances at the Bank of England and worked with the Bank in clearing transactions. Unlike continental European banks, they did not engage in long-term lending or holding industrial securities: they generally lent on overdraft or at most for a two-year term. They thus did not really do profound or long-term maturity transformation. There were discount houses, which took on the treasury (cash management) functions of the clearing banks. There were accepting houses, merchant banks which dealt primarily in foreign trade finance and which guaranteed bills through their signature (acceptance) and, in this way, made the bills useable in the money market. There were building societies, which handled consumer mortgage finance funded through customer deposits. There were finance companies, which specialized in consumer lending for hire purchase and which often funded themselves through credits from the clearing banks. The segmentation made the London market 'respectable', 'orderly' and safe.[28] The British system became the envy of the world: 'Possibly the British banking system did find the holy grail of financial stability without sacrificing the contribution it made to savers, borrowers, and the economy as a whole.'[29] From the 1970s, and much more rapidly in the 1980s, these old distinctions started to break down. Clearing banks began their own treasury operations, often on the Euromarkets in foreign currencies, and moved into the mortgage business. The discount houses were undercapitalized, and handled smaller shares of the clearing banks' money business. Some tried to expand into new areas of business. The accepting houses in the 1980s teamed up with large banks, sometimes British, but in most cases foreign. The building societies competed with banks in lending, and under the 1986 Building Societies Act were allowed to demutualize and become banks themselves. The 'orderly' quality of the London system eroded, and a new City came into being.

From the point of view of the Bank of England, dealing with money and with banks required a quite different organizational and managerial structure for both cases. Money needed a clear overall policy, clearly articulated and communicated. The Bank could not afford to speak with multiple voices. There was a premium on consistency and discipline. But in the late 1970s and early 1980s, the Bank often behaved as a talking shop, and one that was unguided by any consensus on what constituted professional economic expertise. When the government after 1979 started to formulate a policy based on monetary targets, different senior Bank officials disagreed with that policy in different ways. Banking regulation and supervision, on the other hand, required a large number of line managers paying attention to the details of the particular banks for which they were responsible, and quickly communicating their doubts and anxieties. Each bank had its own very individual problems, but also interacted with other institutions in a web of market transactions. But in the 1970s and the 1980s, the Bank was much too hierarchical for such communication to be easy, and in consequence the Bank appeared to 'miss' one problem case after another, Johnson Matthey, BCCI, Barings. In reality, it got the broader financial stability issues right, and there was never in the period covered here any prospect of a general threat like 1931 or even more devastatingly 2007–2008. The Latin American debt crisis might have developed into a general world crisis, like 1931, but was well handled by central banks, and the Bank of England played a major role in building an effective response. But because the Bank could not communicate well, not many people noticed the major success and everyone pounced on the smaller-scale failures.

The different management issues or problems of the different Bank functions inevitably affected the conduct of Bank officials. No one was ever sacked or even discredited within the Bank for espousing the 'wrong' view on monetary policy, although targets were not met and the formulation of targets was profoundly flawed. A possible exception is Andrew Crockett, who might have been sidelined because of his views on exchange rate policy. The Bank was not unique in this way: no Fed official has been straightforwardly fired for a mistaken approach to monetary policy – though Arthur Burns, who gave in to President Nixon's political pressures in the Great Inflation, was not reappointed by President Carter. In part the failure to punish monetary error is a product of the fact that economics is rarely black and white, and even long-discredited theories such as the highly influential nineteenth-century real bills doctrine (that central bank issue should be issued on the security of sound commercial bills) actually may be good policy guides in some circumstances. But, by contrast, supervision of banking is full of pitfalls. Middle-ranking Bank of England officials did lose their jobs because of mistakes in banking supervision. In addition, supervision took on many rather demoralized and disgruntled employees who had previously worked in exchange control, and brought little enthusiasm into their new specialization. The result was an obvious response by young and ambitious officials: money was both more intellectually prestigious and less professionally unsafe. In the 1970s, the most dynamic area of the Bank seemed to be the Overseas Department and then the International Division, and, then, in the 1980s Markets became the hot part of the Bank and in the 1990s Monetary Analysis. Going into the banking supervision side of the Bank was consequently an unattractive and unrewarding career move.

After 1979, the demands on the Bank both in terms of monetary policy and in terms of banking supervision changed. The year 1979 can be thought of as a major caesura. This is not just the case with central banking and finance. Some analysts – including the present author – think of the late 1970s as the hinge of the twentieth century, the moment when the world moved decisively into a new phase of globalization. In China, Deng Xiaoping began a series of reforms that introduced the principles of the market. The year 1979 was the year of the Iranian Revolution, when the Shah was overthrown and he fled Teheran on 16 January. A theocratic and militantly anti-Western regime replaced the modern but cruel autocrat. In March 1979, some members of the European Community (without the participation of the UK) launched the European Monetary System (EMS), a stepping stone on what would be the road to the most problematical aspect of European integration, the creation of a monetary union. On 6 October 1979, the Chairman of the Federal Reserve Board, Paul Volcker, announced the outcome of an unscheduled meeting of the Federal Open Market Committee: 'By emphasizing the supply of reserves and constraining the growth of the money supply through the reserve mechanism, we think we can get firmer control over the growth in money supply in a shorter period of time.' On 3 May, in the UK, in the general election the Conservatives won a forty-three-seat majority, ousted the Labour government of James Callaghan and installed Margaret Thatcher as prime minister.

All these events transformed the economic environment of the UK, including the framework in which monetary policy was made. The results of the Chinese reform were perhaps the slowest to make themselves felt, but produced the most profound transformation of the world's geopolitics and geoeconomics. The spread of manufacturing into areas with an enormous supply of cheap labour exercised a long-term disinflationary influence. The Iranian Revolution immediately produced a new surge in petroleum prices – the second oil price shock, following that of 1973–1974 – at a moment when British North Sea production was beginning to come on line. The UK was becoming a major oil producer, and the pound took on some aspects of a petro-currency: the result transformed the UK balance of payments, reversing the near-continuous downward pressure on the currency that had characterized the 1960s and 1970s. The US monetary revolution and the surge in interest rates had an effect elsewhere, as globalization was beginning to connect financial markets. On 23 October 1979, the UK government announced the immediate removal of virtually all remaining exchange controls.

The Exchange Rate. One of the reasons that the Bank, the politicians, and the public had so much difficulty focusing on the management of money and banks was that because of history, the topic that appeared most prominently and immediately at the top of the political agenda was the exchange rate. In his important contribution for the Bank of England's tercentenary, Stanley Fischer noted, 'Monetary and exchange rate policies cannot be independent.'[30] Monetary crises had come to mean primarily exchange rate crisis arising out of balance of payments problems. There, the great caesura had been the weekend of 20–21 September 1931, when the government – at the advice of the Bank of England – took the British pound off the gold standard. The post-war devaluations of 1949 and 1967 also stood out as political landmarks, as did the humiliation of 1976 when the International Monetary Fund (IMF) had been called in and a set of monetary targets adopted explicitly as part of the IMF agreement. Exchange rate shocks, rather than movements of the inflation rate, were the real stuff of political traumas.

The sensitivity to the exchange rate meant that monetary discussions had a quite different context than they did in the US. Monetary theory there evolved without much need to reflect on the international dimension. By contrast, theorists understood quite well that in 'small open market economies' the exchange rate was the most important price. But the UK at this time was neither a large closed economy nor a small open one. It was somewhere in between, and the inbetweenness affected theory and made it less robust than in the extreme cases.

The exchange rate was obviously more dramatic as an influence in the 1970s and 1980s, in the aftermath of the breakdown of the par value system, with very different macro-economic and monetary stances in the major countries. In the 1980s, but much more in the 1990s, monetary policies started to converge internationally. After major traumas in 1992–1993, large exchange rate movements (with over- and under-shooting) did not stop, but they were less dramatic and destructive than in the past. That fact made it easier to concentrate on monetary policy, and that made for a general improvement in the policy environment, so that a virtuous spiral set in as a backdrop to what became known as the 'great moderation'.

The exchange rate obsession is the backdrop to the interpretative debate over how important monetary targets were. The conventional view is that monetary targeting came in with the 1976 IMF programme (or perhaps just before it) and lasted until 17 October 1985, when Chancellor Nigel Lawson announced in a landmark Mansion House speech, 'The aim of monetary policy is to ensure sustained and steady downward pressure on inflation. [...] But to achieve this, it remains operationally necessary to conduct monetary policy through the use of intermediate targets – taking account of relevant information such as the behaviour of the exchange rate – rather than by attempting to target money GDP directly.' But in fact, monetary targets (in particular M0) remained in place as part of the government's Medium-Term Financial Strategy until 1997, though they were over-shadowed by other policy goals – first the stabilization of the exchange rate, including ultimately membership in the EMS's Exchange Rate Mechanism; and then, after the ignominious collapse of that experiment in yet another exchange rate crisis in September 1992 (Black Wednesday, 16 September), the adoption of an inflation target. Inflation targeting, in a world in which inflation rates were converging, proved to be a much more stable policy orientation, and it allowed a consistency in the pursuit of monetary policy objectives that had been lacking for the past thirty years.

Reflecting on this experience, it is easy to adopt extreme verdicts. In one version, 'monetarism' was followed for only a few years at the beginning of the Thatcher government, producing a severe recession and internal tensions within a government that became massively unpopular and survived only because of the chance of the Falklands conflict. In the pure 'monetarist' interpretation of the advocates of monetary base control, monetarism in the form of its proper application was never practised in Britain, or indeed anywhere else apart from Switzerland, and thus the only failure of monetarism was the failure to put it into practice. (This seems a little like arguments put forward by some Marxists, that the problem of communism was that it was never properly implemented.)[31]

STATUTES AND PURPOSE

It is not surprising that the Bank's communication strategy at the outset of the period covered here was so veiled. Even at the end of the 1970s, there was no way of really knowing what the Bank was supposed to do, apart from giving general advice to the government. The most obvious way of trying to identify the function of an institution is to look at the legislation that creates it and which should govern its operations. But this is not always an easy exercise. In 2009, a report of the BIS's Central Bank Governance Group noted the multiple functions of modern central banks, and observed that 'difficult trade-offs often must be made between multiple objectives in relation to specific functions and between objectives for different functions'. It also commented on the absence of legislative precision: 'Older treatises on central banking had a lot to say about functions but relatively little about objectives; the same was the case for legislation.'[32] The Bank of England legislation is indeed obscure about objectives until very recently (1998).

The Bank of England had been established in 1694, as a mechanism for 'the carrying on the Warr against France', by an Act of Parliament 'for granting to theire Majesties severall Rates and Duties upon Tunnage of Shipps and Vessells and upon Beere Ale and other Liquors for secureing certaine Recompenses and Advantages in the said Act mentioned to such Persons as shall voluntarily advance the summe of Fifteene hundred thousand pounds'. The stockholders were granted some privileges in return for the advance of the £1,500,000, in that, although barred from trading in goods, they were licensed to deal in bills of exchange and bullion:

Provided that nothing herein conteined shall any wayes be construed to hinder the said Corporation from dealeing in Bills of Exchange or in buying or selling Bullion Gold or Silver or in selling any goods wares or merchandize whatsoever which shall really and bona fide be left or deposited with the said Corporation for money lent and advanced thereon and which shall not be redeemed att the time agreed on or within three moneths after or from selling such goods as shall or may be the produce of Lands purchased by the said Corporation.

The Bank's charter, however, did specify that 'we being desirous to promote the publick Good and Benefit of our People'. The next two and a half centuries did not bring much clarification of purpose. The modern Bank of England dated from the Peel Act of 1844, which clearly defined (and separated) the relationship of the functions of issuing banknotes and doing general banking business:

The issue of promissory notes of the governor and company of the Bank of England, payable on demand, shall be separated and thenceforth kept wholly distinct from the general banking business of the said governor and company; and the business of and relating to such issue shall be thenceforth conducted and carried on by the said governor and company in a separate department, to be called 'the Issue Department of the Bank of England'.

But there was no specification of a particular task, apart from the issuing of banknotes, of which the Bank in practice after 1844 had a monopoly, and a general banking business.

Some central banks had a clear mission statement at the outset. For instance, the 1913 US Federal Reserve Act gives a straightforward definition of the purposes of the new institution: 'to provide for the establishment of Federal reserve banks, to furnish an elastic currency, to afford means of rediscounting commercial paper, to establish a more effective supervision of banking in the United States, and for other purposes'.[33] Post-war Germany was not dissimilar, in part because it had an explicit American model after 1945. The September 1948 Allied Military Law 62 created the Bank Deutscher Länder, the predecessor of the Deutsche Bundesbank, with a clear mandate: 'The Bank deutscher Laender is hereby granted the exclusive right to issue monetary symbols in the specified area.' It specified the details – including minimum reserves – of its relations with financial institutions. Article 88 of the 1949 German Basic Law, in effect the constitution of the Federal Republic, gave the new German government a mandate to replace the Military Law with a central bank governed by statute. Paragraph 3 of the 1957 Bundesbank Law echoes the Federal Reserve Act in providing a principal goal – regulating the circulation of money and the supply of credit to the economy, with the intent of 'securing the currency' (*die Währung zu sichern*). The 1989 Reserve Bank of New Zealand Act specifies the goals of 'formulating and implementing monetary policy designed to promote stability in the general level of prices, while recognising the Crown's right to determine economic policy; and promoting the maintenance of a sound and efficient financial system'.[34]

In mid-twentieth-century Britain, there might also have been an opportunity for rethinking the fundaments of central banking. There had been major policy failures in the interwar period, in particular a controversial and costly exchange rate regime after 1925, and the political mishandling of the thorny issue of the relationship between monetary and fiscal policy in 1931. Those mistakes produced a widespread conviction that a nationalized Bank would do better, but there was no statutory explanation given of the reason for the shift. The 1946 Bank of England Act that set the framework for the operation of the Old Lady of Threadneedle Street in the new post-war order had no overall definition of the purpose, and was mostly concerned with the obviously pressing tasks of regulating the ownership – transferring the privately held shares in the Bank to the Treasury – and specifying who could issue instructions: the Treasury to the Bank, and the Bank to the banking sector. There is a whiff of central planning about the statute, in its refusal to state an overall rule, and its insistence on the importance and centrality of (ruleless) instruction. The key parts came in Section 4 of the Statute:

4 (1). The Treasury may from time to time give such directions to the Bank as, after consultation with the Governor of the Bank, they think necessary in the public interest.

4 (3). The Bank, if they think it necessary in the public interest, may request information from and make recommendations to bankers, and may, if so authorised by the Treasury, issue directions to any banker for the purpose of securing that effect is given to any such request or recommendation.

The Governor, Lord Catto, insisted during the House of Lords debate on the bill that in giving directions to banks 'the initiative is with the Bank of England'. His successor as Governor, C. F. Cobbold, had the pages of the Official Report of the Lords debate copied and placed in the Bank's archive with the instruction that the documents were to be 'made available to, and read by, every occupant of the Governor's and Deputy Governor's chairs'.[35] How long that practice lasted is unclear, and the documents now lie untouched and forgotten in the historical archive.

Not everyone was happy with this approach, needless to say; the unhappiness certainly extended to most of the Bank and its senior managers, who saw the destruction of the old institution. Humphrey Mynors, then an Adviser to the Governor, proposed as a function 'to control the currency credit and banking system of the UK and maintain and protect the external value of the pound sterling', a formulation not far removed from the later Bundesbank law.[36] But there was no such phrase, with the result that the act was 'eccentrically devoid of any reference to the wider purpose and responsibilities of central banking'.[37] The uncertainty remained. In 1990, the recently retired Deputy Governor George Blunden reminisced: 'Nowhere in our legislation is the Bank of England described as the central bank of the United Kingdom and indeed it is my recollection that it was not until well after I joined the Bank in 1947 that we started regularly so describing ourselves.'[38] Blunden also sometimes expressed the thought that the lack of legal provision gave the Bank more rather than less power and that it was in consequence 'the most independent because all other central banks are constrained by articles and acts that have established for them what they may do and what they may not do'.[39] Gordon Richardson, Governor from 1973 to 1983, also noted that the Bank 'was almost unique among central banks in the breadth of its functions'.[40]

Section 4 of the 1946 Bank Act was constantly discussed, but never used: indeed, it became the sort of analogy of a Treasury nuclear weapon, a deterrent which was so terrifying that it could never be employed. The Treasury periodically but inconclusively debated what was really meant by the power to give directions to the central bank. The Bank meanwhile believed that the Governor would have no choice but to resign were this clause ever to be implemented. Occasionally, the Bank even used an invitation to the Treasury to issue a directive as a weapon in its power struggle with the government.

By the end of the twentieth century, the Bank had reached a completely different view of its place, and denied that economic management required in any way giving directions. On the contrary, the Governor (Eddie

George) put the case that 'not only were we not telling economic agents what to do, but we never had'.[41]

The Bank of England seemed to be engaged in a constant quest to determine what its real function might be.[42] Only at the end of the century, with the growth of a conviction that public responsibilities needed to be explained, so that public institutions could be held accountable, the 1998 Bank of England Act spelled out clearly only its responsibilities in regard to monetary policy (in Section 10): 'The objectives of the Bank of England shall be – (a) to maintain price stability, and (b) subject to that, to support the economic policy of Her Majesty's Government, including its objectives for growth and employment.' The mandate was clear, but there were open questions. Why should 2 per cent inflation (or any other numerical speci-fication) constitute price stability? What was the relationship between stable consumer prices and other price developments (asset prices, in particular housing)? Was bank supervision and regulation best handled outside the framework of a central bank, since it might lead to compromises in monetary stability in order to preserve banks?

THE GOVERNANCE OF THE BANK OF ENGLAND

The governing body of the Bank of England was the Court, composed of a Governor, appointed for a five-year term, a Deputy Governor, with the same (not concurrent) term, and sixteen Directors, appointed for four-year terms. Traditionally, it met weekly, on Thursdays at noon (the weekday when in the old days changes in Bank Rate had been voted). From 1946, the Directors were appointed by the government, and the non-Executive Directors came from a variety of industrial backgrounds (including from trade unions) and from the City, mostly from merchant banks, but not by tradition from the major clearing (commercial) banks. Until 1998, four of the directors were full-time – Executive Directors – who worked in the Bank in a senior position, but until 1980 without a formal line of manage-ment responsibility. Some of the Directors contributed little to policy formation: others were crucial in positioning the Bank in British politics and society. In particular, in the period covered here, Hector Laing (from 1978 Sir Hector) of United Biscuits was Director of the Bank of England from 1973 to 1991. Since Margaret Thatcher often stayed in his country residence in Dunphail in County Moray, Scotland, he became a crucial behind-the-scenes link between the Bank and the government; he was close to George Blunden, who was brought back from retirement as Deputy Governor to provide a steady pair of hands; he quickly identified Eddie

George as the future of the Bank of England; and in addition, he allowed Governor Robin Leigh-Pemberton to use his private aeroplane (neatly named 'The Flying Biscuit'). The members of the Court were appointed by the government, formally by the Crown on the advice of the prime minister; but this rather formal mechanism ensured that the prime minister could rarely force eccentric choices through. Margaret Thatcher had strong feelings about suitable personalities, and wanted to appoint the economist Patrick Minford and the American banker Harry Taylor of Manufacturers Hanover; but neither in fact were selected.[43] She did succeed in appointing Brian Griffiths to the Court in 1984, and he became the first academic Director of the Bank since Keynes, but he left the next year to head the Downing Street Policy Unit.

The Court traditionally began with a presentation by the Governor on note circulation and the fiduciary issue: as the veteran George Blunden liked to put it, in order to remind the outside Directors that 'we are a bank'.[44] But unlike the institutional arrangements that had prevailed under the Gold Standard, when Bank Rate had been agreed and announced after each weekly Court meeting, the Court at this point had no formal responsibility in preparing the Bank's approach to monetary policy, which was basically left in the hands of the senior officers of the Bank, and where of course the ultimate authority lay with the Treasury – until the 1998 Bank Act came into force. It is hard to determine how influential or wide-ranging were the discussions that took place in and perhaps also around the Court, as the Bank believed that Court minutes were 'discoverable' documents in the event of a legal enquiry, with the result that the minutes were brief and 'even the Secretary's manuscript is destroyed'.[45] By the early 1990s, there was a demand for a reform of the proceedings of the Court, with some longer in-depth meetings taking the place of some of the short regular but routine meetings.[46] The timing of the Monetary Policy Committee after 1998, with decisions announced monthly on a Thursday at noon, indicated the extent to which the modern MPC might be seen as a functional replacement of the older Court of the Gold Standard era.

Within the Bank, the 'Committee of Treasury' constituted an inner committee for the Court, with the Governor and Deputy Governor and five senior Directors elected by the Court. Its main task lay in reviewing contentious items ahead of the full Court and in dealing with remuneration issues. It continued to function until 29 February 1992, when it was 'stood down'.

The Chief Cashier acted as a de facto chief executive, and the Chief Cashier's Office dealt with market operations, for the Bank, the Treasury, as well as for foreign central banks and other customers. A weekly bill tender was handled by the Securities Office. At a daily 'books' meeting, the Governor and the senior staff were briefed on market developments. Within the Cashier's Department was the Discount Office, which was responsible for the money markets, and for dealing with the discount houses, and the Principal of the Discount Office reported directly to the Governor. These offices were located on the ground floor of the Bank, to the left of the main entrance, and represented the interface with the world of the markets, while the Court met on the grand *piano nobile* of the first floor.

An Exchange Control and Overseas Section, established in 1948, supervised the very cumbersome foreign exchange control regulations, but also managed relations with the rest of the world, in particular other central banks, and the Washington IMF. By a tradition dating back to the 1950s and ending only in 2004, a young and promising Bank of England official served as assistant to the Managing Director of the IMF. In the 1960s, the Overseas Section was separated from exchange control and eventually became the International Divisions, located on the third floor of the Bank, along with the Economic Intelligence Department.

The Bank also had branches in major cities – Birmingham, Bristol, Leeds, Liverpool, Manchester, Newcastle and Southampton; there was also from 1940 an office in Glasgow. It maintained a printing works in Debden, on the tube Central Line, constructed in 1956.

The Bank's Governor throughout the later 1970s was Gordon Richardson, who replaced the first Governor to have risen in the ranks of the Bank of England, Leslie O'Brien (who was given a peerage when he retired in 1973, and became Baron O'Brien of Lothbury). Richardson had been a non-Executive Director of the Bank from 1967: he was a Cambridge-educated lawyer who had joined the merchant bank Schroders and became Chairman in 1965. There had been other candidates, including Jeremy Morse, but Richardson looked like the commanding figure, and had indeed even been thought a leading candidate in 1966, when O'Brien was appointed. He, more than any other twentieth-century Governor, looked like a Governor of the Bank of England from central casting: elegant, with silver hair and a patrician manner (see Figure 1.1). One verdict recorded in his obituary had it: 'Very handsome man; he seemed to be quite tall but he wasn't. Very elegant, very imposing. A god.'[47] The journalist Bill Keegan, who liked him greatly, commented shrewdly: 'Like [Prime Minister Edward] Heath he was very much a meritocrat, although he looked every inch the aristocrat.'[48] When the journalist Stephen Fay asked him whether he inspired fear, he rephrased

Figure 1.1 Gordon Richardson: The Patrician Governor
(Central Press/Stringer/Hulton Archive/Getty Images)

the question to say that the position of Governor 'commands a certain degree of respect and goodwill. It's true of Prime Ministers and Popes too, isn't it?'[49] Forrest Capie goes even further in describing him as the last Governor to be treated as an 'Eastern potentate'.[50] The popular author Anthony Sampson claimed that Richardson 'guarded the Bank's traditional secrecy as carefully as if it were the financial arm of MI5'.[51]

In fact, Richardson managed by consensus, and spent an inordinate – and to some senior officials irritating and frustrating – time on bilateral consultations. In consequence, to his closest advisers he appeared indecisive and irresolute. Christopher Dow, the Bank's chief economist, who maintained a diary (arousing considerable suspicion from the Governor) which was posthumously edited and published and became one of the most interesting inside accounts of how a central bank works, wrote of his position in the 1980s: 'He hankers after discussions of high policy, but in practice he does not like the directions in which such discussions are likely to lead.'[52] He was a natural conservative, which meant that in the climate of the 1970s he found relations with Labour Party politicians easier than with Conservatives, and he came to have a very antagonistic relation with Margaret Thatcher. He liked the aphorism, 'All change is bad, especially change for the better.'[53]

Like every Bank Governor in the period covered in this volume, he saw the world in terms of sports analogies. He told the staff when he opened a new squash court for the staff sports club in Roehampton that squash was a much better analogy for central banking than the complex, overstaffed and rule-bound game of cricket (which his successor, Robin Leigh-Pemberton, adored). 'Squash, like the City of London, depends largely on self-regulation. Just as in this country we have no bank inspectors and no Securities and Exchange Commission, so squash players generally sort out their differences without the need for a referee's whistle or an umpire's white coat.'[54] All of that would change, and within five years the Bank would be heavily involved in the establishment of the Securities and Investments Board ('SIB') in 1985, a half-way house, and not a statutory body, but a step on the way to systematic financial regulation. The Department of Trade was empowered to delegate some statutory powers to the SIB. A debate started as to what sort of rules were required. One influential member of the Bank's governing Court, Sir Hector Laing, used the prevailing sports metaphor (here presumably tennis), saying, 'Don't you think, Mr. Governor, that what we need to run the country is a few white lines on the court.'[55]

By the end of the 1970s, there was a widespread sense that the Bank was out of date, or, as Rodney Galpin, the Chief of Establishments (i.e. responsible for the Bank's internal administration), more circumspectly put it: 'The Bank has not been insulated from the changes in society which have occurred at an increasing pace over the last decade.'[56] The Bank had not found an appropriate management style. In the 1960s, consultants from McKinseys swirled around the Bank, eager to give advice on how to make a new Bank. In the 1970s, the Bank turned instead to its own, and asked a former head of the civil service, Lord Croham (Douglas Allen), who had come to the Bank as an adviser on industrial policy, to conduct an organizational review. The aim of the reform was to give responsibility for particular areas of the Bank's activity to the Executive Directors, who had previously been rather free-floating: in the old system, they had not, as Croham concluded, been 'properly integrated in the management structure'.[57]

Within the Bank, the driving force for change was an Executive Director, George Blunden, who felt in particular that the Chief Cashier was responsible for too much, and that the Cashier's Department functions should be subject to extensive pruning. Christopher Dow felt that 'the post was a sign and symbol of everything wrong with the Bank'.[58] John Page had been Chief Cashier for ten years, was respected in the City, but was not adept at thinking or speaking about monetary theory. Forrest Capie describes him as 'reserved in character and quiet [...] not a strong communicator'.[59] He was actively hostile to economists, whom he saw as threatening his view of the Bank and its hierarchy; and – as the historian Elizabeth Hennessy describes him – exuded a 'somewhat dour and humourless impression'.[60] The first cohort of graduate economists had only been recruited to the Bank in the late 1960s, and they had had an acutely unhappy experience. Sir Angus Deaton later recalled starting off in 1967:

I felt like I'd been taken back to my infant school in Scotland. It was called 'Cash School' and the two men who ran it really despised us, and thought that adding up columns of figures by hand, in ink, was a good way of cutting us down to size. No wonder so many of us quit. Many of the people who worked there felt trapped, because the starting salaries were low, but then rose (as did the perks) without much increase in qualifications, so there was no way out. And it was widely believed (perhaps incorrectly) that the Establishment Department (the personnel dept) decided within a year of your arrival exactly what your future promotion would be up to retirement, but only revealed it a year at a time on a fixed calendar date, much dreaded.[61]

A completely new structure of the Bank was rolled out at the beginning of 1980. The main practical part concerned the stripping away of the functions and importance of the Chief Cashier's Department, which was broken into two. The announcement stated bluntly: 'The chief cashier will in future be responsible only for banking work and will no longer be concerned with monetary policy and its execution, and will cease to exercise administrative responsibilities ranging more widely over the Bank as a whole.'

There would now be three organizational areas of the Bank, an anticipation of the Wings structure adopted in the 1990s:

- Policy and markets (including monetary policy, market operations, research)
- Financial structure and supervision
- Operations and services

The first of these rapidly came to be seen as the intellectual centre of the Bank, where the best careers could be made and reputations honed.

But the reform was limited in the sense that the interactions with the large London banks (clearing banks) were not really formalized. The old-style bank managers could see 'no reason' why clearing banks should be represented on the Court of the Bank.[62]

The Bank's employees seem to have been largely distrustful. They saw the move as 'divisive', and as 'an economists' charter'. A staff minute summed up the response: 'There seems to be a body of opinion forming – although I cannot say how representative it is – which describes the changes proposed as "divisive", "an economist's" charter and "dismemberment"; all this is unhealthy.' The reform coincided with the lifting of exchange controls and consequential redundancies and movements of staff. 'Morale in the Bank is presently very low, largely because of the big redundancy program which we have just gone through.'[63]

Ultimately, what shifted was the relationship with what might be described as the stakeholders. In the late 1970s, the Bank thought primarily in terms of its relationship with the government (in particular the Treasury) and with the markets (in particular the discount houses, which served as an intermediary between the Bank and the financial system, including the large commercial or clearing banks).

The Treasury. The Bank of England Executive Director John Fforde described the UK as governed by 'a centralised macroeconomic executive'. 'This includes … both the Treasury and the Bank of England. The latter is institutionally and operationally separate from the Treasury but is best regarded as the central banking arm' of that executive.[64] The underlying policy concept of this institutional set-up was Keynesian, with both monetary and fiscal policy envisaged as tools of macro-economic demand management. But the relationship between Treasury and Bank remained permanently haunted by potential or actual controversy. One way of thinking about the institutional dimension of policy-making at this time is as a continuous tussle for influence and control by the Treasury and the Bank, in which the Treasury was initially dominant, but was so humiliated by policy failure in 1992 that it began to cede intellectual leadership to the Bank. The economist Fred Hirsch described the relationship as a 'distance, and often an "atmosphere," which together have undoubtedly diminished the effectiveness of Britain's post-war financial policy, both in its external impact and domestically'.[65] The brightest minds of both institutions gravitated to the fissure between the two, expending intellectual and organizational energy on trying to clash with the other. Some participants hoped that an end of the conflict meant that the fine intellects of officialdom could turn to a higher purpose than a turf conflict.

In the course of the 1980s, a formalized process developed around regular monthly meetings chaired by the Head of the Treasury (a civil service position). The Treasury and the Bank both prepared papers for this meeting, and the Bank team was headed by the Director of Home Finance (i.e. the Markets Division); the Governor and the Deputy Governor were usually not there. Reviewing these arrangements, the Bank explained to other central banks that it

chooses to provide its advice to the Government on monetary policy, as indeed on almost all other areas in private, believing this to be a more effective and productive channel of communication than through public statements. It also assists the credibility and perceived coherence of policy if the monetary authorities – by which is meant the Bank and the Treasury in combination – are seen to be at one. The Bank of course makes its views known, sometimes opaquely and in coded language, most particularly through its Quarterly Bulletin and through frequent public speeches by the Governor.[66]

Opacity was a product of the Bank's subservient role – and it was a characteristic that could only be shed once the Bank had a well-defined task.

The Markets. In the City as it operated at the outset of the period covered in this volume, there was a network of institutions between the Bank of England and the large banks. It constituted what was referred to as the 'markets'. In Walter Bagehot's 1873 *Lombard Street*, the key actors appear to be the bill brokers, who are described as an 'anomaly', in that they were rivals to the Bank of England but the Bank always provided advances to them on good security. Bagehot concluded that they were 'an inevitable part of the system of banking which history has given us'.[67] By the twentieth century, the anomaly persisted and was even greater. The bill brokers had evolved into principals, as 'discount houses' which had a monopoly in dealing with the Bank of England in bills of exchange and acceptances. They were proud of their status as 'sole recipients of lender of last resort facilities at the Bank of England' (i.e. access to end of day facilities at the Bank against good collateral: the term 'Lender of Last Resort' also has a broader meaning of support for distressed institutions, which was not usually applicable in the case of the discount market).[68] The discount houses took money from the banking system – above all from the clearers – and also lent to the banking system. They had the obligation to 'cover' the weekly

Treasury bill tender, that is, to bid for the entire amount on offer. They constituted the key intermediation between the Bank and the monetary system at large. The close relationship with the Bank is demonstrated by the requirement that no Director of the Bank of England could be either a Member of the House of Commons or connected with a discount house.[69] In 1941, they organized in the London Discount Market Association, whose chairman or deputy chairman went every week on a Thursday afternoon to a markets meeting, often affectionately referred to as 'the Governor's tea party'. The meeting was strategically timed between the usual announcement of interest rate changes by the Bank's Court on a Thursday and the weekly Treasury bill tender on a Friday morning. By 1997, only seven of the discount houses were left: Gerrard and National, Union Discount, Clive Discount, Alexanders, King & Shaxson, Seccombe, Marshall & Campion, and Cater Allen. These sessions – which had started in the 1920s – looked very ritualistic to the outside, especially as the market makers entered the Bank wearing traditional silk top hats, which they then left outside the Governor's room and into which occasionally the Deputy Governor would light-heartedly toss a few pennies (or sometimes also foreign coins). But they were also the occasion of a surprisingly frank exchange of views about the likely future developments of markets; and the Bank then relayed these views as those of 'the market' in discussions with the Treasury. The frankness – and the insider quality – made the meetings more and more controversial, particularly when the Bank started dealing with banks directly. The small capitalization of the discount houses made them potentially quite vulnerable when interest rates rose unexpectedly (they had no way of hedging against the consequent fall in the value of their interest-bearing securities, at least until the London International Financial Futures and Options Exchange, or LIFFE, was established in 1982). From 1986, with the major stock market reform ('Big Bang') a wider range of gilt-edged market makers (GEMMs) were admitted to the market in gilts. The role of the discount houses began to fade as the bill market atrophied. The weekly meetings ceased in 1994, and the discount market itself was abolished in 1997 as monetary policy shifted to using treasury bill sales and repurchases (repos).

In the course of the 1980s, the Bank saw its stakeholders in a broader perspective. Parliament, but also the public, began to be much more important.

Parliament. British constitutional tradition emphasized the responsibility of ministers to parliament. The Chancellor as a member of the government was by convention also necessarily a Member of Parliament, and set out and defended government policy at great set-piece occasions such as the Budget presentation, but also on a regular basis. The Bank's Governor was of course not a politician, so political accountability placed the Chancellor in front of the Governor. The Thatcher government, however, introduced a process for a regular parliamentary examination of the Bank as well as the Treasury, in a reform that went back to a Procedure Committee recommendation of 1977 that had never been implemented by James Callaghan's government.[70] The Bank's principal interlocutors were on the Treasury and Civil Service Select Committee (TCSC). The initial results were disappointing, and the process brought little light, edification or real accountability. In the 1980s, much of the interaction was on the lines of a Punch and Judy show, with particular MPs building their reputation by bashing and needling the Chancellor and the Governor of the Bank. The Chancellor was usually the target, except after bank failures, and the main exercise in needling was to try to establish contradictions between the Chancellor's position and that of the Governor, or between that of the Chancellor and the Prime Minister. Austin Mitchell, the Labour MP for Grimsby, was the master of this sort of exercise. One comment, at the height of the exchange rate drama created by the dollar appreciation of the mid-1980s, became notorious for its sexism, but is characteristic of some of the tone of the meetings:

The Prime Minister interfered – as women do – and created a climate of uncertainty which is the cause of our present problems. In the face of that, you panicked, as no one else has done. You have hiked up interest rates to a level where they are well over double those in West Germany, our major industrial competitor. You are crucifying the people of this country on a cross of high interest rates, and the pound is still overvalued as against the Deutschemark, our major industrial competitor. In short, Chancellor, you have made a balls-up![71]

Another Labour MP, Jeremy Bray, was a PhD mathematician and an economist with a background in operations research, who had also worked in the Cambridge Department of Applied Economics and who developed a powerful and highly sophisticated line of questioning about the Bank's econometric models. Though the Bank replied carefully and conscientiously to his letters, in practice it ignored him. Bray, unlike the Bank economists, was fascinated by feedback loops and, thus, by the establishment of expectations and reactions. Another helpful and important voice was that of the Conservative MP Nicholas Budgen, who used the Committee to deliver some early warnings in the mid-1980s about what would become the Lawson boom, and combed Bank publications for references to 'risk'.

Thinking about how a more independent Bank might be accountable to parliament revolved more and more around ex ante control: debate about a clear mandate such as a price stability objective. The Bank and the government then might be accountable for their performance in relation to that objective. In time, the quality of parliamentary oversight improved, and comparative research began to suggest that Britain performed much better than the US, with less grandstanding, less process and more opportunity to pursue consistent lines of inquiry.[72]

The Public. The Bank also became more interested over this period in how it was viewed by a much broader audience. In 1984, it asked a journalist, Christopher Fildes, to prepare a popular history for its tercentenary (though it never materialized: in 2010, a new history was commissioned in its place from David Kynaston).[73] The next year, in the aftermath of the Johnson Matthey collapse and the controversy over the Bank's involvement, Deputy Governor Christopher ('Kit') McMahon and then his successor George Blunden hoped that another journalist, Stephen Fay, would write a sympathetic portrayal of the Bank from within, but they were rather disappointed with the result. Fay's book had concluded: 'The Bank was really independent only as long as people inside the Bank believed in its independence. These days, not many do. They are nearly all new Bank men now.'[74] Another journalist, Philip Geddes, was asked to make a television programme on the Bank for Television South, and he later also produced a book.[75] In the early 1990s, the Bank started to train its senior officials in how to manage their appearance on television.

There were also more speeches. In the 1960s, there had been around five speeches by the Governor and the Deputy Governor each year; in the 1990s, there were thirteen.[76] The number and length of Bank publications increased at an even faster rate, as did the provision of data. At the beginning of this period, the main vehicle for Bank communications was the *Quarterly Bulletin*, launched in 1960, which was controlled and even censored by the Treasury. Then in the 1990s came the *Inflation Report* (1993), then a *Financial Stability Review* (1996), as well as an annual gilt market report. From 1997, the minutes (but not a transcript of discussion) of the Monetary Policy Committee were published. This quest for openness is not of course unique to the Bank: it was shared by many governmental organizations and by international institutions (such as the IMF). Gradually, all the producers of information began to wonder whether their products were being read by the target audience and whether a Bankspeak (or Fundspeak) impenetrable for most outsiders was not limiting the effectiveness of communication.

The Bank had to explain itself more: but it also functioned in a world where norms were changing. The two most important forces driving the rethinking of the Bank and its mission were professionalization – and in particular the rise of economists – and internationalization. In the 1970s, the Bank was still fundamentally inward-looking; it needed to find better ways of communicating with the world.

Economists had played some role in the 'old Bank'. Montagu Norman had, in 1927, hired W. W. Stewart and then, in the autumn of 1930, a Harvard Professor, Oliver Sprague, as economic adviser as the interwar depression – and the financial crisis – began to worsen. The Governor had particularly insisted that it was 'essential' to appoint an American, and his staff in the Bank had agreed that the appointment 'had avoided the difficulty of electing an Englishman'. The American economists were supposed not only to explain and interpret the policies of different central banks to each other, but also to defend the Bank's policy 'against criticism'.[77] In the same year, 1930, the Bank also recruited Henry Clay, an economics professor at Manchester University, as adviser: doubtless Norman thought that he needed professional advisers to help him combat the onslaught of John Maynard Keynes' arguments and rhetoric. In 1969, the Bank created an Economics Division, and the chief economist of the 1970s, Christopher Dow, recruited a number of economists to senior positions. The role of economists shifted greatly in the 1980s and 1990s. At the beginning, the major contribution of economists had been seen as providing what were already then rather old-fashioned conventionally Keynesian macro-economic models. For a long time, Charles Goodhart was the sole – though loud and persuasive – voice of monetary economics in the Bank. In the 1980s, the new literature on time consistency and credibility made expectations and the management of expectations the centre of a new policy focus. The bank needed to respond. In the summer of 1987, the Deputy Governor George Blunden (who later liked to complain that there were 'too many bloody economists' in the Bank) stated: 'It was perhaps time for a step change in the Bank's attitude to the recruitment of economists. We had clung for too long to an approach to staffing which favoured the amateur, generalist recruit as against the specialist. This contrasted strongly with the policy of many other central banks, where an economics background was regarded as virtually essential.' In his vision, three quarters of graduate recruits should have a formal economics training.[78]

A persistent problem in the Bank's relationship with economists was that academics did not understand, and their models could not encompass, the complex institutional features of the differentiated elements of the British banking system. So, academic economics did not drive policy action until relatively late. But at a much earlier stage, academic arguments provided a retrospective justification for two major policy shifts. The first was the time consistency argument that looked like the most important theoretical justification of central bank independence. The second was the new Keynesian (or perhaps more accurately neo-Wicksellian) consensus that the interest rate could be independently targeted, a step that took monetary management out of its old institutional setting of the interplay between the Bank and the markets.

International examples could provide a powerful way of arguing for policy change. The UK looked in the 1970s – with Italy – as the poorest performer in regard to price stability. It was natural for critics to look to other countries with greater monetary stability. In the late 1970s, Germany or Switzerland served as a template. But imitating Germany would require a compromise with a new frame-work of European cooperation, the EMS, initiated in 1979. The UK had participated in the initial discussions, but then sidelined itself. The chief British Treasury negotiator, Ken Couzens, minuted: 'I am clear that it would have been better for the UK in every event if this plan had never come forward', and laid out his view of how Britain could live outside the EMS.[79] Switzerland was a much more attractive model, which offered even greater stability than Germany, and had not made exchange rate commitments (with the exception of a short-lived and rather disastrous episode in 1978). Margaret Thatcher felt that the UK could learn monetary policy from the Swiss. Later, as the success of Paul Volcker's anti-inflationary strategy became clear, the US looked like the best model. Volcker's successor, Alan Greenspan, played a critical role on two occasions: in June 1990, persuading Margaret Thatcher that the rule-bound discipline of the EMS looked like the gold standard and was hence desirable; and then in 1996 and 1997, advising Gordon Brown on the economic benefits of central bank independence. On both occasions, the Bank worked carefully with Greenspan. The Bank itself did not generally like to think of big rival central banks as models of management, but appreciated and referred to New Zealand's experiment in inflation rate targeting.[80]

From 1992, a further element of managing contact with the outside world was added. It was only then that the Bank employed its first lawyer, and a small legal team was built up under Peter Peddie, a Freshfields partner who had long experience of working with the Bank in sensitive areas (such as the unfreezing of Iranian assets in the US after the hostage release in January 1981) and in channelling the Bank's response to the BCCI failure. The major challenge was how to address new regulatory problems: when the 1998 Bank of England Act took away financial supervision, most of the Bank's lawyers moved to the Financial Services Authority (FSA); only four remained in the Bank. The demand for legal expertise really exploded after 2008 and the Global Financial Crisis, and supervision was also transferred back: by the late 2010s, there were some 150 lawyers employed by the Bank.

In the 1990s, the Bank began to specify essential or core purposes, in particular initially three: currency or price stability, financial stability, and the promotion of the UK financial service sector. There was inherently a tension between these goals, as they represented fundamentally different kinds of responsibility. Monetary stability was a task that could be efficiently delegated by parliament to an autonomous authority, a view that was supported by a large academic and theoretical literature on the benefits of delegated monitoring. Financial stability on the other hand entailed detailed regulatory powers that could only be derived from sovereign authority. And the promotion of UK financial services looked more like an activity appropriate to an interest group, and not to an arm of a sovereign that had a universal and not a particular responsibility.

These three purposes were simplified and, at the same time, made more complex in the process of operationalizing them. The third was the first to fade (it looked a bit like old-style protectionism or the traditional City orientation of the Bank), and was completely dropped in 2004; and the second was increasingly assumed to follow automatically from the first (until the 2008 crisis gave a profound shock to thinking about central banking). So, three dwindled down to two and then one. But as the Bank tried to devise an operational implementation, the number of policy goals also multiplied. By 1998, fourteen high-level strategic objectives, twenty-seven area strategic aims, forty-nine business objectives and fifty-five management objectives were specified in the 'Budbook'. One official noted drily: 'It was inevitable that there were inconsistencies.'[81]

2

Foreign Fetters

The 1970s were years of crisis everywhere, but especially in the UK. The breakdown of the fixed exchange rate system of Bretton Woods and the two oil price shocks, in 1973–1974 and in 1979, made for substantial instability. In the 1970s, the UK's relations with the outside world were recast, with three decisive developments: in 1973, membership of the European Economic Community (later the European Community, then after 1993 the European Union); in 1976, the conclusion of a programme with conditionality negotiated with the International Monetary Fund (IMF); and, in 1979, the ending of exchange controls. The combination of these changes decisively altered the framework for monetary and economic policy-making. The drama can be thought of as the UK's initial encounter with globalization in its late twentieth-century form.

HUMILIATION

Turning points are emotional. The British policy caesura was the consequence of a struggle between differing parts of the British economic establishment, a clash in the macro-economic executive of Treasury and Bank. The policy discussions of the UK in 1976 were dramatic and humiliating. They turned into an indictment of a Britain that had failed. Because of the foreign exchange crisis, the Governor of the Bank of England and the Chancellor of the Exchequer could not make their scheduled journeys to the IMF Annual Meetings, held that year in Manila, and on 28 September turned back from the trip after a turbulent discussion in Heathrow Airport. Chancellor Denis Healey instead of flying to Manila went to the Labour Party Conference in Blackpool, where he explained: 'I do not come with a Treasury view. I come from the battlefield.'[1] The resulting IMF programme, at a turning point in British history, has understandably been the subject of multiple fine eyewitness and historical accounts.

The background to the problem was instability in the international monetary system, and in particular the collapse of the fixed exchange rate world of Bretton Woods. The negotiation of a new parity grid in December 1971 proved to be not lasting, and in June 1972 the UK started a float of sterling. An attempt to restore a new system failed in 1973, and in 1974 the UK withdrew from a European exchange rate grid that had been set up as an initial European response to currency instability.

The financial crisis began with a sharp decline in sterling on 4 and 5 March 1976. Three events combined to feed a market panic. Nigeria ran down its sterling balances; the Bank sold sterling; and on 5 March, it lowered the minimum lending rate (MLR) to 9 per cent. The Treasury had concluded, months before, that sterling was overvalued, and that some depreciation was needed, and Permanent Secretary Douglas Wass met Governor Gordon Richardson on 1 March to explain that the Treasury had decided on a depreciation (but not on the timing or how it should be handled both technically and politically).[2] There was no clear roadmap to explain how a gradual devaluation that might boost the UK economy could really be accomplished. The markets concluded that the fundamental driver was a Treasury policy organized primarily against the preferences of the Bank. Treasury officials told the government that they had wanted a lower rate for sterling, 'but the Bank of England messed it up with a total botch on the technical side'.[3] Disagreements about policy continued, as the Bank intervened to halt the slide of sterling, and Healey and Prime Minister James Callaghan appeared to be taking action to stop intervention.

Wass later chronicled 'this confusion of attitudes – in the Treasury and between the Treasury and the Bank – which led to a decision on positive action being delayed and postponed over a period of nearly two years and, when the depreciation which the Treasury wanted came, it came fortuitously, not as a result of a policy decision'.[4] He rightly presented policy incoherence as the central cause of the British malaise. It was also an intellectual incoherence, and bad policy-making and uncertain ideas combined together in a fatal brew. Later, looking back, a Treasury Minister, Edmund Dell, the Paymaster General, explained that 'economic forecasting was not then and is not now sufficiently reliable to provide a firm basis. [...] Economic policy ideas are free as the wind and indeed often consist of little else.'[5]

In June, the Bank for International Settlements (BIS) agreed a $5.3 bn standby arrangement, but the United States made it clear that it wanted the

UK to go to the IMF and negotiate a package that would include a substantial amount of adjustment. In July, Healey announced a number of measures, including £1 bn in cuts and a 2 per cent addition to employers' National Insurance contributions. But the adjustment was not enough. At the end of September, in a new panic, the pound fell quickly through the psychological barrier of $1.70 and closed at $1.6365 on 28 September. The next day, the UK announced that it was applying to the IMF for a standby credit. The Bank wrote a letter to the Chancellor strongly recommending a packet of measures to improve the balance of payments and reduce the public-sector borrowing requirement (PSBR).[6]

When the IMF mission arrived in London, the mood was tense. The IMF was upset that the UK seemed to be trying to use political pressure, in particular by appealing to German Chancellor Helmut Schmidt, to soften the IMF. Its mission head, Alan Whittome, was a former Bank official and a British national, counter to the convention that a mission should not be headed by a national of the country involved. He believed that his delegation was being spied on, and he conducted most of the internal discussions walking around London parks. The left of the Labour Party, and the influential Economic Policy Group at Cambridge University's Department of Applied Economics, urged a rejection of the IMF terms and the introduction of radical trade measures to correct the balance of payments (a 'siege economy' or, more mildly, 'an alternative strategy of protection').[7] In the government, only the rather junior minister Dell was sympathetic to the idea that adjustment was needed, and Healey at one point was close to submitting his resignation. Executive Director Kit McMahon in the Bank of England complained about the unrealism of much of the policy advice and wrote that 'none of the economists who have been writing for the papers, nor the people in the National Institute [for Economic and Social Research], have any significant experience of or feel for markets'. He stated, 'What *we* can see is that the country is at the end of its financial tether unless some radical change is brought about.'[8] From the Bank's perspective, the economists and the markets could not understand each other.

The change indeed came from the government, and the Prime Minister very boldly confronted the malaise of the 1970s. His party conference speech was subsequently described as the 'words which effectively buried Keynes'.[9] James Callaghan, whose words had in fact largely been penned by his son-in-law, the *Times* journalist Peter Jay, set out a radically new doctrine, which Jay himself then wrote of as 'the most breathtakingly frank public pronouncement since St Paul's First Epistle to the Corinthians'.[10]

Britain has lived for too long on borrowed time, borrowed money, borrowed ideas. We live in too troubled a world to be able to promise that in a matter of months, or even in a couple of years, that we shall enter the promised land. The route is long and hard. [...] I did not become a member of our Party, still less did I become the Leader of our Party, to propound shallow analyses and false remedies for fundamental economic and social problems. When we reject unemployment as an economic instrument – as we do – and when we reject also superficial remedies, as socialists must, then we must ask ourselves unflinchingly what is the cause of high unemployment. Quite simply and unequivocally, it is caused by paying ourselves more than the value of what we produce. [...] We used to think that you could spend your way out of a recession, and increase employment by cutting taxes and boosting Government spending. I tell you in all candour that that option no longer exists, and that in so far as it ever did exist, it only worked on each occasion since the war by injecting a bigger dose of inflation into the economy, followed by a higher level of unemployment as the next step. Higher inflation followed by higher unemployment.

The IMF letter of intent spelled out the new programme, substantially less radical than the one demanded originally by the Fund's negotiating team: the PSBR would be reduced from a forecast £10.5 bn in 1977/78 to £8.7 bn, with a lower figure for the next year. Domestic credit expansion (DCE) was to be maintained at £9 bn in 1976/77 and reduced to £7.7 bn the next year and £6 bn the year after that. There would be £1.5 bn in spending cuts in 1977/78 and £2 the following year. The Chancellor affirmed that the 'course of sterling M3 will be consistent with reduction of inflation'.

The Bank had already argued for publicly announced monetary targets in a letter of 21 October. The Treasury had been persistently sceptical. In July, Wass had written that the UK had 'come very close to overdoing the targetry business'.[11] The critical point, as Healey spelled out in his cabinet paper, was not the targets in themselves but rather the fact that the markets had become obsessed with them:

There is no doubt that unless we take decisive action to improve our balance of payments and to get the monetary expansion under firm control, we shall not raise the funds we need to maintain stability at home and abroad. We need in this context to keep the role of the IMF in perspective. Quantitatively it is not as important as the market itself. But it is the bellwether. If the Fund accepts that our policies are credible, the market is virtually certain to follow suit, and the amounts potentially available to us are large. Per contra, if we fail to reach agreement with the Fund, we are unlikely to be able to raise funds on any significant scale in the market.[12]

Looking back on the development of the crisis since July, Healey had convinced himself that a crucial mistake in the presentation of the July measures was that he had not stated a specific money supply target, though he had said 'For the financial year as a whole money supply [growth] should amount to about 12 percent.' But he now believed that the markets wanted to hear a very specific message on the money supply.[13] In fact, the monetary targeting was less central to the Fund negotiators than other parts of the package, in particular the fiscal cuts (which Healey tried to resist and then weaken), but also the exchange rate. The Fund argued that a competitive exchange rate would increase the profitability of exports on a scale that was 'unprecedented in the post-war world'.[14] An IMF note read:

As regards tactics, we want to know the range within which policy now seeks to operate, and we most decidedly want an upper limit – I think that $1.65 is as high as is acceptable. We accept that the theoretical idea of a steady downward path may present difficulties – though the operators have not always spoken with one voice on this subject. Nevertheless, we want to be assured that the seductive appeal of exchange-rate stability will not be allowed to keep the rate on a plateau for any length of time.[15]

When a newspaper reported that the IMF thought $1.50 would really be needed to launch recovery, the markets became even more jittery.

In addition, on 25 October, Callaghan in an interview on television for the *Panorama* current affairs programme called for the elimination of sterling balances, the substantial official claims on sterling held mostly by Commonwealth countries:

I would love to get rid of the reserve currency. I am not sure that everybody in the Treasury would or maybe in the Bank. [...] From the Bank's point of view I see no particular advantage of being a reserve currency at all. [...] I would very much like to see us get into a situation where these liabilities of ours which we have as a reserve currency were taken over in some form or other. Whether that can be achieved of course isn't only for me. [...] If the IMF were to try to force us into policies which would be harmful to the economy, that we would go into a downward spiral, then we would have to say to some of those other countries 'Look, the IMF and you yourselves must accept the political consequences of what you are doing.'[16]

At the beginning of 1977 the UK agreed a $3 bn G-10 facility for the orderly winding down and repayment of sterling balances. Forrest Capie correctly states that the sterling balances issue was logically not connected with the balance-of-payments problems and the IMF support,[17] but a large set of claims on sterling obviously constituted a potential danger to orderly exchange rates.

In the course of 1977 and 1978 there was a substantial recovery of sterling, especially when measured against the dollar: the US currency had its own version of the British crisis, and indeed the United States drew on IMF resources (though without a programme) for the first time in the IMF's history. The pound had bounced back to $1.70 by the beginning of 1977, before the IMF programme was formally concluded, and then remained stable for some months. In the second half of the year it soared until it was close to $2 at the beginning of 1978. There was also a massive accumulation of foreign exchange reserves in the second half of 1977.

The IMF resources were needed to plug a gap in the UK balance of payments in 1976 (an alternative might have been an equilibrium at a much lower exchange rate), but a subsequent confidence-building dynamic then seemed to make it less needed. As was often intended in IMF programmes, there was a catalytic effect, and the catalyser quickly appeared redundant. Healey misinterpreted that development to argue that the whole fiasco had been a consequence of misinformation: 'we could have done without the IMF loan only if we – and the world – had known the real facts at the time. But in 1976 our forecasts were far too pessimistic, and we were still describing our public expenditure in a way which was immensely damaging to our standing in the financial markets.'[18] Wass took a similar line and concluded: 'the actual Fund drawing was superfluous and indeed the Treasury's anxiety during the negotiations about the adequacy of the initial drawing proved to have been groundless'.[19]

The more accurate lesson was that some framework was needed to reassure and convince markets. But a monetary targeting regime appeared hard to implement because most economists were unsympathetic and the practical management of such a scheme would require a radical overhaul of the position of banks in the British financial economy. A more immediate lesson was that exchange rate management was not working well. A rethinking might involve the end of exchange controls. The exchange rate continued, however, to play a prominent role in thinking about policy-making, up to 1997, and possibly even beyond that new caesura.

The immediate response to 1976 was a sense of failure, 'Goodbye Great Britain', as the title of an influential *Wall Street Journal* article of 29 April 1975 had it.[20] But, in fact, the outcome was 'Goodbye, bad policy' and 'Goodbye, bad economics'. But not at once.

THE ABOLITION OF EXCHANGE CONTROL

A central part of the pre-1979 influence and effective power of the Bank of England rested on the fact that the British domestic financial market was self-contained or cut off from the rest of the world, through the use of capital and exchange controls, applied to UK residents (corporations and individuals) but not to international holders of sterling. The consequence was that the Bank had a much greater leeway in setting interest rates, in that British-domiciled money could not flee to other jurisdictions. Exchange control shut off one way in which banks could expand their activities in the face of the application of administrative measures to control domestic lending. In particular, after 1971, restrictions on bank credit were lifted (Competition and Credit Control), leading to an explosion of bank lending and an inflationary development, and the authorities reacted by imposing quantitative restrictions on banks' balance sheets (the 'corset'). Those limits were applied from December 1973 to February 1975, from November 1976 to August 1977, and from June 1978 to June 1980.[21] The last year of that experience showed how exchange control was fundamentally at the core of a whole system of monetary control and management, because it shut off ways in which commercial banks might expand their liabilities or their off-balance-sheet activities despite the corset restraint.[22] Once exchange control was lifted, the corset became ineffective as a limit of bank action.

But exchange control relied on a large and unwieldy administration that was inherited from a quite different era. A large part of the work of the pre-1979 Bank consisted in the operation and application of the exchange controls, set out in a complex code of 'Regulations', and that work appeared ineffective and redundant. The development of London as an offshore financial centre since the 1960s (though there had been some anticipatory developments in the decade before) meant that there was in London a powerful source of credit and lending but not in the British currency.[23]

The original drafting of the Regulations on exchange control had occurred in the months preceding the Second World War. The only precedent that the Bank had was the strict system of controls applied in Nazi Germany and associated with the controversial central bank president and economics minister Hjalmar Schacht. But control survived the War, and a substantial part of the Regulations was incorporated almost word for word in the Exchange Control Act passed in 1947. Enforcement was much more of a problem in peacetime as normal commercial transactions resumed. The absence of effective penalties clearly encouraged large-scale evasion of the control system, and the development of offshore financing made direct evasion unnecessary for those borrowers and lenders who were not UK residents.

There were only a very few detectives in charge of enforcement. In August 1947, three detectives were seconded to the Treasury to work on exchange control, headed by a Chief Inspector Tarr, but, except for a few trips right at the outset to some attractive European destinations, to Paris and the French Riviera, they usually did not go out into the field for investigations. The enforcers relied on a flow of information from the Bank of England, Customs and Excise, the banks, as well as casual informers. The number of enforcement officers reached a peak in 1951, when there were nine. After that the numbers declined, and it was difficult to prosecute even obvious cases. By 1952, there had been 300 investigations with 9 prosecution and 37 official warnings. Where the officers acted, it was because they were forced into action by public opinion. The most high-profile case was that of Sir Bernard Docker, Chairman of Birmingham Small Arms (BSA) and of the Daimler Company, and his wife. The Dockers had attracted a lot of publicity. Docker was a glorified version of the post-war 'spiv', and his wife, a former showgirl known as 'Naughty Norah', liked driving in the couple's five Daimlers (one of which was gold-plated) and life in general on the French Riviera (she was later banned from Monaco by Prince Rainier). Newspaper gossip columns were filled with accounts of their high life, their yacht and their dispute with the Casino at Monte Carlo. All this was at a time when the annual travel allowance was £100, later reduced to £25, and there was inevitably much speculation on how this style of living was financed. The exchange control case against the couple was concluded after a three-day hearing in Bow Street Magistrates' Court with a £50 fine. That made the process of control look quite ridiculous.

There was an upswing of activity of monitoring in the 1970s, as international capital movements resumed and as governments tried to restrict them, but enforcement remained chronically understaffed. The high premium on investment currency had led to illegal transactions on an unprecedented scale, and the extension of exchange control to the Sterling Area had added considerably to the number of minor cases. There was a backlog of cases. By the end of 1976, two more officers had been recruited, bringing the total strength to seven, at which it remained until 1978 when one officer died and two retired. There were additional problems in that in 1976 a member of the Bank of England's staff was accused, and eventually convicted, of involvement in a conspiracy of stripping the dollar investment premium from sales of foreign securities: the case was promptly exposed by the satirical magazine *Private Eye*.[24] By 1979, some 750 employees of the Bank were working on exchange control (an increase from 490 in

1970), but there remained an enormous disproportion between the numbers working in administration and enforcement.[25]

In 1976, as part of the IMF rescue package, exchange controls had been tightened, with a prohibition on the use of sterling in trade financing that did not involve the UK. As adjustment in the framework of an IMF programme proceeded, the discussion changed radically. The major pressure for relaxation initially came from the banks, with the Bank of England initially sceptical but coming round later to advocating decontrol. By the end of the 1970s, a major argument in favour of decontrol concerned the impact of the increasing flow of North Sea oil on the balance of payments. In large part, there was a hope that the end of controls would stop the inflow of funds and the exchange rate appreciation that was hurting British manufacturers. The clearing banks in particular also pressed for a bonfire of exchange controls, on quite different grounds, as they wanted to extend their business and emphasized 'the urgent need for a return to the situation where London can do international business in its own internationally acceptable currency'.[26]

The new Conservative government started with a partial decontrol in July 1979, when restrictions on direct overseas investments were removed, and portfolio investment also became easier. This step created an uneasy halfway house, and pressure from the Treasury and the Bank to implement further changes mounted. The decisive meeting was held on 17 October, with rather short notice given to the Prime Minister, who was not enthusiastic about the proposal, even though it fitted with her view of the importance of markets; but the Chancellor, Geoffrey Howe, and the Governor of the Bank were now strongly in favour of relaxation.[27] The Bank itself now regarded the abolition of exchange control as long overdue. The main argument as set out by the Bank's Head of Exchange Control was that 'If our experience of the last forty years has taught us anything, it is that exchange restrictions do not cure problems. It has also shown that restrictive systems usually have a bias towards becoming more restrictive.'[28] That was a radical change from even 1977, when Kit McMahon had noted that

there remain weaknesses in the UK balance of payments and many uncertainties about our domestic prospects, especially in regard to inflation. The hard-won improvement in confidence could prove fragile; there is a huge overhang of debt to be paid off; and there are grave uncertainties about the long-term viability of the UK's non-oil external balance. Moreover, the UK is publicly committed to a further running down of one aspect of sterling's international role as part of the Basle arrangements.[29]

A remarkable feature of the final discussions on exchange control is that the effects on domestic monetary policy of terminating exchange control were barely considered. Dow commented that 'although they could plead preoccupation with base money, their long unawareness was hardly excusable'.[30]

Exchange controls were completely scrapped in October 1979 (except with respect to the special controls involved in relations with Rhodesia, where the white settlers had in 1965 pushed through a unilateral declaration of independence that had been met with the imposition of economic sanctions). The word used at the time was 'lifted', implying that the government retained the power to reimpose them, but the response to the end of exchange controls made a reimposition look increasingly implausible. Announcing the change, Howe stated that 'they have outlived their usefulness. The essential condition for maintaining confidence in our currency is a government determined to maintain the right monetary and fiscal policies. That we shall do.'[31]

The Bank responded with a widespread voluntary severance scheme for its employees. It documented the story of exchange control and enforcement, in case controls would ever come back. But fundamentally, the Bank now believed: 'never again, and particularly so should it relate to portfolio securities. This may be a correct reaction. The massive, costly and time consuming, bureaucratic machinery built up both here and at A.Ds [Authorized Depositories, i.e. banks] needs questioning as to what it achieved.'[32]

The end of exchange control deeply affected monetary management. In 1973, the Bank had tried to deal with rapid monetary growth by imposing a supplementary special deposit scheme (SSDS) on banks if their interest-bearing eligible liabilities (IBEL) grew too quickly: they were then required to deposit a proportion of their deposits interest free at the Bank of England. This control scheme, soon known as the 'corset', could easily be circumvented. Borrowers could issue commercial bills instead of taking bank loans, and sophisticated depositors would hold bills rather than bank deposits. After the end of exchange control in October 1979, circumvention was even easier, as all that needed to occur was for borrowers to take euro sterling loans and depositors to maintain euro sterling deposits. A bon mot attributed to the journalist Anthony Harris suggested that 'a corset is a device for producing deceptive figures'.[33] Thus, in practice the end of exchange control meant the end of an attempt to control banks' expansion by administrative measures. By the middle of 1980, the controls were abandoned. In the future, only the interest rate and government debt sales and purchases could be used as policy tools, and thus the debate switched to one over the appropriate form of monetary management.

The possibility of exchange controls remained as a policy option, if the fundamental political situation were to shift. At one moment, Margaret Thatcher contemplated controls on inflows as an answer to policy perplexity. In 1983, the Bank prepared contingency plans in case of a Labour election victory, which would probably lead to large sterling outflows, with a new Labour government likely to respond with exchange controls. The Bank drew up an emergency plan, to which it did not want to give an official codename (that would have needed to be approved by the Ministry of Defence) but instead simply called the plan 'CE'.[34] As long as a Conservative government stayed in power, however, and short of a dramatic and unexpected crisis, there was no going back, and the Bank did not want that either.

3

The Performance of the UK Economy

How far did the policy caesura of the later 1970s change the UK's economic fortunes? The central bank is not just part of an economic executive: it is expected to produce results that are generally beneficial to the people to whom (through parliament) it is accountable. That expectation raises a new and broader issue: What is the role of a central bank in the making of economic policy in the broadest sense? In what ways can monetary policy contribute to economic success or growth? Over the period covered in this volume, the belief that monetary policy was a tool in fighting short-run economic problems (low output or high unemployment) gave way to thinking about monetary stability as providing a framework within which better-informed judgements about long-run decisions could be made. There was a growing recognition that short-term monetary stimulus, often driven by political and electoral concerns (so that there seemed to be a 'political cycle'), was damaging rather than beneficial to overall welfare. For the new policy approach, the key to long-term success was to establish a greater sense of predictability that would be impossible in a world of high and volatile inflation. Monetary stability was crucial in establishing a fundamental security for the functioning of markets.

Even after the erosion of the view that monetary policy might fundamentally and in the long term determine the output level, it remained and remains common to think that an important role for monetary policy lay in avoiding major economic fluctuations. The economist and member of the Bank of England Monetary Policy Committee Andrew Sentance begins a survey of macro-economic policy by stating as a given that: 'It is clearly beneficial to long-term economic performance to reduce fluctuations in output and employment – increasing the predictability of the business climate and avoiding the destruction of human and physical capital that occurs in prolonged downturns.' But he then acknowledges the difficulty of 'fine-tuning' to ensure a 'steady growth path'.[1] The Governor of the Bank of England from 1983 to 1993, Robin Leigh-Pemberton, spoke of the temptation 'for governments to intervene much more in economic policy in the name primarily I think of establishing full employment. This was a perfectly legitimate aim but it may show up considerable difficulties in the side effects it has had on the rest of the economy.'[2] This was also the verdict of Christopher Dow, the Bank of England chief economist, who was deeply unsympathetic to the Thatcher revolution. Both before and after his work in the Bank, he argued that 'budgetary and monetary policy failed to be stabilizing, and must on the contrary be regarded as having been positively destabilizing'.[3]

There may be circumstances in which there are so many distortions that a galvanizing shock may be needed. A response to an accumulation of previous failures, with poor growth outcomes as well as poor inflation performance, cannot simply be accommodated within a general framework of 'stability'. The Thatcher government wanted to reverse economic decline, placing an emphasis on supply-side approaches, with privatization and deregulation, and the limitation of trade union power. A key part was to be played by tax reform and limits on the growth of public spending. Existing very high marginal rates of income tax, which had been a major disincentive to growth, were cut. Increases in VAT compensated for the reductions of income tax, bringing about what amounts to a 'fiscal devaluation', whereby imports become more expensive, although the exchange rate is held constant.[4] The public sector was pruned back, with the aim of preventing public-sector activity crowding out private investment. Controlling government spending also meant limiting subsidies, which had produced substantial distortions to economic incentives. The role of the trade unions was scaled back. There was a substantial amount of financial deregulation, notably 'Big Bang' on the stock exchange, which ended restrictive practices and which made London much more attractive to foreign financial institutions. Institutionally, both in financial markets and in labour relations, the UK began to look more like the US. There was a paradox, in that many of these goals involved radical shocks to expectations that went against the theory that what was needed was a stable framework of expectations.

A key part of the revolution lay in the opening up of the British economy to competition. There had been financial competition, after the 1971 move to Competition and Credit Control, and after 1979 there would be more; but there was also external trade competition. In the 1960s, the level of trade protection was at the same level as that of the highly protectionist 1930s. The average effective rate of protection, which had already fallen to 4.7 per cent in 1979 (from 9.3 per cent in 1968), went down further to 1.2 per cent in 1986. A major part of the dramatic reduction in British trade costs occurred in the 1970s, in other words before the Thatcher government.[5] Some recent economic analysis indeed has identified the UK's accession to the European Economic Community in 1973, rather than the policy changes of the late 1970s, as the key structural break that set the country on a better growth trajectory.[6] The distinction between British association with Europe and the drive to improve competitiveness may be artificial, in that both are part of a policy response to economic stagnation and failure and of an effort to use competition as a driver of reform. In 1986, the Single European Act, which was given a decisive liberalization twist by Thatcher and the European Commissioner she had appointed in 1984, Lord Cockfield, spurred a further opening of the UK economy. By this time, the discussion of where the UK might specialize had shifted away from the previously protected manufacturing base. An area where the UK had particular advantages was in services, notably in financial services, which grew as the City, freed of exchange control and other restrictive regulations, developed a new dynamism. A competition-based view of a dynamic society was passed on to Thatcher's successors, John Major and the Labour Prime Ministers Tony Blair and Gordon Brown, who can be seen as 'Thatcher's children'.[7]

Compared to the comparatively very weak performance of the 1970s – in terms of output but also in inflation – the 1980s and particularly the 1990s were much more successful years for the UK (see Figure 3.1). According to an often-quoted dictum of Paul Krugman, 'Productivity isn't everything, but in the long run it is almost everything. A country's ability to improve its standard of living over time depends almost entirely on its ability to raise its output per worker.'[8]

Productivity increased significantly (see Table 3.1). But the performance was scarred by two very severe recessions, beginning in 1980 Q1 and 1990 Q3, where the collapse of economic activity was much more severe than in continental Europe (though in the second recession, Germany faced its own quite peculiar collapse in the aftermath of the 1990 unification of West and East Germany). The output loss in 1980–1981, 4.6 per cent, was also worse than that in the aftermath of the oil price shock of 1973 (see Table 3.2).

The two recessions were traumatic, but considerably less severe than either the extreme events of the interwar Great Depression or the

Table 3.1 *Productivity growth compared*

	United Kingdom	European Median	West Germany
1960–1973			
GDP/head	2.6	3.6	3.4
TFP in business sector	2.3	3.0	2.5
Manufacturing labour productivity	5.0	–	6.1
1973–1979			
GDP/head	1.5	2.0	2.5
TFP in business sector	0.6	1.4	1.8
Manufacturing labour productivity	0.7	–	3.4
1979–1989			
GDP/head	2.1	1.9	1.7
TFP in business sector	1.5	1.2	0.8
Manufacturing labour productivity	4.2	–	2.3

Source: Crafts 1996, p. 174.

recession associated with twenty-first-century Global Financial Crisis (see Figure 3.2). The two late twentieth-century downturns also had quite different origins. The early 1980s collapse in large part was the intentional result of a radical change in macro-economic strategy; the second was a product of the aftermath of a loose money period with excessive credit growth and then a collapse of a housing bubble. Both occurred in a wider international economic setting: in the early 1980s, in the wake of the second oil price shock and of the 1979 anti-inflationary turn in US monetary policy; in the early 1990s, the responses to the fiscal and monetary shock of German unification, a US slowdown, and a new oil price spike after the First Gulf War. But in both cases, the UK output performance was significantly poorer than that of other major industrial countries.

The Thatcher period after the 1980 recession was sometimes interpreted as a new phase of dynamism, with higher rates of productivity growth. Bean and Symons, for instance, reported an annual productivity growth rate of 2.2 per cent for the Thatcher government's first nine years in office.[9] While labour productivity growth was substantially poorer than that in other west European economies in the 1970s, in the 1980s the UK looked

Table 3.2 *UK GDP in previous recessions*[a]

Date recession began	Output loss (per cent of GDP)	Number of quarters of falling output	Number of quarters to recover output drop[b]
1973 Q3	−3.3	6	14
1980 Q1	−4.6	5	13
1990 Q3	−2.5	5	13

[a] For the purposes of this box, recessions are defined as two consecutive quarters of falling output (at constant market prices) estimated using the latest data. The recessions are assumed to end once output began to rise, apart from the 1970s when two separate occasions of falling output are treated as a single recession.

[b] Number of quarters from the start of the recession until output regained its pre-recession level.

Bank of England Inflation Report, February 2009, p. 20.

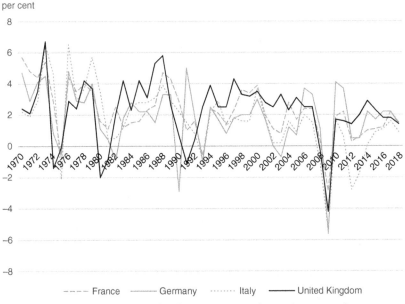

Figure 3.1 Growth of real GDP, per cent change (1970–2018)

better in an international comparison – a strength that continued until the late 2000s (see Figures 3.3 and 3.4). Even noted sceptics about monetarism such as Permanent Secretary Sir Douglas Wass were impressed. He told

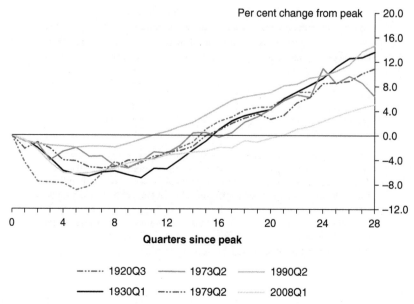

Figure 3.2 GDP behaviour during major twentieth-century recessions
From *BEQB* 2010, 4, p. 279, updated: the dates marked are output peaks

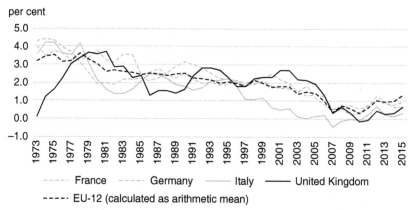

Figure 3.3 Growth of labour productivity per person employed (per cent change)
Conference Board data

The Times as he retired from the Treasury in 1983: 'What has emerged in
shop-floor behaviour through fear and anxiety is much greater than I think
could have been done by more co-operative methods. That is a surprise to

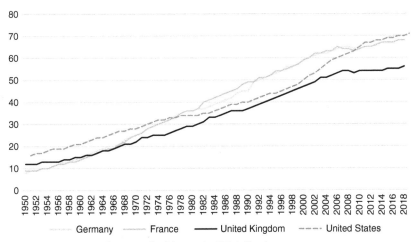

Figure 3.4 GDP per hour worked (2015, in US dollars)
Source: Conference Board, Total Economy Database

me. There is a potential for productivity growth on a scale we have not had in this country.'[10]

There was a particularly dramatic improvement of productivity in manufacturing, but that in part is a product of the severe contraction of manufacturing employment. It is appropriate to think of the experience of the early 1980s as a shaking-out process (see Figure 3.5). A severe recession might lead viable companies to be able to lay off their least productive workers, so that productivity would increase when demand recovered. Secondly, the recession put pressure on trade unions, and helped in particular to end the particularly powerful British culture of multi-union industries and companies, in which unions competed with each other to ratchet up demands and settlements. Thirdly, the economic downturn would cause poorly managed companies to fail, so that there would be a shake out of firms as well as of employees. Some of the loss of skills involved in that process might be avoided if management could be changed – and thus, fourthly, the recession might be a catalyst for a rethinking of the role of management. The end of what Nick Crafts termed the 'trade union veto' on policy took a long time to affect the trade-off between inflation and employment;[11] it was only very slowly that the natural rate of unemployment fell from its very high levels of the early 1980s. From the mid-1970s, it became common to analyse the non-accelerating inflation rate of

Table 3.3 *NAIRU (per cent)*

1969–1973	3.8
1974–1981	7.5
1981–1986	9.5
1986–1990	9.6
1991–1997	8.9
1997–2000	5.7

Stephen J. Nickell and Glenda Quintini, 'The Recent Performance of the UK Labour Market', *Oxford Review of Economic Policy*, 18, (2002), 202–220.

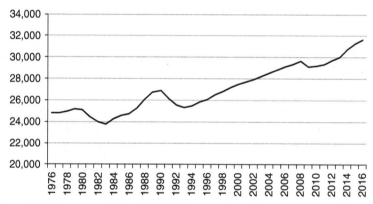

Figure 3.5 UK persons employed (in 000s)
From: Conference Board

unemployment or NAIRU: contemporary calculations show a long high plateau of this rate through the 1980s (see Table 3.3).

Crafts concludes his definitive account of the policy caesura of the Thatcher era: 'The policy reforms of the 1980s, while imperfect and leading to disturbing outcomes in other respects, probably raised rather than lowered the long run growth potential of both the economy overall and manufacturing compared with a counterfactual of trying to continue with the (ultimately unsustainable) policies of the 1970s.'[12] The macro-economic consequences of Thatcherism were undoubtedly damaging, in regard to the two episodes of sustained recession; but the micro-economic consequences were beneficial. Was the latter 'good' result possible without the former 'bad' one? The experience of both the big recessions leads to an uncomfortable conclusion that in some circumstances, shocks – or 'disturbing outcomes' – are an inevitable preliminary to an adjustment of both policy and expectations that makes for a new long-term dynamism.

If that is the case, the position of a central bank in the middle of the shock period is necessarily ambivalent. It is not possible to know what will come, or to be certain that the result of a shock will be a new dynamism. There is as a consequence plenty of room for policy debate. In 1988, Stanley Fischer, the MIT economist who trained a new generation of central bankers, argued: 'There is greater not less confusion at the business end of macro-economics, in understanding the actual causes of macro-economic fluctuations, and in applying macro-economics to policy-making.'[13] One of the outcomes was a profound uncertainty about the potential growth path of the economy; conventional central bankers often assessed growth too pessimistically, whereas mavericks such as the Conservative Chancellor Kenneth Clarke – or the great US central banker Alan Greenspan – did better.[14] The clash on this issue between Clarke and the Bank will be examined below (pp. 363–375). Another consequential uncertainty lay in the management of recessions. Maybe it would be better to allow more room for adjustment, so that the cost of the recession might not be as high. But alternatively, for a central bank that had a rather broad conception of its role, it could use its position as a banking authority in parallel with efforts to stimulate and enforce a British managerial revolution. That is precisely how some figures in the Bank of England in the 1980s came to see their role in reviving British industrial capacity (see Chapter 9). In the aftermath of the 2008 crisis, and particularly after 2013, the Bank refocused again and began to use big data to work on the solution to micro-economic rather than macro-adjustment issues.[15] This new course picked up elements of a much older concern with how economic performance might be improved.

One way of judging the overall performance of monetary policy is to think about the extent of uncertainty. The direction of causation between uncertainty and economic performance is obviously complex.[16] Bad performance and recessions increase the extent of uncertainty, and good performance makes for a more certain environment. But certainty also facilitates longer-term investment decisions and might be expected to increase growth rates. A recent study by Bank of England economists uses a variety of measures to assess economic uncertainty since the mid-

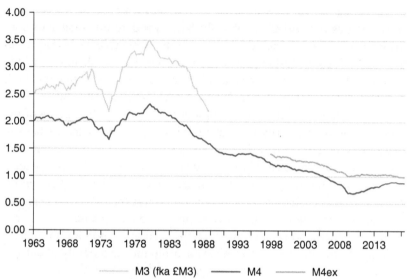

Figure 3.6 Aggregate uncertainty measure (1974–2015)
From: Haddow, Hare, Hooley, Shakir, 2013, extended back by Ryland Thomas

1970s (see Figure 3.6).[17] It is closely correlated to economic performance, but there are four eras that are quite striking in terms of enhanced certainty. The first occurred in the aftermath of the 1976 IMF programme; the second is the period from the mid-1980s to 1988, when policy was driven by the exchange rate considerations; the third followed Black Wednesday, 16 September 1992, when a new monetary policy environment (with inflation targeting) improved performance; and finally again after 2003. The early 2000s saw in particular a dramatic reduction in global uncertainty in the wake of the Iraq war. But it is hard to read the results as solely the result of policy formulation. The general pattern appeared in other countries, too, with different politics and institutional arrangements for setting policy. In that sense the policy improvement is hard to differentiate from an international convergence, which we might well think of as produced by globalization.

4

The Inexplicable in Pursuit of the Uncontrollable

Monetary Strategy

Monetarism was at the core of the ideological and policy wars of the 1980s. Margaret Thatcher's government made it the centrepiece of macro-economic policy, with the 1979 Queen's speech announcing: 'My Government will give priority in economic policy to controlling inflation through the pursuit of firm monetary and fiscal policies.'[1] The crucial third paragraph of the key policy document of the Thatcher era, the Medium-Term Financial Strategy (MTFS) of 1980, stated: 'Control of the money supply will over a period of years reduce the rate of inflation.'[2] Nigel Lawson, the chief intellectual architect of the MTFS, told a television interviewer in 1980: 'I just happen to believe, and the government believes, that the monetarist policy is the right one and it's the only one which will bring inflation down.'[3] There was no doubt about the depth of the policy commitment, but the analytical framework was always controversial.

The British policy-making community could not agree whether money should be an overall *objective* of policy, or simply a *target* for an indicator that might be a temporary expression of how far the objective was being met, or an *instrument* for the conduct of policy in pursuit of the target. The government – and especially the key shaper of its approach to monetary policy, Nigel Lawson, a former financial journalist who had been appointed as Financial Secretary at the Treasury – began by envisaging the use of the monetary base (which it could control) as an instrument. The Bank was sceptical about quantity instruments, and its senior officials were divided as to whether a broad money measure should be a target or simply one of many indicators of economic performance.

Monetarism as monetary targeting had several origins, all of them foreign (unless the genealogy is traced back to Henry Thornton's writing at the time of Napoleon). That characteristic in itself seemed largely to discredit the doctrine in the eyes of the British establishment. In July 1979,

Sir Douglas Wass, then Permanent Secretary of the Treasury, wrote a memorandum warning of a backlash against policies which were 'relatively strange to a British audience'.[4] There was in the UK always a reluctance to see ways in which the doctrine could practically be implemented, and some academic and practical monetarists then complained that their theories had never really been tested. The period of 'high monetarism'[5] did not last that long – just 1979–1980 – and was accompanied by intense policy clashes; after that a rather eclectic process of policy determination began.

Strictly speaking, monetarism refers to the policy of using a measure of a monetary aggregate in order to generate a policy response with the aim of controlling price developments so as to reduce or eliminate inflation. In practice, however, the concept was often used in a restricted – and in reality perhaps often even contradictory – manner, as relating to a restrictive approach to *fiscal* policy. In the first and general sense, monetary control looked like a profound shock to the central worldview of what the Bank of England's John Fforde liked to describe as Britain's 'macro-economic executive', because there was no obvious mechanism to force an aggregate on a system which worked by responding to banks' demands for funds; but also because after the failure of the prices and wages policies of the 1970s, the authorities began to see price behaviour as driven by a complex social process with which they did not want to tamper. But in the second narrowly fiscal sense, it could be accommodated within a sort of commonsense view that was really deeply entrenched in the Treasury mindset – though it would then decidedly not provide a substantive foundation for making monetary policy. The doctrine also appealed to a government that was averse to using an explicit interest rate policy because of political concerns about the effects of high interest rates on mortgage payments in a country with a high level of homeownership.

RESPONDING TO INFLATION

Monetarism was a response to failure: both to the political flaws of a policy process and to the theoretical flaws of an explanatory mechanism. The central and correct insight of monetarism was that the inflation of the 1960s and 1970s was driven by demand, and that there was over the long run a clear link between the growth of money and the development of prices, and no clear association between higher output and higher levels of monetary growth. But a great deal of discussion centred on the short-term relationship between monetary growth, inflation and output.

One 1960s policy insight postulated a trade-off between inflation and unemployment, which could be plotted in the famous Phillips curve first presented in a 1958 paper. The choice about the trade-off then became the basis of policy responses, in that increased inflation would bring higher growth and higher employment. Inflation looked like an easy and indeed desirable way of buying social stability.[6] The new monetarist doctrines were a response to a fundamental and persuasive empirical observation that undercut the basis of what had been the policy consensus of the 1960s. Relatively quickly, it became clear that while the Phillips relationship held for the short term, when there might indeed be a temporary capacity to boost growth and reduce unemployment, in the medium or long run the curve took a different shape: in fact, it was vertical, with no relationship between higher inflation and reduced unemployment. In the 1990s, a report of a panel headed by the economist Eric Roll concluded that even the short-term relationship, over a three- to five-year business cycle, was 'far from proven'. The extent and duration of the trade-off was, Roll's experts concluded, 'a matter of long-standing dispute, not resolved after 40 years of active debate and statistical excavation'.[7] And more extended experience with inflation gave a new empirical result, that the short-term relationship was not so much between inflation and unemployment, but between the change in the rate of inflation and unemployment – in short, a second-order rather than a first-order relationship, so that attacking unemployment with monetary tools would require constant increases in inflation. What mattered for economic behaviour was the extent to which inflation was unanticipated: thus, even the second-order relationship was unsteady. It was also unclear what duration was implied by short-term gains in employment and output: One or three or more years? The consequence was that it no longer made sense to think of inflation as an instrument for soothing social pain, and it was much easier to set a goal for monetary policy as reducing inflation to a low level, in short to target price stability. The academic formulation that discussed an inflation–unemployment trade-off was present in UK debates, but policymakers professed to dislike it.[8]

The confusion arose as to how precisely a reduction in monetary growth could bring down inflation. Monetary policy would need to target some intermediate nominal variable which then affected price behaviour. By the end of the twentieth century, a new consensus held that the key policy instrument lay in the short-term interest rate, and that it might be directly controlled by a central bank. But in the 1960s and 1970s there were still many other levers that could be used to determine monetary developments, including exchange rates and attempts to control the quantity of bank lending, and it was not clear what might be the appropriate nominal variable.

The economic consensus of the 1960s and 1970s, including most senior officials at the Bank of England, explained inflation as a phenomenon driven by wage and other cost increases (the cost-push view). The most appropriate way to tackle it was through measures that led to voluntary or imposed constraint. Neither Conservative nor Labour policy-makers and their major economic advisers believed that any monetary mechanism generated inflation, and they had not believed that there was a short-term trade-off in the Phillips curve between inflation and unemployment.[9] The influential economist Roy Harrod even believed that stronger demand growth might reduce inflation.[10] Edward Heath in consequence thought that his government could boost demand without inflationary consequences. The Labour party adviser Thomas Balogh saw a 'completely new situation' in which 'prices and wages chase each other at widely different levels of employment. In the absence of deliberate policy and deliberate agreement, which is likely only through government intervention, there is no determinate solution.'[11]

In 1972, as inflation surged, the Conservative government of Edward Heath made a U-turn from its election manifesto rejection of 'the philosophy of compulsory wage control'.[12] Following the model of Richard Nixon, it now laid down a statutory prices and incomes policy, with an initial ninety-day wage freeze. In Stage Two, pay rises were limited to £1 a week plus 4 per cent, and then Stage Three, unveiled in October 1973, limited pay rises to £2.25 or 7 per cent per week, up to a maximum of £350 per year. The greater scope for flexibility, and a provision for extra payments for 'unsocial hours', and then a strike of coal miners, led to the disintegration of the policy. The Heath government fell after an election in February 1974 that the prime minister had proclaimed to be about 'who governs' the UK. After a short interlude, in which prices and wages surged, the new Labour government adopted its own version of prices and incomes policies, namely a 'social contract' with the trade unions which replaced statutory regulation with cooperation. The historian Peter Clarke rightly terms the concept 'vacuous', although the initiative may have been destroyed by the international surge in inflation driven by oil prices rather than by purely domestic calculations.[13] In practice, pay guidelines were enforced by the use of price controls, where increases were forbidden to companies that exceeded the pay norm. In the initial approach, in July 1975, increases were set at £6 a week, with no increases for those earning over £8500 annually; in the next round, in 1976, pay rises of £2.50–£4 were allowed, with a maximum of 4 per cent; the third phase allowed 10 per cent rises; and a fourth stage, in 1978, a maximum of 5 per cent.[14] As with the Heath approach, the later phases of the policy broke down, in the 'winter of discontent' of 1978–1979, with widespread strikes and public-sector settlements substantially above the guidelines. Both the Conservative and Labour governments had been destroyed by incomes policies: the humiliating attempt to enforce guidelines that were ignored brought the process of government in general into disrespect. Government arbitration had to reflect on how the claims of miners, or policemen, or nurses, or teachers compared with each other, and which groups should be allowed a special consideration. The process also encouraged trade unions and other interest organizations to assert the claims of their particular stakeholders. It was inevitable not only to think that there should be a better way of dealing with inflation, but also whether the explanatory mechanism might be flawed.

In the 1970s, the Bank of England was largely sceptical about the use of interest rates as an indication of policy stance, in part as a consequence of experience with high rates of inflation that distorted market signals to such an extent that expectations were in constant flux and it was thus impossible to work out what the real interest rate was that in turn guided financial behaviour. Governor Gordon Richardson stated this doctrine very clearly and completely coherently in his Mais lecture, delivered on 9 February 1978, at the City University, which was at the heart of monetarist theory in the UK. But as will become clear below, the Bank did not really know how to translate the new thinking into an operational strategy. Richardson first explained the desirability of a monetary target:

What swung the argument in favour of choosing a quantity rather than a price as the best indicator of the thrust of monetary policy was the acceleration of inflation. Since 1970, not only have prices risen much faster than in the 1950s and 1960s but the rate of inflation has varied considerably from year to year. With increased inflationary expectations, interest rates also have risen greatly. We can, if we like, think of the nominal interest rate as having an 'expected inflation' component and a 'real' interest element. But we can never observe expectations, which are in any case likely both to differ from person to person, and to be volatile. The real rate of interest is an abstract construct. This has made it very difficult to frame the objectives of policy in terms of nominal interest rates.

It is essential for this purpose that monetary targets should be publicly announced, and that the authorities' resolve be sufficient to make that announcement credible. Our acts have, I believe, given observers cause to regard our resolve as strong. This in itself has dampened fears of worsening inflation and provided an appropriate backdrop against which we can continue the struggle to bring inflation steadily down. I would not claim that monetary policy can or should be left to fight inflation singlehanded – I shall turn to this subject again later. But monetary targets have an important place in the relevant armoury.

Monetary targets represent a self-imposed constraint or discipline on the authorities. This can at times seem irksome, the more so perhaps because the permissible thresholds cannot be precisely and scientifically set, involving a considerable element of judgement. Yet the layman's apparently intuitive perception of the broad relationship between monetary growth and inflation – clearer perhaps to him than to the professional who knows all the necessary qualifications – may well make it easier to explain and justify measures necessary to achieve the goal of stability but with immediately unpopular effects. We need a basis of public support and understanding of the limits to prudent action. Furthermore, quantitative monetary targets can provide a useful trigger for more expeditious policy decisions.[15]

The Bank's chief economist at the time, Christopher Dow, noted, 'I was simply impatient with the Bank, as was the Governor, for never having any clear intention regarding its monetary policy: any intention there was shrouded in cautionary phrases and faded as the situation changed.' Dow, whose own prose was replete with what his friends called 'Dowisms', or obfuscations, complained that Richardson's Mais lecture was 'full of vague but suggestive phrases'.[16] Richardson, a lawyer who had become a partner and then chairman of the merchant bank Schroders, was a man of substantial charm, even charisma, and a confident and aristocratic manner. He had substantial political skills, had an excellent relationship with the Labour Chancellor of the Exchequer Denis Healey, and then also managed adroitly to talk with leading Conservatives in the run up to the May 1979 general election. Under both the Labour and Conservative administrations, he was admired in the Bank as skilfully protecting it against political intrusions. But the price was a fuzziness in the Bank's stance. As Dow put it, echoing Evelyn Waugh's celebrated denunciation of charm as 'the great English blight': 'One can grow very tired of charm.'[17] One of Richardson's closest collaborators, who had come with him from Schroders, Anthony Loehnis, commented in a similar vein that his intellectual curiosity combined with 'a lawyer's belief that rational rather than intuitive processes were likely to lead to solutions to problems [. . .] sometimes led to indecision'.[18] At his memorial service in 2010, his son explained in a moving tribute, 'I imagine that all of our lives would have been easier without him.'[19]

Policy decisions cannot be effective unless they influence markets, and for that to happen, they need to be explained correctly and the intended impact understood not only by market participants but by voters who will

decide elections and by unions and employers who determine the outcome
of wage bargaining. A modern central bank consequently needs
a communication strategy. The Bank of England in this period began to
develop an understanding of the role of information in its relationship with
markets. It had operated with unpublished broad money (M3) targets from
1973, and from 1976 published these.[20] But at this moment there was
substantial uncertainty about what the targets really meant. In addition,
the Bank started to contemplate working with other targets, including
a narrow money indicator, perhaps in order to wrest more control over
interest rates from the Treasury.[21] But, as Richardson made clear, the link
between an indicator and action on nominal interest rates remained very
uncertain.

THE INTERNATIONAL SOURCES OF MONETARISM

Three different external sources fed the controversy about monetary targets in Britain, and each produced a different and incompatible method-
ology. Wavering between these approaches then led to policy chaos.

First, there was an international monetarism: in the late 1960s, the IMF
had tried to impress on British officials, especially in the Bank, the need for
a coherent intellectual framework to address monetary policy. The Fund
organized a highly influential seminar at the Bank. Its favoured concept
then, and also in the big inflationary crises of the mid-1970s, was Domestic
Credit Expansion (or DCE), because the main policy objective was stabilization of the balance of payments.[22] In 1969, an article on DCE appeared
in the Bank's *Quarterly Bulletin*, and it was sometimes interpreted as
'giving the signal for a new way of thinking'.[23] This tradition focused on
credit as the best way of understanding monetary processes, and looked at
the build-up of liabilities as a constraint on business or personal action
rather than thinking about money as an asset or as purchasing power and
hence as a direct shaper of price developments. The new vision came to
Britain in the wake of severe balance of payment crises: the first set of
discussions incurred in the aftermath of the 1967 devaluation, and the
emphasis on DCE became embedded in policy in the wake of the 1976 IMF
crisis. The key conditions set out in December 1976 in the British government's letter of intent for the Fund concerned the public-sector borrowing
requirement (PSBR), on which the IMF moved considerably in the direction of British wishes, and DCE, on which the IMF successfully maintained
its stance, with a required reduction from £9 bn in 1976/77 to £6 bn for
1978/79. Healey stated: 'I am satisfied that the resultant course of sterling

M3 will be consistent with the reduction of inflation.'[24] In May 1977 after the London G-7 Summit, the communique stated: 'Inflation does not reduce unemployment. On the contrary, it is one of its major causes.'[25] Healey did not draw the conclusion that the pursuit of disinflation depended on monetary policy alone: on the contrary, he believed that lower monetary growth would mean lower nominal income growth, but an incomes policy was still required to prevent workers pricing themselves out of jobs. The letter of intent for the IMF agreement indeed emphasized the role of 'the social contract with the trades union movement' in reducing wage growth. Gordon Richardson at the Bank made a similar point when he spoke in January 1977 of how 'monetary policy should therefore aim to act in concert with other branches of policy, including incomes policy, in slowing down inflation'.[26]

Secondly, monetarism of a different type came from Europe. Within the European Community there was a pressure to ensure convergence of inflation rates as a stepping stone to further integration because price differentials would lead to debates about unfair competition and pressure for protective measures. The French economist and long-standing vice president of the European Commission and Commissioner for Economic and Financial Affairs Raymond Barre talked explicitly about monetary targets and about what measures of money should most appropriately be used, over two years before the Bundesbank introduced its policy innovation of a public monetary target. The poster child for monetarism European style was Germany, where the Deutsche Bundesbank reacted promptly to the collapse of the Bretton Woods or par value system in the early 1970s with a monetary target (Central Bank Money) as a new anchor for monetary policy when there was no longer an exchange rate peg. But Germans tended not to really believe in the mechanism of monetary control as such: they saw the announcement of a target rather as an effective way of guiding expectations, and in particular the wage bargaining behaviour of employers and trade unions. In that sense, a target was more a psychological manoeuvre than a real policy constraint. Otmar Emminger, the Bundesbank president most associated publicly with 'monetarism', and the man who over decades shaped the Bundesbank's philosophy, stated: 'A monetary objective is only an instrument of monetary policy in the sense that it constitutes a discipline which leads monetary authorities to examine the causes of monetary growth, and also an obligation to justify policy to the public, even though this sometimes has inconveniences.'[27] In this tradition, monetarism focused on the guiding of expectations.

Thirdly, there was US-style monetarism, usually associated with the great Chicago economist Milton Friedman. Friedman's insight depended on a massive empirical investigation, conducted with Anna Schwartz, in the *Monetary History of the United States* (1963). There he showed how remarkably stable over a long period of time was the 'money multiplier', the ratio of the percentage change in income to the percentage change in the money stock: in the US this figure had been around 2. The reserve base fixed by the central bank determined the money stock (via the 'money multiplier'), which in turn determined nominal income (via the velocity of money). The ratio between currency and deposits was also quite stable over long periods of time.[28] The view that there was a highly stable money demand function could also be derived – rather more tentatively – from historical UK data.[29] But from the 1970s, the relationship shifted in an unpredicted way, and velocity became highly unstable (see below, pp. 84–85).[30] The Chicago vision thus concentrated on a measure of reserve base, whose relation with other monetary aggregates was historically clear but where the relationship became unsteady as it began to play a part in policy.

The Bank and its staff almost unanimously regarded the Friedman view as wrong, and dangerous. Chief Economist Christopher Dow later prepared a study of *Major Recessions* in which the role of money was conspicuous by its absence.[31] Christopher ('Kit') McMahon (Executive Director from 1970 to 1980 and then Deputy Governor) in a letter of 1970 had said that the outcome in price behaviour 'depends on being able to ensure that a desired rate of growth of nominal incomes is in fact achieved. Since Friedman believes you can do this through the quantity of money, he is happy. Since I don't, I am not.'[32] He never changed that view, and, as Deputy Governor in the Thatcher period, quite consistently tried to question and resist a policy that had become a principal plank in the government's strategy. It is plausible to see the strong consensus in the Bank of England as the product of a long tradition – that reached its highpoint in the 1959 Radcliffe Report – which downplayed the importance of monetary policy and of the stock of money.[33] Radcliffe focused on asset prices, as determined by liquidity (a broader concept than the money supply, involving a wide range of liquid assets). The report argued that the asset prices that shaped aggregate demand were not specifically or significantly influenced by monetary policy actions. Central banks could not affect liquidity because open market operations only changed the composition of liquidity and not the overall amount.[34]

The problem in applying the 'foreign' theories or doctrines to Britain was that in the UK there existed a quite different institutional history of the financial system, and that banks played a very different role, and that the Bank of England was intricately associated with the day-to-day operation of the banking system. In the UK setting, money was managed through non-transparent market manipulations. In the 1970s, in the aftermath of the 1971 liberalization of bank lending through the new approach of 'Competition and Credit Control', a broad money objective was a better proxy for a wider liquidity measure than it had been before, in the days of Radcliffe.[35] Then came a new influence, internationalization. The openness of the UK increased dramatically in 1979 when exchange controls were taken off. The US had a large number of small banks, and – when Friedman was writing – few internationally exposed banks. In short, the US was a substantially closed economy. It was not at all obvious how the Friedmanite view could ever be translated into British practice in what was becoming an ever-more open economy.

On the other hand, there were many signs of how poor the macro-economic outcomes of British practice and of the simple belief in the efficacy of the Phillips trade-off had been. The UK had the highest rate of inflation in the industrialized world. By the 1970s inflation was tearing the British social fabric apart: especially in its interactions with a government-imposed prices and wages policy. It was also clear that the high levels of inflation were not generating superior levels of employment or of economic growth. It was not surprising that many people in Britain should look to other countries with better experiences of inflation (Germany and Switzerland in particular) and better theories.

BRITISH MONETARISM

Academic monetarism in Britain was represented above all in a discussion group, the Money Study Group, launched in 1969 by Harry Johnson from Chicago, with David Laidler and Michael Parkin from Essex and Bob Nobay (LSE and Southampton); and a little later at the London Business School where Jim Ball and Terry Burns and then Alan Budd developed a monetarist model of the economy as an alternative to the prevailing Keynesian models that depended on an income–expenditure analysis that ignored money. The new type of model provided an essential component after 1979, as the new Conservative government started to formulate an MTFS.

One aspect of British monetarism seemed peculiar and perhaps contributed to its poor image with academic economists and the Bank of
England: its major advocates were journalists and stockbrokers, groups
instinctively predisposed to cranky theories. Monetarism became famous
because its public champions were journalists, in particular Samuel Brittan
at the *Financial Times*, but most influentially Peter Jay – the son-in-law of
Prime Minister James Callaghan – at *The Times*, who then recruited Tim
Congdon as an economics writer. Both Brittan and Jay were very open
about their intellectual debt to Friedman. Sophisticated writers in the press
seemed to be at odds with the academic establishment, which was on the
whole fiercely resistant to the new interpretation. Moreover, some stockbrokers played a prominent part in thinking about the best or most
appropriate instruments of monetary policy. In British debates, the closest
doctrine to Friedmanism was the concept of monetary base control, pio-
neered above all by an influential stockbroker and analyst at W. Greenwell
& Co., Gordon Pepper.[36] He had been impressed by an American private-
sector economist, Beryl Sprinkel, at a conference in the US, had come back
determined to use a monetarist approach as a basis for forecasts, and had
been outstandingly successful. Pepper, backed by a strong reputation as an
economic forecaster, came into contact with Margaret Thatcher as leader
of the opposition. One of the consistent claims of British monetarists was
that their forecasting performed better than the Keynesian alternative.[37]
Stockbrokers concentrated their attention on how asset and other price
movements were generated, but they might not reflect deeply on the
institutional characteristics of the financial system and the institutional
problem of how bank behaviour might actually be controlled.

From the perspective of the Bank, the Monetary Base Control (MBC)
approach appeared hopelessly theoretical or academic. It ignored the
structure of the British banking system, the knowledge of whose complexities and intricacies formed the core of the Bank of England's professional
competence. The Bank remained a centre of a more general claim of what
Nicoletta Batini and Ed Nelson critically call 'UK exceptionalism', where
a non-standard approach is justified by very peculiar institutional
features.[38] As Charles Goodhart, who had moved to the Bank from the
LSE in 1968 as adviser on monetary policy, and who in effect built up the
Bank's approach to monetary economics, put it, 'Academics tended to
believe both that the money stock was adjusted by injections, or withdrawals of such base money, and that this was the correct process. Whereas
Central Bankers knew that their own banking system was constructed on
the basis of a system whereby banks could *always* get additional reserves at

the interest rate set by the Bank.'[39] Every morning, senior officials met at 'Books' in the Bank of England in order to be presented with the positions of the banking system that they needed to accommodate by operating in the market.

As early as 1968, Goodhart had dismissed Pepper's idea of holding M constant as a means of frightening the Treasury into reducing public borrowing: that could not be done in the UK 'because the need to maintain an orderly gilt-edged market limits our ability to put this kind of pressure on the Government'.[40] Obviously, it would ultimately have to be the Treasury that took the decision to hold M constant, and why should the Treasury frighten itself? Dow (in joint work with Ian Saville) later explained the basis of an approach which held that authorities were power-less to influence money as 'the growth of the monetary aggregates has to be regarded as the response of the banking system to market forces'.[41] Only later would the Bank step away from the management of the gilt-edged market.[42] There was in fact a powerful argument that the market reaction could be shaped by monetary policy signals.

In line with the prevailing Bank doctrine, Andrew Crockett produced a paper listing all the reasons why the UK could not learn from US experience:

- The overdraft system for banks meant that banks would expand their lending independent of control
- The convention by which the discount market covers the Treasury bill tender
- The lower priority given to profit maximization by British banks
- The different asset structure of British banks
- The relative interest-inelasticity of many types of expenditure in the UK.[43]

In an article in the *BEQB* in 1979, Goodhart – with the Bank economists Michael Foot and Anthony Hotson – argued that the base is very difficult to use as a practical tool of management:

Under the present institutional arrangements, there are unforeseen swings into and out of central government balances of up to several hundred million pounds a day, and the first requirement for day-to-day control would be either that the Government moved its business to the commercial banks or that the banking system moved to a next day settlement basis for all transactions.[44]

Since government debt played such an important role in the operation of the money market, the conclusion appeared obvious that the major task could be reformulated as the reduction of the contribution of government debt in the building up of debt claims.

A further peculiarity of the policy-making environment after 1979 was the way that the prime minister intervened in what appeared to be the technical minutiae of monetary policy issues. Thatcher revelled in details. Later, she attempted to write a script for a vignette in what was her favourite television show, *Yes Minister*, in which she ordered the fictional minister Jim Hacker and permanent secretary Sir Humphrey to 'abolish economists' as a first step towards cutting the budget.[45] She also distrusted the British establishment and preferred to talk with people from the outside whose judgement might be expected to be objective and disinterested, namely Milton Friedman and Allan Meltzer and later Alan Greenspan from the US, and Karl Brunner and the central banker Fritz Leutwiler in Switzerland. She had met Greenspan at a dinner in Washington in 1975, and had engaged in a deep conversation about monetary targeting, beginning her dialogue with the striking (and apposite) question, 'Why is it that we in Britain cannot calculate M3?'[46] One of her ministers was quoted as complaining, 'Can you imagine [Prime Minister Harold] Macmillan inviting two foreign economists to No. 10 to explain the obscure details of monetary control?'[47] Alan Walters, whom she employed as her economic adviser from 1981, was British but was working at the Johns Hopkins University in Baltimore, and was habitually irreverent about the establishment and profoundly sceptical of the orthodoxies at the Treasury and the Bank of England. Walters in the end played a positive role in bridging the gap between Thatcher's ideas and what might be practical policy in the real world. The consultations did not fit easily with the traditional sense of how bureaucratic politics work – they weren't supposed to – and the result generated considerable friction that reached a peak in 1981 (it would flare up again in 1989). In August 1981, Sir John Hoskyns, the head of the Downing Street Policy Unit, sent the prime minister an excoriating memorandum, with the title 'Your Personal Survival':

You break every rule of good man-management. You bully your weaker colleagues. You criticise colleagues in front of each other and in front of their officials. They can't answer back without appearing disrespectful, in front of others, to a woman and to a prime minister. You abuse that situation. You give little praise or credit, and you are too ready to blame others when things go wrong.[48]

Thatcher's first visit to the Bank, when she had still been leader of the opposition, was remembered by Bank officials as 'disastrous'. Christopher Dow was frustrated that she did not want to be instructed by the Bank. He reported, 'We were of course polite but did not take to her – because she spoke her mind in very broad and sweeping terms, and gave little opening for anyone to tell her things which we could have told her and which in fact would have been useful for her to know.' And she found the Bank officials supercilious and condescending, and later complained to Richardson, 'I saw them smiling.'[49] Initially, Richardson was quite captivated by Thatcher, who liked handsome and good-looking men. George Blunden commented, 'He comes back from meetings in No 10 almost as much in love with her as Hector [Laing, a member of the Bank's Court].' Richardson returned from his first dinner with the new prime minister in 10 Downing Street, when Chancellor Helmut Schmidt was visiting, saying, 'What struck you was how much better everything was done. Even the food was better. It's a great advantage having a woman as host, someone to make the party go.'[50] The warmth in the relationship, however, soon cooled. She referred to him in speaking with the government's Chief Scientist as 'that fool who runs the Bank of England'. In November 1979, she wrote in the margins of a note about the Bank, 'I must put someone there I can rely on'; and she told her loyal adviser Adam Ridley, 'I just don't know how you can trust them.' Hector Laing spelled out the difference of styles, 'He was feline; she was canine.'[51] But she disliked the Deputy Governor, Kit McMahon, much more, largely on policy grounds since he was much more unabashedly Keynesian and noted that 'he'll never be Governor of the Bank of England while I'm Prime Minister'.[52]

THE MEDIUM-TERM FINANCIAL STRATEGY

Geoffrey Howe as Thatcher's new Chancellor launched his first budget in 1979 with an analysis of British economic decline, and then addressed the issue of inflation: 'It is crucially important to re-establish sound money. We intend to achieve this through firm monetary discipline and fiscal policies consistent with that, including strict control over public expenditure' (see Figure 4.1).[53] The target range for £M3 growth to April 1980 was set at 7–11 per cent. The 'keystone' of the new approach to stimulating aggregate supply was the reduction of income tax rates, with the top rate being cut from 83 to 60 per cent, and the basic rate from 33 to 30 per cent. The revenue shortfall was made up by an increase in VAT (previously at a standard rate of 8 per cent and a luxury rate of 12.5 per cent) to a uniform 15 per cent. That immediately affected consumer prices and wage bargaining. The budget was also linked to a 2 per cent rise in MLR, to 14 per cent.

Figure 4.1 Sir Geoffrey Howe and Margaret Thatcher in 1984
(on their way to China) (Mirrorpix/Contributor/Getty Images)

The Conservative government's new approach to monetary and fiscal stabilization – the MTFS announced in 1979 and implemented in 1980 – was accompanied by a joint Bank–Treasury Green Paper on 'Monetary Control' (Cmnd7858), which came down against the idea of MBC, and which the Bank's pragmatists could celebrate as their victory, in which they killed a coherent, but in their eyes foolish, Treasury policy idea. According to the final document, the main instruments or tools for establishing control of money should continue to be fiscal policy and interest rates. It was sufficient to control money supply growth in the medium term, say over a year or more. The government would make its contribution by bringing down over time PSBR as a proportion of national output. The paper did consider monetary targets, and thought that the most suitable was £M3 as target, but in its view, account should also be taken of other aggregates. Policy would be directed to a reduction in the growth rate of all the monetary aggregates. The document also investigated what it termed the impact of policy on the 'Ordinary Man'. This was a critical consideration, as ordinary people were thought to be highly sensitive to moves in interest rates, and ordinary people were the voters whose choice was vital every four or five years. The optimistic view was that a fundamental reliance on fiscal policy and interest rates would mean that the 'proposal for smoother monetary growth' would have a lesser impact on general level of interest rates. But within this generally enhanced stability, there might be temporarily greater interest rate fluctuation; and individuals and institutions would have to accommodate to this.[54]

Concretely the document set out a series of liberalizations or simplifications: in particular, the 'corset' or supplementary special deposits scheme (SSDS) that imposed penalties on banks whose interest-bearing liabilities were growing too quickly would be phased out;[55] the 12½ per cent reserve assets ratio for banks ended; a cash requirement extended to all banks; while the special deposits scheme (where a proportion of bank liabilities had to be placed at the Bank of England at a rate roughly equivalent to Treasury bill rate) was retained. Instead, the growth of money could be limited, above all by controlling public borrowing.

The core policy problem lay in the understanding of the drivers of monetary growth. The most important approach in the UK, known as 'credit counterparts', was based on an accounting identity derived from the balance sheet of the banking system, and provided a dramatic alternative to the US theory of the money multiplier. In the credit counterparts approach, there were three quite separate sources: public borrowing, private debt (driven by bank lending), and the overseas sector (which took on a new importance after the removal of exchange controls). In the official view, the public component was the key: if public debt was not adequately controlled, the effect would be that high interest rates in a monetary control experiment would squeeze private borrowers. Reducing the PSBR meant that there was less need to sell government debt in the market, and consequently the interest levels needed to control private borrowing could be both less volatile and lower. The implication was that, as the December 1977 *BEQB* put it, 'fiscal and monetary policy need to be decided as part of a single policy'.[56]

The Green Paper built up its approach on a concept of the major credit counterparts which fuelled monetary growth, government lending, private lending and international movements. Interest rate movements would affect each in different ways. An increase in rates would immediately raise the cost of government funding and increase the budget deficit; would crowd out private-sector borrowing; and would attract foreign inflows, making it easier to finance the official sector. An anti-inflationary strategy that relied on interest rates might thus in the first instance weaken the private sector. The dilemma was made worse by the liberalization measures, the end of the corset and the removal of foreign exchange restrictions.

The logic of the Green Paper appalled Friedman, who told the Treasury and Civil Service Select Committee:

I could hardly believe my eyes when I read . . . 'The principal means of controlling the growth of the money supply must be fiscal policy – both public expenditure and tax policy – and interest rates.' Interpreted literally, this sentence is simply wrong. Only a Rip Van Winkle, who had not read any of the flood of literature during the past decade and more on the money supply process, could possibly have written that sentence. Direct control of the monetary base is an alternative to fiscal policy and interest rates as a means of controlling monetary growth. Of course, direct control of the monetary base will affect interest rates . . . but that is a very different thing from controlling monetary growth through interest rates.[57]

There was some rather similar pushback against the Green Paper in the Bank's panel of Academic Consultants, where Brian Griffiths took a Friedmanite stance and was particularly critical of the Bank's standpoint: 'The chain of causation was thought by the Bank to be from monetary base to interest rates to money supply. In contrast Professor Griffiths was of the opinion that the chain ran from monetary base to interest rates and money supply simultaneously.'[58] A critique of the Green Paper, with several co-authors, was published as an article in *The Banker*.[59]

But in fact, the approach of the Green Paper was very close to the original political version of monetarism in Britain as expounded above all by Sir Keith Joseph, the major political intellectual behind the Thatcher Revolution. He was especially sensitive to the argument about the peculiarities of the UK and laid great emphasis on the need to reduce public borrowing and the public sector if monetary control was to have the effect of stimulating private-sector activity:

In other words, the monetary process is both a cause of inflation and a link in a wider chain of cause and effect. Monetary contraction in a mixed economy strangles the private sector unless the state sector contracts with it and reduces its take from the national income.[60]

At the Bank of England, Charles Goodhart noted the widespread support for a strong emphasis on fiscal consolidation, with Friedrich von Hayek having written to *The Times* to explain that without structural reform of wage bargaining processes, in particular of union monopoly powers, reduction of monetary aggregates could result in such excessive unemployment as to be politically untenable. And the already-influential Fed chairman Paul Volcker had said, 'We must develop a co-ordinated set of policies designed to attack inflation from a number of directions rather than placing the entire burden on monetary policy. [. . .] I believe it is imperative to keep the goal of budgetary balance in the forefront of our thinking about spending and revenue decisions.'[61] Goodhart concluded that 'this emphasis on the need for consistent fiscal policy, though shared by the present Government, is not fully accepted by monetarists'.[62]

In consequence of these considerations, there was an obvious way of doing monetary targeting. As Alan Budd put it: 'M3 is the preferable measure amongst those available because of its direct link with the government's fiscal and financial policy.'[63] The Treasury made it clear in public testimony how important was the direct connection between the size of the budget deficit and monetary growth. A domestically financed budget deficit increased the net assets of the private sector, leading to a greater demand for all assets, including money, bonds and real assets. Since the wealth increase derived from the issue of bonds, yield on bonds should rise relative to the returns on other assets, and the money supply would increase to preserve portfolio balance.[64]

The MTFS was launched in March 1980, specifying over a four-year period a series of declining target ranges for £M3 on the principle that 'control of the money supply will over a period of years reduce the rate of inflation'. In fact, the original target for monetary growth was only met much later in 1983/4, although the revised ranges were already met in 1982/3. The result was four years of constant questioning of policy, with major tensions between the Treasury and Bank, a critique of policy by most of the British economics establishment but also by parliamentarians, including many leading Conservatives, and a continual engagement in the minutiae of monetary policy management by the prime minister, Margaret Thatcher.

This new approach was fundamentally a brainchild of Nigel Lawson, and then developed by a team of Treasury economists, in particular two academic figures coming from the London Business School, Terry Burns, who became the Treasury Chief Economic Adviser in 1980 at the age of thirty-six, and Alan Budd. Most of the Treasury establishment, with the exception of Peter Middleton, since 1975 head of the Monetary Policy Division, was sceptical. Sir Douglas Wass, the Permanent Secretary of the Treasury, as well as Anthony Rawlinson, William (Bill) Ryrie and Kenneth Couzens were firmly opposed to monetarism. Middleton seemed to be a lone 'Thatcher spy' in the Treasury, as Margaret Thatcher's official biographer Charles Moore puts it; in particular, he derived a great deal of institutional strength from the close and trusting relationship that developed between him and Thatcher's principal economic guru, Alan Walters.[65]

THE TREASURY AND THE BANK

Though the Treasury and the Bank can be considered as a 'macro-economic executive', and though they were 'joined at the hip', the relationship was uncomfortable throughout the 1980s, and often very tense. The Treasury complained on occasion about the 'Everest Complex' of the Bank, especially in the Richardson era, because they thought that all decisions had to come from the Governor, and that senior staff were constrained if they could not have a line that was dictated by the Governor. The tensions appear in the meetings, where – in the words of the mandarin Sir Humphrey of *Yes Minister* – 'the actual meeting is a mass of ingredients for you to choose from', and minutes could be written by selecting 'from a jumble of ill-digested ideas a version which represents the Prime Minister's views as he would on reflection have liked them to emerge'.[66] A characteristic of this kind of process is that there is no consistency, and the policy-making process in the first half or the 1980s remained astonishingly blurry. And since there was no obvious clear response to a particular set of data – in modern terminology, no transparent or explicit reaction function – the monetary authorities were pushed to and fro by other events and other data, in particular from exchange rate movements.

The House of Commons Treasury and Civil Service Committee later observed that 'many believed that the relative power of the Bank diminished in the 1980s'. Nigel Lawson, in his appearances before that Committee, did everything in his power to affirm that impression: 'We take the decisions but they [the Bank] do the work'; or, more dramatically, 'When I think they [interest rates] ought to go up they go up and when I think they should come down they come down.'[67]

In the 1970s, there had not been such a great intellectual gap between Treasury and Bank, but neither institution had clear views or a doctrine of monetary policy. Christopher Dow records for that period that 'a third, or more, of the Treasury is on the same side as the Bank – those in charge of monetary policy in the Treasury are as much like the Bank as Departments of Agriculture are on the side of the farmer'.[68] But the Treasury was pushing back on the Bank. It consistently suspected the Bank's position, complained that Bank papers were not sent to the Treasury, and thought that the Bank was always 'itching to intervene' in foreign exchange markets (which was largely untrue) but also in spending public money in bank rescues (which was partially true, and explains why a momentum built up in the 1980s and above all in the 1990s to separate bank supervision from the Bank and from monetary policy).[69] It also thought that the Bank was politically naïve: as the journalist William Keegan put it, in the Treasury view, it was 'no good saying the monetary base proposal was ridiculous – governments are always doing ridiculous things'.[70]

Peter Middleton wrote a ferocious condemnation of the 'dramatic changes' in the new deregulated banking sector that had pushed the new wave of dangerous monetary expansion. In the Treasury view, the Bank was destroying monetary policy not only by intellectual Keynesian and anti-monetarist orientation, but by its peculiar role in the City as the defender of banking interests:

The banking system has been freed from all restrictions of a monetary policy kind. Lending has expanded vastly in total. It has also expanded into all sorts of fields – some desirable, other not – which were never even thought of in 1977. Apart from lending for housing and an expanding variety of financial services, banks also engage (or did) in foreign to foreign leasing, £ lending overseas on a massive scale (£1 bn in March and April this year to overseas non-banks) and they appear to be about to become estate agents. Indeed, the concept of a bank as an organisation which offers a comprehensive list of financial services seems to have no limit – presumably casinos and betting shops would come under the same definition. And this expansion has come at a time of recession both at home and overseas.

Much of this change has been facilitated – I would say institutionalised, though the Bank would not agree – by equally important changes in the scale of the Authorities' own operations. The Reserve Asset Ratio has gone for monetary purposes but, presumably, is still enjoying a half life in the prudential field. And the Authorities have provided £8 bn of assistance [i.e. sales of government debt, see below, pp. 123–127] in order to hold the interest rates on which this explosion of banking lending is based.

This means that the nature of the prudential problem must have changed – both in scale and kind. We have no concept – prudential or monetary – of a limit to the growth in the stock of bank lending. I suspect the main risk is of an abrupt change in government policy, but it could also be of a further change in economic conditions more generally. If, for example, assistance came to an end – or an attempt was made to recoup it – the resulting difficulties in the private sector (from higher and more variable short rates) would be bound to impact on the banks even though they match variable lending with variable borrowing. The scale of resources involved in any attempt to prop up the system would greatly exceed the resources of the Bank.

I am not sure whether this counts as a prudential worry or not. Or, if it does, whether we are allowed to mention it to the Bank. I am sure that the nature and scale of changes in the banking systems has been such as to make it desirable for someone to ask whether the prudential arrangements are adequate. The question is, should it be us, and how far should we go if so. These are the sort of questions which will be raised in the paper which HF [Home Finance] are working on. It would be useful to know if it is worth proceeding with this work.[71]

The Treasury thus felt strongly motivated to push back against the Bank, and its top officials, though somewhat sceptical of 'monetarism', realized that they might well use the policy views of ministers as a mechanism of realizing their institutional pushback against the Bank.

Within the Treasury, the key intellectual leadership came from Nigel Lawson. He explained in a 1980 lecture that the distinctive feature of the MTFS was that it was 'confined to charting a course for those variables – notably the quantity of money – which are and must be within the power of governments to control. By contrast, governments cannot create economic growth.'[72] In effect, the crucial element of the MTFS was the control of public-sector borrowing, since that would be financed either by borrowing from banks, and thus adding to the money supply (if lending did not come at the expense of private-sector loans), or by borrowing from individuals and institutions, in which case there would be an upward pressure on interest rates. It was very much a Treasury-driven concept, and in the first half of the 1980s the result was a continual tension with the Prime Minister, who thought in terms of a different kind of monetarism, and with the Bank, where the focus was primarily on the management of government debt sales to the City. For the Prime Minister, the main source of inspiration was an engagement with foreign models of monetary management; for the Treasury, the application of the counterparts approach; and for the Bank, the continual dialogue with the markets – in particular the discount houses – that were sensitive to developments in the gilts market.

Margaret Thatcher was initially suspicious of the MTFS and referred to it as revealing a 'graph-paper economics' approach.[73] She was convinced largely because it offered the possibility of bringing down interest rates – a politically motivated concern to help her supporters, in industry as well as homeowners, and which became 'her obsessive desire'.[74]

Faced by the Treasury offensive that was flanked by the arguments of Lawson and Thatcher, the Bank felt shut out of the process of policy formulation. Lawson later explained that 'the tension was undoubtedly exacerbated by our making it clear that the Chancellor was now in unequivocal control of monetary policy'.[75] Goodhart expressed his irritation in a caustic letter he drafted to Treasury Special Adviser Alan Budd (but apparently never sent).[76] The central document laying out future policy simply bypassed the Bank. Richardson complained that he 'had received late last evening a copy of the Chancellor's minute to the Prime Minister on the plan. [...] There had *not* [emphasis added] been discussions between the Governor and the Chancellor or between HMT and Bank officials.'[77] In a meeting with

Geoffrey Howe in February 1980, Richardson set out the specifics of the Bank's case, in an argument that was clearly drawn from Goodhart:

The medium term financial strategy was of vital concern to the Bank, and he was surprised that the Prime Minister should have been shown a draft before the Bank had been fully consulted. For his part he had serious reservations about the credibility of the sort of document produced and about the wisdom of publishing it; he was particularly concerned that the Government should not adopt a posture of complete inflexibility about the monetary targets to be followed in each successive year. Changes in 'monetary technology' could well require substantial revisions to the figures.[78]

The Green Paper on Monetary Control of March 1980 stated in paragraph 4:

No single statistical measure of the money supply can be expected fully to encapsulate monetary conditions, and so provide a uniquely correct basis for controlling the complex relationships between monetary growth and prices and nominal incomes. [. . .] In assessing the monetary conditions, the authorities have to have regard for a range – including not only the narrow measure (M1) but the wider measures of money (M3, £M3) and various still wider measures of private sector liquidity.[79]

This passage was later cited by Treasury officials as evidence of a qualification to the endorsement of £M3.[80] Thatcher later noted that the Budget Red Book constituted 'an important qualification'.[81]

Howe pointed to the problem of interest rates in a minute submitted to the Prime Minister:

The key question on which we have to make up our minds eventually is whether we are willing to assign to the markets a greater role in the determination of short rates. The authorities are of course always part of the market, whatever the technique used. Under a monetary base regime we would still be left to decide when and how the base should be changed if money supply deviated from the target. But would there be much point in going through all the upset which would be involved if we intend to exercise the same degree of discretion as we do at present? In circumstances such as those of the past few weeks, a regime under which the Government worked under predetermined rules, would have caused the market to carry interest rates up; that would have been the justification for the scheme in the eyes of its proponents.[82]

John Biffen, MP and Chief Secretary to the Treasury (i.e. a political figure), a key political ally of Thatcher who saw himself as a loyalist, was very critical of the whole new monetary approach. He noted in a minute submitted to Howe: 'Our monetary policy is still at the stage of apprenticeship. The Financial Strategy, on the other hand, will suggest a certainty about pace and direction that we do not possess, either technically or politically.'[83] Howe's answer set out the basic rationale of the new strategy:

The business world, financial institutions, labour markets and ordinary people (particularly our supporters) must have a vision of how we intend to proceed hereafter. They want to know the course we intend to steer in relation to expenditure and taxes, and what our commitment to monetary discipline might mean. Furthermore, the way the policy works implies that they <u>need</u> to be given a clear indication of the limits within which we intend to manage public spending and the money supply, so that they can adjust their behaviour rationally to fit in with those limits. But they also need demonstration that our intentions and the policies which will realise them are consistent, technically sound, and will bear fruit. At present there is a measure of uncertainty about all of these.[84]

There were three layers to the operational implementation of the MTFS in terms of timing: the annual laying out of monetary targets based on the Treasury model of the UK economy; monthly meetings between the Bank and the Treasury to discuss interest rates; and the daily operations of the Bank. The crucial part of the coordination of strategy with its translation into practice came in the monthly meetings. Bill (later Sir William) Ryrie, the Second Permanent Secretary of the Treasury, had suggested the process at the beginning of 1980, after consulting with Kit McMahon:

The purpose of the meetings would be to review developments in monetary policy over the previous month and consider the short-term outlook and the actions which may have to be considered in the following weeks. That will emerge from our meetings will depend on the circumstances. Sometimes, I imagine, it might lead to an immediate submission to the Chancellor on some point, but we would not expect to do this as a routine. Rather we would expect the discussion to help us all to be clear in our own minds about how we shall approach events over the succeeding month.[85]

These regular meetings were known as the Ryrie meetings, and continued as the Middleton and then the Burns meetings as Peter Middleton (in 1983) and then Terry Burns (in 1991) became Permanent Secretary in the Treasury.

Another way of thinking of the implementation was in terms of the policy instruments available: fiscal policy (obviously determined by the government, with a major input by the Treasury); funding policy (official sales of long-term securities to the non-bank public); and interest rate policy. In particular, the sale of government debt could be used to absorb money and thus keep to the targets for the broader aggregates – particularly £M3, but also PSL2.[86] More and more in the first half of the 1980s monetary policy became in practice the Bank's funding strategy, where the Bank took the lead as the manager of government debt, a role it kept until 1997, and where in the first half of the 1980s the key element was over-funding, or selling too much government debt so as to drain money from the markets. Most Bank of England officials believed that the demand for broad money was not a stable function of income and short-term interest rates, and that short-term interest rates were not an effective means of controlling broad money growth.[87] Almost all participants wanted to take a broad rather than a narrow target, chiefly because it was obvious that the budget deficit (PSBR) was the central counterpart to broad money changes. That was not the case with a narrower target, and thus the broad money target had a greater and direct political impact on the fiscal stance.

McMahon formulated his view – which he presented as the Bank's view – of monetary policy in highly sceptical terms. He wanted – in the terminology of *Yes Minister* – to cook from a mass of ingredients:

Most of us, however, attach some weight to Goodhart's Law: i.e. that in many cases the act of publicly controlling one particular aggregate may tend over time to decrease the value of that aggregate both as an indicator and as an instrumental variable. This reinforces the case for looking at several aggregates even while targeting only one. It also underlines the point that the form of any controls and the manner of their implementation should disturb as little as possible existing market preferences for the type of assets to be held and channels within the funds are moved. If we were starting afresh, and therefore could disregard entrenched views of commentators and markets, and if the Bank was in more or less sole control of operations to meet whatever targets and had been laid down, most of us might incline towards M1 target. The arguments which might be particularly stressed would perhaps include: the likelihood (maybe not very strong) that it is more amenable to control at least by monetary means than M3; that by distancing ourselves from 'counterpart variables' of the PSBR, bank lending and external flows, we might be spared the problems of slow reactions in these areas and especially the self-defeating phenomena of 'buyers' strikes'; and the fact that, in the absence of exchange controls, complications from the external sector and especially the growth in euro-sterling might be less troublesome.[88]

Goodhart himself saw the issue as being primarily a question about uncertainty about the way in which the economy should be modelled. 'If,' he wrote,

we really believed that our models represented 'the truth', there would be no case for the adoption of intermediate targets, such as the exchange rate, – we would (simply!) ask Jeremy Bray [a mathematician and MP] and his supporters to run a policy optimisation exercise. It is largely because there is doubt about the form, stability and accuracy of economic models that intermediate targets are adopted.

Such a target was best conceptualized as 'a rough limit, in the absence of greater knowledge, to the expansionary tendencies' of governments pushed by political preferences.[89] As long as continued doubt – and political contestation – existed as to the appropriate model to apply to the determination of monetary policy, there could not be a high degree of confidence that the UK had either the right policy apparatus or the right policy stance.

5

'A Good Deal of Advice'

The Battle over Policy Control

Against the background of the intense debate about how 'monetarism' might be applied, policy debates in practice followed a rather traditional line. That approach involved sporadically but surprisingly often responding to exchange rate movements, even when the exchange rate was specifically not designated as either a policy goal or an instrument, and then raising interest rates as a way to cool down inflation but also economic growth. Initially, the Bank of England resisted the idea of using interest rates to establish control. The background was the increase in the minimum lending rate (MLR) on 15 November 1979, from 14 to 17 per cent, where the rate remained until the beginning of July 1980 (see Figure 5.1). The problem was that in the open economy, after the end of exchange controls, the rise in interest rates led to an inflow of money, in particular driven by foreign purchases of fixed interest securities: so money supply did not respond to interest rates in an easily predictable way. The inflow of money then had an obvious and immediate impact on the exchange rate, whose appreciation made business conditions worse and thus intensified the severe recession.

In February 1980, in a discussion with the Treasury, the Bank stated that it would prefer 'to intervene if necessary to prevent a further rise in short-term rates'. It used gilt operations explicitly to forestall a need to increase the lending rate (so, for instance, on 13 February, it bought and resold £500 m gilts in order to ease the monetary squeeze on the clearing banks).[1] At a meeting with Chancellor Geoffrey Howe in March 1980, Gordon Richardson expressed his objections to the government's financial strategy by referring to the political impossibility – and hence the lack of credibility – of high interest rates:

(i) Monetary policy reduced inflation both directly and through its effect on expectations; but it was doubtful whether the strategy would achieve the

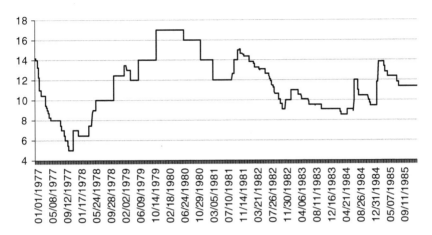

Figure 5.1 Bank of England lending rate (1977–1985)

hope for improvement in expectations given the present difficulties and the clear indications that the authorities were reluctant to see the increases in interest rates required to meet monetary targets in the short-run. This being so it would be very hard for the authorities in practice to achieve a steady reduction of one percentage point a year in the rate of monetary growth, come what may; such a posture was undesirably dogmatic, mechanical and rigid. [. . .]

(ii) The medium-term outlook for the economy revealed by the document was very bleak, and although the figures were presented as only illustrative, the Government might find itself regarded as committed to them, and in some sense responsible for them. Industrialists would be far more worried about the implications of the strategy for output and unemployment than they were reassured by its commitment to the fight against inflation.

(iii) Although the primary objective of policy was to reduce inflation, the document was silent on the reduction in inflation for which the Government was looking. On the other hand, there were difficulties about stating specific objectives, not least because there was no clear relationship, even in the medium-term, between changes in the money stock and changes in the price level.[2]

On 3 April, the Governor told the discount market, 'We have made clear our judgment that monetary objectives do not require higher rates. Of course we could be wrong.'[3] On 3 July, even though monetary growth was outside the target range, the Bank cut MLR by one point to 16 per cent (see the discussion below). Richardson had presented the following argument:

The money supply figures on their own would scarcely justify a reduction and the new Bank forecasts due the following week could well reinforce his doubts. Bank lending did appear to be moving down as the recession deepened. But the case for a reduction, rather than waiting for some further improvement in the money supply figures, was that the pressure on the corporate sector caused by high interest rates and the high exchange rate had become too great and needed to be moderated.[4]

Howe and Thatcher agreed with this argument as laid out by the Bank of England, as it obviously captured the political concern with the popular impact of the high interest rates. The Bank's announcement stated that 'there are signs that monetary growth moderated last month and also that the underlying demand for credit from the private sector may be beginning to ease with increasing evidence of downturn in the economy'.[5] The London *Times* concluded that 'the period of almost eight months of record interest rates in the United Kingdom is over'.[6] The *Financial Times* considered the move 'an augury both that the Government believes that its monetary policies are at last working, and of what may come later this year and next'.[7] The Deputy President of the CBI (Confederation of British Industry) welcomed this 'step in the right direction'.[8]

After the July cut, equity markets surged, with the biggest one-day gain in fifteen months, while the pound fell on the foreign exchange market. At the markets meeting with the discount houses, Richardson explained that 'there are indeed signs that monetary growth has moderated, as bank lending is beginning to do, with the different and worse conditions of industry'. And one week later, Deputy Governor Kit McMahon made a similar point in his discussion with the discount market: the Bank took into account 'the worries of industry' even though money supply was still above range. He believed that lending would fall and hence he was prepared to 'give it the benefit of doubt'. But he saw that central government borrowing would rise, and concluded 'we are less euphoric than you', and warned 'if you get carried along you might not carry us along with you'.[9] In fact, bank lending surged rather than collapsing, in the view of the Bank largely as a result of distress borrowing during the deep recession. Mostly the case for the rate cut was accepted: the Bank noted some 'insults' from the *Financial Times* (where Peter Riddell had been quite critical), but also that the rest of the press 'tacitly or explicitly' (in the case of the *Economist*) endorsed the logic.[10] Chief economist Christopher Dow was fundamentally an old-style Keynesian who was highly critical of the Thatcher government and liked the easing of policy.

He thought of a potential way of placating the monetarist critics by bringing them into the Bank. In a memorandum with the title 'Defence of the Bank's Position', he suggested:

1. Would it be possible to solicit the advice of a number of outside monetarist critics as to what went wrong and more particularly what is the right course now? – Griffiths, Pepper, Brittan? Perhaps with a view later of offering one of the first two an inside post?
2. Pressed for monetary targets in first place. Before that had an unpublished monetary target. Policy has thus for years not been different in kind from present Government's policy.[11]

In other words, Dow thought that the Bank could legitimately defend its institutional view and its stance vis-à-vis the Treasury by saying that it had been monetarist all along, before Thatcher and Howe and Lawson had become monetarists; it was simply that the Bank knew a different monetarism. John Fforde wanted to take a quite different tack, recommending a 'de-rating' of 'the charmed life' of £M3, cutting it 'down to size' and 'in the process, aligning ourselves more with mainstream economic thinking than with people like Friedman, Laidler, Minford and Griffiths'. The Bank should attempt to 'steer by a broader range of indicators, including £M3, in most circumstances, i.e. except when the short-run arrest of inflation is the objective of policy'.[12] The Bank's staff, in diverse ways, pushed against a single indicator and even more against a monetary target.

THE EXCHANGE RATE

An alternative lens to monetary targetry was provided by the analysis of the exchange rate and its influence on financial behaviour but also on the performance of the real economy. Through the high interest rate period, the pound surged against the Deutschemark (DM). From a rate of 3.69 on 5 November 1979, it reached a peak of 5.04 at the end of January 1981 (see Figure 5.2). With the exception of a brief period from February to April 1980, the pound also rose against the US dollar. The exchange rate movement was good news in terms of a strategy of reducing imported inflation, but imposed a major cost on exporters and producers of goods competing with imports. But the Treasury, in particular Financial Secretary Nigel Lawson, was at this stage quite resistant to any corrective action to attempt to reduce sterling's appreciation. The monetarist economists at the Treasury, Terry Burns and

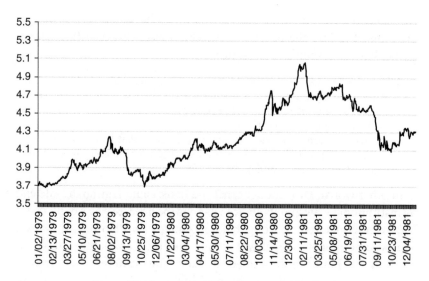

Figure 5.2 Deutschemark–sterling rate (1979–1981)

Alan Budd, thought of themselves as committed to an 'international monetarism' where the exchange rate rise held down costs and inflation, and the pain inflicted on business by the higher exchange rate might be eased by using North Sea oil revenue to reduce tax burdens (and in particular end the employer's national income surcharge). The Treasury–Bank divide over exchange rate policy, which had been a major feature of the 1976 debacle, reappeared again in the setting of the monetary policy debate.

At a meeting in late February 1980, when the pound was moving through the psychologically important 4.00 DM level, Lawson explained that he was also exercised about the scale of the Bank's attempts to moderate changes in the exchange rate. On the latter point, he referred in particular to the Governor's remarks to the Forex Association in mid-January, as reported in the *Financial Times* of 11 February, when Richardson had talked about the 'obvious danger that smoothing, to be effective, might have to be so substantial that it could pose a threat to monetary targets'.[13] Lawson was concerned about the suggestion that foreign exchange intervention should go beyond smoothing and could play an important part in supporting other policy measures. He worried 'about the inherent circularity of the picture which seemed to be emerging: a positive intervention figure helped to boost monetary growth, to which the Government were forced to respond with higher interest rates, thus increasing inflows still further which caused further upward pressure on the exchange rate'. McMahon tried to defend the Bank: 'short of a really massive external counterpart, he thought it difficult to believe that the amount of intervention the Bank had been practising, or were likely to practise, could be such as to force the Government's hand on interest rates'.[14]

Throughout this dramatic move in the foreign exchange rate, government policy-makers emphasized that they did not care about the development. Geoffrey Howe made clear to a parliamentary committee: 'We have said very often that it is our policy to leave the exchange rate to be determined primarily by market forces.'[15] From the Bank's perspective, Charles Goodhart had earlier told the same parliamentary committee that 'the level of the exchange rate is not an element of the Government's policy objectives'.[16]

By July 1980, the situation had become impossible. Britain looked as if it was following the US, where the federal funds rate had been falling quickly since April, as the targeted monetary aggregates fell sharply, and Fed chairman Paul Volcker reversed his high interest rate policy. But then the British monetary indicators went wild, and moved in the opposite direction to the American data. From the beginning of 1980, monetary growth had risen. The really strong surge in £M3 started in April 1980, when the annualized growth rate had been 10.4 per cent, and went through to April 1981, when the level was at 21.5 per cent. On a seasonally adjusted basis, £M3 grew by 34 per cent from 16 January 1980 to 15 July 1981 (while M1 grew only by 15.5 per cent).[17] The explosion most obviously reflected first the end of exchange control, which had initially in 1979 given an opportunity to 'disintermediate', or direct lending through non-sterling channels in order to escape credit controls, and then in the summer of 1980, the abolition of the effective tax on bank deposits represented by compulsory bank reserves with the Bank of England. In consequence, a 'reintermediation' then occurred, with credit expansion via the banking system, as lending moved onshore again. At this point, incidentally, it became impossible to calculate the old money measure in terms of credit expansion, domestic credit expansion (DCE).[18] The credit counterparts suggested that businesses were borrowing more as the corporate sector moved into deficit in the recession, and the government was also borrowing. There may also have been short-term effects that played in, with civil service strikes in the spring of 1980 altering the timing of tax receipts.[19]

Analytically, the monetary surge posed a problem. While before the mid-1970s the velocity of money had been relatively stable, there now started to be large swings (see Figure 5.3). The velocity of narrow money soared. A broader aggregate, however, shows a steep rise to 1983, but then an equally dramatic retreat. The best explanation is increased financialization: as a consequence of liberalization, banks' and building societies' balance sheets expanded more rapidly than nominal income. A larger share of the workforce was now paid monthly, through bank deposit, rather than weekly in cash. The higher balance-sheet-to-income ratios for individuals and corporations meant that it was hard to read inflationary consequences out of higher monetary growth aggregates.[20]

The price effects of the monetary surge were alarming. In a meeting with Howe, Richardson explained that the latest figures suggested that although interest rates had been high, they had not been high enough in relation to the rate of increase in earnings which had actually been experienced.

With hindsight, it was possible to say that MLR could with advantage have been pushed even higher in order to slow the rate of monetary growth, although if the short-term assistance to the financial markets were to have been avoided, MLR could well have needed to be over 20 per cent. Notwithstanding the fact that the

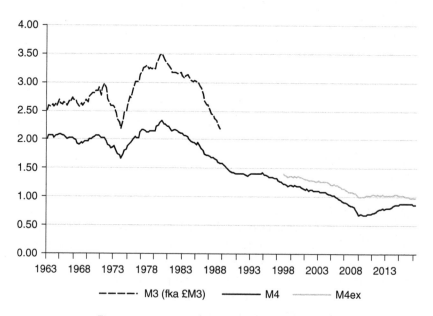

Figure 5.3 Income velocity of money (1963–2015)

money figures had not been within the target range, policy had still borne very harshly on the corporate sector; and there would be the most serious difficulties for UK industry if interest rates had now to be increased in response to recent monetary developments. The Chancellor confirmed that he would wish to avoid any immediate response to the July figures, either by way of fiscal action or through an increase in MLR. The exchange rate should continue to be determined by market forces. The authorities would provide the best explanation they could of the July figures, drawing attention to all the exceptional features, and at the same time emphasizing the firmness of their control over public expenditure and their determination to stick to the monetary strategy.[21]

In a note at the end of August for the Chancellor, Peter Middleton set out what he interpreted as the Bank's view of the problem:

On some analyses, the Bank could be involved in giving special assistance to the short term markets for the whole period of the medium term strategy. We have to reach a judgement about the extent to which this is desirable. If there is a continuing need for these operations we must decide how they are to be implemented and find a way to presenting them which avoids adding to the criticism from some quarters that Government policy is designed to control interest rates rather than the money supply, and that we are unwilling to take any steps which will bring pressure on the banks to restrict lending.[22]

By October 1980, relations between the Bank and the Treasury had reached a crisis: the money supply (£M3) had grown at an annual rate of over 26 per cent in the previous six months (compared with the current target range of 7–11 per cent pa) (see Figure 5.4). There was exceptional growth in bank lending in July and August, after the end of the Supplementary Special Deposits scheme (the 'corset') in June. The corset had

given rise to substantial disintermediation as the private sector increased its holdings of 'near-money' (assets not subject to corset penalties). With the end of the corset, the banks have been able to restructure their balance sheets; and there had been a surge in money supply growth as business that had been forced into non-bank channels returned to the banking sector.[23]

William Ryrie at the Treasury commented that the problem antedated the removal of the corset:

The present system of control seemed to be existing increasingly unhappily alongside a tight monetary target regime. This has become more obvious. Since monetary targets were first introduced in 1975, we have not succeeded in achieving any sustained reduction in the rate of growth of the money stock as measured by £M3; if anything, there has been an acceleration. The more government policy has become predicated on tight monetary policy, the less we have succeeded.

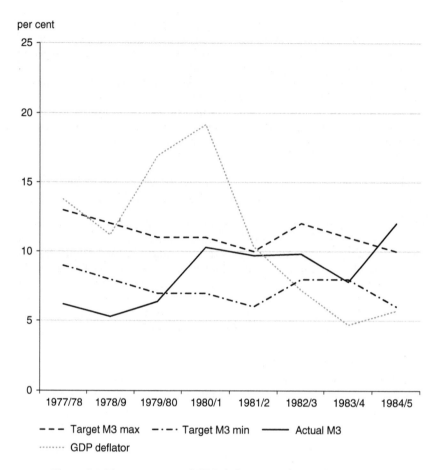

per cent

Figure 5.4 Money targets and GDP deflator growth rates (1977–1985)

The various monetary base, flexible interest rate regimes do this to varying degrees. Shocks feed through on to interest rates rather than money. The price you pay is in fluctuating interest rates. The recent surge in the money supply would have brought about such higher interest rates. This applies to all interest rates; you cannot fix one rate such as the mortgage rate or base rates and expect a monetary base system to work.

The choice is therefore a fundamental one. Do you want a system which will automatically give short-run control and bring you back towards your target, irrespective of the consequences?

If you do, an effective monetary base regime is the direction in which to move. If the Public Sector Borrowing Requirement (PSBR) gets out of hand, or if fiscal policy is imbalanced, interest rates will go up until you do something about it. The banks will not be able to lend as readily as happens at present; they would generate higher interest rates while adjusting their assets to the available base. The regime for interest rates would be very similar to that for the exchange rate. So it would become very important indeed to get the monetary targets right.

If you do not, and you want the money supply to act as the absorber in the economy in the short term – a position taken by the great majority of those involved in our consultations – then you must be prepared to pursue monetary targets in a longer-term sense. That means relying on making changes aimed at getting rid of the source of the disturbance by accommodating swings in monetary growth in the short term and perhaps in the longer term if measures are inadequate or insufficient.

It is easier said than done to manage without short-term control. You have to somehow get the balance between the target, fiscal policy and external policy to generate the level of interest rates you are willing to live with. Yet almost any move to improve short-term control will involve institutional changes. These include tightening up on lender of last resort facilities, with implications for the discount market, encouraging the banks to move away from the overdraft system.[24]

At this point, a new set of considerations came into play. The exchange rate against the DM surged through the 4.50 level on 21 October. From the end of October, both the Bank of England and the Federal Reserve increased their interventions in the foreign exchange markets, with the Bundesbank selling $130 m on the American account on 3 November and the Bank of England selling sterling for $53 m.[25] The Bank's policy was not completely consistent, and by the end of the first week of November, as the dollar soared, the Bank started to sell dollars and hence try to prevent the pound from falling further against a rising dollar.

There was academic criticism of intervention. Alan Budd was particularly vocal in a meeting of the Bank's Panel of Academic Consultants, where he stated that he wished to take issue with one of the conclusions of the Bank paper:

Was it correct to conclude that one could not understand the current level of the £ and still argue that the rate ought to be bought down? A confession of ignorance does not provide any grounds for asserting that the exchange rate is either too high or too low, or that intervention is necessary. Certainly, one could list several theories which suggested that the real exchange rate was above its 'long-run equilibrium' level, such as the Dornbusch account of 'overshooting'. But such theories were purely ad hoc, in that they relied on ad hoc assertions about private market behaviour. Moreover, they possess no more empirical basis than any other theory. Despite the total failure to forecast the UK exchange rate since early 1979, there was nothing, according to Dr Budd, to suggest that the market for foreign exchange was inefficient. He personally believed that, if there were problems for economic adjustment, they existed in other markets (such as labour markets). It followed that the case for exchange rate intervention could only, at best, be as a second-best policy, made necessary by inefficiencies elsewhere in the system.

The counter-case was put by John Flemming, who would succeed Christopher Dow as chief economist:

Commenting on the supposed adverse effects of a high exchange rate on the real economy, Mr Flemming pointed out that current policy should be judged in terms of its main aim – the reduction of inflation by deflating the economy. Several proponents of the current approach believed that the best way to achieve this was by a restrictive monetary policy which had precisely these effects on the exchange rate. Such adherents believed that exchange rate intervention would actually weaken the impetus of the anti-inflationary policy. Moreover, the argument that the foreign exchange market behaved like a casino merely implied that there was scope for profits and losses in such a market – it did not in itself provide a case for intervention on social welfare grounds. Mr Flemming argued that intervention might be justified as a second-best policy if it were accepted that the exchange rate was now higher than anticipated when the present monetary policy had been adopted. It would, though, have been better to have adopted a less stringent policy originally rather than alter current policy now. Moreover, Mr Flemming believed that intervention might be counter-productive if governed by an exchange rate target.[26]

In other words, for Flemming, the need to intervene in the forex market came as a consequence of a mistaken monetary policy stance.

THE PRIME MINISTER'S SEMINARS: THE BANK AGAINST THE FOREIGNERS

Were there any alternatives to the Treasury-Bank strategy? The summer of 1980 constituted the real testing point, the moment of truth, for British monetary policy design. Margaret Thatcher was closely involved in the discussion, and shifted the outcome decisively. The irony was that the Prime Minister, in apparently insisting on a foreign model of monetary base control (MBC), undermined the case for £M3, the most practicable form of British monetarism. In the late summer of 1980, a number of dramatic sessions with the Prime Minister shook the institutional setting of British monetary policy: on 3, 8 and 18 September, and then a 'seminar' on 30 September (without Bank participation) and on 8 October.

James Callaghan had introduced the idea of a prime minister's monetary seminar as a way of managing the aftermath of the 1976 IMF crisis. At the time, the Bank liked the initiative, because it seemed to increase its intellectual impact on policy-making and its prestige. Margaret Thatcher held her first prime minister's seminar on the possibility of using MBC as the fundamental policy instrument on

18 July 1979. It was a relatively restrained and academic affair. The meeting discussed papers prepared by stockbrokers (Gordon Pepper's Greenwell paper), by academic economists (Brian Griffiths and Geoffrey Wood) as well as a Treasury paper and the *BEQB* June 1979 paper of Goodhart, Foot and Hotson that was in practice a pre-emptive attack on the MBC concept.[27] The Treasury's Middleton made it clear when he sent his first draft that

> he has been under great pressure from the Chief Secretary (Nigel Lawson) to complete this. He tells me that he is going to recommend that certain aspects of monetary base control deserve 'further study' – 'given the way the wind is blowing' (his words), this was, he said, the least that he felt he could do. He also has a copy of Professor Griffiths' paper (probably sent direct to the Chancellor), which Middleton said was also a hurried piece – full of typing errors.[28]

Middleton suggested a way of trying to make MBC more 'flexible'. He started off by observing: 'A rigidly enforced MBC would be inflexible probably leading to very sharp changes in interest rates in the short run. The Bank of England, rightly in our view, criticised this sort of scheme in the current Bank of England Quarterly Bulletin.' In particular, he tried to devise a mechanism that would bring the commercial banks into the process of monetary control. A 'Negotiable Base Asset scheme' might transfer the onus of sterilizing external inflows from the authorities to the large banks, mostly the clearing banks, themselves.[29] John Fforde from the Bank set out a sceptical view of such attempts to shape bank behaviour, arguing that money could only be controlled through its price, and not by any quantitative restriction: 'Consequently, attempts to do so by "direct" controls on banks, or by such direct controls on inflows of exchange as may be practicable, are inclined to prove foolish and institutionally damaging.' The key to traditional British monetary policy was its foundation in debt management:

> Next, it is helpful to remind ourselves that British monetary policy relies heavily on debt management conducted within the money markets mentioned above and a bond market of comparable breadth and sophistication. There, the lenders are kept fully at arms length from the borrower, and a completely free market has thereby been preserved despite the strong tendency to corporatism shown in other governmental relationships both in the financial field and elsewhere. But the bulk of debt management is conducted through marketable bonds of a conventional character unindexed against inflation. It has then to be said that there is <u>no</u> way in which such a bond market can be effectively shielded from sharply fluctuating fears, hopes, and uncertainties concerned with the future pace of inflation, the future rate of monetary growth, the size of public borrowing, etc. But by timely

adaptation of tactics and techniques, their effect can be mitigated or softened. Beyond this, there remains either a radical change in market structure or a radical change in the instrument marketed.[30]

The 1979 seminar had taken place amidst considerable optimism about the effectiveness of policy, but marked a clear victory for the opponents of the radical schemes for MBC. The Treasury's overall outlook paper on 'Monetary Objectives and Prospects' explained that the Chancellor's target range of 7–11 per cent for £M3 in the ten months ending in April 1980 was attainable: 'This was deliberately chosen as a tight monetary target, although there is no single way of measuring "tightness" in this context.' And 'while £M3 is the target variable, account will need to be taken of the development of the other monetary aggregates'.[31]

In the summer of 1980, the situation looked uncontrollable. Thatcher expressed her serious concern about the 'out of control' money supply and the urgent need for a government response.[32] Before the 3 September 1980, meeting with the Prime Minister, the Chancellor had held a preparatory meeting in 11 Downing Street, where the Bank had powerfully expressed the view that the monetary aggregates were creating a delusory impression. Richardson started by commenting on the divergence between develop-ments in the 'real economy' and in the financial markets. 'Undoubtedly this divergence made for presentational and political difficulties, given the government's commitment to monetary targets.' But he saw the present situation as promising better for the final objective of policy – a reduction in the inflation rate – than for the intermediate objective (the monetary aggregate). Although, he said, monetary growth had apparently been much faster than the authorities had intended, the economy nevertheless was exhibiting the symptoms of a tight monetary squeeze (as well as those of earnings having grown much too rapidly). The behaviour of the exchange rate was thus for him a very clear indication of the tightness of monetary policy.

Charles Goodhart explained that changes in £M3 were not reliably related to movements in the real economy; £M3 in recent years had been much influenced by structural shifts in the financial sector. In the UK, M1 was currently behaving rather better, but the corresponding indicator had proved substantially misleading in the US and could not be relied on in the UK to give an adequate indication of the present situation or the immediate prospects for the economy.

M0 at this time was slowing down precipitately with the recession, so a narrow money concept did not look very useful either as a guide to price developments. Richardson concluded 'that the £M3 excess would have somehow to be "disowned"'. If a new £M3 target were to be set, there would remain a risk that the authorities would again fail to meet it. On the other hand, if the £M3 target were to be 'de-emphasised', there could still be difficulties with alternatives.

Future movements in £M3 might in the event be much closer to the Government's target range without any further action on the part of the authorities; but for the time being it appeared that we should have rest heavily on a general assessment of movements in the real economy and of the way monetary forces were operating rather than on the current monetary figures.[33]

Richardson had prepared a long draft letter to the Prime Minister arguing against base control. It began with a lament of how the debate had developed:

I have become increasingly concerned in the course of recent discussions that there has not been a full meeting of minds between us. I feel, unhappily, that I have not been able to present before you in full the position as I see it. Moreover, I am worried that certain interpretations of past events, which I believe to be incorrect, may become entrenched. Nevertheless I would like to emphasise two points. First, the decision both to act in this way and with respect to the particular level of MLR to maintain, was not taken by the Bank alone, but was a policy decision taken with the Chancellor and yourself. Whether right or wrong with the benefit of hindsight, it was not just the Bank's policy. Second, the choice of interest rate has continually been made with the overriding purpose, above all, of setting rates at a level that would achieve the target rate for £M3.

Even at the best of times I have doubts and reservations about the merits of monetary base control, especially if applied to the achievement of a £M3 target. Under current circumstances, I believe that it could be counterproductive, not only for the economy more generally and the disturbances that it would bring to the financial system, but also because I doubt whether it would achieve any greater reduction in the growth of £M3 over the next few months than our present techniques.[34]

Wisely, this draft letter was never sent to the Prime Minister, and Richardson eventually dispatched instead a rather anodyne memorandum on alternatives for monetary control, which laid out how the Bank saw the 'theoretical attraction' of base control, with a brief covering note that stated that 'whatever may be the attractions of monetary control, its adoption would necessarily involve a long transitional period before we know enough about the way in which the new system worked to be able to establish meaningful control'.[35]

In fact, on 9 September, Thatcher talked with the Chancellor and Treasury officials, but without the Governor or the Deputy Governor, who were both away from London. The two Bank officials who were present were John Fforde, whom she found incomprehensible and inarticulate, and the at-that-time relatively junior Eddie George, who exuded confidence and competence and delivered a market-based view on why interest rates should be cut.[36] She started the session with an attack on the Bank:

The Prime Minster said that she understood that the underlying rate of monetary growth was now reckoned to be 15 per cent or higher. This was extremely disturbing – given that the 7–11 per cent target was the centre-piece of the Government's economic strategy. It seemed to her that the Bank had been pursuing an interest rate policy rather than a policy to control the money supply. With hindsight it might have been better if the Bank had not undertaken the continuing money market relief measures, even though this would have meant still higher interest rates in the short-term. As long as the clearers could rely on the Bank to relieve any pressure on their liquidity, they would surely be all too willing to maintain a high level of lending to the private sector.

The Bank's representatives tried a defence:

In discussion it was pointed out that if the Bank had not provided relief to the money market, interest rates would certainly have risen including in all probability the mortgage rate. But this had effectively been ruled out. As to the effect of interest rates on borrowing, the net effect of high rates was almost certainly to restrain the level of lending – for the crediting of quarterly interest payments to overdrafts was likely to be offset by the demand elasticity factor. This was reflected in the large amount of destocking that was currently going on. High interest rates were helping bring down the rate of inflation both through their effect on lending and on the exchange rate. As regards methods of monetary control, it was important that the discussions on the Green Paper with interested parties should be completed before final decisions were taken.

But the Bank officials did not convince Thatcher.[37] Keegan rightly notes that it was this meeting above all that 'brought relations between Prime Minister and Bank, and Bank and Treasury, to a very low ebb'.[38] At the same time, George's effective performance at the meeting helped to convince the Prime Minister that he was the future of the Bank.

Another meeting occurred on 18 September, this time with the Governor and the Deputy Governor present. Thatcher's initial preference was to introduce a new set of exchange controls, on the basis of Swiss and German practice in the 1970s, to penalise the capital inflows that were pushing UK monetary growth:

She still felt that the Swiss experience showed that action to restrain inflows could be effective. More generally she found it somewhat ironic that the monetary aggregates were running well above target and yet the exchange rate remained very strong. The failure to control the money supply rather undermined the Treasury's argument that intervention would put the monetary strategy at risk. Nonetheless she was not disposed to any further undermining of the strategy, and was therefore opposed to large scale intervention to get the rate down. If inflow controls would not work, she wanted to know what other measures would.[39]

But both the Treasury and the Bank disliked the idea of inflow controls (officials had previously characterized that as 'a leap in the dark').[40] Thatcher then set out a very explicit view on the exchange rate: 'In conclusion, the Prime Minister said that she was clear that the present exchange rate was too high and that a rate of between $2.20 and $2.30 would be desirable; anything below $2.20 would jeopardise the fight against inflation.'[41] The issue became highly political when at the Conservative Party conference the Paymaster-General Angus Maude and others launched attacks on the Chancellor's stance – and Howe in turn became 'very angry'.[42]

The outcome of the clashes was to water down the centrality of £M3:

Mr Middleton noted that the present system worked off a medium-term control, directed towards £M3. A move to a mandatory MBC would probably require a new aggregate in addition to £M3 or PSL1 [a private sector liquidity aggregate that includes private sector holdings of money market assets with original maturity of under one year, local authority temporary debt, Treasury bills and bank bills]. The Governor agreed that £M3, which was controlled through interest rates and funding, was uncontrollable in the short-term; more precise control pointed towards M1 as the target. However £M3 had its own attractions: it could be analysed in terms of its credit counterparts and could be linked directly to the PSBR.[43]

At this point Thatcher brought a new element into the discussions: a foreign model for monetarism. She had met the Swiss monetarist economist Karl Brunner while staying at Schloss Freudenberg on Lake Zug, at the house of a wealthy retired former Conservative backbench MP, Douglas Glover. Brunner argued that the Bank of England could control money in the UK by adopting Swiss techniques. Switzerland had had a brief but unsatisfactory period in 1978 when a foreign exchange anchor – an informal peg to the DM – produced high inflation, and since then the country had adopted a monetary target. At present, Brunner thought, in the UK, bank reserve requirements frustrated any attempt at control, and the Bank should abandon its discount window operations:

The Bank should abandon its lender of first resort attitude and concentrate on controlling the monetary base. I had the opportunity to ask this summer an official of the Bank of England about their attitudes and procedure. I inquired in particular why the Green Book [*sic*: Paper] essentially attempted to sell the traditional procedures and customs under the pretense of a monetary control policy. The answer I obtained emphasized that the announcement of a monetary control policy was really sufficient and any adjustments of external institutions or internal procedures would have 'confused' the financial markets. This is in my judgment just a camouflage justifying an essentially rhetorical attention to monetary control. It is noteworthy in this context that the Green Book [*sic*: Paper] on Monetary Control thoroughly failed to address the central issues and crucial requirements for an effective monetary control. I find this particularly distressing as some members of the Bank's staff, at the request of the Governor, engaged in regular discussions with the Swiss National Bank bearing on these issues. Whatever observations I may have on the behaviour of Central Bank suggest that we cannot expect a change in attitudes or procedures developed by an entrenched bureaucracy without a substantial outside pressure. I find it difficult to believe that the Bank of England will on its own initiative attend to the two recommendations made above.

Brunner went on to suggest a new sort of academic seminar in which monetarist economists – he mentioned specifically Alan Walters, Michael Parkin and David Laidler – should instruct and correct the Bank's staff.[44] The first such meeting, on 30 September 1980, involved neither the Chancellor nor any Bank official. Instead Thatcher, with Peter Middleton and Tim Lankester from the Treasury, met foreign experts: Brunner, Allan Meltzer from Carnegie Mellon University Pittsburgh, Kurt Schiltknecht, the director of the economics department of the Swiss National Bank and its principal monetary guru, as well as the young Italian economist Mario Monti, who saw monetarism as a central weapon in the struggle against fiscal irresponsibility. There was also a Bundesbank economist, Hermann-Josef Dudler, who did not like the idea of MBC, but was largely sidelined in the discussion. Dudler said, 'If the aim of the MBC advocates was to allow greater variations in interest rates to control the quantity of money, that could in principle be achieved under the present system. It could not be achieved perfectly, but it was not clear that MBC would be any more reliable.'[45]

Dudler in fact was something of star witness against American-style monetary control. A few months later, he told the Commons Treasury Select Committee, 'As to why Germany had been successful in its monetary targets, [...] the basic reason was beyond the Deutsche Bundesbank's control: that the population was very opposed to inflation.'[46]

The advocates of MBC at the Prime Minister's seminar were more numerous, and probably also more persuasive, at least with the Prime Minister. Karl Brunner said:

Either, the Bank would continue with its present instruments, and M3 would continue to be out of control, or we would move over to MBC. In designing the present monetary strategy, the authorities had virtually made it certain that the strategy would fall. The only viable way forward was for the authorities to set a target for the monetary base; he was confident that over a period the other monetary aggregates would follow a similar path. In any case, he believed that there was a good relationship between M0 and inflation.

Brunner also made sure that his views were transmitted to a broader public. He told the *Wall Street Journal*: 'From the start we told her it was in part a data problem. M1 is too narrow and M3 is much too broad .... So long as there is this data problem, the central bank should focus on the monetary base.'[47]

Allan Meltzer was more circumspect about ways of meeting the government's inflation objective:

But the recent jump in sterling M3, even though some of it was due to the end of the corset, underlined the difficulties which the authorities had in controlling the money supply. Under the present control arrangements, there was a tendency to 'procyclicality': the Bank was slow to respond to changes in monetary conditions in its manipulation of interest rates, and this simply made the cycle worse. The Government should free interest rates right away, and move over controlling the monetary base. The M3 target should be dispensed with, and replaced by a new target. For M0 it was particularly important to move quickly so as to get the monetary aggregates under control before recovery appeared. He admitted, however, that there would be a problem of political credibility in moving from one target definition to another: somehow it would have to be explained that the new target was a continuation of existing strategy.

Mario Monti gave an Italian lesson: 'The Italian authorities had used MBC for some time. Although Italy's monetary performance had been less than satisfactory this was not because of inadequate instruments; rather, it was because the Government had not been prepared to take interest rate consequences of the monetary base targets. In other words, they had right levers but not the political will.'[48] The seminar was thus directed against both the Treasury and the Bank.

Thatcher also made no secret of what she had learnt at the seminar. On a television programme hosted by her favourite interviewer, Brian Walden, she explained that she was 'not relying on M1' and that rapid M3 growth had been due to the fact that 'we took off that thing known as the Bank of England corset'. So she concluded that the 'monetary base happens to be [...] extremely important. [...] We do look at monetary base.'[49]

Thatcher's seminar had been preceded by a similar Treasury-organized seminar, held in Church House, with the Bank, with a much broader range of mostly non-foreign economists, where Middleton kicked off by stating that 'there was general agreement on Monday that £M3 could not be controlled in the short term – ie less than six months but that it would be possible to control the base over much shorter periods'. Later in the morning, Anthony Courakis (Oxford) made a similar point: 'The markets were currently suspicious of the authorities. In Germany overshooting did not damage the markets' expectations because of their underlying confidence in the authorities' ability to hold down inflation. The main issue therefore was whether MBC would improve confidence in the UK.' The key issue at stake was the extent to which interest rates would need to spike in the anti-inflationary strategy: the US had undergone a similar problem, and experienced analogous monetary policy debates, after October 1979 when Fed Chairman Paul Volcker tried to implement an anti-inflationary strategy. Tim Congdon pointed out that a shift to MBC could mean an once-and-for-all increase in £M3 arising from a number of factors. Gordon Pepper, the guru of applied monetarism, was 'sceptical about some of the arguments about interest rate volatility; over the medium term interest rates might fluctuate less. Moreover, excess reserves and other buffers would moderate fluctuations; there was no need for short run control. At the moment a central government surplus tended to push interest rates up; the opposite of what was required for monetary control.'

The second topic of debate at the Treasury seminar concerned the stability of the banking system and the dangers that existed if the Bank were to restrict support for commercial banks as part of its anti-inflation strategy. Griffiths pointed out that 'the banking system's record was not very good', and that there existed 'no feasible alternative to MBC that would both control money supply and allow competition'. Charles Goodhart retorted that Griffiths' suggestion of pegging MLR to interbank rates could lead to spiralling interest rates (at least until bank lending adjusted) as it would 'always be worth an individual bank borrowing in the interbank market, rather than from the Bank. Penalties could have a similar effect.' The monetarist Tim Congdon argued that: 'The present LLR arrangements meant that there was no risk of a banking crisis. There was a danger that a change in the control system could risk a banking failure.'[50]

Another iteration of the monetary seminar occurred at 10 Downing Street a few weeks later, on 13 October 1980, with the Chancellor and Treasury officials and with the Governor and Deputy Governor of the Bank as well as Eddie George and Charles Goodhart. Dow later described the event as a 'great inquisition on what had gone wrong with monetary policy in the summer'.[51] Richardson began with a presentation of the Bank's view:

Recent developments gave rise to considerable anxiety. The underlying growth of £M3 after allowing for the unwinding of the corset had accelerated in the late spring and summer to well outside the target range. The reasons for this were, firstly, the very high PSBR – which had been running at an annual rate of about £15 billion in the first half of the financial year. This had proved beyond the authorities' funding capacity, even though gilt sales to domestic non-banks had been very substantial. The Bank had hoped that the high PSBR in the first few months would be offset by lower figures in the second half of the financial year so that the Budget forecast was achieved.

[...]While there were theoretical attractions in some of the [monetary base control] proposals, no one could ignore the practical difficulty that – if MBC or a variant of it were to be introduced now – interest rates would undoubtedly have to rise. This would put further pressure on the exchange rate and add to the pressure on industry. It was hard to see how this would be an appropriate response to the present conjuncture. Indeed, if it was decided on industrial grounds that interest rates should be reduced, this could only be achieved by an <u>administered</u> reduction. The critics of the present system argued that the money supply could not be controlled unless interest rates went up. The Bank's response to them was that, provided the fiscal balance was right, the present system was capable of producing a satisfactory £M3 profile.

Howe agreed with much of the Richardson presentation, also focused on the PSBR, and thought about ways in which the marketing of government debt could be improved. But he added a note about the financial system:

The Lender of Last Resort (LLR) function of the Bank needed to be modified. The present system did not engage the banks in curtailing the rate of monetary growth: on the contrary, they benefited from seeing their lending expand, and by in effect acting as 'Lender of First Resort' the Bank were accommodating this. At least, the Bank ought urgently to consider ways of making the LLR function less as a matter of course.

Howe instinctively saw that – as the Bank was always pointing out – the process of modern monetary management was incompatible with the historic relationship between the Bank and the City of London. Thatcher responded with the observation that 'the present system was plainly not working adequately and that it had to be improved. She was most concerned about the apparent loss of control of the monetary aggregates over the summer, which could put at risk the Government's anti-inflation strategy.'[52] But in regard to policy, she was quite restrained, and did not explicitly press for MBC.

A few days later, in the Mansion House speech, Richardson noted that the Bank had 'received a good deal of advice', a coded reference to the Prime Minister's seminars (in the draft of the speech the wording was the Bank had 'been under a good deal of attack').[53] But part of the 'advice' was also the continued criticism on the part of Milton Friedman, who was quoted in a *Newsweek* article as saying the Bank should attempt to control monetary growth directly and that Mrs Thatcher should 'kick out the people who have been running the money supply and replace them with people who know how to do it'.[54]

In October 1980, a relatively junior Bank of England economist, William Allen, suggested an approach, dubbed an M0 scheme, which would offer a way out of the dilemma, in that policy did not need to target – or even think about – bank lending, and which might fit in rather better with Thatcher's approach:

It would be possible to move towards a kind of M 0, or monetary base, system while maintaining the same degree of control over interest rates and £M3 as we have now. £M3 might, however, be de-emphasised. The basic feature of the scheme would be as follows:

- Monetary base would consist of bankers' balances at the Bank of England. These balances would not bear interest.
- There would be no reserve asset ratio, and no primary liquidity requirement
- The market would be supplied with Treasury bills through daily open-market operations, and not through the weekly tender, which would be abolished.

The initial object of introducing the system would be to learn something about the banks' demand for excess base money and about the relationship between banks' holdings of base money and the monetary aggregates, without losing control over interest rates. The system would evolve to one in which the monetary control was exercised not through setting interest rates, but through setting and hitting a target for the monetary base, if what we learned in the initial stage led to us believe that this was possible.[55]

This was a proposal for squaring the circle of working through targets to affect interest rates. But it would need to rely on finding a stable relationship between different aggregates: the simple demand function that underlay Friedman's model. Dow commented, rather helplessly, that 'we have lost faith in M3, but are publicly committed to M3 targets', and then added a question: 'Would prefer exchange rates?'[56]

THE APPRECIATION OF STERLING AND THE QUESTIONING OF TARGETS

In practice the debate over targeting was overshadowed by discussion of exchange rates, and by a dramatic rise in the value of the pound. The Bank's economists, and many others, concluded in the face of the large fluctuations in the foreign exchange markets that movements could not easily be explained in terms of traditional economic models. Alfred Sherman from the Thatcherite think tank the Centre for Policy Studies asked a Swiss economist, and former colleague of Alan Walters at Johns Hopkins, Jürg Niehans, to report on the causes of sterling's appreciation. Niehans rejected the Treasury view that this was the consequence of the effects of North Sea oil on the trade balance, and instead argued that the root was a monetary contraction; M0 had been shrinking in real terms since 1979. The report was presented on 7 January 1981.[57] Niehans thought that interest rates should be cut at once and M0 allowed to expand. William Keegan aptly describes the Niehans report as 'extremely embarrassing to the monetary evangelicals'.[58] Walters thought of the report as a 'bombshell' and noted that Thatcher now became very defensive: 'No one must know about it. Especially Bank of England. Why? Frightened of calls for relaxation and signs to the wets!'[59] Niehans' critique strengthened the position of those who wanted to see interest rates come down.

The contemplation of an interest rate policy reversal had in fact already begun. In November 1980, the Chancellor and the Treasury began to think about a possible two percentage points cut in MLR, and started to argue that such action might even have a favourable impact on the monetary aggregates:

The short run effect depends crucially on expectations. The monetary, PSBR and public expenditure background are of course not good and we shall need to see how recent press reports are taken. But I think we can convince the markets that a cut in interest rates of this size will not exacerbate monetary growth in the short run. They are clearly getting ready to believe it. And if they do believe it the consequences for £M3 could even be favourable. Reducing interest rates will increase the growth of £M3 over a year to 18 months, so the prospects for the strategy are concentrated heavily on the forthcoming budget. Moreover, to get a neutral effect between now and then depends on putting a difficult series of announcements in a wider context in which the Government's medium term intentions for the money supply and inflation are seen to survive.[60]

This Treasury paper set out the basis of the budgetary strategy that was implemented in the next year. At the following monetary seminar in 10

Downing Street, on 18 November 1980, the elements of a new approach to interest rate setting were laid out:

It was explained that the Treasury and the Bank agreed on the need to move to a more flexible system of operations in the money market. This would include allowing short-term interest rates to be free to move within a predetermined (but unannounced) band, and the disappearance of MLR as such. Greater flexibility in interest rates could ease the political and technical tensions in our monetary operations. Moreover, the possibility of considerable fluctuation of short-term rates could encourage the banks to move towards more variable pricing for their lending, which would also be helpful for maintaining monetary control. The purpose of the band, rather than letting rates move completely freely, would be to avoid undue short-term volatility which might arise from technical factors and which might not be warranted by the underlying movement in the money supply. But it would be possible to change the band quickly if it appeared that the monetary target was not being achieved. The authorities would continue to intervene mainly by open market operations.[61]

The cut in MLR to 14 per cent was announced on 25 November. A further reduction of 2 per cent followed on 11 March 1981, to coincide with the budget. The step had to be rationalized at a new seminar with the Prime Minister on 11 February, where Howe set out the logic. The reduction was also supported by Alan Walters. At a late stage in the discussion, Richardson pushed the case for interest rate reduction with two arguments that he felt might sway Margaret Thatcher, one concerned with moving away from the M3 focus, but the other – more powerful – persuader being the Swiss example:

The Chancellor said that this was a very difficult decision. The Governor had advised that a 1% reduction would be desirable and possible provided we could be satisfied that we could justify it in a credible way. By this he meant –

(i) Acknowledging that the exchange rate was a factor in the decision;
(ii) Praying in aid the fall in inflation (the 12 month RPI figure to be announced on Friday will be 13.01%);
(iii) Acknowledging that M3 is no longer the sole guide to interest rate determination (though in effect we had already done this when we decided to reduce MLR in November);
(iv) Indicating that from now on we would be looking not only at M3 but at the narrower monetary aggregates in determining interest rates and other policy measures.

The Prime Minister said that the exchange rate and inflation considerations were, in her view, very important; and she wanted to give industry a boost. But she appreciated the Treasury's anxiety. She would want to consider the matter further with Treasury Ministers and officials before taking a final decision.

As the meeting was breaking up, <u>the Governor</u> told the Prime Minister that the Governor of the Swiss Central Bank had told him in Zurich that the UK was faced with a similar situation on the exchange rate front to that which he had been confronted in Switzerland in 1978. In other words, he would put getting the exchange rate down as having immediate priority over money supply considerations. He had also told him that our monetary base had been growing, if anything, too slowly.[62]

From the point of view of the Bank, this operation demonstrated the futility and irrelevance of the monetary targeting exercise. The discussion was followed by a flurry of bitter memoranda, all arguing that policy needed to shift to thinking about the exchange rate. The monetary economist Charles Goodhart noted:

I begin, however, by stating a position that I hold, and, I believe, is widely held. That is that the path of £M3 does not provide a good guide, certainly not by itself, possibly not at all, to the selection and determination of short-term interest rates. This is partly because £M3 is not a good indicator of current/future economic developments and partly because its behaviour, at least over periods of up to one year, is notably insensitive to variations in short-term interest rates.

Its only effective use was as a 'prop to fiscal restraint'.[63]

The most critical memorandum was prepared by John Fforde: 'I get a feeling that the foundations of policy are beginning to disintegrate and that we risk becoming operationally entangled with a Cheshire cat monetary policy which would begin and end by satisfying almost nobody, particularly the markets.' The Cheshire cat was a 'fierce looking £M3 target (6–10% for 1981/2), a borrowing requirement regarded as too high by market opinion, and a thoroughly imprecise but strongly-worded kind of conditionality along the lines expressed by the Prime Minister in her T-V interview with Brian Walden'. Fforde concluded 'with apologies to Oscar Wilde, it could be described as the inexplicable in pursuit of the uncontrollable'.[64] His recommendation was that conditionality should refer to the exchange rate. That point was taken up and endorsed by Kit McMahon, who wanted 'a positive and specific conditionality for the monetary target in terms of the exchange rate', but at the same time 'not giving any specific commitment about the lever or range of the exchange rate'.[65]

The 1981 budget produced a massive wave of academic criticism. The undoubted highpoint of the intellectual campaign was the statement signed by 364 economists (including the future Governor of the Bank, Mervyn King) and published by *The Times*: 'There is no basis in economic theory or supporting evidence for the Government's belief that by deflating demand they will bring inflation permanently under control and thereby induce an automatic recovery in output and employment . . .. [P]resent policies will deepen the depression, erode the industrial base of our economy and threaten its social and political stability.' The letter and its aftermath – some signatories later confessed that they had been wrong in their assessment – proved an intellectual or academic challenge to the Bank: Should the Bank associate itself with the criticism of the government?[66] On 7 April 1981, Thatcher wrote on the back of a menu card at a dinner, 'Don't get pushed into a corner by economists.'[67]

ECONOMISTS AND THE BANK OF ENGLAND

The controversies of 1980 and 1981 raised the question of how far the Bank should rely on professional economists, who seemed generally opposed to the government's policy and also deeply divided over analytical and policy issues. McMahon commented on a paper by Goodhart noting that the two major difficulties the Bank suffered from in respect to its use of economists were 'the state of the art these days' but also 'the extreme and controversial nature of the government's policies'. Since McMahon was sympathetic to much of the criticism of the government, he felt it would be wrong to 'block them out by thought control', even though 'things here at some times got a bit out of control and I fully take the point that relationships with Whitehall can suffer from this'.[68]

The problem about economists and how their advice should be viewed and used went deeper. Many senior officials were concluding that the Bank's approach to the use of economic models was flawed. A memorandum in 1981 concluded that the short- and medium-term models 'lag behind current best practice in many ways. The models in no way embody a house view, but are estimated according to the whim of the sector expert, restrained (if at all) only by a hard-pressed model manager who is responsible for data, programmes and model maintenance and forecasts. As a result, they embody quite a lot of inconsistences and can at best be described as heuristic attempts to keep up with the field.' Senior economists felt a 'disillusion with models generally', and the three major Bank models were in 'near dereliction'. Nevertheless, the paper concluded, there should be an annual Keynesian model for the Bank.[69]

The Lucas critique of models suggested that the fundamental flaw was that they had no way of incorporating expectations ('rational expectations'). In general, the mood was turning away from the macro-models that had been developed in order to understand and predict the economy in the 1960s, and to lay the basis for effective policy control, but that had fared badly in the economic turbulence of the 1970s. In a survey of *Who Runs the Economy?* in 1979, the journalists William Keegan and Rupert Pennant-Rea summed up the criticism of models as 'underestimating growth rates and the scale of fluctuations'.[70]

When the issue of model use and abuse was put to the Bank's Panel of Academic Consultants there was a great deal of scepticism. Terry Burns spoke of 'the conflict between models designed for forecasting and monitoring, on the one hand, and for policy analysis on the other. The former requirement militated in favour of large models but this might well produce a rather clumsy framework within which to provide policy advice. The latter might well depend on a smaller number of key relationships. However, the basic reason why large models have contributed less than was hoped to the resolution of disputes as to how the economy works was the pressure from users for regular short-term forecasts.' Angus Deaton, then at Cambridge University, added,

One could design various types of model, internally but not necessarily externally consistent, suitable for analysis of different economic processes and types of economy. But much of the apparent greater detail provided by larger macroeconomic models was in fact spurious – several sections of the HMT model were simply required to print out huge portions of the National Accounts. This implied that it was not necessarily the case that the reduced form of a model would be enhanced by simply introducing more detail and complexity into its structure.[71]

The Bank also found publicity about the stance of its academic economists and in particular about the work of the Panel of Academic Consultants embarrassing. A particularly sore point came when the *Guardian* reported that a member of the panel, David Hendry, had severely criticized the econometrics of Milton Friedman and Anna Schwartz's *Monetary Trends in the United States and the United Kingdom*, a much less satisfactory sequel to their monumental *Monetary History of the United States*.[72] The Bank worried that the government might draw the conclusion that its economists were embarking on a public campaign against the foundations of monetarism.

The lack of self-confidence of Bank economists remained a feature of the Bank during the whole decade and allowed an intellectual ascendancy of figures who looked up to Eddie George and David Walker and to the areas where there was a clear contribution to policy. Both George and Walker had undergraduate degrees in economics, but were not academics. George thought that the work of economists was important, but that their priority should lie primarily in sketching out scenarios for market developments rather than in working with large macro models. In 1985, John Flemming as chief economist considered – if only eventually to reject – a scheme that would distribute economists more widely through the Bank:

Despite the mixture of pros and cons set out above, I am clear that I would not welcome such a radical change: not merely because it would mean a loss of 'turf' but because I believe that the risks of a loss of professionalism and technical competence are too great, given the general tendency towards professionalism both in the City and in Government. (These trends ought, perhaps not to be taken for granted. In the new City without fixed commissions, and with research separately billed, there may be less room for the Paul Nields, Gavyn Davies, Paul Thomas and Tim Congdons. In HMT, and the GES [Government Economic Service], more generally, economists and especially macro-economists feel vulnerable. A recent (factually erroneous) Lombard column [in the *Financial Times*] on shifting from macro to micro touched a raw nerve.) [...] The alternative to ED [Economic Division]'s dismemberment (and the establishment of colonies of economists in other areas), is persistence with the present strategy of 'infiltration and feedback'. This is the process by which graduates, who join ED in disproportionate numbers, move out into other areas (mainly with Supervisory and Administrative rank).[73]

This view that a coherent and harmonious concentration of Bank economists was the best way of improving the Bank's expertise and political leverage proved incorrect (or perhaps premature). In the 1990s, eventually informed economic commentary became more rather than less central to the policy debate; but for the moment and in the midst of the Thatcher experiment such a clear articulation of economists' demand for attention reflected the extent to which the 'markets view' had become triumphant in the Bank.

THE 1981 BUDGET AND A NEW APPROACH
TO INTEREST RATES

In the 1981 budget – the most controversial of the Thatcher years – there was an attempt to take the pressure off manufacturing industry by lowering interest rates.[74] But because of the presentation of the budget – with the fiscal side set out in parliament by the Chancellor – the critics of fiscal deflation missed the possibility that lower interest rates might bring monetary easing (although the move had little effect on real interest rates). 'Monetarism' as a political concept involved the jettisoning of monetarism as a real tool of economic management. On 11 March 1981, MLR was cut further to 12 per cent, but MLR looked increasingly like a distraction because it focused attention on a single figure, whereas in messy reality, borrowers with different risk profiles clearly faced a diversity of interest rates. The reduction had been signalled to the market long in advance by the Bank, with the Governor asking 'what is expected?' from the Budget decisions and the discount houses replying 'it looks like a 2% reduction [in] MLR'.[75]

The Prime Minister was not happy about the slowness with which changes in the monetary regime were implemented. In June 1981, she complained:

It was envisaged in the progress report that the various changes in money market management and in the Bank's role as lender of last resort (including, I thought, the abolition of MLR) could be implemented at Budget time. I understand that progress has been made in that the Bank has substantially reduced its discount window lending and is now operating primarily through open market operations; but the interest rate band apparently still remains to be put into effect, and MLR is still with us.[76]

Richardson was anxious and depressed. He felt 'considerably blasted' by Thatcher and asked, 'Can you give me one good reason why I should stay in my job?' The only consoling thought was that the government would not last for ever, and he looked forward to a general election.[77] Alan Walters was conspiring against the Bank, and in May 1981 recorded in his diary how he met with Allan Meltzer and Brian Griffiths to 'set up an attack on B/E' in the *Daily Telegraph*.[78] The Keynesians in the Bank continued to think about a reversal of the government's fiscal course. In May 1981, at the first meeting of a new policy forum, the Deputy Governor's Committee (DGC), McMahon said: 'If there was still no sign of recovery by the autumn, the Government might be more susceptible to suggestions for stimulatory action, provided they could be presented in a way which did not seem too grossly in conflict with the broad strategy.' And a few weeks later, he came back to the same theme: 'The Government might, in due course, be looking for a rationale for a less rigorous policy stance.'[79] Richardson told William Keegan of the *Observer*: 'In those days one only had to look out of the window to see that monetary policy was too tight.'[80]

In fact, the trough of industrial production had been reached in May 1981, and the (initially weak) recovery was already beginning to set in. At the same time, the growth rate of £M3, which stood at 21.5 per cent on an annualized basis in May 1981, fell continuously until early 1983, when it was below 10 per cent (see Figure 5.5). A wider measure, including building society term shares (a common form of retail consumer deposit), fell rather less dramatically.

per cent

Figure 5.5 Twelve-month growth rates of sterling M3 and a wider sterling aggregate, per cent (1981–1985)

THE OPERATION OF MONETARY POLICY

Douglas Wass supervised the preparation of a memorandum in July 1981 on the Bank's relations with the Treasury, in response to an inquiry from the Chancellor. While the covering note talked about better relations than those existing 'when I first had dealings with the Bank', and commented that the partnership 'seems a remarkably open, friendly, and cooperative one', in fact there was a good deal of tension. 'The Bank should not misuse its accepted and traditional "independent" status to argue publicly, whether explicitly or implicitly, for a weaker attitude to the restraint of inflation and monetary growth. That would be turning the conventional argument for independence on its head.'[81] The document then listed the specific controversies that had flared up: the failure of the Bank to give warning of the impending bid of Standard Chartered for RBS, and the way the Governor had put his authority on the line in turning down the rival HSBC bid. Treasury officials also complained about the 'painful' negotiation of alterations in drafts of the *BEQB* and the 'irritating' way that the Bank did 'not take proper account of our points'.[82] In the clash of great rival bureaucracies, there was no doubt at this stage that the Treasury was absolutely dominant.

There were some areas where the Bank asserted itself. In 1981, under pressure from Nigel Lawson, it began to make narrow money (M0) an official monetary aggregate, and now included a historical data run in the *BEQB*. The practical operation of monetary policy was also modified in 1981, in an indication that the long period of Treasury hegemony was beginning to crack. The decisive signal was the abolition of a single Bank Rate (or MLR). The regular monetary policy operations of the Bank of England traditionally occurred through the intermediation of discount houses (organized in the London Discount Market Association), which acted as the main market makers in bills, and stood between the banking system and the Bank of England. Commercial banks operated by borrowing from discount houses or drawing down deposits or selling securities if they needed funds, and by depositing or buying money market instruments from the discount houses if they had surplus funds. The Bank added liquidity by buying bills (often commercial bills) and reduced money in circulation by selling bills (mostly Treasury bills).[83]

The daily process followed a very long-established course that was given a new daily timetable for market actions in 1981. At 9:45 a.m., the Bank told the market of its estimate of the day's position – a judgement on the interaction of government payments and revenues with the banking system, plus the transactions of other bank customers. It then received reports from the discount houses and the banks. If there was a substantial shortage of funds, there could be an early round of bill purchases by the Bank at 9.45. Banks generally drew money from the discount houses before noon, and the Bank then responded to shortages in the houses by buying bills through its broker (Seccombe, Marshall & Campion, one of the discount houses). The houses offered bills specifying a discount rate for each category of instrument offered, classified into four maturity bands, and the Bank could accept or reject those terms. The transactions (the quantities and the rates) were then made public, and at 2:00 p.m. the Bank offered a new estimate of the market position for the day. The Bank then could deal with a surplus of money in the houses by inviting the discount houses and clearing banks to bid for Treasury bills at specified maturities. Generally, 2:30 p.m. lending was used only when the Bank wanted to announce a change in interest rates. As with the morning operations, these transactions were published. On the other hand, the Bank's lending through private facilities (securitized on collateral) was not. A final round of operations, at 3:30 p.m., could be used to square the positions.

Quite frequently, when the clearing banks and the discount houses had insufficient Treasury or local authority bills, the Bank also operated with commercial bills (which had been the main focus of its activity in the nineteenth century, in the gold standard period: in the 1920s, the Bank had struggled to drive treasury bills out of the regular operations). In the 1980s, the holdings of commercial bills both by the discount market and by the Bank increased dramatically, and these became the central focus of monetary policy. They could be created almost infinitely by the accepting houses (they then became 'eligible bills' with a superior status to the 'trade bills' that had just been accepted by a first-class company rather than a bank). All that was needed was some revenue stream that could be securitized as an eligible trade transaction. The Bank generally tried to keep the market short of money, so that it could make its rate effective, by adjusting the quantity on offer at weekly auctions of Treasury bills. The rates achieved at these auctions were then used to guide Bank operations over the subsequent week. Knowing the market meant being able to judge how the demand at the auctions would price bills, but above all expectations about Bank of England dealing rates. The Bank lent to the discount houses, normally at the rate fixed (conventionally known as Bank Rate, and then the minimum lending rate, or the MLR): but if it wanted to influence the market, it would refuse to buy bills and lend at a penalty rate. These lending operations occurred at 2:30 p.m. The Bank could offer different terms, both as to maturity of lending and as to the interest rate, and indicated in this way the policy stance that it wanted the discount houses to adopt (and how it reacted to the quality of the collateral presented). By the 1980s, the discount houses sold relatively few bills to the Bank, but instead borrowed on collateral. The Bank was also taking bills on repo.

Twice a day announcements were made about the extent of the Bank's operations needed to respond to changes in discount houses 'and clearing banks' operational balances at the Bank or to changes in previous estimates of the Exchequer position.

The discount market thus formed part of the Bank's system of monetary control. But it was also a kind of bank supervision, because the Bank's officials would regularly visit the discount houses and inspect their accounts. The Bank also looked at the bills offered for sale, or more usually as collateral. On occasion, the Bank refused to take some signatures, but its officials would also sometimes note that a particular acceptor or even an issuer of bills appeared too often, and the discount house concerned would then restrict or shut off its dealings with that institution. Overactive institutions would show up in a particularly obvious way, and could thus be indirectly disciplined.[84]

Up to this point, the Bank believed that it operated a 'classical' system that had remained basically unchanged since the nineteenth century. That order ensured a very strict separation of the money market and the capital market, and established a money market that privately generated safe assets through the commercial bill or bill of exchange.[85] That system made the Bank's chosen interest rate, Bank Rate, 'effective' by open market operations, in which securities were sold to absorb money from the banking system, and when the banks then needed to resort to borrowing from the Bank in order to make up their liquidity – at Bank Rate. That was known as 'keeping the houses in the Bank'. Or alternatively, if the Bank believed it needed to enforce a lower rate, it bought securities, so that the market no longer needed to borrow. If the market expected a rate cut, it would offer bills at below the previous rates. The long-serving interwar Governor Montagu Norman had given a fine – and quite threatening – exposition of this classical position when he told the discount houses: 'He was not at all satisfied with the way the market had been conducted in the past six months – they had allowed 3-months' rate to be affected by temporary conditions – this would not do and they must keep it firm and stable. He knew how to deal with them if they didn't and could keep them in the Bank as long as he liked. [. . .] Market could never force Bank either to raise or lower Bank Rate whereas the Bank could force the market to keep rates firm.'[86] That classical system was still working in the early 1980s, as the Bank official Tony Coleby pointed out in an article in the *BEQB*: 'That involved the setting, and periodic variation, of an official discount or lending rate, which, when necessary, is made "effective" by open market operations in the money market. Making Bank Rate "effective" means restraining a decline in market rates from an unchanged Bank rate, or bringing them up to a newly established and higher Bank rate; it is accomplished by limiting the availability of cash to the banking system so as to "force the market into the Bank" to borrow at the somewhat penal rate of Bank rate.'[87] The new approach was aimed at giving a greater role to open market operations (OMOs), with the suggestion that the market's collective choices would shape the rate-setting process. Paul Tucker later referred to the debate as 'clouding the Bank's thinking' about the feasible role of OMOs.[88]

In the early 1980s, in the middle of the deep recession, commercial bank lending expanded. In an attempt to control monetary growth, the Bank then sold more government debt to the non-bank private sector. As a consequence, with cash shortages, banks needed greater reserve balances in order to maintain their cash ratios, and in consequence sold more bills to the discount houses, and thus indirectly to the Bank of England. But since the balances produced as a result of the bills bought by the Bank were with banks, and not with the public or non-banking corporations, they did not show up in the measurement of the money supply. A shortage of Treasury bills thus emerged, and a greatly increased number of commercial bills were bought by the Bank.

The Bank noted the problem that the discount houses' obligation to provide the system with call money against bills had 'denied them the effective freedom to reduce the size of their book substantially should they have wished to do so'. It calculated that some £3 bn of suitable private-sector paper was needed over the economic cycle to accommodate the banks' demand for call money, an amount that put the discount market under great strain. In this view, there was a need for dealers to have a substantial inventory of their own, rather than being purely brokers. It would be better to encourage a wider group of banks to share in the 'package of rights and duties attaching to the function of "sterling money market bank"'.[89] Middleton, who was clearly concerned about the close relationship between the Bank and the discount market, told John Fforde, 'It is important that in your discussion it should be made clear to the discount houses that some increase in variability is expected and that the new arrangements do not give them any guarantee of survival.'[90] By 1988, the Bank had been pushed to provide some codification of the rights and responsibilities of the discount houses.

The 1981 measure followed the 1979 liberalization in expanding the significance of the discount market. One of the leading houses, Gerrard and National, concluded that 'the relationship between the Discount Market and the Bank of England is closer than ever'. It explained this development by the extent of financial turbulence: 'Periods of instability and crises in financial markets have encouraged greater use of the Discount Market and its assets.'[91]

The aim of the reform measures was to increase the extent to which the money market operated as a genuine market, and that would mean involving more participants. But in fact that reform was not realized until 1997 when a completely different money market, based on repos, became fully operational.[92] In March 1981, in *Monetary Control: Next Steps*, the Bank announced that it would increase the number of eligible banks from which it might buy commercial bills. This was the beginning of a reform or liberalization process that lasted until the 1990s, when the anomalous position of the discount houses was finally abolished. In 1981, the Bank made it very clear that it wanted to continue to work with the discount house system, and the houses stated that they were 'grateful for Bank's efforts on Mkt's behalf'. To which the Deputy Governor replied, 'Don't make last point too much outside Bank!'[93]

A new seminar with the Prime Minister was held on 31 July 1981, to cement the policy framework for a complete revamping of the interest rate setting system. MLR was scrapped and replaced by dealing rate corridors that allowed a great deal more flexibility than the highly politicized setting of MLR. It looked as if the result would be a much wider diversity of terms offered in the Bank's dealings with the discount market. A governance consequence was that the formal approval of the Court of Directors for rate changes was no longer required.[94] From the point of view of the government, the new system may have appeared more of a radical break with the old system than in reality it was. In the lead-up to the new policy schedule, Thatcher in a letter to the Chancellor had reiterated her demand for a new form of monetary control: 'I am more than ever convinced – especially after my conversations with [Netherlands central bank president] Dr [Jelle] Zijlstra – that we must change over to some such system of quantitative control and sooner rather than later. I believe MBC <u>could</u> be introduced and implemented provided it includes a suitable discretionary element.'[95]

The new policy envisaged a range of bands for interest rates, in which the actual policy stance would emerge out of the interaction of the discount market and the Bank:

It is agreed that official policy should be expressed by setting a quantitative range for the discount rate on Treasury bills (and from that rate for eligible bank bills) with 1–14 days to maturity, that the width of the band would be 2% initially and that the Bank would aim to keep the appropriate Treasury bill rate, averaged over a week, within that 2%. On any day, the Bank would be free to allow the rate to go as far as 1% in either direction outside the band. None of these parameters are known to the markets and it is important that this remains the case.[96]

The aim of the exercise from the Bank's point of view was to gain control over interest rate setting, because this was a day-to-day operational response to the money markets, rather than the product of a model-based debate in the Treasury:

Official influence over short term interest rates became less overt and is now exercised largely by operating in bill markets (rather than by lending to the discount market at MLR). When the system is short of cash, the scope for influencing short term rates (up to three months) is little different from under MLR: the authorities have always had most leverage over rates at the shortest maturities (up to seven days), and it has always been easier to use this to push up longer term short rates than to push them down. But in the conditions of persistent and heavy market surplus, which are the likely result of a substantial increase in the Central Government's borrowing requirement, the scope for influencing three month rates is likely to be much less than under MLR.[97]

As it was designed, the new system was discussed with the discount houses: on 9 July, the market representatives expressed their concern that M1 may be supplanting M3 and 'may be going wrong. Can Governor help?' The Governor's reply is striking: 'Cannot help on rates – but our own actions have been rather visible. Rate movement over the week was a little short of 1%. Was it not delicate and gentle?'[98]

The new system was launched on 20 August 1981. There was no more MLR; instead, the Bank operated through very short-term interest rates within an unpublished band, set by the Treasury. Any lending would normally be at a rate above comparable market rates, but within the band. There were four dealing bands ranging from Band 1 to Band 4 with respective maturities of 1–14 days, 15–33 days, 34–63 days and 64–91 days. Most frequently the Bank dealt in Band 1. The old agreement with clearing banks on average balances at the Bank of England – which had been one of the tools of monetary management – was replaced by a cash ratio system, which was simply designed to guarantee a consistent flow of income to the Bank as the recipient of unremunerated bank balances. The Bank continued to act primarily through bill operations, but also with lending. There were no longer predetermined dealing rates; instead, the Bank stated that it would influence the market by responding to demand. The idea was that short-term interest rates could be changed much more quickly in response to changing market conditions. The OMOs were used to signal the change in the desired policy rate. The London Clearing Bank's base rate – which in effect became the standard quoted 'interest rate', the successor to Bank Rate – was set in response to the signals, thus allowing the fiction that the market rather than the government set 'the interest rate'. The new arrangement was thus intended to give the impression that it was no longer targeting an interest rate, but instead allowing the market to respond to a quantitative limit on the money base. At the time, the Bank explained that 'the new arrangements may facilitate study of the relationship between monetary base and other economic developments, in particular by allowing the banks freedom to determine, given the prevailing monetary situation, how much of the stock of monetary base they hold'.[99] Retrospectively, Paul Tucker characterized the move as an 'act of folly', a sort of deliberate intellectual confusion 'regarded by Bank officials at the time as the best compromise they could reach given government policy that it should be consistent with transitioning to monetary base control'.[100]

McMahon put a different spin on the new regime, and made it clear how in his eyes the new regime presented a fine chance of recapturing Bank authority on interest rates back from the Treasury ideologues. What looked to outsiders as a new market-friendly orientation was thus a camouflage for a new control system, carefully managed above all by Tony Coleby, the intellectual madrigal-singing official who as Head of the Money Markets Division in practice managed the interaction of the Bank with the discount houses:

I am sure we would all agree that it is important for the Bank to insist, in a substantive as well as formal sense, that changes in the interest rate band (or indeed, I suppose, the continuance at existing levels) should be only on the recommendation of the Bank. The question arises, therefore how best to achieve this.

That ambition was for the moment unrealistic and vain, but it formed the subject of a debate that would continue until 1997, when the discount market was finally killed off. In fact, the 1981 arrangements with the moving rates did not last that long, as the Treasury wanted to be in firm control of interest rates. Thus, the old-style Bank Rate emerged quite quickly again (in November 1982) as a de facto reality, and both the Bank and the Treasury became more open about the fact that short-term rates were really after all a policy-determined variable.[101]

THE BANK'S INCOME

The new system reduced the balances that banks were required to maintain at the Bank of England. Under the old regime, banks had held 1.5 per cent of their eligible liabilities at the Bank of England, which had produced around £500–£530 m in bank balances. The Bank estimated that these balances would fall under the new regime, with ½ per cent of eligible

liabilities deposited at the Bank, to £330 m, but that the decline would go on
as banks learned to manage their liquid balances more effectively.[102] The
outcome was a shock to the Bank's income model; and that in turn led to
a new tussle with the Treasury about the dividend paid by the Bank to the
Treasury. From the Bank's perspective, it looked like a threat to the Bank's
'independence'.[103] Some within the Bank – especially Christopher Dow –
thought that the move had been a result of pressure from the ideologists,
the adherents to 'the purer version of monetary base control' who thought
banks should be free to hold whatever level of deposits they liked with the
central bank, and that 'Charles Goodhart, in particular, gave away the
Bank's income in a fit of absence of mind by agreeing to the force of this
logic'.[104]

McMahon and Douglas Wass eventually agreed to a formula under which
one-third of the Bank's income was paid in tax, one-third was paid as
a dividend to the Treasury, and one-third was retained. But initially the
Court rejected this agreement, on the grounds that the Bank needed to
increase its loan-loss reserves, which had been eroded away by inflation.[105]
It was only in 1983, with a new Governor and a new Chancellor, that an
agreement on this formula – which then proved to be quite stable – was
reached.[106] The oddity of the system was that there was no statutory compul-
sion on banks to hold balances at the Bank of England, but they did because
of the vague threat of 'directions' under the 1946 Bank of England Act.

The new approach remained a satisfactory basis for funding the Bank's
activities until the 1998 Bank of England Act regularized the process (see
Table 5.1). The major spikes in its income came from some sales of Bank
stakes in companies – above all of Portals the banknote paper producer in
1990 and of the industrial financing company 3i in 1995–1996 (see Chapter
9), the proceeds of which going mostly to the Treasury.

THE EXCHANGE RATE AGAIN

At the time, in 1981, when the approach to monetary policy implementation was changed, the exchange rate began to enter into the debates. In
June, Margaret Thatcher had had a discussion with Alan Walters, who
tried to persuade her against forex intervention, though she thought that
might help £M3: as Walters pointed out, 'It would only be very transitory –
and she would lose her shirt.' She also thought that Britain's foreign
exchange reserves (which were controlled by the Treasury, not the Bank)
could eventually be used to buy Trident missiles. Walters then recorded,
'We win – no intervention – I hope we can hold this. But she relents and

Table 5.1 *Bank of England income (1980–2005)*

	Operating profit(£ m)	Exceptional items (sale of shareholdings)		To HMT	Pre-tax profit (after deduction of to HMT)	Tax	Post-tax profit to reserves
1980	25.6			6.5	19.1	7.9	11.2
1981	62.6			15.0	47.6	30.2	17.4
1982	53.2			18.0	35.2	16.0	19.2
1983	70.3			23	47.3	22.6	24.7
1984	65.3			21.75	43.6	31.8	11.8
1985	37.7			25.3	12.4	4.9	7.5
1986	106.3	11.528	CDFC	39.4	66.9	23.0	43.7
1987	82.5			30	52.5	18.3	34.2
1988	66.5			26.1	40.4	14.2	26.1
1989	86			56.6	80.6	13.1	67.5
1990	122.9	41.765	Portals	72.8	91.9	17.0	74.9
1991	161.8			81.5	80.3	18.1	62.2
1992	166.2			67.6	98.5	30.9	67.6
1993	88.3	8.3	AMC	38.1	50.2	12.1	38.1
1994	114.2			48.4	65.8	22.4	43.4
1995	225.9	119.5	3i	102.2	123.7	32.7	91.0
1996	214.4	118.4	3i	88	126.4	38.1	88.3
1997	121			48.7	72.3	23.8	48.8
1998	179			70	109.0	39.0	70.0
1999	172			70	102.0	32.0	70.0
2000	123			50	73.0	23.0	50.0
2001	156			68	88.0	20.0	68.0
2002	103			42	73.0	19.0	42.0
2003	89			34	55.0	21.0	34.0
2004	72			30	42.0	12.0	30.0
2005	100			38	62.0	24.0	38.0

gives Governor £1 bn to "play with."'[107] The discussion in August about rises being principally motivated by exchange rate considerations: the DM rate for the pound had already come down appreciably since February, and was back to 4.56 at the beginning of August.[108] On 4 August, a meeting with Middleton, and then on the 5th a meeting between the Governor and Douglas Wass, reflected the extent of government confusion. The Bank was upset about a ministerial briefing that the exchange rate needed to come down, and Middleton explained that the story originated not from the Treasury but had been pushed by Thatcher's economic adviser, Adam Ridley. The problem was that Ridley seemed to be relaying the Prime

Minister's views. Wass began a masterly exposition of government doublespeak by stating that 'he was keen to persuade me that nobody in the Treasury wanted to reduce the exchange rate. In practice, however, I think this statement is a little nuance . . .. Very privately, he told me that the Prime Minister had a few days ago told the Chancellor very firmly that she wanted no depreciation in the exchange rate at all – though I am afraid she also said that she wanted significant further reductions in interest rates.'[109]

The market quickly detected the stance:

It has now been made clear to the markets that exchange rate movements are an important influence on official decisions about interest rates, even though there is no official exchange rate target. As a result it is likely that the influence exerted on the exchange rate and market interest rates by external developments, and in particular US interest rates, will be stronger than in the past. This means that the immediate prospects for the financial markets seem to depend to a large extent on how the monetary situation in the United States develops following the FOMC meeting on 6 October.[110]

On 12 November 1981, McMahon explained: 'While M3 does not quite have its former significance, it has not quite been given up, and outlook for target period suggests some overshoot. Bank lending has been going at a terrific clip. Inflation seems to have stabilized rather than resumed its decline.'[111] Walters recorded a later meeting with Thatcher, when she told him that she was 'very annoyed that Bank is trying to sell indexed gilts by tender'. And that she was 'now convinced that M3 is no good'.[112]

The Treasury set out its approach in a series of papers:

Behind the preparation of the papers, they appeared to have two main objectives. First, they wanted to explore with Walters and ourselves how strong a case Walters might make for paying more attention to the narrow aggregates in general, and to the monetary base in particular. Second, they were dissatisfied with the state of uncertainty about how the determination of interest rates was to be approached, and wished for a much clearer blueprint in advance of the new arrangements coming into operation.

In particular, a paper by Andrew Britton from the Treasury seemed to support the Bank position in moving away from a rule-based approach. The Bank's evaluation concluded: 'Despite some clear hankering, especially from Middleton, to obtain such a rule-book, Britton's original paper refreshingly concluded that it was possible to itemize those developments that the authorities should consider but NOT to apply quantitative weights to them, i.e. there was no alternative to discretion.'[113] William Allen at the

Bank concluded: '£M3 has, since early 1980, been taken progressively less seriously as a guide to policy, and it seems certain that it will lose further ground in the 1982 budget.'[114]

UNCERTAINTY ABOUT MONETARY AGGREGATES

There was no mention of the EMS in these Treasury papers. But there was a substantial confusion about which monetary aggregate was most appropriate. In Middleton's view:

Ministers could be presented with a number of options for the determination of interest rates:

(i)   A highly discretionary system of the kind outlined in Mr Britton's paper
(ii) Primacy to £M3
(iii) Primacy to the narrow aggregates (M1 or the monetary base)

There was a discussion of the kind operating rules which might govern a more mechanistic approach, whether related to £M3 or M1. Mr Britton said such rules would be very difficult to formulate as there was a wide range of estimates for the relevant interest elasticities.[115]

The new approach was explained in the *BEQB*:

The money market arrangements now in place provide a framework within which it might be possible to operate some form of monetary base control, although it is not currently being so used. Control of the monetary base implies giving priority to the amount of official money market intervention rather than to the rate at which it is transacted. In its extreme form, where the control is sought over a very short period, the authorities would be obliged to forgo all control over interest rates. As was made clear following the discussions which led to the introduction of the present monetary control arrangements, the repercussions of changing to such a system in the United Kingdom would be uncertain. Nevertheless, the new arrangements may facilitate study of the relationship between monetary base and other economic developments, in particular by allowing the banks freedom to determine, given the prevailing monetary situation, how much of the stock of monetary base they hold, i.e. their holdings of notes and coin plus their operational balances at the Bank of England.[116]

From the Bank's point of view, the new approach was brilliantly successful. It was first tested with some small rate increases in August, when the Prime Minister was away in Australia, and the rate went up to 12.6875 per cent (25 August). The Chancellor sent a cable to Brisbane with the message: 'In the present circumstances none of us saw scope for resisting the market movements.'[117]

Interest rates rose, as the overhigh exchange rate no longer seemed a problem. The pound dollar rate by September had fallen 14.6 per cent since the election, and 28.1 per cent from its peak on 24 October 1980, while the Mark rate had appreciated a little since the election but was still 17 per cent below its 16 February 1981 peak, As Richardson put it:

The external arguments for raising interest rates were now very strong. The fall in the exchange rate had persisted over many months: in view of the inflationary impact it was now necessary to act. Intervention alone would not be enough. We now needed to do more on interest rates than had been agreed earlier in the summer, when the external situation had not seemed to call for a rise in bank base rates, and the prospect of lower American rates seemed both stronger and more likely to be sufficient. The rapid fall of sterling this morning added to the force of these arguments. [...] Domestic monetary arguments pointed in the same direction, though there the situation was less clear-cut. The most threatening element was the rapid increase of bank lending particularly for housing.[118]

By September, the fog around which monetary target was appropriate had only increased. Eddie George concluded: 'We have at present so little idea of where we are with regard to the monetary target, and indeed whether the £M3 statistic tells us anything about the current policy stance, that it is by no means obvious at this stage that we need to do more.'[119] On 15 September, the London clearing bank rate was increased to 14 per cent.

Walters was also changing his mind, as the Bank noted:

In earlier discussions, monetary base control had been seen essentially as providing a constraint on the growth of banks' cash reserves, to force monetary growth to follow some predetermined path. Walters' approach has been rather different and somewhat more relaxed, seeing the broad monetary base, which mostly comprises currency in the hands of the public, more as a target indicator to be achieved over several, say six, months. Such distinctions between the use of the monetary base as a target, or a control technique, or a mixture of both are not, however, clear-cut.

The conclusion is that M1 is both more stably related to nominal incomes and easier to control than M0. Alan Walters has, at our meetings, apparently accepted that conclusion. Without giving up the possibility of moving towards monetary base control at some longer-term future date, he appears to accept that for the immediate future the first steps in that direction would involve giving more weight to M1 in the determination of interest rates, perhaps via a quantitative formula.[120]

Howe was also beginning to think of joining the EMS, because it offered a clearer anchor for policy than the constant uncertainty about targets. There had been no reference to the exchange rate in the budget speech, and Nigel Lawson was believed to have been responsible for deleting any overt reference.[121] But on 18 September 1981, Howe wrote to Thatcher:

The case for joining is now probably stronger than it was last year, not least because of the deceleration of inflation and, more important than that, the much lower level of the exchange rate. But our petro-currency status still differentiates us from our partners. The key point is that EMS membership would not of itself provide an additional buttress to our counter-inflationary policies: the success of which would still depend on policy action. Certainly the case for policy decisions could be reinforced by the wish to avoid a realignment within the grid. But it might become politically harder to take the necessary action in what the public would see as a more European context. There would be new constraints on our decisions, which would sometimes conflict with the monetary constraints we have already accepted, and we would have a more direct responsibility for exchange rate levels and movements. In short, entry would not be a soft option. But neither of us would wish to join it for that reason. On the contrary.[122]

Already in July 1981, a note summarizing the Bank's stance on the new monetary arrangements had the handwritten note: 'The possibility of our entering the EMS within the next 12 months reinforces the view against an early change of new target/targets.'[123] Dow thought Richardson had 'always emotionally been half in favour'.[124]

Richardson a few months later sent an even more enthusiastic endorsement to the Chancellor. As he put it:

In my view, joining the exchange rate mechanism of EMS would help to underpin the level and stability of sterling. At the same time I believe entry would enhance rather than undermine the anti-inflationary stance of Government policy at a moment when £M3 has become an unreliable guide to policy.[125]

THE FALLING EXCHANGE RATE

The background to Richardson's new enthusiasm for a more stable exchange rate was that from mid-October 1981, despite a new rate increase to 15 per cent on 12 October, the exchange rate began to fall quite suddenly, both against the dollar and the DM (see Figure 5.2, p. 82): by the end of October, the DM rate was 4.163. That seemed to hold out the opportune moment to join the European Exchange Rate Mechanism. So the exchange rate and its management loomed much larger in debates. The Bank now spoke of substantial tactical intervention in the foreign exchange market.[126] On 9 October, as the pound 'scaled new heights', the Bank was still intervening to sell sterling; from 12 October, it took quite heavy interventions to support the pound, $35 m on the 12th and $63 m on the 13th, with even heavier operations the next week ($86 m on the 20th, in part a response to a conversion of government debt).

The new concern with exchange rate policy left the monetary aggregates discussion in confusion. Fforde noted: 'The only convincing credible and acceptable reason for policy action to raise rates is the external one.'[127] At the Ryrie meeting on 13 October, in the wake of the interest rate hike, Terry Burns discussed 'the problem of how Government should steer now that the pre-eminence of £M3 as an intermediate target had been whittled away'. He was 'clearly uneasy about what is to determine our attitude to short-term interest rates and also funding policy, but as yet his [Burns's] views are not coherent. He noted, for example, that the M1 target which is favoured earlier this year would not have necessitated the 4% rise in base rates last month – a statement implying dislike of such a sharp rise.'[128] From 5 November 1981, a series of interest rate reductions in small steps were undertaken, with the Bank's dealing rate being taken down to 9.625 per cent on 12 October 1982 (the London clearing bank rate then fell to 9.5 per cent, but rose again to 10 per cent the next month).

At this stage, a foreign exchange rate anchor began to look like a plausible alternative. At the DGC meeting in November 1981, two arguments were presented in favour of EMS entry: 'The MTFS numbers may be considered to imply too tight a policy and to be "crucifying the economy," so the EMS is seen as a way to permit some reflation.' In addition: 'With the demise of the MTFS the Government is left with no theoretical framework on which to hang its policies, and in the absence of some constraints there are fears that it may permit excessive expansion.'[129]

Some large interventions days occurred in December 1981: in particular $140 m on 11 December, in response to a blizzard of sale orders that started in Asia; in April 1982, at the beginning of the conflict in the Falklands, after the attack on South Georgia; and in January 1983, in the context of a realignment discussion in the exchange rate mechanism (ERM). On 6 January, the Bank supported sterling to the tune of $90 m, with further interventions the next day, a Friday, and then into the next week. Margaret Thatcher stepped into the debate after discussing the scale of foreign exchange interventions with Walters:

The Prime Minister – who was seeing Walters on something else – had seen the day's intervention figure (then 60) and asked about it. He'd said it was too much for a day on which he 'would not have thought' that the pressure on the pound was heavy and intervention could not continue at 60 a day.

George responded with sympathy, but little support, from Middleton:

I [George] remonstrated about generals taking decisions when they don't know what's actually happening at the front: had he troubled to find out he would have realised that Thursday was a particularly heavy day, quite untypical of recent experience, because of professional reaction to the reserve figures, which he'd totally forgotten. I don't suppose it did much good but he knew he'd been wrong.

George noted that:

what impressed me most was the way in which both Walters and Middleton are locked into their rhetoric about domestic monetary conditions being all that matters. They really do think totally in those terms. Once you accept that, the going becomes easier: and the practical effect need not – in the present situation at least – be very different from our own approach – Middleton at least would be generally very close to the position discussed at the Governor's meeting on monetary tactics on Friday. Similarly it was easier to make headway, with them both, on the question of taking control of interest rates by discussing it in terms of their rhetoric: whereas they both recoiled in horror at any suggestion that we need to show the market that the authorities had decided that the exchange rate had fallen far enough, they both appeared to accept that there would be risks of exaggerating the weakness in financial markets if there were any suggestion of official unconcern when domestic monetary conditions were perceived to be too slack.[130]

George had in fact formulated an effective strategy for subverting wild Treasury ideas: trying to understand the background of how 'they really do think', and then reformulating the Bank's approach in that terminology so as to make the going 'easier'.

The Bank was also isolated on whether the UK should start to offer indexed gilts, a course that the government favoured, in large part because such a step might offer some security to middle-class savers who had been massively expropriated in the high inflation of the 1970s, but which the Bank regarded with scepticism. It feared in particular that foreign purchases of such bonds as an inflation hedge would drive up sterling, and tried to restrict ownership, issuing Restricted Indexed Gilts. Thatcher then countered by arguing that the acronym for the new instrument would lead to accusation of 'RIGging the market'. After a new seminar with the Prime Minister, Richardson wrote a memorandum to record his stance, which he felt had been left out of the official record:

What I said was that we too are totally committed to getting and keeping inflation down but consider that derestriction [i.e. permitting the sale of inflation-indexed bonds], far from contributing to that objective, would prove to be a further major step towards institutionalising inflation. I pointed out that the attitude of the authorities in those major countries, which have been most successful in their fight against inflation, was one of resolute opposition to indexation, which they saw as a progressive process towards accommodation to inflation. It was our concern too that each step would lead to another (as had already happened with granny bonds and was happening with the tax structure and now in the gilt-edged market).[131]

At the beginning of 1982, the Prime Minister demanded a reduction in interest rates, while Burns argued that the monetary aggregates did not suggest that there was scope for a marked loosening of monetary policy. In his view, 'The squeeze which Gordon Pepper's most recent bulletin made much of was exaggerated by the rise in inflation at the end of 1981 which followed the earlier exchange rate depreciation; it would not be right to adjust monetary policy to accommodate this temporary increase in inflation.'[132]

Thatcher said that it had 'sometimes appeared to her in recent weeks that our high exchange rate (when it was, say, above $1.90 with an effective rate [i.e. the trade-weighted rate] above, say, 91) was maintained at this level purely by a high interest rate policy. She wanted the desired reduction in rates to take place this week, and she would then wish to consider whether conditions were suitable for a further reduction of the same order.' Richardson replied that the analysis of monetary policy in his letter concluded in favour of announcing a less specific target for £M3 than hitherto; it might be described as a guideline or 'an expected range'; and it might be right to go for a wider (PSL2) and a narrower aggregate (M1) in addition. It was important to describe any change very carefully to make clear the reasons for it.[133] Burns supported the case that the high exchange rate made a focus on attaining the monetary objectives less urgent, at least for the moment: 'It is important that the excess monetary growth this year should be clawed back at some stage over the lifetime of the Medium-Term Financial Strategy (MTFS). The speed at which this is necessary may be governed by the extent to which the exchange rate falls to a more normal relationship with monetary factors.' He also specified the range that he thought would be appropriate for a decline in the exchange rate: 'Some decline in the nominal exchange rate would be welcome although no active steps should be taken to bring it about. Because of the inflation objective ideally any such depreciation should be limited to about 10–15 per cent.'[134]

The faith in particular in monetary aggregates as a guide to policy eroded further. In 1982, the indicators were diverging very strikingly, with the rate of £M3 coming down very quickly, while at the same time M0 was growing. The danger of monetary targeting now could be described as the dilemma of the cross-eyed policy-maker. The confusion was widely discussed in the press. The *New York Times* reported that even Thatcher's 'most vehement supporters' believed that the 'strategy has not worked out as intended.

What is now widely discussed is why it hasn't worked, and monetarism is drawing much of the blame.'[135] Even Walters appeared not to dissent from the new pragmatism: 'Part of the aim in adhering to monetary targets was to convince the markets that the Government had a real discipline and was following it. The other part was to sustain steady but not excessive downward pressure in practice. He agreed that there had to be a reasonable latitude for interpretation where the evidence was unreliable.'[136] In other words, the cooks would mix and match their ingredients.

OVERFUNDING

How should the Bank respond to the surge in broad money that could not really be effectively controlled by the management of short-term interest rates? The answer was overfunding, that is, selling more than the amount of long-term debt (mainly gilts and National Savings instruments) required to finance the government. The idea was to sell as much debt as possible to non-banks and, in this way, absorb from the private sector the liquidity created by bank credit. More and more ingenuity was spent in thinking of ways of making government debt attractive to private non-bank investors. If the calculation about bringing down inflation were correct and credible, there would be an expectation of large gains from gilt holdings, especially at the longer end of the market. The calculation depended heavily on the credit counterparts approach: some sceptics argued that the operation made no difference at all, as the reserve position of banks was unchanged, and they would offset the effect on their asset side of less government debt by expanding loans to the private sector.[137]

Overfunding had already been conducted in 1977/78, following the credit counterparts approach, but the practice was revived again on a much larger scale in 1981/82 (see Figures 5.6 and 5.7).[138] The exercise can be thought of as the inverse of post-2008 quantitative easing, where the aim is to inject liquidity by purchasing assets, including government but also other securities (mortgages and corporate bonds). The overfunding of the budget deficit proved to be an effective way of offsetting the expansionary effects of bank credit on broad money growth.

When the Bank needed to intervene in the market because banks were short of cash, it bought commercial bills. As these accumulated, they became known as the 'bill mountain'. It looked like a very old-fashioned operation, with a return to nineteenth-century practices: each bill needed to be scrutinized to see whether it was a genuinely commercial transaction

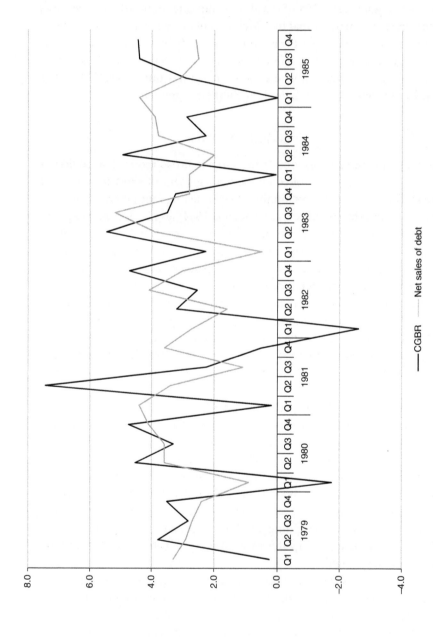

Figure 5.6 Government debt sales and borrowing requirement , £ bn (1979–1985)

———— CGBR   ——— Net sales of debt

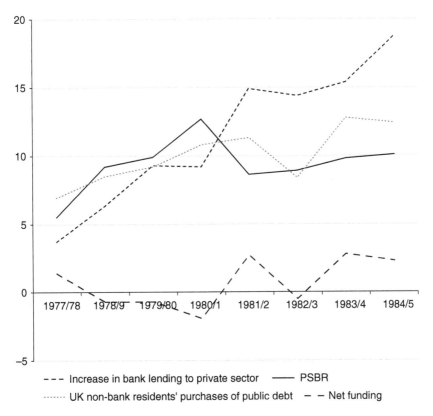

--- Increase in bank lending to private sector   —— PSBR

······ UK non-bank residents' purchases of public debt   – – Net funding

Figure 5.7 Overfunding £ bn (1977–1985)

or a 'pig on pork' affair when the drawer and the acceptor of the bill were related through a shareholding link, that is, in practice identical. One official who was engaged in the evaluation of bills bought by the Bank recalls, 'Sometimes we were sober.' The discount market and the accept-ance houses knew that they had to increase their production of bills. Sir John Chippendale 'Chips' Keswick of Hambros liked to joke that he could create an eligible bill out of the receipts of a Lahore taxi driver. The number and value of the bills was staggering. A recent estimate by William Allen, one of the architects of the operation in the 1980s, calculates by adding the withdrawal of outstanding Treasury bills and the accumulation of commercial bills by the Bank of England, arrives at a total between the end of March 1978 and the end of March 1984 of £12.4 bn, or 4.9 per cent of average GDP.[139] The mountain itself reached £15.1 bn, or 4¾ per cent of GDP, at the end of March 1984, and at times within the financial year even exceeded £20 bn.

The size of the mountain was something of an embarrassment, as well as presenting a problem for day-to-day management as the bills continually needed to be renewed as they matured. But more fundamentally, the overall effect of the policy innovation was to artificially reduce bank deposits (which were a vital component of the monetary aggregates), but at the same time to allow bank credit to expand at fast rates. It was the management problem rather than the theoretical incoherence that drove the retreat from overfunding.

As the practice of overfunding began to develop as a response to the emphasis on M3, Middleton commented:

Fiscal measures of the traditional kind, increases in personal taxation or cut in public spending, could be used to counter the expansionary effect of the increased supply of credit. Some of the fiscal measures taken over the past two years will indeed have had a substantial effect in that direction. Other ways of reducing the PSBR, asset sales for example, have a much weaker affect. The economic effect of funding, in the form of gilts or national savings, has to be fitted into this spectrum.

The economic effects of higher sales of gilts are likely to include:

- capital losses for existing debt holders which may reduce consumer spending;
- higher long-term interest rates, which may deter companies from investing;
- an exchange rate appreciation, reducing prices, but damaging competitiveness;
- a reduction in the liquidity of the economy, which may slow down activity of all kinds as well as inflation.

In the broadest terms we could respond to the situation in three ways:

1. by reducing the emphasis we place on £M3 or any other broad aggregate;
2. by taking measures designed to reduce the growth of bank credit;
3. by legislation to allow the National Loan Fund to run a surplus.[140]

A Treasury paper on 'Influencing Interest Rates' noted the 'danger that massive open market operations to keep rates down may not only fail but may adversely affect expectations'.[141] The new initiative was self-consciously aimed at improving Bank/Treasury relations. Middleton explained: 'The Bank must share equally in the strategy and have over-whelming benefit of the doubt on tactics. He also incidentally volunteered recognition, in the Treasury's own interest, of the need for a strong Bank.'[142]

The discussion about funding also drove a search for other ways of reducing banks' contribution to monetary growth. In the early 1980s, the Bank began to argue that it would be desirable for corporations to issue short-term bonds on a rolling basis. Ian Plenderleith saw the development of such a market as a way of taking pressure off monetary policy as it would lead to a reduction of bank lending: 'In relation to monetary policy, it can greatly assist us in the task we face in exercising monetary control if companies are able to finance their long-term capital requirements outside the banking system by borrowing directly on the capital market.'[143] A working party chaired by John Fforde reported in 1983. The obstacles were that the Bank traditionally reserved issues in the one- to five-year maturity range for local authorities and building societies, and that the disclosure requirements of the Companies Act would need to be modified, as well as that the exercise might be seen as constituting unlawful deposit taking under the 1977 Banking Act. But Fforde also noted that the segmentation of the market ran 'counter to the trend towards deregulation'.[144] From 1985, such issues were permitted, though there was only one small issue (an unlisted issue for Brierley investments in 1987) in the early years. The market really took off only after 1988.

FLEXIBLE INTERPRETATION

Largely free of monetary targets, the Treasury and the Bank could justify their positions by pointing to the course of the great American monetary stabilization experiment. On 14 October 1982, McMahon insisted, 'Volcker has not thrown targets overboard, any more than we have', but also that Volcker liked to assert his freedom to 'interpret' many numbers. On 11 November, he specified the problem: 'We are all tied to the tail of the U.S. They have a problem of how to steer. They are off strict targets, but cannot disregard the aggregates completely.'[145]

George, in response to a Treasury inquiry, marked himself out as the advocate of an anti-inflationary and stability-oriented approach in the Bank. He pushed back against an idea floated by the chief economist, John Flemming, of boosting the economy with a stimulus of capital expenditure on the order of 5 per cent of GDP. He pointed out that both the Chancellor and the Prime Minister 'have made it unequivocally clear that they would not retreat from the PSBR targets'. Instead, it would be better to take more modest steps: 'We have already proposed some limited easing of the interest rate constraint imposed by monetary targets.'[146]

In February 1983, ahead of the Budget, and with interest rates going up again after October 1982, Richardson wrote to Howe:

With a number of important surrounding uncertainties, concerning developments in the oil market, the German and French elections, and the direction of US policy even after Volcker's testimony, any suggestion that we are actively seeking the earliest possible opportunity to bring interest rates lower would carry the risk of again unsettling the exchange rate. That in turn would provide a damaging background to the budget.[147]

In March 1983, a small cut of less than half a percentage point in interest rates was taken on Budget day (15 March), and the exchange rate recovered, and then remained quite stable against the DM (with the dollar strengthening). There was clearly an end-of-term feeling, and this was generally taken as Geoffrey Howe's last budget. The Bank feared that exchange rate might move and prove a vulnerability in the election that seemed imminent.[148] George spoke about the 'now considerably more pressure from HMT for lower interest rates, partly because of concern about the effects of a rising exchange rate, partly because of the mortgage rate, and possibly partly ahead of local elections'.[149]

In a briefing prepared for Labour, should they win the general election that had been called for 9 June 1983, Treasury officials contemplated the possibility of a dramatic U-turn:

We are urgently reviewing:

(i) The scope for influencing short term rates under the new arrangement introduced in 1981, in the very different money market conditions that are likely to obtain after the introduction of an emergency fiscal package, and the case for re-introducing an administered MLR.
(ii) The implications of imposing mandatory ratio on financial institutions, in respect of their holdings of Government securities, and how this may relate to the reimposition of exchange controls.[150]

But even in discussions with Howe, Richardson was worried about a new exchange rate crisis:

He thought it conceivable, and some in the Bank were fairly confident, that, even given a Conservative victory, attention post 9 June would switch to the underlying issues, and sterling would fall. While it had been worrying in recent weeks to watch sterling rise above the level which had brought relief to industry (at the cost of some increase in future inflation) and back towards levels which industry had previously found excruciating, the level even of last November had not in fact yet been regained.

Richardson pressed for a major study, after the election, on 'how much weight should be given to exchange rate considerations if furthering industrial recovery were to be the major aim'. Littler thought that it might be worth comparing UK and German interest rates in recent months. His impression was that theirs had been closely in line, but that ours had risen in the last couple of months, and were now closer to US rates.[151]

LEIGH-PEMBERTON AS GOVERNOR

With the election, and the Conservative victory, came a major change of personnel at the Treasury, but also at the Bank. The transition had been prepared for some time. At the beginning of 1982, Thatcher told Walters both that she wanted to replace Howe and that she needed to change the leadership of the Bank, though 'she knows that Kit McMahon is hanging on'.[152] After the 1983 election, Geoffrey Howe moved from the Exchequer to the Foreign Office, and Nigel Lawson, the principal architect of the MTFS, became Chancellor (see Figure 5.8). On 1 July, Robert ('Robin') Leigh-Pemberton succeeded Richardson as Governor (the appointment had already been announced in December). This was a surprise appointment. He was the chairman of a clearing bank (National Westminster), which was not an obvious or traditional route to the governorship. He had an established pedigree: Eton, the Grenadier Guards and qualification at the bar. He listed his recreations simply as 'country life'. At his funeral, the Dean of Canterbury Cathedral listed his commitments as encompassing 'the bank, the bees, the bible and the Book of Common Prayer'. He kept bees on the roof of his Bank of England flat overlooking St Paul's Cathedral.[153] Some people (wrongly) thought that even when he moved to Threadneedle Street, he regarded the honorific position of Lord Lieutenant of Kent as more significant than being Governor of the Bank of England. Thatcher liked and trusted him, while she had come to dislike Richardson and suspect McMahon, and had been determined to block any prospect of his succession to the Governorship.

Howe and the Treasury had not initially considered Leigh-Pemberton as a serious candidate. To most of the commentariat, he lacked 'intellectual authority and experience to undertake the central role in international

Figure 5.8 Nigel Lawson and Robin-Leigh-Pemberton (Crown copyright)

banking talks'.[154] He was an easy target for derision in the terms used by former Chancellor Denis Healey, as 'an excellent cricketer and avid pheasant shooter'.[155] Samuel Brittan in the *Financial Times* described the new appointment as 'a major blunder': he would have preferred Sir Phillip Haddon-Cave, Chief Secretary of the Crown Colony of Hong Kong, a friend of Geoffrey Howe and a frontrunner for the job, or Eddie George, Peter Middleton or Gordon Pepper, the veterans of the debates about monetary aggregates.[156] The City would have liked Jeremy Morse, who had had a brilliant career at the Bank and then at the IMF, and had chaired the Committee of Twenty Deputies that prepared a reform of the international monetary system, before moving to Lloyds Bank, where he quickly became chairman. The popular novelist Colin Dexter had modelled his fictional donnish detective on Morse, and used the name. Almost universally described as 'fiendishly clever', Morse's obvious mental ability coupled with his reluctance to hide it prevented him from becoming managing director of the IMF – where he was a serious candidate on two occasions – but where the senior US Treasury official Robert Solomon complained that he was 'too clever'. Similar considerations might have applied to the governorship. Geoffrey Howe was worried that Morse would be too argumentative and too skilled. He had also crossed Margaret Thatcher.[157]

Early interviews did not help to build Leigh-Pemberton's position, as the new Governor announced: 'I am monetarist in the sense that I regard sound money as fundamental to civilisation. If you had a sort of scale between the Left and Right extreme, monetarist on the Right and Keynesian on the Left. I am undeniably right of centre. Inflation was vastly more dangerous to Western democracy than communism.'[158] He also upset the Labour Party leadership with what they interpreted as a threat to undermine their policies in the event of a Labour victory: 'It is the prime duty of the Governor of the Bank of England to protect the currency, and if policies were proposed which were likely to devalue it seriously – not technically, but in the eyes of the world – obviously it would be my duty to advise the Government of the consequences of that policy and, I think, to resist it.'[159]

At a very early stage, Leigh-Pemberton made it clear that a major aim of his leadership would be better relations with the Treasury, as well as with the Prime Minister where he needed to unthaw the chill of the Richardson years. He told McMahon, after a meeting with Lawson on 17 June, that he had agreed that the Bank should be 'more forthcoming' in supplying papers to the Treasury, and also that Lawson had proposed holding regular monthly lunch meetings with the Governor of the Bank of England.[160] Dealings with the Treasury would come out of the frost box.

A consensus view soon developed among younger officials in the Bank that the new Governor was a perfect example of the hands-off 'chairman' type, who might work well with an able chief executive. Leigh-Pemberton in fact was very effective at picking the new men, who would bring about an institutional and generational change: in particular Eddie George, who could manage relations with the Prime Minister very well on the basis of his deep acquaintance with the money markets, and David Walker, a former Treasury official who had moved to the Bank as Head of the Economic Intelligence Department primarily to deal with international issues but then rapidly moved into the demanding tasks of reinventing the British approach to corporate management as well as the reform of the stock exchange. George in 1982 had told Alan Walters that 'he does not agree with many in B/E who see the job as expanding demand increasing output etc. B/E should be primarily the Guardian of the currency.'[161] This view, expounded by George and Walker, was correct: Leigh-Pemberton became a highly successful Governor, a pillar of stability who skilfully navigated the Bank through the economic and financial revolution of deregulation in the 1980s, a revolution that called for a fundamental reinvention of the role of the central bank.

By contrast to the younger and more appreciative men who rapidly reached the verdict that Leigh-Pemberton was precisely what the Bank needed, the top level of the Bank hierarchy, including many on the Court, shared the press and political suspicion about the new Governor. Oddly, his salary was set initially slightly below that of Gordon Richardson (whose pay had been increased to £78,600 in August 1982; his successor was initially paid at £75,000, although in August 1983 the figure was increased to £80,000 and by July 1986 it was at £120,000).[162] Soon after the announcement of the appointment, and with press speculation that he would be the effective Governor, McMahon drew up a memorandum on how the Bank might be run through what was in effect an executive committee: indeed, many years later, the DGC was renamed as the Executive Committee.

My central idea is to revamp the Deputy Governor's Committee. This has never worked very well for a number of reasons. I take as a starting point the fact that the Governor-designate will not wish – at least until he has gained experience – to involve himself in as much detail as the present Governor, nor perhaps in as much of the argument and evolution of policy. I imagine he would welcome it if as many of the major decisions he has to take as possible are put to him in the form of either agreed recommendations or, where we cannot reach agreement amongst ourselves, clear statements of differing views.[163]

The [. . .] concern was the much wider one of getting the balance right between keeping work from the new Governor and involving him in it. We discussed many aspects of this and I think our agreed view was that we should encourage him, even beyond what may be his initial inclinations, to involve himself directly in the technicalities of monetary (and exchange rate) policy. A symbol of this would be that the Monthly Financial Review/Middleton Letter would continue to be taken by the Governor himself.[164]

McMahon also wanted to limit the Governor's speaking programme: 'The Deputy Governor felt that the Governor had taken on too many informal speaking engagements: he thought that the number of speeches made by the Governor placed too great a burden on him and their frequency could devalue their impact.'[165]

In fact, Leigh-Pemberton was very personable, and developed a relationship with a substantially larger number of Bank of England officials than had his predecessor. One later commented that 'by the time he took over he knew more people in the Bank than Richardson did after ten years'.[166] By September the new Governor was telling an interviewer, 'I find my days here extremely agreeable.'[167] And the press quite rapidly became much more positive: 'Leigh-Pemberton may well prove to be the most affable Governor the Bank of England has ever had. Since taking over in July as Governor of what is probably the best-run central bank in the world, Mr Leigh-Pemberton has posed gracefully for countless photographs and has already, according to Bank insiders, managed to promote a more relaxed atmosphere at Threadneedle Street.'[168]

The idea of using the DGC as in effect the Bank's Politbureau set it in rivalry to 'Books', the daily meeting that had as its major focus the developments of the three major markets in which the Bank was active: the money market (bills), gilts, and foreign exchange. The new key policy committee would meet regularly on Thursdays, and prepare decisions for the Governor to take on Fridays and lay them out at a Governor's meeting on Monday. In fact, the idea of the transition to the new control mechanism was never fully realized, in particular because a group of younger officials, led by Eddie George, could see that markets were at the heart of the Bank's activity, especially after the change of the interest rate regime in 1981, and Leigh-Pemberton appreciated the same point very quickly. 'Markets' acquired a new prestige within the Bank, and it was clear that the dynamic younger staff was concentrated there. There was also something inexplicable to the outside about the way 'markets' operated: responses relied on an assessment of complex probabilities that made policy seem more like a complex card game. The new Bank that was later run – and reorganized – by Eddie George (who was a very talented bridge player) was already thus taking shape in 1983 with the change of Governor and the departure of Richardson.

The character of the new policy regime is reflected in a minute prepared by George:

The 'right' response in present circumstances is for early fiscal policy action to bring the PSBR back, to under £10 billion for the current year, with credible assurances for next year. Failing that there will need to be a sharp upwards adjustment – of 2% – in interest rates. The markets will become more aware of the policy disarray – though not of its full extent – as a result of the publication of monetary and CGBR statistics in the next week.[169]

The DGC in fact had little impact on the most crucial of the Bank's relationships, namely with the Treasury. The critical issue of preparing the Governor's speaking notes for meetings with the Chancellor and the Prime Minister – thus effectively formulating the Bank's policy – was handled by George, with brilliant success.

THE BEGINNINGS OF A U-TURN

It was clear that the monetary policy approach was being rethought, and that Lawson was the commanding figure who would finally attack the centrality of £M3. A Bank memorandum on the new 'indistinct sense of dissatisfaction' is characteristic of the shift to a new pragmatism. It concluded that monetary 'experts' could not be relied on, and that there was now no longer a compelling overarching narrative:

My [George's] impression is that he [Lawson] is looking for only limited change in the present policy framework – having ruled out EMS on political grounds at least for the time being. What is left is a somewhat indistinct sense of dissatisfaction with the degree of emphasis which £M3 continues to attract, though the Chancellor apparently accepts the £M3 cannot be dispensed with as a target aggregate. He has an inclination, encouraged by Burns and Middleton to give more emphasis to non-interest-bearing narrow money (whether notes or coin, the wide monetary base – M0, or NIBM1) as a guide to short-term interest rate policy.

Some of the technical experts believe that they have found, in the more recent data, more reliable relationships between some of the very narrow, non-interest-bearing aggregates and nominal income, and that these aggregates should therefore play a more prominent part in determining short-term interest rates. But it seems that there is disagreement between the experts themselves on the significance of the latest findings: the improvement in the relationship is evidently very small; and the results are highly data-specific, that is, they swing about if measured over slightly differing time periods. What stands out above all from all this is that the sands are constantly shifting. One area in which policy has been clearly unsatisfactory in recent years has been the medium-term volatility of the exchange rate, as for example in 1980/81. This problem might be addressed in the context of EMS, though we accept the immediate political constraint on this. Short of that, we believe it would be helpful if more substance could be given to 'taking account of the exchange rate'.[170]

From the Treasury perspective, Middleton noted that 'M1 had become unsatisfactory because of the growth of interest-bearing sight deposits and M0 was the best available alternative.'[171] Kit McMahon was meanwhile telling the discount market that 'it is ridiculous how dependent we have all become on the M1 lottery'.[172] And George pointed out that although M0 had been thought of as a possible policy indicator in the 1980 Green Paper, M0's 'pedigree' derived from its potential role as an object of official control, not as an indicator of monetary conditions. In fact, there was no intention of adopting monetary base control in the foreseeable future. That being so, the government would create unnecessary confusion in the financial markets if they chose to target an aggregate which was so clearly constructed as a control variable rather than an indicator variable. Indeed there had already been some market comment on this point (the Treasury seemed surprised by this). A target for M0 would be a conceptual nonsense which could cause damaging doubts about the authorities' competence in their conduct of monetary policy.[173]

The Bank canvassed its views widely. In the Books meeting, McMahon asked 'whether the Chancellor and Sir Terry Burns were aware of the dangers of adopting a less discretionary approach to setting interest rates'.[174] Leigh-Pemberton made a point of asking the discount market how it would react to a change in the form or composition of monetary targets, and was told that 'the market had grown used to such changes and realized the imperfections of any specific measure. The time scale adopted by the market for viewing progress to a target was sometimes too short.'[175] The market had not been adequately brought into the previous manner of influencing and stabilizing expectations. It also set out its views on monetary policy in two books: one a collection of the most important *BEQB* papers, with new introductions by Bank officials, including George and the economist William Allen; and a survey of the UK's monetary experience by Goodhart.[176]

In these circumstances, Eddie George began to build his credentials as an anti-inflationary hero, who would define the essential agenda of the Leigh-Pemberton governorship. In July 1983, responding indirectly to an earlier memo by Charles Goodhart that suggested that the case for a rise in interest rates 'seems dubious', he noted: 'In relation to the intermediate objectives set by the Government, policy is now in considerable disarray.' There was a danger of a new inflationary resurgence. The best response would be fiscal. A £2 bn reduction in the PSBR was required. But

if no fiscal response is possible, so that the weight of credibility has to be carried wholly by monetary policy, it would be important – especially at the beginning of a new Governorship – for monetary action to be seen to be decisive. This would mean, in my view, an immediate 2 percent rise in short-term interest rates. Anything less would carry an undue risk of failure to carry conviction with the markets, which could ultimately mean even higher rates.[177]

A week later, George elaborated the case that should be put to Lawson. He explicitly started by worrying about asset prices as well as consumer prices: 'Asset prices, notably home prices, are not yet running away, but there is beginning to be excited talk which could damage inflationary expectations.' The comment also referred to the exchange rate problem: 'The outlook for inflation in particular would be likely to be a good deal worse than in the forecast if the fiscal and monetary overshoot went unattended, especially if, as is also likely, this was associated with a lower exchange rate.' Nothing more could probably be done on the fiscal side until autumn, though there might be a possibility of absorbing some liquidity by selling off the balance of the Bank's holding of convertible index-linked government bonds (£388 m).[178]

The market uncertainty was reflected in a lack of clarity of the direction of interest rate moves. On 10 May 1984, a new interest tightening occurred, but by July the rate was back at 12 per cent, on the understanding that it might be cut later in the month. The result was that by 1984 there was a sense that the policy was failing. The 1984 MTFS would include a move to two target ranges. Discussion then centred on the choice of the target aggregate(s). Leigh-Pemberton and George argued in meetings at the Treasury for a new measure, that M2,[179] which had been introduced as an official monetary aggregate by the Bank in the 1982 *BEQB*, was

conceptually the best measure of transactions balances. But, because its track record was as yet very short, it would be rash to go for M2 as the single narrow money target aggregate. It would however be no less rash to choose M0 alone, for, just as it had proved useful to refer specifically to PSL2 as a cross check on £M3, so it would be useful to have two narrow money target aggregates.

Lawson thought that 'targeting either carried risks, but they would not be reduced by targeting both'.[180] In fact, M0 and M2 were now chosen.

The vulnerability, and a key element of strain in the Bank's relationship with the Treasury, came from the discussion of foreign exchange intervention. Eddie George noted: 'Unless and until we get back to monetary robustness we're exposed.'[181] Later, in November 1986, forex intervention was transferred to his area of responsibility. The exchange rate continued to be a topic of concern. In the summer of 1983, with interest rates rising again in response to exchange rate weakness, Frank Cassell (Treasury) minuted:

   (i) <u>Monetary control</u>. Last week's experience has raised a number of questions about the 1981 arrangements. It is time for a cool look both at the arrangements themselves and the way we are operating them. Those arrangements were intended to give the markets a bigger role in setting interest rates; but have we over-achieved that objective?

(ii) The role of the exchange rate. As the paper argues, the sensitivity of domestic interest rates to exchange rate pressures are worrying. It may be that, by emphasizing that we take the exchange rate into account in assessing monetary conditions, we have made it more difficult to achieve the interest rate level we desire. We need to consider whether some more precise formulation of how we take the exchange rate into account would be helpful (though, as we have found before, precision in there matters is not easy).[182]

In October 1983, Anthony Loehnis, the director then responsible for the International Division, asked the Treasury about expanding the leeway for Bank interventions.[183] Leigh-Pemberton wrote to Lawson:

Overall we still believe that underlying monetary conditions leave room for a further reduction in interest rates and, as for several weeks now, we will continue to look for an opportunity to encourage a fall as soon as we can do so with reasonable confidence that a fall would stick. That possibility has again been set back by recent developments in the miners' dispute, and in the oil market.[184]

These hopes were shaken by international developments. A major exchange rate movement came with the dramatic appreciation of the dollar. On 14 January 1985, a new interest rate increase was undertaken, in large part as a response to the soaring dollar rate, that had become the predominant focus of the foreign exchange markets; but the pound was also weaker against the DM. The attention focused increasingly on intervention strategies, which demanded some measure of international coordination.

In December 1984, the Treasury imposed on the Bank a new set of guidelines for the management of foreign exchange reserves. From the beginning of 1985, reserves were not to vary by more than ±$200 m during the course of a month, and more than ±$100 m at the end of the month with respect to the end of 1984. In June, the Chancellor wanted to use the exchange rate as a way of lowering interest rates, but the guidelines prevented appropriate action. At the end of July, the Chancellor was worried that upward pressure on the exchange rate would develop if interest rates did not fall with good monetary figures, and was now prepared to contemplate acquiring reserves in German Marks up to the amount of $1 bn.

The intervention discussion then took place on the international level. In January 1985, Leigh-Pemberton reported on a G-5 discussion where Treasury Secretary Don Regan and Lawson had been supportive of intervention (though the influential Under-Secretary Beryl Sprinkel was 'obdurate' in his opposition); and Bundesbank President Karl Otto Pöhl had led a push for concerted intervention if the DM/$ rate fell by more than a Pfennig (German cent) on one day (see Figure 5.9).[185]

On 28 January 1985, in the face of continuing sterling weakness, and with the pound approaching parity with the dollar, the Chancellor and the Bank agreed to increase dealing rates by two percentage points, and the London clearing bank rate reached 14 per cent. There followed a meeting in No. 10 with Margaret Thatcher, in which she agreed with this course but felt it was important to establish the way in which it would be publicly presented.

She accepted that the Government did not have a specific exchange rate target but nevertheless she felt that sterling at its current level was a serious cause of concern for the Government. Not only did it put at risk the Government's inflationary objectives but it did not reflect accurately the true state of the British economy. She accepted that there was little that could be done through use of foreign exchange reserves. It was necessary, therefore, to deploy higher interest rates. As had been the case last July, she believed higher interest rates need only be temporary. The Prime Minister was particularly concerned that expectations about sterling in

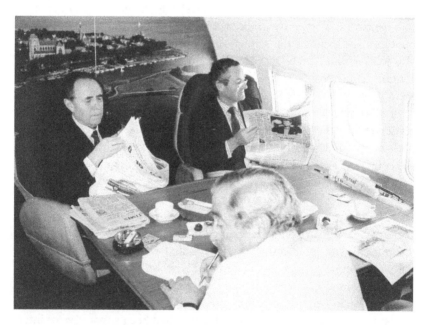

Figure 5.9 The internationalization of central banking: Leigh-Pemberton (at window), with Carlo Ciampi and Karl Otto Pohl (Deutsche Bundesbank)

foreign exchange markets all ran one way. She hoped something could be done to make speculation against sterling a more risky proposition.

The discussion then turned to the EMS. The Prime Minister said she had asked [Netherlands Prime Minister] Mr Lubbers why the Netherlands as a major energy producer was not experiencing similar problems to the United Kingdom. Mr Lubbers thought that the EMS gave some protection as no major change in the exchange rate was expected, other than in the context of re-alignment.[186]

At a meeting with the Treasury in February 1985, George said the onus was on the £M3's critics to establish their case, given £M3's prominent and widely accepted role within the successful counter-inflationary strategy.[187] On the other hand, a Treasury paper stated: 'The velocity of £M3 has not behaved in a regular or predictable way over recent years. Research covering recent years has shown £M3 to be one of the least satisfactory aggregates for predicting future inflation or money GDP growth.'[188] Consequently, the Treasury as well as Lawson began to concentrate on the exchange rate once again. Middleton argued that there 'was a good case for clearer internal and external expositions of the Government's view of the exchange rate'. He held out two possibilities, one of a unilateral shadowing of the EMS or, alternatively, an unpublished effective exchange rate band. 'Without some new objective trigger, however rough, it was difficult to be confident that giving greater weight to the exchange rate within the existing policy framework would in practice lead to earlier decisions to change interest rates.'[189]

In March 1985, a Bank paper for the Court of Directors recorded a 'developing difference of emphasis between the Bank and HMT over the significance of the broad money indicators', but then also concluded that 'the Chancellor's change of attitude to the role played by the exchange rate in monetary policy was welcome'.[190] There was a sharp clash between the Bank and the Chancellor after Tony Coleby told the Treasury Select Committee that monetary conditions were 'out of control' and that 'if the Treasury had been following a clearly understood exchange rate policy within the European Monetary System, interest rates might not have needed to be so high for so long'. Lawson was clearly irritated and told the House of Commons the next day that he 'totally disagreed' with what Coleby was reported to have said.[191] The uncertainty continued. In May, at the Treasury Bank meeting, in discussion, it was agreed that

the sterling M3 and bank lending figures were something of a puzzle. They could not be fully explained away in terms of special factors. Nor was it possible to be confident that their rate of growth would slow down in the short term. But the measures of broad money showed less acceleration than £M3 whose behavior might be reflecting an improvement in the banks' competitiveness. Other indicators were more reassuring.[192]

Treasury officials were perplexed by the attitude of Lawson, who seemed to them to have internalized the full volatility of the foreign exchange markets. Leigh-Pemberton recorded his impression:

We opened by discussing the movements in the foreign exchange market and this led to Sir PM [Peter Middleton] commenting on what he had seen recently to be a growing volatility in the attitude of the Chancellor to various policy matters. I [Leigh-Pemberton] said that we had felt that the arrival of the instructions from [Treasury Second Secretary Geoffrey] Littler on Wednesday morning, about the permitted extent of our operations in the foreign exchange market, might be seen by us to be an illustration of this and I emphasised how mean the scope that we were allowed was felt to be by other colleague central banks in these operations.[193]

Burns was increasingly sceptical about the use of the overfunding strategy, and at a discussion with the Bank laid out the following argument: 'It could be that, other than in the very short term, additional funding did not reduce £M3, but tended to increase the other counterparts – either bank lending or the externals. In that case we might be facing a vicious cycle of overfunding (and money market assistance), higher bank lending (or higher externals), more overfunding (and more MMA).' Coleby and George from the Bank tried to defend the view that overfunding had been helpful in reducing the growth of £M3, and that if the government did less funding the result would be an impact on the exchange rate and on inflationary expectations.[194]

The problems actually came not so much from No. 11 but from No. 10 Downing Street, where Margaret Thatcher revived the notion of a 'seminar' to examine the overfunding issue, and her fears of a new inflationary surge: the meeting was eventually scheduled for 25 June 1985, with a further meeting on 16 July. The Bank and the Treasury both tried to explain away Margaret Thatcher's strong views, and presented targets for different monetary aggregates as simply alternatives. But there was a fundamental conflict between the Bank (in particular Eddie George) and the Treasury. The Bank's review of monetary policy concluded that upward pressure on inflation was likely to come from higher unit labour costs, but also stated that the Bank did 'not consider that the excessive growth of £M3 can be ignored'.[195] The Treasury was much more optimistic: 'We believe that current conditions are tight enough to bring inflation back to a downward level.' It also directed its attack on the £17 bn bill mountain, which 'looks absurd; represents a large structural distortion in financial markets; and complicates official day to day market operations'.[196]

In these discussions, George emerged as the inflation hawk and the inflation Cassandra. The Bank's document warned that the rate of growth of costs

which in manufacturing has risen from below 1% in late 1983 to over 5% now, much faster than our major competitors overseas. We fear the persistence of this trend as wage settlements, and earnings, have now begun to edge upwards again while the exceptional gains in productivity of 1983/84 have not been maintained. It seems that the recovery in profitability may have weakened management's position in pay negotiations; and the labour force – which has achieved a persistent increase in real earnings in recent years for those remaining in work – is likely to respond to the upturn in the RPI with higher wage demands. Although we may be helped in the period ahead by weak world commodity prices, the underlying rise in unit labour costs may make it difficult to get back to, and stay on, the recent plateau of around 5% in the underlying rate of inflation. And we are certainly not confident that we are on course for a further gradual decline from that rate in the period up to 1988.[197]

In preliminary meetings, Lawson expressed his anxiety:

[Lawson] was however clearly anxious that the news would get out that the Prime Minister had called this meeting about monetary policy and that there would be an immediate inference that not only were things off the rails but that the Treasury and the Bank were at loggerheads. He said that he doubted whether the Prime Minister had any particular objective in mind but the combination of seeing the inflation figure going up and the price she had been asked for the new house she was buying in London had triggered anxieties which invariably took the form of hankering after monetary base control. At a later stage in the meeting he said that he would like to be left to choose the timing of our meeting with her because it was important to choose a moment when her temperature was at a non-critical state.

We then moved on to discuss the possibility of a system of control in which if we retain £M3 we should settle for a realistically higher target zone which would obviate the need for overfunding. This manifest weakening of policy at one end would be compensated by a lower range for M0, and acceptance of sharper variations in interest rates which in turn would lead to a higher exchange rate. At some stage it might be more effective to look to NIBMI [M1 excluding interest bearing sterling sight deposits of UK private sector residents with the UK banking sector (including discount houses)] rather than M0 as the best indicator of narrow money, if we could establish credible boundaries between that and interest-bearing M1.[198]

Lawson was also keen to damp press speculation about policy divides:

The Chancellor said he was anxious to avoid further Press stories about rifts between the Bank and the Treasury. The Prime Minister's initiative on monetary policy made this particularly sensitive, though his concern was a general one. The Governor commented that this was a perennial favourite with the Press, nevertheless it was important not to feed their interest indirectly by inadvertent remarks, and he would put his officials on their guard.[199]

In order to understand the source of the Prime Minister's inquiries, the Treasury turned to Alan Walters, who had left his full-time Downing Street position in 1983 but remained as a part-time adviser to the Prime Minister. And he complained about failures on all fronts, especially in regard to the concern with the exchange rate. George wrote up the concerns voiced at the meeting in the Treasury:

> (i) Overfunding and the bill mountain – which he does not see as a great economic problem, though it looks absurd and affects the credibility of policy
> (ii) Too much attention is paid to the exchange rate
> (iii) Short-term rates are too heavily determined by the Bank's bill rates and not left sufficiently to market forces
> (iv) We have made no progress towards monetary base control.

At the end of the meeting, Middleton, Walters and [George] continued discussing some obscure idea of Walters for providing money market assistance in tranches at progressively higher rates, but agreed that the substantive question in this area was Ministers' unwillingness in practice to accept more volatile base rates.[200]

Lawson's response to the Walters argument was:

We had driven into over-funding as a result of our attempts to control sterling M3. As it had become apparent that sterling M3 was a highly imperfect measure of monetary conditions, so the justification for over-funding had become weaker. Conversely, de-emphasising sterling M3 was a necessary condition for ending the over-funding/bill mountain 'merry-go-round'.[201]

These concerns were immediately reflected in a missive from the Prime Minister's office, in which she wanted Walters to discuss the funding issue with the Treasury and the Bank, and her 'concern about monetary policy'. In June, she intervened, at a meeting with Lawson, where she expounded the view that monetary conditions were too lax.

£M3 was persistently above the top of the target range; inflation had ceased to decelerate and, even allowing for the distortions caused by mortgage interest rates, might now be accelerating; house prices were rising rapidly. Secondly, she was concerned that the monetary arrangements introduced in 1981 were not working properly. £M3 was contained only by persistent over-funding, leading to the creation of the bill mountain. The Bank had originally intended to operate only at the short end of the money market, keeping the seven day rate within an undisclosed band. The band had become a point and the Bank operated all along the yield curve. It, rather than the market, was the dominant influence in setting the bill yield curve which was often inconsistent with rates in the inter-bank market, thereby setting up opportunities for arbitrage. The Bank stood ready to relieve cash shortages at a known interest rate without penalty. There was thus no restraint on bank lending. She believed this perpetuated many of the weaknesses which the studies in 1980–81 had sought to eradicate. Whatever view one took of current monetary conditions, these weaknesses of monetary control created the risk of higher inflation in the future.[202]

When the Bank staff prepared a draft document which began with the observation that the Bank shares the Prime Minister's concern about the present rate of growth of £M3 and about the prospect for inflation, the Governor wrote 'must remove' in red ink over that phrase.[203]

At the seminar meeting with Margaret Thatcher on 16 July 1985, Lawson stated that he believed that overfunding was no longer helpful in maintaining monetary control. He therefore recommended that funding should not exceed what was necessary to meet the PSBR, and effectively obtained the consent of Thatcher to end overfunding.[204] The Bank had never worried so much about the distortions arising from overfunding, but it had become more and more of a bugbear for the Treasury.[205] That decision meant that a major instrument for controlling monetary aggregates, the Bank of England's management of the stock and maturity structure of government debt held by the private sector, was effectively discarded. At that moment, the idea was to go back 'as far as possible to the spirit of the 1981 arrangements, under which the Bank confined its operations to short-dated bills. It was recognised that this could not be achieved immediately but was dependent upon first ending the growth in the bill mountain and secondly on reducing it.'[206]

Looking back, the Bank recognized that now 'in practice the authorities are largely dependent on a single instrument – the short-term interest rate'. Coleby explained: 'The dropping of broad money targets meant that funding no longer had a role as an active instrument of monetary policy. Short-term interest rates became the sole instrument through which the authorities actively sought to influence monetary conditions.'[207]

By the end of July, Lawson seemed to have taken up a new stance, driven largely by exchange rate considerations and leading McMahon to comment on his 'weather-cockery':

Apparently the Chancellor is worried that there may be a further upward pressure on the exchange rate next week in the wake of Tuesday's announcement of good £M3 figures, particularly as he will wish to signal that he does not want interest rates to fall further for the time being – being particularly concerned that any further move down could become an uncontrollable slide. He is, however, acutely conscious of the pressures caused by the level of the exchange rate for industry, as expressed by the CBI, and in order to avoid these is prepared to contemplate sizeable intervention in the first half of August, which should be aimed particularly at producing a lower sterling/deutschemark rate (ie we should accumulate deutschemarks). The amount he has in mind is apparently $500mn equivalent, but if $1bn equivalent is necessary in order to achieve the desired results, he is prepared to go that far. An additional reason for this astonishing volte-face (astonishing in the context of the stubborn resistance to intervention to June and July), so [Geoffrey] Littler [Second Secretary in the Treasury] implied, is that the Chancellor is becoming considerably warmer about the idea of joining ERM sooner rather than later.[208]

This seemed to be accepted and the Chancellor went on to say that he hoped that we could get through the period between now and the Mansion House speech without the need for any explanation of the working of policy as practised at the moment. This led to the new initiative about the ERM, on which the Chancellor emphasised the need for absolute security about the proposed meeting with the Prime Minister to take place in the last week in September. I said that it was likely that the Bank would be able to present a concerted view, and he went further to the extent of wondering whether we could agree a single paper to put before the Prime Minister although it would be understood that we would each wish to speak to it.[209]

The approach to monetary policy changed completely after the signal given in Lawson's Mansion House speech (17 October 1985). The substantial part of the speech began with a discussion of the New York G-5 meeting at the Plaza Hotel, where exchange rate coordination to drive down the US dollar had become the major issue. Lawson naturally emphasized the need for a stability-focused monetary policy, but he explained the way that it could be achieved in a completely new way: 'But to achieve this, it remains operationally necessary to conduct monetary policy through the use of intermediate targets – taking account of relevant information such as the behaviour of the exchange rate – rather than by attempting to target money GDP directly.' With this speech, Lawson abruptly ended the practice of overfunding. ('We are no longer seeking to control the recorded growth of £M3 by systematic overfunding.') In effect he had set an end to the first era of Thatcherite economics. 'By the time of my Mansion House Speech [. . .] the position had become ridiculous.'[210]

Ten years later, looking back on the 1980s, a Bank official concluded in a survey of the Bank's relationship with the Treasury that the Bank 'has never given much weight to M0 in its policy advice and seemingly no more than that given to broad money'. 'It is unclear to me whether the Bank actually believed in a black box type of monetary transmission from broad money to prices, but I think not.'[211] The comment was an exaggeration, but one that reflects the extent to which by the end of the 1980s the Bank (and the Treasury) had staged an intellectual retreat from monetarism. The first stage in that withdrawal came in the first half of the 1980s, when monetary economics had fundamentally been destroyed by the conjunction of three powerful forces: the intervention of the Prime Minister in the decisive summer of 1980 with her militant advocacy of a Swiss style of MBC that was at odds with the Treasury's preference for £M3; the refusal of the Bank in 1981 to move to a broader-based system of bill dealings with the entire financial sector rather than with the narrow club of the London discount market; and finally and most decisively, the wild international exchange gyrations of the 1980s and in particular the dramatic dollar appreciation. Graham Hacche gives a slightly different – but compatible – set of reasons for the retreat from monetarism: 'Three problems – of unstable velocity and demand for money relationships, different behaviour of different aggregates, and difficulties of control – would not go away, and would be important in bringing about the later demise of monetary targeting.'[212]

The debates of 1985 terminated the centrality of £M3, while M0 continued to play a role until 1987. It is thus not correct to claim that 'the monetarist system was still largely intact at the beginning of 1985'.[213] Monetarism died or faded slowly; but the practical evisceration started in the early 1980s. Lawson was just nailing down the coffin lid.

At the same time, many commentators contended that 'monetarism' had won. Philip Stephens of the *Financial Times* spoke of 'the triumph of monetarism over Keynesianism in the industrialized world'. Samuel Brittan, the doyen of monetarist journalism, wrote a column under the title 'Monetarism: Far from Dead', explaining, 'Policy is now based on a "nominal framework."' Peter Jenkins commented that it was 'in some ways misleading and unfair' to say monetarism failed or was abandoned, because 'it could not be denied that inflation had been brought down'. A policy success went along with doubting that was both intellectual and practical.[214]

In an interesting survey of the development of central banking produced for the Bank of England's tercentenary, Forrest Capie, Charles Goodhart and Norbert Schnadt describe a battle with an intellectual victory of monetarist theory, both in the nineteenth century and in the late twentieth century, as the giants of the profession, David Ricardo and Milton Friedman, argued about 'how to reform the monetary system'. But then, the essay concludes, the monetarists 'lost the war'. The currency school, the nineteenth-century predecessor to modern monetarism, was vanquished by the banking school. The defeat came because 'the rules, which had been carefully worked out, depended for their efficacy on an underlying, implicit assumption that the structure of the monetary system would remain unchanged. But the very introduction of these new rules helped to change that structure.'[215] A similar revolution occurred in the 1980s, with monetarism apparently victorious, but defeated by the practice of banking.

Paul Volcker in 1990 gave a retrospective view of the successes of central banks and monetary policy in promoting stabilization, explaining, 'The record is quite clear that, despite varied efforts here and abroad, central banks did not discover any monetarist holy grail. In the end, no country in which inflation had become embedded seemed able to moderate that inflation without a painful transitional period of high unemployment, recession, and profit squeeze.'[216] Monetarism delivered a policy framework, and a spectacular success in bringing down inflation rates, and consequently in improving the operation of price discovery in the market mechanism; but it did not in any sense provide a precise toolbox for dealing with the monetary management of an increasingly open economy.

6

The Long Shadow of the Deutschemark

The Exchange Rate Alternative

In the aftermath of Nigel Lawson's de facto abandonment of monetary targets, the focus shifted to exchange rates. Instinctively, many figures in the Bank disliked the idea of fixed exchange rates and of returning to the world of the 1960s. The Executive Director responsible for markets, whose domain from November 1986 included foreign exchange dealings, was Eddie George, who had a quotation from Richard Cobden hanging in a frame in his office, 'Managing the currency, and regulating the currency, is just as possible as the management of the tides, or the regulation of the stars, or the winds.' It did not include the following sentences, also from Cobden's remarks to the House of Commons proceedings of the Select Committee of Banks of Issue, where the great free trader had also said, 'I object to any body of men having the power to increase or decrease the quantity of money.'[1]

The lack of monetary control in the second half of the 1980s produced a new upsurge of inflation. In the discussion of the UK, especially with the benefit of hindsight, the outcome is almost always attributed to the peculiarities of the 'Lawson boom', but the uptick in inflation after 1986 is characteristic of all major industrial countries – including the two that usually served as a reference point for UK discussions, the US and Germany (see Figure 6.1). In fact, the U-shaped trajectory of US inflation in the 1980s very closely mirrors that of the UK. Some part of the story can be explained in terms of the sharp 1986 fall in oil prices and their subsequent recovery. The rise in inflation, and the international environment, inevitably pro-duced a debate about what sort of exchange rate regime was appro-priate, and also how any exchange rate objective could be squared with the monetary targets that still appeared in public policy state-ments, notably in the annual formulation of the Medium-Term Financial Strategy (MTFS). The approach adopted in the UK after

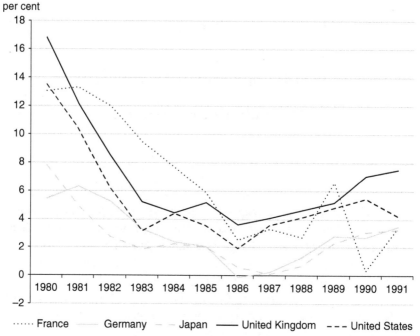

per cent

Figure 6.1 Comparative inflation in the 1980s, annual per cent changes

1985 first assigned a 'greater importance' to exchange rate objectives, without specifying any rule; then, between early 1987 and March 1988, an unannounced policy of linking the pound to the Deutschemark (DM) at the rate of 3 DM/£ was pursued. Subsequently, the exchange target was abandoned. In the first phase, M0 still played a prominent part in Treasury thinking, while in the later phase it was practically ignored.

All three phases of this regime were incoherent, and probably inferior to an alternative policy of visibly associating the pound with European currencies in the European Monetary System's (EMS) Exchange Rate Mechanism (ERM). Indeed, some econometric analysis on central bank credibility suggests that conclusion, namely that an external anchor is the most credible anti-inflationary tool in periods of great uncertainty in more open economies (but not in the US, a much more closed economy). The dramatic instability of the dollar ruled out the most obvious anchor, and thus the UK turned instead to the European Community country with the strongest record of price stability, Germany (see Figure 6.2).

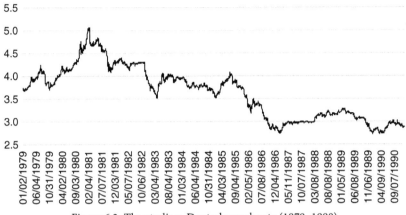

Figure 6.2 The sterling–Deutschemark rate (1979–1990)

THE EUROPEAN BACKGROUND

Were exchange rate targets the appropriate response to international monetary disorder? The EMS, and the associated ERM, had been devised in 1978 as the outcome of a bilateral Franco-German initiative, launched by France's President Valéry Giscard d'Estaing and German Chancellor Helmut Schmidt in the aftermath of a period of dollar weakness which some Europeans saw as 'malign neglect' or even competitive devaluation. The new European mechanism recreated the Bretton Woods system of fixed but adjustable exchange rates – with a margin of fluctuation 2.25 per cent each way of a central rate, and a possibility of wider bands for currently floating currencies of 6 per cent. Britain had participated in the initial negotiations, but was always hesitant and suspicious. On the eve of the decisive Copenhagen summit of 7–8 April 1978, the Cabinet Secretary, John Hunt, minuted:

> Some of the disadvantages to us are fairly clear. This could however be a move towards a two-tier community. The Prime Minister [James Callaghan] will obviously bear in mind the political and other implications if this happened and we were not in the top tier. Thus there is a case for ensuring either that this is a scheme that we can live with or that it founders.[2]

The Treasury suspected the plan as a German exercise in power projection and sketched out a plausible interpretation of German motives: 'If other EEC countries stick with the mark more and with the dollar less, that helps intra-EEC German trade and also helps Germany in competition with its EEC partners in other markets.'[3] Chancellor Denis Healey, who shared many of these concerns about the EMS as a plan for German control, soon made it clear that the UK would not participate in the ERM. But the debate lingered on in the UK, and the issue resurfaced regularly in Whitehall, in the Treasury and the Foreign Office, but also at the Bank of England.

In the first official statement of the new Conservative government's position, in the Queen's speech of 15 May 1979, the government welcomed the ERM and promised to 'consider afresh the question of participation of the UK in its various modes'. But Thatcher later explained that she would not make a decision 'for some time'.[4]

The debate about membership of EMS/ERM, but also about the softer form of an exchange rate target, had always polarized the Bank. From the beginning, exchange rate commitment was frequently cast in terms of an alternative to the MTFS. In the difficult months in the autumn of 1981, some bank officials argued that 'with the demise of the MTFS the Government is left with no theoretical framework on which to hang its policies, and in the absence of some constraints there are fears that it may permit excessive expansion'.[5] An external source of stability looked like an obvious alternative.

Discussion of an exchange rate anchor in the Bank resurfaced in 1983, because of two circumstances: the appointment of a new Governor and the general election, which the Bank (and financial markets) feared might produce a sterling crisis in the event of a Labour victory. In fact, the aftermath of the Falklands War and the split in the Labour Party as the Social Democrats defected produced a dramatic victory for the Conservatives. In the new government, with Lawson as Chancellor, the tone in the Treasury changed. Sir Peter Middleton reported to the Bank that Lawson was 'open-minded about the possibility of joining EMS. He wants to make an early move to help industry in a revenue-neutral way.'[6] The attraction lay in the idea that EMS membership might bring anti-inflationary credibility while allowing a cut in interest rates.

Immediately Lawson became Chancellor, in June 1983, he asked for a paper on ERM membership as well as a review of monetary policy. The product, prepared by Geoffrey Littler, the Second Permanent Secretary, with responsibility for Overseas Finance, argued that membership might be feasible and attractive if (and when) the dollar fell against the DM; but, for the moment, the dollar was appreciating sharply and so the European stabilization option looked less attractive. Littler reported that Lawson wanted to 'patch in something to support the control of the money supply, whatever that might be'.[7] In July 1983, the Deputy Governor, Kit

McMahon, noted that the Governor had asked the Deputy Governor's Committee to look at the question of UK entry into the EMS, on the grounds that: 'It seemed to be the first time for some years that there might be a decision by the government in favour of entry.'[8] Lawson retrospectively complained that it was 'sad' that the Bank 'had no contribution to make to the answer' on ERM membership.[9] The Foreign Office took up the case again.[10] Most senior officials in the Bank now saw a transition to the ERM as a disruption to the existing policy framework. In 1984, McMahon in a discussion in the Deputy Governor's Committee

noted that membership of the unholy alliance [on exchange rates] in the Bank seemed to have remained very much the same, but they had switched from being predisposed in favour of entry, to being against. Since 1982, when entry into the ERM was last considered, the credibility of the MTFS had improved, and the prospect of a better aligned exchange rate also seemed to be more likely.

There was a stronger case for some sort of exchange rate commitment, but outside the ERM. Even that idea encountered scepticism. The associate director responsible for international policy, Anthony Loehnis, thought a change of policy along these lines might 'prove to be a more difficult intellectual switch for HMG than membership of the ERM'. The Bank's chief economist, John Flemming, expressed his concern that a policy of exchange rate management combined with the MTFS might 'reduce understanding of the Government's policy and give rise to some loss of confidence '.[11] Eddie George, the Executive Director responsible for markets, noted that 'one reason for opposing entry was that it would complicate the pursuit of national objectives for monetary policy'; but there was also the possibility that the MTFS might prove unworkable, and in that case the EMS might provide an alternative mechanism for discipline.[12] But he was pretty consistent in his opposition, at this stage, to the idea of moving into the EMS. At the beginning of 1985, he minuted:

As far as monetary management is concerned and indeed economic management more broadly – we do ourselves and HMG a disfavour if we encourage the idea that EMS would in any general sense make life any easier. The fact is that we can, if we choose to, do virtually anything in the monetary/economic management field just as well outside the EMS as inside. I personally come out against membership (as do without exception, all the Bank's senior people on the domestic monetary side with varying degrees of vehemence.)[13]

The Treasury was also divided. Towards the end of 1984, Sir Peter Middleton characterized himself as 'still very doubtful' and added that 'he represented in that position the advance guard of those who were in favour in the Treasury'.[14] At the beginning of 1985, as the dollar soared and it looked as if sterling was very weak, a European solution began to look more attractive. But there was an urgent need to put pressure on the US to change its position on the dollar, and Middleton wanted to urge the Prime Minister to intervene with President Reagan to persuade Treasury Secretary Don Regan to collaborate with the others in a collective attempt to restore reality to the markets.[15] For Lawson, there were 'political ex rate objectives'.[16] In these circumstances, more European cooperation might be helpful. In a bizarre telephone conversation, Thatcher appeared to be 'berating' Lawson for not joining the EMS. In February, at a seminar which included the Prime Minister and Leigh-Pemberton, Lawson then argued that the government 'should not close the door' on the ERM, and Howe presented a similar case. Terry Burns and Eddie George were sceptical. Thatcher stated that she thought 'superficially membership attractive but when looked into in detail it looks less attractive'. She ended the meeting thinking that it 'ended amicably enough'.[17]

THE PLAZA MOMENT

In September 1985, in the middle of a new discussion of how to manage the global problem of the dollar (this time overvalued, in stark contrast to 1978, when the EMS had been conceived in the middle of a dollar crisis), a new push began from both the Treasury and the Bank. They met to discuss the 'new initiative about the ERM', with the Chancellor emphasizing the need for absolute security in the lead-up to a meeting with the Prime Minister at the end of September, as she was 'apparently' 'still against the idea in principle, but it can now at least be discussed with her in a way that still does not apply to certain other topics'.[18] The common position emphasized that both the Treasury and the Bank were 'advocates for joining but not without a sense of realism, of the validity of the old arguments against joining'. In the end, perhaps quite predictably, Thatcher said that she 'was not convinced that the balance of arguments had shifted in favour of joining. A further discussion would be needed, to which other colleagues should be invited.'[19]

In private, Lawson used the type of sporting metaphor beloved by successive Governors of the Bank of England. Leigh-Pemberton reported the conversation:

When I commented that we were confronted by some exciting and fundamental issues, he said that he saw himself as a bowler hoping for a hat-trick: the first wicket would be a useful decision in New York, the second a fall in UK interest rates against a stronger exchange rate and the third our entry into the ERM at the £/DM level which could be more favourably aligned as a part of the changes in the $ rates.[20]

The background to these debates was a major international coordination exercise: the first real attempt at such action since the 1971 Smithsonian meeting. The G-5 finance ministers and central bank governors at the Plaza Hotel in New York on 22 September 1985, convened at the initiative of Federal Reserve Chairman Paul Volcker, agreed to use coordinated intervention with large sums ($18 bn over a six-week period) to drive down the dollar. There was no specific target for the dollar rate, and the final communique merely referred to 'orderly appreciation' of the major non-dollar currencies. There was also no discussion of interest rate policy, and the German Bundesbank in particular was sceptical of the whole exercise and fearful that there would be a pressure applied to German monetary and fiscal policy. The meeting in fact drove central bankers from the participating countries closer together, and it became much more realistic to speak of the 'international brotherhood' of central bankers. They now quite regularly saw each other as allies in their struggles with their own governments. This intensified cooperation indeed became the dominant theme of policy for the next seven years (from the British perspective, it ended spectacularly on 16 September 1992). As William Keegan put it, 'The aftermath of the Plaza "profoundly" affected Lawson's thinking and his policy reactions.'[21]

The Germans tried to communicate their post-Plaza anxieties about foreign exchange intervention to the Bank of England. At a lunch with the Chancellor, Leigh-Pemberton said he had found Bundesbank President Karl Otto Pöhl 'very disillusioned'; he thought it would 'take a lot to get the Bundesbank to intervene in the foreign exchange markets in a major way without a further political initiative of the G-5 type'.[22] The Bank also seemed to push for some measures that ran counter to the spirit of the Plaza because it worried about the sterling–DM exchange rate and wanted to bring sterling down against the German currency (see Figure 6.3).

On 26 September, the Bank of England sold $54 m, and $74 m the next day, but the pound also weakened against other currencies: the yen surged especially in the post-Plaza period, but there were also market rumours that the UK was about to enter the ERM.[23] In October 1985, the Bank suggested to the Treasury that it should buy dollars when there was an opportunity, but the Treasury worried that dollar purchases would be seen as contrary to the Plaza Agreement. In mid-November, the Bank acquired $100 m at a time when there were several orders in the market

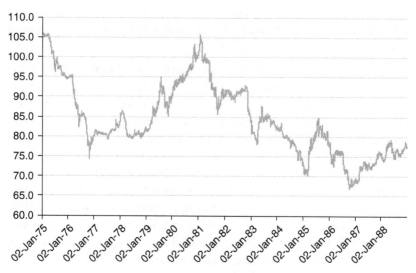

Figure 6.3 Exchange rate index (1979–1988)

to buy sterling, and the Treasury again warned that this was contrary to the Plaza, which had been envisaged primarily as a coordination exercise to drive down the dollar.[24]

A full ministerial meeting to discuss the EMS/ERM possibility turned into a disaster for the Europhiles, when Margaret Thatcher felt that she had been bullied by an orchestrated Treasury – or Lawson – campaign, and she expressed herself in words that are variously reported. In one version, it was: 'I'm not going in on run-up to the election and put interest rates in someone else's hands.' Leigh-Pemberton thought she said, 'I'm afraid we're not going to do this. I'm sorry.'[25] The Bank at this point noted 'it seems that we may have overplayed our hand at the last meeting and appeared to be "ganging up" on the Prime Minister'.[26] Thatcher's reaction made the EMS possibility into a complete political impossibility. The difficulty was that Lawson had been arguing a 'when the time is ripe' case for ERM entry, and Thatcher was now rejecting the case on principle.

Treasury–Bank relations continued to be problematical, with tussles about fiscal issues as well as about exchange rate interventions. In early 1986, Lawson 'was highly critical, indeed astonished, at the contents and style of our Budget submission', which tried to propose shifting the burden of stabilization from monetary to fiscal policy; and also expressed his concern at the frequency with which the media suggested Bank–Treasury relations were bad.[27]

The Treasury now pushed the Bank to intervene in forex markets in new ways. At the beginning of 1986, the Treasury recommended intervening in New York and in the Far East, a step that the Bank resisted on the historically inaccurate argument that tradition laid down that central banks should intervene primarily in their own domestic markets.[28] George in particular pressed for a more coordinated use of intervention:

Eddie George this morning expressed [...] his concern that we did not appear to be giving any support by judicious use of intervention, even within the current limits allowed us by HMT, to the sterling inter-bank market, which was still showing extreme fragility despite the apparent success of yesterday's measures. He wondered whether this was because the dealers did not feel such intervention would have any effect, or because we felt we were under even tighter constrains from the Treasury regarding intervention.[29]

There were different techniques in managing intervention. The Germans liked a 'big bang' with large-scale interventions, 'not seeking to hide their activities and aiming for maximum impact'. By contrast the Federal Reserve liked a lower profile, and officials, including Chairman Volcker, now began to play down the role of exchange intervention as the Plaza receded into memory.[30] The Bank of England wanted more regular and frequent interventions to nudge rather than shock the market. It was not public about its intervention, or about the effects on monetary policy. In the Commons Treasury Select Committee, the Conservative MP for Kettering, Roger Freeman, asked about the Bank of England's policy towards intervention: 'Is it the practice now to sterilise intervention, or do you leave it unsterilised?' (i.e. to conduct offsetting open market operations simultaneously with the forex intervention, so as to prevent the intervention having an effect on the money supply). The Chancellor simply replied: 'It is the practice not to talk about it.'[31]

The background to the most serious policy clashes lay in the new Treasury interest in joining the ERM. Middleton explained to the Bank that he was 'toying with' the renewal of the ERM question 'and seemed clearly to want to engineer a further meeting with the Prime Minister before the Budget'.[32] At an early stage, the Bank recognized that the external policy was threatening the attainment of domestic objectives. Interest rates were being cut in the spring of 1986. The action clearly posed the risk that the action would reignite inflation, but that danger was sidelined because of the debate about international stability. Treasury officials were more hesitant than was the Chancellor, with Middleton laying out 'doubts about the argument that UK interest rates should be reduced in line with reductions in other countries'.[33] Lawson explicitly downplayed the role of broad money aggregates:

More important, broad money is only part of the picture. The exchange rate continues to be remarkably firm against the background of weaker oil prices. M0, which you do not mention at all, is expected to remain well towards the bottom half of its target range. These other indicators tell a rather different story from the broad aggregates you emphasise. And, for reasons set out in both the MTFS and my Budget speech, we have recognised that the target for broad money does not have the same operational significance as that for narrow money.[34]

The Treasury felt frustrated by the three-month monetary forecasts ('the accuracy of these forecasts was pretty unimpressive'), and pressed for a more comprehensive assessment of the current stance, with likely developments of the international situation and the fiscal stance.[35]

This was also a message that Lawson set out in public. In a speech at the Lombard Association, he stated:

But we must never forget that monetary targets are a means to an end. Their use depends on the robustness of a relationship between a particular measure of money on the one hand, and money GDP and inflation on the other. In the real world, no economic relationship is perfect. So monetary targetry was not and never can be a substitute for making an intelligent assessment of monetary conditions, based on all the evidence.[36]

The leadership of the Bank went along with the new emphasis on exchange rate influences. Leigh-Pemberton wrote in a letter to the Chancellor of 25 April 1986:

At our meeting on Friday 18 April we agreed to sanction a ½% cut in base rates, to 10 ½%, which duly occurred later that morning. It was common ground that the main argument in favour of this move was related to the exchange rate and interest rate movements abroad. In particular, the exchange rate had been strengthening, so that, taken together with the lower oil price, the prospect for inflation had improved. With the strong probability of an imminent cut in interest rates in the United States and Japan (as subsequently took place), there was a risk of a firming of the exchange rate to an uncomfortably high level if we did not move as well.

On domestic grounds alone, however, our view was that the case was not convincing. £M3 and bank lending growth were high in banking March, and early indications for banking April are not reassuring. M0 growth has accelerated slightly. In addition, house and equity prices have been rising fast and there is no sign yet that domestically-generated cost inflation is falling significantly, despite the reduction of RPI growth in prospect.[37]

In May 1986, when the Bank's Court discussed the EMS/ERM, 'it was concluded that the arguments were finely balanced and that any decision on membership would be more likely to be political rather than economic'.[38]

The Bank's briefing note for the Governor's meeting with the Chancellor clearly demonstrated the concern about the inflation implications:

The most disturbing features of the current situation are the continuing acceleration of unit labour costs, and signs that house prices are now rising more rapidly across the country as a whole. If, as seems quite likely, the Chancellor is insistent, the situation is such that I do not feel we are on strong enough ground to dig in our heels, i.e. to insist on taking the latter to No 10. I would hope, however, that we could achieve –

(i) recognition by the Chancellor that a further ½ per cent to 10 per cent is the most that he can reasonably expect, without some definite sign of progress on unit labour costs and pay, or on the domestic component of inflation generally;

(ii) his acceptance that the ½ per cent cut should not be imposed upon the market immediately, but should be allowed to emerge from the market during the course of the week.[39]

In July, Lawson indicated that he now expected the major action to come from exchange rate intervention, which as he now saw it might play a role in stabilizing inflation expectations:

At the right tactical moment when the markets were thin we should launch an ambuscade and intervene to buy sterling. This would have a salutary effect in showing the markets that the pound could lurch up as well as down. The interpretation we would want to get across was first, that we were not indifferent to the exchange rate nor were we seeking a fall; and second, that it should be seen as a warning signal that we were liable to act.[40]

The pre-summer holiday meeting with the Chancellor to discuss markets took place on 30 July. The Governor then suggested that 'if the pound rose through August we should look for the opportunity to get interest rates down by ½ per cent. This would be much easier if Germany or Japan made a move, though this was unlikely before mid-September at the earliest.' The Chancellor's position was that 'we should be on the lookout for an opportunity to bring interest rates down by ½ per cent', to which end he proposed more active and overt intervention in the foreign exchange market to strengthen sterling.[41]

But then the exchange rate did not move in the 'right' direction. The Bank arranged a swap agreement with the Bundesbank, which helped to reassure markets and somewhat eased the foreign exchange pressure, even though the swap line was not initially drawn. On 15 October, interest rates were raised by one point, from 10 to 11. But that was all. The markets thought that this was too little and too late, and the pressure on sterling continued. The Treasury was relatively optimistic about the inflation outlook:

Sir Terry Burns said that even with a 1 per cent increase in interest rates the rate of inflation by the end of 1987 should be no more than 4 per cent, raising to perhaps 5 per cent by the end of 1988. We had always acknowledged that we would see some upward pressure on inflation, but he did not see any reason from events already in the pipeline to expect 6 per cent or 7 per cent. It could of course happen if there was a combination of a sharper fall in the exchange rate, a larger increase in domestic demand, and a major increase in commodity prices – but, equally, things could go the other way.[42]

In fact, there was substantial political attention to interest rates as a consequence of the unfavourable exchange rate move at the same time as the Conservative Party Conference met. The *Sunday Times* explained how 'Lawson is also coming under increasing criticism from within his own party. One senior Tory yesterday described his Mansion House speech as "a pathetic performance."'[43] The political interventions kept pressure on the Treasury and the Bank not to tighten policy. The initiative on continued monetary ease did not originate in Threadneedle Street or in Whitehall, but in Downing Street. In December 1986, Margaret Thatcher questioned the need for an interest rate rise that was being contemplated at the Treasury:

The Chancellor said it was his considered view, shared by the Governor, that monetary conditions were now a little too lax. This view was widely shared in the financial markets. It would be appropriate to increase base rates by 1 per cent at a fairly early opportunity, though the timing need not be settled yet. It was a matter of great regret that an increase was now needed. But without it there could be a serious break of confidence. Whilst there could be no guarantee, it might well be possible to reduce interest rates again after the Budget.

The Prime Minister questioned the need for an increase in base rates. A surge in M0 (not seasonally adjusted) had taken place in the summer but it had declined thereafter until November's 1 per cent increase. The cause of the present problems had, with hindsight, clearly been a PSBR which had been set too high in the 1986 Budget. The result had been excessive consumer spending.[44]

In fact there was no base rate rise.

THE LOUVRE AND EXCHANGE RATES

In the circumstances generated by the political logic of 1986, the Bank engaged on a major public reorientation of its policy. The occasion, Leigh-

Pemberton's Loughborough speech, on 22 October 1986, was the Bank's counterpart to Lawson's Mansion House performance, the announcement of a fundamental shift in philosophy in regard to monetary policy. It had been drafted by Eddie George, whose new views on monetary policy it now largely reflected. The Governor now set out a pronounced scepticism about broad money targets in the case of what he called Anglo-Saxon countries. Germany and Switzerland were sheltered from competitive pressure by their strong tradition of universal banks. The whole speech was cast in terms of learning lessons from international experience:

In common with other countries, that framework has been one of targeting the rate of growth of a monetary aggregate. This intermediate objective was chosen in the belief that there was a reasonably predictable relationship between the rate of monetary growth and the rate of growth of nominal income. But in practice our ability to use an estimate of that relationship for target setting, and to meet those targets, has, quite frankly, been less than impressive. Broad money in particular has all too often grown faster than expected or intended. Targeted aggregates have been periodically redefined, and target ranges revised upwards or even suspended for a period. Only two of the past six annual target rates of growth for £M3 have been achieved and, of those two, that for 1982–1983 was achieved only after the target range indicated in the previous medium-term financial strategy had been raised in the 1982 Budget.

There is, I suspect, a connection with the difficulties that these and other Anglo-Saxon countries have experienced in operating a policy framework of monetary targets.

Canada and Australia, for example, have both given up this approach; and the United States has found it necessary, as we have, to redefine and rebase its monetary targets, and has even so had similar difficulties in meeting them. Some other countries, such as Switzerland and Germany have been more successful, perhaps in part because their long-established structure of universal banks has sheltered them in some degree from the particular competitive energy released by the process of blurring the distinctions between different types of specialist financial intermediary.[45]

Leigh-Pemberton only modified the Loughborough conclusions slightly in discussions with the Treasury:

The Governor accepted that there was no case for broad money targets if that carried the connotation of an intention to hit the targets or to take action if it looked like they were not being hit; all agreed that was impracticable. But he thought further discussion was needed about the possibility of ranges or projections.

Mr George was somewhat concerned that having a target for M0 alone might imply that movements in M0 would be of even greater significance to monetary policy. He was not sure that M0 could bear that sort of weight. The Governor noted that it was possible we might be over the top of the target range at the start of the year, even though we might expect growth to fall back within the range later in the year.[46]

The Treasury was increasingly worried about the appropriateness of £M3 as a target or a measure, because

£M3 as at present defined has been increasingly distorted by shifts in relative competitiveness between banks and building societies, and switches in the way that societies chose to hold their liquid assets.[47]

In fact, the problem was that £M3 was now growing very quickly, with the twelve-month growth rate, which had been below 10 per cent at the beginning of 1985, rising to 14.4 per cent in December and close to 20 per cent in late 1986.

The critical issue that dominated the debate continued to be the exchange rate, not monetary growth. As the dollar fell in 1985 and 1986, the DM rose – also against other currencies, including sterling. George in November 1986 stated in a discussion in the Treasury that it 'would be highly damaging if we did not respond to a fall in the exchange rate. He recognised the uncomfortable constraint of an exchange rate target. But at some point we did need to stop saying that additional flexibility was helpful.' In other words, there should not be an exchange rate target, but that abrupt shifts should be smoothed. Lawson indicated that he agreed with this assessment – which indeed formed then the basis for a much harder approach to exchange rate objectives.[48]

By 15 January 1987, in the week following an EMS realignment in which the DM was revalued by 3 per cent, the sterling DM rate was down to 2.761. That fall put pressure on the UK but there was no serious discussion about a rate rise. Instead, the issue seemed to require global coordination. The new initiative started with French papers on reform of the international monetary system, and then with Franco-American discussions about the most appropriate way of halting the dollar depreciation. The culmination was a striking proposal by the French Finance Minister Edouard Balladur at the G-5/G-7 Finance Ministers' meeting in Paris at the Louvre (21–22 February 1987) for a system of target zones with a 5 per cent range, and a mechanism for triggering coordinated interventions as exchange rates moved to the boundaries of the zone. But the proposals for specific figures ran into heavy criticism, above all from Germany and Japan.

The Louvre meeting had its moments of high comedy. Leigh-Pemberton took them as an indication that coordination was fundamentally a quixotic French exercise, and that it was not just the Germans and the Japanese officials who were sceptical. He recorded his observations on the meeting:

The documents emerged from these meetings in final form after various amendments produced during discussions, which were well conducted by Edouard Balladur, largely in English, in the splendid surroundings of the Palais du Louvre and much improved by a superb dinner and lunch. Outside the window of the room in which we met was a large crane with an enormous placard on its side displaying G-5 in large red characters. As will be seen this proved too much for the Italians.

This dinner discussion took place at a long table with all the distractions of a superb meal and bad acoustics in the gilded salon in which candidates for the Inspectorate de Finances have their viva voce examination; and thus lacked precision. It was however understood that of the figures mentioned in 'Understandings on Intervention', 1/3 would be for the United States, 1/3 for Japan and 1/3 for 'Europe' with some uncertainty about $ transactions for intra-EMS purposes would rank, and I don't know whether this was ever resolved.

Volcker left half way through Sunday morning's meetings to 'catch a plane'. His attitude, while there, seemed to me to leave nothing to be desired; he was casual; cynical even and lolled about in a way beyond the conventions of the Palais du Louvre. More than once during the discussions, differences between him and [US Treasury Secretary James] Baker made one wonder whether the US wanted this agreement or not.[49]

It was thus not clear whether there had indeed actually been an agreement, and the Bundesbank in particular remained keen to deny that a meeting of finance ministers should or could prescribe the course for central bank interventions and monetary policy. The critical point that Leigh-Pemberton's note brings up is that dollar transactions for intra-EMS operations might be problematical.

But there was a substantial amount of intervention by the Bank, at much higher levels than after the Plaza (see Table 6.1). On Monday, 2 March, the Bank bought $89 m, the next day $17m, and on Wednesday $77 m. Then the levels surged to $447 m on the Thursday, and $564 m on Friday, 6 March; and the next week began with $713m on 9 March. The high levels of intervention continued into April. Most of the Bank's interventions were in dollars. That drove the dollar down against the pound, but also strengthened the pound against other currencies, and by the middle of March the DM rate was close to 3, closing on 11 March at 2.966. The Bank also started at this point – on the instruction of the Treasury – to intervene substantially also in Deutschemarks.

The policy of shadowing the DM started as it were as an accidental by-product of the Louvre coordination project. Thatcher famously complained that she did not know about it at the time; from the point of view of the Treasury (and the Bank) it came about as an outcome of the international agreement.[51] In fact, the Treasury worried greatly about the effect of the intervention policy:

Middleton thought it was always difficult to know if the exchange rate was at its right level, and that was particularly true at present. We had got strong upward pressure on sterling, but whether that was because the economy was looking strong, or because the dollar was weakening further or because of the Election, was difficult to tell. Normally, we would have taken some of the pressure on different fronts, including some on the exchange rate and some on interest rates. It was clear that intervention alone was not proving obviously successful in holding down the exchange rate; it was also producing a major distortion of our funding, with intervention now totalling as much as the PSBR itself. He felt it was right to let short-term interest rates fall now: they were still somewhat high in relation to the underlying position. But he thought we would get into difficulty if the pressure continued for much longer.[52]

On 8 April 1987 at a new G-7 meeting, the size of the intervention pool was raised from $12 bn to $15 bn.[53] But the meeting was rather downbeat, with Treasury Secretary Baker opening with a remark that 'things looked

Table 6.1 *Comparative intervention*
(A) Post Plaza 1985 (B) Post Paris 1987 $ equivalent, billions
(A) POST PLAZA: 23.9.85–31.1.86; (B) POST PARIS: 23.2.87–
6.4.87. (of which 23.9.85–31.10.85) cob

UK	−$0.6	+$4.3: +0.5DM
	(-$0.3)	(of which +$3.0:
		+0.4DM reported)
		+0.1
USA	+1.9DM; +1.4 yen	−2.9 yen
	(+1.8DM; +1.3 yen)	
JAPAN	−$3.1	+$10.0
	(-$2.7)	
GERMANY	−$1.2 and +$0.1 forward	+0.2$/yen
	(−$1.0)	
CANADA	−$1.7	+$1.5
FRANCE	−$0.6; +0.5 yen; −1.6DM	+$1.7; +.3 $/yen
	+0.6 ECU; +0.1 BFC	+5.1DM
	(−$0.8; +0.4 yen; +0.2DM	
	+0.4 ECU)	
ITALY	−$4.5. −3.3DM; −0.3 ECU	+1.0DM; +0.4
	(−1.8; −0.1DM; −0.2 ECU)	

+ country purchases (currency shown for domestic currency except where indicated)
- Sells Foreign Exchange Division HO-2 6 April 1987[50]

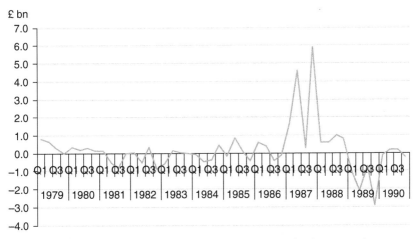

Figure 6.4 Changes in foreign exchange reserves, £ bn (1979–1990)

worse' since the Paris meeting, and the German Finance Minister Gerhard Stoltenberg commenting that it 'would be a bad failure to give up the Louvre now'. Only his French colleague, Edouard Balladur, the real architect of the Louvre agreement, tried to claim that the accord 'had worked well'.[54]

The Treasury worried about the increased amount of intervention (see Figure 6.4). At the regular meeting with the Bank of England, Treasury Under-Secretary for Monetary Policy David Peretz observed that the Treasury 'can't go on intervening at $½ – $1 bn a day until the elections', and Frank Cassell, the Deputy Secretary in the Treasury, replied, 'Why not?'[55] Peretz then brought the debate back to the exchange target, 'DM 3 is crucial.' With that, the discussion shifted to the EMS, and George stated, 'If we want to go into EMS after realignment we'd want to go into it at higher rather than lower rate to give us more room for manoeuvre.'[56] The 3 DM level was clearly established as the market expectation, and George noted the 'clear evidence that the market itself is reluctant to test a cross rate of DM3.00, fearing our intervention!'[57] The goal of a specific DM exchange rate would make sense fundamentally only as part of a wider strategy of entering the ERM: the credibility generated by that policy announcement would take the pressure off from the need for forex intervention.

DM3 continued to be an obsession with the Chancellor and with the Treasury, and Lawson saw it as crucial to policy, and felt that prospective inflation was tolerable, and that the pace of economic expansion 'would tail off before too long and this would provide an appropriate moment for the next onslaught on inflation'. He also saw the exchange rate policy as a way of building the case for EMS membership, and that the September ECOFIN meeting would be an ideal opportunity to join.[58]

George was more sceptical, and worried more about the way the exchange rate obsession was getting in the way of price stability: 'There is a question about the balance of objectives of policy and whether or not our current stance is consistent with making further progress against inflation.'[59]

INFLATION WORRIES

At this point, the UK was growing vigorously, with 3.2 per cent real GDP growth in 1986 and 5.6 in 1987, and showed some signs of overheating. But measuring the degree of policy room at the time – without the statistical benefit of hindsight – is hard. In retrospect, we know that in 1987, for the first time since the early 1970s, there was a positive output gap (indicating that the level of economic activity was over the long-run trend). An easier way to judge the overheating was the external balance: the current account deficit rose to 1.7 per cent of GDP in 1987 (in 1986, it had already been 1.0 per cent).[60] Judging the current account balance is not easy either: and there were many voices that followed Nigel Lawson's belief that the large inflows that financed the current account deficit were simply a sign of the new dynamism of the British economy. The *Financial Times* wrote:

The apparent policy of shadowing the DM remains correct. To the extent that one is concerned about the current account, however, a policy of pegging the exchange rate is no help. High interest rates to support the exchange rate ensure that the current account deficit is financed rather than reduced.[61]

The Bank explained the policy to the market in the same way, saying that the ½ per cent cut (on 28 April) had been 'overtly in response to exchange rate pressure alone'.[62] In other words, the domestic argument would not have been for easing at this point.

The exchange rate focus of British policy coupled with the extreme difficulty of actually implementing the international agreement concluded by the G-7 pushed Lawson to think again more explicitly about ERM membership, and he told Leigh-Pemberton in June that he intended to raise the question once more with Thatcher 'at the first appropriate moment'. He envisaged the September ECOFIN meeting as the most appropriate moment for the UK to join, and argued that the membership would give much greater leverage: 'In doing all that is required of us to strengthen the EMS we would have leverage to require contributions from others, such as the Germans.'[63]

The Bank worried most about monetary growth and a possible inflationary resurgence (see Figure 6.5). M0 targets remained a part of the official approach to monetary policy, but M0 looked quite stable until 1987 (see Figure 6.6). In the second half of 1986, the growth rate of M0 increased slightly, and consumer inflation, which had fallen, began to nudge upwards from August 1986, and in the spring of 1987 crossed the 4 per cent threshold.

George at a meeting with the Treasury set out a rather alarmist view. He said:

he was extremely keen to see monetary conditions tightened. The weekly bank lending data for July was showing continuing very large increases. But he saw potential difficulties in tightening monetary conditions without breaching the 3 DM cap, though he fully understood the reasons for wanting to hold it. He thought the chance of a ½ per cent increase sticking was slim, and would prefer to do 1 per cent, even if that meant waiting. The Chancellor thought that there would be no harm in doing ½ per cent now, and then reconsidering the position in September; we would not lose credibility if we subsequently moved rates up by a further ½ per cent.[64]

The message to the markets was slightly mixed, as at the same time the Governor was telling the discount houses that 'it's a minority view that these interest rate cuts are taking undue risks with inflation'.[65]

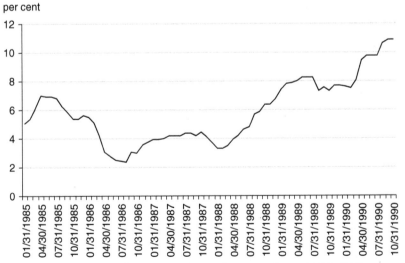

Figure 6.5 CPI inflation, annual rate of per cent change (1985–1990)

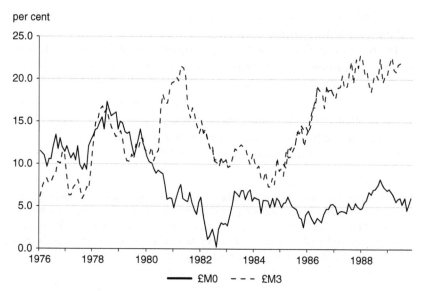

Figure 6.6 M0 and M3 growth rates (1976–1989)

The Bank worried about the consequences of continued intervention to keep the pound from rising:

Meanwhile we have seen renewed upwards pressure on the exchange rate. Since the renewal of the Louvre accord we have experienced renewed strong demand for sterling, and have had to buy something approaching $2 billion of dollars and deutschemarks to keep sterling below the DM3 ceiling. It may be that these inflows represent no more than a one-off adjustment following the renewal of the accord, and we think it right that our initial response to them should be through intervention. But plainly if they were to be sustained we should again be faced with the dilemma which we contemplated earlier in the year.[66]

Some of the inflow was concealed, on instructions from the Treasury, by forward transactions: the Bank sold foreign exchange as a future transaction within the month, with a parallel contract for a repurchase some months later, so that the movement would not show up in the published reserve figures.[67] The pressure increased. At a meeting in the Treasury on 14 October, Leigh-Pemberton reported

that we had bought $2 billion over the previous two days and $4¾ billion since late September. The question now was whether these inflows would be sustained or reversed. He saw no reason to believe that what we were seeing was just a short term flurry; it might instead be part of a steady, longer term diversification into sterling.[68]

There was now a risk, Leigh-Pemberton thought, of inflation rising above 5 per cent, and he suggested, probably at the urging of George, that the best response was to let the exchange rate rise. The Treasury officials pushed back against this view. Burns thought:

This scenario made the policy problem difficult. A rise in the exchange rate would be a perverse response to worries about the external side; and while it might lead to slightly lower inflation, it would produce <u>faster</u> growth in domestic demand.

Sir P Middleton said he had come to the same conclusion, but via a different route, one less derived from the forecast. We had now come to base our policy on keeping the exchange rate stable. He thought we should try to maintain that unless there were very very strong reasons for changing it. We would lose all credibility about our determination to resist downward pressure on the exchange rate if we give in to upward pressure.[69]

Lawson concluded with the thought that it would be 'perverse' to let the exchange rate rise.

The more the international system looked precarious or strained, the greater the concern with the exchange rate and its stability became. Strains in the G-7 constituted a trigger of financial turbulence in October 1987, with a dramatic stock market crash. The markets concluded that international policy cooperation was disintegrating. At the IMF Interim Committee meeting of 27 September, Baker had enraged the German Finance Minister with a statement of only a slightly veiled demand for more German monetary expansion: 'The largest countries have a special responsibility to pursue sound and consistent policies.'[70] At a press briefing on 15 October, Baker suggested that the US would push down the dollar as a response to the German interest rate hike. In the Bank of England's account, he had said that the Louvre would die 'if the Germans kept raising interest rates'.[71] In October 1987, in the aftermath of the stock market panic, international monetary economics, domestic monetary policy and financial stability policy all converged with each other.

Leigh-Pemberton told Lawson about what he now saw as the major monetary policy dilemma, but basically came round to the rather benign view of Lawson and the Treasury:

One strand of thought was that monetary conditions before the Stock Market collapse of October 19 had been satisfactory; conditions had been eased since then to counter the expected impact of the market collapse, but it now seemed that – partly as a result of that action – the collapse was not having a real major effect on the real economy. This implied that conditions now rather lax, and that an increase in interest rates would be appropriate. But it was clear that we could not raise interest rates in present circumstances without breaching the 3DM ceiling, and on balance he felt it was probably better to hold on to our entrenched position now, rather than tightening conditions and running the risk that we might have to ease them again later.[72]

In September 1987, Lawson tried to embed the concrete policy of the UK in a broader rethinking of global monetary arrangements. His set-piece speech at the IMF meetings included an appeal for a return to a generally fixed exchange rate system based on wider bands: a similar concept to the target zones discussed at the Louvre and also promoted by Baker.[73] Thatcher was deeply irritated. She 'wanted to know what was going on, why had she not been told, how was it that something always went wrong when the Chancellor went abroad?'[74]

By September, the Bank's daily foreign exchange and gold reports emphasized the 3 DM rate as the key exchange rate objective, often recording 'robust intervention' in its defence.[75] On 29 September, Bank bought \$634 m foreign exchange, and on 26 October, \$912 m as the 'DM 3 level was under siege throughout the second half of the day'.[76] There was a problem, though, as Middleton actually acknowledged in a discussion with the Bank in late July, that the Prime Minister 'doesn't want interest rates up at all and hasn't endorsed DM3 cap'. While the Prime Minister was fundamentally concerned with interest rates, Lawson was determined to hold the exchange rate.[77]

THE POLITICAL ROW OVER EXCHANGE RATES AND INTERVENTION

From March 1987 to March 1988, the pound–DM rate remained almost completely stable, at just below 3 DM. This was the period in which the unannounced policy of 'shadowing the DM' became apparent to market participants. By September, the *Financial Times* trumpeted, 'It is no secret: the British Government has been living in sin with the EMS.'[78] It was also evident that inflation was creeping up again from the spring of 1987 to the last months of the year (though then retail price inflation fell back). At the beginning of 1988, the Bank observed that 'our judgment remains that, as we agreed last month, monetary conditions are too loose', that the result was a surge in demand, and that, however, 'there remains nothing that monetary policy can do about this, given the proximity of the exchange rate to DM3'.[79] George at the regular meeting with the Treasury said that he was 'more concerned about inflation than the external balance'.[80]

Thatcher by contrast was arguing for a lower interest rate and a lower exchange rate – both would stimulate British growth further. She explained at a meeting in Hector Laing's Dunphail country house that her feelings on this matter were 'inspired by her disapproval of the fact that the Chancellor was successfully shadowing the ERM without being a member of it'. Leigh-Pemberton's account of the meeting added the comment, 'I did not venture to remind her that, not so long ago, she was on record as saying that devaluation was no respectable way of becoming competitive.' But it was clear that he, like Lawson, was leaning to an exchange rate anchor.[81]

The question of holding the exchange rate became highly charged politically, but the fierce clash only erupting two months later. It started with an interview by Thatcher in the *Financial Times* on 23 November 1987, when she denied that there was any exchange rate target, any 'specific range', and stated that 'we are always free'. It was at this interview that the journalists confronted her with the obvious proof that the pound had been 'shadowing' the DM.[82] The evidence of deliberate miscommunication between the Treasury and the Prime Minister's Office now was laid out. As the Chancellor's Private Secretary informed the Bank at the end of November 1987: 'The Prime Minister has not been told about the secret "intervention" side-letter to the G-7 agreement; Taylor [the Chancellor's Private Secretary] told me that he was under firm instructions not to let that go across to No. 10.'[83]

Eddie George objected to the target – or as Treasury officials later termed it 'blew the whistle' on the policy of shadowing the DM. Lawson's interpretation was not just that George instinctively did not like fighting the market, but that 'Margaret Thatcher had been getting at him'.[84] George told Terry Burns that there had been 'excessive intervention'.[85] At a meeting before the internationally coordinated interest rate cuts of 4 December 1987, a response to the stock market crash, and one of the last pieces of international coordination in the spirit of the Plaza and the Louvre, George stated that the Bank's major focus was the inflation threat – which would be fanned by an interest rate cut. At this discussion, he explained that it was 'increasingly clear that qu[estion] was what objective is. Not putting downward pressure on inflation. Clearly answer to strategic qu[estion] is you won't be allowed to use mon[etary] policy to pursue the objectives we thought we were aiming at.'[86] The Governor explained to the discount houses in a similar way that 'we are in a dilemma where we have had to choose between intervention and lower interest rates'.[87]

Leigh-Pemberton continued to be concerned about the exchange rate objective. In a meeting in the Treasury in December, he argued:

Policy for the last few months had been dominated by the 3DM cap. The greater prominence given to the exchange rate had developed gradually since April; the cap had originally been seen as a temporary measure before the Election, but in the autumn it had become increasingly dominant. He saw two ways forward:

(i) We could formalise our policy of pegging sterling to the deutschemark, recognising the implications not only of stopping the rate rising but also of stopping it falling. He had strained very hard to cap sterling rising at 3DM and we should correspondingly have a firm plan of action if sterling came under downward pressure.

(ii) The alternative was to revert to a more pragmatic policy, where the effective exchange rate was one of the factors taken into account in forming judgements about monetary policy. This could imply uncapping if that proved necessary, but with any rise in the rate against the deutschemark being offset by a cut in interest rates.

Middleton thought: 'We should stick to our existing policy for as long as we could. We had considerable capital invested in it, and it was a genuine long-term counter-inflation policy.'[88]

At a Bank–Treasury meeting, when George subversively asked, 'How did we get to the figure of DM 3? Answer: Pure chance', Middleton replied. 'DM policy is the only one we've got. Best chance of getting lower inflation is to stick to it. Must make sure Stock Exchange problem doesn't become a disaster.'[89] The Treasury was locked in: looking back, Burns thought that the exchange rate had been too high for too long (two to three years), but 'now embarked on this policy we need to get on with it'.[90]

In December 1987, a major conflict broke out, fuelled by the contention generated by the *Financial Times* interview. At a meeting in No. 11 Downing Street, on 4 December, the Chancellor had 'asked the Bank to do a significant burst in non-dollar currencies this afternoon, perhaps £100 m worth, with a further £100 m if necessary'. That meant large-scale intervention, but not primarily in the dollar market, since the dollar rate seemed irrelevant to British discussions, and the Bank was principally buying DMs. Heavy intervention occurred in order to defend the 3 DM level, with $694 m of foreign exchange bought on 4 December, $192 m on 10 December and $883 m on 11 December, with additional overnight purchases. Leigh-Pemberton promised to explain to the Bundesbank why the British did not want to see sterling rise against the DM. The brotherhood of central bankers at this moment exploded. Bundesbank President Karl Otto Pöhl reacted 'extremely negatively'.[91] A conversation with the Governor of the Banque de France, Jacques de Larosière, went no better. Paris was just as shocked by the action as Frankfurt, as the moves meant a weakening of non-DM ERM currencies.[92] The Bundesbank legal experts presented the British action as a violation of Article 15 of the Agreement between Central Banks, which limited cross holdings of European currencies to 'working balances' and effectively excluded the possibility of large scale use in intervention policy.[93]

Leigh-Pemberton in a dramatic telephone call early on 9 December tried to warn Lawson of the fundamental incoherence of his policy, and of the likelihood that it would destroy the European cooperation on which the approach rested:

The Chancellor telephoned the Governor at 8.30am today. He said that he had heard accounts of the meeting in Basle, and understood that Pöhl continued to be reluctant to allow us to purchase DM or other strong currencies.

The Chancellor went on to say that he had spoken to the Prime Minister last night. He had explained that the problem was a 1979 agreement, and that the Bundesbank was wholly opposed to our purchasing DM. The Prime Minister said that we had got to go ahead. We should tell the Bundesbank that they were being unreasonable, given the vast amount of dollars that we had taken in.

The Governor said that the Chancellor should not under-estimate the scale of opposition in Europe to what we were proposing. It was not only the Germans, but the French too would regard it as a great affront. De Larosière had been very clear on this. The Governor urged the Chancellor to speak to Stoltenberg and Balladur before going ahead. The Chancellor said that he would try to get a message to both.

The Governor asked whether the Prime Minister really understood how serious a problem this would create for monetary relations in Europe. The Chancellor said that she was entirely clear about that, and would be quite happy to field any protest that might come from Kohl or others. She was very clear that we had borne more than our share of dollar support, and that had to stop.

The Governor asked whether the Chancellor had considered further declines in interest rates as an alternative; the Chancellor did not offer any response.

The Governor said that it was entirely possible that the Germans would not only complain, but would take action to neutralise our intervention. Why would they not buy sterling for deutschemarks to neutralise our transactions?[94]

So, on 9 December, the Chancellor wrote a letter to the Governor setting out the policy most clearly: 'The overriding objective of our foreign exchange market intervention remains to hold the sterling cross-rate against the deutschemark below 3DM. From now on, all intervention to achieve that should be in deutschemarks, and not in dollars.'[95] He added that since the Louvre, British market intervention in dollars had been $25 bn compared with the very modest Bundesbank figure of $3 bn. There then followed a telephone conversation between Thatcher and French Prime Minister Jacques Chirac, in which Chirac warned that if the Bank of England operation selling dollars to buy DM went on, 'the EMS would blow up' because of the pressure against the franc. Thatcher replied, 'The purpose of such calls should not be to tell us to stop what we were doing. There was no option of that. [. . .] She would like to see the Bundesbank doing more to support the dollar.'[96]

On 10 December, Leigh-Pemberton and Lawson met the Prime Minister and agreed that intervention should now be not in dollars, but in French francs, as well as Yen and Swiss francs. When the Governor reported on these fraught discussions to the Bank's Court, the non-executive directors of the Bank 'asked me formally to record their anxiety that the Bank of England should be compelled by an act of policy to renege on an article contained in a formal agreement between itself and other central banks'.[97] The incident was not least remarkable in that it seemed to turn Thatcher in favour of currency intervention, a policy that she strikingly and continually resisted in public.

The incident clearly profoundly damaged the notion of global and also European economic and monetary cooperation. Loehnis discussed the case with his opposite number, Sam Cross of the New York Fed, and the manager of the international operations of the Federal Reserve System, who called the British action 'an unfriendly act'. Loehnis diplomatically explained that intervention policy had 'changed on the instructions of the EEA [Exchange Equalisation Account]'s principals [i.e. the Treasury] and contrary to our advice and wishes'.[98] Cross recorded that 'central banks intervened in concert aggressively, visibly and noisily'. Hans Tietmeyer of the German Finance Ministry complained that the DM purchases 'undermined the whole co-operative approach in international economic affairs which we had been striving for. The US Government could not understand what we were doing.' 'The UK is playing with fire . . .. By the Grace of God the change in our policy had not become public knowledge, but if it did, the deutschemark would strengthen against the dollar even more, and other central banks would be encouraged to join the fun.' And Jean-Claude Trichet, the Director of the French Trésor, said the manner in which the policy change was handled was 'incroyable'.

Matters got worse as the whole intervention controversy was exposed in public. The spat broke with a story that appeared initially in a rather obscure Italian publication, *Il Mundo*, under the by-line of a young journalist called Emilio Galli-Zugaro, who reported that the Bank had bought $1bn of DMs in December against the express wishes of the Bundesbank. The report was quickly taken up elsewhere. The Bank's investigation of how the leak occurred established that Galli-Zugaro had called the Bank's press office, to say that he had 'heard a story'. When asked for the source of his story, he claimed to have 'discussed the matter with a friend at the bank when he was in London'.[99] So the Bank of England dealers fell under suspicion. But in fact, the information did not come from any London source, but rather from the Bundesbank, which had close relations with Galli-Zugaro, and was using the publicity in order to discipline London.

On 12 January 1988, the controversy was discussed in Basel, at the Committee of Central Bank Governors. In the end, the outcome was a new agreement, 'Understanding of the G-7 Countries on Intervention and Consultation', in which the emphasis on consultation prior to intervention was restated.[100]

In the immediate wake of the controversy, in a memorandum of 15 December 1987, George set out two alternatives for what was now termed 'monetary strategy':

(i) to formalize the present 'unofficial' policy of pegging sterling's exchange rate to the DM; or

(ii) to revert to the more pragmatic approach of earlier recent years when the exchange rate (in effective terms) was one, important, element in an assessment of monetary conditions, alongside monetary developments and developments in the real economy, guiding short-term interest rate policy. In present circumstances this would involve 'uncapping'.

He emphasized much more the dangers of keeping to the cap:

(i) it threatens to generate excessive strain on the economy and upward pressure on domestic costs, especially labour costs which are still the principal weakness in our economic performance and which, once they have started to rise, will prove on all past experience to be extremely difficult to stop; and

(ii) it sends the wrong signals about policy to the wider economy and to financial markets, with the apparent message that we are willing to sacrifice counter-inflation to maintaining industrial competitiveness.

There effects are already apparent: in the unsustainably rapid growth of domestic demand; in the worsening trade balance; in accelerating monetary expansion; in higher wage claims coupled with a greater willingness to pursue them through industrial action and a greater preparedness on the part of management to avert disruption through higher settlements; and in a steepening yield curve and concluded:

(iii) The stable DM approach effectively pre-empts monetary policy for maintaining the exchange rate, and precludes the exchange rate as a transmission mechanism. Doing away with the exchange rate target would enable monetary policy again to concern itself directly with counter-inflation, working, where necessary, through induced movements in the exchange rate itself. This in turn would reduce the need for fiscal policy to carry more of the short-term stabilisation burden identified in paragraph 9 (iii) above.[101]

I still remain totally baffled as to what national interest the Chancellor or the Prime Minister thought that their unilateral intervention policy change would achieve. The record of your meeting at No 10 suggests that the Prime Minister is mainly concerned about the risks to inflation caused by the scale of our intervention. She presumably thought that if we intervened directly in deutschemarks the inflation-inducing liquidity creation might be less than that caused by intervening in dollars. You quite rightly warned her that this was unlikely to be so. Even if she had been right, the relatively small gain on that front would have been bought at the cost of undermining the whole of what one had thought to be HMG's policy for international economic co-operation (cf the Chancellor's speeches passim) and the deliberate affronting of all our European Community allies, particularly Germany and France, by showing first an intention to change policy without consulting, then consulting, and then proceeding nonetheless.[102]

Leigh-Pemberton wrote in hand on the memorandum: 'I agree.' He had agreed with Middleton at the bilateral meeting that the end of the exchange rate link was the key to 'getting the Govt off the hook'. It was clear that there was an overheating problem, but the Treasury was unwilling to reconsider the basic approach. Lawson in January 1988 had said that he was 'keen to find the opportunity for a rise, especially one of ½% that would not be followed rapidly by a further half. But he felt that any move had to be in the context of the 3DM cap, not an alternative to it.'[103]

ENDING THE CAP

The aftermath of the December 1987 conflict resonated at an even higher political level – and in the public eye – in the spring of the next year. Sterling rose again, and by the beginning of March in the middle of the preparation for the budget, it was back at nearly 3 DM. As far as possible, the Bank initially tried not to intervene. On 4 January, there was a massive burst of central bank intervention, but not from the Bank of England, which explained that 'we'd already done our share and weren't close to DM3'.[104] Then, on 2–3 March, $1.8 bn intervention was required to stop a surge in the pound, and both Bank and Treasury officials recommended uncapping the pound and letting the exchange rate rise. The proposed actions brought the same problems as before:

The Governor explained that we had taken in $450mn overnight, and were in the process of understanding instructions from the Treasury of converting that principally into ECUs. He wanted to alert Larosiere to this situation and to say that should upward pressure on the sterling/DM rate continue during the course of today, then we might find it necessary to intervene directly in deutschemarks and French franc. If we did that, then we would do it as equal amounts as between each currency.[105]

The New York Fed's officer also protested:

(a) they were most concerned that we had used the dollar last night as an intermediary to buying European currency today. This only gave strength, in her view, to the market perception that central banks were keen to switch out of the dollar. If we wished to pursue a DM cap we should intervene directly in European currencies and not via the dollar.

(b) also she heard in the market-place in New York that we had been switching dollars into marks. This too was 'unacceptable'.[106]

Lawson wanted to delay over the weekend.[107] But Thatcher, who had been informed of the scale of the intervention, was extremely upset, and complained that the intervention was fuelling inflation and wanted to monitor the scale on a half-hourly basis. On Friday, 4 March 1988, large exchange interventions – including big overnight purchases – had failed to hold sterling down. At 2:00 p.m. Lawson was summoned to see Thatcher. When he returned to the Treasury, at 3:30 p.m. in a stormy meeting, George set out the scale of the interventions – $2 bn, mostly in DM but also in French francs – and explained that the pressure was likely to continue.

If we kept the 3 DM cap, we should have to be prepared to intervene heavily. If we were ready to remove the cap, he would very much rather do it soon, rather than waiting and being clearly seen to be defeated by market pressure. He would prefer to make a move in London, where it could be controlled in a more orderly fashion, and so would recommend resisting further pressure that day and on Friday night in Tokyo and then considering the position on Monday morning.

Burns stated the fundamental conundrum of the exchange rate link:

Our hands were tied: we could not raise interest rates because we were tight up against the 3DM cap; but nor could we lower them without an undesirable easing of monetary conditions. He was pessimistic about our chances of holding 3 DM, and thought the strong upward pressure would continue. He thought it more sensible to move now, rather than just before or just after the Budget, when it would be more clearly a defeat and when it would be known that the references to exchange rate stability in the Budget documents would have been written before we uncapped.

George warned against getting 'hooked' on a new rate, such as 3.10, and Lawson countered that he 'could not just allow the exchange rate to rise unchecked'. So the meeting agreed on intervention should the pound rise above 3.05.[108] Lawson then went back to No. 10 Downing Street, and on returning told his officials, 'I have decided that we can't hold on for any longer.'[109]

Thatcher had been upset by the appearance of a defiance of market logic when in December – in the immediate wake of the intervention spat – Lawson had told the Treasury Committee, 'Obviously interest rates are something which I watch carefully all the time and when I think they ought to go up they go up and when I think they should come down they come down.' The use of 'I' looked like hubris. When the MP Nicholas Budgen pressed further, 'I thought [rates] were decided by markets', Lawson retorted, 'No, that would be an abandonment of monetary policy and that I am not prepared to do.' Thatcher's riposte in parliament came on 9 March, with the statement: 'The Chancellor never said that aiming for greater exchange rate stability meant total immobility. [...] There is no way in which one can buck the market.'[110] The next day, the Governor explained to the market that 'the decision was taken quite amicably. The Chancellor saw that it was impossible to go on intervening on that scale and had in any case never said the level of the £ was immutable.'[111]

So as sterling went above the 3 DM level, there were still interventions to stop the pound rising too much, with $488 m sterling sales on 7 March, in order to stop the rise being too abrupt. The exchange rate now rose, moving through the 3 DM level. On 17 March, a half percentage interest rate cut was made in order to slow the appreciation.

Relations between the Treasury and the Prime Minister continued to be very bad. Middleton was, George noted, deeply 'depressed':

This was somewhat different from our usual meetings. We did not spend much time on specific issues but most of our meeting was taken up with him sharing with me his problems arising from the Prime Minister/Chancellor imbroglio. He says that, despite the pleasantness of the lunch after the No 10 meeting, there is still great resentment on the part of the Chancellor and great distrust on the part of the Prime Minister. The Chancellor is showing signs of lack of confidence and testiness; this was evident in his relatively poor performance before the Treasury Select Committee. He also fears this will mean that the Chancellor will not be as willing as he should be to combat [David] Young's [Baron Young of Graffham, the Secretary of State for Trade and Industry] intrusions into Treasury/Bank matters.

Another cause for concern is that Major and some of the junior Ministers in the Treasury have felt the lash of the Prime Minister's tongue and are inclining towards blaming the Chancellor for putting them in this position. This obviously makes intra-Treasury workings more difficult. Middleton said that he was as depressed as he had ever been in his present job.[112]

On 25 March 1988, George accompanied the Governor to a meeting with Margaret Thatcher to explain the principles of the policy: from the Bank's perspective, the overriding objective of monetary policy was to 'exert sustained and gradual downward pressure on inflation'. But there were also the international considerations that followed from the G-5/G-7 exercise: 'Subject to this, exchange rate stability is desirable in itself, and as a part of wider international exchange rate management in the G-7.' Lawson would argue that 'the objective of exchange rate stability should not be seen as subordinate to that of counter-inflation, but as the means of ensuring counter-inflation over the longer term'. But – and this was the major message – there was a problem that arose when fixed rates came under market pressure, and it was impossible then to tell whether the pressures were transient or persistent.[113] Burns' position was much more emphatically in favour of the exchange rate focus: 'There is a lot to be said for conducting policy towards the exchange rate in a way that can be understood.'[114]

The Governor told the market on 31 March that 'we haven't given up exchange rate stability but regard it as an important sub-objective, subject to the overriding objective of lower inflation'.[115] In April 1988, the exchange rate appreciation by contrast drove a new discussion about cutting rates:

With meeting of OPEC and G-7 coming up, and with US trade figures the following Thursday, it was obviously necessary to consider the scope for further intervention, or interest rate changes. The Governor said that he saw little prospect of bringing the pound significantly lower by intervention in amounts of $50 or $100 million – although heavy intervention around 3.15DM might be more effective. Clearly there was scope for a cut in interest rates as the exchange rate firmed, but the Governor saw a case for holding it in reserve for Washington.

Sir T Burns said that he thought the case was finely balanced on monetary policy grounds. At the last monthly monetary meeting, the consensus had been that at around 3.15DM an interest rate cut would be appropriate. On past form, the aftermath of the G-7 meeting would serve to exaggerate whatever trend was already present in the market: in the present climate, that would mean a further strong upward push.[116]

On 13 May, sterling appreciated when Thatcher refused to endorse Lawson's view that a further rise in the pound was unsustainable, and the Bank again took very large intervention action, buying $405 m foreign exchange.[117] On 19 May, the Governor told the markets that 'one of the consequences of the exchange rate having a major role is that interest rates may have to be more flexible – ½ point upward moves are a sign of this'.[118]

The 1988 budget was a stunning political success – with the 1981 budget, it defined the macro-economic framework of the Thatcher years. The tax cuts, reducing the basic income tax rate to 25 per cent and the top rate from 60 to 40 per cent, were wildly cheered by Conservative MPs. The *Financial Times* noted that Lawson was 'a pretty engaging fellow who may even be the next Prime Minister'.[119] But the political triumph was overshadowed by the exchange rate discussion, and then by the discussion about interest rate strategy.

By June, the market situation had reversed, as the Governor explained in the regular Treasury meeting:

If we only did a ½ per cent [increase], he thought it unlikely that the exchange rate would strengthen markedly, and this should leave scope for a further ½ per cent in the very near future. A 1 per cent move now would have attractions from a domestic monetary point of view, but the risk of the exchange rate 'bouncing back' was not in his view, worth taking.

Middleton then endorsed the Governor's preference for a ½ per cent move.[120]

In June 1988, a series of gradual interest rate increases began, which also drove the pound initially higher, so that it went well above the old 3 DM target. Was that enough to curb a potential inflationary boom? In the meeting to discuss the rises, Middleton had stated that 'the main thing is to get interest rates up', and George concurred that 'we were oversensitive to competitiveness for too long', or, in other words, had been too much driven by thinking about the exchange rate. It was not, he thought, 'an independent objective to get the exchange rate down'.[121] Thus, sterling soared against the Mark. But there was still substantial policy uncertainty. George regretted that the interest rate rise was not more decisive, and thought that the half per cent rise gave 'wrong signals', 'creates confusion about seriousness of purpose', and just 'lets people think [we are] concerned about exchange rate and industrial confidence'. Middleton wanted three more half per cent moves in July.[122] Thatcher was now complaining that 'nothing had been done since 1983 to get inflation down'.[123]

The market saw a division between the Bank and the Treasury, with 'some feeling that Bank would like to go up to 11 while Treasury prefers to stick to 10 ½'. The Governor then denied this, 'We are not divided in that way.'[124] On 8 August, the interest rate was increased by a half point, and then, on 25 August, by a whole point. The discount houses complained that the first move 'was the most unexpected of all', and the Deputy Governor explained the move in terms of the softness of the pound/dollar rate, and added, 'It's hard to know when you've overdone it. Each move gets closer to the point at which inflation comes under control.'[125]

In September, with Lawson explaining that devaluation was not 'a possible answer' to the balance of payments problem, the Bank intervened on a large scale ($150 m on 28 September), with continuing sales in October and November.[126]

Reflecting on the rise to 12 per cent, Leigh-Pemberton asked the discount houses, 'Does the market feel that the longer we stay at 12 per cent, the better our chances of not being driven higher?' The reply was: 'Yes, we don't understand why you are buying gilts and foreign exchange at a time when you want to tighten.' In reply, Leigh-Pemberton said, 'It is simply part of the full-fund policy.'[127] But in fact, the need to raise rates continued to press on policy, and the market worried that Charles Goodhart (by then no longer at the Bank, but an influential voice from the LSE) was talking about 15 per cent rates.[128]

At the end of a series of gradual increases, the interest rate was 13 per cent (25 November), but Middleton was continually expressing worries that 'we haven't done enough'.[129] The market interpreted the outcome as evidence that the government was 'looking for a hard landing and subsequent recovery rather than a soft one', to which Leigh-Pemberton rather helplessly replied, 'I don't think that is right. I'm disappointed we had to give up 12%.'[130] The EMS possibility kept on coming back. Middleton in September 1988 started referring to a new initiative from Lawson:

He reckons now to know him well and he was left with the firm impression that the Chancellor has some strange new initiative in mind which he was not yet prepared to reveal to Middleton. He is very puzzled as to what it will be. Incidentally, the Chancellor, in their conversation, had asked Middleton whether he thought the time was now ripe for a new attempt to persuade the Prime Minister that we should join the EMS. Middleton had told him that he thought this was an absolute non-runner.[131]

By the last months of 1988, as inflation rose, Middleton was asking whether 'we were being ambitious enough in our inflation objectives. He wondered whether we ought not to be aiming for 0% by the time of the next election.'[132] The Bank and the Treasury both looked back on the last years of the DM experiment with regret. Burns at the beginning of 1989 argued that the exchange rate had been too high for too long (two to three years), but 'now embarked on this policy we need to get on with it'.[133] George thought that the biggest mistake would be 'any kind of indication of relaxation'.[134] In fact, inflation continued to accelerate with a rise in the RPI of 4.1 in 1987 and 4.6 per cent in 1988 (with a dramatic surge to follow in the next year). Although Leigh-Pemberton began the year by hoping that '13% will hold',[135] and later that 'my desire is that we should get through at 13% and not be forced up',[136] interest rates continued to be increased until they stood at 15 per cent (6 October 1989).

By the spring of 1989, things were looking better from the Bank's perspective, and George was happy about the extent of the economic slowdown. Real GDP growth, which had been 5.9 per cent in 1988, fell back, and the eventual 1989 figure was a more sustainable 2.5 per cent. This looked like a soft landing, and policy-makers could not see any indications of the recessionary cliff that lay ahead. George thought that adjustment was 'proceeding in a more classical way than I can ever remember'. Middleton agreed that the high rates should be maintained, and 'Don't contemplate cut'.[137] From October 1989, interest rates remained at a high plateau of 15 per cent (where they stayed until October 1990).

George remained quite critical of the legacy of the strategy of shadowing the DM. When an appreciation began, he told the Court: 'The strength of the exchange rate was not a conscious objective of policy but a consequence. [. . .] And it was a price that had to be paid if we were to achieve our essential counter inflationary objective. Indeed undue emphasis on a stable exchange rate had been an important cause of our present problems.'[138]

At the beginning of 1989, the economy looked on track for a smooth soft landing, with a gradual tapering of demand. As Leigh-Pemberton put this view in a letter to the Chancellor:

The latest indicators on the monetary and economic situation tend to confirm the impression of slower monetary growth in the fourth quarter of last year and of some moderation in the growth rate of domestic demand, though there is still little sign of any easing of inflationary pressures other than in the housing market. The exchange rate has been steady in effective terms. These indicators have been interpreted very positively in the financial markets. Indeed, some participants are now anticipating an early cut in interest rates.[139]

As monetary growth continued to grow sharply through 1989, however, there was a need to rethink, and the Bank started to contemplate moving away from the full fund rule, so that overfunding might be used once more, primarily as a way of influencing the exchange rate. George set out the proposal in a letter to the Treasury:

As I mentioned to you on the telephone, we have been thinking about what options are available for protecting ourselves against the contingency of continued sterling weakness in the near term, and possible associated market pressure for yet a further rise in short-term interest rates. We think that the most practical option on the domestic side would be to amend funding policy by suspending the full-fund rules. The most natural opportunity for the Chancellor to announce such a change would be in his Mansion House speech next Thursday, which is also the day on which the provisional money figures for September will be published. I thought that it might be helpful to set our ideas on paper now, in time for a decision to be taken in that context. The purpose of making the proposed change would not be to try and restrain broad money growth in the way Tim Congdon has suggested. Indeed one of the effects would be to leave less room for private sector borrowers in the bond market, forcing them back into the banking system, and it is not clear in present circumstances that the overall effect on broad money would be very large or even favourable. Rather, the objective would be to provoke a rise in bond yields, and also falls in the prices of other sterling capital market assets, increasing their attraction compared with other assets, including foreign currency assets, which would provide indirect support for the exchange rate, and help to contain the upward pressure on short-term interest rates.[140]

Tim Congdon, the most consistently powerful critic (from a very early moment) of what was now generally dismissively termed 'the Lawson boom', had held that the move away from M3 – linked to the abandonment of overfunding – had been at the root of the subsequent policy error. An alternative might have been fiscal tightening, but that would have been politically hard to implement, given that there was already a fiscal surplus.

In May 1989, the Bank intervened 'aggressively' as sterling moved down through DM 3.18, with $194 m of sterling purchases on 9 May, and then $209 m on 22 May and $311 m on 23 May, and $156 m on 24 May. George raised the possibility that the Chancellor 'might tell us to intervene as did not want to go below 3.17'. In relaying this report to the Court, in the midst of an intense intervention period, he added that he was 'very concerned'. 'It would signal the collapse of the G-7 concerted approach and would open old wounds.'[141] But on Tuesday, 13 June, there was $603 m of intervention and $226 m the next day, and similar levels for the rest of the week. In fact, despite large-scale continuing intervention operations, the exchange rate went on falling through 1989, from 3.25 in February to 2.72 by the end of the year.

By 1989 and 1990, it was clear that inflation was surging. A retrospective debate ensued that traced the policy mistake back to the mid-1980s. On 19 May 1989, Thatcher had in a BBC interview blamed the inflation rate on Lawson's foreign exchange policy.[142] The Bank also reflected on the lessons of the inflationary surge:

By mid-1986 policy had successfully brought the rate of inflation down to 2½%, at substantial cost in terms of earlier unemployment and lost output; but since then inflation has returned to the current level of nearly 11%. Some have suggested a direct causal link with the abandonment of broad money targets after the 1986 financial year. The Bank does not share this view, but the looser formulation of policy and the acknowledged essential judgmental element in its public presentation may have provided the authorities with greater freedom for manoeuvre, allowing priority not always to be wholly attached to the counter-inflation objective.

Most recently the UK economy now appears to be responding to the pressures induced by the maintenance of a high interest rate policy and to be entering recession. But inflation has yet to respond and cost-push pressures remain strong.[143]

In a widely ridiculed comment, in the early 1980s, Leigh-Pemberton had once stated that he thought that inflation was more of a threat to the UK than was communism.[144] By 1990, communism had collapsed, but inflation was surging. It looked as if policy had lost its orientation. Monetary targeting had fallen from its central role in policy-making. As interest rates soared in 1989, and as monetary aggregates seemed to be still increasing, Alan Walters responded to Middleton's concerns with a dismissive: 'Why waste time bothering about them?'[145] The discount houses lamented after the 1989 abolition of the official M3 series (which had formerly been the politically vital £M3) that 'we're sorry to be losing M3, which some people still think important'. Leigh-Pemberton's reply was: 'It's an indication of the structural changes that have occurred in the banking system.'[146]

Looking back, in one of those sporting metaphors beloved by every recent Governor of the Bank of England, Leigh-Pemberton thought of the problem as lying in the wrong balance of fiscal and monetary policy, a 'criticism of playing golf with one club wrong'.[147] It was in reality a question of having too many clubs in the bag, and then confusing the driver for the putter. Could modern technology have offered a solution, with an easier-to-hit hybrid?

JUDGING MONETARY POLICY

Is it possible to reach a judgement on the quality of British monetary management in the 1980s? What criteria should be used – macro-economic growth, macro-economic stability, price stability? The judgement itself was at the centre of the intense political debate. The best approach might be to think of a way of testing whether monetary authorities could convince the other players in the game. The problem lay in the rapidity with which the political view – of the government and of the Treasury – flipped between and blurred objectives and instruments, ending in a muddle that generated constantly changing and confusing market signals.

Policy thus consistently undermined stability in the 1980s. If macro-stability is the goal, it is hard to give a very enthusiastic verdict on the policy regime of the 1980s, as the monetary policy experiments of the 1980s contributed to two big recessions. If, on the other hand, inflation-busting is the goal, then the most successful period is the Chancellorship of Geoffrey Howe with the Bank under the agnostic leadership of Gordon Richardson, when, as Tim Congdon puts it, Howe 'achieved the largest fall in Britain's underlying inflation rate in peacetime'.[148]

In the 1980s and 1990s, an intellectual revolution occurred in economics, which largely overturned important elements of the consensus that had seen macro-economic management dependent on large macro-models, such as the iconic one operated by the UK Treasury. Finn Kydland and Ed Prescott's work on time consistency and Robert Barro and David Gordon's examination of commitments or reputation led to a renewed search for a rule-based approach to monetary policy.[149] Two alternative routes could be taken as part of the rule-based approach. Target rules are a way of constraining policy – in an extreme version of making policy entirely automatic so that it cannot respond to changing political but also economic circumstances. The best-known variant is Milton Friedman's k-per cent rule, according to which the central bank should increase the money supply by a constant percentage rate every year, irrespective of business cycles. More 'real' versions of a rule include inflation targeting. These target rules involve an optimality condition implied by an objective function together with a specified model of the economy.[150]

The rules approach is vulnerable to the objection that the choice of model is somewhat arbitrary, and in practice most rules that look like target rules are – because of the way that they are dependent on a particular model – more accurately described as reaction functions or instrument rules.[151] Mervyn King observed: 'Simple, or for that matter, complicated, rules for setting interest rates do not exist. They would be undermined by new research on better and improved rules which got rid of the bugs in the first rule as frequently as software packages are released.'[152] Instrument rules depend on a formula prescribing instrument settings as a function of currently observed variables, of price changes and output or employment measures. They are driven by the search for a rule that performs as Bennett McCallum and Edward Nelson put it 'at least moderately well – avoiding disasters – in a variety of plausible models'. The most important variants of this approach look at a response to developments in the monetary base (McCallum), or to inflation and output (John Taylor).

Taylor's approach in a 1993 paper was highly influential.[153] He modelled a way of deriving a nominal interest rate from observed or predicted values of inflation and the output gap (i.e. the difference between output and a reference value calculated from longer-term growth trends). The result was:

$$r = p + 0.5y + 0.5(p - 2) + 2$$

where

    r is the federal funds rate,

    p is the rate of inflation over the previous four quarters

    y is the per cent deviation of real GDP from a target.

Taylor based his calculation on an assumption that the long-term real interest rate was 2 per cent, and a target inflation rate should also be 2 per cent.

An obvious problem in this approach is that the output gap is hard to assess, especially in times of volatility or after large shocks: thus, the 1970s and 1980s might not seem to be an ideal subject for the application of a Taylor rule. Edward Nelson and Kalin Nikolov tried to deal with this issue by calculating two Taylor rule prescriptions: one on the basis of contemporary real-time observations, or from the data that was available to policy-makers at the time; and the second, on the basis of ex post data.[154] In particular moments, there were clear misperceptions that may have influenced policy. Thus, in the second half of the 1980s, there was an over-assessment of the extent of potential output, and the output gap was thought to be much larger than it was, so that Taylor rule calculations on contemporary data give a lower policy rate than those that are based on today's ('final') data. After 1991, this effect is much less pronounced.

The Taylor rule calculations also depend on an assessment of what should be an appropriate or desirable rate of inflation. In the course of the 1990s, a consensus developed that a rate of around 2–3 per cent would be desirable, so the following calculations, drawn from an updated version of Nelson and Nikolov's data, use an inflation goal of 2.5 per cent. Taking a higher inflation level – perhaps a more realistic assumption in the light of the experience of the early 1980s – would give a higher desired policy interest rate (although in 1985 Thatcher spoke of a 3 per cent inflation target, and in 1990 Leigh-Pemberton seems to have had a similar level of inflation in mind).[155]

The results derived from this retrospective assessment are quite striking for the traumatic period in British monetary policy in the first half of the 1980s (see Figure 6.7). The ex post application of the Taylor rule suggests that from 1979 Q2 to 1982 Q3, in other words in the period when 'monetarism' was at its intellectual peak, the policy rate was well below the level suggested by inflation and output data, and that a more restrictive interest rate policy would have been appropriate. One possible explanation is that there was a 'base drift': each time a target was missed, the base for the next period was reset at a higher level. The rationale was that returning to the pre-announced target level as a new base would require a higher variability of interest rates.[156] Given the controversy about the exchange rate, and about the collapse of British manufacturing in the recession of that time, the restrictive retrospective advice looks rather unrealistic.

Even more strikingly, perhaps, after 1982 Q3 and right up to 1987 Q4, when the economy was growing strongly, the policy rate was well above one that might be derived from the Taylor rule: in short, there should have been more easing. That assessment apparently contradicts the frequently made criticism of the Lawson boom, which suggests that over-lax monetary conditions set the stage for a resumption of inflation, and then for a collapse in output when monetary policy tightened as a correction

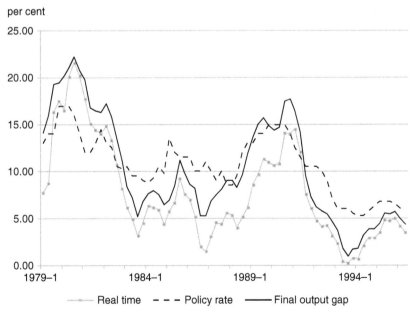

Figure 6.7 Taylor rule calculations (1979–1997)

in 1988. The calculations do suggest that monetary policy should have tightened earlier, in the last quarter of 1986, but from 1986 to 1987 the actual policy rate is still strikingly above the recommended Taylor rule application.

McCallum takes a similar rule-based approach but instead uses monetary base as the policy instrument in the formula:

$$\Delta b_t = \Delta x^* - \Delta v^a t + 0.5(\Delta x^* - \Delta x_{t-1})$$

where

Δb_t = change in the log of the adjusted monetary base, that is, the growth rate of the base between periods t−1 and t

Δx^* = a target growth rate for nominal GDP, namely change in the log of nominal GDP

$\Delta v^a{}_t$ = average growth of base velocity over the medium term.

McCallum sums up the policy implications of his version of a rule as applied to the UK as similar to an approach following from the Taylor rule until the early 1980s (see Figure 6.8); but after that his approach suggests that policy stayed too loose until 1990, when the UK joined the ERM. After the departure from the ERM, on the other hand, policy 'became just about right' until 1997 (when the Bank of England became independent). That verdict – based on an

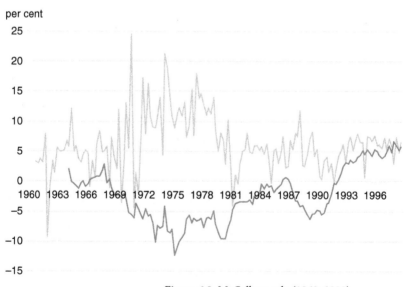

Figure 6.8 McCallum rule (1960–2000)

approach that takes the monetary base as the policy instrument – seems to fit better with the kind of discussions that actually occurred in the 1980s than the simple Taylor rule.[157]

Another recent approach is provided by Michael Bordo and Pierre Siklos, who examine different sources of potential credibility for central banks, an interest rate instrument, a money supply target and an exchange rate target (see Figure 6.9).[158] Since these three were in fact used by monetary authorities in the course of their experimentation in the 1980s and 1990s, this looks like a suitable way of testing the UK's policy credibility in different operating policy environments. The exchange rate instrument very closely follows the inflation rate, while the other two

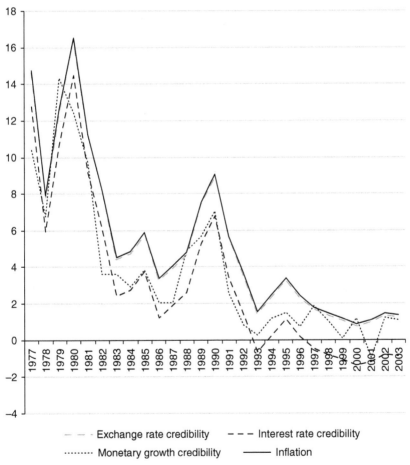

Figure 6.9 Exchange rate, interest rate and monetary growth credibility (1979–2003)

suggest a substantially quicker credibility gain until 1986, and a loss of credibility after that – in other words, in the period of the Lawson boom, and then with the most substantial gains occurring in the period 1991 to 1993, that is, in the period of EMS membership as well as in its aftermath.

By this measure, policy attained a high degree of credibility between 1983 and 1986, and regained even more credibility in the EMS period. The result is striking in that it implies that both the policy shock of the early 1980s, with the confused policy debate, and the policy shock of the ERM period, with an equally fraught discussion about the benefits of membership, laid a foundation for an era of better monetary management. The suggestion is that without these shocks that later stability would have been impossible to achieve, and in that sense a debate about whether a move to inflation targeting in the early 1980s would have been preferable is deeply anachronistic. The inflation targeting approach requires a prior stabilization of expectations in order to make it possible to approach any estimation of real interest rates, and in extreme situations, at the end of great inflations, exchange rate pegs are the most obvious ways of achieving that prerequisite.[159]

7

Hong Kong

Bank Crises and Currency Crises

In the mid-1980s, the Bank of England needed to wrestle with the problem of the relationship between banking stability and monetary stability, but in a place where the economic and political climate was even wilder than that of Big Bang London, and where ultimately also the exchange rate lay at the centre of the debate (and a fixed exchange rate, with the hardest possible peg, through a currency board, was the solution). More directly than in London, there was a clear link between monetary instability, exchange rate turbulence and the precariousness of financial institutions. The Bank of England was heavily involved in the management of Hong Kong's banking and currency arrangements. The shadow that continually hung over both was the prospect of the termination of the lease on the 'Crown Colony' in 1997.

Hong Kong's destiny was driven by economic dynamism as well as by political risk. At the same time as Hong Kong's political future seemed uncertain and unstable, there were tremendous commercial opportunities, and a lending and property boom at the beginning of the 1980s, with a large number of new banks being established. Broad money supply and domestic loans grew at average annual rates of 35 and 43 per cent, respectively, between 1979 and 1982.[1] At first, the Hong Kong administration deliberately restricted new banking licences to branches and subsidiaries of first-class overseas banks. This policy had an unanticipated consequence. These outside institutions did not have time to build their activities slowly on the basis of deepening knowledge of viable local lending circumstances. Rather, they aimed to ramp up their balance sheet as quickly as they could. The Bank noted how the new foreign banks 'tended to send out sharp young managers who were under some impulsion to prove their mettle by bringing back a slice of the profits which, as everyone knew, could be earned in Hong Kong'. Long-established banks in Hong Kong found themselves faced with aggressive competition, and had no option but to trim their margins in order to retain the business.

The Bank of England saw the major problem as lying in weak bank regulation, and sent two of its leading bank supervisors, Brian Gent and Richard Farrant, on secondment to Hong Kong to improve the quality of financial supervision. The Bank also reflected generally on the nature of Hong Kong business:

Operators in the property sector range from sound conservatively managed companies to outright crooks. The eagerness of banks to lend undoubtedly made it easy for crooks to flourish. The most meteoric star on the Hong Kong market was the Carrian Group. Carrian had its registered headquarters at a letter box on a piece of wasteland with the ruins of a hotel. It had started a meteoric expansion in 1979, and crashed in 1982. Its leading figure, George Tan, was able to spirit huge amounts out of banks simply by suggesting that he had backers with limitless resources behind them.

The Bank of England recorded the response of an American banker who did not want to be drawn into the speculative madness:

The local manager took the bank's President, who was on a tour round the area, to see the charismatic George Tan. All went well until the President, in his innocence, asked George Tan who were his ultimate backers. Apparently George Tan said 'When bankers start to probe into my private affairs I tell them to (expletive deleted).' Following this, the President apparently decided that this was not the class of business that he wanted for his bank, and instructed the branch to have no further dealings with Tan. Unfortunately this sort of reaction does not seem to have been very common.[2]

Banking in Hong Kong was dominated by the Hong Kong and Shanghai Banking Corporation (HSBC), which was not just a powerful commercial bank but also in practice, as a note-issuing bank, an essential part of Hong Kong's monetary management, in effect a sort of central bank. It was also acutely aware of its weaknesses, which its dynamic and well-connected chief executive Michael Sandberg sought to counter by internationalizing itself, first with the rather problematic acquisition of the US bank Marine Midland. In the early 1980s, HSBC saw the Bank of England, at this point still firmly opposed to a large foreign presence in London, as its major enemy. The issue flared up after Standard Chartered in April 1981 announced that it had made an agreed bid for Royal Bank of Scotland (RBS), and HSBC launched an aggressive counter-bid. Deputy Governor Kit McMahon immediately responded by saying that that offer would not be approved by the Bank of England because HSBC was not a British bank, because the Bank liked the arrangement with Standard

Chartered, and also that the position of HSBC posed 'a particular problem' for the Bank.[3]

McMahon set out his position at the Bank in a forthright memorandum:

We are not against HKSB tout court. We have allowed them to buy three British banks: BBME, Mercantile and Antony Gibbs. In these cases, they followed our procedures on consent. However, even here some queries arise particularly in relation to BBME. HKSB could be criticised for drawing off too much in dividends and not injecting enough capital and management leading finally to the withdrawal of BBME's head office (see also the point on supervision below). We do have some doubts about the nature of HKSB and its management. It is often said to be buccaneering, a term which contains some implicit doubts as well as praise. We do not know very much about its structure and activities but it is not perhaps difficult to become very profitable if you occupy the position HKSB does in Hong Kong. And in relation to the present case, we have the apparent incompatibility of many of Sandberg's remarks or undertakings. He wants a partnership and is prepared to get it even if he is to take over RBS against its Board's wishes. He promises an 'arm's length' relationship and at the same time that RBS will be HKSB's 'flagship in Europe'. We frankly do not know what weight to give to Sandberg's promises.[4]

In fact, neither bid for RBS succeeded, as the Mergers and Monopolies Commission turned down both bids, with some speculation that it was the Bank of England's position that – as one HSBC banker put it – 'made any other recommendations inconceivable'.[5]

By the late summer of 1983 a crisis broke out in Hong Kong that obviously had a strong political dimension. There might have been an economic cause in the strengthening of the US dollar, but the most obvious root of the nervousness lay in continued Chinese threats to Hong Kong. Property prices fell by half, dramatically raising the prospect of bank vulnerability as over a third of bank lending was for property. The Hong Kong dollar fell by 10 per cent against the dollar from 21 September to the 24th, and the stock market also collapsed. The Treasury minuted:

The FCO [Foreign and Commonwealth Office] have stressed to me that in their view any move by HMG to support the Hong Kong dollar would not only carry the financial consequences discussed below (the logic of which points towards HMG in some sense assuming control over the Hong Kong economy) but would also represent a radical change in the nature of the current political negotiations with China. As I understand it, the constitutional position is that in the last analysis HMG would carry ultimate responsibility for Hong Kong (the FCO will provide further advice on this); but in the negotiation with China we are trying to demonstrate that in practice we can offer Hong Kong a more effective autonomy than they can. There is also the risk that if we become financially committed to supporting the Hong Kong dollar the Chinese might themselves seek to exploit this in the negotiations; they would be able to put a direct financial squeeze on us through further statements and actions affecting confidence in the Hong Kong dollar.[6]

On 25 September, the Governor of Hong Kong and the Acting Financial Secretary Douglas Blye (the Financial Secretary Sir John Bremridge was in Washington at the annual World Bank/IMF meetings) announced that the government would use the Exchange Fund to intervene in the foreign exchange market. Blye in fact was quite distracted from the currency issue, as he spent a great deal of time with daily meetings concerning the micromanagement of the government rescue of Hang Lung Bank. Bremridge had repeatedly stated that no large bank could be allowed to fail. The uncertainty continued, and Hang Lung Bank, which had already experienced a bank run in September 1982, was taken over by the government on 28 September after it had been unable to meet its clearing house obligations with regard to customers' cheques. George Tan of the Carrian Group, the Hang Lung Bank's largest borrower, was arrested. Bremridge stated: 'The government believes it would be unacceptable, both domestically and internationally, to allow this bank to fail, which would involve considerable loss to depositors. [...] The depositors' interests override those of the shareholder.'[7]

Tony Latter, Deputy Secretary of Monetary Affairs in Hong Kong (and a Bank of England official on secondment to Hong Kong), suggested a currency board arrangement, a revival of the pre-1972 arrangements, when the Hong Kong dollar had been linked at £1 = HK$14.55 (after the British devaluation of November 1967, which had produced a revaluation of the HK$):

He went on to talk about the exchange rate which was at present a main and indeed almost over-riding concern. His own studies had convinced him that the whole monetary system in Hong Kong was indeterminate and potentially unstable. There was no effective monetary control which was possible with present mechanisms. His own conclusion was that the only way to regain control, especially over the exchange rate, was to revert to a mechanism closely analogous to a colonial currency board, in which the board stood ready to convert Hong Kong dollars into US dollars and vice versa on demand at a fixed price. We had a short discussion of this idea, which he said was too complex to describe fully over the telephone. But he did show himself aware that this mechanism would probably throw the burden of adjustment on to interest rates, and that surges of confidence would probably be reflected in surges of interest rates.[8]

The major initial input was given by John Greenwood, an economist in Hong Kong at GT Management, and set out in the *Asian Monetary Monitor*, of which he was the editor. Greenwood had had extensive telephone conversations with Milton Friedman and Alan Walters.[9] Friedman had already developed a passionate attachment to Hong Kong as an experimental site for the realization of free market economics. Charles Goodhart, who spearheaded the Bank of England's reconstruction of Hong Kong's financial arrangements, described Greenwood as the Hong Kong equivalent of Gordon Pepper. While the Governor of Hong Kong, Sir Edward Youde, proposed to peg in dollars, Greenwood envisaged a sterling link that was much more robust than a mere currency peg. His main consideration was not really economic, and he stated indeed that a peg to the yen, the Deutschemark or the IMF's basket currency, the SDR, would have been just as feasible, but he saw a mostly political logic. A sterling peg would demonstrate to Beijing that 'Britain was continuing to demonstrate a colonialist attitude to Hong Kong' and that would affect the 1997 talks, while the Japanese currency was ruled out by the memory of the occupation of Hong Kong and the 'long rivalry between the Chinese and the Japanese'.[10] The answer was a return to Hong Kong's traditional currency board arrangements, in which the note-issuing banks were required to hold non-interest-bearing Certificates of Indebtedness (CI) issued by the Exchange Fund to provide backing for banknote issuance.

Both schemes were vulnerable in the view of Goodhart because:

The total amount of foreign exchange that the Hong Kong authorities might have to provide to residents trying to escape from the Hong Kong dollar amounts, not only to the total outstanding volume of bank notes, but also to the total outstanding volume of existing bank deposits, and beyond that to such further claims on Hong Kong monetary assets as could be obtained by borrowing Hong Kong dollars from the banks at any future time when the scheme remained extant. So, the potential total sum at risk is a large multiple of the outstanding Hong Kong currency.[11]

Goodhart arrived in Hong Kong on 4 October 1983, along with David Peretz of the UK Treasury. Their first report explained that the key issue lay with the banks, and with investor uncertainty: the banks required a government guarantee to stabilize confidence and expectations, but if the guarantee were in place with an adequate external plan, the guarantee might not be needed.

If there are pressures therefore they will fall not on the exchange rate or on the Exchange Fund, but on banks. We assumed, and this assumption was shared by all who we spoke to, that banks at all costs would want to maintain convertibility between Hong Kong dollar bank deposits and bank notes. This is the raison d'être of banking. And in a society like Hong Kong's, where queues to withdraw cash are not uncommon at times of uncertainty, no bank could risk the blow to public confidence in it that refusal to permit cash withdrawals would bring.[12]

The Chief Secretary of Hong Kong, in effect the Prime Minister, Sir Philip Haddon-Cave, had been responsible as Financial Secretary for breaking the link with sterling in 1972 and floating in 1974, and resented Greenwood's public attacks on the system he set up. He tried at first to block the Greenwood proposal, and then to look for alternatives; and he consistently emphasized the risks that were being run. A critical role would be played by the note-issuing banks. HSBC was in a strong liquidity position, and well able to absorb the initial shock of a transition to a pegged rate. But Goodhart added, 'We do not have the information to be quite so sure about the SCB [Standard Chartered]. Also there could, perhaps, be a question in their case about prudential willingness to allow the SCB to replenish its foreign currency liquidity.'[13]

After the Governor of Hong Kong returned from London and discussions with the Chancellor, he gave a press conference in which he stated that the Chancellor had given no advice on the currency. The Hong Kong executive announced the decision to implement the currency board scheme on Saturday, 15 October, after a chance closure of the markets because of a typhoon, and complemented the new regime with the removal of tax on interest on HK dollar deposits at financial institutions. In anticipation,

The Exchange Fund purchased from the FRBNY [Federal Reserve Bank of New York] US$100m in large-denomination notes, using a contact established by Mr Loehnis: the notes were lodged in a vault in Hong Kong less than 48 hours from the dispatch of the telex request. This sum was thought sufficient to supplement the relatively high stock of US$ notes already held by the Hongkong & Shanghai Bank and by Hang Seng Bank.[14]

Interest rates soared. The overnight interbank rate, which had closed at around 13 per cent on Monday, hit 30 per cent at one point on Tuesday, though it fell back to close at 19 per cent. The pressure continued the next day, and the interbank rate hit an all-time high of 41 per cent (HK$10 m was dealt at that rate). Clearing accounts with the banks, especially HSBC, were very heavily overdrawn on both the Tuesday and Wednesday. But then the tension fell, and with a more relaxed mood in the market, among the banks and among the public, the Exchange Fund was able to return to the FRBNY US$75 m of the notes obtained as a reserve in advance of the currency board announcement.[15]

Initially, the exchange rate weakened, and the uncertainty meant that banks were not willing to quote a rate for the dollar close to the new peg, and there was a substantial arbitrage between the market rate and the pegged rate for notes. The local Chinese banks without direct access to foreign currency, except through the free market, felt that the system was working against them.[16] William Purves of the HSBC was particularly critical of the chaos:

Purves was at pains to emphasise that his comments should be regarded as strictly confidential – and in particular that they should not get back to the Hong Kong authorities. The burden of his tale was that, contrary to the common market perception, the new arrangements were not working well; arbitrage was not proving sufficiently flexible to keep the rate close to 7.80 and as a result the Hong Kong Bank felt obliged to intervene to support the rate. They had on three occasions been as much as US$100mn short and, now that the London market in HK$ was operational again, had to provide their London branch with up to $50mn overnight. The costs involved were considerable and they felt that further official action was necessary – suggesting in particular the imposition of fractional reserve requirements – to improve the responsiveness of the system: they offered no suggestions as to how such a scheme would operate, expressing confidence that 'our economists' could work out the details.[17]

There was a substantial risk of political shocks. If conditions in Hong Kong were to deteriorate seriously as a result of a turn for the worse in the talks with the PRC, the Hong Kong authorities would find themselves drawn into more extensive support operations for Hong Kong banks, and the British Treasury worried that it might in those circumstances be called on to provide a backstop to the Hong Kong Government's unlimited bank guarantee. It minuted in alarm:

The extent of contingency financial liability that might come into question is of course a matter of concern to both our departments, particularly since it would be a liability that, as we understand it, could fall to be met by HMG should it exceed the resources of the Hong Kong Government. We are not comforted by the doubts we know the Bank of England have about the quality of banking supervision in the Colony, or by Blye's references to what is being uncovered at the Hang Lung Bank as the new management looks through its books. Blye also suggested that, in the worst case, if a substantial portion of the property sector in Hong Kong were to collapse, some form of support might have to be considered for the Hong Kong and Shanghai Bank.[18]

Greenwood set out an eloquent account of the virtue of what had essentially originated as his 'plan'.

The beauty of the plan is that it harnesses market forces in the private sector to bring interest rates, bank credit, the money supply, the various components of the balance of payments, and output and prices (including wages) all into line or 'into equilibrium' at the new 7.80 exchange rate. And all this occurs automatically, that is, without the need for official intervention. In short, Hong Kong does not have a 'pegged rate' but a convertible banknote system that employs the automatic adjustment mechanism to ensure equilibrium at the chosen exchange rate. But only by publishing the now secret accounts of the Exchange Fund can the government prove that there has been no need for intervention.[19]

But that scheme too depended on the restoration of confidence in the banking system. The Bank would play a central role in contingency plans in the event of a Chinese attack or invasion (referred to under the code name Denham), where authority over the Exchange Fund would be transferred from the Finance Secretary in Hong Kong to the Foreign Secretary in London.

The Chinese Government have stated that they do not intend to resume control of Hong Kong before 1997. However Deng Xiaoping told Mrs Thatcher in 1982 that, if there was trouble in Hong Kong meanwhile, their timetable might be revised. It is thus possible that even a pragmatic Chinese government might decide to take Hong Kong over either by direct force or through mobilisation of pro-communist elements in the Territory. Alternatively, a more radical government in Peking might decide to reverse Deng's policies. In such circumstances the prospects for genuine autonomy of a Hong Kong SAR under Chinese sovereignty would almost certainly disappear.[20]

There were indeed continual moments of doubt. Thus, for instance, in the summer of 1984 there was a threat of a new collapse in the exchange rate when on 6 July the HK dollar weakened in London, after the closure of the Hong Kong market, from 7.82 to 8.00, after the collapse of a major Hong Kong property deal and a more militant attitude to Hong Kong negotiators in Beijing. The banks initially proposed to respond by a 1 per cent interest rate hike, but the Hong Kong authorities persuaded them that a much more decisive 3 per cent was needed, and on 7 July the exchange rate came back to 7.86. HSBC was selling Hong Kong dollars on a large scale.

At this time we were reminded by Latter that the Hong Kong Bank had never been fully committed to, indeed, had probably never fully understood, the workings of the new exchange rate system. What they knew was the responsibility for its effectiveness fell to a large extent on their shoulders and that to adhere to its requirements was costly in terms of foreign exchange, ready supplies of which were fast coming to an end. They also stressed the dangers for their, and others' borrowers of ever-higher interest rates.

By 16 July, when there was soothing news about a visit of the British Foreign Secretary, the exchange rate came back to 7.8225.[21] Later another explanation was offered for the sudden July weakness: it derived from the perceived weakness of HSBC's trading position, where one dealer managed to find himself with an unmatched book, over his allowed limit, at the end of the dealing day in Hong Kong. In order to square his position, he sold HK$ for US$ in London, where, not only was the market much thinner, but he was apparently also spotted. The sight of HSBC selling HK$ when the currency was already weakening rapidly, then stampeded everyone else.[22]

The 1983 regime shift and the 1984 panic both raised the issue of how the position of HSBC, which was central to Hong Kong's monetary regime, could be strengthened. The old arguments about the desirability of a London connection came back. HSBC saw it as stabilizing, while the British government saw the political downside as outweighing any gain in financial stability and security. In a meeting in the Foreign Office,

Sir Antony Acland [the Permanent Under-Secretary] said that if, as seemed to be the case from the Governor of Hong Kong's letter of 11 May, the Hong Kong Government would turn down any proposal that the Hong Kong and Shanghai Bank should transfer its headquarters elsewhere, we needed to ensure that no such proposal were made. If it were, it would certainly leak to the press, and the effect on confidence in Hong Kong would be almost as great as transfer itself. The question was how to prevent a proposal. One possibility would be to speak to the Chairman of the Hong Kong and Shanghai Bank, Mr Sandberg, on the subject, though it should be borne in mind that Mr Sandberg was a member of EXCO, and critical of HMG's stance in the negotiations with the Chinese on the future of Hong Kong, and might not be disposed to be helpful.[23]

In March 1985, the chairman of HSBC visited Leigh-Pemberton.

He wanted a preliminary and informal reaction from me on a proposal to form in London a bank holding company which would de facto become the headquarters of the Hongshai Group worldwide. It was no part of his intention to remove the Hongshai Bank Corporation from Hong Kong, but felt anxious to prevent the ownership and strategic control of not only the Hong Kong bank but its other assets throughout the world drifting into a communist state. While the Hongshai Banking Corporation would be a wholly owned subsidiary still incorporated in Hong Kong, other banks and offices throughout the world might well be directly owned from London. He then went on to say that it was still part of his strategy to seek an acquisition in the United Kingdom, and such an acquisition could conveniently again be a directly-owned subsidiary of the new holding company.

The Governor of the Bank was much more sympathetic than his predecessor had been. Leigh-Pemberton noted:

I find the idea of a British-based holding company an attractive solution to the problem of what is to happen to the Hongshai Bank as 1997 approaches and I hope that we may be able to resolve the supervisory aspects of this in a way that could be positive to Hongshai. The question of a UK acquisition is ancillary to this, although it is clearly a very substantial element in it, and I think it would be useful if we could clear our minds about what our reaction would be if some such idea, as I have set out above, is put to us as a proposition.[24]

But the Foreign Office was sceptical:

The PUS[Permanent Undersecretary] said that the real problem was a mismatch of timing. It was generally accepted that in the longer term some readjustment of the HKSB's structure and role would be necessary, but the present moment was much too early. Very careful handling would be necessary vis-à-vis the Chinese and opinion in Hong Kong. I said that the Governor [of Hong Kong] would probably not want to see action on this front until the end of the decade at the earliest.[25]

A paper from the Hong Kong authorities in 1985 suggested:

Although the present exchange rate system appears to be working well and providing monetary stability, beneath the surface it does not operate in the best textbook manner; HSBC's quasi-central-banking role is crucial to the system's success. While this cooperative stance may be depended upon for the time being, at some stage such dependence will no longer be appropriate: the bank itself may wish to disengage, and it would anyway be politically difficult to continue with HSBC at the core of the system. Anyway the system as it is may not be capable of surviving a significant economic, financial or political crisis.[26]

At the Treasury, both Chancellor Lawson and Sir Peter Middleton were convinced that it would be in the interests of the UK to have HSBC's headquarters in London. In part, this may reflect a feeling that the bank constituted a huge potential liability for the Hong Kong government and perhaps ultimately for the UK Treasury. By contrast, the Bank of England pushed back:

There could indeed be advantage in an eventual move by HKSB to this country, even though it is not easy to define the nature of that advantage precisely. We are clear that advantage, such as it is, would accrue only if HKSB remained a fully operational and profitable bank. A HKSB which moved here in a way which generated severe problems in its Hong Kong heartland would land us with a can of worms.[27]

Instead, the Bank suggested that HSBC should buy a British building society, a solution which the Treasury disliked.[28] The Bank did not want

being drawn into a situation of having to support HKSB as a lender of last resort, but if the UK authorities collectively feel that the Bank should accept a lender of last resort role vis-à-vis HKSB, then we should certainly get a comprehensive handle on all its business.[29]

HSBC's Sandberg met Margaret Thatcher in a forty-five-minute-long discussion in Downing Street, when Sandberg explained that he did not want HSBC to become a 'Chinese takeaway'. The Prime Minister argued that the Chinese would regard a change in the status of HSBC as a breach of faith, and would see a British plot to move the bank's assets out of Hong Kong. If confidence in the colony's future were jeopardized, there could also be grave consequences for its financial stability.[30] There were also extensive discussions with the Treasury and the Chancellor:

The Chancellor felt that Sandberg's wish to move out of Hong Kong was very understandable, and that he and his successors could be expected to continue to work towards this objective. If we appeared too obstructive and negative, a time would come when he or his successors would make a move which we would be powerless to prevent, and which would certainly do grave damage. He visual-ised that Sandberg might move to New York, which would leave us looking foolish.[31]

Within the British government, it was the Foreign Office that was consistently cautious about rebuffing Sandberg:

We therefore need to steer a very careful course. We suggest that the Prime Minister should go on to say to Sandberg that she acknowledges what he has done to make HKSB a major international bank: that circumstances may change and that she does not necessarily rule out any possibility of change at some time in the future, though he should be under no illusion that it would be easy (or necessarily even possible). He must appreciate the complexity and sensitivity of the issues to be resolved. She well understands it will be disappointing for him to have to accept that within the span of his chairmanship it will not be possible to resolve these longer-term issues, but what he has achieved for the HKSB will stand as a tribute to his chairmanship.[32]

At the Governor's discussion in Downing Street:

The PM also asked whether there were, in fact, powers to stop the proposal. The Foreign Secretary said that there were two views about this and while the PM doubted whether we could take powers, the Chancellor referred to paragraph 17 of the paper as indicating that the very act of doing so would be destructive. There was some feeling that Deng Xiaoping would not be moved by the argument that it was preferable for the Hong Kong bank to merge with a British one to avoid the possibility of a hostile takeover by Japanese or Germans. It was thought that he might regard them as less likely asset-strippers than ourselves.[33]

There was also the question of the UK's relationship with Japanese banks. By 1986, there were fears of a Japanese bid (from Nomura) for HSBC. But the Bank was still blocking a takeover of Midland by HSBC which would protect the Hong Kong bank from Asian pressures:

The Foreign Secretary is most grateful for the action which the Governor has taken, in accordance with the conclusions of the meeting at No 10 Downing Street on 2 October, to dissuade the Midland Bank and the HKSB from bringing their discussions to any conclusion at the present time. It was a further conclusion drawn from that meeting that the banks should be warned of the Government's view that the consequences of going ahead with the merger could be very damaging.[34]

Additionally, a possibility of a takeover attempt for HSBC from prominent Hong Kong Chinese posed another kind of challenge.[35] Securing the engagement of a large UK bank would make HSBC much more resilient, and in consequence the Bank began to modify its position on the association of HSBC with Midland. In November 1987, in the aftermath of the October 1987 worldwide stock market crash, the Bank saw no reason to object to HSBC taking a 14.9 per cent interest in Midland.[36]

In 1986–1987, the post-Plaza weakness of the US dollar set up a new problem: there were large speculative flows anticipating a possible revaluation of the Hong Kong dollar. The government introduced legislation allowing a defence through the imposition of negative interest rates (based on the strategy that Switzerland had followed in the 1970s to deter inflows). In fact, the powers were never used, and the Hong Kong government just used intervention outside the framework of the currency board arrangements.[37] In July 1988, a new accounting arrangement required HSBC to maintain an account with an Exchange Fund, so that HSBC could no longer have a credit policy that might undermine the official interventions in the dollar rate.[38]

After the Tiananmen Square massacre in Beijing (4 June 1989), the uncertainties facing the colony increased. Credit lines to HSBC were cut. William Purves, who had succeeded Sandberg as chief executive of HSBC in 1986, tried to enlist the Governor of Hong Kong, Sir David Wilson, in his campaign to press for a merger that would secure HSBC with a base outside the colony. In order to do that he had to paint a dismal picture of vulnerability, with lines of credit being cut and the name refused in Tokyo, London and New York 'often by leading banks who knew Hong Kong and HSBC well' because they now believed Hong Kong to be 'high risk'. The Governor told Purves in return: 'The wrong move could bring the house down. The matter could not be seen as primarily commercial.'[39]

The Bank of England's principal bank supervisor, Brian Quinn, reported on Purves' new initiative:

In addition, he thought that HMG could now be less anxious about upsetting the sensitivities of the Chinese who had shown themselves how little they cared about

Western opinions. Willie Purves therefore thought there was a window of opportunity which he should seek vigorously to use to advance his ideas about some kind of merger between the Midland and Hongkong groups.[40]

And Purves believed he had a more sympathetic ear in Whitehall:

Following a conversation with the Chancellor, he now had a sense that HMG could be more receptive to an acceleration of the timetable for closer links between the two banking groups. It was felt that the recent events had strengthened the case for exploring more quickly routes by which HSBC might reduce the threat of damage arising from uncertainties in the run up to 1997 and beyond.[41]

The issue of a merger was easier now that most of the central banking functions of HSBC had been transferred to the Hong Kong Monetary Authority, leaving HSBC responsible only for note issue and settlement. The tie between banking regulation and monetary and exchange rate stability had been decisively broken.[42] In 1989, the only reason for delay was fear of the attitude of the Chinese authorities.[43]

The discussion of an HSBC merger with a large British bank emerged again in 1990, largely because of the problems that emerged at Midland Bank. The Bank described Midland as a 'troubled institution' where – in Leigh-Pemberton's term – 'Sir Kit [McMahon, the chairman of Midland] had introduced too many changes and had not ensured that an agreed strategy and management team were given time to make things work.' On the other hand, it was also apparent that Thatcher wanted 'to get Hongshai into the UK somehow'.[44] In March 1991, the Bank engineered the replacement of the Midland management, with Leigh-Pemberton putting tremendous pressure – with repeated appeals to patriotic duty – on Sir Peter Walters of British Petroleum to become Chairman and Brian Pearse of Barclays as chief executive (see Chapter 13). In late 1991, Lloyds Bank approached Midland with the suggestion of a merger, and Eddie George seemed to take a favourable position and was still in December 1991 telling Pearse that the Bank would fight the HSBC proposal on 'the grounds that they were not financially suitable to own a major bank in the UK'.[45] But by the beginning of the next year, as it became clear that the Lloyds approach would need to be submitted to the Monopolies and Mergers Commission, and might well be turned down, the Bank began to view HSBC with more sympathy. By June 1992, HSBC had won and obtained the agreement of British, European and US regulators, as well as the support of Midland shareholders. It had now fully disengaged from the monetary management of Hong Kong.

8

Shaved Eyebrows

Banking and Financial Supervision

Modern central banking practice distinguishes between macro-prudential supervision, which is concerned with the stability of the financial system as a whole and with the interaction between financial institutions, and micro-prudential, oriented towards the monitoring of particular institutions. But this distinction is rather new. The US House Committee on Financial Services Subcommittee on Domestic and International Monetary Policy, Trade, and Technology in 2008 spoke of 'the newly rediscovered macro-prudential, supervision and regulation of the financial system'. The concept of an overall regulatory approach only really started to emerge in the 1980s, when the word macro-prudential appears for the first time. The very first use that is recorded was in the 28–29 June 1979 meeting of the Cooke Committee in Basel (chaired by the Bank of England's banking supervisor, Assistant Director Peter Cooke); and the term resurfaced in an October 1979 background paper by the Bank of England for a Basel Working Party chaired by Alexandre Lamfalussy of the Bank for International Settlements (BIS) (who later became one of the most articulate proponents of this approach).[1] There is thus a good claim that modern thinking about a more general financial supervision came out of discussions in the Bank of England, in the context of a dramatic uncertainty about financial developments in the late 1970s, as capital controls were relaxed and banking faced a new, internationalized, environment. In addition, bank lending was a key part of the debate about monetary policy, and one tradition examined the 'credit counterpart' as a key part of monetary expansion.

Macro-prudential supervision had not been needed before. The new concerns were quite different from old-style concerns with particular institutions which still continued to dominate the popular treatment of how the Bank looked after financial markets. The fundamental vision with which this period began was that the City of London was essentially a highly responsible self-regulating regime whose effectiveness would be reduced by outside intervention and regulation. The key was that functional separation of roles between discount houses, acceptance houses and banks, or between stockjobbers and brokers, created a mechanism that made for constant monitoring. The compartmentalization meant that each market participant was under continual and close observation. That classical world of the City produced a system that was secure and stable.[2] Many commentators think of this as the central attribute of the phenomenon of 'gentlemanly capitalism'.[3] Bankers and banks that conformed with the code of behaviour would be protected even in adverse circumstances, while those who misbehaved would be excluded. Even famous houses would not serve as a protection against bad behaviour by bad bankers. The modern concept of lender of last resort operations by the Bank of England really began in the crisis of 1866, when the most prominent London discount house, Overend Gurney, was allowed to fail because its new managers had been reckless, and the house could not provide bills of adequate quality, and was clearly insolvent; but the Bank responded to the collapse of Overend by discounting securities from all the other banks in order to prevent a systemic failure, and injected large amounts of cash, both gold coins and high-denomination bank notes, that banks faced with the panic kept instead of other assets.[4] Walter Bagehot then presented the Bank's response as a template for future action in *Lombard Street*.

Sometimes modern accounts present a very stylized version of Bagehot's doctrine, that the central bank should be completely blind to the question of *who* was presenting the securities, and simply make the decision based on the *quality* of those securities, as if there were a frosted pane in the hall that obscured the sight of the lender of last resort.[5] But in fact, there were for a long time quite particular rules in respect to those houses whose partners were members of the Court of Directors of the Bank of England, and directors' banks were treated differently until the 1930s. The basis of this peculiar practice lay in a decision of the Court of Directors in 1841, ordering that 'the Amount of Credit, usually affixed to Parties having Discount Accounts, be omitted in the case of Bank Directors or the firms in which they are partners'. The decision was only revoked in 1935, when the Committee of Advances and Discounts considered and rejected the previous practice whereby the Bank 'gave unconditional and unqualified reports upon all Directors' firms and took their acceptances and discounted their bills without limit'. There had been only small-scale operations – notably the long-term support given to the small house of Frederick

Huth & Co. – but 'the present practice is known to the Market and is undoubtedly regarded by them as establishing an obligation on the part of the Bank to carry such "firms" should they get into difficulties'. The Governor, Montagu Norman, had repeatedly intervened, telling the Committee of Treasury that 'in the interests of the Banking and commercial community, Huth & Co. must not fail'. In October 1935, finally the Court ruled that such special treatment should stop.[6] In the case of Huth, the special advances had been kept secret from the Court.[7]

Normal operations in the classical tradition, analysed above (pages 107–113) consisted of the discount houses as intermediaries between the Bank and the wider financial system coming to the Bank with their financial requirements. The Bank set the rate at which discount houses could borrow, and thus determined the general interest rate structure: except at moments when the Bank Rate went above the market rate, with the result that customers did not take bills to the Bank and the Bank's rate was thus 'ineffective'. Thus, in practice, in some circumstances, the Bank became not just a lender of last resort, but the lender of first resort. The old rules and the classical system were easier to apply after the Second World War, because the constant juggling that was required between domestic conditions and the international requirements of the gold standard no longer applied. Instead, the 1950s saw a long period of 'financial repression', in which the British economy was at least partially sealed off by extensive capital controls.[8] In these circumstances, it was easier for the Bank in a fixed exchange rate regime to make its rate 'effective', as in- and outflows of funds could not either provide alternative resources – at below the Bank's rate – or divert the Bank's financing away from British borrowers.

A segmented financial system was replaced by one in which functional divisions broke down, because of the opening up of the system to competition, which included increasingly foreign competition, above all from American but then also Japanese and to some extent also continental European institutions. The outcome of that competition raised new questions about how supervision should be managed, as stockbroking was no longer separated from jobbing, banks might acquire stockbrokers, commercial banks took over merchant banks, building societies might demutualize and become banks, and insurance companies might offer a broad range of financial services that made their products look like banking products. In addition, as the volume of transactions soared, the pressure to automatize or computerize payments systems intensified: the old methods of clearing and settlement were inadequate and posed substantial risks of failure, accidental or deliberate. The large US house Goldman Sachs would not join the gilt market until the settlement system was made more secure. The resulting world was entirely different to that of the old City. It looked as if it was the outcome of competition, but it created monoliths of gigantic financial power. How could the Bank's supervision and regulation cope with such a radically changed environment?

EYEBROWS

The legitimacy of Bank supervision derived from its role as the ultimate financier: and that gave effective power to the Bank's admonitions (what became known in City jargon as 'the Governor's eyebrows'). Looking back on the post-war era from the perspective of the late 1970s, a Bank paper surveyed the financial stability and security of the 1950s, and the complacency which it had produced:

The 'system' of bank supervision, in the 50's and 60's, was in practice operated by the two Governors in person, the Principal of the Discount Office and not more than two or three assistants (whose own knowledge of events was circumscribed), together with some limited help from the senior official on the foreign exchange side. Everyone else in the Bank was excluded from the supervisory field, in large part because information, quantitative or qualitative, was supplied to us by individual banks on the understanding that it was for the eyes and ears of the Governors only and their designated lieutenant (the Principal of Discount).

As time went by, the atmosphere of gentlemen and servants engendered by this system was not such as to endear it to an oncoming generation of Bank officials whose educational background and habits of thought were rather different to those of their predecessors. We understood the system but were somewhat sceptical of its pretensions and suspicious that it was unduly protective of an established and well-heeled order. But the Bank may be to blame for portraying itself in public (or allowing itself to be portrayed) as being responsible for general health of the financial system when it should have known, if it asked itself frankly, that it did not possess the power to exercise any such responsibility at all closely, in the event of serious trouble developing, until an open crisis occurred. Indeed, some of the ex-post criticism may be due to people having thought, or retrospectively thought they had thought, that safeguards were in place when they were not, and never had been. Perhaps the Old Lady was too susceptible to flattery, and herself came to believe that she possessed some mysterious influence which was self-exercised without being fully aware of it.[9]

The critique developed in these lines still – regrettably – largely applied to the Bank in the 1980s. The Bank did not manage to solve the question of how to apply safeguards. The great problem cases of the 1980s and beyond – Johnson Matthey Bankers (JMB), Bank of Credit and Commerce International (BCCI) and Barings – had their roots in the old regime, and in fact those institutions started their extended metastasis years or even decades before they exploded into public consciousness.

The old world was substantially challenged in the 1970s, as international lending and wholesale banking developed, and as Britain was shaken by major financial crises following from poor monetary policy. In the aftermath of the secondary banking crisis of 1973, the Bank coordinated a 'lifeboat', technically the 'Control Committee of the Bank of England and the English and Scottish clearing banks', and composed of senior representatives of banks under the chairmanship of the Deputy Governor of the Bank. The mechanism involved an assessment of fundamental solvency, and then a commitment of the banks to recycle deposits so as to keep temporarily illiquid banks alive. But the potential losses became ever bigger, and there were even rumours circulating of difficulties in one of the big clearing banks, National Westminster. As property prices crashed, fears of solvency increased; by August 1974, the support amounted to two-fifths of the estimated aggregate total of the capital and loan-loss reserves of English and Scottish clearing banks, and the private-sector banks withdrew from their unlimited commitment, leaving support for rescue operations over £1,200 m entirely in the hands of the Bank of England.[10] The Bank also directly supported some banks outside the lifeboat system, in particular Slater Walker Limited, and Edward Bates & Sons Limited, which had already been the subject of a recapitalization with Arab money. The aftermath of the 'lifeboat' and in particular the exhaustion of its resources made it clear that there would need to be major change: but the system that the Bank had developed was not really well suited to produce that change.

With bank rescue operations, there always remained an uncertainty about who would – and who could – bear the cost of support. The Bank recognized that in the end, if it lost money, the burden would fall on the government; but it was unwilling completely to accept the logical consequence about who should accept the ultimate responsibility for regulation to reduce the fiscal burden following from banking failure. It took a long time after the lifeboat operation before the issue was ultimately clarified in an exchange of letters between the Treasury and the Governor. Richardson initially insisted that the Treasury could not have responsibility to parliament for the Bank's decisions. Initially, he simply ignored the Treasury's letters. But eventually he gave in, and Sir Douglas Wass recorded the agreement: 'I am grateful for your confirmation that you will tell the Chancellor and myself of any situation where either the Court as a whole or you yourself have a sense that the risk could be on a scale which it would not be reasonable for the Bank to carry on its capital and reserves.'[11]

In the old world, the Discount Office had functioned as the 'eyes and ears' of the Bank. It was disbanded in July 1974, and its functions absorbed by an enlarged Banking and Money Market Supervision Division within the Cashier's Department. But at this stage, the interview ('prudential interview') remained 'the cornerstone' of the Bank's system of supervision, and the Bank's regulators remained proud that they could 'smell' bad character and potential misbehaviour.[12]

There were four elements that drove what amounted to an institutional revolution, the end of the old City, and the creation of a radically different and internationalized world of finance.

First, the removal of exchange control in effect brought the world into London, as well as London into the world. There was now a flood of prospective foreign banks attempting to enter the London market, and the Bank of England shifted from being an obstacle to playing a major role as a facilitator of the process. It began to view foreign management and foreign competition as a way of bringing new dynamism to the British economy. It started a carefully controlled deregulation in stages. In 1981, it announced that it would restrict access to the London market to thirty new overseas banks a year, with a queuing system operating for the next in line.[13]

Second, banking supervision was redrawn with the 1979 Banking Act, which instituted a two-tier system of recognized banks and licensed deposit-taking institutions. The 1979 act for the first time gave the Bank statutory responsibility for bank supervision, and also for the first time restricted the use of the labels 'bank' and 'banker'. The act also gave small depositors some protection if banks went into liquidation. At this time, the Banking Supervision Division had some seventy staff, responsible for supervising 150 UK banks, 200 branches of foreign banks and around 150/200 other deposit-taking institutions.[14] So simple arithmetic indicated that one Bank supervisor could not concentrate on a single institution. The most conspicuous failure of the 1980s arose in a case where the official responsible for an originally small London house connected with the bullion market was also supervising the London operations of one of the most fragile US banks, Marine Midland.

Third, a new approach to public ownership envisaged large-scale privatizations, with a first phase of £1.4 bn of assets sold from 1981 to 1983, beginning with British Aerospace and Cable and Wireless, and including Britoil and Associated British Ports, and generating some

£25 m in fees from the government. This process required careful management, and coordination, especially when the privatizations involved foreign purchasers. The aim of many of the privatizations was to involve widespread (citizen) ownership, with British Telecom in 1984 attracting 2.3 m individual shareholders. The privatizations were underwritten, but the underwriting could be problematical in volatile market circumstances. It was only the stock market crash of October 1987 that really highlighted that problem in the case of the international underwriting of a further tranche of BP privatization. The new global financial environment required a degree of coordination with other supervisors, with the Federal Reserve and the Bundesbank and the Bank of Japan, but also with the supervisors of small financial centres, notably Luxembourg and Gulf states such as Kuwait and Abu Dhabi.

Fourth, in 1983 an agreement on liberalization was reached between the government and the London Stock Exchange. In order to escape a case under the Restrictive Practices Act, the stock exchange would drop fixed commissions, end the single-capacity principle that separated stockbroking (for retail customers) from market-making (stock-jobbing), and open itself to competition. The result in 1986 was generally called 'Big Bang'. Foreign acquisitions of major City firms became a central part of the preparations for Big Bang, and of the aftermath, even though the Bank of England at first seemed rather opposed to an end of the old protected domestic sector. In March 1984, the new Governor, Robin Leigh-Pemberton, stated: 'We could not contemplate with equanimity a Stock Exchange in which British-owned member firms played a subordinate role.'[15] But in practice, he soon came round to a quite different position: here too the principle of competition was opening London up. Nigel Lawson's budget speech in 1986 described the reform as 'essential if London is to compete successfully against New York and Tokyo'.[16] The large number of shareholders – between 1979 and 1987 the estimated population of UK shareholders tripled to 9 m individuals – made for a greater need for consumer protection. Regulation was organized within a framework of a new Securities and Investment Board (SIB), a forerunner of the Financial Services Authority, whose chairman and members were appointed by the Governor of the Bank and the Chancellor; under the SIB were sectoral Self-Regulatory Organizations, initially five, for futures broking and dealing, financial intermediation, investment management, life assurance broking and securities broking.

INTERNATIONAL LENDING AND THE LATIN AMERICAN DEBT CRISIS

At the beginning of the 1980s, the major challenges were still primarily domestic. The end of quantitative controls in 1979–1980 still left a prudential problem, and banks needed to be brought in line so that they would not be vulnerable to liquidity shortages. Bank profitability fell during the recession, while the government blamed banks for the credit expansion, and imposed extra taxes, largely at the insistence of Thatcher, who had been highly irritated by the lending explosion. The government also saw banks receiving a windfall from the spread between high lending rates and their unremunerated current account liabilities. Sir Geoffrey Howe had been a little hesitant on taxing banks, explaining that he 'had no desire to initiate a great anti-bank campaign'.[17] When a newspaper article suggested that relations between the clearers and the Bank had deteriorated in consequence of the debate about the excessive expansion of bank lending, Jeremy Morse (Lloyds) protested that 'quite the reverse: relations have improved over the last two or three years, not least because of our [the Bank's] stance on bank tax last year'.[18] In 1982, the Bank set out its policy towards the big four clearing banks in a paper on 'The Management of Liquidity', in which it laid out a philosophy of having sufficient cash or liquefiable assets immediately available to meet liquidity demands, but also setting out a future cash flow strategy.[19] To some bankers, it looked as if credit controls were being reimposed with a prudential motivation. The initial plan was withdrawn after publication, as it seemed inconsistent with the new monetary regime; but it was revived some years later and the fundamental concept was eventually implemented as the Liquidity Coverage Ratio under the Basel III international agreements.

As foreign lending developed, there was also the possibility of an international transmission of crisis. The first major test came with the outbreak of the Latin American debt crisis, which raised the possibility of a breakdown of the whole global financial system. The problem was not wholly unanticipated. In the late 1970s, the BIS had been worried about the growth of international lending, especially to developing countries (what would later be called emerging markets). The Bank joined in this reflection. In May 1980, Pendarell ('Pen') Kent, the head of the Bank's International Division, reflecting on the possibility of a massive loan default, argued that 'because of the very large imbalances expected to persist during the 80s, the strains on the international recycling process may be of an order hitherto unknown. This could lead in turn to great strain in the relationships between North and South.' Continued recession in the industrial world would depress development assistance, and democratic governments would not be able to pursue the enlightened self-interest of transmitting savings to what were then termed Less-Developed Countries (LDCs) and stimulating world demand. 'In that situation heavily indebted LDCs might well come to the view that they would gain more from individual or concerted debt default than from depressing their level of economic activity further to finance the burden of debt service.'[20]

The debate about possible sovereign default produced a major exercise in risk anticipation. In August 1980, the Bank prepared an extensive analysis – which it dubbed 'Apocalypse Now' – on 'Consequences of Debt Service Failure by a Major Borrowing Country'. It looked at the surge of capital flowing on the basis of an annual $110 bn net financing needs for non-oil-developing countries, and concluded that the 'risks of such difficulties cannot be safely discounted and that they could be increasing'. It took BIS data on the exposure of large countries, Brazil, Mexico, Argentina and Korea (ranked in order of size of borrowing). The cautious conclusion was: 'There do not yet seem to be structural reasons why the world's private capital markets should not in general be able to cope with the new volumes of recycling, although they could emerge in say two years' time.'

The paper then drew lessons from already-existing crisis cases, in smaller countries such as Zaire: 'a storm can blow up very rapidly', and 'obtaining good information quickly on amounts of banking debt outstanding and in arrears, and on banks involved, can be difficult'. A shock to a big country such as Brazil would affect the inter-bank market and damage confidence. Even small banks would be sucked in because of the prevalence of cross-default clauses which turned a default on one syndicated loan into a general default. The paper also calculated the exposure of UK banks to Brazil as a share of capital base, 8 per cent for Barclays but 17 per cent for Midland, 26 per cent for NatWest and 28 per cent for Lloyds, and much higher for some merchant banks (Standard Chartered 38 per cent; Morgan Grenfell 44 per cent). It warned about funding problems for banks without a natural dollar base. It noted, 'We have a tradition, which we would presumably not likely discard, of support for banks if it appeared to be in the interest of the market as a whole (cf lifeboat)', and set this against a view attributed to governor Henry Wallich of the Federal Reserve that banks should pay for their own mistakes. As a remedy, it suggested a closer cooperation with the IMF and in particular penalization of lending to countries that had borrowed more than a certain amount, unless they had a standby line with the IMF. But this 'would be interference in the commercial judgment of the banks and would bring with it considerable difficulties'. The Fund's Managing Director, Jacques de Larosière, and some of the IMF staff had pushed for greater coordination between Fund lending and banks, but they did not 'have the support of the membership as a whole and their relationship with the banking community does not lend itself naturally to such a role'. The LDCs would be opposed to coordination of lending. A safety net might be arranged but 'if it looked like an arrangement to bail out the commercial banks it would be politically unacceptable in the United States and perhaps here too'.[21]

The paper was circulated internationally and discussed – notably at the November 1980 meeting of the Euro-Currency Standing Committee, where it produced an initiative to produce and distribute international data more speedily. It was a remarkably prescient anticipation of the Latin American debt crisis, that only missed one important aspect, namely that a debt problem in one large borrower would almost inevitably trigger problems elsewhere as lenders refused to roll over loans to other borrowers, and in that case it would be useless just to think of the risk of exposure to a single borrower: what mattered was banks' vulnerability in the sector as a whole.

On 21 July 1982, at a meeting of the 'External Developments Committee', the paper was discussed again with a proposal for a revision, since 'recent events have shown that against a background of general malaise, events rather smaller than those evoked in the note might be sufficient to cause a crisis of confidence'.[22] It produced some more concrete risk assessment exercises. In early 1982, the Bank submitted a paper to the Treasury on country risk indicators, but was quite cautious about the implications of the exercise (the calculations showed the major Latin American debtors as having a decreasing vulnerability after 1981: see Figure 8.1): 'The Committee discussed this at length and some felt that such a system gave few new insights for countries which are monitored already. The upshot was that the indicator will be introduced only for a limited range of countries.'[23]

On 12 August 1982, the Mexican Finance Minister called the US Treasury Secretary, the Chairman of the Federal Reserve and the Managing Director of the IMF to say that Mexico's foreign exchange reserves were exhausted and that the country would default on its debts; and on 18 August, there came a public announcement that foreign debts would no longer be serviced. This action threatened to bring a collapse of

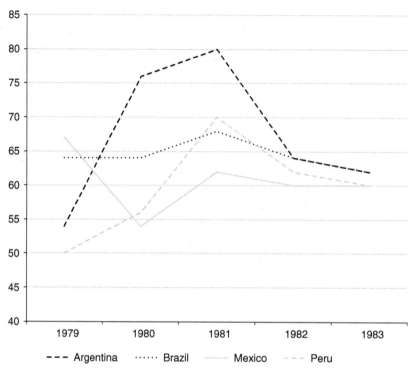

Figure 8.1 January 1982: Bank of England country risk indicators

large US banks, and a breakdown of the whole international financial system. The solution worked out in New York consisted of three elements: an IMF programme with a sharp fiscal adjustment, official credit for Mexico from the IMF and from individual Western governments, and new money from the lending banks so that there would be no formal default, and hence no need to write off banks' exposures. The idea of 'concerted lending' or 'involuntary lending' was quite revolutionary, and ran counter to the normal instincts of bankers. One leading German banker, Wilfried Guth of Deutsche Bank, argued sensibly enough that 'normally a bank says "stop" when it is stuck'.[24] But since there were a relatively small number of large creditors, the concertation of lending was possible, and in each lending country, the major task of corralling the bankers and getting them to agree to the process fell on the central bank. In Europe, Gordon Richardson, together with Fritz Leutwiler of the Swiss National Bank, played a central role in arranging meetings between the IMF and the commercial bankers.

Thatcher was also sensitized to the risk that the debt crisis held for the British banking system. 'She had been worried by Mexico and "by what lies beneath the iceberg," and about the exposure of British banks. She had been reassured in Switzerland that British banks had perhaps been more prudent than those of some other countries and hence had a lesser exposure.'[25] Another version of the Prime Minister's seminar – the forum devised to push the Bank to adopt better monetary policy – was held in the wake of the outbreak of the Mexican (and then general Latin American) debt crisis. But, unlike the monetary discussions, the debate was unsatisfactory and unproductive, incoherent in the view of Anthony Loehnis, the Associate Director in charge of the International Division:

The style of the exposition of the problems and possible solutions was that of Jackson Pollock rather than Rembrandt. There was little or no opportunity given to deploy any ordered response. The Governor had the floor for some five minutes during which he sought to draw out the distinctions between the aftermath of the first and second oil shocks, to point out that we had consistently advocated the need for the international institutions to take a greater share of the recycling burden being borne by the banks, the consequences of the move from negative to positive real interest rates, the effects of the world recession both on the ability of indebted countries to repay and on banks' domestic corporate customers, the importance of banking confidence and its erosion before the Mexican blow-up, the impossibility of getting international agreement on any holistic solution and therefore the need to deal with each problem case on a pragmatic basis as it arose. This was not complacency.[26]

Thatcher wondered

at the rapidity with which the Mexican crisis had arisen. She wondered whether the seriousness of the present situation was properly understood internationally. It was her impression that although the international financial community recognized that high interest rates and continuing recession were producing serious effects, they hoped to muddle through without any clear idea of the action necessary to preserve the integrity of the international financial system. It was regrettable that the recent group of high level international meetings, in particular the Versailles [G-7] Summit, had taken place when it did, rather than in the coming weeks, since she believed that the meetings would have been put to better use if they had been aimed specifically at an appreciation of the situation in the wake of Mexico.[27]

Richardson's successor, Robin Leigh-Pemberton, had moved from the National Westminster Bank, which had a considerable developing country debt exposure, but seemed rather complacent about the crisis, having stated in December 1982, after the announcement of the deal between Mexico and the IMF, 'I think the crisis is over, if there ever was a crisis.' But once he was at the Bank, Leigh-Pemberton continued the Richardson approach, with only slight modifications. He made his opposition to debt write-downs clear: in 1985, in a speech to the British Chamber of Commerce in São Paulo, he attacked those 'who hanker after a more dramatic approach which would relieve countries of a sizeable proportion of their debt burden at a stroke'.[28] But as the crisis receded, he also became less enthusiastic about pressing lending banks to put up 'new money' as part of the bailout operation. By the summer of 1984, the Bank was explaining that it should be less 'forthcoming' in 'dragooning' banks.[29]

Already by this stage, sovereign debt was no longer the only threat to bank stability. In 1984, the Chancellor asked the Governor about the Bank's contingency plans 'should a "Continental Illinois" happen in our country'.[30] The large US bank had collapsed and required the biggest bank rescue of US history prior to the 2008 crisis, as a result of losses on energy loans after the purchase of a smaller institution, Penn Square Bank. But equally, there was always a possibility that one large sovereign debtor could go into open default even with just one creditor and thus trigger cross-default clauses for others. Peru, which was relatively small, experimented with default; but so, from January 1987, did Brazil, an obviously much more systemically significant debtor.

In April 1987, the Bank introduced a matrix system for identifying fifteen criteria determining the likelihood of partial or total failure to repay debt and then setting an overall country score, as part of an explanation of what provisions against losses would be acceptable to the British tax authorities. The next month, Citicorp publicly announced an increase in debt provisioning, a move that put pressure on other (weaker) banks to follow (in Europe, Deutsche Bank, with a much stronger position than its main German rivals, followed the same strategy). Central banks began to talk about 'macho provisioning'.[31] As a consequence of these moves, the large British banks increased provisioning to about 30 per cent of their loan exposure.

PREPARATIONS FOR BIG BANG

In 1983, when the Stock Exchange reached an agreement with the Department of Trade and Industry (DTI) on deregulation and the end of fixed commissions, it would almost certainly bring also the ending of single capacity. Big Bang was originally envisaged as coming in 1985, but the date soon moved to the autumn of 1986, as it became ever more evident to participants quite how unprepared was the City. Stockbrokers in particular looked vulnerable. Americans started to mock London's amateurish and old-fashioned mindset. The *Wall Street Journal* quoted the stockbroking house Laing and Cruickshank talking about 'hand-cranked adding machines that people wheel around on trolleys'.[32]

The Bank consistently saw itself, and acted, as the defender of financial interests of the City. When in 1983 the Inland Revenue suggested treating income from Channel Island offshore funds as income, 'the Bank considered that such precipitous action might be disruptive to markets'.[33] The Bank also on occasion intervened with the Prime Minister to make the case for strengthening the City and its institutions. It tried to make an economic case, telling Thatcher that the City was 'an organization bringing home the bacon'.[34] At the outset, it was hostile to foreign takeovers of City institutions, most spectacularly in 1981 when it blocked the high-profile effort of HSBC to acquire RBS (see Chapter 7). Executive Director David Walker, who had managed a corporate lifeboat in the early 1980s, was now particularly charged with responsibility with City matters. He had skilfully pushed through a reform of Lloyds insurance, imposing an outsider, Ian Hay Davison, as chief executive. He then turned to the importance of reform, holding a large number of lunches and other meetings, and urging City figures to 'think the unthinkable, think radical'.[35]

Within the Bank there was some caution and fear of radical change. A Green Paper on 'The Future of the Stock Exchange' prepared by the Bank worried about the consequences of 'wholesale deregulation', and worried that the market might become 'less liquid and prices more volatile'.[36] In fact, the Bank also realized the economics of the absurd in the case of the City. Charles Goodhart put the issue simply in a draft paper, 'the alternative to "Big Bang" was, and remains, the attempted imposition of even more comprehensive exchange controls'. He concluded: 'Even if secondary trading was no more than pure gambling, there would still be a case for having it provided competitively and efficiently rather than by a high cost oligopoly.'[37]

Consequently the Bank did nothing to stand in the way of foreign acquisitions of London stock brokers as the outlines of Big Bang became clear, and the future of single-function firms looked doubtful. Foreign investment looked like the best way of dealing with the chronic problem of undercapitalization.[38] In July 1983, Brian Quinn (Assistant Director, Banking Supervision) reported on 'well advanced' discussions for Citibank to take over 29.9 per cent of Vickers da Costa's UK business as well as all their overseas business; Citibank was also pressing for membership of all of the Vickers' clearing arrangements, an application which the Bank supported in the face of considerable opposition from British competitors.[39]

Citibank also bought Scrimgeour Kemp-Gee; Security Pacific bought Hoare Govett and Charles Pulley & Co. HSBC bought James Capel, and UBS Phillips & Drew. There were of course British banks that also stepped into the takeover frenzy, with Barclays buying Zoete & Bevan (as well as the jobber Wedd Durlacher), NatWest Bisgood Bishop and Fielding Newson Smith, and Midland Greenwell. When the discount market complained about worries about 'names' and that 'Canadian banks were unwelcome and some US banks too', in late 1983, Leigh-Pemberton responded. At the end of the year, he told the discount houses that 'it was becoming more and more difficult to take a purely chauvinistic line. And indeed that was not really consistent with the City's traditions.'[40]

Leigh-Pemberton set out the Bank's objectives – fundamentally a strengthening of the capital behind stock trading and financial markets in general – in a letter to Chancellor Lawson:

I have little doubt that improved competitiveness of the British securities market and firms in world securities trading activity will depend in part on a substantial strengthening in the capital base of Stock Exchange member firms, and this will almost certainly require some further opening up in the entry provisions. But it is far from clear precisely how this might best be achieved given the need to maintain both adequate protection for investors (for example, it would probably not be possible to retain the unlimited compensation fund if the unlimited liability at present required of Stock Exchange members is modified to encourage the entry of banks) and effective regulatory arrangements in other respects (for example, the Stock Exchange capability to regulate its membership could be significantly attenuated in circumstances in which an important part of the membership consisted of, or was in fee to, major banks or, say, large financial service groups). Separately but not unrelated to all this is what view is taken about the desirability of an outcome in which a large part of our securities trading capability, including that in government debt, was foreign owned. The possibility of such an outcome is not wholly academic.[41]

It was not just stockbrokers that might find themselves with foreign owners. Merchant banks (also known as 'acceptance houses', from their role in trade finance) were vulnerable too. In April 1984, a banker from Morgan Grenfell visited the Bank to sound a warning about the approach from Deutsche Bank (the Morgan bankers were very hostile to the move, and only gave in – later – after Morgan Grenfell was almost brought down by a share ramping scandal). The Governor was thinking in terms of protective measures and wanted to know whether there was a possibility of 'politicians, probably at some time in the future and under a Labour Government, raising the issue of whether there should not be some form of Glass-Steagall [the US Depression-era legislation that separated commercial from investment banking] here'. He also asked: 'Had the Bank of England ever thought of a statement of policy, express or implied, which extended to the major Accepting Houses the inviolate status of the clearing banks?'[42] The Bank did not want to do anything to ward off this approach.

In January 1986, the Governor told the Chancellor that an individual foreigner had expressed interest in acquiring one of the Big Four clearers. Leigh-Pemberton added that the Bank had also been 'warned that one of the major accepting houses was considering moving its domicile to Switzerland'. Both developments raised wider issues which the Bank would like to discuss at some stage. Lawson simply commented that the question of possible foreign ownership of one of the Big Four was 'very difficult'. There were no statutory powers to prevent it; and he added that he 'was not persuaded that a foreign take-over would be entirely disastrous – providing the new owner was "fit and proper"'. More generally, Lawson saw 'a problem in appearing to make banks immune from the sort of take-over activity which they themselves helped to promote'.[43] Leigh-Pemberton then documented the new position of the Bank on the issue of clearing banks: 'He recalled that the Bank was widely believed to be opposed to any overseas takeover, and he himself had said as much in a press interview shortly after becoming Governor. He noted, however, that the Chancellor felt it was difficult to justify adopting a more protective attitude to banks than to the rest of British industry.'[44]

The Bank became more distinctly hands off on the issue of foreign take-overs. In response to the continued discussion about whether there should be a 'national interest' clause in the new Banking Bill in order to protect against foreign competition, Eddie George pushed back:

Mr George agreed that it would be useful to seek additional powers, although he doubted whether Parliament would be prepared to grant them without prescribing reasonably precise circumstances in which they could be used. Yet it would not be in the Bank's interest to see those circumstances specified in any detail. For instance, he could envisage a situation in which we might actually welcome a foreign takeover of one of the CLSB [Committee of London and Scottish Bankers].[45]

The greatest tension came later in the decade, when it came to a discussion of Japanese participation in the City. The government was largely sceptical, because it wanted to use the issue as an opportunity to negotiate for the access of British firms to the restricted Tokyo market, widely at that time seen as holding the key to the future of global capitalism. Japanese authorities at that point were pressing for banking status to be granted to Japanese securities houses. The British government formulated a bargaining strategy of not denying Japanese firms access in London, but of moving quite slowly as long as the Japanese authorities were unhelpful. This policy was known internally as 'stickiness without sticking points'.[46] The Bank was more willing to be obliging in the interest of greater openness, and decided that it would not prevent the sale of Guinness Mahon to Tokai Bank, and the Governor noted that 'this was a matter where we had to take a principled stand against the Treasury, and the Court should be aware of it'.[47]

The new position of the Bank was most fully set out by Leigh-Pemberton in a speech in 1987 to the Northern Ireland Chamber of Commerce:

We are now seeing London emerge as a focal point of the world's financial markets; and this is due, in no small part, to our willingness to see foreign companies come to the UK to do banking business and, on occasion, to take control of British institutions. In my view that policy invigorates the London markets and their participants. Overseas participation in a British bank or financial institution may increase the opportunities available to it, just as foreign participation in a manufacturing company may serve to introduce new capital and technology or to open up overseas markets. As a general rule we would certainly not wish to stand in the way of a bank that sought to make such an alliance. [. . .] But I also believe that it is of the highest importance that there should be a strong and continuing British presence in the banking system of the UK. It runs counter to commonsense to argue that the openness of the London market must be carried to the point where control of our financial system – the payments system, the supply of credit – may pass into the hands of institutions whose business aims and national interest lie elsewhere.[48]

The issue that most directly concerned the Bank was the way the end of jobbing as a separate activity would overturn the old-style gilts market. There were in the old system in the early 1980s seven jobbers in gilts, though in practice the market was dominated by two, Akroyd & Smithers and Wedd Durlacher, who controlled four-fifths of the market. The jobbers were often woefully undercapitalized, producing the constant threat of liquidity shocks in increasingly volatile markets. In the new regime, twenty-seven market makers were approved by the Bank as Gilt-Edge Market Makers (GEMMs). Basically, any firm with a reasonable business plan and sufficient standing was accepted, but it was clear from the outset that the market would in practice soon be dominated by large high-volume American houses that had acquired most of the old brokers and jobbers. The new arrangement was complemented by stock exchange money brokers (SEMBs, who enabled GEMMs to borrow particular gilts if they went short) and inter-dealer brokers (IDBs, enabling GEMMs to deal among themselves).

In January 1986, the Bank launched a new Central Gilts Office (CGO), replacing the clerically maintained certifiable balance accounts in Jobbers' Counter with a computerized system. Gilts could now be pledged as collateral for overnight loans. The Bank also began gilt operations from its own dealing room at this point rather than limiting itself to operations through the discount market and through Mullens, the Government Broker. In October 1988, Nigel Althaus of Mullens, the last individual to hold this historic position, which had been established in 1786 as part of Pitt's financial reforms (with the title of Senior Broker to the Commissioners for the Reduction of the National Debt Government), moved into the direct employ of the Bank. From May 1987, the Bank started auctions for gilts on an experimental basis, as a complement to the existing processes of tenders for treasury bills from the discount houses, and taps, where existing instruments were sold at current market rates. As part of Big Bang in October 1986, payments arrangements were assured by providing for irrevocable instructions for payment to be generated simultaneously with the movement of stock between CGO accounts. The stock exchange reform thus marked the beginning of a long process of replacing the very peculiar London fixed interest and money market by a much bigger, open, in short genuine, market in government debt. There was one major limitation: the US system depended on gilt repos, but there had been a number of scandals in New York, and the Bank of England resisted the establishment of a London gilt repo market until 1996.

A memorandum produced in the Bank at the start of the debate on 'Big Bang' stated the different negotiating positions of the Bank and the Treasury: The Government is:

(i) against restrictive practice;
(ii) favours the full play of market forces;

but

(iii) has political reasons for wanting to be able to say that the small investor will be adequately protected;
(iv) should be concerned about the effect on its own borrowing of any changed arrangements;
(v) has a national interest in seeking an effective machinery for securities dealing.

The Bank:-

(i) is without any formal powers to control the Stock Exchange;

    (ii) sees itself as an adviser to Government and an influence on the Stock Exchange;

    (iii) needs to be sure that there is no impairment of its operations in the gilt-edged market;

    (iv) might not be an acceptable body to police the Stock Exchange;

but

    (v) may attract criticism if things go awry.

The Stock Exchange:-

    (i) has existed, and developed, for a period of over ? years without direction from outside;

    (ii) values its independence – and self-regulation;

    (iii) already has dual capacity to some limited extent.[49]

It is striking that point 3 in the Bank's characterization of its own position referred to the centrality of its operations in the gilt-edged market: after 1986, it was operating in a market in which both gilts and equities trading were substantially opened up or liberalized, with large foreign houses now playing a major role in the market. The Bank of England seemed to switch its position dramatically in the course of the 1980s, starting as the champion of the old City and ending as the enforcer of new market principles. The shift may have been in part a matter of the personalities at the top of the Bank. Leigh-Pemberton was more favourable to the general idea of competition than the much more managerial Richardson. David Walker always liked the idea of a management shake-up as a way of enforcing efficiency and dynamism. There was also a general sentiment in favour of adopting US market practices. The change would raise the question of how well placed the Bank was to supervise financial markets.

JOHNSON MATTHEY BANKERS

The first sign that there was a major flaw in the Bank's approach to supervision came in the case of a relatively small house, Johnson Matthey Bankers. JMB was established in 1965 to conduct the banking and bullion business of Johnson Matthey and Co Ltd. It became an authorized bank under the Exchange Control Act in 1967 and obtained exemption under the Protection of Depositors Act in 1970. JMB was supervised by the Bank before the Banking Act come into effect in 1980. Before 1980, it had been on the receiving end of several possible takeover bids (which did not come to fruition), and it also incurred several sizeable losses arising from its bullion business. The losses were met by charges against profits and through the support of the parent. The link with bullion was obvious, and bullion was a big bet in the late 1970s, as the second oil shock drove gold prices up, and as the Texan oil investor Nelson 'Bunker' Hunt and his brothers tried to corner the silver market (and suffered a spectacular reversal, with a $1.7 bn loss).

JMB was granted recognition under the Banking Act in April 1980. At that time, its activity was heavily concentrated on bullion and foreign exchange dealing, with the banking side specializing in trade finance. But diversification looked like an obvious response to the turbulence in bullion markets – and in the world economy. The Bank was informed about JMB's new strategy and the increase in lending at the end of 1981. Its officials found dealing with JMB tricky: they consistently noted, and complained about, how they had been harangued by the 'garrulous' and 'unstoppable' chief executive, Roy Wheeler.[50] JMB's traditional trade finance business had tended to be concentrated in Pakistan, the Middle East and Nigeria, and these areas provided a number of the customers for their expanding lending operations. In November 1981, JMB executives spoke about Pakistan as an area where they wanted to develop business. In January 1983, the first references to Abdul Shamji occurred, a free-wheeling figure, with contacts high in the Conservative political world, including with Norman Tebbitt and Norman Lamont as well as with the Prime Minister. The JMB executives seemed tranquil, while the Bank's verdict became increasingly critical and concerned: 'Wheeler did not seem to consider that the "venture" risks attached to this type of lending involved any different credit assessment procedures than for his other advances.'[51] By the end of 1983, the Bank's officials were quite worried: JMB's 'abilities in credit assessment have always been weak. But the jewellery losses have uncovered weaknesses in control procedures as well.' They recommended further action, with a 'full prudential' interview at an early date, and 'if we do not get assurance from this interview, then higher authority will need to speak to them'.[52] But this intervention of the Bank's higher authorities does not seem to have occurred.

By the beginning of 1984, other figures in the City were warning about JMB. Early in 1984 Loehnis had a conversation with Peter Hambro of Mocatta International about the unsupervised character of the bullion market. The official responsible for JMB recognized that 'our supervision of bullion banks is not what it should be (we do our best with JMB)'.[53] In

April 1984, JMB was categorized as regularly late in its reporting without an excuse.

The balance sheet of the bank more than doubled between March 1980 and March 1984 by which time footings (i.e. the final balance of debits and credits) stood at £2.1 bn (see Table 8.1). The bank was quite profitable until 1984, when after a bumper year in 1983, there was a sharp decline.

The large commercial exposures which gave rise to the need for the rescue operation first appeared on the returns made to the Bank late in 1982 and in 1983. The exposure to the El Saeed Maritime Holdings Corporation group of companies, a loose association of companies with no formal group structure, rose from £7 m in November 1982 to £19 m in December 1983, at which time it was equivalent to 27 per cent of the bank's capital base. El Saeed was primarily engaged in ship chartering but increasingly became engaged in other activities, including film-making. It was primarily the vehicle of Mahmud Sipra, known to his friends as the Cobra and to his enemies as the Devil, a larger-than-life figure who financed films and led every aspect of the jet-set life (he had his own brand of perfume, named 'Arrogance').[54] The second loan was to another loosely structured Pakistani group, the Altramar Holding and Investment Corporation group of companies. The owners of the two groups were related by marriage, a fact discovered by the Bank of England only after the rescue operation. The exposure to Altramar, whose main business was also shipping, first

Table 8.1 *Johnson Matthey Bankers (1980–1984)*

					£m
End March	1980	1981	1982	1983	1984
Loans and overdrafts	34	78	135	184	309
Holdings of bullion and customers' bullion-related accounts	678	786	804	1,226	1,359
Total footings	874	1,040	1,183	1,735	2,089
Year to March	1980	1981	1982	1983	1984
Pre-tax profits (£m)	14.4	11.6	16.6	24.3	9.4
% of shareholders' funds*	35	22	23	26	9
% of total assets*	1.6	1.1	1.4	1.4	0.4
* as at year end					

appeared in the returns in December 1983 at £13 m (20 per cent of the bank's capital base). The total exposure on these two loans in March 1984, at the end of JMB's financial year had risen to £50 m. The capital and reserves of the bank at that time were some £82 m and of the banking group £102 m. On 9 August 1984, a worried Bank note concluded that the two problematical exposures were 30 per cent of the adjusted capital base: 'Do they have any limits at all?'[55] And a few weeks later, commenting on how 'accident prone' JMB was: 'we managed to uncover some rather worrying features on credit control and the bank's large exposures'. A discussion of credit assessment and control 'did nothing to convince us that the bank's assessment procedures were adequate'.[56]

The actual movements in these loans are shown in Table 8.2: the figure of 30 per cent was a grotesque underestimate. The total loan book continued to expand rapidly in 1984 from the March figure of £309 m to £400 m in June and £460 m in September. The two large loans also grew reaching a combined 72 per cent of capital base by June. At this time a £12 m loan to a related company of El Saeed, Eurostem Maritime, was reported for the first time, bringing the three exposures up to 89 per cent of the bank's capital.

The Bank's internal post-mortem on the debacle concluded:

We interviewed the bank regularly and between October 1983 and February 1984 met with them three times in an effort to improve our understanding of their policy and practice with regard to liquidity management and intra-group lending. Discussions with management were not always easy, not because of any overt resistance to enquiry on their part, but partly because of the complexities of the bullion business and partly because of the personality of the Managing Director, who attended the meetings regularly and who tended to talk

Table 8.2 *Johnson Matthey Bankers' large credits (1983–1984)*

£m	1983			1984			
	June	Sept	Dec	Mar	June	Sept	June 1984 figures as % of capital base
El Saeed	10	13	19	29	27	48	38
Eurostem Maritime	-	-	-	-	12		17
Altramar	-	-	13	21	24	30	34

at great length and single-mindedly about what was preoccupying him. Interviews tended to be very long and detailed.

Initially, when it became clear that JMB was failing, the Bank tried to organize a repeat of the 1970s lifeboat operation, with a private-sector rescue. The initial hope was that JMB might be taken over, either by NatWest or by Charter Consolidated, though a memorandum of 26 September 1984 noted that 'neither was more than a gleam in the eye' and that in fact 'things might develop in such a way as to call for a Bank of England guarantee'.[57] In fact, it should have been clear long in advance that the circumstances that allowed the lifeboat had disappeared, and that, as a Bank memorandum of 1982 already put it, 'the clearing banks now had less in the way of resources and inclination for discretionary lending of the sort associated with the lifeboat, large international debtors, home customers to be carried through the recession and now a fellow member of the banking system'.[58]

Frantic negotiations with other prominent firms in the bullion market then took place over the last four days of September, when Leigh-Pemberton and a substantial number of the Bank's senior staff were in Washington at the annual IMF/World Bank meetings. As a consequence, the Deputy Governor, Kit McMahon, coordinated the Bank's response. He was convinced, largely by the other members of the London gold market, especially Sir Evelyn de Rothschild, that a failure of JMB would be a catastrophic blow to the credibility of the London bullion market. In consequence, the Bank bought JMB for £1, and then injected £100 m into JMB. JMB was in many ways the opposite of 'gentlemanly capitalism', but the manner of the rescue looked very much like the old City at work. The extra guarantee from the Bank occurred without any consultation with the Chancellor, Nigel Lawson, who assured the House of Commons that public money was not involved in the rescue. When it was clear that he had been misled, he was not surprisingly furious with the Bank's leadership. In a bilateral meeting with Leigh-Pemberton, Lawson asked whether 'we would have rescued JMB had it not been a member of the gold market. I said we would not and that I had been at some pains to express our policy on at least one occasion in public.' In particular, he thought that the Treasury 'ought to know at an early stage when we had anxieties about a bank'.[59]

Brian Quinn went rather further than Leigh-Pemberton in drawing up his verdict on why Johnson Matthey was rescued. Certainly membership of the London gold market was the 'primary reason', but there was a risk that contagion might spread from bullion traders to parent banks: Samuel Montagu was owned by Midland, and Mocatta and Goldsmid by Standard Chartered.[60]

The aftermath of the collapse only added fuel to the political debate. Rodney Galpin, an associate director on the administrative side of the Bank, and as a veteran of the 1974 lifeboat operation 'the Bank's safest pair of hands',[61] was sent in as the new executive chairman of JMB. He dismissed the top three executives, who continued to mount an extra-ordinary (and naïve) defence of their actions. The Finance Director of JMB, Ian Fraser, explained that his 'conscience was clear'. He thought that 'the problem was only with two bad clients, but the rest of the portfolio was in good shape. [...] Everyone could make such a mistake.'[62] Fraser, dismissed from JMB, moved to Deechan Finance, whose main shareholder was a prominent customer of JMB, Daswani. The whole episode was ventilated in public a year later as a Labour MP, Brian Sedgemore, used the legally privileged space of the House of Commons to tear into the Bank for its handling of the affair. 'Mr. Ian Fraser says that Mr. Rodney Galpin, a director of the Bank of England, told him, "You keep your head down for three years and you will be back in banking."' And Daswani himself was then also quoted by Sedgemore: '"A couple of call girls at night clubs, a few Xmas presents, birthday presents – don't make bribery. Everyone in bank-ing does it." The fraud squad has discovered that Mr. Ian Fraser had a couple of mistresses who needed expensive entertainment. Mahmoud Sipra told us that Mr. Abdul Shamgi [*sic*: Shamji] provided the flat for Mr. Fraser in Mayfair.'[63] Sedgemore then quoted David Walker describing Galpin's conduct as 'daft and inexplicable'. [64] He was not the only MP to use the case against the government: Dennis Skinner, a radical dissident, joined in; and the former Foreign Secretary and leader of the Social Democrats, David Owen, mounted an even more persuasive case from the political centre. The Conservative backbencher Jonathan Aitken asked: 'Where are the guilty men?' Lawson replied: 'I think what has gone wrong is that there is prima facie evidence of a weakness in the way the banking supervisory system works.'[65]

Inevitably, the Bank itself was wiser after the event. In a memo on credit limits submitted to McMahon, one official simply reported: 'The short answer to your enquiry is that JMB have certainly since 1959 and particularly since 1970, always been regarded as a poor risk.'[66] 'We should have been more alert to the political sensitivities,' Galpin later explained.[67] But the Bank was defensive, conservative and fundamentally unpersuasive. On 27 November 1984, the Governor appeared for a rather awkward meeting with Lawson, who started off by saying that 'this is a complex and serious business', and noting that the Bank did not receive a copy of the auditor's management letters as a matter of course. There was a need for a comprehensive review to find out whether 'there should be a different way of doing things, have you got the right staff and the right techniques and are auditors doing their work'. Leigh-Pemberton conducted this review under his own supervision. Asked about the repercussions of the failure of JMB, he replied to Lawson rather feebly that he 'personally doubted whether the result of the review would be to suggest any radical change in the existing structure of banking supervision'.[68] The Chancellor then bluntly said that the Bank 'can't sit back and say everything is all right'. Leigh-Pemberton agreed that 'perhaps we should have been more aware', but then added wistfully, 'how do you prevent foolish lending?'[69]

In the aftermath of the JMB failure, Margaret Thatcher involved herself personally in the reorganization of the Bank's approach to banking supervision. By July 1985, she was arguing that banking supervision should be taken away from the Bank, while Lawson was claiming that he had successfully dissuaded her 'on the grounds that it would distract from the Bank's standing'. But she focused then particularly on the role of Peter Cooke, Assistant Director and Head of Banking Supervision. Lawson, as Leigh-Pemberton noted, 'rather concerned me by referring to the weakness of my own position should Mr. Cooke's not be seen to have been changed'.[70]

Cooke has to bear, in the Prime Minister's view, substantial responsibility for the Johnson Matthey debacle. It would therefore be quite wrong, in her view, for him to retain responsibility for general policy and preparation of the new Banking Act, though she would not object to his continued involvement in the international aspects of supervisory co-ordination.[71]

The most visible result of the JMB affair was the removal from the Bank of Deputy Governor Kit McMahon, who was compensated with the position of Chairman of the Midland. When Leigh-Pemberton told Lawson, the news 'was received blandly and with an expression of good will'. Leigh-Pemberton proposed to appoint as his successor the dynamic David Walker, but Lawson thought him 'far too young' and made an alternative suggestion for a weathered (and retired) warhorse: 'Why not put in G. Blunden.'[72] Blunden had a good eye for what was wrong with the Bank's existing culture (see Figure 8.2). In particular, he saw that the Governor's office needed to be strengthened rather than weakened, so that the prominence of the Deputy Governor's Committee, a feature of the McMahon period, was quickly reduced.

Figure 8.2 Bank of England repent, (Kenneth Mahood, *Punch*, 8 July 1988)

In the aftermath of JMB, the Treasury proposed a Banking Commission on a French model, as the Bank thought largely in response to Thatcher's 'strong desire' to separate banking supervision completely from the

Bank.[73] The commission bancaire had been created as a supervisory body in 1984, and had seven members including the Governor of the Banque de France, the Directeur du Trésor, that is, the senior Finance Ministry official, and the insurance regulator. It was thus linked to, but organizationally outside, the Banque de France. The adoption of such a model would symbolically separate the supervisory and monetary policy roles of the Bank of England, retaining a central role in both of the Governor as a 'pivot of responsibility'. The Bank pushed back: in its response to the Treasury paper, it noted that 'when one asks how the responsibility or accountability will be exercised everything becomes foggy'.[74] The French model was indeed unclear, as well as alien to the City's traditions, and the Bank kept its role, but with a cloud hanging over Threadneedle Street.

The Banking Supervision Division was now reorganized and put under Rodney Galpin, returning from his brief spell as chairman of JMB, who after a few months drew a preliminary conclusion:

JMB has left its imprint; and particularly among the younger members of the Division there is a desire for more bureaucracy and more ratios with a consequent loss of flexibility – and some danger of eroding one of the strengths of the system. No proper management information system is in place. Although it probably exists, it is not in a form which can be readily accessed by senior management. It should be and Banking supervision is ideally suited to electronic systems, depending as it does in large part on the analysis of statistics. A start has been made on this.[75]

The response to the JMB saga was the government's appointment of a committee (Committee to Consider the System of Banking Supervision), chaired by Leigh-Pemberton, whose report formed the basis for new legislation.[76] The 1987 Banking Act unsurprisingly left banking supervision with the Bank of England, but eliminated the two-tier system of banks and deposit-takers, put stricter controls on lending exposures (including limits to large exposures) and instituted a compensation mechanism for the victims of fraud. The major institutional innovation was a Board of Banking Supervision, which met regularly to consider the operation of supervision, and issued annually a report. Some thought it did not go far enough, and that it was no more than a 'cosy luncheon club', in the words of the Conservative MP and former banker Anthony Nelson.[77] The Bank formulated a clear new policy, that exposure to a single counterparty should not normally exceed 10 per cent of a bank's capital base without thorough justification, and that no such exposure should exceed 25 per cent of the capital base other than in 'the most exceptional circumstances'. These limitations had existed before, but only with respect to the lower tier of banks under the 1979 act; the consequence of the JMB imbroglio was to make the supervision of banks equivalent to that of the former 'deposit-takers'. The specified exceptions to the 25 per cent rule were: exposures to other banks with a maturity of up to one year; exposures to overseas central governments; exposures of up to one year to group financial companies; exposures secured by cash or British government stocks; and, in the case of bank subsidiaries, exposures guaranteed by the parent bank. The new act also strengthened the position of the Bank in respect to auditors: proper control was now a part of the criteria for recognition as a bank; and the auditors should report concerns to the Bank of England without being in breach of customer confidentiality. Finally, the act also (in section 22) required the Bank to object to individuals controlling banks if it was not satisfied that 'the person concerned is a fit and proper person to become a controller of the description in question of the institution'. The Bank continued to maintain a list of financial undesirables, or, as it put it, the 'Men Not For Jobs' list.[78]

But the legacy of JMB continued to represent a major vulnerability for the Bank. In July 1988, Ian Fraser was arrested on a likely charge of 'corruptly receiving gifts'. Leigh-Pemberton at this point asked as to 'how this squared with our previous assertion that there had been no evidence of fraud by JMB staff'.[79] Already in March 1986, George commented on the phenomenon of 'people becoming less responsive in the City climate to "eyebrows"'. That mattered because the pace of takeovers and – in general – of innovation in the City was accelerating.

The JMB episode left the Bank quite vulnerable. It attempted to explain more of what it was doing, and encouraged a journalist, Stephen Fay, to write articles and then a book about the Bank in an attempt to lift the veil of secrecy. But inside the Bank, the result was felt to be a disappointment. George described the employment of Fay as an 'attempt to "sell" the Bank'. But Fay's output had been 'very unsatisfactory and a more traditional, reticent approach would be followed in the future'.[80]

A SUCCESSION OF SMALL SCANDALS

The problems for banking and financial supervision more generally continued to come in dispiritingly regular dribs and drabs. In some cases, the Bank was quick and effective. After the Guinness affair, which involved an illegal share support operation in a successful 1986 takeover bid by Guinness for Distillers, Deputy Governor George Blunden quickly demanded the resignation of two directors of Morgan Grenfell. In response to the Department of Trade and Industry (DTI) Inspectors' Report, the Board of Banking Supervision declared five Morgan Grenfell employees 'unfit for positions' – four had already left, but one was still in place – as well as a banker at Ansbachers.[81] Blunden explained the Bank's stance in an off-the-record discussion with Lawson and Sir Peter Middleton, in which the Chancellor asked whether the behaviour of Morgan was 'in our opinion common among merchant banks'. Blunden responded that 'the general opinion among the "first division" of merchant banks was that Morgan Grenfell had of late been going beyond the bounds of what was acceptable'. Lawson asked what the Bank would do if Morgan Grenfell were to come under pressure, and Blunden explained that he was requiring a purge: 'They could not expect assistance from us so long as there was a possibility of their being found a "guilty institution." If systemic problems arose because of a loss of confidence in them, we would support the innocent but not them.'[82]

But the application of new law in the post-1987 regulation posed a fundamentally insoluble dilemma to the Bank's former approach. Freshfields, the Bank's solicitors, advised that the traditional moral suasion applied by the Bank was problematic as it seemed to exclude a recourse to legal action. The Bank's Banking Supervision Division worried that the legal advice 'seems to come dangerously close to "shaving off your eyebrows" in the area of banking supervision. If so, this would be a quantum change in the Bank's position in relation to the banking industry and in its role as a supervisor.'[83]

There were also cases where – as an internal Bank document later analysed – the work of the Banking Supervision Division had been impeded by considerations about the need to 'trim' when passing recommendations up to the senior levels of the Bank. The paper gave examples, but only from the Richardson period, of tensions: Brian Gent, the star supervisor of the 1970s and early 1980s, had felt unable to take energetic action in the case of the small London house of Knowsley, which was run by a brother of the Labour Minister Harold Lever and which was thought to be protected by Richardson; or Peter Cooke, the next supervising star, suffered from a period of disapprobrium in the Bank as he refused to give recognized status to the also-well-connected Commercial Bank of Wales, run by Sir Julian Hodge, with close links to Prime Minister James Callaghan.[84]

Some critics in parliament, above all in the Labour Party, and in the press, above all in the *Financial Times*, argued that the task of financial regulation more generally required the creation of a statutory body. But the solution of 1985 was much less than that: the new SIB was a private body with powers delegated by the government, whose members were jointly appointed by the Bank of England and the DTI. The DTI was the ultimate supervisor. This outcome was widely regarded as a 'victory for the City lobby'.[85] From the City view, however, the SIB seemed too bureaucratic. Its first head, Sir Kenneth Berrill, was an economist and economic historian who had run the Central Policy Review Staff before moving to be chairman of Vickers da Costa in 1980. He looked like a mandarin from Whitehall who had come to enforce rules, stating that 'there is no such thing as a friendly rulebook'.[86] Some City figures considered his approach confrontational. Since the Bank was partly responsible for selecting the members of the SIB, clashes about Berrill's style dominated a great deal of discussion in the City and the Court. The influential merchant banker John Chippendale 'Chips' Keswick, the chairman of Hambros, spoke of 'an ever-increasing bureaucracy of supervisors, motivated half by fear and half by good intentions'. Leigh-Pemberton tried to come up with a solution that was much more personable and flexible: it relied on applying the David Walker principle of finding the right personalities. That proved to mean replacing Berrill by Walker. The Governor's private secretary noted that there was a need to find 'balance' between 'Goodhartism and Berrilism', i.e. monetary policy formulation and rule-based regulation, and that the 'perfect solution is Walkerism and Leigh-Pembertonism'.[87] As Leigh-Pemberton put it, 'Adam Smith's theory of the "invisible hand" does not quite lead me to believe that ideal payments and settlement systems will emerge just from competition between the banks. Some of the invisible handiwork may again have to be the Bank of England's.'[88]

The Bank often warned when it could not act directly. Barlow Clowes, which did not take deposits and hence was not a bank but was a financial company which bought and sold gilts with notional tax advantage implications ('bond-washing'), was shut down by the High Court in May 1988, owing £190 m, with some 18,000 customers losing their money. The investigation by the DTI completed in 1989 showed up how the DTI had ignored warning signs – including those coming from the Bank – from 1985.

Market supervision became much more political as a consequence of a new era of popular capitalism, in which privatizations resulted in large-scale sales to a new and largely inexperienced investing public. A central question related to the business underwriting in securities markets in times of substantial volatility. Because of the dramatic stock market collapse on 19 October 1987, the handling of the privatization issue of £7,250 m of BP shares that had been fully underwritten the week before the crash became immensely controversial. The BP offer clearly flopped. Only 250,000 applications for shares were received out of an expected six million. But the cost was born in different ways in different countries: the seventeen major British bank underwriters had shifted a significant portion of their risk to 400 sub-underwriters, but the US underwriters, by agreeing to British rules, were unable to shift any of the risk. There was in consequence a widespread demand, especially from Canadian and US investors, to invoke the *force majeure* clause, cancelling the issue if 'adverse overriding circumstances' intervened between the impact day (15 October) and the date on which the offer would become unconditional (30 October). Did a major stock market collapse constitute such a circumstance? David Mulford from the US Treasury telephoned the international Executive Director, Anthony Loehnis, to say that the BP issue threatened global financial stability. It was 'no longer simply an underwriting problem'. The 'world's largest equity issue ever made' in the new conditions would 'reduce the market's already vulnerable liquidity and postpone for a very long time the hopes of a restitution of equilibrium'.[89] The Treasury was initially reluctant to give a guarantee as there was in its view no adverse change since 15 October that should not be regarded as a proper under-writing risk.[90] On 27 October, the Tuesday after the crash, newspapers reported that there was an expectation that the government might cancel the share issue, which 'now hangs like an albatross around the City's neck'.[91] The Bank – and in particular George – was sympathetic to the case that the markets needed to be stabilized, and George proposed to buy the shares at 20 pence below the issue price (120 pence).[92] He discussed the question first with Rothschilds, and then at the Treasury, where Lawson began by arguing that the Bank's scheme 'went well beyond what was necessary to deal with the problem of BP shares going into free fall. It implied support at a level substantially higher than the market price. It could not be defended in the House of Commons.'[93]

Immediately after the meeting with the Bank, Lawson went to the House of Commons to announce that the Bank of England would buy the interim rights (the Partly Paid Shares) at 70 pence, through the Issue Department of the Bank (i.e. leaving the risk with Treasury). The Labour Treasury spokesman John Smith made an alternative case, that the issue should have been cancelled. In fact, the floor worked brilliantly, in that dealings opened at 85 pence on 30 October. The initial cut-off for the buyback scheme had been set at 11 December, and by December the market was buoyed by large-scale Kuwaiti purchases of BP stock.

The operation was a financial success, but threatened to be a political disaster. Lawson was angry because he thought that Bank officials had briefed journalists that the scheme was originally the Bank's and that Lawson had only accepted it after Prime Minister Thatcher pressed him.[94] A few days later, with the share price falling to the Bank's 70 pence floor, at the annual Mansion House dinner, both Lawson and Leigh-Pemberton tried their best to smooth over the clash, and Leigh-Pemberton enthused: 'In this connection I would like to take this opportunity to congratulate the Chancellor on the wise and effective choice that he made last week to resolve the unprecedented dilemma of having launched the largest ever internationally-underwritten equity issue and then being faced with market [sic] more dramatically disturbed than at any time in the present century.'[95]

The most problematical late 1980s case involved a bank. County NatWest, the merchant bank subsidiary of NatWest, had advised Blue Arrow, a British employment agency, in its 1987 bid for Manpower Inc., an analogous but much larger US company. Blue Arrow needed to raise capital to complete the transaction, and announced on 29 September 1987 that the £837 m rights sale operation had been successfully completed, though the press noted that 'a sizeable portion of the issue was left'.[96] Only 48.9 per cent of the stock had been taken up by the existing shareholders, and 13 per cent had not been taken up. County NatWest did not force the sub-underwriters to take up shares. In fact, its subsidiary County NatWest Securities had bought 4.6 per cent and County NatWest 4.9 per cent of the stock; the rest of the non-taken-up stock was held by Philips and Drew, a stockbroker owned by the Swiss bank UBS. The idea was to split the stock into packets of below 5 per cent, so as to keep the holdings undisclosed. The engagement was not reported because County NatWest claimed an exemption for market makers under the 1985 Company Act, but in fact the engagement amounted to a large exposure that should have been declared under the Banking Act.

The issue was brought to light in an investigative article in the *Economist*, which quoted Charles Villiers, the chairman of County NatWest, as saying that he 'saw a chance to make a profit'.[97] Deputy Governor George Blunden wrote to Peter Middleton that 'Even with the benefit of hindsight, we do not believe that we could have done anything different', either in September 1987 at the time of the operation or after 17 December 1987, when County NatWest closed out the indemnity it had given to UBS. 'It would not be practicable to conduct our supervision on the assumption that senior members of our largest banks are not to be relied on,' Blunden concluded.[98] An internal report produced in May 1988 by Sir Philip Wilkinson, a deputy chairman of NatWest and a member of the Bank of England's Board of Banking Supervision, was fundamentally reassuring, and the Bank of

England took it at face value, but passed it on to the DTI. At a meeting on City issues, the Bank basically accepted the argument that the shareholdings were below the 5 per cent threshold.[99] The *Economist* kept up its pressure on the case, asking, 'Why was the bank's senior management, rather than outside investigators, allowed to conduct an inquiry into a possible breach of company law?'[100] Eventually, in December 1988, the DTI very belatedly launched its own investigation under the terms of the 1985 Companies Act Section 432 (relating to fraud). NatWest deputy chief executive Terry Green told the DTI inspectors: 'Crucially, I was told that County NatWest Limited had taken legal advice (on the indemnity), that the Bank of England was in the picture, and that Blue Arrow was fully aware of the shareholdings.' There had been meetings at the Bank of England on 30 September and 4 December 1987 with County NatWest representatives.[101] When Leigh-Pemberton saw Charles Green, another NatWest executive, in February 1988, he discussed the 'moral and ethical quandaries' of the City, and suggested that Alan Webster, 'the recently retired Dean of St Paul's Cathedral, could have helped more in his pastoral capacity'.[102] Webster, a 'Red Dean', had been a fierce critic of City ethics. The DTI report was published on 20 July 1989, when three NatWest directors, including Charles Green and Terry Green, resigned, as did the chairman of NatWest, Lord Boardman, who had written to the Governor of the Bank to complain of the unfair criticism of the DTI report, and to say that 'he could not accept the resignation of these three loyal colleagues of great integrity and remain'.[103]

The affair had an aftermath, with a trial convicting four men, three from County NatWest, of misleading the market. They appealed, and the result (in August 1992) was a not guilty verdict. A new DTI report repeated the criticism of the Wilkinson report as 'the product of inefficiency and inexperience. It was not the product of dishonesty.' It also concluded, 'At no stage did the Bank of England obstruct or impede the DTI in relation to its investigations into the Blue Arrow transaction.'[104] The inspectors looked at the notes of meetings between Boardman and Leigh-Pemberton, in which the Governor was reported to have said that 'some of his senior colleagues at the Bank had told him that they regarded the Wilkinson report as a whitewash'.[105] The *Economist* continued to treat the issue as an indictment of the way bank regulation worked. In February 1992, after the first trial, it wrote that 'it emerged during the trial that directors of both NatWest and the Bank of England had known about the secret parcelling-up of Blue Arrow shares from the start'. But on 22 January 1993, the *Economist* printed an 'Apology', stating that there was no suggestion that the Bank of England was involved in a conspiracy to 'hush up' the Blue Arrow affair.[106] As on 22 January, it was also announced that the editor of the *Economist*, Rupert Pennant-Rea, was moving to the Bank of England, the 'apology' had a slightly peculiar flavour.

This was a go-go period, and there were accusations of sleaze everywhere (including in the protected gilts markets: see below). Post-Big Bang London looked like late 1980s Reaganite America, with loud City excesses of the type depicted in Oliver Stone's iconic 1987 film *Wall Street*. The rather old-fashioned Bank did not really know how to deal with the new mood: but there was a political pressure to do something. An issue emerged in the late 1980s which later became even more central to debate over finance and its role in national life: excessive compensation. The new City appalled the inherently rather thrifty Margaret Thatcher. Already in 1985 she told a television interview that top salaries in the City 'fair make one gasp, they are so large'.[107] The old-style Leigh-Pemberton felt sympathetic to that view, and reported a conversation with the Prime Minister in the relaxed setting of Sir Hector Laing's Scottish residence.

When we were at Dunphail the Prime Minister drew my attention to a report in the Times of how dividends of £19 million were paid to two individuals [...]. The Prime Minister understandably disapproved of such a level of personal reward but I was unable to tell her anything about the history of the firm. On investigation it appears that the report in the Times is reasonably full and accurate. What is bad is that two young men, by very aggressive and frankly questionable sales methods, should have been able to make profits on such a scale at the expense of their clients in the futures market; what is better is that the firm has had to improve its methods and standards in order to comply with the Financial Services Act and that, in spite of a sharp fall in profits and the absence of Hughes and Walsh from the management of the firm, it has not yet been accepted by the SRO [self-regulatory organisation] to which it has applied.

At the same time, the Bank increasingly shared the conviction – intrinsic to the political climate of the late 1980s – that heavy regulation would destroy London's competitive advantage. As Leigh-Pemberton put it, there was 'a degree of dissatisfaction with life in the City', and he then added 'that we may not be successful in preserving London's position as a major financial centre during the 1990s if the criticisms about over-regulation were not taken seriously and carefully examined'.[108]

STABILITY ISSUES

One of the results of the combined fallout of JMB and the aftermath of the spectacular innovations, takeovers, uncertainties and reorganizations that followed Big Bang was that attention was concentrated on the small-scale scandal. The big systemic issues, which had been so prominent at the time of the 1970s stagflation and then the early 1980s recession and the Latin American debt crisis, seemed to pale into significance, because perhaps they were unthinkably large or perhaps because they were less picturesque than crooks and frauds. But there was still a possibility of a need for large-scale loan-loss reserves at the Bank in order to deal with potential bank insolvencies. In the words of Blunden:

In the 1960s we had let two banks fail once it had become clear that they were insolvent rather than merely illiquid, although in the late 1970s the Bank had stepped in to support some insolvent banks because we did not want a UK bank to be the first to falter in the evolving euromarket. Meanwhile, assistance from the commercial banks had been sought only in cases of illiquidity, most notably during the 1974/75 lifeboat operation. The JMB case might therefore best be seen as an exception to a general rule. The problems at JMB appeared at first to relate to liquidity and it was at this stage that we had engaged the assistance of the commercial banks. When it became clear that there was a solvency problem we did not take the decision to disengage these banks. It would be unwise to count on the banks being prepared to underwrite an insolvent institution in the future.

Eddie George set out a rather different philosophy in response:

We needed to be much clearer on what we meant by help in this context. It would be quite wrong for the Bank to carry sufficient reserves to bail out one of the major clearing banks and he would want to resist any suggestion that we should seek to ensure that the Bank's reserves should grow at the same rate as the liabilities of the banking system. If an institution became insolvent we ought to approach the Government, who are after all our own shareholders.

The implications of this assertion, a version of the too-big-to-fail doctrine that had clearly emerged in the US in the 1980s, was that if the government really had to bear the ultimate liability, it should also manage the supervision. It also meant that there could be no advance preparation for resolution procedures: the critical point was to secure a management of liquidity to ensure that liquidity problems did not spiral out of control and a management of the payment system to minimize the systemic impact of particular bank problems. Since the topic of Bank loan-loss reserves and the size of the balance sheet raised such potentially politically controversial issues, it was better just not to touch them. As George put it:

The existing level of reserves was sufficient for any support operation which we might contemplate and that it would be very difficult to argue the need for any additional reserves for this purpose. He also pointed out that it was certainly not the case that any increase in the Bank's reserves was unambiguously a good thing. As the level of reserves increased, either the Treasury or the commercial banks became more likely to question the justification for this. The Deputy Governor expressed surprise that we heard so little from the banks about this, since they were subject to a tax which had not been voted by Parliament. It was important to note that the Bank was making a loss if one excluded the income derived from Cash Ratio Deposits (CRDs). Mr Quinn thought that from the perspective of a commercial bank he would also be troubled by the level of the Bank's expenditure, since this had increased in real terms.[109]

When, with the recession and potential bank problems worsening, Leigh-Pemberton raised the issue of a fiscal backstop with the Treasury and the Chancellor (now John Major), and when it was clear that some of the problem cases might not even be British banks, the Treasury was scared.

The Chancellor said that he shuddered somewhat at the idea of a Treasury guarantee to the Bank should it come to a rescue operation on the basis of the Deputy Governor's manuscript note to me at the end of last week, particularly in circumstances where we had not done the same thing for a British bank. I said that our first step was to ensure that the bank's shareholders should put the provision of appropriate liquidity to this subsidiary at the top of its priority allocations of hard currency and that we had an opportunity to put this forward at the end of the week.[110]

The potential vulnerability of the government had become a sensitive issue by 1990, because it was clear that there were major weaknesses in some very important financial institutions. All kinds of stories and uncertainties circulated in the wake of the property price collapse. Standard Chartered was described by Brian Quinn, the official primarily in charge of banking supervision, as having a 'deficient credit culture', while Midland was 'once again a potential problem case . . . a troubled institution'. Leigh-Pemberton believed that Kit McMahon had 'introduced too many changes and had not ensured that an agreed strategy and management team were given time to make things work'.[111] Banking looked very vulnerable, and in fact Britain was lucky to avoid a Swedish- or Norwegian-style general banking collapse in the early 1990s.

INTERNATIONALIZATION

An obvious way around the problem of deficient or dangerous British banking was to look for a more robust international framework for banking regulation and supervision. This quest had begun in the 1970s; and it was and probably never could be complete, because bank rescues – the aftermath of failed supervision and regulation – required national fiscal resources. At the same time, altering rules affected the playing fields between different national financial industries. Governments were torn between wanting to avoid potential fiscal liabilities and attempting to maximize revenues (and maybe political influence) by allowing powerful banks to expand.

British bank international regulatory endeavours went forward on two completely separated fronts. One front was the negotiation of the Basel accord on capital adequacy, a process that took part almost exclusively between London and New York, with the continental Europeans and the Japanese being deliberately excluded. Fed chairman Paul Volcker and Gerald Corrigan of the New York Fed had become concerned about burgeoning off-balance-sheet finance (through guarantees and derivatives) as they only applied a simple leverage ratio, and Volcker initially suggested to Leigh-Pemberton that the Fed should adopt the risk–asset ratio approach created by Richard Farrant at the Bank of England in the late 1970s.[112] The outcome of a long bilateral exercise was the 1988 Basel agreement, which gave a very simple standard, with risk weights for sovereign debt of 0 for OECD countries and 100 for other borrowers, 20 for bank borrowers of OECD country banks and 100 for other banks, and 50 for property loans fully secured against mortgages.[113]

The second framework for discussion was a legacy of European banking discussions from the 1970s. Debate about supervision and the definition of banks had always had a European dimension. One of the reasons that the 1979 Banking Act was required was that a European directive stipulated that 'Member States shall require credit institutions subject to the Directive to obtain authorization before commencing their activities'.[114] A possible answer to British dilemmas – that was driven in addition by the 1986 Single European Act and the prospect of a completely integrated European capital market – was that banking might be Europeanized. That would deal with the question of establishing 'domestic' firms of adequate size to combat the American and the Japanese challenges. In the aftermath of the Big Bang, it was clear that the traditional City was changing very quickly. In 1987, in regard to the prospect of an EC Single Market, Deputy Governor George Blunden noted, 'It was now clear – as it had not been at the time of the Big Bang – that not all UK firms active in financial services could remain competitive internationally across a wide range of business. We should therefore develop a line in promoting European groupings which would be large enough to do so.'[115] By July 1988, Blunden remarked, 'the threat of takeover, in the City at least, had been shown to do good. But the general conclusion to be drawn from this discussion was that the Government's present mergers policy was indefensible, stupid and inconsistent with the implications of 1992 [i.e. the completion of the single European market].' Leigh-Pemberton agreed completely with this verdict, and 'noted that the Government had consistently ignored the Bank's advice on this matter and had in fact moved in the opposite way to our recommendations. We would continue to press for change.'[116]

In response to the Delors Report discussions of a possible European monetary union, and the aftermath of the Committee's Report, the Bank of England pushed for some European coordination, and conceded that 'in the long run there might be a banking supervisory role for the European central bank, especially if the detailed supervision continued to be carried out by national bodies'. At the end of 1989, Lamfalussy at the BIS predicted that 'there would be something like a European Central Bank within 5 years'.[117] But Anthony Loehnis, the Director of the International Division, added that 'some of those who supported this move saw it as hurrying up the creation of a European central bank, and this was something which HMG was likely to resist'.[118] His successor after 1989, Andrew Crockett, was more enthusiastic about the European prospects, arguing that 'the trend was toward fewer, larger, multi-national institutions', and that 'competition between cultures could be beneficial to the UK'.[119] But actually the concrete results of European coordination were highly disappointing. Quinn characterized the Brussels Banking Advisory Committee as 'unsatisfactory, with no real dialogue between the participants'.[120]

A reminder of the problems of European interconnectedness came with the Ferranti affair in 1989, with a loss of some £176 m as a result of fraud in the issuing of commercial paper by the Italian electronics group. The problem showed up the weakness of Italian banking supervision and also exposed some City banks. Barings needed to coordinate some thirty US and European as well as other UK banks in a Standstill Agreement.[121]

Faced with supervision trapped between obsession with scandal and inability to confront systemic issues, and between a need for international coordination and its practical and political impossibility, the Bank clearly needed to give up on its old sense that it was a part of a City protective network. In 1993, at a meeting to discuss a new study of financial regulation (the Norton Study on Banking Supervision), Eddie George, now Governor, expressed his surprise at the conclusion 'that the Bank was in some sense motivated by a desire to protect the banking system', and he now went back to the principles of Competition and Credit Control, which he said was 'an attempt to break up the cartel rather than protect banks'. He also expressed his worry about an increasing emphasis on consumer protection, which 'was leading to the expectation that banks would never fail'.[122] When they did fail, the fallout would inevitably produce criticism of the banks themselves, but also of the supervisory and regulatory framework that tolerated them.

9

Tunnelling Deep

The Bank and the Management of British Industry

The Bank as it reconfigured itself in the 1980s had two new faces, Eddie George and David Walker. Both were widely tipped as the future Governor of the Bank of England. Both were highly effective verbal communicators, with a very wide range of contacts. They represented a radical break from the Bank of the 1960s and 1970s, which had been dominated by the written word and by men such as John Fforde or Christopher Dow, who wrote elegant and complex papers, memoranda and letters. Both Fforde and Dow had been quite shy, and some interlocutors describe Dow as charming but fundamentally inarticulate or tongue-tied. The Bank on the other hand was becoming an institution that worked by oral persuasion, by mellifluous rhetoric. George was often described as 'silver tongued', and Walker was 'Walker the talker'. Spoken persuasion was replacing elegantly worded memoranda in the internal processes of the Bank.

On the one hand, Eddie George built up a group of young Turks who derived their power from their familiarity with markets and who spoke the same language and shared the same sensibilities. The ability to interpret markets gave George a substantial leverage in dealing with the Treasury, where there was no direct contact with financial institutions, but also with the Prime Minister. George had spent virtually his whole career at the Bank, arriving at the age of twenty-three with a degree in economics from Cambridge. The 1967 devaluation of the pound convinced him that he wanted to go into policy-making. After that he only spent relatively short periods in the BIS and the IMF before returning to Threadneedle Street. He also looked socially distinct from the old Bank of England elite: the son of a postal clerk, he was visibly not grand or patronizing, and was the antithesis of the 'guilty public school boys' (i.e. patricians who felt ashamed of their status) who populated much of the upper ranks of the British civil service and whom Margaret Thatcher despised.

The other new face of the Bank was David Walker, who had come to the Bank from the Treasury, where he had worked on the international side and had spent a considerable amount of time at the IMF. He had too an economics degree from Cambridge, a double first. His initial position was as Head of the Economic Intelligence Department. Walker's appointment was primarily intended to strengthen the Bank's international work, but rapidly was diverted into dealing with the impact of the recession on British manufacturing and industrial life. In 1980, as assistant director he moved to head the new Industrial Finance Division, became executive director in 1982, and was then in overall charge of the Finance and Industry area of the Bank. British industry became his métier in the course of the 1980s: he knew how to fix a problem. When he left the Bank in 1988, he became chairman of the Securities and Investment Board. Whereas George spoke the language of conjunctural economics and the markets, Walker spoke the language of managers. He also thought of the fundamental British problem as lying in poor management quality, and spoke of the need for

freeing the enterprising, technologically qualified manager from the safety-first cocoon which he at present inhabits, with its BUPA [i.e. private health insurance], motor car, security and pension promise. The principal constraint in this area is with the man who is at present secure in a large firm but, perhaps, frustrated because of the frequency with which his project is shelved.[1]

The discussion of how micro-economic and organizational reform is an essential element in dealing with recession and poor productivity performance seemed to fade away, but it revived in the twenty-first century in the aftermath of the Great Recession.[2]

Christopher Dow had a quite different view to Walker of how the fundamental industrial problem should be addressed. He thought that British industry was being destroyed by bad monetary policy, and wrote a fiercely critical memorandum to Richardson objecting to a Mansion House draft speech that pushed for disinflation.

It would, after all, be very ironic if in the search for ways to help industry, you fastened policies on it which might well damage it beyond practical remedy. The Bank crucified British Industry in 1926 [actually 1925] by returning to gold as the old parity and no doubt in other ways. And, in general, a lot of the policies the Bank is tempted to follow are heavily influenced by considerations relating to finance or market reactions and frequently short-term.[3]

As Dow recalled it, the problem of how the Bank should respond to the plight of industry was an important part of British economic history.

A HISTORY WITH INDUSTRY

The initial involvement of the Bank of England in British industry – in effect in industrial policy – came about as a result of severe economic downturn. In the interwar era, the world of banking was often seen as opposed to the world of manufacturing. Winston Churchill, not an admirer of Montagu Norman, wrote in a letter, 'I would rather see Finance less proud and Industry more content.'[4] The impetus came from the Great Depression, and the Bank developed a considerable activism. In 1930, the Bank coordinated the creation of the Bankers Industrial Development Co., or BIDCO, of which it held a quarter of the capital (the rest came from other British banks), which was intended to finance the rationalization of business. At the same time, the Bank also began a system for regular reporting of business conditions throughout the country by the agents from the Bank's branches: the local reports were then synthesized into a report circulated to the Bank's management. The Macmillan Committee report in 1931 highlighted the issue of a 'gap' in which smaller companies, which could not issue their own shares, were also unable to access bank credit.[5] As an alternative to a banking structure or financial market that was allegedly not as developed to support industry as that of Germany or the US, the Committee envisaged as an alternative 'a company to devote itself particularly to the smaller industrial and commercial issues. [...] We see no reason why with proper management and provided British industry in general is profitable, such a concern should not succeed.'[6]

In the 1970s, in the aftermath of the oil price shock and with both leading Conservative and Labour figures demanding an increase in industrial investment, the theme of industrial finance became central to policy-making again. Gordon Richardson had worked at the Industrial and Commercial Finance Corporation (ICFC) and pressed it to merge with the Bank-run Finance Corporation for Industry (FCI), a relic of the Norman initiatives of the 1930s that had done little except some rather desultory work with the British nationalized steel industry. The resultant Finance for Industry (FFI), established in 1973, was 15 per cent owned by the Bank, with the rest of the capital held by large banks. It was intended to facilitate industrial investment through the provision of loans, originally up to £1 bn for two-year maturities. In 1983, FFI was rebranded as 'Investors in Industry', and renamed as 3i.

3i

3i continued to be owned by the Bank of England and six clearing banks (Barclays, Coutts, Lloyds, Midland, National Westminster and RBS), but from the middle of the 1980s the Bank of England wanted to sell its holding. The company developed more and more into resembling a successful venture capital fund. It sold off most of its property portfolio in the late 1980s, and also withdrew from management consultancy. By the early 1990s, it held stakes in some 4,000 British companies; but it had also begun to diversify internationally, with an office in Paris from 1983 and then in Frankfurt (1987) and Madrid and Milan (1990), as well as substantial activity in the US. Its management argued that the 'Macmillan gap' in which adequate financing was not available to small and medium-sized companies was not merely a British peculiarity, but also constituted a structural barrier to growth in all of Europe. The company saw itself more and more as a commercial enterprise, run in order to galvanize entrepreneurship.

The attempts by the Bank to launch a public offering constantly ran into suspicions from the major bank shareholders. In 1984, Midland, in trouble because of its US engagements, tried to push for divestment, but the other banks blocked it; and as Pen Kent later concluded, 'That episode may have sown the seeds of discontent which some of the shareholders have exhibited subsequently.'[7] In 1989, the charismatic and dynamic Sir John Cuckney, a tall and handsome former spy who had come to prominence as Chairman of Westland Helicopters in the mid-1980s, was appointed Chairman with the explicit goal of selling the company. The goal became more important after the 1987 Banking Act, since the two arms of 3i, a longer-term investment vehicle and a shorter-term lender, had banking licenses, putting the Bank of England in the uncomfortable position of being both shareholder and supervisor. In 1990, RBS proposed to buy out the other shareholders together with a group of institutional investors, and NatWest responded by stating that both they and Barclays were unlikely to approve new dominant shareholders of 3i.[8] By the early 1990s, the issue of a sale had become urgent as the opposition Labour Party looked set to win the next general election, and Labour politicians had both expressed an interest in 3i because of its extensive regional coverage, and realized the conflicted nature of the Bank's position. Cuckney told the Bank that the Labour MP Mo Mowlam was 'intelligent, mendacious and untrustworthy', and had 'spotted the Bank's dual role as supervisor and shareholder, and had cast a wary eye on our 14.9%'.[9]

But then 3i seemed to run into difficulty in the severe recession of the early 1990s. The share price fell, so that the owners wanted to delay the divestment operation.[10] Cuckney then stood down as chairman. The next year looked even more problematic. An association of borrowers from 3i formed a '3i Club', whose Committee complained about the service that they were receiving and about the possibility of deterioration after an effective privatization. The Bank as supervisor, perhaps more vigilant in the wake of the BCCI fiasco (see pp. 378–386), noted that 3i seemed badly run, in a stunning contrast with its smooth operation in the 1980s. As the Bank's supervisor noted after a Strengths, Weaknesses, Opportunities and Threats (SWOT) meeting, 3i seemed to have a 'casual attitude to regulation', 'exemplified by the recent failure to even know what their RAR [Revenue Accounting and Reporting] was, still less to be in a position to prevent a breach of it'.[11] Cuckney's successor as chairman, Alan Wheatley, ran into hostility from the banks, which disliked his ambitious expansion plans, which they may have seen as constituting unpleasant competition, and was forced to stand down in April 1993. A new chairman (Sir George Russell) was appointed.

The long-delayed flotation occurred in two stages, in July 1994, when the holdings were reduced (the Bank's was now 6.5 per cent), and a second phase in June 1995, when the remaining stake was sold.[12] The Treasury made it clear at the outset that it expected the full profit from the sale to be paid as dividend by the Bank to the Treasury.[13] It looked as if it had been very successful: in the ten years before the sale, the company's value had risen fivefold.[14] 3i then continued as an independent company, with the status of investment trust bringing tax advantages when it came to liability for capital gains.

INDUSTRIAL FINANCE UNIT

The Bank in the 1970s played a large part in the Committee on Finance for Investment under the auspices of the National Economic Development Council. A paper on 'Budgetary and Monetary Policy 1974–75' started with the observation that in the 'postwar years we have not seen anything like the present liquidity crisis in industry'.[15] A stockbroker seconded to the Department of Industry, Anthony Gray, who was also the son-in-law of the Bank's former Governor Lord Cromer, suggested establishing an industrial finance unit (IFU) in the Bank. Against the background of major company problems – in Burmah Oil and British Leyland Motor Corporation – the proposed initiative looked more and more appealing. In 1975, a prominent accountant, Sir Henry Benson (later Lord Benson), was appointed as Adviser to the Governors, and the existing industry group within the Bank renamed as the Industrial Finance Unit. It was intended to 'obtain a more systematic flow of financial intelligence from industry and assist in identifying the financial problems of particular industries, and to establish a looser liaison on these matters with the financial community'. But it was also supposed to act as an 'active catalyst' in raising industrial funding.[16] In 1975, Equity Capital for Industry (ECI), whose capital was subscribed to by insurance companies, investment trusts and unit trusts, and a parallel Equity Capital Unit Trust, where the units could only be bought by pension funds, were created. Benson joined the board, and the new company announced that it would not fund lame ducks.[17] But in practice, ECI did rather little, and many of its investments proved quite problematical – or, in other words, lame ducks, such as the disastrous carpet company Bond Worth, or the textile equipment maker Stone Platt. Nevertheless, the Bank continued to believe in its industrial mission, and Bank representatives told the Wilson Committee (for Review of the Functioning of Financial Institutions) that 'there seems no option but to continue with this worthwhile task'.[18]

The IFU was engaged in some of these problematical companies, but it had a rather broader remit. It essentially coordinated bank lending in cases where there was a financial challenge. The first large case, British Dredging, in 1977, went badly as the banks chose a new chief executive who had a history of fraud. In 1978, the IFU organized the first of what was called a 'group arrangement' or workout. Spillers, a large flour milling and baking company, had borrowed from a number of British and foreign banks in what was termed 'multibanking'. It needed to be reorganized.

When the Bank structure was reshaped in 1980, industrial finance was shifted to a new Industrial Finance Division under David Walker. The reorganization coincided with the severe recession of the early 1980s, and the question of how to manage industrial borrowing became acute. Some bankers took a straightforwardly Darwinian approach to the problem, with Michael Wallis, who was in charge of problem loan cases at Midland, saying that the recession had 'sorted the men from the boys'. However, other bankers explained that 'the chairman is very conscious of the [worst recession for fifty years] and wouldn't want me to put a receiver in to any company that could survive, given reasonable support. But he doesn't expect me to be a buffoon and lose the bank's money.'[19] In 1983, British banks held £88 bn loans to industrial borrowers; in 1982, the big four had set aside a mere £363 m in bad debt provisions for domestic customers.

Walker's new division needed to employ new technologies in order to determine the extent of the new industrial problem. An online data service, Datastream, would be combed to identify potentially problematic companies by a set of criteria (profit before tax less than 15 per cent of current liabilities, current assets less than 1.5 times current liabilities, current liabilities greater that 80 per cent of total assets, and immediate assets less current liabilities less than half of operating costs). These were then assessed according to a rating procedure – known as a 'Z score' – developed by the American academic Edward Altman in 1968 as a way of predicting whether a company might go bankrupt over a two-year time frame.[20] In March 1979, the recently formed Company Appraisals Group identified some twenty companies as problematical, including Westland Aircraft and the Weir Group (engineering). The Bank then started to make enquiries with the banks and large shareholders of the companies at risk. As an example, after the CAG meeting on 19 November 1979, the Bank decided that Benson should speak to Lord Weir.

Interventions in companies that were problematical followed a standard procedure: the Bank corralled creditors into agreeing to a short-term standstill; that measure provided time for a set of proposals to be developed for a long-term restructuring of the organization and management as well as the finances of the company; and then additional funds might be provided by the existing lenders on a pro rata basis. Exactly the same general type of approach was applied after 1982, in coordination with the IMF and the Federal Reserve, in the case of over-indebted sovereign borrowers in the Latin American debt crisis. The exercise convinced many of the Bank officials involved that the fundamental problem of the British economy was poor, outdated, or incompetent management. Restructuring enterprise, in the setting of the severe recession of the 1980s, would provide a basis for a new economic dynamism.

The problem was not just one of bad industrial management. The Bank was also struck by how often British banks had very poor credit assessment policies and how in some cases they knew nothing about the total of the credit facilities used by one of their customers. In general, both in their knowledge of the business of their customers and in their flexibility in the face of problem cases, the foreign banks, in particular large American banks such as Citibank, appeared much more competent.

The restructuring of the Weir Group – a Glasgow-based engineering company – was arranged at a meeting chaired by Lord Benson on 12 March 1981, in which a large number of foreign banks (SBC, BNP, HSBC and Bank of Nova Scotia) participated as well as RBS and Lloyds.

Bank debt was converted into £10 m of preference shares, and a further £5 m shares were underwritten by the Finance Corporation for Industry and the Scottish Development Agency.[21] Part of the personal awkwardness involved asking Lord Weir, a Director of the Bank of England, to step aside as chairman. Or there was the reorganization of heavy steel forgings businesses from the nationalized British Steel Corporation and the privately owned Johnson and Firth Brown, as a new jointly owned company, Sheffield Forgemasters, in a new sort of joint venture between private and nationalized enterprises. The rubber manufacturing giant Dunlop was another company where the financial solution required asset sales and a new chairman.

Technology on its own was not enough to really solve the issues. Walker spent much of his time on the personalities who would clean out antiquated management in vulnerable companies: in finding new managers, but also in appointing able and active non-executive directors.

There were some conspicuous failures, the most striking of which were Stone Platt and Laker Airways. Stone Platt, a textile machinery producer, ran into problems with one of its banks in 1980 because of a breach of a covenant. A refinancing arrangement involved £10 m in new equity and £50 m banking facilities, but the trading performance continued to be poor, and in March 1982 the company went into receivership. The case provided a shock that emphasized the desirability of coordination. As the journalist Margaret Reid put it, 'It served to remind the banks of public sensitivities on such matters and, on a practical level, seems to have encouraged closer inter-bank and bank-shareholder consultations on difficult large problem cases.'[22]

Laker was a much higher-profile case, with more political involvement. In the summer of 1981, Midland Bank brought Laker to the attention of the Bank's Industrial Finance Division. From the late 1970s, Laker had started to operate a highly innovative no-frills airline service across the Atlantic at low prices, undercutting the established carriers. It looked like the perfect embodiment of a new entrepreneurial spirit in Britain, an incarnation of Thatcherite economics. But it rested on a financially fragile basis. It expanded its aircraft fleet with bank loans and supported these with loss guarantees from the manufacturers, McDonnell Douglas, General Electric and British Aerospace. When the dollar surged, fuel costs increased, and at the same time other airlines cut their fares: in consequence, it looked as if Laker required a financial restructuring. The initial discussions estimated that £5 m would be required, and that the company could be helped by a sale and leaseback agreement on its aircraft with Airbus. The junior

Treasury minister John Biffen set out the scheme and noted that 'the work of the Bank of England in bringing everyone together and facilitating communications' was 'extremely helpful'.[23] The denouement occurred at a meeting in 10 Downing Street, where Walker represented the Bank. Thatcher made no secret of her wish to rescue the company ('leave no avenue unexplored in the attempt to find a way of saving Laker Airways. The travelling public would be ill-served by the demise of Laker: there must be a suspicion that the big airlines, once Laker was eliminated from the scene, would raise their fares'). Alan Walters was in despair about this sort of interventionism. ('PM was considering putting in £5 million or so. NEVER it would be quite stupid.')[24] David Walker explained that the January traffic figures had fallen sharply, and that a much larger sum than £5 m was now needed. But above all there was the problem that if the government injected money, it might be hard to avoid the 'accusation' that the government was inducing others to give credit. So at the end, Thatcher sadly concluded that 'she was satisfied that Departments and the Bank of England had done everything they could reasonably do to assist Laker Airways; nothing more could be done'.[25] The company failed on 5 February 1982.

Walker tried to systematize the lessons derived from the workouts. In 1981, he produced a memorandum spelling out how

We have been depressed over the past twelve months in particular by the frequency at which, in cases that are brought to us, a first task of the Bank has been to assemble the reliable body of up to date information which, in well monitored lending, would be part of the basic material available to a bank. That it is commonly not available, and that the banks are frequently surprised or disturbed at what our quite simple but persistent probing brings to light e.g. the number of other banks, the nature of guarantees given in respect of overseas borrowing, security given to some banks but not others etc. reflects a general sloppiness that many bankers have said to us privately marks a substantial deterioration on the practice of a decade ago. [...] But there is I think now sufficient soreness among the clearers, particularly to some of the American banks, to be encouraging them to take a tougher line with corporate clients who have gone for multiple banking.[26]

The Bank thus took an initiative in developing guidelines for bank lending; and Walker also formulated guidelines to the banks involved in Bank-engineered support operations.

In some cases, new capital was required. That was provided mostly from the banks and large institutional investors, but a part came from FFI, whose role had been envisaged as a catalyst in mobilizing bank credit.[27]

There was some pushback against the new industrial activism from Dow, who sent a handwritten note to the Deputy Governor asking whether this was 'really a Bank function' and whether 'DAW [Walker] (though he loves it) best used in this way?' 'Walker is almost continuously in session seeing bankers about the affairs of ailing companies. Is this the best use of his time?'[28]

With the end of the recession, the number of cases fell after 1982. By the beginning of 1984, the Bank had involved itself in around 150 cases, one-third of which it classed as 'major involvements', involving meetings at the Bank. The total 'case list' of the Companies Appraisal Group was somewhat larger (around 250). One-fifth of the cases in which the Industrial Finance Division became involved had not been picked up by the Z score monitoring, including the large UK computer company ICL.[29] As the Bank explained it, 'Where possible, banks should be supportive of companies which face financial problems.' 'We can act as an honest broker and are regarded, I hope by all sides, as an independent and neutral mediator. We have the advantage of being detached from the immediate pressures of crisis which can sometimes lead to misunderstandings and strained relationships on a personal level.'[30] Or as Leigh-Pemberton put it:

In practice, the Approach is of most help in cases where a diverse group of banks has become involved in providing a range of facilities, linked to particular facets of a company's business, rather than to situations in which a long-term relationship has been established with one bank, which is close to a company and which can normally be expected to be in possession of the information required to reach a proper commercial judgment of the situation.[31]

This approach became the basis of the actions of the Bank in the next sustained recession, in the early 1990s.

PORTALS

The Bank also had a direct stake in some companies. In 1949, it bought 60,000 shares from the estate of a former director of Portals, and in 1950 extended its holding. Portals was a maker of paper suitable for printing bank notes, and its paper mill at Laverstoke in Hampshire had supplied the Bank since 1724; back in 1815, the Bank's Committee of Treasury had cautioned the partners of Portals 'not in future to make any other Note paper than for the Bank of England'. In 1984, the Treasury noted that the Bank's stake in Portals made 'no sense in the light of the Government's policy on privatisation', and in particular noted that Portals had become a broader conglomerate that now did much more than simply produce paper for Bank of England notes, so that the Bank had 'a 29 percent interest in every Permutit water softener that is sold'; but the final embarrassment came from Portals' political contributions: 'The fact that Portals are naïve enough to make donations to the Conservative Party whilst having the Bank as such a major shareholder only confirms my view that the shares should be sold.' And in addition, the Bank had 'carpeted' Rothschilds, the merchant bank chiefly involved in the government's privatization programme, for drawing the attention of the Portals shareholding to the Financial Secretary of the Treasury.[32] The Bank pushed back energetically, arguing that it depended on Portals as the only supplier of high-quality banknote paper in the UK, and that the stake allowed the Bank to get a better price on banknotes, and also helped Portals do a better business in overseas markets. In 1986, it resisted an approach from De La Rue to buy Portals from the Bank, on the grounds that that would not be the end and 'sooner or later they are likely to turn their attacks on our note-printing business'.[33] The Bank sold the holding only in 1989.[34] De La Rue indeed did also secure, eventually, the printing contract at the Bank's own printing operation at Debden.

THE CHANNEL TUNNEL

The most high-profile engagement of the Bank in reorganizing business corporations was also largely a matter of personalities, arising out of the chance that Leigh-Pemberton and Walker had acquired the reputation as the public servants who had the best nose for managerial talent. In 1986, the British and French governments signed a treaty establishing the Channel Tunnel project as a purely privately financed project, with government financing prohibited. The tunnel would be owned and operated by Eurotunnel plc and Eurotunnel SA; and built by a consortium of builders and banks, Trans Manche Link (TML). Originally, the cost of the project was estimated at £4.8 bn (including an inflation allowance). The financing was to come from three sources, 'Equity 1' from the original shareholders, 'Equity 2' from financial institutions and, finally, 'Equity 3', a public share offer. The project raised obvious coordination problems: between the contractors and the financiers, and within the group of 210 financial institutions in the syndicate. The problems started with 'Equity 2', which was first delayed, and then, when supposedly nearly complete in October 1986, seriously undersubscribed. The response of Lord Pennock, the joint chairman of Eurotunnel, was to go to the Cabinet Secretary, Sir

Robert Armstrong, with the message that only £54 m of the UK share of £75 m was in place, and suggesting that the Prime Minister should intervene.

Armstrong thought the Governor of the Bank was a more appropriate figure, and David Walker set to work energetically raising more money. The Bank described assistance as 'another illustration of the way in which the Bank is called upon as a last resort'.[35] Walker quickly discovered that the existing commitments were not really firm, and quickly came to the conclusion that Morgan Grenfell had been very ineffective. He also thought – characteristically – that the management of Eurotunnel was weak and that a new chairman was needed. By 29 October, Walker could tell the Books meeting at the Bank that the UK financing was complete and had been accomplished 'without the need for excessively strong arm tactics'.[36] Walker's original suggestion for the chairmanship, the chairman of one of the large tunnel contractors, Trafalgar House, Sir Nigel Broackes, turned out to be flawed: there was an obvious conflict of interest, and Broackes immediately demanded a guaranteed 5 per cent share for his company in the work; and in addition, Broackes seemed to be heavily under the influence of alcohol when he discussed the question with Leigh-Pemberton and Walker. Walker then went through a number of alternative candidates, and in the end selected Alastair Morton, whom he had already used in the financial reconstruction of Massey Ferguson in 1982. Morton had been managing director of the British National Oil Corporation 1976–1980, and then chief executive of Guinness Peat Group from 1982. He was a dynamic and highly effective executive, but was also often seen as an abrasive and confrontational personality. The *Economist* obituary described him as: 'Towering and irascible, with piercing blue eyes and, at one time, a bandit's beard, he should not have been dealing with British civil servants and City types at all. He was really a voortrekker, like his South African forebears on his mother's side.' He defied the 'sullen hopelessness' of the British establishment 'as an optimist and, in his secret heart, a socialist'.[37] At the same time, as it were as a counterweight to Morton, Sir Kit McMahon was appointed to the board.

The public share offer was also delayed, with the consequence that it seemed to compete with a large privatization tranche of BP; it too took place in the aftermath of the October 1987 stock market crash. Although half a million individuals and institutions had registered an interest, only 112,000 applied for shares, and the issue was 20 per cent undersubscribed.[38]

The difficulties of the project were clearly not over, as it suffered – like almost every large-scale construction and investment endeavour – from cost overruns that set the construction consortium against Eurotunnel. Late in 1989, Leigh-Pemberton warned Chancellor John Major that there was a risk that the equity might be lost, the banks might foreclose and the project might come to a halt.[39] In 1990, the banks agreed to give a waiver if TML accepted some reduction of its claims, but TML as part of a deal pressed for a new chief executive of Eurotunnel, who would leave Morton to concentrate on his functions as chairman. McMahon supported this position. At this point, Leigh-Pemberton intervened, and held a long discussion with Morton.[40]

On 16 February 1990, Leigh-Pemberton chaired the meeting of Eurotunnel, TML and the banks. The meeting was very raucous; at one point as participants spoke over each other, Leigh-Pemberton said 'sssshhhh'. Morton engaged in a strong defence of his position, but in the end agreed to stand down as chairman, while continuing as chief executive and deputy chairman.

The Bank continued to be involved, first in pressing Lloyds Bank to come in to raise more equity – as this was a precondition for bringing in Japanese money. Then in August 1990 Margaret Thatcher wrote to Japanese Prime Minister Toshiki Kaifu, and Eddie George, as Deputy Governor, to the Governor of the Bank of Japan, enclosing the Thatcher letter and asking the Bank of Japan to press the Japanese banks. To the Japanese banks, this high-level engagement looked like an implicit guarantee of the British government.

Leigh-Pemberton had a high level of personal commitment to the project, perhaps heightened by his position as Lord Lieutenant of Kent. He repeatedly complained to Major about the 'tiresome and difficult' negotiations, but at the same time thought that it would be a 'disgrace' if the City failed on financing. There was a great deal of brinkmanship. Pendarell (Pen) Kent, who had taken over David Walker's functions as the driver of the process, spoke of a 'serious risk of an accident because those playing brinkmanship miscalculate how near they are to the edge'. The problem was that the agent banks wanted to avoid building the 'unquenchable expectation that they would always stump up', and in consequence they threatened to pull out their financing.[41] The Bank of England had become central to the effective financial management of the vast Chunnel construction project.

THE BANK AND INDUSTRY

3i looked as if it was a dynamic success. But elsewhere there were still lame ducks – an issue that was closely related to the old question of finance for industrial development. In 1990, at the start of a new recession, Pen Kent presided over a revival of the Walker method, which now became known as of the 'London approach' to banking coordination. As Leigh-Pemberton explained it, three principles were essential:

The first is that, when difficulties arise, a lending standstill should be considered so that a proper analysis can be made of whether continuing support – and particularly additional financing – is justifiable. Secondly, the fullest possible information should be gathered to support that analysis and the subsequent judgement. And thirdly, there is a very important role for the lead bank. Whatever its size or home base, the lead bank needs to ensure that all interested bank creditors are informed of the company's position at the earliest possible stage, and are kept informed. This is of help to all creditors, and particularly the smaller banks. No one should be – or feel – disadvantaged through lack of information.[42]

The fifty new cases included Nissan UK, hit by the recession as well as tax investigation; the Vestey Group, a shipping, insurance, retail, property and food group with a big exposure to property and £450 m in debts that needed restructuring, and which was turned round by Terry Robinson, a former Lonrho director; as well as Maxwell Communications, left with £1.3 bn of bank debt after Robert Maxwell's suicide and which crumbled as Swiss Bank Corporation demanded repayment. These were all cases of spectacularly poor, and in some cases criminal, management.

Kent, looking back on the experience of the London approach, suggested that the best way of eliminating the problems that had led to the Bank's intervention and crisis management was a return to more old-fashioned banking, as it were an undoing of the go-go years that followed 1986. He wanted, as the 'most important and key step', ' a return to some kind of relationship banking' in order to make for 'a major improvement in information flows and the use that is made of them'.[43] The problem was that that was not going to happen. In effect, what had been characterized as 'Walkerism' was failing as the British economy was becoming more complex, more dynamic and more financialized. All that was left was 'Georgism', ensuring that markets worked efficiently and securely and that a proper combination of monetary policy and supervision delivered stability.

10

Great Leap in the Dark

The Bank, the Delors Committee and the Euro

Robin Leigh-Pemberton was always instinctively pro-European as well as pro-establishment. His continental orientation prepared the ground for another altercation between the Governor of the Bank of England and the Conservative Prime Minister. His stance was not simply, however, the reflection of his personal views. The new policy orientation after 1985 – and the world environment – had brought him into the international central banking community that some participants liked to term the 'brotherhood'. The discussions on a common European currency that developed after 1988 were the natural outcome of a new approach that developed through dialogue in that brotherhood.

Europe's modern monetary order was the outcome of global debates about currency disorder in the mid-1980s. In practice, nothing came of a global plan for nearly fixed exchange rates proposed by Edouard Balladur, the French finance minister, but then he formulated a much tighter European scheme. When German foreign minister Hans Dietrich Genscher appeared sympathetic, and drew up his own plan (with a significant input from the Bundesbank), the president of the European Commission, Jacques Delors, proposed asking Europe's central bankers to prepare a timetable and a plan for currency union. The result was a report, presented in April 1989, when no one in Bonn or Paris was thinking about any possibility of a profound geopolitical transformation of Europe, that laid the basis of the Maastricht Treaty negotiated in 1991.

In May 1988, the chairman of the EC Monetary Committee, Geoffrey Littler (UK Treasury), concluded his discussion of a report to be presented to the EC ministers with the observation that the Exchange Rate Mechanism (ERM) worked well, that there had already been some modest improvement in coordination procedures, but that there was a substantial problem with the ultimate objective of monetary union. 'The question was raised as to how far towards these goals progress might be made without the prior or parallel assumption of a willingness on the part of Member States to submerge their fiscal and political autonomy.' The report had also made clear the centrality of the central banks to any reform discussion in recognizing 'that the EMS was based on an agreement between central banks and that changes to it were the preserve of the Governors'.[1]

At the Hanover meeting of the European Council (27–28 June 1988), the European leaders not only agreed to set up a committee of wise men, but also recommended that Delors himself would chair the committee. Delors' chairmanship came as the result of Chancellor Helmut Kohl's personal insistence, and infuriated the British government. Nigel Lawson later referred to the 'disaster of having Jacques Delors as the committee's chairman, or even as one of its members', since the presence of the Commission President would carry an authority in the EC for the committee's eventual report which would not exist if the report had simply come from the technocratic Committee of Governors.[2] Bank of England officials also minuted their alarm. Nevertheless, Margaret Thatcher consented in the belief that the powerful presence of Bundesbank President Karl Otto Pöhl would mean that the committee would not reach any dangerous conclusion on European monetary integration.

The members of the committee were the central bank governors, acting in a personal capacity, rather than as representatives of their institutions, and they would not be accompanied by any staff who might restrain them. For both the Banque de France and the Bundesbank, this was an important decision, in that the governors were highly forceful personalities who did not necessarily represent the institutional consensus of the bodies over which they presided. There were also three independent experts, the general manager of the BIS, Alexandre Lamfalussy, the Danish economics professor Niels Thygesen, and the Spanish economist and former finance minister Miguel Boyer. Delors also insisted on including as a fourth external member the EC Commissioner in charge of agricultural policy, Frans Andriessen.

Leigh-Pemberton saw the Prime Minister shortly after his nomination to the Delors Committee. She clearly expressed her scepticism of the enterprise, and her sense of how Leigh-Pemberton should negotiate. But, as the Bank's record of that initial discussion reveals, he never thought that he could avoid discussion of a single currency and a central bank:

The terms of reference of the Delors Committee quite deliberately make no mention of a central bank or a single currency. Consequently, these are not topics on which the Committee should feel obliged to give a verdict. Their purpose is to see 'whether and to what extent there are practical steps that can be taken towards monetary union'. If in doing so they have to consider possible institutional structures so be it – but that is not their objective. [The Governor accepts all this but foresees great difficulties in maintaining such a position in the Committee!]

It is entirely premature to talk about a single currency or a central bank when there are still capital restrictions as between Member States. It may be that after 1990 it will be possible to study the position again. [The Governor judged this to mean that she would see the possibility of further steps being taken after 1990 once capital restrictions have been removed and the consequences of their removal have been properly assessed.]

Thatcher privately warned the Governor to be extremely careful of Delors, whom she described as a 'Jekyll and Hyde' character. 'He will appear to be very co-operative at the meetings and agree to confine the discussions to pragmatic steps – but will then make public speeches or work in the background to achieve quite a different objective.' And finally she added: 'Don't forget Delors is a socialist.'[3]

The Prime Minister said that she had only agreed to appoint the four wise men on the basis that two of them, she was assured by Kohl, were 'on our side'. She seemed to think that the two were Thygesen and Andriessen, and to regard Lamfalussy and Boyer as 'visionaries' – the Governor thought (correctly) 'this was probably wrong and that Lamfalussy and Thygesen should change round!'[4] On the other hand, from the beginning he felt sure that Karl Otto Pöhl was a loyal ally who would support what was thought of as the British position, as did Thatcher, who advised him that he might sign anything that Karl Otto Pöhl agreed to. Pöhl had been outraged by Delors' and Kohl's initiative at the Hanover Council meeting, and felt that he had been deliberately left out of the policy loop. In July 1988, Pöhl had called Leigh-Pemberton to say 'how unhappy he was about the formation of the Committee and the fact that Delors was Chairman'. In particular, Delors' wish to appoint the federalist Italian economist Tomaso Padoa-Schioppa (along with the German BIS official Gunter Baer) as one of the rapporteurs, who would presumably have a decisive role in the formulation of the report, boded ill from Pöhl's point of view: it meant 'that the report would immediately get a strong bias in the wrong direction'.[5]

Once the Delors Committee had been set up, an interdepartmental group composed largely of Treasury and Bank of England officials was set up to monitor progress and detail the UK's approach to EMS issues.[6] The Treasury wanted to make sure that it was kept well informed about the state of the negotiations. Lawson formulated a distinct sabotage plan: 'It was clear to us, too, that Robin's tactics should be to assemble the widest possible opposition within the Committee both to any early treaty amendment required to achieve the full EMU objective espoused by Delors, and to anything that smacked of a recommendation to take any particular course of action.' But he was frustrated, he believed, largely because of the inconstancy of Pöhl, who 'proved a broken reed [who ...] made a number of sceptical interventions in the Committee's deliberations, but he never really engaged himself'.[7] At a lunch in September 1988, just before the first meeting of the committee, Lawson simply recommended that Leigh-Pemberton should 'adopt a Japanese stance' (presumably smiling politely but not agreeing to anything). Leigh-Pemberton replied, with a rather different spin, that he had 'no intention' of adopting a high profile, 'but would wish to make my contribution to keeping the Committee on the rails'.[8]

Within the Bank, a smaller group of officials, in particular John Arrowsmith and Lionel Price, from the international division of the Bank, worked extensively on preparing meetings and, in the later stages of the Committee's work, on drafting. The only other native English speaker on the Committee apart from Leigh-Pemberton was the Irish central bank governor, Maurice Doyle, and for the most part central bank officials then were less fluent in English than they are in the twenty-first century: so Leigh-Pemberton and the Bank had a great advantage. But the group preparing the Committee work within the Bank had little interest in keeping the Treasury briefed, and so in practice they worked very much on their own. Anthony Loehnis, Executive Director at the Bank and head of the International Division, complained that the Treasury's view was 'over-influenced, I think, by fear of the Prime Minister's dislike of a common currency, a European Central Bank or (horror of horrors) a United States of Europe'. And Leigh-Pemberton doled out simple reassurances: after the first meeting of the Committee, he wrote to Chancellor of the Exchequer Nigel Lawson that all was going well and that 'the pragmatists were well to the fore and seemingly in a strong majority; the idealists relatively muted; and Delors himself neutral'.[9] In February 1989, he wrote to Margaret Thatcher, after a meeting with the Prime Minister as well as Lawson and Sir Geoffrey Howe, that 'difficult as it may appear, I shall do my utmost to achieve the outcome that we all want'. He also wanted to keep the Prime Minister as quiet as possible, and added: 'From my own personal viewpoint it is extremely important that the members of the Committee should not know that you have seen drafts of our report, or that you have heard detailed accounts of the Committee's proceedings.'[10]

There were in all seven meetings of the Delors Committee, 13 September 1988, 10 October 1988, 8 November 1988, 13 December 1988, 10 January 1989, 14 March 1989 and 12–13 April 1989, amounting to some sixty-five hours of debate and discussion, as well as numerous informal bilateral meetings.

Leigh-Pemberton's willingness to act unilaterally increased because of his growing doubts about the Prime Minister's position. In September 1988, his private secretary noted:

(i) She is apparently giving a major speech shortly in Bruges, though for security reasons this has not yet been given publicity. At present she has it in mind to use the occasion to try to lead the Community away from closer integration towards being a 'loose confederacy'.

(ii) She is apparently asking questions in No. 10 about the possibility of our moving from full membership of the Community to an 'associated' membership.

The Governor wrote in the margin, in red ink, an exclamation mark and the comment 'Terrifying'.[11] When Thatcher gave her speech at the Bruges Collège d'Europe, on 20 September 1988, it indeed became the defining statement of British resistance to Brussels centralization:

It is ironic that just when those countries such as the Soviet Union, which have tried to run everything from the centre, are learning that success depends on dispersing power and decisions away from the centre, there are some in the Community who seem to want to move in the opposite direction. We have not successfully rolled back the frontiers of the state in Britain, only to see them re-imposed at a European level with a European super-state exercising a new dominance from Brussels.

On the issue of monetary unification, she actually said rather little, merely:

The key issue is not whether there should be a European Central Bank. The immediate and practical requirements are:
- to implement the Community's commitment to free movement of capital – in Britain, we have it;
- and to the abolition through the Community of exchange controls – in Britain, we abolished them in 1979;
- to establish a genuinely free market in financial services in banking, insurance, investment;
- and to make greater use of the ECU [the basket currency, European Currency Unit].[12]

The Delors Committee had been given a clear brief: not to discuss the desirability of monetary union, but rather to focus on the institutional question of how it might be achieved. That might indeed involve, as Thatcher thought, a greater role for the synthetic basket currency European Currency Unit (ECU). The report was to be crafted as a technical exploration of what was possible, and not as a political manifesto on integration. In fact, some members expressed their doubts about the extent of the political commitment of their governments to monetary union. As Maurice Doyle put it, no one in Europe believed the European Council when it said it wanted Economic and Monetary Union.[13] As a result, even sceptics in the committee could believe they were achieving their goals by just spelling out precisely what monetary union would involve (and thus precisely showing how difficult it would be).

When Robin Leigh-Pemberton started his work as a member of the Delors Committee, he thus had no idea that it would produce a report that would serve as a blueprint for European monetary union. The issues concerned were repeatedly and extensively discussed at the Bank. Eddie George warned that the Bundesbank in particular was 'under strong political pressure, and it was conceivable that they could respond by accepting a "great leap in the dark"', to which the Governor replied that 'this was very alarming, as he was relying on Pöhl's support' in the committee.[14] Lawson by contrast realized at an early stage the 'fundamental weakness' of the UK's position:

> He said that there was a fundamental weakness in the UK's position, namely that we had committed ourselves to the ultimate goal of economic and monetary union (and he said he wondered whether the Prime Minister fully realised what she had done in this respect) and it was therefore very arguable for Delors to press for the means as well as for the end.[15]

At the first meeting of the Committee in September, Leigh-Pemberton had begun the discussion with a note of caution: 'I don't say that I am against monetary integration, I am arguing about forcing the pace of it.' In November, Leigh-Pemberton assured Bank officials that on the Delors Committee there was 'a solid majority for pragmatism, and that Pöhl during the meeting had made it clear that he could not associate himself with any prescriptive report: all he would be prepared to do would be to continue to discuss hypothetical situations'.[16] And at the end of the year, the Deputy Governor, Sir George Blunden, told Treasury officials that 'it was possible, perhaps even probable, that working with Pöhl and the Danish governor Erik Hoffmeyer and others the Governor could ensure that an acceptable report will emerge'.[17]

But in fact, once the first draft or skeleton report emerged at the 2 December 1988 meeting of the committee, all the alarm bells rang at the Treasury. Baer and Padoa-Schioppa circulated a document in which they laid out possible mechanisms through which the ECU could evolve into a common currency. One was simply to extend the private use and market acceptance of the private ECU. But there was a more dramatic and radical path: 'a second option would be to alter the present arrangements and to introduce the ECU as an additional currency, which would no longer represent a weighted average of Community currencies, but would be independently defined, have fixed but adjustable exchange rates vis-à-vis national currencies and be managed under the responsibility of the European system of central banks.' Lawson called the skeleton document 'an appalling document': 'It was clearly wholly unacceptable. It handed over to the Community the conduct of monetary policy, budgetary policy, and tax policy, and required a whole new Treaty. But it had to be said that if the Community was really serious about EMU, then much of what was proposed was perfectly logical.' Lawson also saw that Pöhl could be won over by the enthusiasts of a single European money by a promise to make the new central bank 'an image of the Bundesbank'.[18]

The tensions between Governor and Chancellor continued in January.

The Chancellor said he had been disturbed to read the Governor's account of the latest Delors Group meeting. He thought the compromise which had been reached went significantly too far, and well beyond what the Prime Minister's meeting had agreed would be acceptable. That applied in particular to the commitment to draft a new Treaty, even if the timetable was unspecified.

The Governor said that the remit agreed at the Prime Minister's meeting had proved impossible to meet: Poehl had accepted the compromise on a Treaty amendment, so that the option of sticking with Poehl and avoiding a Treaty amendment had disappeared. If he refused to agree to a commitment to start work on a treaty, there was a danger that de la Rosiere would resurrect pressure for immediate institutional change. The Chancellor said it would be well worth seeing if anything could be done to persuade Poehl to change his line.[19]

It was by this stage clear that Pöhl could not really be what Thatcher and Lawson had hoped for, the bulwark against a positive recommendation on monetary union, and that he was 'drifting away' from a position sympathetic to the UK government. Thatcher's private secretary phoned the Governor's private secretary to try to adjust Leigh-Pemberton's bargaining strategy: 'The PM's immediate reaction, as you might guess, was that the Governor faced no dilemma at all, and if the position was indeed as the Chancellor had outlined it, then the Governor's plain duty was to sign a minority report.'[20]

Some of the stormiest clashes were reserved for the penultimate round of discussions, when a full draft report was discussed, on 14 March 1989. This was the moment when many observers believed that the discussion was 'almost derailed'.[21] Pöhl came with thirty pages of quite radical amendments. As a consequence of the German stance, Hoffmeyer stated that he could not sign the report as currently drafted. The Banque de France reported that Pöhl was setting in doubt 'in a radical style all the main points of agreement of the six previous meetings'.[22] The Bank of England recorded that Pöhl would not accept the ECU as a future currency, was not prepared to recommend a treaty change and would not agree to a central bank.[23]

At the beginning of April, Leigh-Pemberton had an indication of the Prime Minister's thinking. Sir Peter Middleton had spent five hours with her at Chequers and – according to the notes of a subsequent conversation in which he relayed the discussion to the Governor – tried to convince her that it was not worth making a fuss: 'The report would attract a lot of attention on publication but that she need not react violently to it and that the publication itself would be followed by a long lull before the European Council starts debating what should be done about it.'[24]

The next round of meetings, on 11–12 April 1989, was supposed to be the penultimate meeting, but in fact the Committee's life was curtailed by the leaking of central points of the new draft report to the *Financial Times*. The publicity generated a fear of increasing political pressure, in particular from Lawson and Margaret Thatcher, with the result that the members of the Committee were reluctant to leave room for another series of discussions. And in one decisive regard, the new draft seemed to meet one of the major thrusts of Pöhl's demands, by including 'price stability' as the major objective of the new central banking system. Pöhl was nevertheless still assertive and truculent:

Mr. Chairman, I really don't know what the . . . is here in this group, I really can't understand that because, firstly, I am not prepared to accept the argument that the external world is looking at us, that they expect us to give a signal and that we are losing credibility if we don't give the signal. We are not politicians, who are we, as Robin rightly said? We are not politicians who have to give signals and we are not losing our credibility. We are losing our credibility if we make proposals which are completely unrealistic.

It was actually Leigh-Pemberton who ended the discussion and produced the definitive argument against deferring the final text for a new meeting and a new round of discussions.

If I show this damned thing to the Treasury they're going to be mad. Now I'm going to be under strong pressure to show this paper to the world. They're going to clamp down on me because of all this independence stuff. If they know that I have a week to reflect, they're going to ask me to make amendments and I'm going to be dead . . . I'm protecting myself.[25]

He felt that he needed to push on with the timetable of what would unexpectedly prove to be the last meeting of the Committee. Thus, in the rush of that final meeting, in a peculiar twist of historical irony, Leigh-Pemberton, and the fear of Margaret Thatcher's rage, made the Delors report happen, and in fact created the euro.

In the final report, there was a clearly laid-out path to monetary union, defined as 'a currency area in which policies are managed jointly with a view to attaining common macroeconomic objectives'. But the Committee also added the rider:

> The adoption of a single currency, while not strictly necessary for the creation of a monetary union, might be seen for economic as well as psychological and political reasons as a natural and desirable further development of the monetary union. A single currency would clearly demonstrate the irreversibility of the move to monetary union, considerably facilitate the monetary management of the Community and avoid the transactions costs of converting currencies.[26]

At the Madrid summit of 26/27 June 1989, the heads of government accepted the Delors report as 'a sound basis for future work'. In particular, Madrid accepted the Delors follow-up procedures (paragraphs 64–66), which entrusted more work to the ECOFIN Council as well as to the EC Committee of Central Bank Governors, the Monetary Committee and the EC Commission, to implement the First Stage, as well as to provide suggestions to serve as the basis for a revised treaty at an intergovernmental conference. Madrid thus really made the implications of the Delors Report clear, explicit, and political.

Margaret Thatcher was furious, feeling that she had been out-manoeuvred by Delors and betrayed by Robin Leigh-Pemberton, whom she never forgave. The British Chancellor of the Exchequer, Nigel Lawson, had consistently argued that Stage One, which envisaged a strengthening of existing cooperative arrangements in the EMS, was desirable but that there was no need for a new Treaty or for further 'Stages' that would move on with creating the institutions of monetary union. But Thatcher could not really disagree either with anything in the first stage, which had emerged as a result of the efforts of Pöhl but also especially of Leigh-Pemberton in the 'softest' possible form. She merely emphasized that 'there is nothing automatic about going beyond stage one'.[27] Britain remained rather outside the process, even after the UK joined the EMS ERM in October 1990. Indeed in November, the Bank of England issued a statement for the other European central banks: 'The Governor of the Bank of England records that the UK authorities do not accept the case for a single currency and monetary policy. He has nevertheless participated fully in the discussions of the Governors' Committee on this draft statute.'[28]

In London, Leigh-Pemberton obviously had a great deal of explaining to do:

> The Governor said that he would like to discuss the question at some point because it was important to prevent divergences of view appearing between the Bank and the Government. He had signed the Delors Report on the basis that Stages 2 and 3 were the necessary means to achieving monetary union as defined in the Werner Report. But he had made plain all along that he considered it would be premature to speculate on what should happen beyond Stage 1 before a lot more progress has been made in developing the single market. He had a great sympathy with the proposal for 'soft union' – i.e. Delors without final locking of exchange rates – that had been put forward by Poehl. Perhaps our support for this would carry more weight if we were inside the ERM. His feeling was that he might just live to see monetary union in Europe but it was quite pointless to start planning it now.[29]

At the beginning, it looked as if the outcome would be minimal. In November 1989, a meeting of the DGC in which scenarios for Europe were discussed listened to Eddie George reflect on how 'the most plausible scenario over the next five years was that we would not see the introduction of a European central bank or of a common European currency'.[30] But a few days later, the Berlin Wall came down, and European diplomacy was transformed. Thatcher now was desperate to derail the drive to monetary union, and looked around quite wildly for plausible alternatives, including a restoration of the gold standard. A Bank of England report discussed the fallout from Delors, and the reaction in the Treasury and in Downing Street:

> the Prime Minister was quite 'distressed' by a Treasury paper on EMU, which she regarded as disingenuous, and [Barry] Potter [the Prime Minister's Private Secretary] thought probably fairly so. The paper had opened by saying that the UK did not want Stage 3 and that that was our position but the following fifty paragraphs or so had gone on to say that we should nevertheless negotiate, impliedly on Stage 3. The Prime Minister had asked whether this would be negotiating in bad faith.
>
> Two developments flowed from this. First, the Treasury is working on a second paper. Secondly, the Prime Minister decided to go and look at some old papers on a possible commodity standard. Downing Street officials had initially thought this might be the Odling-Smee work done last autumn (when Chancellor Lawson commissioned a huge paper which led to the competing currencies idea), but in fact the source was, Barry said, 'from over the water', i.e. Walters. There had since

been contact with Walters (who remained unnamed, but it was quite clear) on this idea and further work was being done on a possible commodity-based standard. Barry confirmed that this would go wider than the EC and be for industrialised nations, or at least North America.

The idea had, as we know, most recently arisen in the context of Greenspan's trip, when Greenspan had explained that the gold standard approach was a genuine alternative to free floating, and had said that the ERM had come to function rather like a quasi gold standard.

Also, when the Prime Minister had pursued the idea with Greenspan, Greenspan had given an ever so slightly patronizing smile, and Potter thought the Prime Minister 'recognised' that this meant the gold standard idea could not be brought off.[31]

The Bank also sought to develop its own foreign policy. In May 1989, the former British ambassador in Brussels Sir Peter Petrie was appointed at the Bank as Adviser on European Issues and Developments. The concrete aftermath of the Delors report was a two-pronged approach, with a frantic search for realistic policy alternatives, but also a need to engage more positively in a discussion of the EMS and ERM as a way of holding up the bigger theme of monetary union.

The Treasury produced a scheme for a hard ECU, fundamentally as a stalling device that would complicate and then hold up the monetary union discussions. Bank officials contributed some ideas to the Treasury alternative, but remained fundamentally unconvinced that this was a truly viable course. In a redesigned ECU, there should be no basket currency, and no reliance on one national currency, but rather a link to the most stable currency at the time. In case of realignments, the hard ECU would thus never be devalued against any participating currency.[32] The idea of the hard ECU had originated in 1989 from the private-sector City European Committee chaired by Michael Butler, first as a brainchild of a Midland Montagu economist, Paul Richards, but was then taken up in the immediate aftermath of the Delors Committee by the UK Treasury as a way of modifying Delors so as to get a common currency without any political appendages, with no fiscal dimension, no regional dimension and, above all, no central bank. The concept was first officially articulated in June 1990, when Leigh-Pemberton circulated it also to his European colleagues with the request that 'I should like to discuss these [ideas] with you at our next meeting of the EC Governors' Committee': that demand was not met. At that time, Leigh-Pemberton advertised the scheme's fundamental attraction as bringing 'collective counter-inflationary pressure to bear throughout the Community, while leaving the ultimate responsibility for national monetary policy decisions in national hands'.[33] That looked entirely compatible with the principles of Thatcher's Bruges speech. Bank of England officials, notably Andrew Crockett, who had replaced Loehnis as the Executive Director responsible for the International Division, were then charged with trying to sell the hard ECU to other central banks, but it was not an endeavour for which they could really muster much enthusiasm.[34] The discussion of the hard ECU in fact provided a prelude to what amounted to a decade-long holding operation, over the course of which suspicions of European monetary projects gradually increased.

Pöhl set out a rather nuanced position in post-Delors discussions with British ministers. He told Lawson's successor as Chancellor, John Major, that he had been 'always' personally opposed to proceeding rapidly to monetary union, and that the push had been a political one with France trying to reduce the weight of the Bundesbank in monetary policy. He also thought, correctly, that the Delors framework was flawed and potentially dangerous because the enforcement mechanism on sustaining convergence was inadequate: 'Under the Delors route a profligate government would be constrained only by loss of competitiveness and high unemployment.'[35] But when he spoke to the Prime Minister, the advice sounded different. On 8 November 1990, Karl Otto Pöhl met Thatcher for the last time. He reported the conversation afterwards to Leigh-Pemberton, and claimed that he had 'tried to persuade the Prime Minister to accept the principle of a single currency and a single Central Bank'. But 'she refused adamantly to countenance such a development'. Nevertheless, Pöhl recorded that he 'remained very impressed by her intelligence and her grasp of economic affairs'.[36] It was a tense political moment. At the beginning of the month, Geoffrey Howe had resigned as Foreign Secretary, and on 13 November he gave a devastating resignation speech in the House of Commons, in which he reviewed the government's European policy and the Prime Minister's interventions: 'It is rather like sending your opening batsmen to the crease only for them to find the moment that the first balls are bowled that their bats have been broken before the game by the team captain.' Soon after, a leadership challenge forced Thatcher herself to resign. But the problems, political and economic, posed by monetary relations with Europe remained corrosive to effective policy-making.

11

The Spine Theory and Its Collapse

The ERM and the 1990s Recession

The short-lived British membership of the European Monetary System's (EMS) Exchange Rate Mechanism (ERM) provided the final twist, or perhaps the *reductio ad absurdum*, of the saga of British exchange rate policy. The UK joined as a recession was developing – one that was not as deep as that of the early 1980s, but which lasted as long, and where the initial recovery was very weak and political anxieties very high. The British ERM experience occurred at a tense moment on the international stage, with shocks emanating from the combination of tight monetary and loose fiscal policy in Germany after German unification in 1990, as well as from the Iraqi invasion of Kuwait in 1990 and the following Gulf War, and from the disintegration of the Soviet Union over 1990–1991. The Kuwait war almost doubled the oil price, and affected sterling as the UK unlike the other large European economies was a net oil exporter. UK membership also (perhaps coincidentally) marked the beginning of a convergence in major industrial countries on a low-inflation norm. In that sense, the longer-term aftermath of what quite soon looked like a disastrous miscalculation might be seen in retrospect as beneficial for the UK.

The high-level political drive to European integration came as a consequence of an economic, a political and an intellectual shift. Economically, it took place in the wake of currency instability and the failure of the Louvre experiment in international coordination. The political atmosphere was transformed in the wake of the end of the Cold War and the aftermath of the shock of German unification. The new European discussion also converged with a turn in academic economics. Thomas Sargent's seminal work on rational expectations and inflation gave a great deal of emphasis to an exchange rate target as heralding a commitment to a new policy regime: 'It is arguable that pegging to a foreign currency is a policy that is relatively easier to support and make credible by concrete

actions, since it is possible to hook the domestic country's price expectations virtually instantaneously onto the presumably exogenous price
expectations process in the foreign country.'[1] When that obvious mechanism proved problematic in the early 1990s, there was a need to rethink the
process by which credibility was established, and to move further in the
direction of a hard currency fix. Monetary union in Europe was one answer
to a world that seemed to be looking for 'corner solutions', either free-
floating currencies or complete and immutable currency rigidity.

THE DEBATE ABOUT THE ERM

British entry into the ERM had long been opposed by the British Prime
Minister, Margaret Thatcher, who had argued that: 'You can either target
the money supply or the exchange rate, but not both [. . .] The only effective
way to control inflation is by using interest rates to control the money
supply. If, on the contrary, you set interest rates in order to stick to
a particular exchange rate, you are steering by a different and potentially
more wayward star [. . .] the result of plotting a course by this particular
star is that you steer straight on to the reefs.'[2] By contrast Bank of England
Governor Robin Leigh-Pemberton had made his opinion clear that ERM
membership was a good way of establishing an external anchor to bring
down persistently high British inflation levels. He had long argued this
case, at first in the Bank, but then in international settings such as meetings
of the EC Committee of Governors, and also in public. In a speech in 1989,
he stated: 'ERM member-countries have dramatically improved their inflation performance in recent years [. . .] the inflation gap with Germany has
been much reduced in Italy and virtually eliminated in France.'[3]

And it was international pressure that Leigh-Pemberton used to push
government policy – but from the other side of the Atlantic. The critical
voice was Alan Greenspan, the world's most powerful central banker, with
whom Margaret Thatcher had struck up an early and warm rapport. In
June 1990, Greenspan met Thatcher again, and immediately after gave
a detailed account of the conversation to Leigh-Pemberton. Greenspan
explained how he had devoted 'a good deal of the meeting' to 'restructuring' the Prime Minister's view of the virtue of floating exchange rates. She
had thought that arrangement was the only one compatible with free
markets, while Greenspan countered that 'this was not right because the
gold standard had been a viable alternative'. Thatcher 'jumped on this,
saying that a gold standard might provide just the sort of set of rules that
were needed as a sound foundation for a market-place'. She then called it

a 'spine', and Greenspan ended by telling Leigh-Pemberton 'that the most important element of the discussion had been the PM's spine theory'.[4] The international central banking community provided a valuable vehicle for the Bank to press the Prime Minister and the government. Greenspan had been a passionate believer in the gold standard in the 1950s and 1960s, and had later moved away from advocacy of gold but still thought of references to gold or commodity currencies as a way of bonding with conservative politicians.[5] His encouragement of Thatcher's longing for a gold spine was at least intellectually irresponsible, but from the perspective of the Bank of England and the Treasury it appeared as the best way of getting Thatcher to fall into line.

The background to these reflections lay in the political and economic repercussions of German unification. The discussion about ERM was also part of the fallout from the painful Delors discussions. Even before the committee had its first meeting, at the regular lunch of the Governor with the Chancellor, when Lawson quipped enigmatically that 'these lunches are the pleasant part, but it is not all like that', Leigh-Pemberton had commented that 'I agree about EMS – if we cd [could] ever change the stance, post Delors might be a good tactical moment.'[6] Bundesbank President Karl Otto Pöhl in the aftermath of the Delors Report was taking an increasingly sceptical stance towards monetary union; but he was equally enthusiastic about bringing the UK – which he thought of as an ally – into the ERM, at least in part in his view in order to frustrate the monetary project. In July 1990, he urged the new Chancellor, Lawson's successor John Major, to join in September or early October of that year, since 'waiting too long would risk disappointing market expectations and that would be disastrous for sterling'. Pöhl proved to be the decisive voice, and his argument about timing prevailed. Major agreed with him, saying that while he 'had not always been an enthusiast for joining the ERM [. . . he] was now convinced that it would be in the UK's interests. We were committed to joining as soon as conditions were right. Herr Poehl said that he had long been in favour of UK membership.'[7] (This was not quite true: he had confessed in 1987 to his Dutch friends that he would not be pushing for British entry if he thought that there was any real chance that they actually would join the ERM.) Major later explained that he was not 'at the outset' committed to the ERM as an anti-inflation mechanism, but 'I became attached to the ERM – and we went into it – because, frankly, we had run out of options'.[8] In other words, Major seemed to recognize that the only policy option left was to delegate monetary policy to a foreign independent central bank, the German Bundesbank.

Margaret Thatcher came round to the view that ERM might be desirable in June and July with inflation moving sharply upwards, to 9.8 per cent.[9] She thought that membership might square a domestic political circle: allow interest rate cuts while pushing down the inflation rate. On 4 May, just after local elections had been held, the Treasury sent to the Prime Minister a list of possible ERM entry days, with the first being 18 May.[10]

The Bank did not have a very clearly formulated strategy on ERM. The most obvious explanation of the problem lies within its institutional structure, and the divide between an Overseas outlook and a Markets vision. The International Division at this point felt ever more at odds with the rest of the Bank. Already in 1987, its then director Anthony Loehnis had complained about what he now called the 'centrifugal' bank that had been produced by the attempt to make policy-making more flexible. He thought that the intellectual gap occurred at the top as well as lower down in the divisions of the Bank, and that it resulted from a 'lack of communication and/or coordination'. The 'Reclassification' exercise in which authority in the Bank was further devolved was likely to intensify the problem. (This 'Reclassification' was the only large-scale attempt at institutional reform between 1979 and 1993, and reduced the number of levels in the old hierarchy by half, to five, and tried to simplify and clarify the pay structure. It was motivated by the reflection that the Bank's role in the economy requires it not only to possess qualities of dependability and stability, but also to be responsive to change.)[11] In Loehnis's view, it risked provoking 'the emergence of differences of opinion among ourselves which make the Bank look, as well as be, divided and hence weaker and less effective'.[12] He left the Bank in 1989, to join the board of S.G. Warburg Group PLC. He had been consistently rather sceptical about European integration arguments, and his successor, Andrew Crockett, who had started at the Bank but then moved to Washington and the IMF, was much more enthusiastic: so eager indeed on Europe that his name had come to Thatcher's attention as a possible troublemaker, and she had tried to block his appointment as Executive Director. But Leigh-Pemberton objected to her candidate, Tim Lankester, who had worked as her Private Secretary, and the Deputy Governor inspired the *Daily Telegraph* to run a story that Crockett was critical of Nigel Lawson, which helped to convince Thatcher that he might be useful. What finally clinched the point was that Leigh-Pemberton told the Prime Minister that while she might appoint Lankester as a Director, the Bank's Court could simply respond by offering a post as Associate Director to Crockett and then giving him the management role. Thatcher backed down in the face of Leigh-Pemberton's determination to work with

Crockett and not Lankester. Crockett turned out to be reliably pro-European.

The much more sceptical Markets view had been very clearly articulated in the *Quarterly Bulletin*, and had led the press to conclude – on the basis of briefings with Eddie George – that

the high rate of inflation, the huge current account deficit and the large gap between British and European interest rates have persuaded the Bank of England that the time is not ripe for Britain to become a full member of the EMS. [...] At a time when the cabinet is reported to be divided over whether to tie sterling to other European Community currencies in the EMS Exchange Rate Mechanism, the Bank has sided with the Prime Minister in saying no.[13]

The story irritated the Treasury, and the Chancellor 'hoped we could prevent further stories of this sort'.[14]

By early 1990, there was a clear gap between the International Division, now under Crockett, and George as Director in charge of Markets. George argued that 'we should not enter until our inflation/interest rates had been substantially reduced and held at that reduced level for some time'. By contrast, Crockett thought that 'we should contemplate going into the system possibly as early as later this year when the current adjustment is well in train and we wish to ease policy for domestic reasons'. This stance was interpreted by the Governor's private secretary as meaning that 'in those circumstances we would not need to be too worried about upward pressure on sterling forcing us to the top of the band and thus forcing us to reduce rates'. To this Leigh-Pemberton added the handwritten conclusion:

I am not optimistic about joining in 1990, although the fact that it is probably the last practical time before an election just makes it a possibility. I think our line probably ought to be the 'George' line [i.e. an insistence on greater initial convergence of the UK with Europe] in public, qualified by the implication that conditions will never be perfect and that entry at any time will involve some bumps – therefore if there are bumps, they could well be accepted sooner rather than later.[15]

Crockett himself had long had second thoughts about the appropriate rate, and on 17 September 1990, on the eve of the UK joining the ERM, minuted that there was a 'significant danger' 'that we should lock in the exchange rate at too high a level, to discover subsequently that the domestic economy was weakening by more than we anticipated, and our external competitiveness was insufficient to permit exports to become the engine of renewed growth. If we did this, and subsequently kept the exchange rate unchanged, it would be a mistake of historic proportions.' This argument – in essence a reprise of the Alan Walters critique of the EMS as 'half-baked' – proved highly prophetic, but essentially it now came too late. And Crockett then added that a 2.80 Deutsche Mark (DM) rate rather than 3.00 would be 'acceptable.'[16] There were obviously parallels in his mind with the still frequently discussed issue of Britain's perhaps misguided choice of parity in going back to the gold standard in 1925, sometimes referred to as 'the Norman Conquest', which had provided the policy backdrop to the Great Depression, and which then produced a political revulsion against Governor Norman and his Bank.

RECESSION

The discussion of the ERM and its constraints was even harder as it became clear that the UK was falling into recession. In consequence, thinking about the Great Depression and its lessons came more naturally. Policy-makers felt trapped as a result of what looked in retrospect like an artificial boom, driven by overinvestment in housing. In the spring of 1990, with clear signs of weakening as the economy moved into recession, Crockett made a characteristically forceful intervention:

He felt that UK policy was effectively in a box on account of constraints that had existed in the past. Looking back, it was possible to see that if policy had erred more on the side of caution, the authorities would now have greater credibility and thus greater room for manoeuvre. In other words, if we had done more sooner, we would have more flexibility now. As a separate matter, the Governor said that he wanted to explore the proposition that a weakening in the exchange rate gave more latitude to wage bargainers and therefore seriously undermined the counter-inflationary strategy. He was inclined to think that in terms of the magnitude of the effect, the increase in the RPI brought about by administered price increases (or for that matter even an interest rate increase) was more powerful. In this respect, he had been struck by a comment made to him by a businessman over lunch in Durham to the effect that exchange rate moves had a relatively small impact on the firm's costs and that indeed wages were also a small item. [Bank of England Chief Economist] Mr Flemming said that he was sure, as the Governor had suggested, that the exchange rate was a far weaker influence on the wage bargaining process than the RPI.[17]

The exchange rate thus came to be a focus for policy debate. William Allen, as part of the George group, argued that 'for technical reasons' the British position in the ERM would be 'unstable', while Crockett used exactly the same argument about instability to justify membership. He said that he was 'more persuaded than before of the merits of early entry. This was because the gap between our position and that of the existing

ERM members had widened and therefore membership would be post-poned for a long time if we were to wait for a reasonable degree of convergence.' George, by contrast, spoke of 'an increasing recognition on the Continent that it would be bad for the system – as well as for the UK – for us to join too early; Pöhl had said as much last week'.[18]

The attraction of the ERM was that it looked like the best way of anchoring anti-inflationary credibility. That was articulated in a Court discussion, where Sir David Scholey of Warburgs, the strongest outside candidate to succeed Leigh-Pemberton as Governor, reflected on a Bank paper which asked, 'might the lesson of the last few years be that not always giving precedence to the inflation objective is a short-sighted policy?' Scholey said:

> He answered this with a resounding affirmative. So far as he was concerned, inflation continued to be Public Enemy No 1, but this was not so much the precise rate as measured by any particular index but rather the underlying substance. If the counter-inflationary battle were relaxed for short-term reasons, the costs would be spread forward for future generations to suffer. He was sure that unless precedence was given to counter-inflationary policy, the country's relative economic decline would continue. Sir David continued that, so far as the balance between interest rate and exchange rate objectives were concerned, in the early days of this Government the exchange rate had been seen as a residual item. There had plainly been a dramatic change in policy since then. The exchange rate was the nearest thing in national terms to a company's share price in corporate terms, not least in that it indicated strength of confidence in the country, internally and externally.[19]

The Treasury was careful to direct the communications strategy of the Bank so as to suppress any wider awareness of the intensity of policy contestation within the Bank. In the lead-up to ERM entry, Middleton explained that he did not want any discussion of alternative monetary strategy management issues. He noted that the next *Bank of England Quarterly Bulletin* was due to include an article on reserve asset ratios and pressed for it to be withdrawn.[20]

The rate at which sterling entered the EMS/ERM should have been, both legally and logically, the subject of negotiation in the European Community Monetary Committee, as the other member countries were taking on an obligation to defend the British rate. But the UK short-circuited the negotiation by declaring its preference for DM 2.95. In weekend talks in Brussels, Bundesbank officials used the large British current account deficit as evidence for the argument that 2.95 was too high, and Hans Tietmeyer argued for a rate of 2.90. Later, Pöhl said that he had thought 2.60–2.65 would be more appropriate. On the other hand, French officials thought

2.95 was too low and would give British exporters an unfair advantage. The result of the Franco-German divergence of views was that there was no effective alternative to the rate proposed by London. The Italian chair of the Monetary Committee, Mario Sarcinelli, suggested that there should be some change in the central rate just to teach the British the lesson that they 'could not dictate to their new ERM partners'.[21] But that rather confrontational view was ignored. The Monetary Committee's report to the European Community Ministers stated: 'On balance, and given that a proposed rate had already been announced, the Committee was led to recommend that rate.' But it did add a warning shot, that the 6 per cent wider fluctuation margins reflected the fact that 'the convergence of the UK economy on best performance in the Community is not yet satisfactory'.[22]

In Britain, there was also some dissension about whether the central rate (at DM 2.95) was appropriate. The Bank and above all chief economist John Flemming made the argument that sterling had been given a short-term boost by the oil price hike that followed from the Iraq invasion in 1990 and that would in consequence not be sustained. The Treasury by contrast held the view that it was impractical to do anything except to use the prevailing market rate.

The political arguments in Britain relied on two potentially contra-dictory positions. First, the maintenance of the exchange rate was seen as a credibility enhancing anti-inflationary tool. Secondly, EMS member-ship was expected to bring down interest rates as a consequence of a gain in anti-inflationary credibility, and would consequently bring a politically desirable and economically expansive growth of credit. In other words, it would produce inflation. Thatcher – always sensitive to the politics of interest rates – saw this as the major part of the political appeal of EMS membership, and indeed insisted that the news of a cut of interest rates from 15 to 14 per cent should be given priority over the ERM announce-ment. A Treasury paper, submitted to the Chancellor of the Exchequer on 1 June and sent on to the Prime Minister on 8 June, argued that 'it would seem a reasonable starting point to suppose that entering the ERM at an effective rate some way above present levels would be desirable if other factors bearing upon the tightness of monetary conditions remained unchanged'.[23] A draft minute to the Chancellor of 3 October 1990 argued that 'to maintain the downward pressure on inflation it will be vital that there is no fall in the exchange rate'. In later papers, the Treasury some-what speciously argued that its officials had been so mesmerized by the political struggle with the Prime Minister over EMS membership that they had not been able to consider properly the technical aspects of membership. When the interest rate part of the British calculation did not work out, it became highly attractive to place the blame on the German policy mix. Thatcher's successor as Prime Minister, John Major, complained: 'The Bundesbank is too formidable an institution not to grasp the effects of its decisions, but neither it nor the German government did more than express sympathy and understanding for the havoc its policy was causing elsewhere.'[24]

MEMBERSHIP OF THE ERM

The announcement of the UK's ERM membership came rather precipitately on Friday, 5 October 1990, and was accompanied by a 1 per cent interest rate cut. The Treasury had planned an announcement one week later, but brought the timing forward so as not to conflict with the Prime Minister's speech at the Conservative Party conference in Bournemouth (where she said 'exactly a week ago, John Major dropped one of his quiet surprises on an unsuspecting press. Well, they surprise us sometimes too'). It is also likely that Major feared that a week's delay would allow Thatcher to change her mind.[25] The final preparation had occurred in a meeting on the morning of 4 October in 10 Downing Street with Treasury officials and Eddie George, as Leigh-Pemberton was on his way to Japan, a trip that could not be postponed because the change of travel plans might alert markets to the impending announcement. Before he left, Leigh-Pemberton sent a letter to the Prime Minister that set out a rather different view to the government's on the right course for interest rates:

I am very sorry not to be able to attend your meeting this afternoon but John Major and I have come to the conclusion that it is probably wiser, from the security point of view, that I should stick to my established programme for my tour to Japan and the Far East. I think that entry into the ERM on the right terms will be seen as a strong policy signal by the market and this will, in turn, provide a good chance of an outstanding result and success for the Government. I mean by this that the exchange rate will strengthen and will provide an opportunity for an early, but justifiable and sustainable, cut in interest rates. Such an outcome cannot obviously be guaranteed and it is possible that the exchange rate will not rise immediately and that the interest rate cut might consequently have to be delayed, although it is my personal opinion that it will not have to be delayed long. [...] I see the fall in interest rates as a deserved and justifiable dividend from entering into the ERM and one that could well be distributed quite promptly after the event. I do think, however, that we should avoid distributing the dividend before we have been seen to have 'earned' it.[26]

For Terry Burns, the interest rate cut was 'like a stag night before the wedding', a pointless but morale-boosting exercise in profligacy.[27] Leigh-Pemberton also delivered a reprimand to the Chancellor at the next meeting, saying: 'There was a general feeling in the City that the reduction in interest rates had been the Prime Minister's condition for joining the ERM. That had occasioned some worry that politics could intervene to prevent a rise in interest rates should it be necessary to hold our ERM bands.'[28]

On 8 October, five days after German unification, the British pound formally joined the EMS/ERM. Welcoming Britain's new exchange rate anchor, Leigh-Pemberton told an audience in Tokyo in October 1990: 'It's a great event in our economic life. It is something I have looked forward to for a very long time.'

The move to British membership had an immediate effect on the discussion of the Bank's relationship with the discount market. Already in 1988 and 1989, the Treasury had voiced its concern that the discount market seemed to have been tipped off about a release of market-sensitive trade figures and interest rate moves. The Bank tried to defend itself by saying that the meeting on the date concerned with the interest rate move (24 November 1988) had actually been cancelled because Bank officials needed to be at the Treasury: but even the cancellation of a meeting might well constitute market information. The Bank noted 'a sort of dissatisfaction that the LDMA were getting advance and private information of this kind'.[29] The case of 5 October 1990 was much more widely discussed. Leigh-Pemberton had avoided going to Downing Street on the morning of 4 October for 'security' reasons, because journalists could easily have guessed the purpose of his visit to the Prime Minister. But there was also something in Threadneedle Street that seemed to give the game away. Some banks, including Midland Montagu, Lloyds Bank, Hill Samuel and Barings, informally complained about losses they made on deals done in Floating Rate Agreements just before the official announcement on ERM membership, and it became clear that one discount house, Gerrard and National, had made a very large profit.

Gerrard and National had expected ERM entry at some point during the summer and had long been cautiously building up a position with longer-term assets which would appreciate with the interest rate fall that they expected to come with the new regime. The discount house believed that it was also likely that the measure would be announced at the end of a week or at the weekend when the European markets were closed. The calculation that ERM membership was imminent had been wrong-footed after Saddam Hussein's invasion of Kuwait, which had given a shock and sent rates up briefly. Characteristically, discount houses were very vulnerable to short-term movements, and Gerrards made heavy losses. Later in the year, matters were different. There were all kinds of vague discussions about the timing of entry into ERM, which was by now looking ever more probable.

Were there more specific indicators of the authorities' intentions? On 4 October, Andrew Crockett had attended a lunch at Gerrards where he had remarked that 'having got to the altar you didn't want to hang around before putting the ring on'.[30] The firm's chairman, Brian Williamson, had been at a retirement party with a Bank official and noticed that the senior Bank officials who might have been expected to be celebrating were not there; when he asked a Bank contact whether anything special was happening, he received an ambiguous reply. But the precipitant for Gerrards to build a big position in forward rate agreements was the visit of another Gerrard director, Henry Askew, to the regular 2:45 p.m. tender meeting at the Bank on 5 October, where he had seen officials buzzing around 'like blue-arsed flies'. This was the meeting where the discount houses borrowed. There was regularly some sort of banter at these meetings, and traders tended to say outrageous things and 'cast flies' in the hope of getting a response from Bank officials. Askew referred to the decision of the Bank to meet the full requirement of the discount market at 2:45 p.m. by stating, 'That's a punchy offer.' He thought that the Bank official was in an 'excited, bouncy mood, in an extrovert mood'. There was some light-hearted conversation in the course of which the Bank official poked Askew in the stomach and said something which was alternately reported as 'I'll slit your throat if you say anything to your colleagues' and 'If you do something stupid, I'll never forgive you.' And finally, another Bank official told Askew to 'have a good weekend', accompanied by a wink. Was all of this normal? Askew returned quickly to Gerrards, by 3:00 p.m., and from 3:30 p.m. over the course of fifteen minutes Gerrards concluded £445 m of forward rate agreements maturing in February 1991: the agreements that generated the large profit. At 4:00 p.m. the ERM membership was announced. Already on the Friday morning, at the Treasury bill tender, Gerrards had very aggressively bought the whole amount (£100 m). There was immediate tension because of a forex contract with Barings, which Barings felt that it was not obliged to settle after the shock of EMS entry; and because of a disaffected Gerrards employee who wrote a whistle-blowing letter. As the news leaked out, Williamson responded to the Reuters news wire: 'I categorically deny we were aware of either UK entry or the reduction of base rates.'[31] He was convinced that there had been a leak, but that it had

not originated from the Bank but from indiscreet remarks at a City dinner
by a Downing Street adviser. A subsequent investigation determined that
there was no 'leak' from the Bank, and that Gerrards had simply drawn
their own deductions about what was likely to occur – and also how it
would be linked to an interest rate move.

The longer-term consequence was that the ambiguity that was created
by the regular presence of the discount market in the Bank ended from
April 1991 and the 2:45 meeting was replaced by a more hands-off process
for arranging Bank lending. Sir David Walker, the head of the SIB, had
written to Leigh-Pemberton to express a fundamental reflection on the
clubbiness of the discount market's operations and on the Thursday afternoon meetings (rather than the daily 2:45 funding operation):

My doubt relates to the long-established tradition for one of the Governors to 'see
the market' after lunch on Thursdays. If the smallest crumb of new intelligence is
imparted, the question arises of why it is not made available to other markets. And
if nothing of substance is passed on, I wonder whether the maintenance of
a courteous and civilised practice offsets the risk that it may be perceived that
something new is liable to be said; even if nothing ever is.[32]

EUROPEAN INTEREST RATES AND RECESSION

At the beginning of the UK's ERM membership, the hope of lower interest
rates receded. At the beginning, perhaps, the worry about the economic
consequences was reduced because the recession at first looked relatively
shallow and harmless.

There had admittedly been a moment of uncertainty when sterling fell
on the exchange markets, in part because of political uncertainty following
the spectacular resignation of Sir Geoffrey Howe as Foreign Secretary and
rumours that this would set off a leadership challenge to Margaret
Thatcher in the Conservative Party. In these circumstances, it was impossible to think about interest rate cuts. The Bank had to devise a covert
intervention strategy:

Continuing, Mr Coleby [Executive Director with responsibility for markets] said
that he thought intervening overtly would be counter-productive at least until the
current uncertainties were over. There was otherwise a high risk that intervention
would be 'swept away' as those political uncertainties increased. But he would
recommend covert intervention at particular points, the natural market 'sign
posts'. In particular, he thought DM 2.90 would be seen as important and
suspected that the market would give spontaneous support to sterling at that
level, although not if the break point were either approached too rapidly or

breached very easily. If sterling did go lower, he thought it would be some time before another break point. He therefore recommended that the Bank intervene covertly up to a limit of £250 million in any single day to support sterling at the level which they identified as the most likely to be effective – probably around DM 2.90. No overt intervention should be done until the full shape of the current political situation was known.[33]

After the start of British ERM membership, after the resignation of Margaret Thatcher as Prime Minister (November 1990), and with a new political team with Major as Prime Minister and Norman Lamont as Chancellor, the economic situation as well as the politics changed. The new Chancellor was increasingly worried. The collapse of the British economy in what was becoming a severe recession appeared to have been exacerbated by the uncooperative stance of both American and German policy-makers on their interest rate policies. At the first Bank–Treasury meeting with the new Chancellor, Lamont seemed to agree that

we should be cautious about reducing interest rates. It could be argued that we should not do so before the underlying rate of inflation began to fall. He asked whether the Bank was sceptical of forecasts that we faced a deep rather than a shallow recession. Mr [John] Flemming [Executive Director and Chief Economist] said that the Bank had not yet finalised their current forecast. But they did not expect the recession to be very deep (unless events in the Gulf led to a prolonged and marked rise in oil prices). They expected consumption to lead the recovery but it might well not turn out to be a strong recovery and it might come about later than forecast in the Autumn Statement. Inflation would also be slow to respond but should come down to 5 per cent during 1992. Sir Peter Middleton agreed with the Governor's assessment of the prospects on interest rates. The underlying economic position pointed to an early reduction and the money figures in recent months were quite worrying. However, the first priority had to be credibility within the ERM. He would not wish to see any reduction linked too closely with the publication of the RPI. He commented that with hindsight the reduction of interest rates on 8 October had clearly been fully justified on economic grounds and, despite a lot of comment about political deals, it had not been badly received in the markets.[34]

Leigh-Pemberton was more sanguine, also speaking only of a 'shallow recession'. There were clearly real constraints on interest rate policy:

Sir Terry Burns said that the monetary situation in the UK justified a lower interest rate but we needed to avoid damaging our credibility within the ERM and there had to be an interval between the Chancellor's appointment and any action on that front.[35]

The subsequent discussion also revealed how deep the politicians' frustration with economic advice ran:

The Chancellor asked what the prospects were for growth in the UK the following year. He had been told that Q4 would be roughly flat, and if anything down slightly. Mr Budd said that 1992 on 1991 growth was now forecast to be 1 ½ per cent, compared with 2 ½ per cent forecast in the Autumn Statement. This was an arithmetic result of the forecast slower growth in 1991 H2. The Chancellor said that he was increasingly convinced by the argument for not publishing a forecast, and possibly dismantling the Treasury forecasting team altogether. Sir Terence Burns said that it would not have helped if there had been no internal forecast: Ministers would still have had to say that the economy was going to improve on the basis of their policies and what other people were forecasting. The problem was the 1975 Industry Act which set out the timing and required detail of the published forecast. Mr Budd asked whether policy would have been different if the forecast had been different. The forecast was not the basis of policy: that would be fiscal fine-tuning.

From Lamont's perspective, the priority of bringing down interest rates was even more fundamental than it had been for Thatcher, and he considerably overstated the risks of the slowdown in growth (which ran at a real rate of 0.6 per cent in 1990, with a negative 1.3 in 1991):

The Chancellor said that if the economy were moving into the worst recession since 1929 then the Government would have to act: it was no good going on about the credibility of government and politicians. Sir Terence Burns said that there were two specific problems. The first was the deterioration of confidence in the US economy; the second was that the ERM was ill-designed to deal with a major economic shock to its leading currency.[36]

The Bank had the substantially negative task of pointing out how limited was the British room for manoeuvre, given substantial continental European scepticism:

On the internal context, Mr Crockett said that, immediately after sterling's entry to the ERM, there had been a certain amount of resentment on the part of other ERM countries at what was perceived as the UK's opportunism. This impression must be corrected. But a reduction in interest rates now would suggest that the UK was giving priority to its domestic economy over its ERM obligations, and, more specifically, to the real economy over inflation. There were already tensions within the ERM. Although the Germans would not, he thought, raise their interest rates before the New Year, it seemed likely that their fiscal position would actually worsen next year to a deficit of around DM180 billion – 6 percent of GDP. France and Italy were becoming concerned at the situation. A UK move could generate more dissension and prompt an unravelling of the current position for which we would receive the blame. In response to a question from the Chancellor, Mr Crockett said that various indications had emerged from Germany that they might wish for a realignment at the time they increased interest rates. Mr [Deputy Secretary Michael] Scholar added that the Germans were not willing to accept an ERM constraint on their ability to raise interest rates.[37]

Treasury briefings made things worse, because of the obsession with interest rates: on 19 December, the markets fell because of an apparently inspired article in *The Times*, with the title 'Treasury ready for interest rate to fall sooner than expected', which explained:

The Treasury is looking not at the pound's precise level, but at its direction of movement and its general stability within ERM. It will give the Chancellor more room for manoeuvre in the face of a recession which officials admit is deeper than expected.[38]

The Bank quickly worked out that the Treasury was behind *The Times* article:

You should be aware of the attached article by [Anatole] Kaletsky in the Times this morning. It has contributed to the softening in sterling during the day, and we now understand was based on briefing given to Kaletsky by Middleton. The Treasury are obviously maintaining that Middleton has been misinterpreted, and Terry Burns has apparently been 'fuming' about the interpretation placed on Middleton's remarks.[39]

Eddie George meanwhile suggested, perhaps rather mischievously, that interest rate cuts were possible, but not in the ERM:

The Deputy Governor said that domestic indicators were now moving in a direction which would permit a cut in interest rates, although they did not suggest that an immediate cut was necessary. The evidence was never conclusive: he pointed to recent stirrings in the housing market and the relative strength of first estimates of broad money (M4) growth in November, although this could be partly due to the electricity privatisation. On balance, the Deputy Governor said that he would be happy to see a cut in interest rates now, were it not for the constraints of the ERM.[40]

The new Prime Minister, who was more cautious on the interest rate issue than Lamont, confined himself to hoping that things would improve:

[Barry] Potter [the Prime Minister's Private Secretary] said that he thought the Prime Minister's current mood was to accept that conditions were not right for an interest rate cut before Christmas. He would, however, want to probe carefully when the timing might become appropriate, and Potter mentioned three questions in particular in this respect:

(1) What economic indicators were coming out over the next period that would have a bearing on timing;
(2) economic conditions abroad;
(3) at what stage would it be right to decide that we had waited long enough for conditions to become perfect, and that we ought to take a risk and reduce interest rates anyway.

Potter mentioned that the Chancellor was likely to argue that we could not cut rates while we were falling against the deutschmark. But when would the relationship with the deutschmark be alright? Would it be enough for the £/DM rate to stabilise or would we be needed to move up against the deutschmark?[41]

It is not clear how aware the Treasury and the Prime Minister were at this stage of the beginning of a transformation of markets, with hedge funds playing an increasing role, with the potential of placing very substantial bets on exchange rate movements. Already in 1990 the Quantum Fund had made a substantial profit betting on the appreciation of the Deutschemark.[42] Any fixed exchange rate regime gave the possibility of an asymmetric bet, as it was highly improbable that sterling would rise, but increasingly likely that a speculative attack generated by the calculation of the political impossibility of an exchange rate might force the pound down off its peg. In January 1991, the Governor spoke with Karl Otto Pöhl by telephone, trying to convey something of the political pressure that was coming from Lamont:

The Governor continued that he would be seeing the Chancellor tomorrow morning to discuss policy and, in particular, the possibility of an interest rate cut. We faced a dilemma in this country given the need on the one hand to maintain appropriate tightness of policy and to stay within our ERM bands, and given on the other hand the biting recession. The dilemma was becoming quite intense and the politicians might now be hoping that we could manage a modest fall. The Governor said that personally he thought that it would be quite difficult to agree to a cut at this point, but a critical factor in this was the likely course of Bundesbank policy over the coming weeks. In New York at the G-7 meetings, Pöhl had suggested that provided wages stayed reasonably restrained in Germany there might not be a need for a further rise in rates.[43]

Pöhl was not responsive to the suggestions from London, and the Bank was in a political trap. In February 1991, the Bank was told by Major's Principal Private Secretary that the Prime Minister was 'gnashing his teeth' over the Bank's insistence on keeping rates up.[44] From February 1991, some of Leigh-Pemberton's hopes were realized and a virtuous circle set in, with British cuts in interest rates demonstrating to the markets that the ERM membership was a success. In the March European Community Committee of Governors meeting in Basel, the Alternates reported that the Bank of England had made it clear that 'a further cut would be undertaken only when it was considered to be consistent with exchange rate stability within the ERM'. But Leigh-Pemberton also made explicit the double nature of British policy-making in that purely domestic considerations continued to play a major part in motivating decisions: 'The possibility of further reductions in interest rates would be linked not only to the position of sterling within the ERM but also to domestic considerations.'

By April, Leigh-Pemberton could write in the Governor's letter to the Chancellor that:

In the space of exactly two months we have achieved four ½% falls in short-term interest rates, so that the general level now stands a full 2% lower than in mid-February and 3% lower than before ERM entry last October. Most importantly these reductions have been universally accepted as entirely justified. [. . .] Yet it was only in January that many saw the ERM as a box from which it would be impossible to escape. Happily this has not proved to be the case.

But the economy was still looking grim: despite some inconclusive evidence of recovery, 'the weight of the evidence however seems to indicate that recession continues, and is likely to do so for some little while yet; but there does seem to have been a change in mood, no doubt reflecting the interest rate reductions'.[45] Both in the UK and the US, the shock generated by a property price collapse had been underestimated. In the US setting, this underestimation led the Fed to maintain a tight monetary policy, even without the ERM constraints that applied in the UK, and that policy mistake may have cost President George H.W. Bush the chance of re-election in 1992.

At the Alternates' meeting of the Committee of Governors in Basel in May 1991, the Bank of England's representative, Andrew Crockett, 'confirmed that the Bank of England was not yet sure enough about inflation to take a lead in the process toward lower interest rates'.[46] However, the policy stance quickly changed. Lamont consistently pressed and pressed hard for rates to be cut. In April 1991, he expressed his concern again:

[Jeremy] Heywood [Principal Private Secretary to the Chancellor] said that the Chancellor had been quite concerned by the recent M4 numbers and was likely to ask you about our interpretation of the monetary aggregates. In particular, the severe slowdown in M4 had given the Chancellor pause for thought and made him wonder whether conditions were tighter than the authorities had believed, so that impliedly (Heywood did not say this) a further easing was needed or, leastways, the 'pause' in policy should not be as long as originally expected. Heywood said, however, that given the weakness in the exchange rate (against the dollar but also against the deutschmark on Wednesday) and given the shape of the yield curve (with long-term rates still quite high), it was probable that the Chancellor would not think that there was a case for going much further with interest rate cuts for the moment.[47]

Every statement by the Bank could in consequence be controversial. When Leigh-Pemberton gave some anodyne remarks at Exeter University in

May 1991, in which he warned against using the headline inflation rate 'single yardstick', and that there might be 'false dawns' in the battle against inflation, the government interpreted this as a subversion of its strategy. Major and Lamont had both played up the significance of April's inflation fall by linking lower inflation to 'greater flexibility' on interest rates, which was a coded phrase for interest rate cuts.[48]

Consequently policy-makers emphasized caution. Leigh-Pemberton insisted that 'the market was currently very sensitive to perceptions of the Government's resolution, and that anything that could be done to persuade the markets that there was no risk of "instant government" would help'.[49]

British interest rates had been cut from 15 per cent in October 1990 to 11 per cent by July 1991. Inflation too fell over the same period, from 10.9 per cent to 5.8 per cent. Business and the political opposition both pressed for even faster and more dramatic cuts in interest rates. By the autumn of 1991, the interest rate differential to Germany had largely disappeared: this was a faster convergence than UK policy-makers had originally envisaged. There was only one fly in the ointment: the position of the Bundesbank.

There were also exaggerated expectations about the extent to which British rates might fall:

Sir Terry Burns said the Chancellor had noted that stories of base rates falling to 9½% by election time were damaging and he would inform senior colleagues. There was a brief discussion of tactics in the event of a November General Election.[50]

The main problem, the fundamental constraint on British policy, lay in German moves in the opposite direction. The German central bank embarked on a series of interest rate increases to deal with inflationary pressures arising from the massive fiscal transfers that followed in the aftermath of German unification. On 2 November 1990, it moved the Lombard rate (the charge on collateralized loans) from 8 to 8.5 per cent, and through 1991 further increases occurred while US rates were being cut and the dollar was weakening. On 1 February 1991, the German discount rate was raised from 6 to 6.5 per cent, and the Lombard rate to 9 per cent. On 16 August, these rates were moved up to 7.5 and 9.25 per cent, and on December 20 to 8 and 9.75, respectively. Finally, on 17 July 1992, as a final step in the drama, the Bundesbank set the discount rate as 8.75 per cent (see Figures 11.1 and 11.2).

Lamont was deeply frustrated by the German action and the influence that it necessarily had on British rates and on the severity of the recession.

per cent

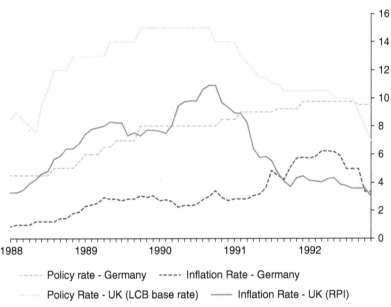

Figure 11.1 Inflation and interest rates Germany and the UK (1988–1992)

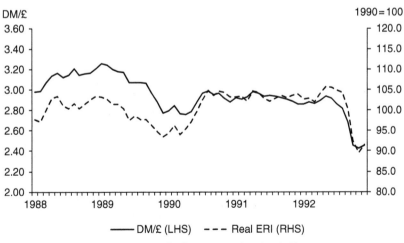

Figure 11.2 Exchange rates (1988–1992)

At the end of 1991, in a meeting with Bank and Treasury officials he vented his frustration, asking whether 'it were likely that the recession would become the most severe downturn since 1929'; and he raised the issue of radical action at the political level, 'perhaps Mitterrand and Kohl would pay more attention if Britain threatened to leave the EMS'. The Treasury official Michael Scholar replied that it was 'unlikely that they would react', and Jeremy Heywood drew a probably correct and quite different conclusion, that French dislike of German policy 'made them seek to move to EMU more quickly in order to have more of an influence'. Terry Burns agreed that there was indeed a risk of a 1929-style event. International cooperation should aim at reducing the level of real interest rates, but was undermined by the German stance and 'cooperation between Germany and the US was not adequate'.[51]

At the meeting of the European G-4 (i.e. the four European members of the G-7) in January 1992, Bundesbank President Helmut Schlesinger, who had replaced Pöhl after he unexpectedly stepped down in May 1991, started with a conciliatory statement in response to a repetition of Lamont's perpetual question about Bundesbank policy:

Schlesinger, in reply to a question from Lamont whether German interest rates might go higher, said that the majority in the Bundesbank council which voted for a ½% increase rather that ¼% did so because they wished to make an increase which would be seen to be 'the last step'. The subsequent fall in long term rates seemed to confirm this as accepted by the markets and he thought that bond prices were likely to rise. In reply to a question as to whether, if there were a realignment, he could see German interest rates falling he said he could not obviously make a promise to that extent but that interest rate differentials could ease in such circumstances. Removing exchange rate tension clearly had the idea of easing interest rate tension.

[French Finance Minister Pierre] Bérégovoy led powerfully when it came to discussing realignment or devaluation. If there were a realignment the French franc would move up with the deutschmark. [Italian Treasury Minister Guido] Carli said that Italy ruled it out and Lamont concluded the tour de table by saying it could hardly be a realignment if it were only the UK which devalued. [German Finance Minister Theo] Waigel went on to say that Germany had not asked for it, Schlesinger had merely mentioned it as a possibility. But once such a clear view had come out round the table I was able to secure agreement from the Germans, which I hope will be observed, that there should not be further public talk about a realignment.

But then came the explosive revelation that the Bundesbank was pushing for more exchange rate flexibility – or for a realignment. Leigh-Pemberton recorded that:

Nevertheless I [Leigh-Pemberton] feel that Schlesinger himself sees this as an appropriate solution to present tensions. He told me after the meeting when we were talking alone that for a situation like that in the UK with recession, high interest rates and a balance of trade payments deficit, a devaluation had to be the classic response. I replied by saying that it was doubtful if the present ERM situation allowed a classic result, since the loss of credibility flowing from devaluation might well mean that interest rates subsequently had to rise to the present or even higher levels . This incidentally was a view which when expressed by me at the table received support from [Banque de France Governor Jacques] de Larosière and [Banca d'Italia Governor Carlo Azeglio] Ciampi.[52]

At the beginning of 1992, the greatest strains seemed to have passed. The Bundesbank had increased its central rates by 0.5 per cent at the end of December 1991, with the discount rate now at 8.0 per cent and the Lombard rate at 9.75 per cent, and the hike produced a strong effect on the DM–dollar exchange rate, but not on European exchange rates. In January 1992, exchange market interventions had virtually ceased and short-term interest rates had declined in most EC countries from the high levels reached at the end of 1991. The width of the narrow band had effectively been reduced to a much smaller range than permitted under the EMS agreement, with exchange rates fluctuating by only about 2 per cent, following a period in which the width had been extended to the maximum permissible limit, with interventions being required at the margin.

One of the major concerns started to be the imminence of a UK general election. At a meeting in the Treasury, with Bank officials present,

Sir Terry Burns said that he did not think that interest rates could be cut after the election had been announced: the only conceivable circumstances would be if there were overwhelming market pressure for a move. Mr [Deputy Secretary Michael] Scholar said that the Labour government had cut the Minimum Lending Rate in the run up to the October 1974 election [the move was repeated in March and April 1979 in the run-up to the May election]. Mr Coleby said that this may have been a simple application of the formula for the MLR which was in operation at the time. The Deputy Governor said that he thought cutting rates would be problematic in the run up to an election, although in the context of the ERM there plainly might be circumstances in which it would be necessary to increase rates in order to honour our ERM obligations.

Lamont seemed to give in, agreeing that an interest rate cut could be virtually ruled out during the election period.[53]

Leigh-Pemberton told the market meeting with the London discount houses, 'I believe the Germans to be well aware of the feeling around Europe that they have been insensitive to the problems they have created, but I doubt that will weigh much with them.'[54]

The major alarm signals in London initially concerned the run-up to the general election, which had to be held some time in 1992. By April 1992, in the context of a discussion of 'Economic Policy and Market Questions Concerning a Possible Labour Government', Crockett summarized a paper (of 2 April) to conclude that 'economically there was a broad consensus that sterling was probably overvalued and that the economic consequences of German unification pointed towards general ERM realignment'. But there were strong arguments against devaluation on credibility grounds and, as Crockett put it, 'an even greater credibility problem [...] if a Labour Government initially stuck with the current parity but were forced off it a year or so down the road on account of economic recovery having failed to emerge'.[55] In the context of this debate, the Bank's new chief economist, Mervyn King, interestingly formulated the idea that a future Labour government might be obliged to set a fiscal rule in order to ensure credibility. He was already beginning to shift the debate from its obsession with externally imposed credibility to internally generated stability.[56]

In the end, however, there was a powerful political pressure to cut interest rates after the election (9 April 1992), in which John Major surprisingly won a narrow majority, especially since the elections were followed quite quickly by a round of local elections. The Bank concluded:

The hasty calling, and re-timing, of the meeting reflects Ministerial desires to have an interest rate cut no later than tomorrow. The running is being made by the Prime Minister. The purpose is not so much to ease the reception next week of the Queen's Speech and the subsequent debate, as to influence the outcome of the local elections on 7 May. There is no good reason why a ½% cut to 10% should not be made in the fairly near future.[57]

Interest rates were cut by 0.5 per cent on the weekend before the local elections. The election had also been accompanied by spectacular movements as money flowed into government paper in anticipation of interest rate cuts. The Bank had uniquely kept its dealing room open through the night of the election, and at 2:30 a.m. and 8:15 a.m., announced two packages each of £800 m of tranchettes, both of which sold out very quickly, the first in five minutes. Including unofficial sales, the Bank sold over £2.5 bn in the immediate aftermath of the election.[58] The election night became a spectacularly successful funding operation.

INSTABILITY IN THE EMS

The gilt surge was quite short-lived. There were five factors now making for increased instability in the EMS, and in particular for renewed British vulnerability. One lay in the development of British labour costs, where there were indications of continued inflationary expectations: in early 1992, a large scissors started to open between Germany and the UK, with UK costs rising at a fast rate. Secondly, policy in the UK had been trapped because of the prominence given to the interest rate issue and because of the perception that Britain was caught in a uniquely severe economic crisis. British interest rates were politically much more sensitive because of the prevalence of adjustable mortgage rates, which ensured that homeowners would be instantly hit by monetary tightening. In July 1992, the British National Savings issued a high interest rate bond, paying over 10 per cent, but the Treasury was rapidly forced to withdraw it after protests from the building societies. This episode was read by the markets as a signal that there was no political possibility of defending the pound with the interest rate tool. Thirdly, inflation in Germany also increased, and with it pressure on the Bundesbank to tighten interest rates. Perversely, though, that rise in German inflation was interpreted by British politicians as a sign of the appropriateness of the policy stance, as UK inflation was now below that of Germany (see Figure 11.1, p. 285). Fourthly, there was a sharp episode of dollar weakness from April to August 1992, in which the dollar depreciated by 20 per cent against the Deutschemark. Despite this, the Federal Reserve cut interest rates on 2 July. The *Economist* cover of 29 August 1992 depicted the falling dollar as the world's main problem. Dollar weakness then, as before in the 1970s and 1980s, produced the effect of 'dollar polarization' in which the Deutschemark strengthened relative to other European currencies. Finally, a new political uncertainty emerged about the sustainability of the Maastricht process and became the trigger of speculative attacks that would not have occurred in the absence of such political 'bad news'.

The precipitant of the collapse came from doubt about the direction of the whole process of European monetary integration and its relationship with political integration. On 2 June 1992, the Danish electorate unexpectedly and by a narrow margin voted against the Maastricht Treaty, with 50.7 per cent against and 49.3 per cent in favour. This rejection was quite widely interpreted as a beginning of a general revolt by the European populace (or rather by profoundly nationally conscious and different peoples) against the technocratic (Eurocratic) elite that had run far ahead of the popular will. The consequence was that there were now grave doubts about the Maastricht Treaty, which inevitably shocked the foreign exchange markets. The focus of market attention shifted from Denmark to France. President Mitterrand announced a referendum on Maastricht that would be held on 20 September, and its outcome looked increasingly precarious. But British anxiety was focused on the Bundesbank, rather than on French voters. The Bank of England recorded:

Jeremy Heywood called me [Paul Tucker, the Governor's Private Secretary] this morning to say that on returning from the ECOFIN the Chancellor was extremely agitated about Schlesinger's remarks about the possibility of a realignment before EMU. The Chancellor regarded this sort of comment as deeply unhelpful to other countries and felt that Schlesinger should respect the positions of other countries. The Chancellor has asked whether you might have a quiet word with Schlesinger at the forthcoming Basle.[59]

In March, at the regular meeting of the EC Committee of Governors, Leigh-Pemberton had talked about 'considerable pressure for an interest rate cut'.[60] In July, in the same forum, he was ostentatiously mild. He began by saying that 'the situation in the United Kingdom was currently difficult'. But he 'welcomed Mr. Schlesinger's understanding approach to the difficulties of Germany's ERM partners, although the situation was made more difficult when the media reported on statements which appeared to have been made by the Deutsche Bundesbank concerning a realignment of the ERM currencies'.[61] The Bank at this time began to suspect that the Bundesbank was playing a double game, and briefing journalists about the need for a realignment. A front-page article in the *Financial Times* quoted a 'senior Bundesbank official' as saying that 'We are not in a fixed exchange rate system yet.' The article continued, 'Although he stopped short of calling outright for a re-alignment, he indicated that the Bundesbank believed market forces might eventually force weaker currencies towards a devaluation. The official did not mention EMS devaluation candidates by name. But he said the Banca d'Italia had been intervening with "considerable" amounts to defend the lira last week.'[62] Since the same issue of the newspaper contained a long profile of Schlesinger, the readers were presumably intended to draw the inference that this was the view of the Bundesbank president. At Basel, Schlesinger and the vice president Hans Tietmeyer were consequently obliged to deny that they had been the source of the article and Schlesinger 'promised to look into what – if anything – had been said'.[63]

Only two days after the Governors' gathering, on July 16, the Bundesbank Council met in what was regarded as a 'historic meeting' and produced a shock: it raised the German discount rate from 8 to 8 ¾ per cent.[64] The vote was preceded by a fierce discussion. Some members of the Council argued that interest rate rises would not put any brake on the rapid growth of M3, which might even be fuelled by speculative anticipation of parity changes; there were even suggestions that interest rate reductions might lower the pace of monetary expansion. Another very obvious, and very familiar, reason for exercising restraint in interest policy was the international situation, in that it was quite possible to imagine that a new conflict would destroy not just the EMS but also the Maastricht process. Economics Minister Jürgen Möllemann attended the meeting, and begged the central bankers to consider the effect of their actions on East Germany and on Europe. But Möllemann was not a heavyweight figure, even though he had just been appointed as Genscher's successor to the position of Deputy Chancellor. He was a showman, who had worked as a lower-grade schoolteacher, before turning to politics, initially as a Christian Democrat and then as a liberal. Within a year he would be forced to resign in the aftermath of a corruption scandal. Möllemann provided a perfect target for the Bundesbank to demonstrate that it would not receive instructions from politicians. The Frankfurt bankers ignored him, and may indeed have believed that a demonstration of monetary discipline was necessary precisely for the sake of the future of the European monetary order.[65] In a previous meeting at the Bundesbank Council in June, Finance Minister Theo Waigel had said that the Bundesbank 'must not be taken over by its partners'.[66]

The British complained about a 'whispering campaign' from Germany pushing for realignment. The British Foreign Office instructed the Bonn embassy to protest to the President of the Bundesbank against 'a particularly unhelpful follow-up to the Chancellor's major speech on Friday evening in which he gave a robust defence of the ERM and the UK's determination to maintain its present parities'.[67] On 29 July, the pound fell to its lower limit against the Portuguese escudo, and – at a very modest level – obligatory interventions began. From 7 August, on the same principle, there were also sales of Spanish pesetas for sterling. But most importantly, on 5 August, sales of DM to support sterling began.

A more efficient way of reducing the strains on the EMS might have lain in intervention on a global level to stop the rise of the DM against the dollar. The Europeans pressed the US Treasury to this effect. On 21 August 1992, eighteen central banks intervened in the forex market buying dollars, but the action had no major effect on the dollar/DM rate. The Federal Reserve, which had been sceptical about this intervention, then pleaded to stop the interventions. One of the reasons that Federal Reserve officials later gave for their opposition to intervention was that the Bundesbank was against it, on the grounds that the crisis represented an opportunity fundamentally to change the EMS by demonstrating that it did not mean a permanent fixing of exchange rates. The President of the New York Fed, William McDonough, later reported:

The Federal Reserve had only two choices: either to have the desk intervene for the Treasury alone, as we had once earlier this year, or to participate in the intervention. If we did not join the Treasury, we believed that it would be even worse than an ill-advised intervention. It would become public sooner or later, that the American monetary authorities were split at a time when the dollar was weak and the European monetary system was showing ever greater signs of stress. We made the decision, approved by the Chairman, that the wiser choice was to join the Treasury. Together we bought $300 million against German marks [...] After a brief lift, the dollar dropped further and set a new low of DM1.4255 later that day. The following Monday, we had a repeat. Against very strong advice from the Federal Reserve, the Treasury again instructed the desk to organize a coordinated intervention. Faced with the same choice, the Federal Reserve chose to keep the American authorities united and joined in the intervention. [...] We had authorization to buy up to $300 million. Even during the intervention, the dollar continued to fall and I stopped our intervention, with the later agreement of the Treasury, rather than risk further damage from a counterproductive effort.

But as the post mortem discussion of the Open Market committee of the coordinated intervention developed, McDonough referred to the position of the Frankfurt bankers:

all during September we were very much in the mode of not wishing to intervene because of the likely counterproductive effect on [our] domestic markets, especially the bond market. Therefore, in fact, I didn't have any discussions of 'What if . . . ?' or 'What do you think we should do?' with them. At that time the main thing that would have inhibited any desire by the Germans to do an intervention operation with us is that they very much wanted the ERM to come apart in order to stop having the monetary policy problems they had and to establish what they think is the single most important principle of the mechanism, i.e. that it be flexible. So, I think the main concern they had was purely internally European.[68]

Before 21 August, there had been little intervention in dollars. There were interventions amounting to DM 9.7 bn in the EMS, mostly (DM 6.5 bn) in intra-marginal support for the Banca d'Italia. But it was clear to many central bankers as well as almost all the market participants who took bigger and bigger bets against them that intervention and foreign borrowing could not really do the job (see Figure 11.3). In a memorandum for the UK Treasury of 12 August, the Bank of England had set out the views of its European and Markets divisions that 'the fundamental defence of sterling had to lie in a willingness to raise interest rates'. On 17 August, the Bank was so alarmed by sterling weakness that it minuted: 'Given the present market sentiment towards both the dollar and sterling, it must be questionable whether we can carry on even until 20 September with our current

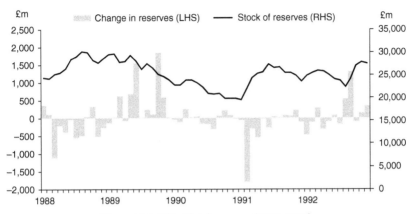

Figure 11.3 UK official reserves (1988–1992)

operational stance, without getting sufficiently close to limit down against the DM for official intervention to defend the parity to be completely on the line.' But significantly in this memorandum, the recommended strategies lay in stepping up intra-marginal intervention, moving to an internationally shared intervention strategy, and in concluding a big foreign loan (£5 bn). Significantly, the paper no longer talked about an interest rate rise.[69] The market consensus at this time was that such a rise in interest rates would run into insurmountable political resistance.

On 24 August, Michel Sapin, the new French Finance Minister in the socialist government headed by Prime Minister Pierre Bérégevoy, invited his British, German and Italian colleagues, as well as the respective central bank governors, to the gleaming new and ultra-modern Finance Ministry building in Bercy. They focused on the European situation, rather than on global dynamics. The British Minister, Norman Lamont, began with an appeal for coordinated interest rate reductions in Europe and an 'activation' of the Basel-Nyborg arrangements for intra-marginal interventions, and France and Italy also pressed for German rate cuts.

The results of the ECOFIN meeting were predictable. Just before, Leigh-Pemberton had told the London discount houses that there would be no realignment, and he also made the point that the UK could not afford to abandon its policy: 'We are on the way to establishing credibility and we can't make this the cornerstone of our policy and then abandon it.'[70] After the meeting, Lamont and his advisers briefed the press about a German 'promise' not to raise rates: 'It's the first time this has been said openly and publicly. Growth in the EC has been slowing, and prospects are not brilliant. Many people would like to see lower interest rates.'[71] Lamont had mischaracterized the actual German commitment, which was reflected in the agreed statement which simply stated: 'The Bundesbank in present circumstances has no intention to increase rates and is watching closely the further development of the economy.'

The apparent promise of German help at first led the markets to concentrate their speculative attacks on currencies with no formal defence mechanisms. Finland was forced to let the markka depreciate on 8 September, and the Sveriges Riksbank raised its marginal lending rate to 75 per cent. Within the EMS, Italy looked like the most vulnerable target of market pressure. On 7 September, the Belgian Secretary of the EC Monetary Committee sent out an abruptly worded note to cancel the regularly scheduled meeting of the Monetary Committee on Friday, 11 September. Andrew Crockett wrote by hand on the margins of the incoming fax, 'It was feared that if the Press found out about the meeting it would fuel speculation on a possible realignment.'[72] In fact, the rotating chair was held by Jean-Claude Trichet of France, who feared that a general realignment discussion would involve France – and that a French devaluation would be a massive humiliation. He therefore did everything in his power to block discussion.

But there was a meeting that was not rescheduled, of the EC Committee of Central Bank Governors, in Basel on 8 September. The Bank of England account of the meeting explains:

Schlesinger took the offensive. [. . .] Public opinion in Germany had interpreted the Bath meeting as further evidence of European pressure on the Bundesbank. Such pressure was being presented as a foretaste of what would come with the ECB and would reduce the willingness of Germany to ratify Maastricht. The Bundesbank couldn't now be seen to give in to this pressure and let interest rates fall. Nor was he able to say anything in public supporting the idea that current parties would/ should hold.[73]

The official minutes make the same point, that 'the interpretation placed by the German press on President Mitterrand's recent statement about the importance of an independent central bank had made it more difficult to gather support for the modification of the Maastricht Treaty in Germany'.[74] The charismatic investor and fund manager George Soros was at Basel and talked to Schlesinger on the fringes of the central bank meeting: that discussion strengthened his conviction that an ERM crisis was imminent, and he added a bet against the Italian lira to his existing bet against sterling.[75]

Interest rate moves on the part of the monetary authorities in the weaker countries were not successful in stemming speculative attacks. In part, this was simply because of widespread doubts about whether such a policy regime could be maintained for more than a brief time: this was a classic problem of credibility that had affected central banks in nineteenth-century and interwar crises. The technology of forex trading made for additional vulnerability in the early 1990s: the new algorithms that were used by some of the most influential and dynamic market participants made the defence moves of the central banks fundamentally unsustainable (although at this stage Soros, who was responsible for the largest bet against sterling, was not using the new methodologies). 'Dynamic hedging', based on the models of Fischer Black and Myron Scholes, depended on a price relationship between the market value of the securities traded (in this case, a foreign currency) and the price of the underlying security.[76] But an active defence of the exchange rate through interest rate rises increased the measure of 'delta' or the hedge ratio, and the formula automatically indicated that positions should be made shorter still. In this case the Black-Scholes calculation was simply replicating an older trading assumption that central banks could be pushed by very volatile markets. Institutionally magnified through large leveraged positions, such bets made the official sector virtually powerless.

THE DISCUSSION OF REALIGNMENT

On 10 September, a handwritten note records a discussion of Leigh-Pemberton with Jeremy Heywood of the Treasury:

'The C/E was at the end of his tether with the Bundesbank. He had the highest regard for Schlesinger personally and professionally but he (the C/E) had no prospect of moving the Bundesbank Council.' In a draft letter the Chancellor proposed to tell the President of the Bundesbank, 'I was very disturbed to learn that sources at the Bundesbank were reported as saying that a devaluation of sterling was inevitable.'[77]

Other countries, especially those with some sterling reserves, were anxious about the UK's commitment. On 11 September, Antonio Borges of the Bank of Portugal called Andrew Crockett to say that his bank's portfolio 'was now severely unbalanced and that they had been taking some steps to reduce the weight of sterling in it'. The Portuguese had then been told that the Bank of England was 'reluctant' to take more sterling off their hands, and so Borges asked, 'What was my assessment of our position in the ERM?' Crockett gave the classic stalling reply:

Our commitment to the present parity was virtually absolute. The Prime Minister's statement in Glasgow last night had left very little room for doubt, and the advice the Government was receiving from the Bank of England was consistent with this. If the Italians were forced to realign that would be regrettable, but we had no intention of using it as a pretext for a more general realignment. We had substantial resources to defend the currency, and intended to make use of them. [...] Of course, nobody could predict how strong market pressures might eventually turn out to be, but that we would not yield without a major struggle.[78]

The qualifiers, 'virtually', 'very little room', 'not without a major struggle', must have functioned as a warning. In fact, even before this Crockett had been authorized by the Governor to start discussions with the Banque de France about the possibility of a coordinated devaluation linked to a declaration of independence for both central banks. This was desperate, and a pipedream: for France, especially before a referendum, devaluation was a political impossibility.

Lamont had prepared a letter to send to the Bundesbank, protesting against 'sources at the Bundesbank', saying that 'a devaluation of sterling was inevitable', but the Bank persuaded him that it would be counterproductive to send this.[79]

On the same Friday, the German Finance Minister told his Italian colleague that the Bundesbank could not continue interventions in support of the lira, and that a realignment, preferably a general one, was needed. Germany sent the top permanent official in the Finance Ministry, Horst Köhler, to Paris and Rome to discuss a possible realignment. But there was no discussion at the highest political level, and Kohl never tried to speak with Amato or with Major as the panic was intensifying. Trichet was reluctant to call a meeting on Saturday 12 September, and the central banks were consulted by telephone, bilaterally. In the course of these discussions, Trichet came to the conclusion that only Italy wanted a realignment vis-à-vis the DM, and that a physical meeting was thus unnecessary. It was certainly correct that Major opposed any such manoeuvre. The UK held the chair of the ECOFIN Council and did not propose any discussion of realignment at the ministerial level. The French Finance Minister Michel Sapin was especially reluctant to undertake any dramatic move before the 20 September referendum. The French position was that calling the meeting would signal a general realignment, but that such a move was not really justified by the fundamentals. In that way, the French and the British were held together by the belief that a meeting would be a very dangerous signal. A devaluation of the franc against the Deutschemark would be perceived as a painful humiliation for France, and would be punished by the voters. On Sunday, 13 September, a last Italian attempt to secure a general realignment occurred. Fabrizio Saccomanni from the Banca d'Italia spoke with Crockett, while Amato spoke to Major, who was staying at the Queen's residence in Balmoral, Scotland. He explained Italy's impossible situation, and that there would need to be a change of parities before the markets opened on Monday. Germany would respond to this move with a small reduction in interest rates (0.25 per cent in the Lombard rate). Amato suggested as directly as he could that Britain might do well to follow this move, but Major was still convinced of the essential strength of the pound and perhaps even remembered his foolhardy claim that sterling would soon replace the DM as the strong currency of Europe. At the end of the conversation, Amato simply stated that he would have to go on his own with a new parity. When Major said, 'Good luck Giuliano,' he replied ominously, 'I should say good luck John.'

The outcome of the weekend profoundly shocked the Bank of England. The pound immediately fell to its floor against the new ERM rate of the Italian lira, and both the Bank and the Banca d'Italia needed to provide considerable support in the markets to defend the limit. Andrew Crockett abruptly summoned a handful of journalists to a background meeting on the Monday afternoon to explain the circumstances of the cancelled Monetary Committee meeting on Friday, since the press had indeed picked up some indications of the French position. The participants in that off-the-record meeting describe the meeting as 'extraordinary' and 'bizarre'. After talking about the non-meeting of the Monetary Committee, Crockett replied, 'Whether I come, or whether I go, what difference can it make.' Some participants interpreted this as a statement that the Bank had given up on the defence of sterling, and one, Anatole Kaletsky, wrote to that effect in an article in *The Times* that appeared on the Tuesday morning under the header 'After the lira, how vulnerable is sterling?' It began with the striking sentence, 'Governments always lie about devaluations and central bankers are paid to deceive investors.'[80] Before joining *The Times* in 1990, Kaletsky had worked with the *Financial Times* in New York, and had got to know George Soros. When *The Times* appeared, very early by New York time, one of Soros's managers, Richard Medley, called Kaletsky to push further about the story. The phone call led Soros to build up his already-established position against the pound very quickly. It was the basis of another story in which an American reporter later claimed, incorrectly, that Soros had a mole, a 'very deep source' in the highest echelons of the Treasury or the Bank of England.[81] A few minutes before Medley had called, Norman Lamont's Special Adviser Bill Robinson had called to express his outrage at Kaletsky's piece.

But the Bank of England was not the main source of the rumours: Bundesbank President Helmut Schlesinger was also talking about his worries with investors, notably Rob Dugger of Tudor Investment, and Soros later explained the basis of his bet in an interview with Kaletsky that *The Times* later published: 'I felt safe betting with the Bundesbank. The Bundesbank clearly wanted the lira and pound devalued, but it was prepared to defend the franc. In the end, the score was Bundesbank, 3–nil; speculators, 2–1. I did even better than some others by sticking to the Bundesbank's side.' Soros built a position of some $10 bn against the pound, and later said, 'In fact, when Norman Lamont said just before the devaluation that he would borrow nearly $15bn to defend sterling, we were amused because that was about how much we wanted to sell.'[82]

In Bonn and Frankfurt, an equally dramatic scene was unfolding. Alan Budd from the Treasury and Mervyn King from the Bank of England had been sent on an emergency mission to explain to the Bundesbank and the German Finance Ministry that the pound was correctly valued and that the UK should and would maintain the ERM parity. Especially at the Bundesbank, where the President (Schlesinger) did not receive them, and where they met instead in the office of the chief economist, Otmar Issing, the German officials could not conceal their incredulity. When the British economists laid out their charts to show that sterling was correctly valued, Issing presented Bundesbank calculations that showed an overvaluation of around a fifth. The Budd/King trip – conducted flying through September thunderstorms that seemed to reflect European monetary relations – quickly became known as the least successful central bank mission ever. The humiliation of having had to stand up for an untenable position contributed to drive King to an intense suspicion of European entanglements.

On Tuesday, 15 September, in the afternoon, starting around 2:00 p.m., the pound weakened again, going significantly below DM 2.79. The Bank provided $500–$600 m worth of support, intramarginally during the afternoon, and internally discussed overt intervention but George decided against it.[83] At the end of a nervous day on the foreign exchange market, with very large sell orders, the Governor went to a meeting in the Treasury with the Chancellor. Leigh-Pemberton explained that 'the Bank had decided against overt intervention because the problem had become severe close to the end of the day; and because there was a danger of bringing the spotlight on sterling'. The most nervous trading had been in lira and Swedish krona. But he was preparing for large-scale intervention at 8:00 a.m. the next morning, and saw overt intervention as a necessary preliminary to the next stage of the defence of sterling, a rise in interest rates. He seemed relatively calm and confident, even adding that 'it was by no means certain that the pressure on sterling would continue. There had already been substantial movement in the deutschemark and it was difficult to say whether the process had come to an end.' Lamont was more anxious and insisted on the climate of 'significant danger'; and George even went as far as to contemplate what would happen if intervention and interest rate hikes did not move the market: 'Then the only option would be, in effect, to float.' Leigh-Pemberton also reported on his conversation with Schlesinger, who had complained that the UK press 'made up quotes and attributed them to him'.[84]

The final blow came after an interview of the *Wall Street Journal* with Schlesinger, which was reported by the German financial paper *Handelsblatt*, in which the Bundesbank President seemed to be calling for a parity alteration for the UK as well: according to the wire report, Schlesinger

commented that the measures taken up to now have, naturally, not definitely resolved the problems. A more comprehensive realignment would have had a greater effect in alleviating EMS tensions. However, in his view, a change in exchange rate parities incorporating other currencies [as well as the lira] was not possible.[85]

The interview was denied the next morning, but it represented the final tipping point for speculators to pour into the attack on sterling. Speculators began selling sterling overnight. The Bank's dealer, William Allen, had instructions for the evening to try to keep the rate in touch with DM 2.78 (it had already gone below that level in late European trading). As the rate fell below 2.78, Allen started intervening in dollars (as that was the most liquid market), then switched to DMs as the dollar strengthened. The news of Schlesinger's comments came in at around 9:00 p.m., and the Midland Bank dealers informed the Bank about heavy selling by Goldman Sachs, who were now expecting the devaluation. Allen after talking to George then asked the Bank of Japan to intervene in the Asian markets for the Bank of England's account if the pound breached the limit. Allen also thought that it would be good if the Bank of Japan were not 'too discreet' about the British interventions, though in the end there was no Tokyo intervention.[86]

In frantic telephone calls between the Prime Minister's office, the Treasury and Leigh-Pemberton, in his flat, British policy-makers tried to think of ways of persuading Schlesinger to retract the statement; but when the Governor's private secretary, Paul Tucker, eventually reached Schlesinger the Bundesbank President simply explained that he did not know how to do that.

Later, the story of the *Handelsblatt* interview would constitute the key argument in the case that this was an unnecessary crisis engineered by the Bundesbank for fundamentally domestic political purposes. The Governor's European adviser, Sir Peter Petrie, reported a conversation with a French official and his wife, a journalist, René and Françoise de la Serre: 'He believes that sterling would have survived in the ERM if it had not been for the BUBA [Bundesbank]. Schlesinger was guilty of criminal negligence, if not worse (i.e. a deliberate intervention to provoke realignment).' There was an additional irritation because Schlesinger's predecessor, Karl Otto Pöhl, was reportedly advising French bankers to vote 'non' in the referendum.[87]

BLACK WEDNESDAY OR WHITE WEDNESDAY

Wednesday, 16 September 1992, or 'Black Wednesday', began with massive official and overt intervention by the Bank of England in the exchange markets. Allen spoke with the Bundesbank and obtained permission for very large-scale interventions, initially speaking of DM 1 bn, but then going to 5 bn and then 7 bn. The Bank bought a further £350 m against DM after 10:00 a.m., and asked the Bundesbank and the Bank of France to buy £100 m and £50 m, respectively (which they did). Allen later reported that 'the Bundesbank and the Bank of France were extremely helpful – not only in doing the business but in refraining from making clear to the press that they were dealing for our account'.[88]

Eddie George took control of operations, and was repeatedly on the telephone with the Chancellor and the Treasury.

The Deputy Governor told Sir Terry [Burns] that the Bank had intervened that morning in two shots of £300 million each. This had temporarily pushed sterling up to DM 2.7825, but it had then fallen back to DM 2.7795. The Deputy Governor said the Bank would shortly buy another £400 million, taking total intervention for the morning up to £1 billion.

The Deputy Governor said that a rate rise was now very likely and the question arose as to the form it should take. One possibility would be to announce a rate for MLR for the next three days. While an increase of 2 percentage points might be sufficient, the best chance of success was with, say, 4 percentage points. The MLR announcement would need to be accompanied by briefing (to the effect that it was a response to pre-Maastricht turbulence) and by a schedule of dealing rates in various maturities of commercial bills. This raised the issue of whether the likely short-term nature of the rate rise should be merely implied or stated explicitly.

Even in the first telephone call, George and Burns contemplated giving up the peg.

Sir Terry and the Deputy Governor agreed that if the initial rate rise did not have the desired effect, the authorities would have to consider either a further rate rise or floating sterling. It was also agreed that, in view of the levels of intervention another concertation among the EC Central Bank Governors would take place at 3.15pm after the Governors had consulted their Governments. Provided this concertation confirmed the views expressed earlier, and the outflow of reserves remained light, then the UK could continue to meet its obligations until 4.00pm; this would be the legal way. The Chancellor noted that the UK would not be able to suspend obligations until 4.00pm in any case, since the Prime Minister wanted to speak to Chancellor Kohl first.

At 11:00 a.m., the Bank announced that it was introducing Minimum Lending Rate, at 12 per cent; and that measure immediately led to an increase in base rates. But the move did nothing to stem the foreign exchange pressure, and the Bank lent heavily to the markets in sterling (some £920 m over the course of the day). At 2:30 p.m., the rate was put up to 15 per cent. In the immediate aftermath of that announcement, the outflows from sterling fell off considerably, in large part probably because of funding issues. The money market rates largely disappeared from the Bank's screens, suggesting great market uncertainty about the price of interbank borrowing and maybe also about its availability. That would have supported the pound, as UK institutions could no longer borrow to conduct their foreign exchange operations.

But in fact the attack on sterling was much stronger and deeper, and the other European central banks seemed, from the British perspective, quite unhelpful. So were the senior British Cabinet Ministers, who considered a range of options presented by Major in a 1:00 p.m. meeting. The Foreign Secretary, Douglas Hurd, argued that the 'rules of the ERM' should be followed. 'It could not be sensible to act in a way which would destroy trust in all our other decisions. Failure was one thing, panic another.'[89] Michael Heseltine and Kenneth Clarke fully endorsed this position. The consequence of insistence on rules, coming both from the British government and from other European central banks, meant that a futile defence and a full-scale haemorrhage went on all day, although the purchases slowed in the afternoon.

The Deputy Governor reported that at the 2.15pm concertation all the other EC Governors had emphasised that the UK should stick by the ERM rules. The Deputy Governor noted that if the rate of outflow of reserves remained low, it would be possible for sterling to get through to 4.00pm, at which point the UK's obligations under the ERM would be ended for the day. Moreover, the UK could then call a realignment conference which would have the effect of suspending its obligations under the rules until new parities could be agreed and the obligations restored. The suspension of the UK's obligations would last until a new parity for sterling had been agreed (i.e. potentially indefinitely).

The Deputy Governor said that on the concertation the other Central Banks had been adamant that the UK could not unilaterally realign and would therefore have to go on intervening and if necessary raise interest rates further until a realignment conference could be called. The Deputy Governor noted that another concertation among the EC Central Bank Governors would take place at 3.15pm after the Governors had consulted their Governments. Provided this concertation confirmed the views expressed earlier, and the outflow of reserves remained light, then the UK could continue to meet its obligations until 4.00pm; this would be the legal way. The chancellor noted that the UK would not be able to suspend obligations until 4.00pm in any case, since the Prime Minister wanted to speak to Chancellor Kohl first.

The Deputy Governor noted that the cost of continuing with the UK's ERM obligations would be to expose the reserves to further outflow for another hour or so. At the moment, the loss of reserves was fairly light, but he warned that it could become much heavier in the last 15 minutes or so up to 4:00 p.m. He added that he would be disposed to continue to meet the obligations until 4.00pm, provided the Chancellor was content.

The Chancellor asked about the prospect for achieving a realignment that evening and the Deputy Governor replied that, in his view, it would be very unlikely. In advance of the Maastricht vote, the UK would have to accept a devaluation of some 15% so as to avoid being put in the position of Italy that week following their realignment the previous weekend.

The Chancellor asked whether the Bank could stand the haemorrhage for the last half hour or so. Did we have sufficient reserves? The Deputy Governor replied that the authorities would be able to raise sufficient liquidity to withstand the outflow, though it would be extremely painful.[90]

There were three rounds of concertation with the other EC Governors on 16 September, the first at 2:15 p.m. The Bundesbank insisted on sticking to the rules obliging central banks to intervene, which obviously cost the UK a large part of its foreign exchange reserves as the haemorrhage continued, while the Bank pleaded unsuccessfully for other central banks to take action in defence of sterling.

The Governor explained that he had been obliged to ask for a concertation following the events in the exchanges during the morning. The drain from our reserves was barely sustainable, running at about £1 billion per hour at our ERM lower limit. Against that background, we had just announced that official interest rates would be raised by 3% to 15% with effect from the following morning. We hoped that this would stem the outflow, but if not we would need to look to the other central banks in the system for help in the form of intervention on their own account in substantial amounts. Otherwise, the UK Government was going to need to contemplate suspending its ERM obligations, and an announcement to that effect might have to be made during the afternoon.

Responding, Tietmeyer (substituting for Schlesinger who was not in Frankfurt) said that, in the Bundesbank's view, it was important to stick to the rules, which meant using intervention and interest rates. They would not support a suspension since that was against the rules.

Larosière said that their first principle was that everything should be done to maintain the EMS. He therefore welcomes the UK's interest rate increases, which were clearly part of the required solution. Intervention at the margin also had to be pursued. Both courses might need to be used vigorously, and in this connection Larosière mentioned the Swedish rise in interest rates to 500%. He would need time to consider what the Governor had said and to discuss the issues with his Government, but his immediate reaction was that the UK might need to face the possibility of a realignment.

A second round of concertation occurred one hour later, at 3:15 p.m., when the Bundesbank still insisted on its position of sticking to the rules, while the Banque de France appeared to change its stance:

[Philippe] Lagayette ([the Deputy Governor of the Banque de France] standing in for Larosière) said that the French Government and the Banque de France were still reflecting but their provisional view was that a UK suspension might be better than seeking to agree a realignment, but that a general suspension would not be good for the ERM at all.

Tietmeyer said that the Bundesbank and Germany would like to keep to the rules of the ERM, but indicated that if that were not possible the Bundesbank might acquiesce in a temporary float, although he emphasized that it was for the German Government to decide. The advice of the Bundesbank to the Government would be that every effort should be made to hold to the rules but that if a realignment were pursued it would have to be credible and that would mean its being a very substantial one. Tietmeyer added that if realignment was discussed, it was important that the possibility of more than one country moving should be addressed.

The Governor invited the views of the other Governors on the UK's position and in particular on the response which the UK might receive if, as earlier suggested by the Governors, we sought a realignment, which he noted would itself lead to a suspension of the ERM if new parities were not agreed by the time the markets would otherwise be due to reopen. He also pointed out that a realignment only a day or two before the French referendum would face particular difficulties.

And finally, in the third round at 6:00 p.m., after the European markets had closed, it was clear that the UK would exit from the ERM:

The Governor said that the UK Government had reached the conclusion that the turbulence in the exchanges was such that there should be a general suspension of ERM obligations and that the UK members of the Monetary Committee would be proposing that at the meeting arranged for later in the evening. If that did not prove acceptable, the UK had decided that it must in any case suspend its own ERM obligations for the time being. It was important that an announcement of the outcome of the Monetary Committee's discussions should be made before the markets officially reopened at 8.00am tomorrow morning.

Larosière said that if would be impossible for the French to accept a general suspension of ERM obligations. That was out of the question. It would have dramatic and negative consequences for the market and for the general climate in France before their Referendum at the weekend. If the UK felt that it had to suspend, then the French would have to accept that conclusion, making clear that it was a temporary measure and the outcome of a concerted meeting and discussion this evening of the Monetary Committee.[91]

The ERM was a vital interest for France. Later, in December, Trichet told the EC Monetary Committee that 'losing faith in the ERM was equivalent to losing faith in Europe'.[92] For the UK, the aftermath of the ERM also amounted to a loss of faith, a new element in what became a progressive distancing of the UK from Europe.

At the end of the affair, Leigh-Pemberton wrote a stinging personal letter to Schlesinger, protesting against Schlesinger's attempt to justify in a conversation with *Financial Times* journalists the actions of the Bundesbank by referring to its agreement to a large UK credit tranche and its willingness to do intramarginal interventions. Schlesinger had produced a document that was released by the German Embassy in London asserting that the Bundesbank had 'treated the pound sterling and French franc alike in all respects' and that the compulsory D-Mark sales in favour of sterling, which the Bundesbank financed, were 'the largest compulsory interventions ever undertaken vis-a-vis a partner currency'.[93] Leigh-Pemberton was outraged: 'As you will be aware, the Bundesbank bought sterling only for our own account, and we were given the very clear signal that you were not willing to do so for your own account.'[94] The Treasury issued its own statement: 'We have simply noted the very public way in which statements of support for the (French) franc were made, in contrast to the undermining statements made in relation to sterling.'[95]

The experiment in European cooperation had ended in failure. But the central banks themselves were conciliatory. The morning after Leigh-Pemberton's letter was sent, Schlesinger telephoned Eddie George, to explain that again he had miscommunicated, and had not intended that his document should be presented as a statement to the *Financial Times*. George in response then set out his view that 'no serious damage had been done to the Bundesbank's reputation', and that 'the Bank had been very understanding in public of the domestic situation faced by the Bundesbank' and that 'when the dust had settled, it would be important

Figure 11.4 Governor Leigh-Pemberton as physician (Richard Willson, *The Times*, 29 October 1992)

to quietly explain how the exchange market tensions had arisen from the very different domestic situations faced by Germany and the UK'.[96] So central bank cooperation could go on, and soon the Bank of England as well as the Treasury moved to a more optimistic interpretation of 16 September, White Wednesday or liberation, rather than Black Wednesday (see Figure 11.4). In 1994, Mervyn King called it 'Grey Wednesday'.[97]

COST OF ERM

Much of the discussion of the UK's ERM experience focuses on the humiliation of Black/White/Grey Wednesday, and draws the conclusion that the episode as a whole was costly – above all in terms of the harsh recession of the early 1990s, but also in the immediate sense of the measures needed to defend the ERM parity – and ultimately futile. The intervention policy that the Bank had followed from August 1992 was indeed a costly exercise. The Treasury's Exchange Equalisation Account, where the interventions were booked, declined by $4.15 bn from August 1992 to April 1993, from $23.63 bn to $19.48 bn. If there had been no intervention at all, the Bank's foreign exchange reserves would have increased to $24.39 bn, because of interest income. The cost of all the interventions could therefore be set at $4.91 bn (or £3.31 bn). If the pound had left over the weekend of 11–13 September 1992, following the Italian devaluation and the bungled discussion of an EC Monetary Committee meeting, there would still have been a substantial loss from the earlier interventions, some $3.62 bn or £2.37 bn.[98] Most of the sterling that was bought was eventually used to reconstitute reserves, though there was a strategic decision to go to a lower equilibrium level of reserves. If as a counterfactual there would have been no intervention in September 1992, and reserves had then been decreased gradually in line with actual post-ERM policy, the cost would have been £3.3 bn at a valuation of February 1994, and a little more with a valuation from 1997.[99] On the other hand, there was the question of whether the UK really would need reserves in a world of flexible exchange rates.

The immediate calculation of the cost thus arose out of the policy of rebuilding the UK's international reserves. Lamont initially asked for a replenishing of reserves at a rate of £3 bn a month. He also telephoned when he felt that on a good day on the markets the Bank had not been buying reserves. This was a very secret operation. On 26 November 1992, Heywood explained the 'secret negative forward book' used to acquire foreign exchange through 'forward swaps' worth around $12.5bn: 'In principle the forward book could be run down either by public borrowing or lower gross reserves; but having consciously disguised this part of the September's operations it would now be very difficult to explain the real reason why we were now undertaking further borrowing or revealing lower gross reserves.'[100] As Leigh-Pemberton put it in one of the phone conversations with Lamont on intervention, 'It was important not to be seen as being in the market; and market perception that the Bank had a target for taking in of reserves or wished to cap the rate for sterling might very well lead to an adverse reaction and make it much more difficult to take in further reserves.'[101] Rebuilding foreign exchange reserves meant that the Treasury was forced to pay a price for the decision to join the ERM.

If the ERM episode is seen as a moment in a struggle for monetary stability, however, the general verdict looks rather different. Alan Budd argued that 'although it was certainly a political disaster, the case can be made that it was an economic triumph and marked the turning point in our macro-economic performance'.[102] This was a widespread view of the political class. In his account of UK relations with Europe, John Major's Private Secretary Stephen Wall notes, 'I still believe that, had we not gone into the ERM, we would never have found the discipline to put an end to the inflationary "stop-go" policies that had bedeviled the management of the economy throughout my life and which largely accounted for the relatively poor economic performance from the 1960s onwards.'[103] Major himself stated, 'the ERM deserves much of the credit. It hurt, but it worked.'[104] This view has some support from modern econometric analysis. The examination of credibility by Michael Bordo and Pierre Siklos shows the strongest gains in the early 1990s.[105] The subsequent generation of a better policy framework through inflation targeting would not have been possible without that gain, since there would not have been an adequate anchor for expectations. In general, there is a substantial literature that suggests that an external anchor is the most suitable policy tool for a disinflation.

THE LONGER-TERM LEGACY

The ERM experience was a game changer in thinking about monetary policy and exchange rates. Before September 1992, the way economists thought about currency crises was largely in terms of responses to bad and unsustainable fiscal policies. The responses of markets had been modelled by Paul Krugman in what was later termed the 'first generation' currency crisis model.[106] The 'second generation' came when expectations about self-sustaining attacks were built in, most prominently in the model developed by Maurice Obstfeld. Such expectations could be applied very effectively to the European crisis. Willem Buiter, Giancarlo Corsetti and Paolo Pesenti explained the origins in terms of a 'disinflation game' with a centre (Germany) committed to stable prices and a periphery, where markets had diverging expectations about the extent and the political tolerability of the output cost that would be involved in keeping inflation down and the exchange rate stable. To economic historians, that interpretation looked very like the traumatic 1931 crisis, when rumours of a naval mutiny at the Scottish base of Invergordon triggered a run on the pound, with the Bank of England being unable to stage a defence with higher interest rates, as that would make the pain of austerity worse.[107] There existed multiple equilibria: markets would believe in the permanence of one exchange rate fix until a momentum developed to push to a different equilibrium. The crisis could thus be entirely explained in terms of the calculations of a George Soros. By the time of the 1997–1998 Asia crisis, when a similar pattern of radically revised exchange rate expectations drove a domino effect of one country after another collapsing, the 'second generation' interpretation became canonical, and Asian leaders demonized Soros. Putting the theory and the history together led to the inescapable conclusion that the intermediate solution of a fixed and adjustable peg was unsustainable, and that in consequence there were only two realistic and stable options, corner solutions: either a publicly announced, credible and time-consistent monetary policy, or monetary unification with only one central bank for a large currency area. By the late 1990s, it was easy to see that the UK was going on the first route and continental Europe on the second.[108] After 2016, that choice began to be referred to as an earlier version of Brexit (as was 1931, and perhaps also the 1532 legislation of the Henrician Reformation). The Asia crisis had seemed to demonstrate to both the Europeans and the UK's policy-makers that their decision was the correct or economically literate choice.

In British politics, 16 September proved to be a constant reference point. It ended the psychological fixation, above all in the Treasury but also for the Bank's Governor, with the exchange rate that had re-emerged in the mid-1980s and that led to Lawson's 1985 Mansion House speech turning away from monetarism and to an exchange target. Eddie George in particular on the other hand had never believed in an external over an internal anchor. The policy shock required the Bank of England to think about a new mode of operation and a new target – almost immediately, the Bank moved to inflation targeting. That required a new relationship with the government. The main driver was Mervyn King, who had been preparing a different framework for ensuring a time-consistent central bank policy, but who had also been humiliated by the last-ditch defence in the mission with Alan Budd to convince Bonn and particularly Frankfurt of the virtues of the old policy framework. And party politics needed to be rethought also. The crisis ended the association of the Conservatives with economic competence. Tony Blair and Gordon Brown reflected on very different ways by which Labour could enhance its economic credibility. Conservative rethinking took longer. In the background of Lamont's television commentary after the 'difficult and turbulent day', there was a young tanned and apparently relaxed-looking political aide to the Treasury, David Cameron.

12

'You Can't Be In and Out at the Same Time':

The Legacy of Delors

Did the Exchange Rate Mechanism (ERM) experience change the UK's relationship with Europe, and should it even be seen as the first 'Brexit'? The Maastricht Treaty was negotiated in December 1991 fundamentally on the basis of drafting by the central bankers of the European Community. The Treaty gave the UK an opt-out from monetary union, and, after the negotiations, Europe's move to monetary union looked less immediately relevant from the perspective of Threadneedle Street. There was, however, still uncertainty about the longer-term possibility of the UK eventually joining the Eurozone, a prospect that few liked, but equally that almost no policy-maker wanted to rule out definitively. At a press conference, Prime Minister John Major explained: 'We have also reserved the right to go in if we think it right for the British economy at that stage. It is not a one-way option. We have a two-way option.'[1] In fact, as the Liberal leader Paddy Ashdown told the House of Commons, Major had created a Britain that was now 'semi-detached' from Europe.[2] The uncertainty meant that the UK needed to think about issues of institutional design to ensure that the euro would not immediately damage British interests: about how non-members should be represented at the European Central Bank (ECB), but also about the question of banking supervision in a single-currency area, about the location of institutions and about mechanisms for ensuring access by the City to European financial markets. But the dynamic was substantially affected by the political turmoil that followed the UK's departure from the ERM.

As Governor from 1993, Eddie George pressed hard – via the sympathetic Dutch central banker Wim Duisenberg, who would be the first President of the ECB, and then with his successor at the Nederlandsche Bank, Nout Wellink – for a membership in the ECB Council for 'outs', including the UK. The Netherlands looked like a perfect intermediary between a British and a German view of economics and central banking. A participation of 'outs' would have transformed the ECB governance, and perhaps allowed a better balance between the objectives of the currency union and the aims of the Union as a whole. But it was firmly resisted by Germany. Bundesbank President Hans Tietmeyer briefly noted that 'you can't be in and out at the same time'. George then told Duisenberg that

the ECB's response could impact on attitudes here in the UK: if the ECB adopted an exclusive approach, it would not be seen as positive whereas a more inclusive approach could help condition the Government, political and more general climate ahead of EMU entry. He added that the German view seemed to be that hostility to the outs would encourage them to join: he thought that the reverse would be the case in the UK context.[3]

The Bank was also involved in attempting to discuss the circumstances in which LLR would function in a monetary union – an issue left largely unresolved in the Maastricht Treaty, and which would only really be tackled after political decisions in 2012 laid out the basis of a banking union. Here was an issue on which British and German philosophies of central banking clashed outright. The Bank view thought of supervision and regulation as an appropriate task for central banks, whereas the Bundesbank held such an arrangement to constitute a mortal hazard to stable and consistent monetary policy. Just before the establishment of the Delors Committee, a subcommittee of the European Commission (EC) Committee of Central Bank Governors, chaired by Brian Quinn, was established to examine the coordination of European banking supervision. Huib Muller, of De Nederlandsche Bank, who was also chairman of the Basel Committee on Banking Supervision, and Tommaso Padio-Schioppa, of the Banca d'Italia, who was also chairman of the Banking Advisory Committee to the EC (and would later follow Muller as chair of the Basel Committee), had argued that there was a satisfactory framework for drawing up legislative proposals on banking supervision in the EC, but no adequate way of drawing up more general policies on prudential supervision.[4]

In the Committee of Governors, Duisenberg stated powerfully the view that banking supervision needed to occur at the European level.[5] Such a move would deal with a strong objection to global attempts by the Basel Committee to evolve what became the 'Core Principles of Banking Supervision'. Brian Quinn, who was also a veteran member of the Basel Committee, repeatedly worried that global rules evolved by a committee of central bankers might lack 'democratic legitimacy'.[6] There was also considerable opposition to the future ECB developing a major competence in this field. The president of the German Credit Supervisory Office (Bundesaufsichtsamt für das Kreditwesen) wrote to Karl Otto Pöhl in early 1989 protesting attempts to Europeanize banking supervision, which he saw as parallel to the initiatives of the G-10 and of the Basel Committee and also as potentially reducing the competitiveness of German banking. At the same time, Tietmeyer argued that banking supervision was a responsibility of finance ministers, and not of central banks, and that the German ministry should be represented in discussions of this issue. Pöhl tried to respond to these domestic German critiques by pointing out that any decision would need to be taken by governments and parliaments, and that such a moment of choice lay in the distant future. There was similar opposition from France's *commission bancaire*, which urged the Governor of the Banque de France to exercise 'vigilance' because Brian Quinn was believed to favour the transfer of supervisory and regulatory authority to the ECB.[7]

In February 1990, at the Monetary Policy Committee meeting in Brussels, there was complete agreement that the different national rules regarding bank regulation should be left in place.[8] Delors was unwilling to force the pace on this issue, and stated that the EC approached the issue of banking supervision with an 'open mind': the ESCB should simply 'participate in the coordination of national policies but would not have a monopoly on those policies'.[9]

But the British representatives consistently pushed for a European approach to regulation. On 29 June 1990, in the alternates' meeting of the Committee of Governors, Crockett proposed that 'a further objective of the ESCB will be to preserve the integrity of the financial system'. Tietmeyer objected that this outcome should be considered a 'task' rather than an 'objective'. At the Governors' meeting to discuss such a goal, the wording was softened, mostly in response to the German position. It was agreed that 'any suggestion that the system should undertake rescue operations in favour of individual banks should be avoided', though there might be a need to deal with (rather vaguely defined) 'sudden developments' in financial markets. The wording changed, so that 'preserve' became 'support', and 'integrity' became 'stability'. That phrasing seemed to preclude any responsibility to act as a classical central bank lender of last resort. In the end, the 'tasks' of Article 3 were watered down to the much less far-reaching and less ambitious goal 'to promote the smooth operation of the payment system'.[10]

In October 1990, when the Alternates discussed the Banking Supervision Subcommittee proposals on draft articles for the central bank statute, Hans Tietmeyer restated the sceptical position of the Bundesbank, which was consistently worried about the moral hazard implications of central bank involvement in supervision. If the central bank took on the responsibility of regulating, it would also deliver an implicit commitment to rescue banks should there be bad developments that it had overlooked. Tietmeyer provided a neat encapsulation of the German philosophy of regulation: 'This did not mean from the view of the Board of the Deutsche Bundesbank that the ECB should not support the stability of the financial system, but that it should never be written down; this would be moral hazard.'[11]

Eventually, Article 25.2 of the ECB statute held out some possibility of the ECB conducting banking supervision: 'In accordance with any decision of the Council under Article 105(6) of this Treaty, the ECB may perform specific tasks concerning policies relating to the prudential supervision of credit institutions and other financial institutions with the exception of insurance undertakings.'

George saw the practical aspects of how banking support might intersect with monetary policy: 'In respect to liquidity, an extension of emergency support to an individual institution could as a practical matter be offset by transactions in the rest of the system for monetary policy purposes. It would be highly desirable, therefore, for the ECB to be notified in advance of a transaction so that adequate offsetting measures could be undertaken.' George did not want the ECB to be required to give a prior consent for such operations:

Forming a judgment about whether systemic risk justified such a transaction would also be controversial given that one could very well envisage circumstances where the issue would be one of regional rather than national or Europe-wide system risk. For instance, preventing the Italians from rescuing Banco di Napoli would perhaps not have very extensive EU-wide consequences but it clearly would result in social and economic catastrophe in large parts of southern Italy.[12]

One of the major issues that had a practical as well as a symbolic significance concerned the siting of the new ECB. The Bank joined City efforts to bring London into consideration as a possible site, but given the uncertainty about British EMU membership that always looked like a rather uncertain prospect. Some were over-confident about the importance of the City and its traditions. The Bank's adviser on European affairs, Sir Peter Petrie, explained, 'in the short run it mattered particularly to the ECB to be in London as there could be operational problems if it was located

elsewhere. In the long run, however, the advantage would be for the UK.'
Sir Brian Corby, the chairman of Prudential and a member of the Bank's
Court, spoke of the pre-eminence of London and thought that 'we needed
to fight to retain this position since others would fight even harder to wrest
it from us'.[13] Jeremy Morse thought at an early stage that Frankfurt would
be the best location 'as it was likely to instil the maximum degree of
monetary discipline in the new institution'.[14] That was clearly a realistic
stance, but also one which made the currency union appear more
'German'.

There remained the issue of looking out for the interests of City businesses, and ensuring that euro business could be transacted in London. The
Clearing House Automated Payments System (CHAPS) for euros was
connected with the European Trans-European Automated Real-time
Gross Settlement Express Transfer (TARGET) payment system. Over the
conversion weekend to the euro in 1999, the Bank kept in close touch with
forty City institutions, and later made the argument that its careful preparation had been responsible for an increase in City business.[15]

The question of careful, very careful, preparation for EMU also seemed
to many in London as a way of slowing down the process. The Bank's
internal watchword was 'Prepare and Decide': that is, the Bank should
prepare so that the UK authorities could make a decision whether to enter
or not without being constrained by any practical obstacles. But many
senior figures in the Bank were consistently keen to highlight the risks.
Mervyn King was particularly outspoken, both in internal discussions and
on academic and semi-public occasions. Thus, for instance, he propheti-
cally told a conference in Rome that

the prize of a strong European currency was great. But the process of getting there
suffered from a problem either of credibility or of legitimacy. Granted the EU's
track record, particularly during the EMS/ERM crisis, the project had a significant credibility problem (ie it had been tried and failed). There was also a real
danger that the conditions and policies necessary to realise the project would be
so tough and unpopular as to render the whole thing illegitimate in the eyes of the
public. It was also hard to see how an unelected ECB could impose its will in, for
example, cases where its decisions (eg over interest rates) were the direct cause of
unemployment in certain parts of Europe. Such decisions might well be contested
politically. The only viable way forward seemed through economic convergence.
And the credibility of that derived from successful domestic, not EU, policies.
The worst tragedy for the EU would be to move to an EMU which failed, thus
imperilling the future governance of Europe. One should be under no illusion
that a hard-core EMU in 1999 would not radically alter the way in which Europe
works. To give policy guidance to the ECB, Finance Ministers would need to form

a mini- ECOFIN which would agree measures, arrangements for the outs, and Europe's monetary stance vis a vis the rest of the world. This would have serious consequences for the way in which the G-7 operated. These would represent major political costs to the outs.[16]

In 1994, a bank official, William (Bill) Allen, head of the Foreign Exchange Division, attended a lunch of the Association for Payment Clearing Services (APCS) at which the Europhile Economic Secretary of the Treasury, Anthony Nelson, set out a view in which the European Monetary Institute (the embryo of the future ECB) would 'take on much of the practical work in the absence of any clear political direction'. Allen together with Theresa May of the APCS (a former Bank of England official, and future Prime Minister) thought Nelson was much too optimistic about the EMI and 'concluded that the Economic Secretary cannot be relied upon to listen sympathetically on this point even to papers that have the backing of the whole of the European Banking Federation (whose French members are as sceptical about the timetable as anybody else)'. Allen also noted that he and May felt that 'there was growing unease at the slender grasp of practical realities demonstrated by politicians and officials around Europe'.[17]

A twin-track strategy from the perspective of London involved both trying to make monetary union more logical and more robust, and slowing down what looked to British eyes like an ill-thought-out stampede into union. Allen worked on an inflation-targeting solution for the 'out' members of the EU, in order to reduce the risks posed by monetary union – and the fear of competitive devaluation by the 'outs' – to the single market.[18] In 1995, it looked as if EMU would be delayed, and the Treasury even started to think that the chance of a 1999 start was reduced (and also that the number of 'in' countries conforming to the Maastricht convergence criteria would be reduced, hence strengthening the chances of a smaller and more convergent monetary union).[19]

The Bank – and the Treasury – began to congratulate themselves as being seen as 'serious players' who were allies of a German push to 'conduct a responsible monetary policy through the ECB and to support this with necessary flanking of economic policy decisions. There is growing recognition of our new-found stability orientation and conduct of monetary policy.' The British embassy in Bonn also recorded that Germany wanted the UK to move formally to making the Bank of England independent, and hoped that 'we will then summon the political will to join stage III in 1999'.[20] Germany began to see the UK as a potentially critical ally in pushing the monetary union to liberalism and the strict observation of market principles. The Bank of England collected examples of 'creative' accounting practices that allowed European countries to qualify under the Maastricht criteria: what was described as 'the French telecom fiddle', involving a French privatization, or gold sales.[21] The Bundesbank encouraged the Bank's research efforts in this direction, with one Bundesbank Council member noting that Frankfurt was 'looking to the Bank to put other countries' performance under the closest scrutiny'.[22]

Some thirty euro-related projects were completed by the Bank before January 1999, including linking CHAPS euro settlement to the ECB's TARGET system, and the provision of intra-day liquidity in euros to members of CHAPS.[23] The preparations were so effective that the conservative Bundesbank began to worry about the creation of an uncontrolled 'soft euro' offshore through CHAPS – analogous to the development of the Eurodollar market in the 1960s.[24] The City saw itself – and the Bank encouraged that view – as the financial centre of a new integrated European market. Lehman Brothers London office argued that London would not suffer if the UK was not in the first wave of euro members, but 'they would be worried if the UK ruled out ever joining'.[25] By 1991, the UK accounted for an estimated 80 per cent of the ECU bond market.

As monetary union approached, and especially after 1997 with a rather sceptical Gordon Brown as Chancellor, it was clear that the UK would be on the sidelines of the project. That position also seemed to have considerable support from across the Atlantic. The British embassy in Washington reported that Treasury Secretary Larry Summers in private 'believes that EMU is unlikely to be a success'.[26] George Soros told the Bank that he felt 'that a rapid drive to monetary union might actually cause serious damage to the European Union as a whole, despite his general commitment to greater political integration in the long run'.[27] The Bank was just as critical. George wrote to Lord Kingsdown (Robin Leigh-Pemberton) in late 1997, 'To be quite honest, I tend to regard the period of the Delors Committee as increasingly part of history. [...] It is not a focal point in the debates of today.'[28] When one of his European counterparts tried to compare the transition to EMU with the French Revolution, Mervyn King called the idea 'bizarre', and wryly noted, 'quite whom he had in mind for the role of Napoleon was unclear'.[29]

Under Gordon Brown, the Treasury evolved five tests to determine whether the UK had converged sufficiently to make joining the monetary union an economically viable proposition. Were business cycles and economic structures sufficiently compatible for the UK to accept

ECB-determined euro interest rates? If problems emerged, would there be sufficient flexibility to deal with them? Would joining the euro encourage investment? How would the City of London be affected? Would euro membership promote higher growth, stability and a lasting increase in jobs? Brown termed the analysis 'the most robust, rigorous and comprehensive work the Treasury has ever done'.[30] The tests were fairly obviously designed to be failed, and to kick the can down the road by postponing a final decision from one parliamentary term to another, while avoiding any decision on principle not to join the common currency. The Bank added its own substantial scepticism, elaborating early on the proposition that the tests about cyclical convergence could never really be decisively or even adequately answered. King as Chief Economist put the point very bluntly to a House of Commons Committee:

I do not think the evidence from one cycle is ever enough and this is why I think the Governor said we shall not ever really know conclusively whether the costs of adopting the one-size-fits-all monetary policy are large or small because they will change over time and it is very hard to draw conclusions. The length of the cycle is probably up to ten years now. The reason why I think one can say you will never really know is that to have enough experience, enough observations, on business cycles to find out whether they have converged – the IMF Study did not cover very long periods – you need 200 or 300 years of data. The reason why that would not be valuable is precisely because the situation would change during that period.[31]

But there was still a wish to be engaged in the project. Remarkably, when Wim Duisenberg's term as ECB President was coming to an end and the question of succession arose, King, who had just become Governor, made a bizarre suggestion to Chancellor Gordon Brown. Should Brown not propose a British candidate rather than the French favourite, Jean-Claude Trichet? King explained, 'There were two British candidates whom he was confident would not only be worth successors but would be better than any alternative candidates from either France or any other member country. He could offer them a choice of Sir Edward George or Mervyn King.'[32] Was that a very peculiar British joke?

There was a curious parallelism in the development of British and European thinking. The same logic, and the same desire for central bank independence, that produced the euro and the ECB, dedicated to price stability, in the UK produced new arrangements under Tony Blair's Labour government for the operation of monetary policy by a central bank that was given a specific mandate. And in both cases, the eventual mandate left out financial supervision, with consequences that became fully apparent only during the Global Financial Crisis.

13

Horses for Courses

The Drive for Independence

In 1990, the greatest central banker of the day, and indeed possibly of all times, the commanding Federal Reserve chairman Paul Volcker, in a lecture at the IMF entitled 'The Triumph of Central Banking?' made the striking claim that 'there is objective reality in my impression that central banks are in exceptionally good repute these days'.[1] This was the beginning of an era when central bankers became godlike figures or rock stars or masters of the universe or alchemists who turned everything into gold. That period lasted until the 2008 financial crisis, when the reputation of central bankers everywhere took a dive, and commentators started to write instead about the 'Futility of Central Banking', and central bankers were held up as the prime example of the illegitimate power of unelected technocrats.[2] The late twentieth-century celebration of central banking produced a drive for independence or – perhaps more accurately – policy autonomy of central banks. But autonomy needed to be explained, and the new era of central banking also necessitated both greater transparency and greater accountability: a move away from the old era of obscurity and secrecy.

The British debate about central bank independence predated the UK's exit from the Exchange Rate Mechanism (ERM), but really took off only after the abandonment of the exchange rate anchor left a policy void. The void was quickly filled by a new objective – an inflation target. But the debate about how best to implement an inflation target triggered a broader discussion of the appropriate relationship between the Bank and its stakeholders: the Treasury, the financial markets, but also parliament and the public. It raised a constitutional issue, since the British tradition saw accountability as the relationship between ministers and parliament. The new environment also required fundamental changes in the way that the Bank organized itself, and of its vision of itself. The discussion constantly revolved around one term whose meaning was open to debate: independence.

The European Monetary System (EMS) crisis was a catalyst for a fundamental rethinking of the role of the Bank, the functioning of monetary policy, but also of its institutional arrangements and its philosophical orientation. The old Bank was pragmatic, and highly integrated in the life of the City. The new Bank would be driven by economic policy-making; and there then started a new debate about the role of economics in the policy approach. The immediate outcome of September 1992 was a push for an intellectual and disciplinary reshaping of the Bank's self-conception. Before 1992, there were also no lawyers employed by the Bank (it relied for legal advice on a firm of solicitors, Freshfields). After 1992, as the question began to be critical of how the Bank related to the general framework of governance in the UK, legal expertise also became more vital, and the Bank began to build a legal department, chiefly as a result of the Bingham inquiry into BCCI (see pp. 384–386). The initial and more pressing challenge was to bring economic thinking into the heart of the Bank's functioning.

INDEPENDENCE

In August 1988, on his return from a summer vacation, Chancellor Nigel Lawson started to refer to the desirability of central bank independence, a move that – as the Bank of England noted – 'caught everyone off balance'.[3] Sir Peter Middleton, at that time Permanent Secretary of the Treasury, later commented, 'Was I surprised? No, I am professionally not surprised by anything that Ministers do. It is certainly an interesting question. [. . .] I have looked at much funnier things than the independence of the central Bank of England.'[4] Some part of Lawson's calculation revolved around improving the credibility of monetary policy, but the initiative was also born out of frustration: frustration with the lack of progress on the ERM issue, but also a personal frustration with the powerful Sir Peter Middleton, who was very opposed to this thought and started to respond with 'Why don't you abolish the Treasury while you're at it',[5] and exasperation with the Prime Minister. The Bank – and the British public – only found out about this discussion over a year later, when Bank independence featured as a proposal in Lawson's pugnacious resignation speech (31 October 1989). It was clear that Margaret Thatcher was opposed to a move that would deprive her of influence over an electorally important policy tool, but she also thought that independence would require a central banker of more stature, a British equivalent to Karl Otto Pöhl or Paul Volcker or Alan Greenspan. She told her friend, the journalist and former Labour MP Woodrow Wyatt, 'Leigh-Pemberton would hardly be tough enough to run a privatized [*sic*; independent] Bank and determine what happens with our money nationally. We would have to have somebody very powerful indeed and I don't see one around.'[6] Treasury officials also liked to point out the unpleasant practical implications to Bank of England staff ('You would have to go before Select Committees quite regularly'). If the Bank wanted to raise interest rates, the Chancellor would see that he would be asked in the House of Commons whether he approved, and so he would want to be consulted – and to have an influence – before the formal decision. Redefining the relationship with parliament would thus be a key part of the move to an independent Bank.

After Lawson's resignation, which shook the Thatcher government, the question of independence flared up once more. Leigh-Pemberton told the *Sunday Independent* on 4 February 1990,

I think that it would be easier for the politicians if this highly contentious matter of monetary policy, and therefore of how resolute the counter-inflationary stance is, were taken out of day-to-day politics and were seen to be the responsibility of the central bank. It would mean that the politicians would have to say to themselves that the aim for price stability is a permanently given element in economic policy, and is not up for grabs in certain circumstances. Whether they are ready to do that is a matter for the politicians.[7]

Deputy Governor George Blunden in his Julian Hodge lecture of the same year made the argument that independence was fundamentally a characteristic of central banks in federal countries – the US, Switzerland, Germany – but then cautiously added that

nevertheless it can be argued that the granting of a specific mandate to the central bank to formulate and implement monetary policy in such a way as to bring about price stability would be of considerable value through its impact on people's expectations and behaviour, rather along the lines of one of the arguments once put forward in support of the setting of monetary targets. The granting of such a mandate might be useful in changing people's expectations by persuading them of the importance placed on price stability by the government.

He ended on a nuanced note, concluding that the 'ideal is a publicly responsible central bank entrusted with effectively maintaining the stability of the currency but in a society where such stability is generally desired, where inflation is widely recognised as a deadly sin, and where government is dedicated to price stability'.[8] It was clearly not obvious to Blunden that at that time British society really shared that objective, in contrast to Germany where there could be no doubt of the depths of inflation phobia.

In February 1990, an informal discussion was held in the Court. Blunden again set out the basic position of the Bank, in which independence was limited to the operational implementation of a specific goal on price stability:

In his view it would be quite wrong in a democracy for a central bank to be totally independent. Rather it was a question of whether a central bank should be given an explicit mandate to pursue price stability with appropriate arrangements being put in place to ensure adequate accountability. As to the precise terms of any such mandate, the Deputy Governor believed that it should be restricted to the pursuit of price stability and should not oblige a central bank to take account of other economic policy objectives, as that would merely replicate the conflicts currently faced by governments. As to accountability, the Deputy Governor felt the best model – for any European central bank or for the UK – was for the central bank to have to report to the legislative assembly along the lines of the US arrangements.

But Blunden also recognized that independent central banks by themselves did not guarantee a low-inflation performance:

The US, where the Fed was 'independent', was hardly one-hundred per cent successful, while in contrast the Bank of Japan had had great success but was extremely unindependent, as was the Bank of France which also had a noteworthy record over the past few years. The two obvious countries where success was combined with considerable independence were Germany and Switzerland, but in both cases it was important to recognize that the population had a strong aversion to inflation. The Deputy Governor did not think the UK public regarded inflation in the same light. On the contrary, public opinion probably regarded a bit of inflation as no bad thing; certainly, a wage offer of less than five per cent was widely viewed as insulting.[9]

Independence for a central bank thus could only make sense in the context of a change in broader political culture and preferences.

TWO OR THREE PURPOSES

In order to make a case for independence, it was clearly necessary to specify what particular goals an independent central bank would work towards. Price stability was not the only goal of the central bank according to its vision of itself. Eddie George, who in March 1990 succeeded Blunden as Deputy Governor, was the central figure in pushing the Bank clearly to define its purposes, which were not mentioned in any statute. He came up with a triple mission, with financial stability and the good working of the financial system added on to the quest for price stability. Thus, the Bank produced what amounted to the first systematic statement of its mission in its entire history, with a document entitled 'Purposes, Responsibilities and Philosophy':

The Bank is committed to public service.

As the central bank of the United Kingdom, it has three essential or core purposes which depend for their achievement on both the quality and the effective coordination of the work of all its various departments and divisions:

- The stabilisation of the value of the currency as the necessary precondition for the achievement of the Government's wider economic goals. This the Bank seeks to achieve through its advice to the Government on monetary policy, as developed from economic and financial analysis of developments both in this country and abroad; by implementing agreed policy through its market operations and its dealings with the monetary system; and by maintaining the integrity of the note issue.
- The maintenance of stability in the financial system. This the Bank seeks to achieve by monitoring the financial health of the various sectors of the domestic and international economy; through the direct supervision of individual institutions and financial markets; through cooperation with other financial supervisors, both nationally and internationally; and through its involvement in payment and settlement arrangements.
- The promotion of the efficiency and effectiveness of the UK financial services sector, both to meet the needs of the rest of the economy and as an important contributor in its own right to employment and to national income whether generated in this country or by British firms abroad. This the Bank seeks to achieve by facilitating competition among financial intermediaries and by acting as a catalyst to collective action where market forces are perceived to be deficient; through advice to the Government; through its own expertise in the market place; and by supporting British interests through its relationships with financial authorities overseas.[10]

The third issue figured very prominently in a rethinking of the payments system that occurred at the same time as the recession of the early 1990s put big strains on the financial system, but faded after that, when a concern for designing a robust system was replaced by a robust confidence that competition alone could make for effectiveness and that the need for a Bank catalyst was no longer acute. Industrial policy, which had still been a core concern of the Bank in the 1980s (see pp. 246–254), was also written out of the Bank's sphere of activities, so that the third core purpose effectively was folded into the second.

The rethinking of purpose also occurred in the setting of a general European discussion, as part of the move to monetary union, about the appropriate role and aims of a central bank, and the relationship of central banking to politics. In July 1990, the Bank concluded that there was little change in its legal position that was likely in the future, but that a general European move to monetary union might include – as indeed the Maastricht Treaty in the event did – provisions about central bank independence in Eurozone members. In those circumstances, it was likely that the focus in mandate would be largely – indeed perhaps exclusively – on price stability, and that financial stability would be excluded from the Bank's remit. In the course of the run-up to the Maastricht negotiations on monetary union, the increasingly intellectually self-confident German Bundesbank again and again emphasized the dangers of central bank involvement in financial supervision, as that engagement would risk at some moments compromising with price stability if it appeared that significant financial institutions were under threat.

In a Court discussion in 1990, Leigh-Pemberton had already set out the issues that would dominate debate for the next decade very clearly:

The Governor opened by saying that he took it as axiomatic that there was no chance of a change in the law in the foreseeable future. The Deputy Governor agreed that fundamental change was unlikely. He nevertheless believed that the Bank could help to improve the climate as regards the Bank's constitutional position by continuing to press the point that price stability was an absolutely essential pre-condition of stable long-term growth and the proper functioning of the economy.

The Governor felt that it might also be possible to improve the Bank's position, within the existing statutory framework, by reaching a better de facto relationship with HMT [the Treasury].

The Governor raised the question as to whether it was possible that, in the event of the Bank being given a statutory mandate to operate monetary policy in the pursuit of price stability, there would be pressures for other functions to be removed from the Bank, such as for example the management of the government debt programme, the industrial finance functions and bank supervision.

Mr Crockett thought that, given the opposition on both sides of the House to making the Bank 'independent', the Bank independence debate was likely to be played out in a Euro-context and specifically as part of the developing EMU debate.[11]

For George, the argument was very different, and there was no need to think of European developments to justify the centrality of price stability, since 'the line that leads from monetary policy to the health of the financial system is pretty clear'. Large institutions did not present a problem, rather 'systemic dangers have tended to originate among the smaller banks'.[12]

THE END OF THE ERM AND THE SEARCH FOR A NEW PARADIGM

The discussion of independence continued in a highly truncated form during the ERM period, where monetary policy was basically set within the framework of an exchange rate arrangement. In the run-up to the April 1992 general election, with opinion polls consistently showing a small Labour victory, Leigh-Pemberton commented that a hung parliament, while politically 'the most unsatisfactory outcome', could 'actually create an important situation and even an opportunity for us, as there may be a need in those circumstances for the politicians to announce that the monetary reins had been placed in our hands'.[13] In fact, John Major won a surprise Conservative majority, and was clearly set against the idea of Bank independence.

But once the ERM crisis had destroyed the exchange rate anchor, there was an urgent need to find a new policy approach. On 16 September 1992, the Treasury very obviously suffered a massive humiliation, and some figures at the top of the Bank saw an ideal opportunity to assert the Bank's position. Almost immediately after 'Black Wednesday', brainstorming within the Bank about new policy options began. The new world felt to some in the Bank like a liberation. On Thursday, Eddie George minuted an immediate response:

> Yesterday was, in an obvious sense, a crushing defeat for policy. But it also presents us with an opportunity to break free from the intense conflict between domestic and external objectives which ERM membership in the exceptional circumstances of German re-unification has involved us in over much of the past year. Because monetary policy has had to be directed solely towards maintaining the exchange rate we have had interest rate at levels which were inappropriately high in relation to domestic inflationary pressure and domestic activity, particularly in the context of the debt overhang. Given that, the Government has relaxed fiscal policy to a degree that would otherwise have been clearly inappropriate; and we have, untypically, ourselves recently advised the Chancellor to undertake further fiscal expansion. The opportunity now presents itself to revert to a more appropriate policy mix.[14]

He went on to state that the Chancellor should be discouraged from thinking of repegging sterling for the time being. What was now required was a relaxation of monetary policy.

Mervyn King produced a similar but more institutionally oriented piece of advice on the same day:

> We should consider how best to argue for independence of the Bank. If we remain outside the ERM, and there is no independence for the Bank, a clear and coherent

framework for the formulation of monetary policy will be necessary, in my view, to restore any semblance of credibility to our policy stance. Otherwise, we shall have no hope that we shall be given the opportunity to build up credibility by the pursuit and achievement of price stability.[15]

There had been some discussion of inflation targeting immediately after it had been introduced in New Zealand in 1990, but at that time most senior Bank of England officials felt that targets would probably be missed regularly and hence be a source of embarrassment rather than of stability. On the other hand, in the summer of 1992 Arthur Grimes, one of the architects of the New Zealand policy and a recent PhD from LSE, had met Mervyn King at a conference in Sydney run by the Reserve Bank of Australia, and King had been impressed by the potential of applying the policy in the UK context. At this conference, King had himself discussed alternatives to pure discretion in monetary policy, without mentioning the ERM, and also commented that a move to inflation targeting might be 'the appropriate direction to pursue' in the UK.[16] Even before that, King had submitted a paper to the Bank's Court on 'Design and Implementation of Monetary Policy', which examined four methods of establishing and enhancing policy credibility: pre-announced policy rules (which would be hard to find); investment in reputation, through the pursuit of tough policies in the short term; incentives such as indexation to prevent future governments being tempted to inflate; and finally, 'delegating monetary policy to an institution charged with the objective of price stability'.[17]

In a relatively open economy, inflation would clearly be affected by the exchange rate, and a drop in the value of the pound would produce more price increases. Accordingly, King believed he needed to think quickly about which models would be most appropriate to estimate the effects of possible interest rate policies. By the end of September, he ran two scenarios through two contrasting models, one a conventional macro-model that showed a surge in inflation in 1993 and 1994, and another more modern vector autoregression model that required less guessing about the forces that shaped variables (see Table 13.1).[18] In the first scenario, the exchange rate was held at 2.50–2.60 Deutschemark (DM), and interest rates maintained at 9 per cent until German rates might fall in the spring of 1993; in the second scenario, there was a more aggressive cut in interest rates.

A few weeks of intense and wide-ranging discussion of potential new ways of making policy began immediately after 16 September 1992, involving both the Treasury – where the debate was centred – and the Bank, which did not want to be left in the cold. King initially raised the

Table 13.1 *Inflation projections (1993–1994)*

	Macro-model		VAR model	
	1993	1994	1993	1994
August 1992	3.0	3.5	3.1	4.8
Case 1	4.6	6.7	4.1	5.9
Case 2	5.9	9.8	3.8	6.4
Outcome	2.25	1.17	2.25	1.17

King memos, King, 28 September 1992 report on inflation; GDP deflator from ONS.

possibility of an inflation target in a regular Treasury–Bank meeting on 2 October 1992, in which he set out the overall vision, and a substantial amount of agreement on the desirability of the approach seemed to have been reached:

A medium-term inflation target, and the public justification of all interest rate decisions in terms of that target, might improve the credibility of policy by making the way in which discretion was used more transparently. The problem with targeting intermediate variables was that they could easily give wrong signals – either signaling a policy change when none was needed or failing to signal policy change when it was needed; ignoring the indicators in such circumstances tended to damage credibility even though it was warranted by the ultimate policy objective. Given the past variability of inflation and the size of forecast errors, the target range might have to be quite large – probably 4 percentage points wide – to have a high probability of achieving an outcome with the range. But setting a range which went as high as 4 per cent would seem to indicate tolerance of inflation rates with which the authorities could not really be comfortable. It might be possible to describe the target in such a way that a firm central objective was distinguished from the outer zones of the target range. The centre of the target range might be based on the objective of price stability or on the achievement of the Maastricht inflation convergence condition. [. . .] It was agreed that the inflation assessment could not simply be based on macro model forecasts even though all the information from the indicators should, in principle, be included in the forecasts derived from macro model.[19]

But when King returned to the Bank, he was heavily criticized by George, and he remembers 'being shouted at' by the Deputy Governor.

On 6 October 1992, George told Treasury Permanent Secretary Sir Terry Burns that he and the Governor were 'exercised about the possibility that future monetary policy would be set in stone before the Bank had had its chance to give its input', and also noted that the Bank would find it hard to support 'specific inflation or monetary aggregate targets'.[20] But the same day, Leigh-Pemberton wrote to Chancellor Norman Lamont with a specific proposal for an inflation target:

As we discussed last night, we do not feel that a credible policy could be erected on the basis of a published 'range of indicators' for the monetary aggregates and possibly other indicators of inflationary pressure, although we do as you know firmly believe that the monetary authorities must take account of all relevant indicators in assessing the position and setting policy. We believe that the best way to do this would be through the publication of a credible inflation objective combined with the publication of a periodic report, which we would envisage being made quarterly, on the outlook for inflation, setting out an assessment of the implications of all the relevant indicators. Attached to this letter is a proposed draft of an inflation objective, and we have separately sent to Terry Burns a copy of a paper entitled 'Report on Inflation' which is the sort of thing we believe could very usefully be published, preferably by the Bank quarterly.[21]

The attached document on 'Price Stability' amounted to a very gradual approach to inflation targeting:

For the period ahead (say over the next three – four years) this might mean that prices, measured for example by the change in retail prices excluding mortgage interest payments and indirect taxes, should fall in a range of 3–5% compared with 4–7% for most of the past decade. And over the longer-term, in the absence of inflationary shocks (such as changes in oil or commodity prices – in either direction), it would imply a range, on the same illustrative basis of 0–2%.[22]

On 8 October, Lamont wrote to the Chairman of the Treasury and Civil Service Select Committee (TCSC) setting out a new framework for monetary policy 'to replace that hitherto provided by the ERM'. It included what in practice constituted an inflation target: 'I believe we should set ourselves the specific aim of bringing underlying inflation in the UK, measured by the change in retail prices excluding mortgage interest payments [the indicator that became known as RPIX], down to levels that match the best in Europe. To achieve this, I believe we need to aim at a rate of inflation in the long term of 2% or less.' For the remainder of this parliament, the objective would be to keep underlying inflation within a range of 1–4 per cent.[23] He also envisaged a target for M0 between 0 and 4 per cent, which looked easy since the latest figures were in the middle of that range.

On the evening of the same day, Leigh-Pemberton presented a vision of how the Bank might draw the right lessons about price stability from the turbulent experiences of the past month. He started by observing:

It would frankly be humiliating – and I mean nationally rather than institutionally or personally – if we had to accept that we could only manage our affairs effectively and responsibly if we were subject to external constraint. It could only mean that we lack either the wit or the determination to manage our *own* affairs. In fact, we came very close in the mid-1980s, *outside* the ERM, to achieving a stable basis for sustainable longer-term growth, until the excessive expansion of some five years ago sparked off the inflation, the consequences of which we are still suffering.

But the speech went beyond a very narrow definition of price stability, and included a strong defence of the need to consider asset prices and also the exchange rate:

Rather, we should utilise all of the information available from the monetary/ financial economy and the real economy. That includes the whole range of broad and narrow measures of money and of credit, not just in aggregate terms but in terms of their components and sectoral composition. It includes asset prices. It includes the whole range of factors bearing directly and indirectly on prices and costs, from the pressure of demand in relation to the supply capacity of the economy, to international influences such as world commodity prices and global demand conditions. And it includes, importantly, the exchange rate, which is far too important a price to ignore, whatever the exchange rate regime.[24]

On 20 October, the Bank developed a proposal for a new format for regular meetings of the Chancellor and the Governor, with an objective 'to make it more difficult for No. 10 to intervene in interest rate decisions, and make it similarly difficult for a non-orthodox Chancellor to make interest rate movements which were – or at least whose timing was – motivated by political considerations'.[25] On 27 October, in a meeting in the Treasury, when Norman Lamont set out his idea of a new framework for monetary policy-making, which he would announce two days later in his Mansion House speech,[26] the Bank reverted to its proposal that it would issue an inflation report in the *Quarterly Bulletin*.

The Chancellor said that his Mansion House Speech would specify a range of proposals for greater openness and accountability in the conduct of monetary policy. This would involve:

(a) Publication of a timetable for monthly Chancellor and Governor meetings;
(b) Publication of the Treasury's monthly monetary assessment, excluding the minutes of the associated meeting and unpublished figures (such as intervention);
(c) Publication of an account of the reasoning underlying each interest rate change.[27]

Lamont made it clear that he did not expect any linkage between the regular meetings between the Chancellor and the Governor and interest rate decisions.

By October, then, a framework was emerging in which there would be regular – and well-publicized – meetings between the Chancellor and the Governor (or what became later known as the 'Ken and Eddie show', once Eddie George succeeded Leigh-Pemberton and Kenneth Clarke replaced Lamont). The mechanism was specifically seen as a form of political insulation or protection. There would have to be much more explaining of the reasons for policy decisions, and much more cultivation of relations with the press. Sir Terry Burns later complained that "openness on monetary policy is creating an awful lot more work for Treasury officials."[28]

The new framework, which included a Monthly Monetary Report from the Treasury and a quarterly Inflation Report from the Bank, and regular meetings between the Chancellor and the Governor, was announced by Lamont in his Mansion House speech on 29 October 1992. He presented the new framework as 'a welcome shift away from the excessive secrecy that has up to now shrouded much of the policy-making process'.[29] King was very emphatic that the Bank's Inflation Report was 'not subject to negotiation with the Treasury'.[30] The major difference of the new system was that – unlike the old articles in the *BEQB* – there was no Treasury input; and in that sense a distinctive Bank input would be clearly visible to markets and to the public. The report was designed to constitute a powerful lever over the Treasury.[31] At the outset, the Treasury was understandably suspicious, and the Bank achieved its objective by packing the *Inflation Report* with charts and figures which effectively could not be quibbled over, and the Treasury rapidly gave up any claim to redact the document (see Figure 13.1). The central projection involved a range of likely outcomes, with a comparison to previous projections.

The first of the new quarterly reports was published on 12 February 1993, and presented by Mervyn King at a press conference. The conclusions were often, especially at the beginning, implicitly critical of the government. The first report outlined that 'the central projection for underlying inflation is in the 3%–4% range', and then observed: 'There is also a risk that large fiscal deficits might create expectations of higher inflation in the future. Expectations of inflation have not yet adjusted to levels compatible with the target range for inflation of 1%–4%.'[32] In May, the tone was similar: 'Both direct surveys of expectations and also the indirect evidence from implied forward market interest rates suggest that many economic agents have yet to be convinced that the target will be met in the long run. But the longer underlying inflation remains within the target range the more credibility will grow over time.'[33]

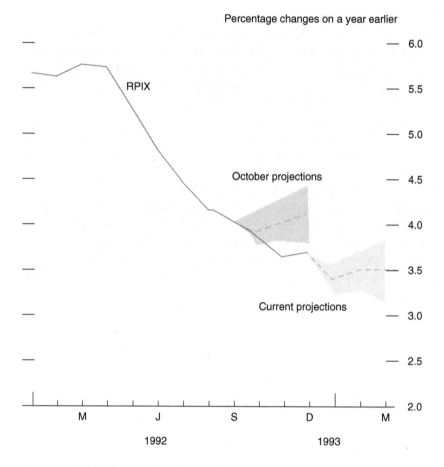

The range is defined as the central projections plus or minus the average
error on such forecasts in the past.

Figure 13.1 Inflation report: RPIX inflation projections and outcomes (February 1993)

The choice of 2.5 per cent was guided by three considerations. First, any
lower figure would be unachievable, and would look absurd and incredible,
and so it would be best to provide a new more ambitious and lower target
only when the 2.5 had been hit. In this way, inflation expectations would be
guided gently down. Secondly, there were substantial wage and price
rigidities in the UK (and other industrial economies), so that a target
choice that was too low would increase cost pressures and could lead to
output losses. Third, measurements of the cost of living ignored the effects
of technology in increasing quality: most obviously, computers or cars are

not the same as those produced and sold five years earlier, and the better performance should be reflected in greater value. This objection was perhaps less powerful in the UK than in other countries, because a more frequent rebasing of the index to adjust for exactly this sort of change took place. One argument that was entirely absent from the British debate of the 1990s was the most common modern (post-financial crisis) argument for a target greater than zero (which might appear to be absolute price stability): that a higher target means that there is less of a problem that interest rates cannot be set below zero (the zero lower bound) and that in consequence a liquidity trap of the type diagnosed by Keynes for the 1930s would emerge.[34]

King was careful to distinguish the Bank's argument from the academic argument that was popular and influential at that time, whereby better policy would result from a contract (with penalties) between government and central bank. One version was the suggestion by Kenneth Rogoff that governments would do better by delegating decisions to a 'conservative' central banker (obviously modelled on the actual example of Paul Volcker), whose inflation preferences were below those of the general public. King saw inflation as determined by occasional shocks that needed to be accommodated, with the consequence that what was important was the distribution of inflation outcomes rather than occasional peaks. In this way, the central bank might deliver a better performance than that of an 'inflation nutter', as he characterized the 'conservative' central banker (in a paper originally given at the very conservative Swiss National Bank).[35] The point aimed at showing that the Bank was no longer the old Bank, chained to City interests, but rather that concern with inflation was only part of a wider commitment to macro-economic stability.

He looked for international applications, and even saw the inflation-targeting framework as potentially a way out of the impasse that the ERM seemed to have sunk into after the Italian and British crises of September 1992 were followed by a general breakdown, in which the French franc became the target of a speculative attack, in July 1993. All European countries might adopt an inflation target, and the ERM might become a way of carrying out a peer review: 'It is, after all, easier to lose weight when one's own family members are on the same diet.'[36]

The Bank's *Inflation Report* had some inherent communications difficulties. The Treasury also worried about supplying the Bank with statistical information for forecasts, out of fear that there might be an issue of insider trading.[37] At the outset, the Bank may not have realized how thoroughly the press would scrutinize the language in order to find clashes or contradictions with ministerial statements. As Alan Budd commented, 'The Bank does not seem to appreciate how nasty-minded journalists are. (Maybe that is because they are never nasty to the Bank.)'[38]

In his original scheme for the remaking of the macro-economic executive, Lamont did not want to see interest rate changes associated with the regular Chancellor–Governor meetings, although Leigh-Pemberton expressed a 'preference' that 'there should be some expectation that interest rate movements would follow closely' from those meetings.[39] In fact, the Treasury wanted to do its best to destroy any impression that Britain was trying to 'mimic' the policy-making arrangements of the US, with the voting processes of the Federal Open Market Committee (FOMC).[40]

The discussion with the Treasury about a new policy framework was followed by an extensive debate in the Court of the Bank. Sir David Scholey, who was widely regarded as the most likely successor to Leigh-Pemberton as Governor, pointed to the need for a reform of Bank governance, in the light of a European move to placing central bank independence into a set of treaty obligations, but warned against 'any serious dash for UDI [Unilateral Declaration of Independence, a reference to White Rhodesia's move under Ian Smith to escape the British Empire in 1965] against the government's wishes as he thought the government would win'. Scholey added a critique of the way the Bank did its business: 'He thought that the structure of Court had become outdated, in particular in the context of external developments in how decisions were being made.' Andrew Crockett made a point that also drew on European debates, and on the role model of the Bundesbank, where the President was really tied by the Bundesbank Council, when he argued that 'the responsibility for monetary policy should be vested in a group rather than in an individual'.[41]

Thinking about the institutional setting of policy might logically include the thorny question of the relations with Treasury. A variety of foreign precedents on how to manage Bank–Treasury relations were discussed. By the spring of 1993, there were discussions with Prime Minister John Major, but the Bank was still groping for a view as to how it should articulate its case. The problem at this point was that, in the aftermath of the bitter struggle over interest rates during the ERM period, the whole issue had become hopelessly politicized.

The most immediate consequence of Black Wednesday was to remove the constraint on interest rates that had been imposed by the EMS. Rates were cut very rapidly – falling in increments of a whole percentage point, with the London clearing banks' base rate falling to 8 per cent on 18 October, 7 per cent on 13 November, and 6 per cent on

26 January 1993. The last move in particular excited attention and controversy. It had been preceded by a political mobilization in which Conservative MPs demanded that Leigh-Pemberton should cut borrowing costs, and was timed just as Major was leaving on a trip to India. Lamont justified it by referring to weak M4 growth in December. When it came, there was a wave of political welcome and financial opprobrium. City economists spoke of 'panic'.[42] The exchange rate immediately weakened.

In the last meeting of the Governor and the Chancellor before the 26 January move, on 13 January at lunch, Leigh-Pemberton

wondered whether the Chancellor might be put in the position of having to reduce interest rates in order to 'buy' an increase in taxation (analogous to the famous 1981 Howe budget where a deflationary fiscal stance had been accompanied by a big interest rate cut). In his view this would be most undesirable and would be badly received by the markets. [...] A cut in interest rates before the Budget would be seen as driven by political rather than economic motives. The markets were not expecting an early cut in rates; and if a move were made the exchange rate might fall sharply.

Lamont replied that 'he was not entirely persuaded that interest rates should not be cut <u>before</u> the Budget'.[43] Leigh-Pemberton's note of the lunch records that Lamont 'wanted to wait and see more evidence', and that Lamont 'appeared to accept the Governor's argument that it would be better to see the reaction of the market to the Budget first and respond to a favourable reaction, if it materialised, rather than offering changes in monetary and fiscal policy as a package'. Lamont seemed to think that devaluation might bring competitive benefits, although he self-deprecatingly talked of this view as 'fool's gold': 'It was an open question as to whether it would be desirable to let the pound rise sharply.'[44] It was this lunch meeting, where Leigh-Pemberton wrongly thought that he had convinced the Chancellor, which ensured that the Bank leadership – Leigh-Pemberton but especially George – refused to conceal their dismay when Lamont cut the base rate.

The discussions and the eventual decision of 26 January showed up a fundamental policy incoherence. At the end of January, the *Sunday Times* reported that Major was planning to sack Lamont and then push 'further big cuts in interest rates after he takes overall charge of the economy'. A 'senior minister' was quoted as saying that 'he had been pressing for a cut for some time but the Treasury was dragging its feet'.[45] Immediately afterwards, Sarah Hogg from the Policy Unit in Ten Downing Street spoke to Eddie George, who tried to insist that 'there should be no public perception of a division between No 10 and No 11 on economic policy', and Hogg tried to say that 'there was absolutely no push from the Prime Minister for interest rates to be taken below their present level of 6%'.[46] Sir Douglas Wass, a former Treasury Permanent Secretary, thought that the long spell of Conservative government had undermined the Treasury's intellectual capacity and that it did not employ enough 'mavericks who would question ministers' own judgments about the economy'.[47] In response to such criticisms, the Treasury had convened a new panel of economic forecasters, four of whom, the intellectually quite diverse Patrick Minford, Wynne Godley, David Currie and Tim Congdon, demanded interest rate cuts at a meeting of the Institute of Economic Affairs.[48]

Thus, the time looked ripe for an initiative that would shift the balance of power between the Bank and the Treasury. George thought it best to work through the Prime Minister, in part because Lamont's reputation had been so damaged by Black Wednesday, 16 September, that he no longer looked like a very authoritative figure. He would in fact soon (on 27 May 1993) be replaced by Kenneth Clarke, a much more politically astute personality. Within the Treasury, civil servants worked on a plan for independence, but without consulting the Bank ('on the grounds that if we were No. 10 would think we were conspiring with the Treasury').[49] In his resignation speech, delivered a few days later, on 9 June, Lamont raised the issue of Bank independence again:

Figure 13.2 Robin Leigh-Pemberton with John Major (from *Daily Telegraph*, 25 November 2013)

Nothing would be more effective in establishing the Government's credibility than if my right hon. Friend [Prime Minister John Major] would have the courage to establish an independent central bank in this country. The time has come to make the Bank of England independent. It is my greatest regret that, after two and a half years of trying, I failed to persuade the Prime Minister of this essential reform.[50]

Following the January debacle over interest rates, the Governor prepared a draft letter to the Prime Minister with a paper on 'operational autonomy of the Bank of England' (see Figure 13.2). The letter appealed to a common understanding of there being no long-run trade-off between inflation and growth, and of the government's commitment to 'reducing inflation to negligible levels and keeping it there'. The Bank welcomed the inflation target and raised the possibility of a statutory change with all-party consent; but even in an 'evolutionary approach', the Bank might decide on the size and timing of changes in interest rates. The government would set the target for inflation – that is, set policy 'and be accountable to Parliament for that policy', but would not be responsible for technical judgements as to particular decisions but 'would have to review the Bank's husbandry of the mandate'. This proposal 'would be consistent with trends in the rest of the world and in particular in Europe'.[51] As eventually formulated in the final letter, the Bank statement said: 'We prefer to use the term "operational autonomy" for a working arrangement in which the Government would continue to have responsibility for setting the objective of policy but the function of operating interest rates would be delegated to the central bank in a way both requiring and enabling it to meet the objective.' Such a move would be necessary if and when the UK proceeded to Stage 3 of EMU.[52]

In the discussion about the precise shape of the letter to the Prime Minister, Leigh-Pemberton said

that he was happy to approach the Prime Minister but the question was how to put the case to him. He envisaged acknowledging that what the Prime Minister did was a matter for him. He would also like to suggest that the Prime Minister might consider reversing the conventional position that the Treasury decides on interest rate moves by adopting a procedure similar to that in the Netherlands. There the central bank operates monetary policy but discusses policy with the Finance Ministry. Mr Crockett said that that would be a fundamental change in the procedure and would in practice give the Bank almost full powers except in certain extreme circumstances. It would not leave the Government with very significant residual powers. The Governor said that his concern about this route was that a disagreement on policy might lead the Treasury to retrieve the powers from the Bank leaving the Bank in a worse position that it was now.

The Governor said the he felt it important to prevent moves being made for purely political reasons. He noted that the timing of the most recent cut in rates had

been determined by the Prime Minister when he was in India. The Deputy
Governor said that it would have been possible for the Bank to resist this if it
had been appropriate to do so, but in fact the Bank had argued the previous week
that there was a case for reducing rates which made it difficult to dispute the
substance of the move. The Governor felt that the timing of the cut had been
unfortunate because it was felt to have been politically motivated.[53]

When the Prime Minister met the Governor and Deputy Governor, on
25 May 1993, he bluntly told the central bankers that parliament would not
agree, and that there could only be an incremental move.

The first step was to convince political and market opinion that the
Government's economic policies were credible in their own right and that
economic recovery was happening because of these policies, not in spite of
them. It needed to be clearly established that recovery had begun before Britain
left the ERM – and indeed that recession began before we joined it.[54]

In short, Major wanted the Bank to use its credibility to make propaganda
for the government – in an ironic way, a powerful example of the reasons
why central banks should be independent.

RETHINKING THE BANK: PERSONALITIES AND DESIGN

The new thinking about what the Bank was and consequently how it
should be organized was fundamentally driven by a dramatic initiative by
the new Chief Economist, Mervyn King. The new initiative marked the
beginning of an era in which economics and economists played a much
greater role in policy formation, and in which the Bank started to think of
its impact practically exclusively in terms of its input into the strategy
behind monetary policy.

On 7 November 1989, two days before the Berlin Wall fell and Europe's
political geography changed fundamentally, the Governor of the Bank met
with the Chancellor, the newly installed John Major, to discuss the imminent reshuffle at the top of the Bank, when Eddie George would succeed
George Blunden, who was about to reach the age of 67, as Deputy
Governor. Blunden had famously liked to complain that there were 'too
many bloody economists' at the Bank.[55] Leigh-Pemberton told Major

that there was one non-executive post to fill on the Court and he was looking for
a successful industrialist from the North of England, if possible one from a small –
medium sized business. He would like to announce the new appointment together
with the new Deputy Governor early in December. The Chancellor agreed that this
would be sensible and said he would consider whether he knew of any candidates
for the remaining post.[56]

Leigh-Pemberton made his push for a business figure the subject of a quite vigorous campaign. At his regular meeting with the Chancellor in January 1990, he 'made it clear that he would be reluctant to see an economist at the Court and stressed that, if an economist were to be appointed, it would be very important that they could make a contribution other than as an economist'.[57] Just over a week later, at lunch with the Chancellor, Leigh-Pemberton noted that he thought that Major really had 'battled' for the industrialist, with Sir George Kenyon, a fourth-generation Manchester cotton manufacturer, as top choice; but the Prime Minister had decided otherwise: 'she would like to have an economist at the Court and Mervyn King is her choice'.[58] King had come to her attention primarily as the author of a paper on tax reform which had laid the basis for Nigel Lawson's spectacular 1988 budget triumph, and Lawson had apparently asked, 'Why don't people have ideas like this *inside* the Treasury?'[59] In the early 1980s, she had also pressed for an economist, and at that time had wanted Patrick Minford, a suggestion that Richardson and McMahon moved quickly to frustrate.[60] In 1990, Mervyn King started at the Bank as a Non-Executive Director.

In 1991, at the insistence of Leigh-Pemberton, who had been highly impressed by King's role in the Court's debates on Bank independence, King succeeded John Flemming as Chief Economist. He immediately tried to improve the quality of the Bank's forecasts, at first by approaching City economists from James Capel, SG Warburg, Nomura Securities and Goldman Sachs. The *Financial Times* now reported: 'For the price of a middling lunch, the Bank's forecasting team, headed by Mr Andrew Brooks, has been trying to add to what it knows about forecasting. This is the bread-and-butter work of City economists, while the Bank has until very recently produced, but not published, only two forecasts a year.'[61]

King found the dominance of the Bank by the Markets Division puzzling, as Markets tended to argue very pragmatically about how policy would interact with the behaviour of a financial market driven by a compulsive belief to focus on one particular story – a story that could and did change radically from time to time. That – from his initially academic perspective – did not look like a very solid foundation for policy. Together with Markets, policy had also been driven by the International Division, which became increasingly visible and important to formulating the Bank's approach as exchange rate issues became the key to monetary policy, first with the shadowing of the DM, and then with EMS membership. After Black Wednesday, the International Division had misstepped by focusing on how the UK might return to exchange rate stability.

At the end of 1992, King prepared a statement for the Court that laid out clearly an argument that a fundamentally new approach was needed:

Taking monetary policy away from the Treasury is necessary to save the Treasury. But the same applies to the Bank. I have been surprised by how limited is the time that we have available to consider monetary policy. Many other issues crowd in. Responsibility will imply specialization. In the last resort, the basic case for independence is simply horses for courses.[62]

The Court paper emphasized a very European – indeed German – view of how monetary policy should work. In it, King rested the case for independence on a number of propositions, the first of which was that 'price stability should be one of the principal objectives of economic policy'. There was no long-term trade-off between inflation and real economic activity, and thus 'the rate of inflation is ultimately determined by monetary policy'. Inflation would be lower when governments persuade employers and workers, but also the financial markets, that they would not exploit a short-term trade-off between inflation and output. And the best way of achieving that goal would be to delegate policy to an institution 'which is given a statutory authority to pursue monetary policy and is made fully accountable for its performance in achieving that objective'. King's proposal included that it was 'quite proper' for the government to 'raise questions' as to whether the central bank that had independence with respect to monetary policy should continue to perform many of its other functions, including 'banker to the government, manager of the public debt, registrar of government securities, printer of bank notes, collector of statistics, and monitor of industrial finance'. The paper concluded: 'The intellectual climate is running strongly in favour of central bank independence.' But it also added a European touch, and a case about political economy.

The Maastricht Treaty requires that the Bank be granted independence before the UK could enter Stage 3 of EMU. And there is no better time for a government to demonstrate its self-confidence and commitment to price stability than when it has succeeded in bringing inflation down. Following departure from the ERM a change in the institutional framework for monetary policy is required to restore credibility. Independence of the Bank of England is the answer.[63]

Independence was a problematical term, however, and Andrew Crockett noted that 'we say in the first paragraph that independence is not an appropriate word', but that 'the paper then goes on to use it throughout the rest of the text'. He tried to use 'operational autonomy' instead – Leigh-Pemberton preferred 'delegated authority'.[64]

The critical question that arose at this stage was the extent to which an independent central bank should continue to be involved in supervision. At an internal discussion, Leigh-Pemberton followed King in distinguishing between 'supervision to limit systemic risks and conduct of business regulation which might be delegated elsewhere'. Andrew Crockett made another argument for the end of involvement in supervision when he talked about 'the suspicion in some parts of the Labour Party [...] that the Bank was representative of an alien interest. The Bank would need to present the case that it would represent the general interest.'[65] In response to that debate, Brian Quinn produced a paper in which he started by outlining the case for separating out supervision, including that 'Supervisory failures, which are inevitable – and sometimes desirable – in a market system, frequently lead to public and political criticism which can damage the central bank's reputation and weaken its authority in the conduct of monetary policy.'

The independence debate was also the backdrop to a new discussion in the Commons Treasury and Civil Service Select Committee, which also visited New York and Washington to study the model of the Federal Reserve, and how it might be applied to British circumstances. The report noted the 'tendency across the world for central banks to be granted a greater degree of independence, or at least autonomy'. In the wake of the BCCI closure and the perception of regulatory failure, the report also noted the contrast with the US, where the committee was struck by 'the more aggressive nature of the authorities' approach by the overlap of supervisors and by the expense of the system'.[66] The former Treasury mandarin Peter Middleton raised some hackles by explaining that the composition of the Court would have to be changed if the Bank were to assume control in setting interest rates. In particular, all the members would have to be committed to fighting inflation, 'unlike the present mob who look rather like a pressure group in the opposite direction'.[67] Despite the powerful appeal of Middleton and also of Nigel Lawson to take banking supervision away from the Bank, the report concluded that there was 'no overwhelming case for separating out the responsibility for prudential supervision to a separate body'.[68] It also recommended creating a strong and independent Monetary Policy Committee.

In November 1993, a group of ex-officials, business figures, international central bankers and academics chaired by Eric Roll of Warburgs published a report with the title *Independent and Accountable: A New Mandate for the Bank of England*, making a case for statutory independence (in line with the Maastricht Treaty), but leaving uncertain whether this goal was part of

a process of conforming with the Maastricht requirements, or an alternative search for a way of anchoring expectations. It argued that price
stability should be the sole statutory objective, but that in order to provide
a response to shocks or emergency circumstances, the government could
be allowed, with the approval of parliament, to suspend for a six-month
term the Bank's objective of price stability. The argument about price
stability presented no advantage in 'any particular target other than zero
inflation', since 'the pursuit of moderate inflation easily becomes the pursuit of rising inflation'. Like the TCSC, the Roll report was agnostic about
whether banking supervision should be hived off; but it argued that the
Bank should no longer be banker to the government with a presumption
that it should purchase government securities. Roll added that a benefit of
a 'clean divorce' between Bank and government was that the Treasury
would lose access to 'various channels of implicit, automatic, or hidden
finance'. The report, however, also recognized that one limit on independence might be that the government would never want to lose complete
control of exchange rate policy: it tried to solve the problem by emphasizing the responsibility of the Bank to advise government and parliament on
the consequences for price stability of any choice of exchange rate
regime.[69] Both the French and the German central banks were represented
on the Roll panel of experts, and their advice played a part in the discussion
of whether and how a central bank needed to accommodate geographic
diversity.

The major speaker at the tercentenary celebration of the Bank of
England in 1994 was Stanley Fischer of MIT, at the time the very influential
First Deputy Managing Director of the IMF. Many of the most prominent
figures in a new generation of central bankers would emerge from MIT:
including Ben Bernanke, Mario Draghi, but also Mervyn King. Bernanke
and Draghi had been Fischer's students. He was in an ideal position to lay
out lessons from other central banks – which Paul Volcker at another point
in the conference correctly described as all 'the Bank's children'. All over
the world, central banks had increased independence: not just in Europe,
where such legislation was required by the Maastricht Treaty, but in Chile,
Mexico, New Zealand and Venezuela. The speech concluded with an
appeal, 'On her 300th birthday, it is time to allow the Old Lady to take
on the responsibilities of independence.'

Fischer's speech laid out a number of the points that had appeared in the
Roll report and would influence the debates of the next years: debt management should be left to another agency than the central bank, because there
might well be a conflict between the government's desire to keep debt

service low and monetary policy goals. But unlike Roll, Fischer did not argue for zero inflation. A positive but low target rate of inflation would be optimal, similar to the ranges specified by the New Zealand and Canadian central banks, and also close to the Bundesbank's practice. So a 2 per cent target over a three-year period announced after consultation with the Treasury would be appropriate, with the Governor held accountable through testimony before a House of Commons Committee (on the model of the US). There should be instrument independence, but not goal independence – the goal should be set as a consequence of political debate and democratic decision-making. In some circumstances, the government should be given the authority to override the Bank's decisions, but such action should 'carry a cost for the government'.[70]

The Bank clearly regarded the TCSC report as helpful to its case. In fact, however, the independence initiative was obstructed within the Treasury by Terry Burns, and finally killed by the Prime Minister: Major argued that 'he could not sell it to MPs, that it would complicate the Maastricht bill, and that the arrangements for accountability were unconvincing'.[71] Burns put the point brutally: 'Ministers hoped and expected that the issue would go away.' As a response, the Bank could only think of trying to use outside pressure, inviting 'weighty figures – central bankers, academics – to look at the UK experience with monetary policy, and report on how it might be improved in the future'.[72] It was exactly those foreign voices – in particular Larry Summers and Alan Greenspan – that would help Labour later make the case for Bank independence.

A NEW GOVERNOR AND AN ORGANIZATIONAL REVOLUTION

The debacle of 1992 provided a severe shock to the UK's 'macro-economic executive'. In order to apply successfully a model-based approach to monetary policy-making, the Bank needed to function in a different way. And then there was the need for a new institutional outlook, a cultural revolution, because of the way that the functions of the Bank were changing. Another set of challenges that arose as a result of the BCCI debacle, in which an obvious criticism emerged, that information was not being shared effectively in the Bank. But there was a great deal of pushback. A cultural shift, let alone cultural revolution, was clearly at odds with the Bank's stiff tradition. After a discussion of some ideas raised by consultants from the Cranfield Management College in July 1991, Andrew Crockett observed that 'even if the Bank's mission underwent a change, its culture was unlikely to change radically'. Brian Quinn and Pen Kent noted 'the difficulty in breeding a Bank-wide culture'.[73] The change clearly needed to begin at the top.

Discussion of Bank independence also affected the succession at the top of the Bank. John Major had wanted to appoint an outsider to replace Leigh-Pemberton, perhaps Sir David Scholey, the chairman of Warburgs and a dominant voice in the Bank's Court, or Sir Dennis Weatherstone, a veteran trader from a working-class British family who had risen to be chairman of the American bank JP Morgan (which had just begun to re-enter investment banking). But Lamont favoured Eddie George, and Scholey modestly said that George was the outstanding candidate. So as a compromise, an outsider was picked at a very short notice, not for the governorship but for the deputy governorship: Rupert Pennant-Rea, the editor of the *Economist*, whom Lamont also liked and trusted and whom Sarah Hogg, the head of Major's policy unit, had worked with at the *Economist*. The abrupt announcement left a peculiar taste, as – hours before the appointment was offered to Pennant-Rea – the *Economist*'s weekly edition had gone to print with an apology for the periodical's treatment of the Bank in the Blue Arrow affair.

The press reception of the appointments – especially that of George – was almost uniformly enthusiastic. The *Sunday Times* was typical in speaking of George's 'uncommon intellect, utter integrity and great experience'.[74] He was seen as an anti-inflation hawk, steady Eddie, who had risen to public prominence by criticizing Lawson's shadowing of the DM. In one of his first pronouncements after the appointment was announced, he had declared that fighting inflation was 'the No. 1 agenda item, the order of the day'.[75] He had reinforced his anti-inflation credentials by adding a personal incentive, declaring that his £227,000 salary would be frozen for the entirety of his five-year term as Governor.[76] He also retired the Rolls Royce traditionally used by the Governor.

George was an ideal Governor for a time of crisis. He had read undergraduate economics, but he always believed he had been recruited by the Bank because of his talent at bridge: and he thought of life as a bridge game. In particular, he treated each morning as a day that presented a new hand to play. He communicated brilliantly with individuals – with political personalities, Thatcher, Major, and Clarke, with the Bank staff, who were completely committed to him and regarded him as the natural leader, with market participants, but also with the general public. In the middle of the BCCI crisis, he appeared on television to explain the Bank's role when the Bank's media advisers thought that Leigh-Pemberton's manner would come across as too patrician, even though he had not been involved in bank supervision and the handling of the BCCI case, and even though exposure over this case might well hurt his chances of succeeding to the Governorship. It was exactly this fierce institutional commitment that bound officials to him in ties of deep loyalty. Looking back on his years at the Bank, all the officials I interviewed started with almost exactly the same phrase: 'The remarkable thing about Eddie . . . .'

George now talked of a change in style, towards a more hands-on management of the Bank. He had a quite different approach to the more distant 'chairman' style of Leigh-Pemberton. Major was not enamoured of his strong personality, and made it clear, while approving the appointment of George, that Bank independence was not on the cards. Indeed, in his vision, Pennant-Rea and George would be Co-Governors, with an exalted position for a Deputy Governor who would forge the government's economic policy vision. In practice, however, Pennant-Rea thought of his contribution as being largely organizational, and left monetary policy-making to the old Bank. He was supposed to bring a breath of fresh air to the Bank corridors, and his first employer, the Labour MP Giles Radice, was quoted describing him as 'very much a child of the 1960s, you know'.[77]

The issue of independence remained very sensitive, and George's Governorship started on a very fragile footing in respect to the setting of interest rates. On the eve of his appointment as Governor, George told the TCSC that rates had been 'adjusted for reasons which have little to do with monetary policy', and that the result had a 'corrosive effect' on the credibility of policy.[78] And on his first day in office, 1 July 1993, George spoke in a *Financial Times* interview of the impression (he qualified it as 'the largely false impression') that the last two interest rate cuts had been 'dictated by political considerations'.[79] Sarah Hogg from the Prime Minister's Policy Unit immediately called the Bank to protest against the Governor's intrusion into politics. But George had also made it clear in the *Financial Times* interview that he was trying to broaden the basis of the Bank's political support:

The thing that I shall lobby for is to broaden the constituency and support for stability, because in a sense unless you actually have public, political support for stability. [. . .] then greater autonomy, statutory accountability, call it what you like, wouldn't be terribly effective. [. . .] I think there is no doubt that the constituency for stability is the horse. The rest is the cart.[80]

His fundamental skill lay in the persuasive presentation of an approach that was quite malleable, so that staff talked about his 'silver tongue', even though it depended on a deeply held underlying philosophy about a stability goal. Others, less sympathetic, thought of him as having 'actor-like qualities'. He later became generally known as 'steady Eddie', although at the time Treasury officials thought of him as prone to tantrums. One explained, 'I could not have dealt with Eddie this day had I not brought up three children of my own.'

In the aftermath of Black Wednesday and of the change of Governorship, the Bank started to rethink its organization, a process that culminated in a retreat of the executive committee (EXCO) of senior staff in Ashridge Management College on 3–5 December 1993. The idea was to think of how 'we would organize the Bank of England again if we were starting with a blank sheet of paper'.[81] The new Governor liked to reflect on plumbing: 'I was quite clearly brought up in the Bank and have been totally involved in what you might call the plumbing. So I shall continue to take an extremely close interest in the plumbing.'[82] That plumbing involved thinking about how the Bank's institutional arrangement should be reshaped in accordance with its new role. The key planning documents for the Ashridge meeting were prepared by Rupert Pennant-Rea, who used the occasion to impose his intellectual mould on the Bank. But Mervyn King also used the retreat to move in a rather different direction, and in practice to build a bridge to a future for the Bank that was more in line with academic economics and less shaped by market familiarity.

The meeting itself was remembered as something of a disaster, with the participants initially stuck in Friday afternoon London traffic, a report by an external consultant on staff disenchantment with the Bank that made George angry, and finally a confrontation between George and Pennant-Rea over Bank redundancies. George was reluctant to dismiss Bank employees, while Pennant-Rea claimed that 'if you've never fired someone, you've never managed'. Other senior Bank of England officials pushed back against the way in which personnel issues were put in the hands of outsiders with 'no experience of the Bank'. Cultural change might be good, but the 'change needed to be handled sensitively, which was easier with an understanding of the Bank'.[83]

The Bank had already shrunk significantly since the late 1970s, when it had employed around 7,500 (see Figure 13.3). Now there were just under 4,000. But it was not clear how the different functions of the Bank related to each other.

King set out his view of the operation of the new Bank in two memoranda. In the first, he argued for the abolition of the International Division, as it 'would be a mistake to consolidate a "foreign office" within the Bank'. In the covering note, he noted, 'I have not circulated this to EXCO members. It

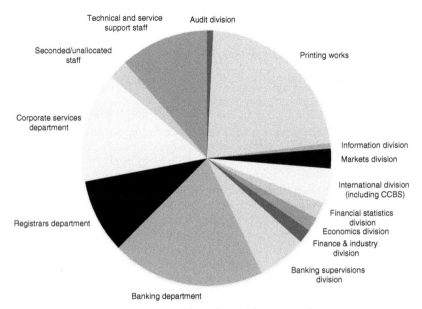

Figure 13.3 Staff numbers (February 1993)

might appear self-serving.' The Governor had long been planning to abolish the International Division, and integrate international work into other parts of the Bank. Even though Crockett had repeatedly warned that the rate of British entry into the ERM was too high and would cause trouble, he had been humiliated by the EMS events, and in particular by his suggestion in the immediate aftermath of Black Wednesday that the UK might contemplate at some time a re-entry into the ERM. His articulation of the view that 'the exchange rate can perform this function [of anchor] as well or better than most of the alternatives', and his opinion that 'an explicit rejection of Community mechanisms (such as the ERM) will do considerable damage to our relations with Community partners', did not seem right in the aftermath of what was now generally seen as 'white Wednesday'.[84] In early 1993, Crockett had proposed that if the ERM were to collapse (as it almost did in July), it could be replaced by a similar arrangement without Germany and the countries close to German monetary policy, so that the UK would be in an exchange rate system with France, Italy, Spain, Portugal and Ireland. King produced a withering comment on that suggestion, 'given that this set of countries is hardly a list of medal winners in the fixed exchange rate regime, we should consider carefully what such an arrangement might achieve'.[85] Crockett had the reputation of being on the centre-left, and if the Labour

Party had won the general election in April 1992, he might have been a favourite to succeed Leigh-Pemberton as Governor. Crockett was then tempted to move to Basel as General Manager of the Bank for International Settlements. The politics – in the Bank and outside – after the re-election of the Major government made it easy to dismantle the International Division.

As King put it:

I argue that part of this work should be moved to other areas in the Bank. I do this not because I believe that international issues are unimportant for the Bank, but because they are too important for them to be segregated into a separate group whose task is to 'deal with foreigners'. All of our work – from economics to supervision and from markets to industrial finance – should be informed by, and integrated with, an appreciation of developments in other countries. The departure of Andrew Crockett creates both a problem and an opportunity. His unique combination of personal and technical qualities, as well as his years of experience on the international circuit, makes him irreplaceable in the particular role which he played. [. . .] On more than one occasion since I came to the Bank, Andrew has suggested that were either of us to leave it would be sensible to merge our positions.

The move would solve some major problems that had bedevilled the Bank in the early 1990s, including in King's view:

Culture: a general problem with the Bank, it seems to me, is that it is a very closed institution.
Morale: of good economists; the perception by good economists in the Bank is that 'serious economics' is done in ED and less technical briefing work in ID.[86]

One of King's assistants made the point explicitly that 'if we are to become more independent we will need to be seen as independent not only of government but also of City interests. This points to shedding much of what FMID [the Financial Market Infrastructure Directorate] and IFD [Industrial Finance Division] currently do.'[87]

In the second memorandum, King drew up a blueprint for the radical overhaul of the Bank, including more details on a clear definition of its mission:

Whatever the outcome of the debate on independence, the position of the Bank has already changed in recent months, and I believe that we should be discussing what I have called 'the New Bank'.

The key questions, it seems to me, are the following:

  (i) what should be the main functions of the Bank in the future, and how do these map into an organisational structure?
  (ii) How can we manage the conglomerate which the Bank has become, and what is the role of Directors in that process?

(iii) Do we have the right staff to deliver the goods, and if not how do we recruit and retain them?

The Bank does too many things. Accountability requires clearly defined responsibilities against which performance can be judged. The basis of our case for independence in the area of monetary policy is not that we are inherently superior at the job, but that it is vital that there should be clear public accountability for policy. Accountability is possible only when there are not too many responsibilities within the same institution. Over time the Bank has acquired a variety of functions, not all of which are core central banking activities. The enthusiasm for these may derive from the failure to acquire the one responsibility which the Bank really wanted, or should have wanted.

King provided a devastating picture of how the old Bank, with its humanistically and non-economically educated bright Oxbridge graduates, had become dysfunctional:

We are not short of numbers. Indeed, we have large numbers of surplus staff. But I am struck by the imbalance between the demand for very able young people, particularly for specialists such as economists, and the low demand for the older generalist group of officials. What puzzles me is that many of this older generation appear to have been the high-flyers of the past who are now underperforming and undervalued. Is this 'internal wastage' inevitable?

Instead, King saw a Bank composed of experts in different areas who together would make something like a football team (he had a passion for soccer): 'A successful team consist of people who are (a) committed to the same objective, and (b) have very different skills and experience which complement each other. No team can comprise only centre-forwards or only goal-keepers. And goal-keepers expect to be assessed as goal-keepers and not as centre-forwards.' He wanted a smaller but organizationally more coherent Bank. He then set out a vision of the Bank with an organization that matched its two fundamental functions, managing monetary policy and providing for financial stability, with two wings. The wing structure was a vital part of Pennant-Rea's plan for the remaking of the Bank:

The first is concerned with monetary policy and the second with stability of the financial system. [. . .] They represent the essence of central banking and complement each other. They are appropriate now and would remain so under independence. They correspond to our first two core purposes.

One of the perennial complaints is lack of delegation to people lower down the chain. This is closely related to the issue of independence of the Bank. In the absence of independence, the Bank plays a largely advisory role in its main and natural core activity. The key to being an adviser is access. But access is a zero sum game and there is rather little to delegate. All this would change with independence, a move which I am sure would sharpen up many of our staff and provide them with as much involvement as they could handle.[88]

The third function of the Bank, as set out by George just a few years earlier in regard to the effectiveness of the functioning of the financial system, was now brought into the second wing. Maybe it just seemed too obvious. The relationship of the functioning of the payments system with the general issue of financial stability and with monetary policy was not explored in this new vision, which had a deliberately narrow view of what financial stability was supposed to ensure. Brian Quinn provided a self-consciously institutional definition of financial stability:

This may appear to be self-evident but it may be sensible to be clear from the outset. Financial stability means the circumstances in which the Bank can carry out smoothly and effectively its first core task of executing monetary policy. This would be interpreted narrowly: the avoidance of difficulties in the banking system; or more widely: the avoidance of disturbances anywhere in the financial system that could impede the Bank in executing monetary policy.[89]

King had a very different vision of economics and economists in the Bank than his predecessors as chief economist. While they had thought that the fundamental task was building a sophisticated model of the whole of the UK economy that might stand in parallel with the Treasury's forecasting model, King saw the work of economists as shedding new light on a whole range of practical policy problems (and not just the estimation of output/GDP and inflation). He wrote to the economist David Currie, a modeller and a member of the new Treasury panel of 'wise men': 'In my experience, large models have concealed rather than revealed ideas about how the economy behaves, and, in particular, have been rather poor in focusing attention on the shocks which hit the economy.' He drew from his experiences in the US, where he found that empirical work 'is driven much more by trying to understand ideas and learning about theories than about the classical statistical approach of testing a single model'. The New York Fed had in particular a section that accumulated market intelligence. He concluded, 'In terms of new ideas about economic policy, or the debate on policy issues, models have played a minor role.'[90]

King was also worried about the markets-oriented approach of George and his team, and in particular by the way in which markets seemed to have powerful but constantly changing and fundamentally economically inconsistent stories that drove their behaviour and expectations. Looking back later, he contrasted the old-style 'haphazard and informal approach to policy setting', in which 'the person round the table with the best anecdote often had the most influence'.[91]

On 14 February 1994, the Court basically endorsed the two-wing structure. The implementation of the administrative reform was handled by Pennant-Rea (see Figure 13.4). The changes inevitably produced a great deal of discontent at the Bank, as the top-heavy administration was pruned back. To the outside world, the Bank explained the reforms as 'the emergence of a leaner, fitter and more professional Bank, reflecting Mr George's 32 years of service, his no-nonsense personality and his determined pursuit of the twin goals of lasting low inflation and a solid financial system in Britain'.[92] The reforms – largely engineered in accordance with Mervyn King's view of the world – were in public attributed to George and Pennant-Rea.

The main target of the reforms was what the Bank now termed 'surplus staff', 'a group of people costing more than £1 m a year, who are surplus to our requirements but are still being paid as if they were doing useful work'. The idea was to create a more general sense of involvement in the Bank: 'It is still far too common in the Bank for individuals to produce pieces of

Figure 13.4 Rupert Pennant-Rea holding sheets showing post-Ashridge bank structure (Ingram Pinn, *Financial Times*, 24 April 1994)

work without having much idea of the underlying purpose or, indeed, ever getting a clear feel for how that information is used. The Bank's hierarchical nature causes work to be pushed up through layers of management.'[93] There was a backlash against the changes, with staff demonstrations on the steps of the Royal Exchange, across from the Bank. George noted, 'it was not the good younger people who complained about the culture change, it was those whose cosy regime was threatened by the new system'.[94] In the end, the outsider who had been brought in to implement the changes was sacked, and a series of measures introduced to rebuild morale: including a downstairs gym that occupied the space previously taken by the Bank's central mainframe computer, but not the swimming pool in the old vault that Mervyn King had dangled out as a boost to morale.

Those within the Bank who felt under attack from the new management reforms and the attempt at a cultural revolution had their opportunity for revenge in March 1995. The Deputy Governor as a young journalist had also dabbled in fiction writing, producing a lurid and indeed in places semi-pornographic novel, *Gold Foil,* about the seduction of a dynamic Bank of England adviser by an unscrupulous American-born journalist working for the *Guardian,* who 'had learnt at an early age that money and sex make fools of intelligent men'. His hero concludes in the end that he'd been 'caught in the web, and would shortly be eaten alive. He'd have to leave the Bank, his career in ruins.'[95] Pennant-Rea presumably chose the Bank, where he had worked as a young man but with which he then had no connection, as a location because it seemed the paradigm for British stuffy conventionality. The old novel seemed a peculiarly prescient prelude to reality, when the *Sunday Mirror,* in March 1995, splashed on its front page the story of Deputy Governor Rupert Pennant-Rea's three-year relationship with an Irish-American journalist, an affair that had been partly carried on in the Bank's buildings, including on the deep pile carpet in the Governor's offices. The headline read 'The Bonk of England'. In a strange echo of his suspense novel about the Bank of England, the exposures started when the journalist tried to sell her story to the *Daily Mail.*

There was no financial impropriety involved, but a sordid story of betrayal and anger. At first, it seemed as if the Deputy Governor – who repeated Montagu Norman's celebrated dictum of central bank haughtiness, the dogs bark but the caravan moves on – would weather the storm. George was initially inclined to support Pennant-Rea, especially because he had confessed to the affair one year before the public scandal. Kenneth Clarke was much firmer in resisting pressure for the offender to resign: 'I personally did not see any reason for him to leave public life. It's absurd to lose a deputy governor of the Bank of England because some newspapers wish to print stories about his private life.'[96] But the affair became especially corrosive because it came after the Prime Minister's ill-conceived programme of restoring old values and morality, 'back to basics'. Sensationalist newspapers could use an argument about public responsibility. Tessa Hilton, the editor of the *Sunday Mirror*, said: 'The Bank is an august institution respected worldwide. The public is entitled to know when high-ranking officials who enjoy privileges and position employ Bank of England drivers to ferry their mistresses around, arrange for their mistresses to use fake names to bypass security checks intended to protect Bank of England staff, and use private apartments of the governor of the Bank of England for purposes for which they were never intended.'[97] One Conservative minister was quoted as saying, 'It's getting ridiculous. It seems there's a policy of one bonk and you're out.'[98] The *Financial Times* leader concluded that the 'depressing departure' was 'in all, a typically British story, about a country that cares far more for appearances than for achievements'.[99] In discussions with the Treasury, in which Clarke's opposition to a resignation was fully set out, George countered that 'the events had damaged the Bank and the issue was not just the extensive publicity but the truth of the allegations'. In particular, he told Clarke directly that the involvement of the Bank 'was more than the staff could accept and it had undermined the Deputy Governor's authority. [...] He had let the institution down badly – one member of staff had said that he had "trashed the Bank" – and he would no longer have the authority to lead in the way he would wish'.[100]

Just over a year after the fall of Pennant-Rea, the outsider who had been brought in as head of personnel, Roy Lecky-Thompson, was also pushed out of the Bank, and was replaced by an 'insider', the deputy cashier Merlyn Lowther.[101] The attempt to fundamentally recast the Bank's organization appeared to be in trouble.

Pennant-Rea was succeeded as Deputy Governor by Howard Davies, the Director-General of the CBI, who had also had extensive experience in the Treasury as well as in the Foreign Office and McKinseys. In 1995, discussing Bank of England appointments with the Chancellor, George explained that he 'hoped to reappoint' King, though he also thought that at some point he would want to return to academia.[102] In fact, the structural reforms that had just been implemented, and the increasingly poisonous public atmosphere around the Bank's financial stability function, ensured that King would stay, and that he would mould and shape the Bank even further.

INFLATION TARGETING

Interest rates were cut very quickly and dramatically after the end of EMS membership, but the exchange rate recovered after the initial fall, and inflation remained low (see Figure 13.5). The surprise shock of 1992, and the surprise that inflation did not surge, led to a rethinking of the centrality of credibility – along with the academic focus on forward-looking calculations, and on expectations. After the emphasis on an inflation target proved a spectacular success, King set out the lessons in a speech at the 1996 annual Federal Reserve conference at Jackson Hole:

When Britain joined the Exchange Rate Mechanism in 1990 inflation expectations did not jump to those in Germany or other 'inner' core members of the ERM. Inflation expectations did fall modestly, and they rose again when Britain left the ERM in September 1992. But the process of learning about the Government's commitment both to the ERM and to price stability did not stop upon entry to the ERM. That shows that a regime shift may be easier to identify in theory than in practice.[103]

Initially, the idea of an inflation target was also controversial, and there was some uncertainty at the Bank. On 10 November 1992, Burns called the Bank to ask how it would feel about a 2 per cent target. George replied that

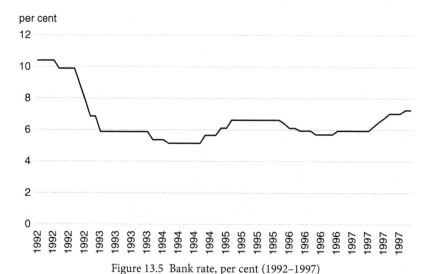

Figure 13.5 Bank rate, per cent (1992–1997)

this was a risk to the exchange rate. ('It would lead to the perception that the authorities had given up all concern about inflation.')[104] In fact, in an open economy such as at the UK, exchange rate considerations continued to play some role even after the successful transition to inflation targeting (see Figure 13.6). Later George explained that he thought 0–2 per cent was 'pretty well synonymous with zero inflation', and that 'what I am pretty clear about is that you actually have to continuously aim at zero' (see Figure 13.7).[105] He later explained, '0–2 percent was a reasonable longer term inflation target. One could not preclude the possibility that inflation might move outside that range but one had to be able to explain why it did so.'[106]

The Bank quickly came to accept the idea of a target as a way of simplifying the communication issues involved in explaining how interest rate policy was set by a response to 400 or 4,000 indicators: 'All the movements of financial markets. All the monetary indicators; not just broad money. What's happening in credit. What's happening to the sectoral behaviour – the personal sector, the industrial sector, the financial sector. All the real economic indicators. The behaviour of the fall in unemployment and what that is telling us about the economy.'[107] The principal attraction in the new approach lay in its obviousness. The different

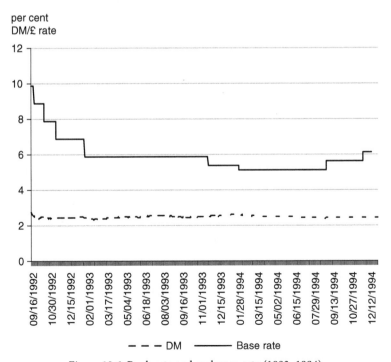

Figure 13.6 Bank rate and exchange rate (1993–1994)

Figure 13.7 Governor Eddie George pruning a tree labelled 'Inflation' with 'Interest Rate' shears and cutting off the green shoots of economic recovery (Ron McTrusty, *Evening Standard*, 6 January 1995)

monetary aggregates had been a source of confusion and poor communication, with the public, with the markets, but even and often between Bank and Treasury. King thought of inflation targeting as a 'coping strategy': as he put it, its great attraction was that 'it is a framework that does not have to be changed each time we learn something new about how the economy behaves'.[108] It was also quite simple to present and understand. As Paul Tucker later explained, 'Targeting inflation by setting an interest rate fitted the bill because it made sense in terms of the day-to-day lives of households and businesses, whereas targeting a monetary aggregate had been incomprehensible to anyone other than the cognoscenti.'[109] Later on, it became clear that even this approach was not completely transparent, and that different measures of inflation behaved in different ways: in particular, how would the British national obsession with houses and house prices be managed? The Retail Price Index included housing costs, whereas the Consumer Price Index did not, and then an RPI excluding mortgage interest payments (RPIX). In addition, 'something new about how the economy behaves' proved to be problematical soon after the transition to inflation targeting in that a combination of technical change and globalization exercised an apparently irresistible downward pressure on prices.

There continued to be some use of monetary aggregates, but they were restyled as less committal 'monitoring ranges': a meeting in the Treasury in February 1993 indicated a 'broad sympathy' with the new nomenclature, although Sir Terry Burns 'expressed a residual feeling that some harm might come from changing the name of the M0 range from target to monitoring range'.[110]

In 1995, the target was modified. In the wake of a controversy about the personalization and politicization of monetary policy (see below), Clarke announced in his Mansion House speech, 'Our aim beyond this parliament will be to continue to achieve underlying inflation, measured by the RPI excluding mortgage interest payments, of 2.5% or less. Setting interest rates consistently at the level judged necessary to achieve the target of 2.5% or less should ensure that inflation will remain in the range of 1 to 4%.' This was accompanied by an acknowledgement of the importance of expectations: 'Monetary policy today influences the level of inflation up to two years in the future.'[111] So the new aim was an inflation rate of 2½ per cent or less over a two-year-ahead time frame.[112] There was still no reference to output or employment as an explicit consideration in the setting of monetary policy.[113] George embraced the 2 ½ per cent target. In response to a question in Court, he said: 'We should get down to 2 ½ per cent before looking for more. And aiming for 2 ½ per cent or less would deliver most of the stability that we wanted to achieve.'[114] There was, however, at this point no idea of symmetry, and of the later notion that inflation under 2 per cent might be dangerous or even deflationary. The later fixation on 2 per cent as a central figure thus had something of an arbitrary or accidental character.

Later, in 1996, the Treasury and the Bank reaffirmed that

it was sensible to retain monitoring ranges for both M0 and M4. One argument here was that it would be unwise to emphasise a single monetary aggregate. This could prove misleading. At the aggregate level M0 has been shown to have good properties as a leading indicator on inflation. But sectoral measures of broad money appear to contain valuable information about consumption and investment expenditure, and hence nominal aggregate demand. Given this, and the arguments above, we assume here, as last year, that the realistic choice this time around is between retaining monitoring ranges for both M0 and M4 or dropping both.[115]

In addition to M4, the Bank also started formally to monitor M4 lending.

MONETARY POLICY AND DEBT MANAGEMENT

The new approach with the adoption of an inflation target also broke with the old way of signalling monetary policy to the markets. The standard practice that had emerged in the course of the 1980s was thought of as 'testing the waters', and was controversial even before September 1992. The regular Thursday meetings with the discount market looked more and more peculiar. The discussion of the 1990 ERM entry leak (see pp. 276–278) prompted a new wave of sensitivity and distrust. The discount market no longer looked like an effective arm of the Bank that reached into the markets. In the penultimate meeting, before the procedure was brought to an end, George in 1994 explained, 'It is also something to do with other parts of the market, we are bound to be sensitive to some of the perceptions of the traditional meeting. That is not good for the market itself.'[116] The issue of operationalizing monetary policy involved a rethinking of the approach to the management of government debt.

In late 1994, Anthony Nelson, Economic Secretary to the Treasury, announced a Debt Management Review. The initiative was motivated by the intention to take up best practice, and to learn in particular from the example of the US government debt market which had also guided extensive reforms in France. The Treasury thought that the better methods would allow cheaper borrowing and the consequent fiscal saving that had been achieved in France and the US, while the Bank pushed back with the observation that differences in inflation performance might be a factor in the pricing.[117] There was also some discussion at the Treasury of the need to consider 'possible future developments in European monetary integration'.[118] The overarching goal was to improve the transparency and predictability of gilt issuance, in line with the more general thrust of Treasury policy to rationalize the division of responsibilities by setting specific remits to the bodies responsible for executing functions on behalf of the government. The Treasury proposals included: an annual statement of the maturity mix of gilts to be issued; a high proportion of gilt issuance to be via auctions rather than taps or unofficial sales; to move to issue some index-linked gilts by auction rather than wholly by tap; and to focus issuance primarily on 'benchmark' stocks.[119] In 1992, the US Treasury, which had been auctioning its debt regularly since the 1970s, started an experimental series of uniform price auctions for two- and five-year notes, which proved very successful. In the UK, the movement from taps to auctions was already taking place from the early 1990s. While in 1992–1993, 37.4 per cent of the sales of debt occurred in auctions, the figure rose to 65.8 per cent in 1994–1995.[120] The average size of individual auctions was simultaneously reduced by scheduling auctions monthly (except around the time of the Budget).[121]

The UK experience of the early 1990s also pushed towards a rethinking of debt management: the fiscal deficit had shot up in 1992–1993, and remained very high (much higher than in the 1980s: net general government borrowing was 5.2 per cent in 1992, 6.7 per cent in 1993, 5.8 per cent in 1994 and 5.0 per cent in 1995).[122]

The Treasury official responsible for working on the Review, Jonathan Portes, saw the change as part of a general move to a financing rather than a funding approach: what was important was how the cash was raised, rather than the deeper accounting question of who ultimately pays. In the new approach, the central government's borrowing needs were covered by selling gilts, National Savings products and Treasury bills. Borrowing by the rest of the public sector would not have any effect on the form of debt issued by the central government. The existing framework in which enough gilts over three years in maturity and National Savings products should be sold to fund the Public Sector Borrowing Requirement (PSBR), and which did not count as funding borrowing from banks, issues of Treasury bills, or gilts under three years maturity, was a construct that was simply designed to stop government transactions having an effect on M4; but, as Portes noted, M4 was no longer a monetary target.[123]

The debate reflected an orientation towards a world in which the Treasury saw itself as managing its debt in order to get best value for the government, rather than using the debt market as a way of running monetary policy. It is also possible that by the mid-1990s the Treasury was already preparing for independence and at minimum wanted to constrain the Bank's independence as part of the package, with the review (along with a later review of the money market) as the tool to deliver analysis which would establish the case.

Some market participants in the City, notably hedge funds, had been concerned at the unofficial sales in 1994, which they felt suppressed profits they had hoped to earn when they bought gilts. The Gilt-Edged Market Makers (GEMMs) were reacting in particular to the February 1994 interest rate cut, just before a gilt auction, which had cost them money. The

GEMMs also expressed their concern that the Bank was avoiding the issuance of longer stocks, demanded by institutions such as pension funds. In fact, the Bank was indeed concerned that long yields were around 8 per cent when there was an inflation target of 2 ½ per cent. It considered instead some one-off innovations such as the floating-rate gilt (with a quarterly interest payment linked to the three-month interbank bid rate) and a convertible (a three-year gilt, with an option for the holder to convert to a long gilt at a specific date and price). The new instruments were issued in the course of 1994. The operation looked like a success, and was contrasted favourably with the experience of Austria, German and Spain, where debt auctions were cancelled in similar turbulent market conditions after February 1994 (see below, p. 360). But the financial institutions that criticized the Bank's gilt market operations could naturally complain to the Treasury as well as the Bank, since after all it was the Treasury's debt, and made the general observation that monetary policy and debt management policy were not properly coordinated.[124]

In late 1996, the Treasury also initiated a money market review, which would have covered treasury bill issuance (it argued that the Bank was issuing government debt to manage money market conditions, rather than considering bill issuance as part of the government's portfolio of debt). However, this exercise had barely started before the announcement in May 1997 that debt management and Treasury bill issuance would be transferred away from the Bank as part of monetary policy independence, rationalized by the avoidance of conflict of interest.

Traditionalists in the Bank pushed back against the Treasury initiatives, arguing that the Bank's historic approach of a mixture of auctions and taps allowed for close contact with the market and the ability to tailor funding to take account of revealed demand.[125] Ian Plenderleith, the Executive Director with responsibility for Markets, feared the prospect of having to issue into an unfavourable market, and he also believed that the less-developed index-linked market was not liquid enough to cope with auctions (rather than taps when there was known demand). The new measures would make the relationship between the GEMMs 'minimal and possibly unsustainable', and the Treasury would have to construct a US-style primary dealer system.[126] Nigel Althaus, the last holder of the traditional office of Government Broker, who had moved into the Bank after Big Bang, wrote from retirement that 'the whole exercise starts from a mistaken premise that what happens in America is best. The American market is in the state it is because of many years of excessive deficits. [...] The trouble with the current review is that it has been conducted from a position of weakness with an over-borrowing government faced by GEMMs and investors still smarting from their over-indulgence in 1993.'[127] By contrast, the Monetary Analysis staff (the Monetary Instruments and Markets Division under Creon Butler) argued on similar lines to the Treasury that auctions were generally preferable to taps, supported a pre-announced issuance programme, and wanted to see index-linked auctions. Mervyn King endorsed this modernizing position, and concluded his observations on the Review with the comment that there is 'Nothing in the Report which could fairly be described as "aggressively iconoclastic."'[128]

The Bank in fact effectively and unproblematically implemented the main proposals of the Debt Management Review. The total amount of issuance for each financial year would be announced in advance together with the broad mix of issuance as between short-, medium- and long-term conventional issuance and index linked, and the intended dates of auctions; then there was a quarterly announcement of the stock to be issued at each auction. Some tap issuance continued, but when proposing taps the Bank was required to explain to the Treasury (by telephone) how an issue was consistent with the annual Remit set by the Treasury. The tap sales should not usually amount to more than 10 per cent of the total issuance. The Bank eventually set out an 'acquis' on understandings between Bank and Treasury on the Bank's operations in gilts and specifying the occasions on which it was expected to seek the Treasury's agreement.

The transition to a new monetary regime, in which repos would become the main monetary policy instrument, had been actively discussed since Big Bang in 1986, and a broad repo market appeared to be in conformity with the underlying liberalizing philosophy. A repo is a sale of securities coupled with an agreement to repurchase the securities at a specified price on a later date. The major advantage offered as compared with simple lending on collateral is that the lender has control – ownership – of the assets, and so can respond directly in the event of a payment incapacity of the borrower. It had been long used as a financing instrument in the US, and the market expanded during the 1970s as government debt grew, and also because of the low interest rates in regulated lending. A critical breakthrough in the use of repo on the US market occurred in 1982 in the aftermath of the failure of a mid-sized government securities house, Drysdale Government Securities, when firms that had lent securities to Drysdale were insufficiently provided with margin and had less cash than the replacement cost of their securities. Another smaller dealer, Lombard-Wall Securities, failed a few months later, and the bankruptcy court treated the repos as secured loans, rather than outright transactions, and issued a temporary restraining order prohibiting sale of the repo securities. Federal Reserve chairman Paul Volcker then pushed Congress to vote an amendment exempting repos on Treasury and other specified securities from application of the automatic stay. He argued that 'repos are a very important tool used in Federal Reserve open market operations' and thus that 'it is important that the repo market be protected from unnecessary disruption'.[129] The outcome was the Bankruptcy Amendments and Federal Judgeship Act of 1984, and after that a new legal security spurred a large extension of the repo market, and a new market developed, with clearing banks acting as intermediaries in transactions.

The Bank of England was in the 1980s somewhat sceptical of the US developments. It argued that the GEMMs were already trading in regulated repos (i.e. those repos intermediated by stock exchange money brokers), and so there was an existing market, but that the upheavals of the US Treasury markets in the early 1980s had been a warning of the dangers of an extended and unregulated repo market. Fundamentally, it took the approach that it would be unwise to 'unleash' further reforms until the dust of Big Bang had settled.

In the course of the 1990s, the Bank's approach changed. The Maastricht Treaty required a new approach, and repos were compatible with the monitoring of secondary market purchases of government debt, and with the Bundesbank's approach to monetary policy. The US market remained quite problematical, however. In particular, an instance in 1991 when Salomon Brothers cornered the market for two-year securities, buying up 90 per cent of all the notes issued in one month and thus becoming the only supplier to short sellers, looked like a warning. Outside the US, the possibilities of the repo market were most quickly taken up in France. Above all, a 1993 memorandum noted that the 'progressive internationalization of markets and competition between financial centres appear to be leading to a convergence of market practices (generally towards a US norm), with repo already being allowed in other government bond markets'.[130] A reform would address the shortage of collateral if the Bank just operated in bills of exchange at the time that the Bank stopped operating via the discount houses.

The urgency was increased with a major market panic in late February and March 1994, set off by the belief that the US was embarking on a tightening of policy, but which was also widely blamed on poor communications by the Bundesbank after German money supply figures showed a surprisingly large 20 per cent increase in the first quarter. There were widespread reports of illiquidity in the bond markets, and rumours of big losses at some major banks (Bankers Trust) and for hedge funds (George Soros' Quantum Fund). For the first time since Big Bang, the Bank of England engaged in large-scale operations in the government bond market, coordinated with other central banks, in particular with the Banque de France. When the French Governor called, George explained the British purchases of £250 m gilt-edged stock on 1 March.[131] In all, the Bank bought £625 m stock in the month after 24 February, at or below the market prices; it resold £250 m of that sum quickly, and intended to hold some part to maturity.[132]

On 27 September 1995, a gilts auction of £3 bn failed spectacularly – the first such failure since the auction system was introduced in 1988. Bids for the auction fell short by nearly £30 m, and even that level of demand was reported to be the result of considerable 'arm twisting' by the Bank of England.[133] The market participants explained that they had been influenced by bad results in US bond sales, and by a similar development on the German government bond market, but also by the fear that the UK government was moving as a consequence of political pressure to tax cuts that would make the management of public debt impossible. The stock market panicked in the aftermath. Discussing the fiasco in the Treasury, where George blamed the 'new transparent approach to debt management', contrasting with the old methods where the Bank had concealed its activities behind a 'number of veils', Clarke responded that he sympathized and that he 'was against open government'.[134]

The new repo market was announced on 21 February 1995, and started operations in January 1996: one of the main attractions was that it looked compatible with international practice, and above all with the Bundesbank's approach. Anyone could borrow gilts, under standard documentation which the market had developed with the Bank, a precondition for the gilt repo market that the tax treatment of interest and capital gains/losses should be the same. That move required co-ordination with the tax authorities. Low coupon gilts were no longer 'expensive to the curve', because they were no longer particularly advantageous to retail holders liable to the higher marginal rates of tax. The discount houses no longer had a monopoly in dealing with the Bank of England in treasury bills. The mechanism of 2.30 lending at the Minimum Lending Rate was ended. A secured borrowing facility replaced the practice under which settlement banks invited the Bank to buy Treasury bills up to 3:00 p.m. The Bank's open market operations (OMOs) were now conducted at the policy rate, which thus regained a strict meaning for the markets. From the Bank's perspective, as from that of the City as a whole, the end of the long tradition was a recognition of reality: 'Their long-run viability as specialist money market traders has in fact been under pressure for some while, and almost all of them have taken steps in recent years to diversify into areas less dependent on position-taking. Nor will the current reforms come as any surprise to them, since they have been expecting us to move in this direction.'[135]

From 3 March 1997, the Bank shifted its money market operations to using gilt sale and repurchase agreements, or gilt repos, as the central tool for the daily managing of short-term interest rates. Gilt repo is both a money market and a gilt market tool: a money market tool because it allows in effect secured lending and borrowing against 'general' gilt collateral; a gilt market tool because of the 'specials' market, allowing a market participant to 'borrow' a specific gilt to meet delivery obligations having sold the gilt short. GEMMs had previously been able to borrow specific stocks from the stock exchange money brokers (SEMBs).

The movement to a more completely securitized market included the availability of 'strips', in which the interest payments on specified gilts could be traded separately from the principal sum. The market spotted that the Bank was preparing a strip market when successive benchmark gilts were given the same interest payment date (7 December), making the interest payments fungible, improving liquidity, although the strips market was not launched until 1997.

The new system worked because of the much larger volume of collateral created by the availability of gilt repo (see Table 13.2). In the early 1990s, the short-term paper market was not growing quickly enough to meet the needs of the liberalized financial system.

Over the next years, a wider set of instruments were admitted as collateral: in October 1998, access was extended to sterling-denominated foreign government and international institution debt that had been issued in the UK ('bulldogs'). In June 1999, there was a further extension to sterling-denominated bonds of European government and international agencies accepted in Euroclear (the delivery vs. payment system initiated in 1968 by the Brussels office of Morgan Guaranty Trust Company of New York), and of euro-denominated securities eligible in ECB monetary policy operations. The British market was thus brought into line with the developing European market. At this moment, the development was also pushed by fears of a liquidity problem that might be created by market infrastructure problems created by data systems unprepared for Y2 K (many dates were set as double digits, and there was a fear of what would happen when computers

Table 13.2 *Collateral eligible in
open market operations
(1990–1999)*

	£bn	% held by Bank of England
1990	37	13
1995	30	11
1996	34	14
1997	320	2
1998	327	3
1999	2325	1

Source: Federal Reserve Bank of Boston, Paper: The Bank of England, 2001 (BoE 17A150/7)

consequently made calculations on the basis of a date of the year 1900 rather than 2000). In late 1999, in consequence, longer-term operations of three months were introduced to give market participants the assurance of liquidity.[136] Even after the new millennium in 2000, the technical advances continued. In March 2000, the restrictions on bank bills were lifted: in the old world of the nineteenth century, that had extended through the whole of the twentieth century, only self-liquidating transactions were believed to be adequate collateral for bills accepted at the central bank. Now what had previously been discriminated against as 'finance bills' became the basis of business as 'commercial paper', and the way was open for the twenty-first century.

KEN AND EDDIE

At Kenneth Clarke's first meeting as Chancellor with the Governor of the Bank, on 2 June 1993, there was a very relaxed atmosphere ('informed and open discussion'), and a rapid agreement on setting up a schedule for regular informal meetings (see Figure 13.8).[137] The Chancellor said that while he shared the ideas of Lawson and Lamont on the desirability of central bank independence, many Conservative MPs did not, and the Labour leader John Smith was opposed to a loss of 'democratic accountability'. 'It was therefore quite difficult to see early progress being made towards an independent Bank.'[138] Instead, Clarke came up with a new formula on how Treasury–Bank relations

Figure 13.8 Ken and Eddie, with George in foreground and Clarke in shirtsleeves (Stefan Rousseau/PA Images/Alamy Stock Photo)

should be handled – and how British monetary policy should be made.

The aim of more transparency about the process of setting monetary policy was to dispel the notion that politics determined the interest rates, and hence that monetary policy was not time consistent. Transparency had become a major theme in central banking elsewhere. Alan Blinder speaks about a 'revolution in thinking'.[139] From January 1990, Australia started to announce its monetary policy stance in regular meetings. In February 1994, the Federal Reserve Open Market Committee moved to announce policy actions with a press statement immediately after the decision had been taken. The effect was to decrease the amount of surprise for markets.[140] The British meetings were intended to represent a non-political discussion of Treasury and Bank expectations on inflation and output. Kenneth Clarke tried to explain that divergences between Governor and Chancellor 'were very rarely black and white'.[141] But in fact, the circus around what became known as the 'Ken and Eddie show' increased rather than reduced the perception of political influence.

In all, thirty-nine monthly meetings occurred between January 1994 and April 1997. In two of them, George recommended interest rates cuts, and the Chancellor accepted; in nineteen he suggested no alterations, and the advice was accepted seventeen times. In eighteen meetings, George advised the Chancellor to raise rates, but that was accepted only on four occasions. Most notably, in the run-up to the 1997 general election, Clarke rejected the call for higher rates, on what seemed to be political grounds.[142] There was a bit of theatre or 'soap opera' about the regular meetings. George and Clarke both liked to present themselves as bluff, normal, smoking and beer-drinking 'blokes', but, as *Financial Times* columnist Martin Wolf put it, 'Clarke plays the bluff man of the people, George the cautious adviser.'[143]

It is too easy to interpret this pattern as a political struggle, in which a vote-seeking populist Chancellor overrode the concerns of an inflation-fixated central banker. There was a genuine intellectual difference, which emerged at the very outset of the new monetary policy process. Estimating the policy implications of monetary actions requires an assessment of the degree of slack in the economy, of the output gap. The Treasury and Clarke had a more optimistic view of the potential for growth – and in the event, they were largely proved right. The debate between a conservative central banker and a more unconventional thinker had its counterpart in internal debates within the central bank in the US, where Chairman Alan Greenspan also had a more optimistic view of economic potential than the Federal Reserve Board staff, and was also correct on the issue, the transformation of productive potential as a consequence of the information revolution.[144] The uncertainty about potential economic performance complicates the picture that came to dominate the academic debate of the time, in which a conservative central banker solved the time consistency problem: there was a suboptimal stabilization bias that the academic literature then began to explore. Right at the beginning of the Ken–Eddie process in the UK, Alan Budd wrote to Mervyn King that 'your estimate that the output gap is 3% is at the pessimistic end of the range' that the Treasury had calculated.[145] Much of the debate thus focused on the most appropriate approach to estimating the relationship of growth and potential growth.

A new aspect of the Bank's approach was the need for transparency in communicating information to markets. There had been some discussion of publishing the minutes of the discussions: the pressure came in particular from the Commons TCSC and its 1993 report, but the initial minutes were produced only for internal use. In September 1993, the Treasury reported that the Chancellor 'sees some attraction in publishing, probably with a lag of six weeks or so'.[146] But it required a public relations fiasco for the commitment to openness to be realized.[147]

In the first, January 1994, meeting, Clarke said that 'the objective case for a further ½ per cent cut in rates was quite strong', but George retorted that 'the risk associated with cutting interest rates now was greater than the risk associated with waiting'. On that occasion, the Chancellor agreed to do nothing. The tensions between Chancellor and Governor were well publicized after a dramatic clash at the second of the new-style meetings, on 3 and 4 February 1994. George began by noting that at the last meeting, there had been agreement on a 'bias towards easing', but that economic evidence published since the January meeting had 'if anything, weakened rather than strengthened the case for an immediate rate cut'. 'The case for an immediate cut in interest rates rested on a view that the Budget measures would significantly slow down the pace of growth', but it would be 'safer to wait for more evidence of the effects of the tax increases before acting'. There was a considerable upside risk of an increase in inflation and 'to cut rates now in advance of this evidence would run a risk of higher inflation and some loss of credibility, and he strongly advised against'. Clarke offered a diametrically contrary view, namely that 'he was concerned that advice was erring excessively on the side of caution. He had been more inclined to cut interest rates last month, and in his view the case for a cut had become stronger since then.' He went on: 'The monetary indicators provided a good case for an interest rate cut. [. . .] In addition, pay settlements remained between 2 and 2 ½ per cent on average, with a significant minority of employees accepting a pay freeze'. There was thus 'little risk of an increase in inflation'.

In the following discussion, as recorded in the published minutes, views were not attributed to officials, but one participant observed that 'there was a danger that an interest rate cut now would be interpreted as being influenced by political considerations'. It was during the discussion that the possibility of a one-fourth percentage point rate cut was raised. On the second day of the meeting, the chancellor said that he 'still favoured reducing interest rates now. He saw little risk of inflation picking up, but a significant risk that the fiscal measures would slow down the recovery. An interest rate cut in April would be too late to offset the effect of the fiscal measures. Although he thought an immediate ½ per cent reduction would be justified, he saw advantage in a ¼ per cent cut. Moving interest rates by smaller amounts was quite common in other countries, and was consistent with the current low inflation and low interest rate environment.' George said that he could 'agree to a ¼ per cent, but not to ½ per cent', and concluded with the observation that 'his concern stemmed from experience that it would be difficult to restrain inflation if it started to rise'.[148] The move of a quarter per cent cut, to 5.25 per cent, was announced on 8 February. It looked odder, perhaps, and evidence of a conscious decoupling from the US because, on 7 February, the Federal Reserve had raised the federal funds rate from 3 to 3.25 per cent.

The press rapidly picked up the difference between the Bank and the Treasury, and in particular an article by Anatole Kaletsky in *The Times* laid out the political character of the conflict. The situation was made worse because the announcement of the interest rate decision came at the same time as the chance sensation of the news of the death of a Conservative MP, Stephen Milligan, who was found naked with an orange stuffed in his mouth. So suspicious minds thought that the Treasury was attempting to bury the monetary story. Burns immediately called the Bank to complain about the reception of the decision: 'Firstly, he felt that the Treasury had not been properly warned about the conclusions of the Inflation Report. Secondly, the press release for the interest rate cut had been mishandled. Thirdly, he was very concerned by an article in *The Times* by Kaletsky which suggested that the Governor would have opposed a ½ point rate cut and, Sir Terry thought, implied that the decision had been a compromise.' Kaletsky wrote: 'Throw in the Bank's cack-handed timing of the [interest rate] announcement and Mr Clarke may finally be starting to understand that he was playing with fire by giving Mr George permission to run a public, political campaign for central bank independence.'[149] George then apologized to the Chancellor for the 'shambolic' press handling. Burns also complained that it 'was now the perception of Number 10 that the Governor was actively campaigning on independence'.[150]

The press response to the rate cut reflected a widespread cynicism about the politics behind interest rate moves. On the afternoon of the rate cut, Tony Coleby, then the Executive Director for Markets, went to Bank underground station to buy an *Evening Standard*. The news vendor indicated the headlines, looked up at what he took to be a City gent, and said: 'Yes guv, would 'ave been an 'ole point if they 'adn't got the donkey aht the 'ouse'.

Once Kaletsky had shown the way, every other commentator piled in. Jim O'Neill, then at Swiss Bank Corporation, called the move 'the first mistake Clarke has made'.[151] Christopher Huhne concluded that 'neither of our two leading economic policymakers is emerging from his present travails with laurels. By digging in his heels against an interest rate cut larger than a quarter percentage point, Eddie George, the Governor of the Bank of England, has revived old suspicions about whether he is – in his phrase – an "inflation nutter".' Within a week of the decision, it was clear that inflation was better than the Bank had predicted. And the recovery may have been weaker because of overly restrictive monetary approach.[152]

George was not hesitant in making the case for the Bank in public. He told the Bankers' Club annual banquet in London's Guildhall that the government needed control over interest rates only if it wanted to 'retain the option of debasing the currency', and acknowledged that the Bank's relationship with the Government was one 'in which there is bound to be tension'.[153] The minutes as prepared for publication were quite sanitized. Thus, in looking back at the February 1994 meeting, the Treasury decided that before publication it would be best to excise the Chancellor's view that this might be the last political opportunity to cut interest rates for some months, and also Clarke's acceptance of the view that there were limits to the pace at which the economy could grow without kindling inflation. The Treasury mandarins also wanted to remove any hint of a further quarter point cut, as well as the Financial Secretary's statement at the meeting that 'our experience in the past of underestimating the strength of recoveries was a strong argument against an activist monetary policy'.[154]

There were models as well as politics behind the Treasury/Bank divergence. In the first meetings of 1994, the Bank was also consistently much more optimistic about economic growth prospects than was the Chancellor, and hence less inclined to press for a monetary easing. In March 1994, Clarke said, 'It would be appropriate to consider a further reduction in interest rates if indicators subsequently suggested that activity was subdued and inflationary pressures remained under firm control.' George was more hesitant: 'There would be a case for a further easing of interest rates if the evidence suggested that activity was slowing', although he concluded 'at this stage there was insufficient evidence to warrant a cut.'[155]

The press picked up every nuance of the policy divergence, even noting that Clarke seemed to be more downbeat about the economy in the Bank discussions than he was in public – because of the need to press the case for lower rates. Thus, the *Financial Times* noted that 'Mr Clarke's utterances in the monthly meetings seem less upbeat than his more public statements on the economy. In March, he said that "anecdotal evidence did not suggest that activity was growing strongly." In February, referring to the fall in unemployment, for example, he said that "much of the employment created so far had been in part-time jobs."'[156]

The *Inflation Report* proved a problematical tool. In particular, it became clear that although inflation estimates 'might suggest the direction in which policy should move', it did not help judge the magnitude of the change that would be desirable. That would require alternative forecasts with different interest rates. Some Bank officials consequently suggested that the forecast scenarios should be accompanied by a range of alternative forecasts assuming different interest rates. They argued: 'Without a medium-term quantitative benchmark of some kind there is a danger that the size of any change will be judged only or primarily in terms of market reactions.'[157] A wider intellectual approach to forecasting was needed in this view to escape from the tyranny of a more casual 'markets' approach.

There was also a substantial discussion of the inflation projections. Goldman Sachs economists noted that the Bank's inflation forecasts had fallen out too high.

In the November report, the Bank forecast that underlying inflation would hover at about 3.3 per cent in the final quarter of 1993. We now know that inflation actually averaged 2.7 per cent over this period. The importance of this is clear. If the authorities can be so wrong about inflation over the next three months, what confidence can investors have in their ability to set policy which, in the Government's words, is 'based on assessment of the prospects for underlying inflation in one or two years' time?'[158]

The 1993 *Inflation Reports* did indeed give trajectories for inflation that were much too high (the subsequent two years were much better).[159]

The fracas over the botched February rate rise led to a decision to publish (with a six-week delay) the minutes of the Ken and Eddie discussions, which considerably altered the dynamic of the meetings. 'The exercise is intended to give the City and the public a guide to the thinking that underlies interest-rate decisions, in the hope that this will prevent damaging speculation about policymakers' motives and future intentions.'[160] A greater measure of unanimity was achieved at the 2 March meeting: the minutes reveal that there was no intention to raise bank base interest rates, as had been feared by some City commentators.

In September 1994, when the interest rate was hiked by half a point from 5.25 to 5.75, Clarke had argued that 'although growth was strong, inflation was low and the main indicators were not showing concern'. George thought that 'notwithstanding the recorded price performance and reasonably reassuring monetary indicators (showing continued slow M4 and M4 lending growth and moderating but still rapid M0 growth), the increasing – albeit anecdotal – evidence of capacity and prices pressures in the pipeline could not be ignored'. The result was that at the Ken and Eddie meeting there was eventually an agreement on the increase, to be timed at the discretion of the Governor (the move was implemented on 12 September).[161] Newspapers quickly interpreted the victory of the Bank over the Treasury as a sign of a fundamental reorientation of policy: 'Part of the explanation for Monday's pre-emptive strike was, according to officials, the fact that the "bottom half" policy has now become "operational". What that actually means is that the Bank of England is forcing the Government to take it seriously, whatever that means for the popularity of the Tory Party and its electoral prospects.'[162] One City economist complained that it was easier to read the intentions of the Fed and Bundesbank. 'With the Bank of England we still live in [John le Carré's fictional spy George] Smiley's world of secrecy.' In his view, the surprise and the wrong-footing of 'some highly respected economists show how the Bank has made confusing and misleading signals to the market'.[163]

At the end of 1994, the issue of how inflation estimates should be communicated flared up. The November report appeared to give a benign view of inflation, but internally many Bank economists had argued that the risk was on the upside. The Bank gave an off-the-record briefing, which so exacerbated the Prime Minister that he blurted out: 'No one would take any notice of the Inflation Report in the future.' George thought that a real press conference might be the solution, but warned that that innovation would 'increase the profile' of the Bank. Clarke accepted that 'the logic of the new approach was greater openness'.[164]

A further half a per cent rate increase occurred in December 1994, when Clarke agreed to a rise on the basis of the 'balance of risks' and explained that he 'wanted to remain in control of events by acting in good time'. George made it clear in the discussion that he was responding to strong GDP figures rather than to monetary indicators, which 'did not give any very clear guide to developments'. M0 had slowed in November, there was not much movement in M4, and consumer spending seemed sluggish.[165] Anatole Kaletsky in *The Times* criticized the 'pedantic legalism' in the status of the inflation target by which the Bank now claimed that the true target range was 1 to 2.5 per cent.[166]

By the spring of 1995, the controversies had escalated once more, with a new rift appearing between cautious Eddie and stimulus Ken. The core of the argument again lay in the interpretation of inflation data, as the yearly change in RPI ex MIPs (mortgage interest payments) rose from 2.7 per cent in February to 2.8 per cent in March, and headline inflation also rose from 3.4 to 3.5 per cent. George stressed, 'The risk to the credibility of the policy approach, if the authorities were seen to be prepared to take risks on the side of inflation. Given this country's history, inflation expectations and inflation itself were likely to accelerate because of that.'[167] But there was also an exchange rate aspect to the debate, as the rate fell to a record low against the D-Mark earlier that week 'amid market concerns about a possible split between Mr Clarke and Mr George'.[168]

In May 1995, an increase in interest rates had been widely expected.[169] The decision not to move took the financial markets and City economists by surprise, as most had concluded that the continued strength of economic growth and the weakness of sterling had made a rise in rates inevitable. At a hastily convened press conference at the Treasury, Clarke said: 'I think there are no new inflationary pressures to justify my raising interest rates in the light of the policy measures already taken.' He said economic growth was slowing and that 'there are no signs of any demand pressures or any earning pressures inside the economy'. Inflationary pressure from higher costs was being constrained by competition. It was inevitable that the move was interpreted as a fundamentally political play. As the *Financial Times* explained, though 'the chancellor insisted the decision had nothing to do with the Conservatives' dismal showing in the local government elections. But Labour and the Liberal Democrats said the move appeared politically motivated. One Tory MP said that leaving rates alone was the "first sensible thing he has done in months."'[170] And the *Financial Times* leader fulminated:

If the chancellor has funked doing the right thing now, people will ask, is he not less likely still to act as the general election comes closer? If the decision to do nothing now means he needs to do still more a few months from now, will he not funk that harder task as well? If he is not prepared to act on monetary policy, for political reasons, will he not also cut taxes next November, with irresponsible abandon, again for political reasons? In short, is the UK not back to its bad old ways? These perceptions, inevitable in the circumstances, are the result of a defective policy regime. If Mr George had made the same decision, on his own, few such doubts need have emerged – and, correspondingly, fewer risks would have been run.[171]

The same division was repeated in the June meeting, with a similar response from City economists, who began to claim that Clarke was overriding the Bank's inflation concerns and that he sounded 'dangerously Lawsonian'.[172] The disagreements between Governor and Chancellor continued. In June, the Bank's judgement was reported as being that 'output was still growing a little bit above trend and that this was likely to continue. But given the conflicting evidence on manufacturing output in particular, no one could be sure about this, and the survey evidence in the past month had softened a bit.'[173]

Critics now began to interpret every policy move in terms of personal manoeuvres. Geoffrey Dicks of NatWest Markets wrote a note about the new 'Kremlinology'. Clarke himself commented: 'Like Kremlinologists in a previous era, "expert" commentators pore over every detail of these minutes to see which indicators supposedly are "in" and which are "out."'[174] Samuel Brittan in the *Financial Times* picked up the term:

In the last published minutes, for June 7, Kenneth Clarke went out of his way to say that interest rates would be determined by the 'economic evidence' and not by financial market beliefs. For this, two and three-quarter cheers. The last quarter is withheld because the remark does not rule out a residual desire to go beyond neutrality towards market expectations and spring a childish surprise.[175]

The principals of the theatrical show realized that credibility was being undermined: Clarke now said 'that it was important that he and the Governor got back into a state of agreement on monetary policy. Their disagreement at the May monthly monetary meeting had been widely discounted but in his view few had guessed that they had disagreed at the June meeting. One way of achieving a soft landing was to agree a ¼ per cent increase at some stage.' They both discussed the way parliament would interpret the central bank's mandate. George said, 'If asked by the TCSC whether he would have preferred a lower target he would say that he would have preferred 2 per cent or less but that if, in practice, 2 ½ per cent or less was achieved that would be just as good.' Clarke said that he 'would also take the line that not even independent central banks set the target for inflation. That was a matter for Government. He would also not depart from the convention that he did not reveal the contents of meetings until the minutes were published. He did not expect his announcement to make major political news. That was more likely to be his affirmation that he was not for turning from his fiscal strategy.'[176]

Low and stable inflation also became a key because it offered a way for the Bank to resist the idea of European monetary integration. In this vision, a foreign anchor imposing policy constraints would no longer be needed as the key to credibility. George told the Commons Treasury and Civil Service committee, 'Britain has a good chance of proceeding to a low-inflation economy with relatively stable interest rates, even if it fails to join other countries in a single currency and a single European central bank around the end of this decade.'[177]

In 1996, the Ken and Eddie meetings were largely consensual, with the Governor repeatedly recommending interest rate reductions, with low-wage pressure and retail prices also responding to the sharp rise in the exchange rate.[178] All that occurred was a discussion of a longer-term possibility that rates might need to rise if there were signs of inflation emerging, and where George argued that monetary policy was not a powerful tool to produce more vigorous economic growth. In April, there was an agreement to make no change in interest rates, as there was 'still a quite high probability of rebound later in the year'.[179] In May, George argued that there was 'little that monetary policy could do to offset the present, temporary, effect of weak overseas demand on manufacturing industry'.[180] In June, Chancellor Clarke imposed a cut in rates even though the Bank 'thought it probable that interest rates would need to rise at some point to protect the inflation target [. . .] did not exclude the possibility of a need for a further reduction in interest rates if there was clear evidence of overall activity slowing significantly over the next months'.[181] Clarke seemed indeed to be more 'relaxed' about interest rates, though John Major apparently was, according to the Bank, 'inclined to take a different view'.[182]

The June reduction was the fourth in seven months and took bank base rates from 6 to 5 3/4 per cent, their lowest level for a year and a half. With economic growth expected to accelerate later, some City economists argued that political considerations had driven the cut. But Clarke dismissed as 'nonsense' the idea that he was preparing the ground for an autumn general election. He added that he 'remained on course' to hit his inflation target of 2.5 per cent or below. The Bank of England refused to say whether the Governor had agreed with the chancellor's decision to cut rates. 'The unusually long meeting between the two to discuss rates on Wednesday raised suspicions of a disagreement, but most economists argued that Mr George was unlikely to have put up too much of a fight.'[183] In fact, George had argued, as the minutes of the June meeting which were published on 17 July showed, that 'The Bank had recognized that there were short-term risks to activity. If those risks were realised that would affect the prospect for inflation – which would also be improved if the recent strengthening of the exchange rate was sustained. But the Bank did not expect activity to turn down even in the short term on a central view – though the Bank was not looking for an acceleration until into the second half of 1996 and 1997.'[184] Clarke was also keen for the Bank to be 'more honest' about declaring foreign exchange reserves, and also that the Bank 'had too many' reserves.[185] That was an indication of a fundamental turning of policy away from forex intervention.

In July, Clarke noted that the publication of the Bank's May *Inflation Report* meant most commentators were expecting a difference of opinion.[186] The Bank started to press its case more powerfully. By the end of the year, it looked as if the cycle was turning, at a rather politically inopportune moment, since a general election was expected in 1997. In December,

George recorded that it was difficult not to recommend tightening in January. Clarke expected a ¼ per cent rise in January, but worried about implications of ½ per cent, which might trigger a flood of 'hot money' into London.[187]

The Chancellor said that, after not raising rates this month people would be very surprised, and wonder what the strategy was given the current conjuncture, if they were raised in February. Moreover, he was not convinced that over the cycle rates would have to go up to the 7–7 ½ per cent level that the markets believed. The Governor noted that, since there was a general expectation that rates needed to go up, and this in itself had an influence on people's expectations, they have in some measure achieved the effect of raising rates. It was for this reason that he attached importance to continuing to press the case for a raise. Nevertheless, in his Edinburgh speech he had been very anxious to explain quite explicitly the genuine dilemma that we faced in setting policy in the context of the tale of two economies. He concluded that the debate was currently within sensible parameters, and it was still really a question of whether we did a bit more later rather than a bit less now.[188]

The Bank in January 1997 recommended a ¼ per cent rise, but thought it likely that a tightening of ½ per cent would be needed soon to moderate growth of domestic demand. Clarke rejected that argument, 'Interest rate decisions were not dependent on the exchange rate, but it was one of the factors to be taken into account.'[189] Many commentators, including the *Financial Times*'s influential Samuel Brittan, argued that the soaring exchange rate would dampen inflation and that on economic rather than political grounds the Bank's push for higher interest rates should be resisted.[190] In public, Clarke always insisted on the priority of the inflation target. On 16 January 1997, Clarke appeared on the *Today* programme and explained that policy 'is set to get to 2 ½ percent or below. I am only doing one thing and that is to keep the best record on inflation for fifty years and to keep it going.'[191]

The arguments were rehashed in February, where the minutes stated: 'There was only a 25 basis point difference between [the Chancellor] and the Governor. But he did not currently see the case for an increase in interest rates, and decided to leave interest rates unchanged for the moment.'[192] And in March, where the minutes record 'a small difference of judgment about the outlook for inflation 1–2 years ahead, and about the balance of risks'.[193] And in April: Clarke was 'not persuaded that the current level of interest rates was inconsistent with achieving the inflation target, and he decided to leave them unchanged for the moment'.[194] Before the April meeting, George had even given a public speech (on 3 April), warning that domestic spending was accelerating at an unsustainable pace, and arguing that rates should rise, even though this would be uncomfortable for exporters crippled by the strong pound. The *Financial Times* mocked the process: 'Like a wicked witch, the governor of the Bank of England popped up to spoil the fun right in the middle of the manifesto fairytales.'[195]

And then came the general election, and a genuinely new regime. On 6 May 1997, the new Chancellor, Gordon Brown, accepted the Governor's recommendation of a ¼ per cent rise, and 'accepted the argument that interest rates may need to rise soon by a further ¼ per cent'. But the main news was the institutional reordering that day, in which the Chancellor gave up the control of interest rates, which would now be set by an independent Monetary Policy Committee located in the Bank. The long-standing debate about central bank independence had been politically resolved.

14

Failure of Internal Communication

The Development of Banking Supervision in the 1990s

The 1987 Banking Act established a new framework for bank regulation in the UK, but the act did not require the Bank of England to prevent bank failures, and the Bank indeed went out of its way to emphasize that it rejected 'the view that all bank failures are supervisory failures'.[1] In taking this line, the Bank was firmly in the consensus of late twentieth-century central banking practice, but also in accordance with its own nineteenth-century tradition that had been cemented during the 1866 panic when the Bank allowed the powerful house of Overend and Gurney to fail. Fed Chairman Alan Greenspan, for instance, sounded very similar when he said, 'We should not forget that the basic function of these regulated entities [i.e. banks] is to take risk. If we minimize taking risk in order to reduce failure rates to zero, we will, by definition, have eliminated the purpose of the banking system.'[2] This view of banking coexisted with an older view, in which the Bank of England had an overall responsibility as what the distinguished banker Jeremy Morse of Lloyds (also a director of the Bank of England) called the 'pater familias' of the City. By the time Eddie George became Governor, the Bank had definitively turned away from that second tradition.

By the 1990s, the Bank was confronting a range of challenges in banking that came from quite different sources, from the internal chaos produced in many financial institutions by the rapid liberalization, amalgamation and internationalization, but also from the overall environment in the unstable domestic macro-economic situation, as well as in the globalizing world economy and in the financial environment revolutionized by the application of IT. How should the Bank shape its regulatory response?

First, the Bank had a clear (but very difficult) mandate to police individual financial institutions. The 1987 act provided some guidelines for supervision: it specifically required reports of large exposures (Section

38); it required the Bank to request an investigation and a report when it felt that the interest of depositors or potential depositors was at risk (Section 41); and it also called on the Bank to reach a judgement as to whether those running banks were 'fit and proper persons' (Section 22). That was an inheritance from the 1979 act, as were requirements on prudence as 'minimal requirements for deposit-taking institutions' in Schedule 2. So there existed a mandate for quite extensive microprudential surveillance.

Second, banking problems might follow from macro-economic shocks. That kind of problem had nothing to do with defective personalities, cowboys in the City, or fraud, neglect and incompetence. The severe recession that began in the second half of 1990 put banks under strain, especially where they had been heavily engaged in property lending. But one of the characteristics of financial stress is that problems that are covered up by the euphoria of good times become harshly exposed, so that the perceived amount of fraud and criminality increases. In a rather overused metaphor, as the tide goes out the swimmers are left naked. The macro shock thus highlights microprudential problems, and leads to even more focus on microprudential regulatory concerns.

Third, many of the banks that operated in the UK also had substantial international activities, or were foreign owned or foreign based; and the regulation of these banks required coordination with banking supervisors in other jurisdictions. The questions raised by overlapping and sometimes conflicting legal frameworks at the time had no obvious answer, and indeed have not really been completely solved even after the 2008 Global Financial Crisis.

The importance of adopting better technology – and the inadequacy of traditional City methods – was shown up in a spectacular robbery in May 1990. The securities that formed the basis of the Bank's monetary operations – Treasury and other bills – were still taken around the City by messengers. The Treasury bills were bearer securities that could be cashed by anyone who held them. That presented a formidable temptation. A messenger of the discount house Cater Allen was robbed of £290 m in securities, £170 m Treasury bills and £121.9 m sterling certificates of deposit. The petty crook who had done the mugging was subsequently found dead with a gunshot wound to the head, and eventually all but 2 of the 301 papers were recovered. But in the meantime, the Bank had felt obliged to protect the owners of the securities against loss.[3]

All the major scandals that erupted publicly at this time, and which produced large-scale criticism of the Bank of England's regulation and supervision in the press and in parliament, apparently involved criminal misconduct and fraud. BCCI, the Bank of Credit and Commerce International, was popularly dubbed the Bank of Crooks and Cocaine International, while the failure of Barings was understood mostly in terms of the spectacular story of the large-scale criminal fraud of the 'Rogue Trader' Nicholas Leeson, whose story produced numerous biographies (including an autobiography) and several films. These bank failures were not systemically threatening, although BCCI led to a major problem for a substantial number of small banks. The one problem case – Midland – that was genuinely systemic (but did not really involve misconduct) was so threatening that it was dealt with in the utmost secrecy, with the consequence that even most of the Bank's senior officials were unaware of the extent of the Bank's involvement. Because the case involved reputation – as the key to credibility and the ability to function in the interbank market – it could not be discussed and certainly not publicized. Instead, the very public debate about supervision in the 1990s revolved around what was from the financial stability point of view a non-relevant or even trivial issue, of criminal behaviour, and entirely avoided the genuine macro-economic implications of the financial sector and its inherent problems. That debate was the background to the decision in 1997 by the new Labour government to separate financial supervision from monetary policy by taking it away from the Bank.

The Bank's supervisory staff was also relatively small – below 150 people involved in operational supervision. It was also relatively young: there were only three supervisors aged 50 or over, and eighty were under 30 in 1992. It was difficult to know how to measure success, and the supervisors complained that 'by and large success went unsung while failures were all too obvious'. Leigh-Pemberton added a peculiar and problematic criterion of success: 'The number of banks who chose to operate in London because they saw London as a clean and efficient market where supervision was effective but not intrusive.'[4] The problem was that the more banks were attracted, the more financial activity expanded, the greater and more complex would be the task of the supervisor.

BCCI

The first spectacular problem case of the 1990s was an international bank. Unlike JMB, BCCI was a very large institution, and it raised a new kind of problem: the coordination between different regulatory frameworks. BCCI had been created in 1972 by a Pakistani financier, Agha Hasan Abedi. By the early 1990s, it had $20 bn in assets and operated in sixty-nine countries. There were two main subsidiaries under the umbrella of a holding company, a company registered in Luxembourg with worldwide assets of $7.4 bn and $3.2 bn in branch operations in the UK, as well as a subsidiary authorized in the Cayman Islands. Many of the worldwide operations were in fact run from London, although the ownership lay elsewhere. The Bank of England thus became involved in negotiating primarily with the Luxembourg authorities responsible for the parent company.

The mechanism for regulatory cooperation was a college of supervisors, one of the first instances of a practice that would become much more common in the 1990s and after. Four supervisory authorities were involved: besides the Bank of England and the Luxembourg Monetary Institute, the Bank of Spain and the Swiss Federal Banking Commission had a responsibility in supervising parts of BCCI's global operations. An initial meeting took place on 22 June 1988. The *Financial Times* reported in the late 1980s that BCCI was the world's 'largest bank without a lender of last resort'.[5] In fact, the experience of attempting to coordinate between the different regulators was regarded as 'a trail for a wider college to deal with supervision more generally'. The question of regulation of the group as a whole remained obscure. The Bank's official responsible for supervising BCCI at this time reported that 'the position of BCCI in London was solid and secure: the question was whether there were difficulties elsewhere. At present there was no reason to think there were.'[6] The reassuring feature was supposed to be that BCCI could not be expected to run into liquidity problems because of the 'strong support from its shareholders, including members of the Saudi Arabian royal family'.[7] Thus, even if there were problems in the bank's lending, there could be no question about the adequacy of the bank's capitalization. The problems in other words might involve complex legal issues, but they were not believed to be capable of bringing a threat to overall financial stability.

There had, however, long been suspicions about BCCI. In 1981, the Bank of England had recorded its 'concern regarding the bank's seemingly opaque shareholding structure'.[8] After the collapse, the press cited a Bank of England memo from 1982 which described BCCI as 'on its way to becoming the financial equivalent of the SS Titanic!'[9] The Bank had in fact at this early stage persuaded BCCI to commission an analysis from a firm of auditors, Ernst and Whinney, but the 1981 report that resulted appeared basically satisfactory, and the Bank's staff felt relaxed: 'The London management continues to be extremely cooperative and following the report of the auditors, who have expressed a high degree of confidence in the quality of the loan portfolio, they will no doubt expect recognition in the future.'[10] In the mid-1980s, after large losses, Luxembourg supervisors asked BCCI to go through a new audit. But Price Waterhouse attributed the problems not to fraud but to 'incompetence, errors made by unsophisticated amateurs venturing into a highly technical and sophisticated market'.[11]

The Bank of England received repeated warnings in the late 1980s, as reports circulated about the engagement of BCCI in drug dealing in the US and political manipulation in Central America involving the Panamanian dictator General Noriega. The Bank discussed the allegations at the highest level – including regularly in meetings with the Chancellor. In March 1988, after news that Abedi had had a heart transplant, BCCI was termed at Books 'a one-man band'.[12] In October 1988, BCCI (along with the Delors Committee) took up most of the Governor's regular meeting with Chancellor Lawson, who stated that he was 'quite content to leave the supervisory side of this to us but asked that we would ensure that he was informed if the political side developed in any way; drugs, financial scandal and so on were obviously sensitive'. The Bank's memorandum on this meeting stated that 'the Governor noted that there were no immediate supervisory worries over BCCI'.[13] The first meeting of the supervisory college, in June 1988, spent most of its time discussing a quite extensive fifty-page report prepared by Price Waterhouse, recommending that BCCI reduce the concentration of lending to a number of major borrowers.

The immediate causes of the collapse of BCCI were problems in the US, which for a long time the Bank of England did not want to think were connected with the UK operations of BCCI. In January 1990, after two years of investigation, a BCCI agency had been convicted of drug money laundering; but that was only the beginning of a much bigger and very sensitive investigation. In May 1991, a very senior Treasury official, Ed Yeo, travelled to London at the request of Alan Greenspan to explain the problem. Greenspan insisted that the visit be utterly secret, and in particular that it should not be revealed to the president of the New York Fed, Jerry Corrigan. The account Yeo gave was so lurid and sensational that Leigh-Pemberton and George were deeply shocked:

He began by suggesting that BCCI could be at the heart of a vast geo-political web designed to influence government policies in South America, Nigeria and Pakistan, as well as parts of the Middle East and the US itself. He cited the intervention of [US Assistant Treasury Secretary] Mulford [...] to scupper an Argentine support program that the U.S. Government was behind in 1987, with the aim of assuring that Menem rather than Alfonsin became President; he spoke of buying the administration in Peru; and he mentioned links with President Assad in Syria, the Saudi Intelligence and various others.

Yeo went on to talk about BCCI's involvement in First American Bank, which he believed to have made large and improper loans to prominent politicians. 'He suspected that even the Administration could be involved through campaign receipts.' And it was also possible that Fed staff were involved.

In London, a new Price Waterhouse report (18 April 1990) declared that lending concentration had not been reduced, and that the auditors no longer placed any confidence in the Chief Executive Swaleh Naqvi's integrity. In October 1990, the meeting of the college of supervisors in Luxembourg was informed by the Bank of England of a Price Waterhouse report on money laundering that concluded that 'general standards are satisfactory, but a lack of vigilance in the acceptance of customers has been noted and back to back financing has been criticized because the origin of these funds has not always been checked'.[14] The Price Waterhouse report for the BCCI Audit Committee was actually much more damaging, reporting that $1.5 bn was needed to cover losses, and including a statement that 'we now believe that the previous management may have colluded with some of its major customers to misstate or disguise the underlying purpose of significant transactions'. The Audit Committee report, however, was not widely circulated in the Bank of England, and neither Brian Quinn nor Roger Barnes, the senior Bank officials concerned with bank supervision, saw it or could read it until after the collapse of BCCI. The Bingham inquiry later heard from Price Waterhouse that the auditors had been surprised that the October 1990 report did not provoke a stronger reaction in the Bank and thought that 'no one wished to grasp the nettle, perhaps from reluctance to be seen to assume a lead role'.[15]

At the beginning of 1991, there was a rapid development after a change of personnel at the top of the bank. Abedi stepped aside because of ill health, and Naqvi was removed because of failures as a banker (but with no accusations of fraud at this stage). After the new general manager at BCCI, Zafar Iqbal, revealed that there were deposits of around $600 m not recorded in the official books, the Bank began discussions about commissioning an audit report under Article 41 of the 1987 Banking Act, and in April the Bank instructed Price Waterhouse to prepare that report, which the Bank received on 24 June 1991. The new Waterhouse report involved access to some 6,000 secret files belonging to Naqvi. The outcome was a damning document, revealing details of widespread fraud, and describing BCCI as 'one of the most complex deceptions in banking history'.

By the end of June, the Bank of England had reached the decision – in consultation with the British government – that there was no alternative to closing the London operations, which constituted the commercial core of the bank. The liquidation was discussed in a phone call with the Luxembourg authorities on 28 June, a Friday; and over the weekend there were discussions in Abu Dhabi, where the ruling dynasty had recently, with the encouragement of the Bank of England, acquired a major investment in the company. There was also a demand by the head of the Luxembourg Monetary Institute, Pierre Jaans, that the major shareholders should be given an 'active and responsible' role in shutting down the bank. Over the weekend of 29–30 June, Ghanim al Mazrui, the secretary general of the emirate's investment authority and head of the private office of the ruler, Sheik Zayed bin Sultan al-Nahyan, explained that the shareholder's support of BCCI could not be open-ended. But when the final meeting of the supervisors with the owners' representative took place in Luxembourg on the morning of 5 July, Mazrui was quite stunned, and delivered a long rambling response. Initially, there were no representatives of the auditors at the meeting, but when it resumed at 1 p.m. with Price Waterhouse present, Mazrui stood up, shook hands with the Luxembourg and Bank of England officials and then walked out. The decision to shut down BCCI on 5 July 1991 was made by the Bank of England's Governor Robin Leigh-Pemberton, with the timing dictated by the Luxembourg requirement to close a problematic bank during business hours (the court closed for business at 5:00 p.m.) and the wish to coordinate the liquidation operation on both sides of the Atlantic, so that the action was brought forward to 2:00 p.m. in Luxembourg. At 9:00 a.m. EST, New York state banking regulators seized $100 m in assets held in BCCI's agency office on Park Avenue in Manhattan. The outstanding debts of BCCI's Luxembourg operation amounted to $10 bn.

One immediate concern was the response of the major shareholder. Leigh-Pemberton needed to fly to Abu Dhabi to reassure Sheikh Zayed. 'There appeared to be a sense of affront in Abu Dhabi at the lack of consultation in advance of the closure of BCCI,' Leigh-Pemberton reported.

All in Abu Dhabi were very bruised by their experience; their pride had been dealt a severe blow by the feeling that they had been deceived by the bank's senior management. He explained that Sheikh Zayed had been a shareholder since the establishment of the bank in 1972 but had originally held only a 20 per cent stake. BCCI's founder, Abedi, had built up a very good relationship with the Sheikh, presenting BCCI as the Moslems' answer to Western capitalism. Abedi had persuaded the Bank of America to take a 30 per cent holding at the outset and when disposed of this went to another wealthy family in Dubai. Thereafter BCCI began to lose money, and the Sheikh had been persuaded to increase his stake steadily until it reached its present size of 77 per cent. Over the years, the Sheikh had put into the bank around $10 billion.[16]

The UK government was taken by surprise by the discussion of closure from the end of June, although it should not have been. Norman Lamont, the Chancellor of the Exchequer, said that

the Governor had, he recalled, mentioned the BCCI case to him at their regular bilaterals on two occasions before the closure of the bank. He had said the bank had been convicted of offences in the US but there did not seem to be significant implications for the London operations; that it was not a very serious matter from the UK point of view; and that difficulties had only come to light because of developments in the US. The Governor said that he would have been basing such comments on the 1990 Price Waterhouse reports. In the US, investigations had been taking place into, for example, the possible illegal acquisition of two US banks, widespread charges of corruption and some suggestions of involvement in worldwide political bribery. But so far as had been known, none of this had gone on in London. He had known nothing about the fraud in this country or elsewhere in Europe until Thursday 20 June when he received the Price Waterhouse report: no evidence of fraud had been received until then.

Lamont was worried that he would be asked about the Section 41 report. 'The Governor said that Section 41 investigations were by no means unusual; a number had been carried out over the past year.' Sir Terry Burns said, 'It would not be easy for the Chancellor to say he did not know that in January 1991 $600 million were missing and a Section 41 report was underway.' Burns went on to observe, 'One problem was that the initial Bank/Treasury action might not be credible.'[17]

The investigatory and legal aftermath dragged on for years. On 29 July 1992, a Federal grand jury in Washington indicted Clark Clifford, the influential former Secretary of Defense, as well as his law partner Robert Altman, accusing them of taking bribes from BCCI to help hide its illegal ownership of First American, but the charges were subsequently dismissed. The New York Fed then informed the Bank of England that the number two figure in BCCI, Abdur Sakhia, was claiming that BCCI 'had a friend' in the Bank. The New York District Attorney's informant claimed that he had seen a briefcase with US dollars being handed over in a hotel bedroom to a Bank of England official. But when the charge was investigated, there were no concrete details and the New York informant was unable to identify photographs of the Bank of England officials he had allegedly seen. Nevertheless, there remained some doubt about BCCI influence on its supervisors, and one of BCCI's Bank of England supervisors, a man with a rather hawkish reputation, 'mentioned in an off-the-cuff way that he had on one occasion been to the Raymond Revue bar [a London nude dancing club] with BCCI and other guests'.[18]

Leigh-Pemberton reported to the Court on his experiences with the House of Commons Treasury Select Committee, where he had tried to distinguish the UK from the US operations of BCCI:

He had told the Committee that the Bank had been aware of BCCI's laundering of drug money in the United States. As a result the floorboards had been taken up in the United Kingdom branches but no evidence of any similar operation had been found. The branches had been very closely supervised and the Bank had required BCCI to provide a daily balance sheet although later this had been reduced to a weekly one. There had been reports of terrorist funds placed with BCCI and details had been passed on to Special Branch but the reports could not be substantiated. The two Price Waterhouse reports of April and October 1990 had not revealed evidence of widespread fraud and certainly not sufficient to close the bank down by revoking its licence.[19]

The Federal Reserve Board proposed a record $200 m fine on BCCI for secretly controlling three American banks – First American, the Centrust Savings Bank of Miami and Independence Bank of Encino, California.

The investigation report on BCCI produced by Lord Bingham was released in October 1992. It criticized the Bank of England for not pursuing 'the truth about BCCI with the rigor which BCCI's reputation justified' (see Figure 14.1). The issue became a political football, with the government largely defending the Bank of England as 'party to no conspiracy or no cover-up'. The Labour Treasury spokesman, Gordon Brown, on the other hand described the Bank as 'a soft touch for a crooked bank'. On the other side of the Atlantic, a US Senate Subcommittee on terrorism, narcotics and international operations complained that the Bank of England had been 'wholly inadequate' in protecting shareholders.[20] Eddie George defended the supervisor most concerned with BCCI, whose name appeared in forty-nine paragraphs of the report: 'If we were to respond to this pressure that blood must be spilled we would be weakening our supervisory capability rather than strengthening it. That is not what we are about to do. Roger Barnes [Assistant Director and head of Banking Supervision] is a world class bank supervisor and is recognised as such by most of the banks he

Figure 14.1 Brian Quinn (DG) in goalmouth front portico of the Bank (Ingram Pinn, *Financial Times*, 14 March 1992)

supervises and by other supervisors. He is also the person delivering the service that Bingham says has served the community well.'[21]

Before the report was released, it had been discussed in the Bank's Court, and Sir David Scholey, the man most frequently mentioned as a successor to Leigh-Pemberton should he resign in the wake of affair, asked whether 'heads should roll' and noted that the report was devastatingly critical of Barnes, but less so of his superior, Executive Director Brian Quinn.[22] But there was general agreement that the senior officials had not failed through either technical incompetence or negligence. Barnes in fact resigned at age 56 in February 1993, but the Bank publicly affirmed that the resignation was not connected to BCCI and that 'no resignations were justified by the report. Our system of supervision was described by Bingham as one that had served the community well and Roger Barnes could take a lot of the credit for that.'[23] Sir David Walker emphasized that the Bank had a 'culture problem' and 'needed to be more street-wise'.[24]

In a meeting with the Chancellor before the Bingham report was released, Leigh-Pemberton had promised to create a special investigations unit (that the Bank liked to term the 'smells' unit), establish a legal division and improve internal communications as well as communications with the Treasury.[25] Bingham endorsed the importance of the new legal unit in the work of the Banking Supervision Division.

In the aftermath of the collapse, the liquidators sued the Bank of England, but their claim was ultimately abandoned after more than a decade, in November 2005, with BCCI's creditors in consequence having to foot the Bank's £74 m costs as well as their own £57 m legal expenses. The trial was Dickensian in its dimensions and complexity. In order to succeed, the claimants would have needed to establish that their losses arose from 'bad faith' rather than negligence on the part of the Bank of England – because of the Bank's statutory immunities. One of the records set was for the longest opening speech ever by counsel: it took over six months. The trial generated a vast documentary mountain, which was built up in court in lever files as a sort of wall between the opposed legal teams.[26]

The liquidators were more successful with a case against the auditors Price Waterhouse and Ernst & Young, who settled for $175 m in 1998. In 1994, the government of Abu Dhabi agreed to pay $1.9 bn into the depositors' pool. But there was an additional fallout from the BCCI affair: by the late 1980s, BCCI had twenty-nine branches in London, primarily to serve the Asian immigrant community. One of the consequences of the BCCI collapse was to give a peculiar twist to the small banks crisis that blew up in the early 1990s.

THE SMALL BANKS

The BCCI collapse came in the middle of the first major post-war collapse in housing prices. From the third quarter of 1989, when the Nationwide calculation of the average UK house price was £54,352 (for London £93,681), there was a fall until the market reached a bottom in the first quarter of 1993 (£50,128; London £66,948), a fall of 7.8 per cent, and for London 28.5 per cent). In the first half of 1991, figures produced by the Council for Mortgage Lenders showed that 221,900 mortgages (2.3 per cent of the outstanding stock) were more than six months in arrears, compared with 109,370 (1.2 per cent of the outstanding stock) a year earlier, and that 36,610 dwellings were repossessed (0.4 per cent of the outstanding stock of mortgages), more than double the number recorded a year earlier. Personal bankruptcies and consumer credit defaults were also at record levels. Over the same period, the first half of 1991, company insolvencies reached 10,833 (4.0 per cent of the total number of companies registered at Companies House) compared with

6,549 (2.7 per cent) in the equivalent period a year earlier. Property and construction firms were particularly hard hit as a consequence of the property price collapse.[27]

Not surprisingly, lenders – especially those focused on the London market – were in trouble. From the late spring of 1991, the Bank started monitoring the small banks' funding position on a weekly basis. It worried in particular that a shock emanating in this area might be contagious, and bring down smaller merchant banks. There were too many small banks in London. Many were disappearing by themselves, but in the early 1990s the Bank estimated that there were still twenty to twenty-five whose long-term future was doubtful. It was also becoming clear that banks which had previously lent to secondary authorized institutions – through syndicated facilities, committed bilateral lines and standbys – were already, even before the BCCI collapse, rethinking their exposure to the sector, and in particular to banks which specialized in property lending. National Home Loans (NHL), for example, lost all but £10 m of the £248 m committed facilities which came up for renewal during June. City Merchants Bank and East Trust also lost a significant proportion of their bank lines during this period.[28]

Many of the small banks had not financed themselves through deposits, but used the wholesale market and borrowed from other banks and institutions. The Bank of England calculated that some thirty small banks relied on non-retail deposits. One immediate impact of BCCI was that local authorities, which had some £5 bn on deposit with the banking sector, became worried and withdrew deposits in smaller banks. As problems began to appear in small lenders such as First National Bank and Finance Corporation, Wintrust, Edington Place and City Merchants, the Bank started to worry about how the problem could be addressed. The solution of the 1970s, a private-sector engagement via a Bank-coordinated lifeboat, looked less attractive, and the Bank believed that that old approach would not be 'saleable to the major UK banks'.[29]

British and Commonwealth Merchant Bank was part of B & C Holdings. It collapsed in June 1990, when three major creditor banks, Midland, Lloyds and Standard Chartered, withdrew from a £70 m standby facility. At its peak in the summer of 1987, B&C had been the UK's second-largest non-banking financial institution, in terms of market capitalization. It was brought down primarily by losses in a leasing subsidiary, Atlantic Computers.[30] Later, looking back, John Gieve, the Chancellor's Private Secretary, described this collapse as a turning point, marking 'a distinct tightening of perceived policy'.[31]

The most shocking development was at Union Discount Company, a traditional discount house and thus at the core of the Bank's traditional immediate sphere of interest. Union had diversified into a problematic office equipment leasing venture, Sabre Leasing, which incurred heavy losses in the early 1990s. But its fundamental business model was also problematical, as the *Financial Times* noted: 'It may be that with the UK in the ERM, the tendency for interest rate cuts to be signalled in advance means Union's core business is inherently less profitable. Just as well, perhaps, that some of its other businesses are making a little money.'[32] The Bank stepped in with support of £350 m, with a penalty rate of interest, and an obvious public demonstration of its association through the appointment of the Bank veteran Sir George Blunden as Deputy Chairman.[33]

The smallest problem banks were simply allowed to disappear quietly. That could not happen with the larger institutions, such as NHL, with two-fifths of its loan book over two months in arrears. Its problems were very public, and the bank responded by laying off large numbers of its staff.[34] Some large retail banks, including Abbey National and Warburgs, had discussed a rescue package with the Bank of England. Sir Jeremy Morse, the Chairman of Lloyds, told the Bank that he believed there was a high probability of another secondary banking crisis. In that event, another lifeboat operation would be required and 'Lloyds would certainly play its part. However, in the case of NHL, the Bank appeared to be asking Lloyds to participate on a commercial basis. Lloyds did not regard the proposed facility as commercial and so had declined to participate.'[35] In consequence, as doubts began to arise over the originally preferred lifeboat package, the Bank had to step in to provide a guarantee to the banks before they would provide a £200 m facility to NHL. The Bank emphasized that it was adopting a case-by-case approach and not putting on a general rescue.

One of the factors that influenced the Bank but especially the Treasury was the fear that if the government were to guarantee NHL it would make compensation for BCCI depositors 'very difficult to resist'.[36] Consequently, the Bank assistance was quite circuitous: it gave an assurance that if the private facility proved insufficient, it would first ask banks to provide further funding, but if that failed the Bank should be prepared to put in the additional funds.[37] In a discussion of the £200 m support facility, the Treasury tried to argue that the solvency of NHL was a separate issue from 'the fact that the bank was part of a much larger group which obtained its funds from the wholesale market, which was unsupervised and had engaged in flashy and fast lending practices in the mortgage market'. Sir

Terry Burns asked, 'What exactly the problem would be if NHL were to be allowed to fail?' George replied that 'it would be a precondition of any sort of public sector support that the institution would not be financed as a going concern'. The other banks were smaller: East Trust Limited, which received a standby facility from Barclays Bank for £7 m, with a Bank guarantee that was undisclosed. City Merchants, the third bank, owned by two investment trusts and with a total balance sheet of £170 m, received a £30 m standby arrangement from National Westminster and Lloyds.[38]

There were also legal problems about the rescue operation, in that the European Commission raised the question of whether it was compatible with European provisions restricting state aid. The Bank concluded that 'if the [£115 million liquidity] support was properly described as aid, it was felt likely that it was state aid. The Bank is, we were advised, an organ of the State.'[39]

But the major argument against acting to save NHL would be that NHL would go under anyway, and that the rescue operation would thus turn into a public embarrassment. The Treasury and the Bank were worried by the question of at what stage it would be necessary to make a public announcement. Burns said: 'The danger not making an immediate statement would be that although NHL might be saved, withdrawals would simply continue from other banks.' Other Treasury officials noted that there was also a propriety question if public funds were involved, and 'worried about a real problem of moral hazard as banks would believe that there would henceforth be no penalties for the risks they took'.[40] The outcome of the discussion was that the Bank's accounting practice was tweaked so that the support operation could be concealed for some time.

The influential Markets Division at the Bank also pushed the moral hazard fear. George as Deputy Governor was worried about the assumptions on which the large clearing banks were operating.

If an individual bank crisis arose on a day when there was a surplus the bank would have to rely on existing market arrangements. The markets may not be deep enough to accommodate their requirements unless the bank is a frequent trader in these markets. Moreover if the big banks continue to marginalise the discount houses, their behaviour will ultimately lead to a reduction in the number of counterparties and a reduction in the depth of the market for the instruments in which the houses traditionally trade. At that point certain liquidity policies will be imprudent. The Markets Divisions argue that, if the bank's perceptions about the Bank's willingness to provide liquidity in circumstances other than system illiquidity are left unchallenged, the Bank will have created moral hazard for itself.[41]

Table 14.1 *Exposure of Bank of England in*
small banks crisis (1993)

	Maximum possible exposure	Current exposure
East	£7 m	£6 m
CMB	£40 m (approx)	£0
NMB	£492 m	£458 m
UDC	£350 m	£160 m
TOTAL	**£889 m**	**£624 m**

By 1993, the Bank calculated that its maximum possible exposure as a consequence of the small banks crisis had reached £624 m (see Table 14.1).[42]

Another dimension of the small banks problem related to community relations. By the beginning of 1993, three of the four privately owned Indian banks incorporated in the UK – Mount, Equatorial and Roxburghe – collapsed and closed. The fourth, Meghraj, was in serious difficulties. The four banks had combined assets of about £400 m, and mainly served the Gujarati-speaking community, making loans to small businesses in the UK while funding themselves to a significant extent from deposits drawn from the Indian community in East Africa, particularly Kenya. Many of these deposits were labelled 'no correspondence' and probably constituted flight money.[43] These collapses raised political fears – that were articulated by a Labour MP close to the immigrant community – that the Bank was not helping in the case of an especially vulnerable community.

Looking back at the chronology of the small banks crisis, the leading figures at the Bank of England began to set out a completely new philosophy of crisis management. The new position was most articulately presented by Mervyn King: 'Over-capacity could build up in any regulated system and would be squeezed out following deregulation, but he was not convinced that this could lead to systemic fragility. He added that the weakness of the clearers was a result of the cartelised market. It was therefore arguable that it was lack of competition that produced financial fragility.'[44]

MIDLAND

The 1990–1991 recession affected profitability at all UK clearing banks, but one was especially vulnerable. For 1989–1990, profits before bad debts fell by 2.5 per cent at Barclays, by 9.5 per cent at National

Westminster and by 17.1 per cent at Midland (while there was a slight profits increase in Lloyds). Midland had long looked weak, and had suffered major losses on its US subsidiary Crocker Bank in 1983 and 1984. By the beginning of 1991, it looked as if there might be a panic and a run on Midland Bank. Estimates for the 1990 pre-tax profits fell from the budgeted £657 m to £300 m in July and £55 m in November, and at the beginning of the new year a loss seemed a real possibility.[45] The problem lay both in the asset side of the bank and in the high level of funding costs. There were bad debts as a result of the UK real estate market, as well as losses arising from the holding of lower-yielding dollar assets against problem country debt. A young American had been appointed to sort out UK Banking and Group Operations, and he set out a plan to cut costs and increase credit checks and controls: but at first it seemed as if he was intent on pushing all the blame on his predecessors, and staff at the bank became even more demoralized. In January 1991, Brian Quinn, reviewing a Bank supervisor's memo on Midland, concluded that he shared 'the view that Midland is in, or rapidly approaching, a crisis'. He suggested that a two-pronged strategy was needed, first to replace the top management, and then find a suitable partner for a merger. 'We must,' he wrote, 'give some thought to considering whether Sir Kit [McMahon]'s tenure as Chairman [and Chief Executive in a combined role] has not been a failure and whether his strategy for the group over the last five years has been fundamentally flawed, both in concept and in its execution.' It would be difficult to merge Midland with another British clearer, but also 'it is not very obvious where a foreign partner might come from but this perhaps comes of the current depressed conditions on the international banking scene'.[46] In a Bank of England meeting on 10 January, Andrew Crockett argued that there needed to be a contingency plan, involving a 'copper-bottomed guarantee', and that 'the situation might even require nationalization'.[47] On 15 January, at the Board of Banking Supervision, Leigh-Pemberton talked of the need for a new chairman and a new chief executive. Other banks started reducing their exposure to Midland in the interbank and foreign exchange markets, and so it appeared as if there might quickly be a liquidity crisis. The Bank's officials thought that Midland – which accounted for some 17 per cent of clearing bank deposits – was 'indeed too big to fail'.[48] The danger was that a half-hearted, or not copper-bottomed, declaration of support, would trigger a depositors' run. In a meeting with Treasury officials, Quinn recalled the experience of Continental Illinois, where a qualified statement of support had been followed after six weeks by a run.

Immediately, the Bank bought as much marketable paper as it could from Midland (it had some £3–£4 bn in liquid bills). But beyond that the Bank prepared a full range of scenarios, beginning with a change of management, though also including public guarantees, finding a bank that would take Midland over, as well as nationalization.

The discussion of Midland's future was highly personalized. The problem lay in the Bank past of former Deputy Governor McMahon, who seemed at least to the Bank to wish to escalate his bank's conflict with the Bank of England. He had repeatedly denounced the high interest rates that followed from the adoption of the ERM as fundamentally responsible for banks' problems. Leigh-Pemberton felt that Midland and its chairman might be getting a light ride because many senior officials remembered and liked McMahon from his time as Deputy Governor. The Governor was also persistently sceptical about Midland's attempts to merge with HSBC, commenting, for instance, in 1990 that 'he did not feel this was terribly solid'.[49] If the merger went ahead, 'it would be a case of two-plus-two certainly not making five or six and struggling to make four'. Eddie George took a similar stance, commenting that 'quite independently of the Hong Kong risk factor, [...] Hongshai was not an appropriate merger partner for the Midland, but the Hong Kong risk factor put this more or less beyond doubt'.[50]

McMahon continued to the last moment to resist the call to step down, and complained that the Bank actions were leading to 'internal risks'. Midland staff had noted that Quinn was absent at the regular prudential meeting with the Bank and above all that the official responsible for Midland supervision was 'markedly less aggressive than he had expected', giving rise to suspicions that a radical plan was about to be launched. The Midland management also complained that another clearer had refused Midland a two-year swap. The Bank of England was in effect 'taking over the corporate governance of Midland'.[51] Leigh-Pemberton's attempt to engineer a change at the top was initially frustrated by the refusal of Bruce Pattullo of the Bank of Scotland to become chairman, and the Governor then turned to a London clearer and approached the deputy chairman of Barclays plc, also unsuccessfully; finally, he asked Brian Pearse of Barclays to take on the role of chief executive, with Sir Peter Walters, a former chairman of British Petroleum, as chairman. The move was carefully sounded out, with a meeting with the Prime Minister, who authorized the Governor to say that taking the job was in the national interest. But the Bank also prepared the way in a highly secretive meeting with partners of Cazenoves, the merchant bank, who were summoned in to meet the Governor, entering the Bank through a rear door and going into a completely sealed-off Parlours: the Cazenoves partners explained that the package would not be credible if McMahon were allowed to stay on until his sixty-fourth birthday.[52] After more meetings with the Treasury, the Bank had a draft letter of support prepared in which the Bank might receive an indemnity from the Treasury for a possible rescue operation, involving 'action to restore the bank's [Midland's] capital position, whether by varying retentions policy or by a capital injection or by some other means'.[53] The Bank also contacted Willie Purves, of HSBC, who felt left out of the negotiations – HSBC had taken a 15 per cent stake in Midland, but now had the intention of reducing it. Purves explained that 'he had not realized the situation was so grave', and worried about taking a chief executive from another clearer.[54]

In the end, the operation to announce the change of management went smoothly. McMahon acknowledged that he had been pushed out: 'The Bank of England was clearly involved in the search for a new chief executive. I admit that over the years we have made a lot of errors. I hope to find retirement a little more relaxing.'[55] Initially, the reaction was positive, and there was no need for the Bank contingency plans. But the longer-term future was only really secured with the takeover by HSBC.

Midland was not the only major bank to have problems in its top management. In 1993, the Bank staged a similar operation in regard to Barclays. Barclays had posted its first ever loss (of £242 m, a consequence of £2.6 bn in bad debt provisions), and there was widespread criticism of the double role of Andrew Buxton as chairman and chief executive, but also of the former Treasury mandarin Sir Peter Middleton as vice chairman. Buxton, a member of one of the nineteenth-century banking dynasties whose banks had come together to form Barclays, had stepped in in 1992 after the resignation of John Quinton, the first non-family chairman, who had tried to innovate, and to expand Barclays as 'the McDonald's of banking', a place where 'you're greeted with a smile and you're not kept waiting'.[56] But the circumstances of this experiment were inauspicious. Middleton had a shrewd political sense, and had insisted on an office at group headquarters 'carefully placed between the chairman and chief executive'. He wanted 'to make sure that conflicts are minimized';[57] but that approach was complex when the chairman was also the chief executive. Leigh-Pemberton thought that 'the Chairman appeared to be seen by his own managers as weak and unable to exercise control over mighty barons'.[58] One Barclays manager told the Governor that if there was no new chief executive in a reasonable time, 'the proprietors would become extremely impatient and would "move in" [presumably try to exert political pressure], perhaps not only into Barclays but also into the Bank of England'.[59] When Buxton announced that there would be a search for an outsider to take over as chief executive, the press speculated that the 'announcement had been made in response to the Bank of England's insistence that Mr Buxton end the uncertainty and take immediate action towards splitting his roles. It is not unknown for the Bank to "suggest" appointments and departures at Britain's leading banks. Barclays denied last night that Threadneedle Street had intervened. The Bank of England declined to comment.'[60] At the annual meeting, the criticism of Buxton continued and Middleton was obliged to explain what shareholders interpreted as public criticism of Barclays. He responded rather lamely: 'You put me on the spot. I certainly wasn't criticising the board.'[61] Buxton remained as chairman until 1999, and successfully presided over a stabilization and then a new expansion of the bank.

The covert Midland rescue operation raised the question of how secure was the settlements system. In the late 1980s, there had been some discussion of contingency planning for the clearing system, but the risks at that time seemed remote. Tony Coleby prepared a paper on wholesale payments arrangements in the UK, in which he argued for the establishment of real-time final settlement facilities in sterling and dollars, but George Blunden, the Deputy Governor, was sceptical and relayed the clearing banks' arguments that 'exposures to them were relatively free of risk'.[62] Paul Tucker was nevertheless asked to prepare a paper on how a new real-time clearing system might operate. He looked at increasing risks flowing from an increase in volumes of trading, unsatisfactory settlement systems, but also from the perception that the Bank might underwrite clearing operations. He called for 'reforms that would leave the banks in greater doubt than at present as to whether we would always stand behind the clearing, as the real damage done by moral hazard is not that we may suffer losses but that the settlement banks might be less vigilant in their control of settlement risks'.[63] The initiative was again shot down by Blunden. The Tucker paper was, Blunden suggested, clearly 'based on US experience', and it was 'not yet in a form in which it should go to the Treasury or the clearing banks'. Indeed, 'we should certainly not imply that there were serious problems about the clearers'.[64] But that was precisely the problem that the Midland experience in 1991 raised. Before that there had been no need to quantify the extent of intraday exposure. The clearers were shaken and agreed that work on RTGS should proceed. In November 1991, Coleby pointed out his concern that 'the banks had managed to convince themselves that the risk they were facing was less than it was in reality'.[65] There was a very clear argument that the investment of some £20 m could eliminate risks that amounted to billions each day. It also looked likely that the risks would escalate as the number of banks, and the involvement of European banks in the City, grew.[66] By 12 August 1992, a decision was taken to move to an RTGS (Real-Time Gross Settlement) system.[67]

The virtue of an RTGS was that it protected market participants from worries about the failure of a counterparty. Bank failures might be possible, then, as long as payments were protected; and there would be no need to rescue an institution purely out of fear of the systemic consequences of failure. That question came up in a Court discussion, and Eddie George replied, 'It was unlikely, though not inconceivable, that we could allow such institutions to fail.'[68] Protecting the resilience of the system was crucial because banking supervision was – perhaps inevitably – still vulnerable. Roger Barnes' successor as head of supervision, Michael Foot, noted that 'not everyone had fully adjusted to the change in ethos required post-BCCI'; and that in particular there persisted 'a rather isolationist mentality within the Division'. There were institutional reasons for that: 'The general perception elsewhere in the Bank was that BSD was a place to avoid, on the grounds that its workload and responsibilities were very heavy and that it was often difficult to get out of the Division.'[69] Then came another blow to the Bank's reputation.

BARINGS

In February 1995, Barings, London's oldest merchant bank, collapsed in the aftermath of trading losses accumulated by a single 28-year-old individual, Nicholas (Nick) Leeson. Just over a hundred years earlier, the Bank of England had coordinated the rescue of Barings after it had overexposed itself to Argentine debt in a bubble that burst in 1890. The complicated rescue operation then – in which the bank's capital was wiped out and new capital put in by other banks – was the first real moment when the Bank coordinated the City of London like an orchestra conductor. The rapid failure in 1995 of a similar attempt at a similar exercise provided a vivid demonstration of how the old clubby City of London had come to a dead end.

The managerial flaws were undoubtedly greater in Barings than in the Bank of England, but the episode shed a harsh light both on supervision within a City firm and that of the City by the Bank. Leeson, who since 1992 had been based in Singapore, had been reporting to four different managers, and he was allowed to run his own 'back office' operation so that he could conceal the fraud by means of an 'error account' 88888. There were some losses that appeared right at the beginning of Leeson's operations, which Leeson hoped to make good by larger bets. His major positions were in futures of the Nikkei 225 index and in Japanese government bonds, both of which were traded in Osaka but also in Singapore on the Singapore International Monetary Exchange (SIMEX). By the end of 1993, the losses stood at £20 m, and rose to over £200 m by the end of 1994. The problem escalated out of control when the Kobe earthquake in Japan (17 January 1995) produced a sharp drop in the Nikkei and other Asian markets. Leeson then made a series of short-term gambles based on the rate of recovery of the Nikkei, and lost even more money. Between 31 December 1994, and 24 February 1995, Barings provided Leeson with £521 m to meet margin calls. On 27 February, Leeson disappeared for some days before flying to Frankfurt, where he was arrested on 2 March. Leeson's losses reached £827 m, twice the bank's available trading capital. Barings was declared insolvent on 26 February. The collapse of the Japanese stock exchange between 24 February, when the losses became known, and 27 February considerably increased the size of the loss.

The regulatory question went back almost a year. In May 1994, Barings was committing so much money to SIMEX via its subsidiary Baring Futures (Singapore) that it was concerned that it might be in breach of the large exposures rule, which limited the amount that could be lent to any single customer to 25 per cent of capital. So Barings asked the Bank of England supervisor, Chris Thompson, whether that rule applied to margin payments posted as short-term 'loans to clients'. Thompson did not respond. On 6 September, Barings' Head of Banking reported that Barings was now beyond the 25 per cent limit. Thompson responded by saying 'that he was aware that he owed us a response but that the matter was buried reasonably deep in his in-tray'.[70] But he was 'relaxed' about the case because the exposure was in reality to all members of the Singapore exchange. This 'informal concession', which was not fully documented by the Bank, was withdrawn in February 1995 as the Baring exposure in Singapore mounted. The Bank later explained that it had not been told about the £760 m cash advance to Barings's Singapore unit in February, and Eddie George explained to the Treasury and Civil Service Committee that it was 'impossible' for the Bank to know 'day to day details of every exposure'.[71]

In the meantime, the Bank's regular SWOT (strengths and weaknesses, and opportunities and threats) report explained on 11 August that Barings had an 'excellent reputation at home and overseas, particularly in the Far East'.[72] On 16 November, Andrew Tuckey and Peter Norris from Barings visited the Bank. A background briefing was again encouraging, noting that 'Barings are having a remarkable 1994 in terms of results, in contrast to other merchant banks'. One day later, a Bank email, written by Howard Walwyn, spoke for the first time about 'issues' with Barings: 'emerging markets competition, especially in the Far Eastern markets which are the jewel in the crown but which everyone else also has an eye on'. In addition, there was a question about 'controls on settlement problems and integrity (of trading or corporate finance advice) in out-of-the-way markets'.[73] Walwyn later, after leaving the Bank of England, explained, 'I always favoured the role of the aberrant City worker: Guardian-reading, left-leaning and secretly subversive, amid the rather patrician and old-fashioned work environment I faced at the time at the Bank of England.'[74] He also confessed, 'Yes, I did wonder why Barings' position had become so substantially profitable. Indeed, I asked questions about it periodically in briefings and things. I was quite keen to know how profitable it was exactly because we did not know, and some of my questions prior to that November meeting were aimed at doing that. I thought about the profitability. I was pleased with it because we were keen for Barings to make profits, given their earlier problems in Barings Securities.'[75] On 18 January 1995, he noted, 'In recent months we have been allowing Barings to exceed 25% consolidated LE [large exposures] capital.'[76]

Other regulatory classifications on the part of the Bank did not show any advance warning either, and in December 1994 the Bank's Credit Risk Analysis Procedures (CRAP) rating put Barings in Category 2, along with old and quite solid banks such as Lazard, Schroders and SG Warburg.

On 2 February 1995, after the Kobe earthquake but before any specific knowledge of the Barings fraud was available, the Bank wrote to Barings about the Japanese stock futures exposure in Singapore, stating that 'we would have no discretion not to enforce the 25% limit'.[77] On Friday, 24 February, Peter Baring requested a meeting with the Deputy Governor, Rupert Pennant-Rea, who came into the Bank with some colleagues at noon, and told his astonished interlocutor that Barings was ruined.[78] Brian Quinn, the head of Banking Supervision, called Singapore to say that a large fraud had been discovered, with an estimated mark-to-market loss of S$650 bn at the close of business on Friday.[79]

Eddie George had been on the way to a skiing holiday but returned to take charge of a possible rescue of Barings. The construction of a rescue was made much harder because the knowledge of the failure of Barings was already public: it appeared on the front page of the *Sunday Telegraph*, which was available to other newspapers already on Saturday evening.[80] On Sunday, 26 February, just before 9 a.m., the Bank of England supervisors worked out that $400 m in new capital was needed, and that the losses were expected to be $510–$570 m. Soon after, the chairmen and the chief executives of major banks appeared for a 10:30 a.m. meeting in Threadneedle Street called by the Governor. George obtained pledges of £50 m from large players (Barclays, Lloyds, HSBC, NatWest, Abbey National, CSB and Merrill Lynch) and £25 m each from medium-sized institutions (Standard Chartered, Schroders, Warburg, Morgan Grenfell, Kleinwort); a little later, the Royal Bank of Scotland (RBS) was brought in as a larger bank and Bank of Scotland (BOS) as a second-tier institution. But there was a great deal of hesitation on the part of the other banks, and one American banker told Quinn that he regarded the Barings controls in London as lax. Then, in the course of the Sunday morning, a further $360 m in losses on written options emerged, and the rescue scheme collapsed. George reported 'some willingness to give support', but he could not see a total of $5½ bn around the table. There were other alternatives that were briefly but unsuccessfully considered, such as selling stakes in Barings to 'natural holders: of Japanese equities and bonds', and the Japanese Ministry of Finance briefly entered the discussion.[81]

The still-open derivatives contracts exposed Barings to 'unquantifiable further losses'. It was also conceivable that American institutions would refuse to post collateral for Osaka and Singapore exposures, and that this action would drive prices down even further. The Bank calculated that Barings' exposure to the Japanese equity market was equivalent to a $7 bn holding, and that the exposure to Japanese interest rates was equivalent to a holding of $20 bn of Japanese government bonds. It estimated that liquidating the position in a fire sale would drive down the Nikkei index by around 10 per cent.[82] The immediate cause of the failure of Barings was the inability to pay the additional collateral required for Monday trading in Tokyo, but in the course of the week, the Osaka stock market paid back £76 m to Barings and SIMEX in Singapore paid back £54 m. The uncertainty about the derivatives exposure made the Sunday rescue impossible, and led to subsequent criticism of the Bank's handling of the attempt at a lifeboat. One market participant was quoted as saying: 'If Rupert Pennant-Rea (the Deputy Governor) and his acolytes understood the derivatives markets as well as they claim, they would have grasped the solution very quickly and found a way of ring-fencing the (derivatives) exposure.'[83]

There existed some concern about contagion. Barings was not in any sense a systemically critical bank. But there were obvious ramifications to a collapse. On Monday, there were rumours in the market that another merchant bank was in difficulties. On Tuesday, the discount house King & Shaxson was supposed to be insolvent as a consequence of the Barings failure. There was also the question of possible depositor losses: the sensitivity was increased as the Lord Chamberlain, Lord Airlie (a former banker with Schroders), expressed the worry that the Queen had very nearly lost some of her funds.[84] The Treasury on the other hand was quite relaxed. The Chancellor, Kenneth Clarke, later looked back: 'I soon realised that it wasn't a risk to the rest of the banking sector, so I went to watch Nottingham Forest play away to QPR [Queens Park Rangers].'[85]

But in the end it looked as if the decision to let Barings go conformed to market logic. The principal debate concerned whether danger signs should have been noted earlier. On 12 July 1995, the Court was informed about the final draft of the Board of Banking Supervision's Report on the Barings collapse: it had been drawn up by the six independent members of the Board, since the Bank officials clearly should not judge their own cause. In discussing the report, George said, 'the criticism was that the Bank had been a longstop and had failed to stop a difficult and bouncy ball. Specifically, we had been less than rigorous on large exposures and on solo consolidation.' In a replay of the discussion of BCCI, Sir David Scholey asked whether the failure reflected specifically on Christopher Thompson, the official responsible for supervising Barings. George said that it did: 'More rigour on his part would have avoided criticism of the Bank, although perhaps not stopped the failure.' Once again there was a discussion of 'a failure of internal communication'. Quinn reported that the large exposures section of the Report was 'the only area where the Board had been unable to come to a view on whether or not the Bank had contributed in some way to the failure'. But he tried to argue, 'Up until the end of January 1995, the large exposures concession could have made no difference: Leeson was not relying on margin payments. The suggestion that by pressing Barings to comply with the 25% rule after the end of January 1995 would have made any difference seems fanciful: Barings, as the Report made clear, were not in a position to know whether they were meeting it or not.'[86]

The soul-searching within the Bank went on much longer than after BCCI, although there was no legal case, as Barings was bought by the Dutch bank ING for £1 (after a few days of uncertainty, when it appeared that the

Japanese stock market had stabilized). Initially (on 1 March) the Nederlandsche Bank, the Dutch central bank, had told Brian Quinn that it was unwilling to let ING proceed with the purchase. It then changed its position and agreed to the deal.

In July 1995, Thompson resigned, commenting, according to a press report: 'I don't feel any sense of guilt. It seems that the Bank didn't take any account of my representations.' The Governor, however, had publicly defended Thompson. George and Quinn appeared before a Commons Committee on 19 July, where George explained that if MPs conducted a 'witch hunt' every time something went wrong, it would make it 'very difficult to find people to do the job'.[87]

One year after the Barings éclat, the Bank was still worried about its bank supervision work, and the deficiencies were highlighted in a report commissioned from Arthur Andersen. The report recommended a more systematic approach to investigations, and an abandonment of the rather unstructured SWOT process towards a new approach under the acronym CAMEL (Capital, Assets, Management, Earnings and Liquidity) and in particular a RATE model (Risk Assessment, Tools and Evaluation) that would deliver qualitative but also quantitative results. The Bank should also extend its use of Resident Accountants who would be engaged in trilateral meetings with the Banks and the regular accountants. Arthur Andersen also investigated the existing structure of the Bank's 380 supervisory staff and noted that they were often doing low-value tasks; it also called for the appointment of more specialists.[88]

Frances Heaton, the director general of the Panel on Takeovers and Mergers, a full-time director of Lazard, and the first female Director on the Bank's Court, explained that

she had been shocked by the Arthur Andersen Report: the cumulative effect of all of the recommendations did indicate the need for a radical series of changes, most significantly in the culture. If the Report were published, the Bank would face another round of criticism.

The whole issue of supervision was still very problematical:

There were heavy pressures on senior management, partly because of the inexperience of more junior staff. Morale was poor. There was still a feeling that the area was a poor relation of the rest of the Bank.[89]

George responded that

the whole subject was in a state of flux and development. There were very significant changes and implications. It was clear that there was a mis-match between the control structure of complex organisations, which was different to the legal and regulatory structure: so that oversight of any group, even just for prudential purposes, was massively complicated. The position was changing all the time.[90]

Quinn reported to the Court that he had doubts about the future of the Financial Stability wing since the 'outside world did speculate that supervision might be taken away from the Bank', although he believed that 'it could not be said too often that it was an integral part of the Bank's job'.[91]

On 29 February 1996, Quinn retired from the Bank. In 1996, the Bank undertook an overhaul of Supervision, on the lines suggested by the Arthur Anderson report. But it was far from being a fundamental reinvention of supervision, and Deputy Governor Howard Davies, who was charged with its implementation, explained that the main strategic move to more on-site work and a more systematic risk assessment was not a 'radical shift'.[92] The move did little to convince the political world – especially the opposition Labour Party – that a central bank whose fundamental responsibility lay in making monetary policy should remain entrusted with supervisory and regulatory responsibilities.

The more significant move by the Bank was the introduction from October 1996 of an annual *Financial Stability Review*, in large part as a defensive measure against criticism in the wake of the failure of Barings and as a way of making the case that the Bank had an important role to play in supervision. The first report spelt out clearly the problems of the new international environment by examining two problem cases: the behaviour of an asset manager in Hong Kong, working for a UK financial group, Jardine Fleming; and Morgan Grenfell, where the fund management subsidiary of a UK group (owned by a German bank, Deutsche Bank) had invested in markets regulated by the US Securities and Exchange Commission. Both cases seemed to show that new and apparently safe areas of financial activity – fund management – could bring threats that were as serious as those that arose in banking operations. It is not clear, however, that warnings such as these were translated into changes in behaviour on the part of financial institutions, or indeed how far documents such as the *Financial Stability Review*, were taken seriously or even read by the financial community.

By the middle of the 1990s, it had become clear that the UK's financial system had been revolutionized, that the old segmented world was gone and that there was a new set of problems coming out of the creation of financial behemoths. Some non-executive directors on the Court of the Bank, especially Sir Jeremy Morse and Sir Christopher Hogg (chairman of

Reuters), wanted to extend the grasp of the Bank's regulatory power to institutions such as Lloyds insurance and the stock exchange; but George pushed back against such thoughts, and could only envisage a narrower version of supervision.[93] The Bank was concerned about how effectively it could really police the new British financial system.

Howard Davies explained that banking supervisors should see themselves much more as doctors than as cops: the Bank wanted to move away from enforcement. He set out how in the modern Bank, supervisors deprecate the cronyism, the cosy chats, the old-school-tie attitude they claim to detect in judgement-based supervision. Regulators should, on this view, keep a decent distance from their clients: personal contacts should be kept to a necessary minimum. Certainly tea parties in the Bank's Parlours 'are out of the question'.[94]

This approach is understandable, but it is also clear that an arm's-length approach and the discouraging of private contacts (tea parties in the Bank Parlours) led in the 2000s to a greatly decreased awareness on the part of regulators of the effects and consequences for overall stability of an unusually fast period of financial innovation.[95] It was a peculiar consequence of a widely acknowledged absence of internal communication within the Bank that the old channels of communication with the outside financial world were shut down. That shutdown corresponded to the new insistence on transparency and openness, since the logical – but unattainable – aim was that all interactions should be visible to all market participants at the same time. The logical outcome of the new thinking was to draw a clear line between supervision and regulation on the one side and monetary policy on other, and to take responsibility for the former out of the Bank. That approach was followed by the Labour government in 1997.

THE PLUMBING OF FINANCE

The Bank was gradually being pushed out of financial supervision and regulation, but an important area of concern remained: securing the provision of an adequate, stable and sustainable platform for trading operations. Facilitating the technical operation of finance became an increasingly important concern of the Bank.

In October 1990, the Bank opened the Central Money Market Office (CMMO) to provide a central depository and electronic book entry transfer system for sterling non-fungible money market instruments. Later, it proposed to develop a separate clone for euro money market transfers, in anticipation of a possible British membership in the monetary union.

The experience of the Bank with the Central Gilts Office from 1986, and with the CMMO, was useful after plans to move to electronic settlement on the London Stock Exchange, labelled TAURUS, collapsed and the LSE Chief Executive Peter Rawlins was obliged to resign.[96] The Stock Exchange had for seven years been working on a highly complex mechanism to replace the slow manual settlement system, which involved a two week period and was conspicuously slower than New York, but also than other European exchanges. There had been more and more problems as share ownership spread in the aftermath of the big privatizations of the 1980s. The average daily number of bargains in UK ordinary shares had risen from 30,000 in 1986 to 54,000 in the first months of 1987. By August 1987, there were some 400,000 unsettled old bargains outstanding.[97] Bankers wrote in to the Bank to warn about the risks to markets arising out of inadequate settlement procedures.[98] The TAURUS plans became a case study of cost overshoots in complex mega-projects. The eventual cancellation of TAURUS, which had multiple non-compatible software systems, was estimated to cost the City some £400 m.[99]

In 1993, in consequence, after TAURUS failed, the Bank set out its own plans for the 'dematerialization' of security settlements. The new mechanism was called CREST, an acronym for nothing at all. In anticipation, settlement times were reduced. It would be cheaper, at an estimated £30 m to £40 m compared with the estimated £85 m for TAURUS. CREST was owned by sixty-nine equity market participants under the umbrella of CrestCo, a private company. The Bank explained that 'the wide ownership base is to insure against Crest's pricing policy, operating regime or development plans giving undue advantage to any one commercial interest or to any one community'.[100] But in fact, institutional investors felt that they were not adequately represented, and that the new institution would be dominated by banks with an interest in keeping up costs. Private investors still had to deal with their share certificates and paper communications. The Chancellor of the Exchequer, Kenneth Clarke, warned against the Bank sending the 'wrong signals' by financing the development of CREST, but Eddie George countered that 'a badly designed settlement system carried risks for the whole financial system'.[101]

The system was gradually modernized in advance of the launching of CREST in 1996. By July 1994, the Stock Exchange's old Talisman system had been adapted to accommodate a ten-day 'rolling' settlement, and by January 1995 it could move to a five-day rolling settlement.

ASSESSING FINANCIAL SURVEILLANCE

It is harder to assess the effectiveness of financial surveillance than of monetary policy. Monetary policy is designed to be forward-looking, and is regularly tested against the outcome in a particular time frame. By contrast, financial stability policy has to be backward-looking, but will be tested against surprise events in the future that are necessarily very rare. Instability in financial markets comes unpredictably and unevenly, and there is a strong cross-country contagion. While it is clear from an inflation outcome whether monetary policy has been successful, we do not really even know what financial stability is. It is an old term that began to be widely used in Britain in the early 1870s, at the time that Walter Bagehot was preparing his great work on *Lombard Street*. At the beginning of 1873, the *Commercial and Financial Chronicle* noted that, 'The fall in gold [reserves], the steady growth of our credit, the progress we have made during the last four years in wealth, in population, and in all the elements of our industrial strength, are due quite as much to this financial stability as to the more conspicuous causes which oftener challenge attention.'[102] The term started to be used more frequently only much later, in the 1990s, at exactly the moment that the globalization and liberalization of financial markets was effecting a dramatic revolution, and making it ever more difficult for governments to control financial flows.

Pierre Siklos compiled a list of meanings of financial stability as used in central banking legislation since the 1990s. The concept refers to policies intended to build and maintain 'confidence in the financial system', improve a country's 'resilience to shocks', prevent 'financial disruptions', or the rise of 'financial imbalances' spilling over into the real economy.[103] These terms are also definitionally slippery. If banks always do maturity transformation, how severe do imbalances need to become to be threatening? Is a threat a failure of surveillance, even if the threatened outcome never materializes? By the 1990s, the Bank was thinking primarily in terms of the regularity of monetary policy-making. Brian Quinn put the new orthodoxy in this way: 'Financial stability means the circumstances in which the Bank can carry out smoothly and effectively its first core task of executing monetary policy. This could be interpreted narrowly: the avoidance of difficulties in the banking system; or more widely: the avoidance of disturbances anywhere in the financial system that could impede the Bank in executing monetary policy.' The problem was that financial activity was changing dramatically, and with unpredictable effects: 'As banks do more things formerly outside their sector, and as they acquire or become part of groups with diverse financial functions, the Bank must have a capacity to understand and keep abreast of what is going on in those areas.'[104]

A famous paper which launched the term 'the Great Moderation' in 2003 apart from the role played by monetary policy also emphasized the part played by 'good luck', or smaller international macro-economic shocks.[105] Andrew Haldane thinks that financial instability could be 'defined as any deviation from the optimal saving–investment plan of the economy that is due to imperfections in the financial sector'. The correct insight here, which derives from both Keynes' and Hayek's contemplation of an earlier era of financial instability in the interwar period, is that the revaluation of financial assets can push an economy into a different equilibrium, frequently a bad one. That definition, however, produced a howl of outrage from the economist Geoffrey Wood, who condemned it as 'a totally non-operational definition. What is the optimal plan? How big a deviation? What are imperfections in financial markets? How do we recognise them? The central bank is bound to fail, for it cannot know what the task is.'[106] Instead, Wood wanted to define financial stability even more simply, in what he saw as an old-fashioned way, as the central bank being a 'lender of last resort to the banking system'.[107] But that role became increasingly problematical as financial activity expanded and internationalized. It is in consequence tempting to define financial stability as the absence of a major financial crisis, but that definition too is not of much use for policy-makers and for practice: by the time the crisis occurs, it is too late to do anything about it.

There is also a relationship between financial and monetary stability. One of the classic arguments for greater attention to monetary stability is that it reduces unpredictability and financial shocks. Anna Schwartz suggested, 'If inflation and price instability prevail, so will financial instability.' The argument was that monetary uncertainty would mask or distort prices, and thus lead to an inefficient allocation of resources. This approach was even termed the 'Schwartz hypothesis' and derived some measure of support from empirical testing.[108] Eddie George suggested something similar even before Schwartz really formulated the position when he claimed that 'the line that leads from monetary policy to the health of the financial system is pretty clear'.[109] But recent experience seems to challenge this view. In the 1950s and 1960s UK, there was a substantial fluctuation in inflation performance, but great financial stability. As inflation performance improved after the 1980s, financial instability came back globally. Some commentators then suggested that monetary stability might produce a false certainty that led to excessive risk-taking. Before 2007, this was a minority view, largely associated with the BIS, but after the global financial crisis it looked almost self-evident.[110]

In the 1990s, as banking became internationalized, every advanced industrial country tried to improve the quality of its banking supervision. A broad statistical cross-national comparison by the World Bank, first conducted in 1999 and then repeated at regular intervals, showed the UK authorities as operating a higher level of supervisory power than in the US, Japan or Germany (only France was slightly higher). The US was also much more restrictive in its control of financial conglomerates than the continental European countries.[111]

The public discussion of the Bank's financial supervision focused on the spectacular failures, Johnson Matthey, BCCI and Barings. However, the UK avoided a systemic financial crisis over this period. Since financial banking crises are often linked to, and amplify, severe recessions (of which the UK experienced two) and currency crises (which the UK also had in 1992), the outcome was fortunate. At least in one plausible interpretation, it reflects a successful tradition of financial supervision. Other major industrial economies did suffer from financial sector problems which an authoritative IMF report on the issue categorizes as 'systemic'.[112] Poor economic conditions clearly expose management and strategy weaknesses, and can produce confidence or contagion effects. In addition, a currency crisis raises the question of asset/liability mismatches, as funding may be largely in a foreign currency. At the end of 1993, in the wake of a recession and a currency crisis, the fourth largest Spanish bank, Banco Español de Crédito SA, or Banesto, needed to be rescued by the Bank of Spain, with the government injecting 180 bn pesetas (£860 m) in new capital, and taking over 285 bn (£1,370 m) in bad assets. In the same year, Crédit Lyonnais required a government rescue that is estimated to have cost the taxpayer £14,000 m.[113] Banking crises in Norway (1991) had an estimated fiscal cost of 2.7 per cent of GDP, in Sweden (1991) 3.6 per cent and in Finland (1991) 12.8 per cent. The Japanese banking problems after 1997 are estimated to have cost 14 per cent of GDP, and the US savings and loans problem after 1988 3.7 per cent.

Put in this perspective, the £144 m gross (£88 m net, after the recovery of funds from the liquidation or administration) paid in the UK through the UK Deposit Protection Fund (funded by authorized banks), or the £105 m from public funds for bank recapitalization and rescue, look relatively trivial.[114] The major financial and banking crises in other countries in the early 1990s only appear in the UK in an attenuated form of the small banks crisis. Midland is consequently not treated in the same breath as Crédit Lyonnais or Banesto, but viewed as an institution that successfully overcame its management problems. This is generally a good record, but it could only be defended in terms of the famous Sherlock Holmes conundrum of seeing dogs that do not bark at night as the key to the problem. But a good record can sometimes be deceptive as a guide to the future. Relatively successful management of financial conditions set the stage for a substantial measure of complacency in the 2000s, especially after 2003–2004 when international leverage increased, and when a new wave of financial innovation resulted in the belief that risk could be better managed than in the old world.

A conscious choice was made for light, very light, or even no regulation. Responding to the 2001 report of the 'Committee of Wise Men' chaired by Alexander Lamfalussy on European securities markets regulation, a key regulatory economist in the Bank commented that 'our message' should be 'keeping regulation to the minimum so that Europe remains competitive globally'. And 'where common rules are needed', the Bank should push for 'reaching a consensus among market practitioners, as far as possible, rather than new legislation'. There should be mutual recognition rather than harmonization, 'driving towards an objective of more subsidiarity, not less, but with enhanced competition among supervisors'.[115]

There were regular meetings with banks, with questions about preparedness for market shocks. For instance, in 2001, Paul Tucker asked Bill Winters of JP Morgan Securities Ltd about the effects of securitization: 'whether non-bank institutional buyers of bank loans had sufficient experience of the credit cycle not to be unpleasantly surprised by the decline in credit quality. Winters felt that European institutions might be less familiar with the market than US institutions'; and he noted that 'sudden, large-scale withdrawals could lead to un-collateralized positions being called as well as creating liquidity pressures'.[116]

In the early 2000s, an internal member of the Financial Stability Committee, the distinguished monetary economist William Allen, produced a memorandum trying to define 'financial stability', but recalled that it evoked little interest in the Bank; he then, with Geoffrey Wood, published the paper as a journal article. The two economists began with an erroneous reflection that the term was quite new, and that they could not find any example of its use before 1994, when the Bank of England took it up (!). Of course, the Bank then was just reprising a much older concept. Allen and Wood finished their case by criticizing the regulatory framework of Basel II as too restrictive:

While we accept that official regulation has played a crucial role in developing risk-management standards in the financial industry in the transition from a controlled environment to a freer market, we do not accept that the maintenance and further development of risk-management standards, once a free-market environment is established, will require anything like the same degree of regulatory activity and involvement. Indeed [...] we think that excessive regulation can unintentionally inhibit the development of risk-management techniques, and thereby retard further improvements in risk-management standards.[117]

The paper, published in 2006, is a testament to a mode of thought that was dominant in the era of financialization, but rightly came under attack after 2008. It was a restatement of the mindset that was complacent about previous successes, and even more complacent about monetary policy successes, and that led to the financial crisis.

15

The New Bank

A University of Threadneedle Street?

The general election of 1 May 1997 produced – as was almost universally expected – a decisive victory for a Labour Party revitalized by Tony Blair's push away from traditional socialism. The outcome was the least surprising UK result in the second half of the twentieth century, largely because the September 1992 currency debacle had destroyed the Conservatives' credibility. That fact focused attention on policy credibility. The British public, but also the Bank, had as a consequence had almost five years to think about how Labour would work in government. Gordon Brown as the new Chancellor almost immediately set about establishing the independence of the Bank. The move was widely anticipated, though its suddenness came as a surprise. The Labour manifesto had promised a new mechanism for setting monetary policy, with a committee structure, but not necessarily Bank independence. What was not really predicted – at least not in Threadneedle Street and certainly not in the Governor's Parlours – was that the new government would also remove financial supervision from the Bank.

INDEPENDENCE AT LAST

The Labour Party manifesto had stated: 'We will reform the Bank of England to ensure that decision-making on monetary policy is more effective, open, accountable and free from short-term political manipulation.' Bank independence initially looked as if it was at odds with traditional Labour thinking, which emphasized the political control of economic processes (see Figure 15.1). The post-war Labour Party had stood under the impact of 1931, when it believed that a 'Banker's Ramp' had imposed deflationary austerity and destroyed Ramsay MacDonald's Labour government. The 1946 nationalization was the payback for the

Figure 15.1 The Bank slips its lead (Richard Cole, *Sunday Telegraph*, 11 May 1997)

Bank's perceived political overreach under Montagu Norman. The Bank could not really defend itself convincingly – an internal history of the 1931 crisis, written by Lucius Thompson-McCausland during the War, indeed gave so much potential ammunition to the Ramp thesis that the Bank never published it.[1] But over the course of the last weekend before the 1997 election, Brown concluded, 'What a release an independent Bank of England would be – a release from a "banker's ramp"!'[2]

The question of Bank independence had been discussed with leading figures of the Labour Party since the early 1990s. In September 1993, Gordon Brown, as Shadow Chancellor, explained to Deputy Governor Rupert Pennant-Rea that he 'would not feel comfortable with Government being in a position to choose to override a particular interest rate decision, because it would imply that if the Government chose not to override it was in full agreement with the action that the Bank had taken although, in practice, this might not be the case'. He also expressed his preference for a single mandate, namely price stability.[3] From 1995, George had been discussing supervision issues with the Labour front bench, and the diplomat Sir Peter Petrie (who had previously been engaged as the Bank adviser on European affairs) began to coordinate a briefing campaign, 'to counter two general beliefs about the Bank: first that it was part of a cosy City club; and second that it was obsessed with counter-inflation policy for its own sake. We had developed ways of explaining.'[4] When at this stage the Bank thought about independence, it saw the move as part of a general European move, as required by the Maastricht Treaty as a precondition for participation in the European System of Central Banks and in the monetary union. The surprise came that Labour wanted to create an independent central bank for its own sake. Such an institution might give the new government a long time to think about how it should handle the question of monetary union – about which Gordon Brown was highly sceptical.

Gordon Brown had come round to the idea of an independent Bank after his former strategy, focusing on managed exchange rates, had been destroyed by Black Wednesday. A young (and very Euro-sceptic) *Financial Times* journalist, Ed Balls, provided a way out in a Fabian Society pamphlet with the title *Euro-Monetarism: Why Britain was Ensnared and How it Should Escape*. The argument set out was that Exchange Rate Mechanism (ERM) membership had failed to give what Britain needed, a 'credible, flexible and transparent macro-economic framework and a medium-term strategy for industrial regeneration'. Balls rapidly became the key strategist in the remaking of Labour policy. William Keegan describes his pamphlet as a 'guide to much of what Gordon Brown attempted to do as Chancellor'.[5] Before working at the *Financial Times*, he had done postgraduate work at Harvard, where he had been taught by Martin Feldstein, and had been deeply influenced by Larry Summers, Greg Mankiw and Alberto Alesina: in particular by their adherence to the new view of the time consistency arguments for central bank independence. By 1995, he had formulated the idea of a Monetary Policy Committee (MPC), as a way of circumscribing the power of the Bank and its Governor: 'We are not in the business of depoliticising interest rate decision-making only to personalise it in one independent Governor. That is a form of independence I reject.'[6]

A final clincher for Labour policy was given by discussions in the US with Alan Greenspan. If there was any foreign model for how the UK should evolve, it was American rather than German (with an independent and powerful Bundesbank with a strong sense of its institutional position, and a substantial informal connection to the banking supervisor but no formal link at all) or French (with a newly independent Banque de France and a separate banking supervisor on which the Banque de France was represented, the *commission bancaire*). It was American monetary policy and American economists, rather than European central bankers, who seemed to represent to Labour policy-makers the most congenial vision of the future of UK policy-making (see Figure 15.2). In a final round of these talks, on 20 February 1997, shortly before the British election,

Figure 15.2 Alan Greenspan and Eddie George at International Monetary Fund meetings (2002) (Alex Wong/Staff/Getty Images News/Getty Images)

Greenspan told Balls and Brown that it was '"unfair" to expect elected politicians to make unpopular decisions on interest rates'.[7] Tony Blair had also floated the idea of Bank independence in discussions with leading British business figures.

Meanwhile, the informal discussions of Labour with the Bank also intensified in the months before the 1997 election, with Eddie George but also with Mervyn King, who was highly sympathetic to Ed Balls' approach to monetary policy questions. A number of principles emerged quite clearly. From the point of view of a left-wing party looking for financial and monetary credibility, it was vital to avoid any risk of a public disagreement of the Chancellor with Bank advice; greater credibility would mean lower interest rates and hence would reduce the cost of financing the government. The Bank of England thought that independence would take about fifty basis points (half a per cent) off the cost of servicing government debt: a very substantial saving, given a market holding of some £370 bn.[8] The Labour Party could also derive a benefit from delivering very visibly on its pledge to remove short-run political influences from interest rate decisions. One of the reasons that Margaret Thatcher had given for opposing Bank independence was that the potential threat to monetary policy by a left-wing government provided substance to a claim that Labour could not be trusted with the economy. Since the 1992 exchange rate crisis, the Conservative claim to superior economic management had looked problematic, and it was now an obvious move for Labour to take away a critical part of the threat discussion.

Brown also wanted to cut down the powerful figure of the Bank Governor as an alternative economic policy-maker. Replacing the Governor by an inevitably more diverse or less coherent committee would be a way of ensuring that he could not be bested in any future confrontation with the Governor. Creating a policy committee that would collectivize monetary policy-making and take it out of the hands of the Governor of the Bank was central to the new vision. The most striking examples of collective or committee-based policy-making came from federal countries, and the Bundesbank Council and the Federal Reserve Open Market Committee (FOMC) were designed to support constitutional federalism. For the UK, there was a brief-lived discussion of whether there should be an analogous regional representation on the MPC, but that course was rejected. Instead, Labour thought that the Court of the Bank might be reformed to give greater regional representation.

In the course of the preliminary debate within the Labour leadership, it soon became clear that the benefits, both fiscal and political, from a strategy of moving to Bank independence would be greatest if it were implemented very early in the life of the administration.[9] In February 1997, Brown, accompanied by Ed Balls, met George and discussed how an MPC might operate in future. From the Bank's perspective, it was important that the MPC's advice should continue to be monolithic, and should not be 'a menu of views of different MPC members'. Brown seemed to be amenable to this case, endorsing the idea of an MPC chaired by the Governor, with its own transparency and publication of minutes, and no meeting with the Chancellor. Balls had a rather different view: the critical feature of the MPC was that it was designed to take power and influence away from the Governor, who would be constrained by intellectually rigorous external members who had an established reputation to defend and would not be expected to give in to subtle or even unsubtle pressure from the Bank hierarchy. From the Bank's point of view, Brown's view of supervision also seemed reassuring: he had noted the 'good cooperation between the Bank and the SIB', and 'stressed that Labour did not favour major change'. But he also added that he and Alistair Darling (who would become Chief Secretary in the Treasury) would want to discuss regulation with the Bank after the election.[10]

Labour also wanted to appoint two Deputy Governors, one with responsibility for monetary policy and the other for financial supervision. Balls noticed that Mervyn King was less than enthusiastic about that part of the Labour agenda, and that he really saw the Bank as developing in the future as what he thought was a modern central bank, and what Balls termed a 'monetary policy institute'.

The differences between Labour and the Bank at this stage looked relatively minor. A speech by Brown, on 26 February 1997, was critical of George; and George looked tougher on inflation, talking about a rate of 2.5 per cent or less, preferably under 2, while Brown wanted to keep to the Clarke formula of 1995, 2.5 per cent or less RPIX, but to make it symmetric so that an undershooting of the 2.5 per cent rate would also require a letter from the Governor explaining why it had occurred, and when a correction might be expected. The notion of symmetry thus came from the political world, not from the Bank. Another issue that concerned the Bank at this stage was that Brown seemed to be sympathetic to the idea of a nominal growth target, which had substantial support from US academics, and Mervyn King in particular wished to resist that as an element of unnecessary complexity, and argued that by 'targeting inflation two years ahead we were taking account of the alleged objective of a nominal growth target'.[11]

Labour also thought about whether the objectives of the central bank should be set to include growth and employment as well as price stability, on the US model according to which the Federal Reserve is set a dual mandate. Brown initially wanted this, but was dissuaded by lawyers who reflected on the conflicts that two primary mandates might imply.[12] In the end, he concluded that a symmetrical numerical inflation target – which the FOMC had never formally adopted – would be enough to produce an environment in which boom and bust cycles would no longer occur. The abolition of the old business cycle became the explicit leitmotif of New Labour economic thinking.

The Treasury staff were intensely involved in these debates about the future institutional framework, successfully seeking to dissuade Brown from being seen to appoint all the members of the MPC.[13] In the end, half of the MPC was Bank; the other half were outside experts appointed by the Chancellor, with the Governor as a ninth member with a vote (and also the capacity to give a casting vote if the absence of one member meant that the Committee was evenly split). The personalities involved constituted an obviously sensitive issue. A sort of precursor to the MPC, from the Treasury side, had been the attempt by Norman Lamont in the wake of the ERM crisis to establish a panel of seven 'wise men'. That initiative turned into a spectacular failure within a year, when one of the 'wise', Tim Congdon, wrote an open letter attacking the others in scathing terms as 'literary critics who read prose but never look at poetry, or mathematicians who understand arithmetic but are bewildered by algebra'. Cambridge Professor Wynne Godley responded that the Congdon letter was 'crazy and possibly libellous'. Gavyn Davies, another panel member and the UK chief economist of Goldman Sachs, commented on the controversy, 'Get seven doctors together in a room and present them with the same patient. They will try roughly the same tests but have different ideas about the right treatment. Economists are no different.'[14] That was why it was crucial to the design of the MPC that it should have a much narrower remit, in particular the focus on the achievement of a specific inflation target.

After the election, the independence plan was developed at breakneck speed, with Brown giving Permanent Secretary Sir Terry Burns the plan on the Friday after the election, immediately after he had been named as Chancellor. Burns as well as the Cabinet Secretary and Tony Blair's Private Secretary pushed for some delay and deliberation in Whitehall, but Brown was emphatic that the new government should begin with a revolutionary move that would enhance credibility ('forever lock in our commitment to low inflation') and deliver an immediate pay-off in terms of lower interest rates.[15] The Cabinet Secretary was surprised that there was to be no cabinet discussion of such an important strategic move. The finalization of the Bank reform scheme by officials came frenetically over the weekend so that it could be presented to the Bank on Monday (5 May, a bank holiday). George was given two letters, both dated the 6th, and both signed in red ballpoint. The first letter was titled 'The New Monetary Policy Framework'. It explained that 'the Government intends to give the Bank of England operational responsibility for setting interest rates', in order 'to achieve an inflation target which the Government will determine'. There would be two Deputy Governors, and 'operational decisions on interest rate policy will be made by a new Monetary Policy Committee' (five internals and four externals), with monthly meetings. The Court would be reformed in order to increase its representativeness. Finally, 'the Bank's role as the Governor's agent for debt management, the sale of gilts, over-sight of the gilts market and cash management will be transferred to the Treasury'.

A major and fundamentally unresolved issue concerned the relationship of fiscal and monetary policy, the core of the operation of the old UK 'macroeconomic executive'. The problem oddly did not figure prominently in the 1997 discussions, but by the beginning of 1998 Eddie George raised it in a meeting with the Chancellor. Brown gave a rather peculiar response: 'It was important that, while the Government did not comment in a second guessing sort of way on the monetary policy process and the Bank in turn did not comment likewise on fiscal policy, there was an open channel of communication between the two to ensure that policy was coordinated and was seen to be so.'[16]

The second letter prepared by the Chancellor was more problematical and much less clear. It was titled 'Banking Supervision' and seemed merely to promise a process of consultation: 'As you know, our Business Manifesto commits us to restructuring the regulation of financial services. It is the Government's intention to introduce the necessary legislation at an early date. I stated that it was the Government's intention to consider transferring part of the Bank of England's responsibility for banking supervision to another statutory body. I am pleased that you agreed that consultation will now start on this basis.' The government was considering the removal of banking supervision, but the letter seemed to suggest that the final outcome was still undetermined.

George initially was delighted: 'I think it is terrific; the nettle has been grasped.' He also realized, approvingly, that the new formula ruled out any exchange target: 'If the government were to commit to a rigid exchange-rate target, you wouldn't have that and an inflation target running side by side.'[17] On Tuesday, 6 May, the outcome was announced to the press, the stock market soared, and gilts surged as the prospect of a monetarily irresponsible left-wing government seemed to have been removed. Brown explained the historical background and the need to shift from a failed policy of the old Conservative government: 'The perception that monetary policy decisions have been dominated by short-term political considerations has grown.' By contrast, in the future operational independence to set interest rates in order to achieve the inflation target would ensure macro-economic stability: 'I want British economic success to be built on the solid rock of prudent and consistent economic management, not the shifting sands of boom and bust.'[18]

On 14 May 1997, George told the Bank's Court about the new proposals:

Turning to the Bank's objectives in the legislation, he said that the current Act and Charter said nothing about the objectives of the Bank of England. The Bank had always found the situation quite comfortable, though for management purposes it had defined its core responsibilities internally. He believed that question [of banking supervision] was likely to be raised on the evidence of a side letter from the Chancellor, and sooner rather than later. The logical sequence would be to make a decision on banking supervision first if the government wanted to remove banking supervision.[19]

There was also some discussion of the name of the institution. In the light of the new government's commitment to a measure of devolution for Scotland and Wales, the name 'Bank of England' might appear odd. George was prepared to consider the rather cumbersome alternative 'Bank of England (Central Bank of the United Kingdom)', but the Chancellor's initial response to an inquiry from Treasury officials was that the 'Bank of England was a good name'.[20] There would have been a need to revise a very large number of statutes and regulations that referred to the Bank of England. The emotional side was as important. Keeping the old appellation was just as important a symbolic gesture of continuity as keeping the Queen's head on the banknotes (even though before the 1920s, the monarch had not figured on Bank of England notes).

GOLD

Part of creating a new Bank involved following a new reserve policy. Traditionally, gold and the Bank of England had been intimately tied: the Bank had for centuries created promises that were as good as gold. That association might look old-fashioned in the twenty-first century. In reality, the gold in the vault of the Bank of England belonged not to the Bank but to the Exchange Equalisation Account set up in 1932 in the aftermath of the British devaluation, with the purpose of providing resources to smooth out fluctuations of sterling. On 7 May 1999, the government announced that it would sell 415 tonnes of gold, with the first 125 tonnes to be auctioned in 1999–2000. The move came very clearly at the initiative of the government, and of Gordon Brown.

In August 1998, Brown had asked the Treasury to prepare discussions with the Bank, and the first meeting occurred on 28 August.[21] The Treasury position combined two arguments: first, gold was unstable and would have little long-term value, and, second, the IMF should sell gold as part of an initiative to give relief to poor high-debt countries. There had been large-scale IMF gold sales (of a total of 730 tonnes) between 1976 and 1980, in similar circumstances; but in practice the new sale was held up by the US until 2009, when the IMF's Executive Board finally agreed to the sale of one-eighth of its gold or 403 tonnes. Other countries also looked as if they might embark on major gold sales: in particular, two traditional large gold holders, Germany and Switzerland. Switzerland was engulfed in a very painful and public debate about its gold policy in the Second World War, when it had bought looted gold from Nazi Germany (including gold directly looted from Jewish and Roma victims of genocide). So it might reasonably be thought that the price would fall, and the UK should move quickly, even though the gold sales were the subject of international coordination. At the time, George described the sale as 'a straightforward portfolio decision' and 'perfectly reasonable'. The step was supported by Mervyn King, but criticized by traditionalists in the Bank, Ian Plenderleith (who had worked out the technicalities of the sale of the gold from the Exchange Equalisation Account) and also the retired head of the Bank's foreign exchange division, Terry Smeeton.[22]

When implemented, the move to dispose of part of the UK's gold reserve was widely criticized by the gold lobby, the World Gold Council, and by many market traders as 'out of left field', 'unexpected', 'bloody unhelpful', 'disappointing' and 'puzzling'.[23] Smeeton also criticized the timing: 'I find it at best ironic that our government, which has tried to seize the moral high ground with regard to the IMF debt issue, then gets in first with its own sales.'[24] As the gold price fell, some central banks hesitated. Germany never embarked on any sales. In early 2000, the Bank noted that the Netherlands and Switzerland had stated that they would scale down the sales if everyone else did, and the Bank memorandum concluded, 'so it was up to us!'[25] Later, when the gold price rose again spectacularly in the 2000s, conservative critics liked to call the market response to the gold sales the 'Brown Bottom'.[26]

FINANCIAL STABILITY

The announcement of operational independence was quickly followed by another surprise: the removal of banking supervision from the Bank to a super SIB, which would be styled the Financial Services Authority (FSA). Gordon Brown had originally prepared just a single letter to the Governor, setting out both the new monetary policy regime and a new statutory approach to financial regulation. In the event, the initial two letters he sent meant deferring for a few days the decision on reordering the approach to financial sector supervision.

Brown had in the past been highly critical of the very visible regulatory failures of the 1990s – BCCI and then Barings. Balls saw the Bank's supervisors as permeated by a 'slightly old-fashioned amateurism', and was worried about the cumbersome and creaky process of multiple self-regulating bodies in financial services. He and Brown also gave a substantial weight to consumer protection issues, as a large number of people had suffered from the misselling of pensions. There was in Labour's view a strong case for a coherent overall financial authority that went well beyond banking supervision alone, and there seemed no particularly strong case to place that single supervisor in the Bank. Treasury officials were also highly sceptical about the Bank's grip on financial supervision.

Within the Treasury, there had been a debate about how best to manage the institutional reordering, with Terry Burns – whose relationship with Brown and Balls was becoming more strained – arguing that to do all the Bank reform in one stage was 'too much for Eddie George to take in', while the Second Permanent Secretary and Managing Director of the Finance, Regulation and Industry Directorate, Steve Robson, thought, more logically perhaps, that 'you don't give the good news now and the bad news later'.[27] Robson was pushing very articulately for the centrality to the reforms of a coordinated and coherent single financial supervisor. The Bank and its staff were profoundly shaken as the central roles of the old Bank of England had been destroyed. Ian Plenderleith, who was especially upset by the concomitant loss of the Bank's responsibility for managing government debt as this was his fiefdom in the Bank, said, 'I suppose it's not *all* bad news. We *have* got independence.'[28]

The creation of the Debt Management Office as an Executive Agency of the Treasury took away one of the central pillars of the Bank's older approach to monetary management, its strategic advice on the funding strategy but also its day-to-day dealing operations in the gilt markets. Since the 1980s, the Bank had been struggling with the issue of how to modernize the market – for instance, by instituting repos – in order to attract international as well as domestic investors. The US – and to some extent French – innovations looked like a model; and in both cases the markets depended much more on Treasury choices than on decisions made by the central banks.[29] In that respect too, Labour's move was a step in the direction of a new international institutional consensus.

The new Brown letter announcing the loss of financial supervision was a shock, but it cannot have been wholly unexpected. Brown was not at all alone in his criticism of the Bank's supervision after BCCI and Barings, and the ex-Treasury official Sir Peter Middleton had told the Commons Treasury Committee, 'I just do not think that supervision should be done by the Bank of England.'[30] The main problem for the Bank was that George had been wrong-footed: he had not been consulted, as he believed Brown had promised, and he had also reassured the Court and perhaps more humiliatingly the Bank's staff that no major changes in supervision were expected. He contemplated resignation at this moment,[31] though his closest advisers felt that it was unlikely that the momentary burst of anger would really lead George to break with an institution that he had identified with all his working life.

On 20 May, the Governor told the Court of his astonishment that the Chancellor had wanted to take out financial supervision and create an enhanced Securities and Investment Board under Howard Davies, which would be shifted out of the Bank:

The Governor commented that this came as a surprise to him. He said that he had made it very clear to the Chancellor that he felt let down, and that it made his position extremely difficult. An element in his decision was that it would make it easier to win acceptance for his Commons statement, because the Conservative Party had come out against independence and some Labour backbenchers would also oppose it. So the removal of supervision was seen as a countervailing step. The Governor said he believed that the Chancellor had presented to the Cabinet a fortnight before, a package combining independence with the removal of supervision. He had sold independence on the basis of removal of supervision. The Governor told Court that his immediate reaction was to hand in his resignation. He was still ready to do that if Court thought it a sensible step. However, the Governor said that, reflecting on it, there were a number of reasons why it was not a sensible thing to do. Firstly, he should stay and hold the Bank together. [. . .]a public statement that the Bank had not been consulted might be construed as a declaration of war.

Sir David Scholey responded, 'There was no need to declare war.' And Mervyn King took a noticeably differentiated position from that of the Governor:

it was clear that it would become public that the Bank disagreed with the Chancellor's decision. It was important that the reasons were made clear in language of the Bank's choosing. The reason for the disagreement was not that the Bank believed there was no case for moving supervision outside the Bank. A decision on whether supervision should be in or out of the Bank of England should follow logically from prior analysis of the supervision of banks and non-banks in the UK. There was no one clear answer. To decide on the structure without clear analysis was to put the cart before the horse.

In the end, George recognized 'how weak the Bank's position in reality had become':

He also commented that, if the Bank drew attention to its great record in super-vision, it would be laughed out of court. The perception was that the Bank had been asleep on the job more often than it should be. The reality was if there were another Bank failure, the removal of supervision would happen immediately. The difficultly was that the Governor could not stand up and give in a positive way the reasons why it was opposed to the decision.[32]

By the beginning of August, George told Tony Blair, 'Many had argued in the past that when the central bank was also the supervisor, there could be an undue predisposition to bail out a failing institution. A clear split between Bank and SIB would remove any suggestion of such bias.'[33] The Bank wanted to maintain some link with the process of financial supervision. The government's argument had been partly cast in terms of the failure of the Bank's engagement in banking supervision, but also in part on the fiscal nature of the process (because it might be linked with the provision of bank support). A Bank memorandum laid out the issue very clearly:

We start from the statement made by the Chancellor to Parliament on 20 May that: 'The Bank will remain responsible for the overall stability of the financial system as a whole. The enhanced SIB will be responsible for prudential supervision.' Our difficulty relates to the nature and size of the limit [on Bank provided financial support] which is proposed. As described, it appears to relate to the quantum of assets that we can acquire without regard to their risk characteristics. In that case particularly, but in any event, the size of the limit is in our view inadequate. In practice what a limit as low as this would mean would be that virtually every decision to undertake financial market operations or to lend would have to be referred to and decided by the Chancellor. That may indeed be the intention, presumably on the grounds that public expenditure is at least potentially involved, and that all public expenditure should be authorised by Ministers, who would then be accountable to Parliament for such authorisation. We understand this approach – indeed in many other contexts it is wholly appropriate. The question is whether it is the right approach in relation to a central bank. Hitherto, as is the case with almost all our counterparts overseas, we have had our own finite capital and reserves, with the use to which that capital has been put being determined by Court. Court has been accountable for its decision in this regard to Government and Parliament through the medium of the Bank's Annual Report and Accounts. Court's responsibility for the management of the affairs of the Bank in this sense has in fact been a major part of its raison d'être. Indeed the real heart of the issue in relation to the Bill as a whole, or so it seems to us, is whether we are to remain a central bank as that has been generally understood, or whether we are in effect to become something akin to a government department.[34]

The new regime made sense from an intellectual perspective – generated primarily by King but fully endorsed also by George – that financial stability could fundamentally be guaranteed by a pursuit of good monetary policy: 'The line that leads from monetary policy to the health of the financial sector is pretty clear,' as George put it.[35] There might be some bank failures, but they would not be systemically important, and – most importantly – they did not constitute supervisory failures.[36] The new FSA entirely appropriated this line of thinking when it acknowledged that a 'zero failure' regime was impossible.[37]

A link with the FSA was preserved by having the new Deputy Governor for Financial Stability sitting on the FSA board, while the FSA's new chairman, former Deputy Governor Howard Davies, was appointed to the Bank's Court of Directors. But the whole arrangement was improvised, and, as Gordon Brown later would admit, rather unsatisfactory: 'sadly [. . .] a compromise, [. . .] less definitive on who did what than it should have been'.[38] The new institution, with the many Bank staff who were transferred, moved to Canary Wharf, which was still largely a construction site (the Jubilee line extension on the London Underground was only opened in 1999). At the beginning, the FSA was a conglomeration of eight separate self-regulatory and statutory authorities, and they did not have powers to act in their own right until the Financial Services and Markets Act of 2001.

Financial plumbing and infrastructure concerns remained in the Bank, however. The Bank began work in 1996 on testing its computer systems for readiness to deal with the problems of New Year's Day 2000, when computer systems that used only two digits to record twentieth-century dates might behave unpredictably. A government-sponsored Task Force 2000 estimated that the cost of changing all systems in the UK would be some £31 bn, and one high street bank estimated that the effort required 900 man years of work, with 50 bn lines of COBOL programming code needing to be checked.[39] In February 1998, the Bank started to circulate widely a Blue Book to help the financial sector prepare. There was a substantial worry, and some economists feared that Y2 K would become a major financial disruption. The chief economist of Deutsche Morgan Grenfell, Edward Yardeni, estimated the chance of a 'severe global recession' resulting at 75 per cent.[40] The Bank both urged extensive preparation and made itself into a reassuring presence. A 1998 memo for the Governor's Committee (Govco) noted that although 'two years from today. We may be asking ourselves what all the fuss was about', 'there are few people today who are prepared to take such a sanguine view'. It concluded that there was a widespread relief in the City that 'someone appears to be taking responsibility'.[41] In 1999, it arranged for open market counterparties to borrow for up to three months at the year end, in addition to the regular two-week operations. In September, the Bank's Court agreed to increase open market operations swaps from the normal £2 bn to £3 bn, with a possibility of up to £5 bn being made available 'in extreme circumstances' over the New Year, up to March 2000.

The Bank suggested that the Federal Reserve open up swap lines in order to prepare for a liquidity crunch, but the Fed pushed back on the argument that there was an 'awkwardness of their reengaging in swap facilities' that they had started in the wake of the Asia crisis but only recently terminated. Such a step would require approval from the FOMC, which would necessarily become public. Similarly the ECB argued that 'they would not want to announce anything because of their decision not to announce any liquidity facility'.[42] Americans were in general convinced in any case that this was more of a European problem than a US one, because, as a participant on credit risk in a New York Federal Reserve conference put it, 'Europeans are distracted by preparations for the euro.'[43]

The removal of supervision transformed a long-running discussion about accountability in the case of bank resolution through the use of public money. The Cruickshank Report (2000) on *Competition in Banking* recommended that the use of LLR facilities should be made public within a year, in the interest of transparency and public accountability. The Bank argued for a more discretionary approach, with the timing depending on whether disclosure could threaten stability, and the government sided with the Bank.[44] There was still room for discreet rescue operations, but neither Bank nor Treasury thought they would really be that significant. This line of argument became more important after the end of George's Governorship. Mervyn King would probably never have succeeded George in the old regime, when the existentially central task of the Bank was management of the City and its interests, as well as of course the interests of the British government. Now that imperative behind that task had faded. King did not particularly care for the work of the financial stability division, and he wanted to 'operationalise' it, which was interpreted as 'simply writing and publishing two financial stability reports every year'. King made it clear that these were in a completely different league to the central work on generating an inflation report, and he did not present the stability reports himself.[45] The Bank would focus on monetary policy, not on banking.

The Bank also came to the conclusion that it needed to become more political. At the height of the controversy with the government over the separation of banking supervision, the Bank discussed a new activism in public relations. George successfully demanded that the major speeches of Bank officials should appear on the Bank's website. Mervyn King chaired an internal working group on 'building a constituency for low inflation'.[46] Others in the Bank emphasized the need to target the press – but particularly the tabloids, especially the *Daily Express* and the *Daily Mail*.[47] The

Figure 15.3 Gordon Brown with the Lord Mayor of London and
Eddie George
(Photoshot/TopFoto)

Bank needed to convince a broad public of its centrality in the economic
policy-making apparat (see Figure 15.3).

THE GOVERNANCE OF THE BANK

The 1998 Bank of England Act created a new structure for the Court. There
were now sixteen rather than eleven non-executive directors, intended to
represent the regional and sectoral diversity of the UK economy. They were
organized in a formal sub-committee, known as NedCo, and initially
chaired by Dame Sheila Masters, a partner of KPMG, who would also
chair the Court in the absence of the Governor. Under King as Governor,
after 2003, the Court was regularly chaired by the senior non-executive
director. Its tasks included reviewing the Bank's performance in relation to
its objectives and strategy, monitoring its financial management, reviewing
the internal financial controls and determining the Governor's and Deputy
Governors' remuneration. It was also charged with reviewing the operation
of the MPC, and in particular ensuring that the work of the MPC adequately reflected the regional balances of the British economy.

The act also set the Bank's income model for the first time on a statutory
basis. The banks' cash ratio deposits were no longer notionally 'voluntary',

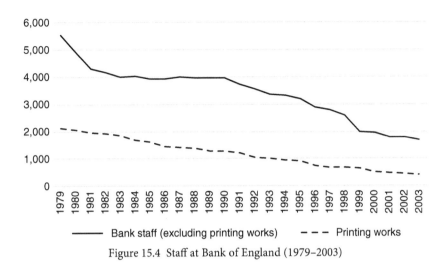

Figure 15.4 Staff at Bank of England (1979–2003)

but were set by the government, and the building societies were for the first time brought into this scheme, a final recognition that they were really also banks.

The Bank had been shrinking in staff terms since the late 1970s (see Figure 15.4). That process continued, with a dramatic shift when 450 staff concerned with banking supervision moved to the new FSA in new offices in the newly developed London Docklands, which rapidly became the visible architectural embodiment of a new world of financialization. In February 1998, before the move, there had been 3,056 full-time and 222 part-time staff employed. With the exodus to the FSA, only four lawyers were left in the Bank.

Some benefits were rationalized, and odd anomalies removed. In the 1999 'Benefitselect' reform to the staff benefit system, the old system of cheap (5 per cent) mortgages as well as the legacy of 2 per cent mortgages for staff joining up to the end of 1979 was ended: the old system had produced occasional embarrassments when low-level Bank staff were interviewed by the press and on television after interest rate hikes and announced that they were not worried because their mortgages were fixed.

The expansion of the Bank's monetary policy role was reflected in a change of the relative prestige and power of the different parts of the Bank's operations. In practice, the dominance of monetary analysis over the rest of the Bank – including the once-dominant Markets Division – is

Table 15.1 *Staff numbers end (May 2003)*

Monetary Analysis, MPC unit & MFSD (including Agents)	319
Market Operations	117
Banking and Market Services (including Printing & Registrars)	431
Financial Stability	174
Central Services	670
Other	71
Total (ex BCCI)	**1782**[48]

Table 15.2 *Number of economists supporting monetary analysis*

	Number of economists
ECB	150
Banque de France	62
Bundesbank	75
Banca d'Italia	124
US Federal Reserve System	500
Bank of England (excluding Agents)	122[49]

clear from the size of the Bank, now very much smaller than it had been in the 1970s or 1980s (see Table 15.1).

It was also clear that the number of monetary economists was similar to those in some European central banks, greater than in Frankfurt or Paris, but very much lower than the numbers of economists employed by the Fed (see Table 15.2).

Looking back in 2003 at the experience of operating for five years under the new framework, the new Governor, Mervyn King, set out some objectives for changing the way the Bank was run:

(i) To move the Bank from an ad hoc and responsive approach, characteristic of some but not all parts of the Bank, to a more systematic and pro-active method of work.

(ii) To introduce greater clarity of objectives to the Bank, and to make it more transparent and accountable.

(iii) To give responsibility for decisions to individuals, not to committees, and to increase personal accountability within the Bank.

(iv) To align the Bank's activities more closely with the Bank of England Act 1998, and the Memorandum of Understanding between HMT, FSA and the Bank, also of 1998.

King was also critical of the multiple purposes of the Bank, and especially of any hint that it should continue in its old role as advocate of the City:

The Bank's core purposes form part of the strategy of the Bank determined annually by Court. It is time for a review. The first two are the essence of a central bank. But, in the view of the Executive Team the Bank's current third core purpose needs to be reconsidered. It has been given a variety of interpretations from 'promoting the City' to 'developing the financial infrastructure', and requires greater clarification if it is to survive. Its future turns on the leadership role of the Bank in the financial community. A paper on this will be brought to Court.

If the Bank were really to be responsible for overall economic stability, it would be inappropriate for it to also be in effect the lobbyist for the City, or for a particular part of the British economy, whose interests diverged from the overall good. Fundamentally, the Bank's major mission was now redefined as the achievement of monetary stability, which it interpreted widely as economic stability, and its key instrument the newly instituted MPC. The MPC far overshadowed the other wing of the Bank, the financial stability function, especially since supervision and regulation had been hived off to the Financial Stability Authority, staffed largely with staff taken from the Bank and located well away from the Bank, in the new financial hub at Canary Wharf. There was a Financial Stability Committee, but it seemed like a very pale rival to the MPC.

The old idea of a UK macro-economic executive was kept on, with a notion of tripartite action, in which the Treasury, the Bank and the FSA would regularly consult and assess the spillovers between fiscal, monetary, and financial stability policies. In fact, these regular consultations were inevitably ill-focused without the pressing need to make a decision (as on interest rates, in the 1980s and 1990s version of the macro-economic executive). The three parts of the triune entity thus in practice moved away from each other, and there was less assessment of the policy spillovers than might have been desirable as financial risk built up in the 2000s.

THE FINANCIAL STABILITY COMMITTEE

Most of the initial work of the FSC focused on the international environment – on the Asia financial crisis, and later on sovereign debt issues in Argentina and elsewhere. UK financial issues were clearly more and more intertwined with the stability of the whole international order. So much of the financial stability work seemed a continuation of the work that had once been done in the old International Division. But it encountered an intractable problem: in considering a large number of potential vulnerabilities, it was never in a position to do more than analyse a succession of problems. It could not really assess their comparative importance, or rank them according to the severity of the threats posed.

UK banking showed a gradual but very slow lowering of capital ratios over this period, and also what the *Financial Stability Review* noted as a 'a greater reliance on short-term wholesale funding – which is likely to be less stable in the event of stress' (see Figures 15.5 and 15.6).[50]

The FSC saw clearly the declining capital ratios of UK banks, but did not really know either how worrying it might be – or what to do about it. Any single capital ratio looked arbitrary: 'Since the consequence of bank failure differ from bank to bank, it is impossible to point a simple "right" figure for bank capital or an acceptable probability of failure.'[51] At a meeting in 2001, George asked how a 10 per cent cut in capital could be compatible with 'the Committee's agreement to maintain the overall level of capital in the

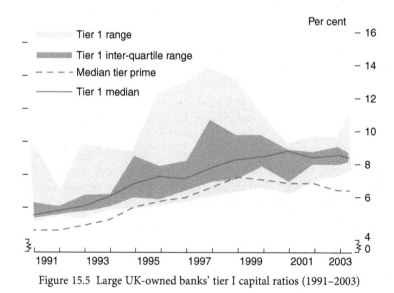

Figure 15.5 Large UK-owned banks' tier I capital ratios (1991–2003)

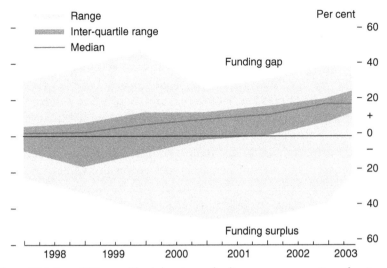

Figure 15.6 Large UK-owned banks' customer funding gap as a proportion of customer lending (1998–2003)

system'.[52] The Deputy Governor for Financial Stability, David Clementi, replied that it was 'acceptable for the level of capital to vary between different banking systems. If banks in some countries, such as the UK, ran less risky portfolios this should be reflected in capital levels.'[53]

Above all, the dynamic to push down capital levels and increase leverage seemed to come largely from the US. In 2000, one participant in the Financial Stability Committee asked incredulously 'whether the US was really prepared to countenance a 40% cut in the amount of capital in the international banking system'.[54] In 2001, Patricia Jackson stated that while the UK, Spain, France and Italy all seemed to be concerned about procyclicality, 'the US did not seem to be'. Because the US banking system was diversified and fragmented, its regulators felt that it was 'less vulnerable to credit crunch'.[55] George thought it right to focus stability discussions chiefly on what went on in the US – but that was clearly an area where the extent of UK influence was limited.[56]

In the immediate aftermath of the 1997–98 Asia crisis, Gordon Brown had called for a 'Global Financial Regulator', but Japan was reported to be agnostic or opposed and the US was not enthusiastic: 'The fractured nature of the US regulatory system would make it difficult for a representative of one entity to have a wider representative role.'[57] There were international agreements: in February 2000, the Basel Committee on Banking Supervision published 'Sound Practices for Managing Liquidity in Banking Organizations', setting out broad qualitative guidelines for liquidity risk management; but different countries adopted a variety of approaches to quantitative liquidity requirements. In 2003, the seven largest UK-owned banks had 'large' exposures to forty-five different banking groups, most of which were foreign-owned.[58]

There were also discussions of the potential problems of winding up large and complex financial institutions (LCFIs). George asked pointedly whether regulators had sufficient information on the LCFIs, and John Trundle replied, 'These groups themselves were not always aware of the range of payment and settlement systems they used; and he doubted the FSA were.' The problem lay in institutional complexity. Patricia Jackson explained that an exercise five years earlier to map the structure of major banking groups had, for instance, shown Merrill Lynch as having 300 different entities, only three of which were considered 'significant' in terms of risk markets. The debate also showed a sensitivity to the issue of banks being excluded from the interbank market and the swaps market as their ratings were downgraded.[59]

Many of the issues that would destroy the financial system in 2007–2008 were identified and discussed, sometimes at length: exposure to international banks, dependence on wholesale markets, management and organizational complexity, complex legal institutions, and problems of the interbank market. But they were disconnected from each other, and not addressed in terms of an overall framework, as a question of inadequate loss-absorption capacity or capitalization. The problems identified looked so very distinct because the linkages or connections could not be straightforwardly addressed in the institutional framework as it emerged in the 1990s. That made the search for effective solutions hard, even impossible.

THE MPC

The MPC, as created by the new Bank of England Act, was composed of the Governor and the two Deputy Governors of the Bank, two members appointed by the Governor after consultation with the Chancellor (in practice the Chief Economist and the Executive Director for Markets), and four outside 'expert' members appointed by the Chancellor: in other words, there existed an even balance between four outsiders and four insiders, with the Governor being able to tip at the fulcrum. Though the legislation only came into force on 1 June 1998, the Chancellor's letter of 6 May 1997 stipulated that all aspects of the new procedure for making and publishing monetary policy would de facto begin immediately. The Committee met at monthly intervals, over a two-day time frame, producing a decision on interest rates that was announced at the traditional time of noon on Thursday. Members spoke in a randomly determined order, so that there was no hierarchy (unlike the Greenspan Fed, where the Chairman conventionally began the discussion), though in the Thursday meeting the Director General for Monetary Policy always went first, and the Governor always concluded. The MPC was accountable through monthly reports to the Court of Directors, and it would also regularly present evidence to the House of Commons Treasury Committee. It would also publish minutes of each meeting within six weeks.

The new process was deliberately set to be transparent, in large part to enhance the credibility of policy, as well as to reflect a new style of governance in the UK. But there was also a consequence that Gordon Brown particularly began to realize quite quickly. The monetary policy transparency was greater than that of the incipient European Central Bank, and 'it would be difficult for the UK to enter EMU and thereby reduce the amount of transparency here'. Thus, the process acted as a defence mechanism against any push from the Prime Minister to join the monetary union promptly. Brown added, 'It was particularly ironic that transparency was being pressed on the Asian countries [by the US and the IMF in the wake of the East Asia financial crisis] but not accepted in Europe.'[60]

One concern that was voiced by some figures in the Bank was that the new format would become personalized and politicized. 'Ken and Eddie' had looked to journalists like a permanent struggle, and the MPC might spawn a 'different personality culture – "the monetary muppets show"'.[61] The first outsider members of the Committee included two non-UK nationals, DeAnne Julius, an American who had been Chief Economist of British Airways since 1993, and Willem Buiter, a Dutch economist who had come to Cambridge University from Yale. They were quite different in character, with Buiter having a strikingly articulate and combative personality, and Julius being rather calmer and assured. They also came with different professional backgrounds: Buiter had an instinct for theoretical economic insights, while the broader and international business background of Julius gave her a more substantial insight into the changes to the policy environment that would be brought by globalization.[62] The other outside members were by contrast veterans of British monetary policy-making and of the monetarist debates of the 1970s and 1980s: Sir Alan Budd, who had been Chief Economic Adviser at the Treasury since 1991, and Charles Goodhart, who had been at the Bank before returning to the London School of

Economics. Budd and Goodhart had been major institutional and theoretical advocates, respectively, of the MPC system, which Budd later described as 'possibly the best system in the world for setting monetary policy'.[63] They were, however, both marginalized in the political process: Alan Budd in April 1999 announced his resignation and a move to become Provost of Queen's College Oxford, and Goodhart's term was not renewed.

The Bank of England Act 1998 stated that the Bank 'shall publish minutes of the [MPC] meeting before the end of the period of six weeks beginning with the day of the meeting'. In practice, the Bank quickly reduced this delay to two weeks. These minutes did not attribute policy positions to particular committee members, and remained in the form 'Members discussed [...], and made a number of points.' But there were also longer records of the meetings. King originally proposed that the transcripts of MPC meetings should be released after ten years, and that the tapes used to produce the transcripts should be destroyed once the transcripts were finalized.[64] In the event, the tapes were destroyed, but so were the transcripts. There was thus no way of really tracking the record of individual MPC members, or of holding them to account – except for what they said in speeches or to newspapers, and that new publicity began to generate a peculiar dynamic. In 1999, George told a House of Commons Committee:

When we first produced the minutes of our meetings it was quite difficult to force ourselves to display the differences. I think we have made a lot of inroads into that now and we do manage to display there was this view and that view and that other view, sometimes all three views being held by the same person, because it is exploring the implications of the different possibilities, which is why we do not attribute individual views to particular people.[65]

But the concern to keep a veil over the proceedings remained. Indeed, the debate about reaching a way of assessing the performance of individual monetary policy setters only took off after the Great Financial Crisis.[66] Only in 2014, after the Financial Crisis, did the review headed by the US central banker Kevin Warsh conclude that 'the ultimate release of these transcripts – together with individual speeches, interviews, and testimony before the Treasury Committee – would ensure that MPC members were held to account for their views'.[67]

The Bank's operational independence and the establishment of the MPC produced an immediate benefit in the reduction of long-term interest rates, a sign of increased credibility (see Figures 15.7 and 15.8). The argument was that investors required a rate of return (interest) that takes into account the expected rate of inflation.

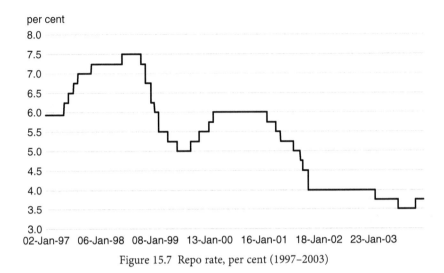

Figure 15.7 Repo rate, per cent (1997–2003)

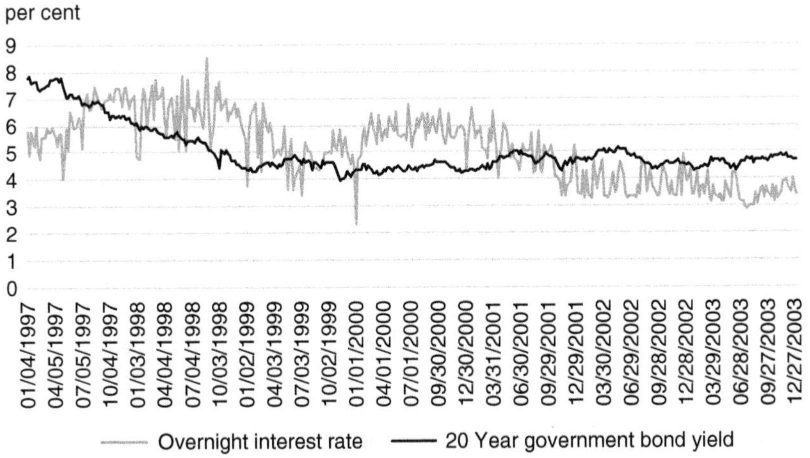

Figure 15.8 Interest rates, per cent (1997–2003)

The MPC's first meetings were highly consensual, with unanimous votes supporting small-scale (1/4 per cent) moves upwards in the repo rate. The first divided vote came in January 1998, in the wake of uncertainty about the worldwide fallout of the East Asia crisis, which had just hit Korea in a devastating shock to confidence. The majority of the Committee agreed to hold rates, while a minority (all outside members), Alan Budd, Willem Buiter and Charles Goodhart, wanted to continue with the course of small rate increases. In February, the debate was essentially repeated, with a consensus that 'near-term uncertainties, including those resulting from the Asia crisis, were unusually large and mainly on the downside'. The three from January were now joined by an internal, Mervyn King, who also wanted a rise: with only eight members, the Governor voted initially in an evenly split vote, and then had a second, casting vote in favour of maintaining rates. This might have been a testing moment in that a senior Bank figure was voting against the Governor, but George actually welcomed the split, which showed that the Committee was working as a genuinely deliberative forum. The March vote repeated the February outcome, and the April meeting was also quite similar, except that there was one defection from the hawkish camp, Charles Goodhart. In May, six members supported keeping rates on hold, while Buiter wanted an immediate rise in interest rates and DeAnne Julius an immediate cut, so that there was a three-way split. The Committee was probably not taking into account sufficiently the risks to global growth from the Asia crisis, and relying too much on backward-looking domestic indicators from the Office of National Statistics. For instance, in the July meeting of 1998, the majority was worried about a rise in average earnings and about the effects of an introduction of a National Minimum Wage.[68]

At this early stage, it was not completely clear that the Committee mechanism was working better than the previous process of Bank–Exchequer meetings. King expressed his frustration very candidly. He thought interest rates would have risen more quickly under the old mechanism in 1997, and it was 'one of the great tragedies' that the first year of the MPC had seen policy that was 'much worse'. He added, 'One can only imagine the frustration at the other end of town [in the Treasury].'[69] He also found it 'amazing' that the Committee had also agreed to a projection for inflation at 3 per cent that would imply that there was a need for interest rates to rise. It was becoming clear that the mechanism for thinking about the inflation projection was not adequately integrated into the policy vote.

There was also a great deal of public criticism of the process of the Committee. Martin Wolf wrote, 'The decision to give responsibility to a monetary policy committee rather than a person, as in New Zealand, was probably an error. Committees procrastinate. Even Eddie George, the Governor, has wondered whether he was wrong to oppose higher interest rates early this year. He was.'[70] One of the most far-reaching indictments was that of Philip Stephens, in the *Financial Times*, who had initially been critical of the uniformity of the Committee's voting, and then, as the splits emerged in 1998, wrote:

The Bank of England's Monetary Policy Committee is more like a senior common room than a real policy making forum. But to put six economists in the same room is to invite what one commentator has called paralysis by analysis. As a result the committee's conclusions are entirely unpredictable. There is no rhythm to the monthly deliberations. The participants seem trapped in the headlights of the latest economic indicators. The Bank finds it impossible to guide the expectations of bond and currency markets. Its quarterly Inflation Report points in one direction, the conclusions of the committee in another. Industry pays the price in unpredictable swings in the exchange rate.[71]

The exchange rate was rising, feeding into worries about monetary policy being too tight. In August 1997, for instance, the committee discussed how the 'appreciation of the exchange rate over the past year is putting severe pressure on businesses exposed to international competition'. But the appreciation continued, in large part after 1999 because of the initial weakness of the new European currency, the euro.[72] By June 1999, the minutes record 'the fact that since the turn of the year, sterling had consistently turned out stronger than assumed each month. And although the May Inflation Report fully reflected the appreciation of the exchange rate in the first part of the year, its persistent rise created a greater sense of underlying strength and weakened perceptions of the likelihood of the sustained fall in sterling that was assumed in the central projection.'[73] By February 2000, there was even a discussion of forex intervention. The MPC had indeed been given the authority to authorize a limited amount of foreign exchange dealings (though that possibility was never actually used). The minutes record how:

Those members prepared to contemplate intervention placed some weight on its use as a signal of concerns about the level of the exchange rate – a more powerful signal than words alone – but most of them concluded that it could be an option only if the Committee decided to leave the repo rate unchanged and, even then, would have to depend on market conditions. Other members thought, first, that it was doubtful whether intervention would be effective as there was little evidence that the market consensus which sustained sterling at its current level was fragile; and that a failed attempt to influence the exchange rate via intervention would damage the Committee's credibility. Second, to the extent that sterling's strength mainly reflected euro weakness, the MPC could do very little about it.[74]

A lower exchange rate and a higher interest rate might have been desirable, also as a way of tackling the incipient house price inflation.[75] By February 2000, Charles Goodhart was calling the exchange rate 'silly', and George was fully endorsing that view, simply saying that he was 'very concerned' about the strength of sterling.[76]

The strength of the exchange rate highlighted the problem of regional disparities in the UK. While London was booming, and seemed to require constant or even higher rates, the North was depressed. Large enterprises, including Fujitsu, Siemens and Vickers, laid off workers and blamed the appreciation of sterling. In October 1998, in answer to a question asked at a London lunch for regional newspaper representatives on whether he thought job losses in the north were an acceptable price to pay for curbing inflation in the south, George responded: 'Yes, I suppose in a sense I am. It's not desirable, but the fact is we can only seek to affect through monetary policy the state of demand in the economy as a whole. It's only through monetary policy that we can determine what happens to the labour market as a whole.' The Labour MP for Rotherham, Denis MacShane, responded in parliament by stating that 'I believe that state-ment exposes the fallacy of having our economy controlled and deter-mined by the values of the City.'[77] He called for the Governor to resign. But Gordon Brown defended George. A few months later, George explained in Newcastle: 'We are not in the business of sacrificing jobs to bring inflation down; we are in the business of keeping inflation down in order to create jobs and higher living standards for the medium and long term. High levels of employment and effective price stability are more like love and mar-riage – you can't have one without the other, at least for very long.'[78] When asked on television in early 1999 about exchange rate movements that hurt exports, George replied, 'I could seek to ease his pain but only by giving him an aspirin, and actually the underlying pain would be worse later on if I did.'[79]

George eventually had to reformulate his view on the relationship of regional policy to overall monetary objectives by explaining: 'Our essential mandate is stability in the economy as a whole but it does provide the right environment for the different parts, the different sectors and different regions to actually prosper.' In other words, financial management needed to be linked to the broader business environment. The Third Core Purpose was now redefined as trying to promote the effectiveness with which the UK financial system generated a widespread national competitiveness and growth.[80]

An important part of the work of the MPC came to be the presentation of the Bank's policy discussions around the country, including in the manufacturing districts that had long felt that the Bank was the creature of the City, with fundamentally antagonistic interests. The Third Core Purpose in the 1990s formulation seemed to refer explicitly to the defence of the City. It became clear that this was an outdated, but also politically unacceptable, way for the Bank to present its role. The wider dissemination of the thinking behind the Bank's policy discussions, and of the fact that there was no single or monolithic vision that shaped the Bank's response, and also no absolutely 'right answer', played a central part in the move to change the whole political climate in which monetary policy was discussed.

The first cut in interest rates under the new regime came only in October 1998, by a quarter point, with two MPC members, Buiter and Julius, voting against, as they preferred a larger cut in interest rates. In November, a half-point cut followed, although some argued that 'taken in isolation, a cut of more than 25 basis points might create the misleading impression that the outlook was worse than implied by the Committee's central projection on the grounds that financial markets thought the most likely outcome of the meeting was a cut of 25 basis points'.[81] Buiter again wanted a larger cut in rates.

DeAnne Julius' position was based on an argument about the deflation-ary pressures on a world level exerted first by the Asia crisis, but then, more generally, by 'globalization', the spread of manufacturing production to emerging markets with large supplies of cheap labour. Only two times did she vote for higher rates. The argument about the impact of geo-economic shifts was novel, and perspicacious, in a setting in which monetary policy had been thought about in much more insular terms. Some business people styled her 'Saint DeAnne of Threadneedle Street', and contrasted her background with that of the rest of the committee: 'In a period where the MPC could have been damagingly dominated by central bankers and academic economists, her influence has been for the good.'[82]

Willem Buiter had the initial record as being the most dissident member: of the thirty-six votes he took part in, he was in the minority on seventeen, in nine cases voting for higher rates and eight times voting for lower rates than the majority. The press initially attacked him as being a remote academic, 'a Dutchman with extensive experience in academia but little exposure to the world of commerce and industry. Arguably the most hawkish member of the Bank's Monetary Policy Committee, he has voted consistently for an increase in rates every month from January to June.' [83] From mid-1998, he turned into a monetary dove. By the end of the year, he was telling newspapers that the MPC had got it wrong, that the MPC 'did too little, too late and the country was now suffering as a result'. 'The committee failed to foresee the worldwide recession and should have acted earlier to raise interest rates in bigger steps than it did.' He was in the Midlands, visiting the Kidderminster carpet-maker Tomkinsons, to show that the committee was aware of the region's problems.[84]

Buiter was also at the centre of a dispute about the resources available to the 'externals'. He recognized quickly that the discussion involved not so much a clash of views or hunches as a testing of different analyses, with the consequence that, in the absence of a substantial research and analytical capacity, the external members would be trapped in Bank thinking, in what Gillian Tett would later term a 'silo mentality and tunnel vision'.[85] A dangerous propensity to groupthink would follow from the limits imposed on the external members. The workflow of the Monetary Analysis Division, including the analysis of labour and product markets, was set by the chief economist and the Deputy Governor responsible for monetary policy, and these figures initially vigorously resisted attempts by external MPC members to speak or engage with Bank economists. A new external member, Sushil Wadhwani, who had replaced Sir Alan Budd, complained that 'these were not the terms on which he accepted the job'. By late 1999, the dispute about resources reached boiling point. Goodhart and Budd, both of whom were in a sense insiders, had been happy with their research resources; the others were not. In particular, the external MPC members who had been away from academic-style research for a long time found the Bank's modern research too technical and the policy discussion cast in unfamiliar terms from academic economics: shocks, rules, commitment, forecast bands. DeAnne Julius later told an MPC staff research adviser that serving as an MPC member was like going back to (graduate) school.[86] In October 1999, the independent members presented a paper to the Court setting out their view that their inadequate research resources made it impossible to stand up to the Bank view and to present really independent analysis. They detected a substantial hostility on the part of King in particular, who suspected that they really wanted assistance with speech-writing in order to make more of a public splash. But the most serious and immediate reaction came from George, who simply said, 'You weren't appointed to pursue your own personal research program or to set up your own publicly-funded research institute.'[87]

George summed up his view of the controversy, telling the Court that the externals appeared 'to see their role as an independent counter weight to the MPC members who were executives of the Bank', and that a 'them and us' mentality was developing. 'The idea that the "independent" members should be supported with a large research capability of their own, account-able to them alone, in order to enable them to challenge a supposed "Bank view," never to the Governor's knowledge featured in the debate leading up to the new arrangements and was not reflected in any of the texts that established those arrangements. Requests on the resources of the Monetary

Analysis division had escalated so as to produce an impossible workload.' King noted that the externals' concept of their resource requirement had gone from one to twelve over a few months 'without any change in the objective circumstances'. He was even more dismissive than George about the idea of building up a separate research capability: 'Contrary to the suggestion that the arrangement now was only suitable for academics, the proposal by the externals would set up an arrangement that was indeed only suitable for academics. It would create a university of Threadneedle Street. It was an attractive option for the externals, but he could not believe that a non-academic would find this a rewarding way to spend time.' He saw the fundamental issue as who would control Monetary Analysis, the area that was the proper heart of a modern central bank:

The Bank was held in enormous esteem for the quality of monetary analysis. A senior Japanese Ministry of Finance official had written in the *Financial Times* earlier in the week that the Bank of Japan might adopt inflation targets, Bank of England-style. That was not an accident. There had been a very clear vision of what the Bank wanted to create and a clear management structure to produce it. Success in that area would be at risk if the Bank had collective management of these resources. If the resource was free there would be infinite demand for it. Monetary Analysis could not be successfully managed by the external members. The quality of the team would not survive under collective management.[88]

Who would guide the economic analysis? The Monetary Analysis economists 'wanted to have a debate, and the MPC wanted to hear their views, but the staff were there to serve nine members, who had differences of view. The staff did not want to be seen to be aligning with one particular member. They had not one but nine bosses. That made it more difficult for them to take up clear positions.'[89] For King, the critical issue was the credibility of the policy outcome.

One member of the Court, Bill Morris (the General Secretary of the Transport and General Workers Union), spoke of 'a chronology of frustration, which highlighted the inertia of the internal bureaucracy, which they believed frustrated their efforts to perform the function for which they were appointed'. He worried that 'a public manifestation of the issue could have devastating consequences'. Another member, Sheila McKechnie (of the Consumers' Association), observed: 'A number of them might say that they were not willing to accept the situation, and might go public or threaten to resign.' Frances Heaton (of Lazard) noted: 'They called themselves independent because they felt outsiders. They felt second class citizens, or pheasants with their wings clipped, because they did not have the resources to do research to reinforce their views where there were differences from the institutional view. At the Treasury, where Mrs Heaton had worked, there was great room for differences of view.'[90]

Eventually, the issue was resolved only because the Governor was worried that the Court discussion would spill over into the public discussion of the Treasury Select Committee. The Governor gave in, and conceded to each external member a graduate economist and a research assistant, but also agreed to spend more time on the discussion of long-term research priorities. George reflected that he 'hoped that over time they would come to recognise that there were nine independent members and their sense of needing to assert themselves would go away'.[91] In practice, many of the research economists allocated in this way realized that they were underused, with some enjoying the opportunity to do more independent academic research on their own. But at least for some members of the MPC, the fierce debate over resources poisoned the climate of the Committee's work.

The process of appointment and possible reappointment also produced some tension. George made it clear in writing to the Chancellor that he would like to see a renewal of the appointments of both Budd and Goodhart, not just for their expertise but 'because the continuity would be extremely helpful at this phase of the Committee's development'.[92] But continuity with the pre-1997 regime, in which Budd had been the Principal Economic Adviser to the Treasury, was precisely what did not appeal to Gordon Brown. Neither Budd nor Goodhart were reappointed to the MPC.

DeAnne Julius was joined by other 'doves': Sushil Wadhwani, from Tudor Proprietary Trading and before that Goldman Sachs, and then Christopher Allsopp, who had been at the Bank in the early 1980s. Allsopp's appointment generated some pushback from the House of Commons Treasury Committee, in large part because some MPs wanted to register a protest at what they saw as the illegitimate nonrenewal of Goodhart.[93] Wadhwani was the most emphatic in wondering about the process, and at the beginning argued that setting monetary policy priorities through majority voting might not give 'the diversity in research that was necessary for good decision-making'.[94] But none of these doves behaved as conflictually as outside members (Danny Blanchflower and later Adam Posen) did later during the Great Financial Crisis. Wadhwani was the only member of the MPC who became really concerned about monetary deflation, feeding into the zombification of the banking system. In 2001, but especially in 2002, the spectre of a malign deflation figured prominently in US discussions. Ben Bernanke, who became Governor of the Federal Reserve System in August 2002, warned of a Japanese-style danger.[95] The

MPC discussed the Japanese experience in March 2002, and in the January meeting of 2002 there was some discussion of inflation undershooting: 'in which case it might be difficult to ease monetary policy by enough to restore inflation to target'.[96] But in the second half of 2002, when the US deflation discussion was taking off, the word 'deflation' does not occur in the MPC minutes.

The press commentary quite quickly liked to stylize the MPC debates as clashes of hawks and doves (see Figure 15.9). So, for instance, in March 1998, Mervyn King was reported to have 'defected to the hawks'.[97] The House of Commons Treasury Committee even devised a score for determining numerically who was a hawk, who was a dove, and how far an individual member was close to the policy consensus. Two internal members, Mervyn King and John Vickers, his successor as chief economist, were on this scale at 1.2, while DeAnne Julius and Sushil Wadhwani, and the Bank's Governors, George and the Deputies David Clementi and Howard Davies were at the central 1.0.[98] Gradually, it looked to the committee as if King was building a hawkish reputation.

The rate reduction response to a business downturn was conducted very much in consideration of the likely response of market psychology. In April 1999, when rates were cut by a quarter point, to 5.25 per cent, the argument was made largely on the basis of signals and expectations.

Figure 15.9 Make your mind up time? That's strictly for the birds (Richard Cole, *Daily Telegraph*, 16 August 1999)

It was possible that a decision to leave interest rates unchanged would be interpreted as a signal that current levels would be the trough of this interest rate cycle. It was also possible that a similar conclusion might be reached from an unexpectedly large reduction in rates. Given that any decision was open to misinterpretation, the Committee agreed that this was not a factor which it would take into account.[99]

By 2000, the Bank's policy credibility had been very well established, and the critical comments in the press largely faded. The Committee now experimented with new ways of assessing the monetary policy stance:

RPIX inflation had now been below 2½% for more than 18 months; without an early policy response it might well continue to be so for the next two years. While current monetary conditions had loosened slightly over the month as a result of the fall in the exchange rate and in market interest rates, a Dynamic Monetary Conditions Index, which took account of the effects of lags and had been introduced largely at the urging of Julius, continued to tighten slightly.[100]

In general, as the recovery from the growth slowdown, and the international shocks of the Asia crisis and the collapse of the dotcom bubble proceeded, there was a measured and cautious response:

While recognising the downside risks from the international slowdown, the fall in equity prices and foot and mouth disease, and while agreeing that it was important to remain forward looking, it was equally important not to over-react. Final domestic demand growth remained robust. The strength of the housing market would cushion the effects on consumption of falls in equity prices.[101]

There was also a rather cautious reaction in an extraordinary meeting after the terrorist attacks on the US on 11 September 2001: the majority favoured a reduction of twenty-five basis points, rather than a more dramatic action to follow the Fed's half-a-point cut on 17 September after an emergency telephone conference.

Such a cut would demonstrate that the Committee was prepared to act in response to the change in economic circumstances. Although a 25 basis point reduction would be less than the cuts made by the Federal Reserve, the ECB and some other central banks, both current economic conditions and the impact of the recent shock differed across countries. That needed to be taken into account when judging the appropriate policy response for the UK. Before the terrorist attacks, demand conditions appeared rather more resilient in the UK than in many other countries. As a result, there was a possibility that a matching reduction of 50 basis points could convey an exaggerated impression of prospective economic weakness and affect confidence adversely.[102]

A preference developed in the MPC for being not too dramatic:

In the current conjuncture, cutting rates would undesirably stimulate an already buoyant household sector; and with price pressures currently so benign, a rate increase would be premature. The best course was to leave rates unchanged. Second, some members emphasised the prospect that inflation would be rising at the two-year horizon. There would be a risk to the effectiveness of policy if the Committee were to cut rates now only to have to increase them quite shortly afterwards even in the absence of news it was preferable for the Committee to build and maintain a reputation for making policy settings which would persist unless economic circumstances changed. That way, repo rate changes would tend to have a bigger impact on longer-term interest rates, the exchange rate and other asset prices, aiding the effectiveness of policy.[103]

As a result of these calculations, aimed in great part at dealing with higher house price inflation, interest rates remained significantly above US levels. The MPC did not follow the sharp cuts in the Federal funds rate. In consequence, the difference in interest rates with the US remained high until 2005.

In 2001–2002, the MPC thought that it had identified a 'key policy dilemma'. Thus, in February 2001: 'With household debt having risen relative to income and net trade having made a negative contribution to GDP growth for five years, there were underlying imbalances in the economy which created a risk of sterling falling at some point.'[104] Or again in June: 'There were major imbalances developing, with increased consumer demand but slower exports, showing up as a balance of payments deficit; but also as a boom in residential and commercial property.' Action to prevent or even reduce those imbalances would require a slowing of the domestic economy and would lower the inflation rate below the target. And then action against the deflation danger would increase the imbalances further.

So with slower output growth and falling production, especially in the externally exposed sectors, the imbalances in the economy – which had been apparent for some time – were likely to persist. RPIX inflation was somewhat below target and projected to remain so for some quarters. If the dampening effects on inflation of the slowdown in world activity and the strength of sterling were to persist, that would have implications for inflation further ahead. Policy action to offset these effects would, however, tend further to stimulate consumption and so to worsen the imbalances. These could then prove more problematic for the control of inflation in the medium term.[105]

The same issue was highlighted in the Bank's *Financial Stability Review*, which related how 'final domestic demand has grown more rapidly than the economy's productive capacity for some while. [. . .] These developments have entailed growing net external liabilities from cumulative current account deficits.'[106]

Some participants in the MPC discussions thought the debate should involve more attention to the development of asset prices. Wadhwani had been a co-author of a May 2000 Geneva report on 'Asset Prices and Central Bank Policy', which called attention to the issue and concluded that a central bank concerned with stabilizing inflation 'about a specific target level is likely to achieve superior performance by adjusting its policy instruments not only in response to its forecasts of future inflation and the output gap, but also to asset prices'.[107] But that view was rejected by the majority of the MPC, by the Bank's leadership and by the British Treasury. Indeed, a Treasury official, Gus O'Donnell, attended the Geneva conference on the report and warned about the 'great dangers' in 'mechanical rules' relating asset prices to inflation.[108]

There could be two approaches. In one version, monetary policy could try to cool down growth and lower the long-term equilibrium exchange rate with a rate hike. But there was a risk that the move would simply increase the exchange rate in the short term and more funds would flow in and prompt more overheating. Faced with this dilemma, it seemed obvious – and safe – to do nothing and let domestic demand grow and the current account deficits remain. At the Mansion House speech in June 2001, George explained: 'The imbalance can not continue to grow indefinitely, at some point, the elastic is going to break – quite possibly through a sharp exchange rate adjustment. And at that point, having deliberately stimulated domestic demand we would need to rein it back, but we could then find its momentum hard to stop.'[109] There was a two-speed economy, with a vigorous domestic side of the economy, but poorer export performance. Some economists in the MPC tried to shrug the problem off by comparing the two speeds to good and bad performances in a cricket match. George simply commented that 'imbalances make life difficult'.[110]

Mervyn King later identified this 'unpalatable choice'.[111] At the time he explained that 'the economic see-saw lurched with external demand falling and domestic demand rising. While the MPC can try to maintain stability in the economy as a whole it cannot prevent movements in the see-saw reflecting swings between external and domestic demand resulting from changes in in the world economy. And lurches in this see-saw produce damage.' Internal imbalances were the mirror of the external imbalances reflected in the current account. But King gave a relatively optimistic explanation of the source of the domestic imbalance: potential productivity gains in the future that led businesses to higher levels of investment in new technology in the expectation of future profits.[112]

Eddie George eventually settled the debate about the correct policy with the explanation:

What we were able to do, given that inflation was under control, by cutting interest rates as we did last year, was to try to compensate for the external weakness by stimulating domestic demand growth here in the UK. Given the weakness of business confidence, and therefore investment, reflecting the external pressures, that meant essentially stimulating consumer demand. [...] We expected the global economy to begin a sustained recovery in the latter part of last year which would allow us to return to better balanced growth in this country, and so we took the view essentially that for the time being at least unbalanced growth was better than no growth at all.[113]

It looked as if this calculation was correct. After 1999, in fact, the current account consistently improved until 2005 (unlike in the US), especially as the exchange rate appreciated considerably after February 2002; thus, the urgency of the 'dilemma' seemed to fade (see Figures 15.10 and 15.11).

The MPC minutes also demonstrate an early concern about the rise in housing prices – a feature that had been at the core of monetary policy

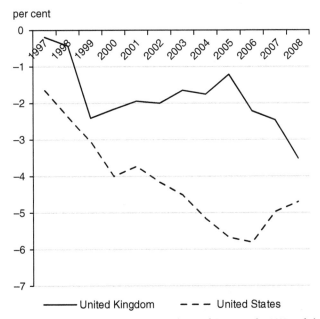

Figure 15.10 Current account imbalances as share of GDP in the UK and the US (1997–2008)

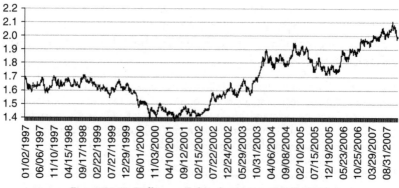

Figure 15.11 Dollar–pound exchange rate (1997–2007)

problems in earlier recovery phases, in particular in the 1980s Lawson boom. Thus, in February 2002, there was a discussion of 'some of the possible implications of a substantial cumulative rise in household debt relative to income and of the position of household finances more generally'. But the debate was inconclusive, and the argument always needed to be tied back to the discussion of likely future consumer inflation: 'In the view of some members, therefore, rising debt levels risked increasing the volatility of output and so of inflation in the medium term, potentially making future inflation outturns more uncertain. Other members placed little or no weight on this.'[114] In October 2002, the committee considered

whether, in the face of continuing slow growth in external demand, monetary policy should now provide a further stimulus to domestic demand. On the one hand, there was a risk of failing to prevent too rapid a slowdown in domestic demand growth before the world economy picked up, which might imply that inflation would fall below target over the next two years or so. On the other hand, there was a risk that maintaining the momentum of the economy would add to the build-up of household debt and house price inflation.[115]

Financial stability thus entered into the discussion, but only sporadically. There was never any explicit discussion about whether it might be desirable to 'lean' against possible causes of financial disruption. Julius at one point lamented to the Court of Directors that 'there was no comparable single indicator for financial stability to the inflation target for monetary stability, and asked whether it would be worth trying to come up with an aggregate indicator of the relative level of financial stability'.[116] But that proved to be a practically impossible task. Maybe the inability to find an adequate measure helped to assure the downward relegation of financial stability in the hierarchy of policy preferences.

THE PERFORMANCE OF THE MPC

Part of the general move to transparency and accountability in the 1990s and 2000s involved a much greater attention to benchmarking performance. The MPC thought about its own procedures, as did the Bank. It also sought outside expertise, and the Federal Reserve by this stage looked as if it was easily the best model for governance and openness, as well as for depth of economic analysis. In 2000, at the Bank's invitation, Don Kohn, a veteran of the Federal Reserve System, Secretary of the FOMC and Director of the Division of Monetary Affairs, advised both on improvements to modelling and to the operations of the MPC. He strongly supported the use of models:

Models play an important role in MPC deliberations on the inflation forecast, in many respects substituting for a staff forecast as a focus for discussion. They help to organise consideration of how developments in the economy had deviated from expectations and how to treat those deviations in the new projections. [. . .] In this process the staff relied on statistical models to a considerable extent, both a main model and auxiliary equations, to organise the analysis and present options for MPC decisions. The use of a variety of models is entirely appropriate – no one model can capture all relevant aspects of every issue the MPC would want to consider. This practice confirms closely to that followed in the United States, where the Federal Reserve Board staff has a large multiequation model.

But Kohn worried about the way that assumptions built into the models could be manipulated to order to achieve a particular desired outcome or recommendation:

Moreover, a number of members perceive some game playing with regard to choices on individual assumptions; that is, members argue for particular assumptions not out of conviction on those assumptions, but rather to shape the overall outcome in a direction they are most comfortable with. Several also saw the process as 'contentious', though in my experience the discussion was fair and civil, if at times appropriately vigorous. And the process is so complex, the Committee tends to shy away from late changes after the MPC meeting that would accommodate the evolution of Committee members' thinking in the course of policy discussions.

The scale and scope of individual approaches to economic analysis was increasing:

In addition, the outcome is not clear. The MPC needs to continue examining what it means by 'best collective judgment' to refine its understanding and possibly to consider alternative approaches. Originally, apparently, the forecast was a consensus of Committee members, forged through compromise and trade-offs. But as views became more diverse, compromise to achieve a single forecast was no longer possible.

The rates discussion had become increasingly diverse in consequence:

If the MPC continued to seek consensus or majority forecast, the problems are even larger. In my conversations on this issue, many MPC members stressed the difficulty of the Committee coming to agreement on a possible future path for interest rates. [...] Experience in other countries suggests that problems arise not so much in reaction to the announcement of a path, as in market responses to subsequent developments. Central banks making announcements about future paths for policy-related variables try to emphasise that they are conditional and contingent on the expected evolution of the economy, and that deviations from those expectations would require paths to be adjusted. However, it is impossible to foresee all possible developments – every situation is different, and the differences, possible subtle, may not be clear to markets, which then react inappropriately. The central banks of both Canada and New Zealand found that publication of expected monetary conditions indexes (which include both exchange and interest rates) tended to produce inaccurate and counterproductive interest rate movements when certain unexpected shocks hit the exchange markets.[117]

Might there have been an even more fundamental issue? Kohn was supporting the Bank's pushback against a new wave of academic literature, driven especially by the work of Michael Woodford and Lars Svenson, as well as by the practical example of New Zealand, whose central bank was – as in the case of inflation-targeting – at the avantgarde of monetary practice. The new thinking suggested that a central bank should provide 'forward guidance' to markets on the expected interest rate path. In its Article IV discussions with the UK, the IMF discussed this issue extensively, and its staff produced a cautious recommendation that the UK should extensively discuss forward guidance. But even this cautious and watered-down suggestion was met by a fierce pushback from the UK authorities. Tom Scholar of the Treasury, then the UK's Executive Director at the Fund, concerted a Board response in which his colleagues attacked the proposal as carrying 'time-consuming coordination costs and the risk of being misinterpreted by the market'.[118] The IMF also suggested that if there was a fan chart of different inflation outcomes, logically the Bank might also provide equivalent materials on other outcomes, notably output. The Bank was reluctant to do that, because such material would immediately lead it back into the mine-filled territory of assessing how likely the government was to hit its fiscal targets and hence to follow the 'Golden Rule' which Gordon Brown had held up as the sure guide to fiscal stability and accountability.

The broad initial policy consensus on the committee that RPIX was the right indicator to look at was not challenged, even by dissidents outside the MPC. In December 2003, the government changed the target from 2.5 per cent RPIX to 2 per cent CPI.

Looking back from the perspective of 2007, just before the Global Financial Crisis hit, the approval was pretty unanimous, even from outside the narrower policy consensus that developed in the committee discussion. The monetarist Tim Congdon said that the MPC's approach had been 'massively successful', while the Keynesian Simon Wren-Lewis agreed that 'the MPC has been very successful', and the veteran voice of Charles Goodhart added that stability in inflation was 'remarkable'.[119]

The new monetary regime was intended not only to be about transparency; it also was supposed to involve continuous control and accountability. The members of the MPC patrolled each other; parliament and public opinion invigilated over them. Paul Tucker commented: 'To be credible, modern monetary regimes rely on many people in different capacities – many audiences – watching what is going on in a 360-degree equilibrium.'[120] But if everyone in that process of surveillance has the same views, participates in a process of groupthink, the practice may be less stability producing than the old practice of a City with carefully segmented interests, in which interests required that each market participant check on each other.

A remarkable feature of the solidity of the new consensus, and hence of its persuasive power for markets, was that the possibility of an explicit mandate to consider responses to asset prices was rejected. Thus, Wren-Lewis argued that the Bank of England 'should be on the lookout for bubbles, that is periods in which asset prices in particular seem to depart from fundamentals, because potentially those bubbles can impact seriously on the economy. However, although in principle it should look out for those things and in principle could act to try and counteract them, in practice actually identifying when bubbles occur is incredibly difficult.' The now ex-Governor Eddie George added, 'If one decided to set a target for house prices and equity prices one would end up in "heap on the floor". One just cannot focus on more than one objective.' And Tim Congdon also did not want a specific mandate to consider leaning against the wind of asset price movements: 'I think there is a medium-term problem out there and the question is whether there will be a bust or a gradual what is called "rust", in other words a long period in which house prices go sideways. My guess is that it is more likely they will go sideways for a period than collapse. Logically, history says there should be a problem of adjustment in the next few years with house prices.'[121] Wadhwani was a partial dissident, and co-authored some papers while he was an MPC member advocating a response to asset price movements.[122] And the question of whether central banks should lean against asset prices is still controversial.[123]

There was an obvious problem of imbalances that could not be covered by the inflation target framework alone. King reflected on the problems at the start of his Governorship:

Since it was set up in 1997, the MPC has been more successful in meeting the inflation target than could reasonably have been expected at the outset. Over that period, inflation has averaged 2.4% and annual GDP growth 2.5%. This outcome was achieved by allowing domestic demand to grow rapidly to offset weak external demand, resulting in part from the sharp appreciation of sterling of around 30% in effective terms. So a successful overall economic performance was achieved at the expense of the build-up of significant economic imbalances between different sectors of the economy. Those imbalances are now likely to unwind. Managing the return to more normal growth rates for consumption, while coping with possibly greater volatility of inflation in the short run, will test our analytical capability. The success of Monetary Analysis is no cause for complacency, and it will not be easy to stay at the leading edge of economic policy.[124]

The success of an anti-inflation strategy was in part a technical one: but it was also, as the Bank recognized, an issue of communications and expectations, not just with the markets but with the public. So the Bank also commissioned surveys of attitudes to inflation, finding by and large that there was support for the idea of a stability culture. Support for the view that higher inflation would damage the economy remained fairly constant, at just under 50 per cent of response. Only 8 per cent thought higher inflation would strengthen the economy.[125]

The success of the MPC was clearly not due solely to its composition, or the (mostly) benign personalities of its early members. There is a possibility, however, that although the process of making policy was well thought out and designed, the actual outcome of the policy process was quite similar to that of other central banks, with entirely different designs. The Federal Reserve and the ECB tackled policy-making in a different way, with more politics, and at the ECB much less transparency. But they achieved the same, apparently also highly successful, results. The outcome might have simply been 'in the air', and not an outcome of the particular design of the Committee. This was also a period of considerable stability and growth in the world economy. As Wren-Lewis pointed out, the committee was 'lucky in the sense that it has not been a very turbulent period, so in that sense it has not been severely tested'.[126] But the lucky or benign circumstances may also have caused the committee to ignore an insight that it was precisely the success of increased monetary (price) stability that might blind the committee to the building up of speculation that was encouraged and pushed on by precisely the overall framework of stability.[127] 'Nor is it hard to imagine that these normal tendencies to boom-bust behaviour might be aggravated by easy monetary conditions. At the heart of the matter is the "search for yield" when nominal risk-free rates are very low.'[128] That was a dissident perspective, formulated largely by the BIS and its chief economist William White, but ferociously rejected by the Fed and in consequence also dismissed by most of the economics profession, the IMF, and indeed also the Bank of England.

Thinking of a scenario in which there would have been no decision for Bank independence in 1997 requires imagination. Some of the alternatives produce worse policy. One striking counterfactual laid out by Ed Balls, a key figure in driving the decision forwards in the Labour Party, involves continued conflict between the Treasury and the Bank, leading to a decision to join the European currency union, and then a greater exposure to shocks in the euro debt crisis after 2009. He put the point very vividly: 'There would have been a big row over interest rates; a lack of confidence in our monetary regime; someone would have been sacked; the CBI and TUC would have said "join the single currency"; we'd have joined the euro; we would have crashed out or been like Greece on steroids; and we would have left the EU five years earlier than we are going to.'[129] This is implausible: if there is any Eurozone economy that resembles the UK, it is Ireland, highly liberalized and highly financialized. After an appallingly severe financial crisis, it then experienced a spectacular recovery – while remaining in the euro. And it is plausible at least to imagine that being in the euro would have made the Brexit debate less attractive or less destructive.

It is equally plausible, however, that given the generally benign state of the world economy in the early 2000s, there would have been no significant conflicts at that time; and Gordon Brown as Chancellor was very keen to signal fiscal responsibility. When severe conflicts arose between government and Bank in 2007–2008, it is conceivable that the Treasury might have handled the initial response to the global financial crisis in 2007 more skilfully than the Bank, and in particular have pressed the Bank to undertake the extensive liquidity provision undertaken both by the Fed and the

ECB. Dealing with the financial crisis required a close coordination between fiscal and monetary measures, and the arm's-length relationship created in 1997 was not helpful from this point of view. Geoffrey Wood in retrospect stated that the tripartite system functioned 'with jaw-dropping incompetence and chaos'.[130]

There are clearly then both worse and better scenarios than the messy historical reality. In many ways, the debate about the outcome of Bank independence is tangential to the issue of a substantial improvement of the policy environment in the early 1990s. That move, and in particular the response to the ERM exit, rather than 1997, was the true beginning of an improved policy framework, and also better macro-economic performance. There was an unanticipated consequence. The better framework and more stable performance led the way into a trap, in which the sense of stability lulled policy-makers and those who were supposed to control them into complacency and groupthink, and set the stage for a new shock emanating from the financial system after 2007.

A division, a glaring gap, opened up between the expectation of market participants that they would always be secure, even when taking ever-wilder risks, because of a 'put' by central banks on asset prices, and the actual capacity of the policy community to gauge the extent of the risk. The Bank would have been well advised to follow the advice that the British public, or at least the London Tube traveller, associates most with Bank: namely, the recorded voice in Bank Tube station, telling passengers to 'mind the gap'.

16

Epilogue

The monetary and financial governance mechanism created by the Labour government in 1997, which appeared to have been functioning so smoothly and satisfactorily, was severely tested after 2007–2008, in what became known as the Global Financial Crisis. Both elements of the new approach to economic governance – the operational independence of the Bank on monetary policy, and the separation of financial supervision – stood as subjects of controversial debate, and a new wave of institutional upheaval set in. Much more than in the 1990s, the new moves were coloured by a blame game, a search for culprits for the severe financial crisis and deep and long-lived recession. The Bank had become widely recognized as a best-practice central bank, but now a shadow fell over international central banking as a whole.

In 1997, the British 'macroeconomic executive' had been neatly split, with fiscal policy clearly the domain of politics and the Chancellor, and monetary policy entirely determined by the Monetary Policy Committee acting in the framework of an operationally independent Bank, with an inflation target defined by the government in a political process. In normal circumstances, that splitting of functions worked well. But in exceptional conditions, the split becomes problematic, and in deep recessions accompanied by financial fragility, fiscal policy can be constrained, so that all the burden of making policy falls on the monetary side. In consequence, it is easy to think that monetary policy is 'over-burdened'. That was the case in the UK, but also across the industrial world, from Japan through the Eurozone to the US.

Policy uncertainty shows up in exceptional times and leads to economic damage as agents postpone decisions. The authorities could only signal a framework for expectations. In the mid-1990s, Eddie George had 'thought it important to emphasize that, not only were we not telling economic agents what to do, but we never had'.[1] That was not quite right as the old Bank had relied extensively on direct or more usually indirect hints (the Governor's eyebrows): but the new Bank as it emerged in the 1990s renounced that way.

In the 1980s, Eddie George and in the 1990s George and Mervyn King had reflected often and extensively on the linkages between monetary and fiscal policy. Weighing the appropriate contribution of each was central to the generation of stability-oriented policy. But it was difficult to theorize how the linkage should work in terms of the new insistence on the carefully delineated democratically sanctioned delegation of decision-making. Thinking about consistency in the approach to macro-economic policy might suggest that fiscal and monetary policy should be subjected to parallel rules, setting up a comprehensive and stable framework for expectations. Thus, for instance, in Norway in 2001 both inflation-targeting and a fiscal rule were introduced as a new policy regime.[2] In the UK, the policy mix was less satisfactory, and would eventually give rise to political controversy. The 1997–1998 move to Bank independence was accompanied by the assertion of Gordon Brown's 'Golden Rule', namely that over the economic cycle the government should borrow only to invest, but not to fund current spending. Very quickly after Bank independence, Brown announced a 'fiscal stability code' requiring the Chancellor to show how Budget measures comply with long-term government objectives for the public finances, and committing the Treasury to publish projections of government borrowing and other key fiscal variables for at least ten years ahead. The fiscal targets would have to be consistent with the long-range projections, and also with the terms of the European Union's 'growth and stability pact' for present and potential euro members. In practice, however, the Golden Rule was not strictly followed. The calculation required assessments of output volatility and asset price volatility. History could be used to calculate the surplus that was needed to assure that the Golden Rule was met. The IMF suggested that a 1.5 per cent surplus was needed to have a 95 per cent chance of hitting the target of the fiscal rule. But assessments of volatilities in order to work out the room for discretionary fiscal measures would lead to a questioning of the rule.[3] The more successful policy was, the more it would be assumed that the cycle would be overcome, and hence that greater resources were available for politically popular discretionary spending.

There are clearly fiscal as well as other influences (emanating from the global economy) that will shape monetary reactions. In the midst of the global financial crisis, and in the politically charged circumstances of a general election in May 2010, the Prime Minister, Gordon Brown, who ironically had been the principal political architect of the 1997 settlement, believed that the Governor's statements about fiscal consolidation constituted an illegitimate intervention by a technocrat into politics. The problem began in 2009, with an appearance before the Treasury Select Committee (on the day that King had also just been granted the first ever audience of a Governor of the Bank of England by the Queen). King seemed to be criticizing Brown's plans for an internationally coordinated fiscal stimulus: 'I think the fiscal position in the UK is not one where we could say, "Well, why don't we just engage in another significant round of fiscal expansion?"'[4] As Brown subsequently put it, 'During a revealing press conference in May 2010, Mervyn [King] claimed it was his right as governor to comment publicly on the overall fiscal position because of its impact on monetary policy. [. . .] Mervyn was thinking less about his remit as governor than his own personal attitude to debt. [. . .] Mervyn King failed to understand the limits of his unelected position.'[5] The irony of the 2009 and 2010 clashes was heightened by the fact that the Governor was the economist, Mervyn King, who had been a principal advocate, and also one of the major technical architects, of the 1997 arrangement and of the shift of the Bank to a nearly exclusive focus on monetary policy-making. By 2017, consultants to the Shadow Labour Chancellor urged moving large parts of the Bank's operations to Birmingham in order to ensure that the Bank was responsive to British industrial rather than purely financial needs. The shadow Chancellor, John McDonnell, commented, 'Our financial system isn't delivering enough investment across the whole country.'[6] His gesture recalled all the interwar polemics, as well as those of the 1960s and 1970s.

That the clash with Gordon Brown was not simply a question of a revival of the old suspicion of the centre-left of the actions of the Bank of England – a replay of the interwar debate about the Bankers' Ramp that brought down Labour in 1931, or of exchanges between Lord Cromer as Governor and Harold Wilson as Prime Minister in the mid-1960s – was shown a few years later. Then a new Governor's advice on the likely economic and financial consequences of a referendum vote to leave the European Union ('Brexit') was interpreted again as the illegitimate political action of 'experts'. Both before and after the June 2016 referendum, the Conservative Right turned to invective against economists, economics, and rationality, part of which was heaped on Bank of England Governor Mark Carney. The MP Jacob Rees-Mogg complained: 'What concerns me is that the influence and the strength of the Bank of England is in its Olympian detachment from day to day political partisanship. And in your evidence, in your letter and in your speech you are getting into political partisanship, removing yourself from your Olympian detachment, damaging the Bank's ability to regulate through influence, which has historically been just as important as the letter of the law.' Two previous failed Conservative Party leaders, Iain Duncan Smith and Michael Howard, spoke of 'startling dishonesty in the economic debate, with a woeful failure on the part of the Bank of England, the Treasury, and other official sources to present a fair and balanced analysis'. After the referendum, the former Chancellor Nigel Lawson called on Carney to resign: 'He's behaved disgracefully. I have known all six of his predecessors as Governor of the Bank of England and not one of them would have thought it proper to behave as he has done, particularly during the campaign when he joined in the chorus of scaremongering.'[7] Most dramatically of all, the new Prime Minister, and former Bank of England official, Theresa May, seemed to dedicate the most vivid and most controversial part of her speech at the October 2016 Conservative Party Conference to an attack on the Canadian Carney: 'Today, too many people in positions of power behave as though they have more in common with international elites than with the people down the road, the people they employ, the people they pass in the street. But if you believe you're a citizen of the world, you're a citizen of nowhere. You don't understand what the very word "citizenship" means.'[8]

May linked the general criticism of cosmopolitan experts to an attack on the distributional consequences of the low-interest-rate regime: diminishing the income of ordinary middle-class savers, while spurring asset price booms (in real estate and stocks) that were in the interest of the cosmopolitan elite. That critique had parallels in other countries: in the US, where Fed-bashing took off, or in Germany, where conservative politicians and economists made similar complaints about the European Central Bank's (ECB) low-interest regime. These arguments were often mounted in a broader context of complaint about economics: that economists and central banks had failed to predict or prevent the 2007–2008 collapse, and that in consequence their subsequent policy stances were similarly flawed.

The Bank of England had become the target of both the major British political parties. A caricature of the 1997 order was that it reduced a complicated policy framework to something very simple – a determination of an interest rate that might be set by a few skilled economists, or even by an algorithm (as in the approach of Stanford's John Taylor), which produced a 'Taylor rule' widely used as a retrospective check on central bank policy decisions. And then in the crisis, central bankers did much more, so that in some versions they appeared to be the rock stars who were saving the world, or in another common phrase 'the only grown-ups in the room'. But they were grown-ups with a distinct view. Some academic analysts began to argue that partisanship of central bank governors had a distinct and measurable policy impact.[9]

The pre-crisis focus on monetary policy had given a concentrated focus for a central bank, which became a hedgehog that was good at doing one thing (in Isaiah Berlin's famous metaphor). The crisis and the return of financial stability issues required central banks to multi-task feverishly, or to become 'foxes'. Paul Tucker noted that this sort of institution could no longer 'be the sole preserve or domain of macroeconomics PhDs'.[10]

The background to the extraordinary range of criticism of central banks was that policy had become more complicated, and that many of the practical steps to combat the crisis involved elements where distributive spillover effects were much clearer than in the case of monetary policy. Rescuing banks obviously involved a fiscal element, and the major initiatives came from the government, from the Treasury and particularly from the Prime Minister. Policies that required buying certain classes of assets on the central bank balance sheet also changed relative prices. As the Bank moved more into financial regulation, and made judgements about what sorts of lending might be desirable, it was also favouring and disadvantaging specific sectors of the economy. Even those close to the centre of Bank policy-making admitted that the environment had become more political. At the conference held to mark the twentieth anniversary of the Bank's independence, DeAnne Julius commented:

Instrument independence was good when people understood what the instrument was and how it worked. Once you go from buying government bonds to buying corporate bonds to loosening credit through things like funding for lending, and mixing that up with what's going on on the macroprudential side – where it can look like the bank is pushing lending with its interest rates policy but pulling it back with its regulatory policy – things get much more complicated.[11]

The new environment produced the conclusion that central bank monetary decisions always have budgetary implications and thus are always fiscal.[12]

In the happy or NICE (as Mervyn King termed it: 'non-inflationary consistently expansionary')[13] pre-crisis years, there had also been little concern with either cross-border or domestic financial stability issues. Instead, the attention of policy-makers, both in central banks and internationally, was focused on current account positions, usually characterized as 'global imbalances', pushed by what Ben Bernanke had called a 'global savings glut' driven by large emerging markets and especially China. Large (and increasing) current account deficits, driven by a housing boom, were financed through the banking system. In fact, the real threat originated with the much larger gross flows. After 2008, by contrast, the domestic financial system appeared threatened by international flows as the interbank market seized up in a sudden stop. Central banks then had to find alternative ways of providing liquidity.

The problem with the international system approach was that policy was not really made in one country, and there appeared to be little that UK policy-makers could undertake. Mervyn King attributed the problem to a bad mix of government policies: 'Across the world, government policies have, whether by design or accident, impeded movements in exchange rates and pushed long-term interest rates down to unsustainably low levels.'[14] When they looked at the domestic financial system, by contrast, there was plenty of observation, and successive Financial Stability Reviews presented a bewildering array of possible risks. The multiplicity of warnings made it hard to produce a clear policy response. In 2006, Paul Tucker delivered a clear analysis of the credit growth involved in the activities of entities labelled as 'Other Financial Corporations', and noted that 'there is little research on the macro-economic significance of OFC money'.[15] But, as Gillian Tett has eloquently noted, there was no adequate language at that time to describe the emergent problem.[16]

There is another derivation of the NICE acronym, by John Taylor, who thinks of the generation in the early 2000s of a Near Internationally Cooperative Equilibrium. The Bank's approach had emphasized good domestic policy. It was only in the financial crisis that a new mechanism for cooperation needed to be established very quickly. But it was clearly partial, and liable to political pushback from authorities who would think primarily in terms of national stabilization.

Faced with asset booms, the conventional wisdom was that it was hard reliably to identify a bubble, and in the absence of general inflationary development, policy should not target asset prices in a particular sector (even in a major part of the economy such as housing). A 'lean' versus 'clean' debate suggested that it would be cheaper and better to deal with possible problems after the events (clean-up) rather than attempt to tackle them pre-emptively (lean against the wind). That was the position taken by the Bank, and by the Treasury, from a very early stage: it is, for instance, evident in the Treasury's response to the 2000 Geneva report on central banking and asset bubbles (see p. 444).

After the crisis erupted, the Bank was criticized – as was the Federal Reserve and the ECB – for emergency measures that seemed to exceed its legal mandate. Former Fed Chairman Paul Volcker commented that the US central bank had 'taken actions that extend to the very edge of its lawful and implied powers, transcending certain long-embedded central banking principles and practices'.[17] Central banks were also heavily criticized for the scale and scope of their international engagement. The ECB's bond-purchasing programme was the occasion of a partially successful lawsuit by conservative German economists in that country's Constitutional Court. On the other hand, economists and economic historians pointed out that overstretch was a characteristic historical response, and one that was desirable in that it produced better outcomes.[18] At the conference on the anniversary of 1997, Stanley Fischer looked back and explained: 'History shows that governors can generally take actions which aren't legally within their remit, in times of crisis.'[19] After 2007, the new necessities were clear. As Alan Blinder put it, 'The principle [sic] objective of the central bank changes. It's no longer fighting inflation, which may be unnecessary or even counterproductive if a slump is imminent, but rather holding the financial system together. That's also the [US] Treasury's overriding goal.'[20]

Meanwhile, the British financial system had obviously become vulnerable. It had moved in the opposite direction to the machinery of economic and monetary policy. While the latter had been united and was then split up, the former had once been functionally separated, and then in the late twentieth century moved more and more to dominance by integrated all-finance giants. Innovation occurred within these large groups, though they often legally arranged themselves so that affiliated 'other financial corporations' remained outside the legal bounds of the parent corporation. In retrospect, it is apparent that the groups lacked both the knowledge and the technology (integrated information systems) to deal adequately with change. The old segmented financial system had relied on self-policing; as separated functions disappeared after 1986, the new order required more and more supervision. Supervisory failures on the part of the Bank of England had been the reason why the Financial Services Authority (FSA) was established in 1997, but by 2008 the new institution looked more ineffective than the old arrangements had ever been, despite a vigorous, dynamic and imaginative new chairman who took over on 20 September 2008, a few days after the collapse of Lehman Brothers brought the most intensive phase of the financial crisis.

The accumulation of risk in large agglomerations was obviously dangerous. Adair Turner, the new FSA chairman, now described banks as 'socially useless' and later explained that 'I think we – as the authorities, central banks, regulators, those involved today – are the inheritors of a 50-year-long, large intellectual and policy mistake.'[21] But there were limits to which the revolution could be remade. The putrid fish soup could not be converted back into the happy aquarium. In some cases, bank mergers looked like the best way of dealing with failed institutions, and in this way larger and more complex organizations were created (such as through the 2009 merger of Lloyds TSB and HBOS).

The best that could be done was to use supervision to enforce separation within entities. There was, in the aftermath of the 2011 Vickers Report, a legislative move to 'ring fence' banks' retail banking divisions from their investment banking arms to safeguard against high-risk activities and protect the consumer parts of the bank that should be safe (and boring).

The 2012 Financial Services Act abolished the FSA and established instead the Prudential Regulation Authority (PRA) as a part of the Bank of England, responsible for the supervision and regulation of around 1,500 banks, building societies, credit unions, insurers and major investment firms. It was also clear that the Bank should think more about the links between financial stability and monetary policy. In 2014, a new strategic initiative, with the slogan 'One Bank', aimed to 'break down cultural barriers with new ways of working and commitment to a different conduct'. It sought to 'promote connectivity' across the Monetary Policy Committee (MPC), the Financial Policy Committee, and the PRA, with more mechanisms for sharing of information and analyses.[22]

By 2017, faced with the institutional and economic challenges posed by Brexit, the Bank of England, the Treasury and also the newly (2013) established Financial Conduct Authority went on what was described as a coordinated 'charm offensive' to reassure European investment banks in the City that the UK would remain as an international centre open for business.[23] Something that looked rather more like the old Bank – and indeed the old macro-economic executive – was being recreated. It was more complex than the simple structure established in 1997, because it had to deal with a wider range of tasks. It was at the same time more modern than the old establishment, and could no longer rely on intuition and an implied code of conduct. It needed more formal rules, but those rules had to be designed for a complicated set of objectives in a complex world. The old theme of the Bank as a provider or guarantor of financial stability came back, with all the conceptual ambiguity over what financial stability really meant. Even advocacy for the City occasionally seemed to make a comeback. Maybe a 'modern' central bank in the sense of an inflation-targeting monetary institution was in the end too narrow a vision.

Both the fiscal and monetary dimensions matter to policy consistency. Sometimes central banks are described, in an analogy that goes back to Keynes, as conductors of an orchestra. There are different styles of conducting. Some famous figures such as Otto Klemperer or Karl Böhm seemed barely to indicate the rhythm that coordinates the orchestra; others engage in histrionic communication of deep emotion. How should a central bank conduct? Is it just a question of indicating the right beat for the economy? There was – and there is – no obvious and easy solution to the question of designing monetary management as part of a broader economic policy-making framework. What is involved in being the very model of a modern central bank is today no longer quite as obvious as it had been at the end of the twentieth century.

Biographies

Allen, William ('Bill') (1949–), joined the Bank in 1972; Manager, Gilt-Edged Division 1982–1986; Head of Money Market Operations Division 1986–1990; Head of Foreign Exchange Division 1990–1994; Deputy Director, Monetary Analysis 1994–1998; Deputy Director, Financial Market Operations 1999–2002; Director for Europe and Deputy Director, Financial Stability 2002–2003.

Arrowsmith, John (1944–), joined the Bank in 1966; Senior Adviser, Western Europe and EU affairs 1985–1994; British Consul Frankfurt 1999–2004.

Balls, Ed (1967–), *Financial Times* journalist 1990–1994, adviser to Gordon Brown 1994–2006; Economic Secretary to the Treasury 2006–2007.

Barnes, Roger (1937–), joined the Bank in 1961; Assistant Director, Bank of England and Head of Banking Supervision Division 1988–1993.

Blair, Tony (1953–), Leader of the Opposition 1994–1997, Prime Minister 1997–2007; Director, Hambros Bank Ltd 1993–1997.

Blunden, Sir George (1922–2012), joined the Bank in 1947; Executive Director 1976–1984; Non-Executive Director 1984–1986; Deputy Governor 1986–1990.

Brown, Gordon (1951–), Chancellor of the Exchequer 1997–2007; Prime Minister 2007–2010.

Callaghan, James, Baron Callaghan of Cardiff (1912–2005), Prime Minister 1976–1979.

Clarke, Kenneth (1940–), Chancellor of the Exchequer 1993–1997.

Coleby, Anthony ('Tony') (1935–), joined the Bank in 1961; Assistant Director in charge of the Money Markets Division 1980–1986; Adviser to the Governors 1986–1990; Executive Director 1990–1994.

Cooke, Peter (1932–), joined the Bank 1955; Adviser to the Governors 1973–1976; Head of Banking Supervision 1976–1985. Cooke joined the

Bank from Oxford in 1955. He was seconded to the Bank for International Settlements (BIS) and was the Personal Assistant to the Managing Director of the International Monetary Fund (1961–1965). After serving as Secretary to City Panel on Takeovers and Mergers, and a spell with the Chief Cashier's, Cooke became an Adviser to the Governors in 1973. In 1976, he became Head of Banking Supervision, and he was an Associate Director from 1982 until 1988.

Crockett, Sir Andrew Duncan (1943–2012), joined the Bank in 1966; Executive Director 1989–1993 responsible for International Affairs; General Manager of BIS until 1993–2003; President of JP Morgan Chase International.

Fforde, John (1921–2000), joined the Bank 1957; Adviser to the Governors 1964–1966, 1982–1984); Chief Cashier 1966–1970; Executive Director for Home Finance 1970–1982; author of 'The Bank of England and public policy 1941–1958' (1992).

Flemming, John (1941–2003), joined the Bank as Chief Adviser 1980–1984; Adviser to the Governors 1984–1988; Executive Director 1988–1991; Chief Economist at the European Bank for Reconstruction and Development 1991–1993.

Foot, Michael (1946–), joined the Bank 1969; Head of Foreign Exchange Division 1988–1990; Head of European Division 1990–1993; Head of Banking, Supervision Division 1993–1994; Deputy Director, Supervision and Surveillance 1994–1996; Executive Director 1996–1998; Managing Director and Head of Financial Supervision, FSA 1998–2004.

Footman, John (1952–), joined the Bank in 1969; Private Secretary to Governor 1986–1989; Head of Information Division 1989–1997; Deputy Director for Financial Structure 1997–1999; Personnel Director 1999–2003; Personnel and Executive Director for Central Services 2003–2013; Secretary to the Bank 1994–1997, 2009–.

Galpin, Rodney Desmond (1932–2011), joined the Bank in 1952; Private Secretary to Governor 1962–1966; Deputy Principal of Discount Office 1970–1974; Deputy Chief Cashier, Banking and Money Market Supervision (BAMMS) 1974–1978; Chief of Establishments 1978–1980; Chief of Corporate Services 1980–1982; Associate Director 1982–1984; Executive Director in 1984–1988, after which he left the Bank in 1988 to become Chairman and Group Chief Executive of Standard Chartered.

George, Sir Edward ('Eddie') (1938–2009), joined the Bank in 1962; Deputy Chief Cashier 1977–1980; Assistant Director Gilt-Edged Division 1980–1982; Executive Director, Home Finance 1982–1990; Deputy Governor 1990–1993; Governor 1993–2003.

Goodhart, Charles (1936–), joined the Bank in 1969; remained as adviser on monetary policy and then Chief Adviser 1980–1985; Norman Sosnow Professor of Banking and Finance at the London School of Economics 1985–2002; External Member of the MPC 1997–2000.

Heaton, Frances (1944–), Director General of the Panels on Takeovers and Mergers 1992–1994; first woman appointed as Non-Executive Director 1993–2001. Previously a Director of Lazard Brothers, she also spent ten years in HM Treasury and some time before that in the Department of Economic Affairs.

Howe, Geoffrey, Baron Howe of Aberavon (1926–2015), Chancellor of the Exchequer 1979–1983; Foreign Secretary 1983–1989.

Jackson, Patricia (1952–), Head of Financial Industry and Regulation Division covering banks, insurers and asset managers; Member of Basel Committee for Banking Supervision 1997–2004; Partner and Head of Banking Risk, Ernst & Young 2004–2013.

King, Mervyn, Baron King of Lothbury (1948–), Professor of Economics at the London School of Economics 1985–1995; joined the Bank as Non-Executive Director 1990; Executive Director 1991–1998; Deputy Governor 1998–2003; Governor 2003–2013.

Kohn, Don (1942–), Secretary of the US Federal Open Market Committee 1987–2002; Member of the Board of Governors of the Federal Reserve 2002–2010; Vice-Chairman 2006–2010; Member of Bank of England's Financial Policy Committee 2013–2018.

Laing, Hector, Baron Laing of Dunphail (1923–2010), Chairman United Biscuits (Holdings) plc 1972–1990; Non-Executive Director of Bank 1973–1991.

Lamont, Norman, Baron Lamont of Lerwick (1942–), Chief Secretary to the Treasury 1989–1990; Chancellor of the Exchequer 1990–1993.

Lawson, Nigel, Baron Lawson of Blaby (1932–), Financial Secretary to the Treasury 1979–1981; Secretary of State for Energy 1981–1983; Chancellor of the Exchequer 1983–1989.

Leigh-Pemberton, Robin (Lord Kingsdown) (1926–2013), Chairman National Westminster Bank 1977–1983; Governor of the Bank 1983–1993.

Loehnis, Anthony (1936–), seconded to the Bank from J. Henry Schroder Wagg & Co. 1977–1979; Executive Director 1981–1989.

McMahon, Kit (1927–), Fellow and Tutor in economics at Magdalen College Oxford 1960–1964; joined the Bank as Adviser to the Governors 1966–1970; Executive Director 1970–1980; Deputy Governor 1980–1986; Deputy Chairman and Chief Executive of Midland Bank 1986–1987; Chairman and Chief Executive 1987–1991.

Major, Sir John (1943–), Chief Secretary to the Treasury 1987–1989; Foreign Secretary 1989; Chancellor of the Exchequer 1989–1990; Prime Minister 1990–1997.

May, Theresa (1956–), joined the Bank 1977; financial consultant and senior adviser in International Affairs at the Association for Payment Clearing Services 1985–1997; Prime Minister 2016–2019.

Middleton, Sir Peter (1934 –), Permanent Secretary Treasury 1983–1991; Group Deputy Chairman Barclays and Executive Chairman of Barclays de Zoete Wedd 1991–1997; Chairman of Barclays Capital 1997–2004; Barclays Group Chief Executive 1998–1999; UK Chairman of Marsh & McLennan Companies 2007–2013.

Morse, Sir Jeremy (1928–2016), joined the Bank as Adviser to the Governors 1964–1965; Executive Director 1965–1972; Chairman of the Deputies of the Committee on Reform of the International Monetary System (the Committee of Twenty or C20) 1972–1974; Deputy Chairman Lloyds Bank 1975–1977 then Chairman 1977–1993; Non-Executive Director of the Bank 1993–1997.

Page, John Brangwyn (1923–2005), joined the Bank of England in 1948; Chief Cashier 1970–1980; Executive Director 1980–1982.

Peddie, Peter Charles (1932–2009), Partner in Freshfields 1992; Adviser to the Governors and Head of the Legal Unit 1992–1996.

Pennant-Rea, Rupert (1984–), joined the Bank in 1973; joined the Economist 1977; Editor of the Economist 1986–1993; Deputy Governor 1993–1995; Chairman, Economist Group 2009–2018.

Petrie, Peter (Charles) (1932–), UK Ambassador to Belgium 1985–1989; Adviser to the Governors on European and Parliamentary Affairs 1989–2003.

Plenderleith, Ian (1943–), joined the Bank in 1965; Governor's private secretary 1976–1979; Head of the Gilt-Edged Division 1982–1990; Assistant Director 1986–1990; Associate Director 1990–1994; Executive Director 1994–2002; Deputy Governor at the South African Reserve Bank 2003–2005.

Price, Lionel (1946–), joined the Bank 1967; Alternate Executive Director, IMF 1979–1981; Head of European Division 1988–1990; Head of Economics Division 1990–1994; Director of Studies at CCBS 1990–1994.

Quinn, Brian (1936–), joined the Bank in 1970; Head of the Information Division 1977–1982; Assistant Director, Banking Supervision 1982–1986; Head of Banking Supervision 1986–1988; Executive Director with responsibility for the Banking and Banking Supervision Departments 1988–1996.

Richardson, Gordon, Baron Richardson of Duntisbourne (1915–2010); Chairman of J. Henry Schroder Wagg 1962–1972 and Schroders 1966–1973; Governor 1973–1983.

Scholar, Sir Michael (1982–), Deputy Secretary Treasury 1987–1993.

Scholar, Sir Thomas (1968–), Principal Private Secretary to Chancellor of Exchequer 1997–2001.

Scholey, David (1935–), Director of Bank of England 1981–1998; Chairman of S. G. Warburg 1985–1995.

Thatcher, Margaret, Baroness Thatcher (1925–2013), Prime Minister 1979–1990.

Thompson, Christopher (1944–1997), joined the Bank 1966; supervisor of the UK merchant banks until 1995.

Trundle, John (1957–), joined the Bank in 1979; Head of Payment and Settlement within Financial Structure (Financial Stability) 1996–1998; Head of Market Infrastructure within Financial Stability 1999–2003; Head of Business Continuity within Central Services 2004–2005; left the Bank in 2005.

Tucker, Sir Paul (1958–), joined the Bank in 1980; Principal Private Secretary to Governor 1989–1993; Head of Gilt-Edged and Money Markets Division 1994–1997; Head of Monetary Assessment and Strategy Division 1997–1998; Deputy Director of Financial Stability 1999–2002; Executive Director for Markets 2002–2009; Deputy Governor 2009–2013; Chair of the Systemic Risk Council 2015–.

Wadhwani, Sushil (1959–), worked with Goldman Sachs 1991–1995 and Tudor Investments 1995–1999; Member of MPC 1999–2002.

Weatherstone, Sir Dennis (1930–2008), Chairman of JP Morgan 1990–1994; member of the Board of Banking Supervision 1995–2001.

Walker, Sir David (1939–), UK Treasury 1961–1977; joined Bank as Chief Adviser 1977–1980; Executive Director 1982–1986 with responsibility for finance and industry; Chairman of Johnson Matthey 1985–1988; Deputy Chairman of Lloyds 1992–1994; Chairman of the Securities and Investment Board (SIB) 1988–1992; Non-Executive Director of Bank 1988–1993.

Wood, Geoffrey (1945–), Special Adviser at the Bank and Professor of Economics at the City University.

Appendix 2

The History of Monetary Aggregates

Date	Measure	Event	Detail
1970	M1	First published	• Notes and coins in circulation with the public; *plus* • UK private sector's (defined as non-bank private sector) sterling current accounts held with banks in the UK
	M2	First published	• M1; *plus* • UK private sector's sterling time deposits held with deposit banks and similar accounts held with discount houses
	M3	First published	• Notes and coins in circulation with the public; *plus* • UK private and public sectors' sterling and non-sterling deposits held with the UK banking sector.
1972	M2	Discontinued	Distinction between deposit accounts with deposit banks and discount houses, and similar deposit accounts with other banks was no longer valid.
1975	M1	Re-defined	'Current accounts' replaced by a more precisely defined category of sight deposits, which included

(continued)

467

(continued)

Date	Measure	Event	Detail
			money at call and money placed overnight. This allowed funds placed by the UK private sector with discount houses that fell within the new definition of sight deposits to be included in M1.
1977	£M3	Introduced	M3, excluding foreign currency deposits
1980	PSL1	Introduced	• M1; *plus* • UK private sector's sterling time deposits with an original maturity of up to two years held with banks in the UK; *plus* • UK private sector's holdings of sterling bank certificates of deposit, money market instruments (banks bills, Treasury bills, local authority deposits) and certificates of tax deposits
	PSL2	Introduced	• PSL1; *plus* • UK private sector's holdings of building society deposits (excluding term shares and SAYE[3]) • UK private sector's holdings of National Savings instruments (excluding certificates, SAYE and other long-term deposits) • Building societies' holdings of bank deposits and money market instruments were excluded.
1981	Wide monetary base (M0)	Introduced	• Notes and coins in circulation with the public; *plus* • Banks' till money; *plus* • Banks' operational balances with the Bank of England, after December 1983 was referred to as M0.
1982	All measures	Re-definition of UK banking sector	The UK banking sector as defined for the calculation of monetary

Date	Measure	Event	Detail
			aggregates was extended and called the monetary sector. It included all recognised banks and licensed deposit takers[4] (LDTs), the National Girobank, the trustee savings banks, the Banking Department of the Bank of England, and those banking institutions incorporated in the Channel Island and Isle of Man which opted to comply with the new monetary control arrangements.
	M2	Re-introduced	• Notes and coins in circulation with the public; *plus*
			• UK private sector's non-interest-bearing sterling sight deposits with banks in the UK; *plus*
			• UK private sector's interest-bearing retail sterling deposits with banks in the UK
			Retail was defined by reference to size, transferability and maturity.
1983	M2	Re-defined	Expanded to include:
			• all shares and deposits with building societies that were within one month of maturity; and
			• deposits with the National Savings Bank ordinary account
1984	M0	Re-defined	Published as a weekly average instead of being measured as a level at the end of each banking month
	M3, £M3	Re-defined	Re-defined to exclude the UK public sector's sterling deposits with banks in the UK
1986	PSL2	Re-defined	Expanded to include:

(continued)

(continued)

Date	Measure	Event	Detail
			• building society term shares and SAYE deposits; and
			• UK private sector's sterling deposits with an original term longer than two years held with banks in the UK
1987	M3, £M3, M3 c	Re-named	£M3 renamed M3 Old M3 renamed M3 c
	M4	Introduced	UK private sector's (for first time defined as the non-bank non-building society private sector) holdings of:
			• sterling notes and coins; *plus*
			• sterling deposits (including certificates of deposit) with banks in the UK; *plus*
			• Building society shares, deposits and sterling certificates of deposit.
	M5	Re-named	New name for PSL2.
	PSL1	Discontinued	PSL1 discontinued Last published in *BEQB* May 1987 Statistical annex
1990	M3, M1, M3 c	Discontinued	Ceased to be published due to the conversion of Abbey National Building Society to a bank, which caused a major break in each series. The non-interest-bearing component of M1 (nib M1) continued to be published.
	M4 c	Introduced	• M4; *plus*
			• UK private sector's foreign currency deposits with banks and building societies in the UK
1991	M2	Re-defined	This was re-defined to form a subset of M4. Deposits with the National Savings Bank and building societies' holdings of notes and coins were removed.
	Nib M1, M5, M4 c	Discontinued	No longer published

Date	Measure	Event	Detail
1992	M3 H	Introduced	• M4; *plus* • UK private sector's foreign currency deposits held with banks and building societies in the UK; *plus* • UK public corporations' sterling and foreign currency deposits held with banks and building societies in the UK
1993	M2	Re-defined	'Retail' deposits were re-defined. Building societies' 'retail' deposits included all shares held by, or sums deposited by, individuals. Banks' 'retail' deposits are defined as those which arise from a customer's acceptance of an advertised rate (including nil) for a particular product. This series is also known as the 'retail' component of M4.
	Divisia	Introduced	The Divisia index is based on the components of M4, weighted according to their liquidity.
1997	M2, M3 H, M4	Re-defined	Any bank in the Channel Islands and Isle of Man that had 'opted in' to the monetary control arrangements was removed from the monetary sector. Business with the Channel Islands and Isle of Man was re-classified as non-resident.
1999	Estimate of euro-area M3 for the UK	Introduced	This measure provides an estimate of the European Central Bank's broad money aggregate M3, but for the UK. This series replaced the M3 H European harmonized aggregate that was previously published for comparison purposes.

This table was prepared by Ryland Thomas. See also: Jagjit S Chadha, Ana Rincon-Aznar, Sylaja Srinivasan and Ryland Thomas, A Century of High Frequency UK Macro-economic Statistics: A Data Inventory, ESCoE Technical Report 03, April 2019.

Notes

Introductory

1 Paul Krugman, 'Money: The Brave New Uncertainty of Mervyn King', *New York Review of Books*, 14 July 2016, nybooks.com/articles/2016/07/14/money-brave-new-uncertainty-mervyn-king/

2 R. S. Sayers, *The Bank of England 1891–1944: Volume I* (Cambridge, UK: Cambridge University Press, 1976), 1.

3 Walter Bagehot, *The English Constitution*, R. H. S. Crossman, ed. (London: Collins/Fontana, 1963, originally published in 1867), 65.

4 Fred Hirsch, *The Pound Sterling: A Polemic* (London: Victor Gollancz, 1965), 145.

5 Fynn Kydland and Edward Prescott, 'Rules Rather than Discretion: The Inconsistency of Optimal Plans', *Journal of Political Economy* vol. 85 (1977): 473–490.

6 Sylvester Eijffinger and Eric Schaling, 'Central Bank Independence in Twelve Industrial Countries', *Banca Nazionale del Lavoro Quarterly Review* vol. 184 (March 1993): 49–89. Sylvester C. W. Eijffinger and Jakob de Haan, 'The Political Economy of Central-Bank Independence', *Princeton Studies in International Economics* no. 19 (1996): International Economics Section, Department of Economics Princeton University.

7 Mervyn King, 'Monetary Policy: Rhyme or Reason?' *BEQB* vol. 37, Q1 (February 1997): 96.

8 See Andrew G. Haldane, 'A Little More Conversation, A Little Less Action', speech given at Federal Reserve Bank of San Francisco Macroeconomics and Monetary Policy Conference, 31 March 2017.

9 Kevin Warsh, 'Transparency and the Bank of England's Monetary Policy Committee', available at hoover.org/sites/default/files/transparency_and_the_bank_of_englands_monetary_policy_committee.pdf (December 2014); N. Dincer and B. Eichengreen, 'Central Bank Transparency and Independence: Updates', *New Measures' International Journal of Central Banking* vol. 38 no. 3 (2014): 189–253.

10 Hirsch, *The Pound Sterling*, 145.

11 Daniel M. Abramson, *Building the Bank of England: Money, Architecture, Society 1694–1942* (New Haven, CT: Yale University Press, 2005), 212–213.

12 ECB Press Release, 13 January 2005: ecb.europa.eu/press/pr/date/2005/html/pr050113_2.en.html.

13 Douglas Holmes, *Economy of Words: Communicative Imperatives in Central Banks* (Chicago: University of Chicago Press, 2014), 54.

14 Chris Giles, 'Damaging Culture at Court of "Sun King"', *Financial Times*, 1 November 2012, p. 3. Alistair Darling, *Back from the Brink* (London: Atlantic Books, 2011), 70.

15 Andrew G. Haldane, 'Halfway Up the Stairs', *Central Banking Journal*, 5 August 2014. Paul Einzig, *Montagu Norman: A Study in Financial Statesmanship* (Abingdon, UK: Routledge, 1932), 150, simply states that Norman was upholding the 'traditional policy' of 'never explain, never apologize'. John Hargrave, *Professor Skinner Alias Montagu Norman* (London: Wells Gardner, Darton, 1939), 191.

16 Andrew Boyle, *Montagu Norman: A Biography* (London: Cassell, 1967), 217.

17 *The Bank of England Today* (London: Institute of Bankers, 1964), 39.

18 David M. Jones, *Understanding Central Banking: The New Era of Activism* (Abingdon: Routledge, 2014), xii.

19 Adam Smith and Edwin Cannan, ed. *An Inquiry into the Nature and Causes of the Wealth of Nations* (Chicago: University of Chicago Press, 1967, originally published in 1776), 341. See also Hugh Rockoff, 'Upon Daedalian Wings of Paper Money: Adam Smith and the Crisis of 1772', NBER Working Paper No. 15594, December 2009.

20 Above all, see Walter Bagehot, *Lombard Street: A Description of the Money Market* (New York: John Wiley, 1999, 1873); Ralph Hawtrey, *The Art of Central Banking* (London: Longmans, 1932); Charles A. E. Goodhart, *The Evolution of Central Banks* (Cambridge, MA: MIT Press, 1988); and the fine modern survey of these theories, Stefano Ugolini, *The Evolution of Central Banking: Theory and History* (London: Palgrave Macmillan, 2017).

21 Curzio Giannini, *The Age of Central Banks* (Cheltenham: Edward Elgar, 2011).

22 A. J. P. Taylor, *English History: 1914–1945* (Oxford: Oxford University Press, 1965), 297.

23 Mervyn King, *The End of Alchemy: Money, Banking, and the Future of the Global Economy* (New York: Norton, 2016), 78.

24 'Economic Commentary', *BEQB* vol. 17, Q2 (June 1977): 151.

25 Capie, *The Bank of England*, 703.

26 Margaret Allen, *The Times Guide to International Finance: How the World Money System Works* (London: Times Books, 1991), 36; also Stephen Fay, *Portrait of an Old Lady: Turmoil at the Bank of England* (Harmondsworth: Penguin, 1988), 87.

27 See Capie, *The Bank of England*, 596.

28 Anthony C. Hotson, *Respectable Banking: The Search for Stability in London's Money and Credit Markets Since 1695* (Cambridge: Cambridge University Press, 2017), 4–5, 109.

29 Ranald C. Michie, *British Banking: Continuity and Change from 1694 to the Present* (Oxford: Oxford University Press, 2016), 21.

30 Stanley Fischer, 'Modern Central Banking', in Forrest Capie, Charles Goodhart, Stanley Fischer and Norbert Schnadt, eds., *The Future of Central Banking – The Tercentenary Symposium of the Bank of England* (Cambridge: Cambridge University Press, 1994), 304.

31 See for a similar analysis Ulrich Bindseil, 'The Operational Target of Monetary Policy and the Rise and Fall of Reserve Position Doctrine', ECB Working Paper No. 372, June 2004, p. 38.

32 Bank for International Settlements, *Issues in the Governance of Central Banks: A report from the Central Bank Governance Group, Chair: Guillermo Ortiz, Governor of the Bank of Mexico*, May 2009, p. 18.

33 On the origins of the Federal Reserve system, see Peter Conti-Brown, *The Power and Independence of the Federal Reserve* (Princeton: Princeton University Press, 2016), 15–39.

34 Available at legislation.govt.nz/act/public/1989/0157/latest/DLM199364.html

35 BoE, G1/264, Official Report of House of Lords Debate, 22 January 1946; Official Report of Committee Stage, 31 January 1946, and 18 July 1949, governor's note.

36 John Fforde, *The Bank of England and Public Policy, 1941–1958* (Cambridge: Cambridge University Press, 1992), 12–14.

37 Fforde, *The Bank of England,* 13; Forrest Capie, *The Bank of England: 1950s to 1979* (New York: Cambridge University Press, 2010), 35.

38 BoE, 7A320/11, 14 February 1990, George Blunden, Julian Hodge Bank Annual Lecture: The Role of the Central Bank.

39 House of Commons, Treasury and Civil Service Committee, Session 1993–1994, 'The Role of the Bank of England, First Report, Evidence', 20 October 1993, 71 (Question 242).

40 House of Commons, Treasury and Civil Service Committee, Session 1993–1994, 'The Role of the Bank of England, First Report', 8 December 1993, vii.

41 BoE, 18A55/1, 9 December 1993, Governor's Bilateral, 8 December 1993.

42 Interview with Paul Tucker, October 2017.

43 BoE, 13A231/1, 19 August 1983, McMahon: Succession at Court.

44 BoE, 13A231/1, 24 June 1983, Kit McMahon: Introductory Remarks at Court.

45 BoE, 13A231/12, 30 August 1990.

46 BoE, 12A110/6, 10 March 1994: The Court.

47 Lord Richardson of Duntisbourne (Gordon Richardson) obituary, *Daily Telegraph*, 24 January 2010: telegraph.co.uk/news/obituaries/politics-obituaries/7066584/Lord-Richardson-of-Duntisbourne-KG.html

48 William Keegan, 'Lord Richardson of Duntisbourne (Gordon Richardson) Obituary', *The Independent*, 8 February 2010: independent.co.uk/news/obituaries/lord-richardson-of-duntisbourne-governor-of-the-bank-of-england-during-the-troubled-times-of-the-1893352.html

49 Fay, *Portrait of an Old Lady,* 69.

50 Capie, *The Bank of England,* 829.

51 Anthony Sampson, *The Moneylenders: Bankers in a Dangerous World* (London: Coronet, 1982), 144.

52 Christopher Dow, Graham Hacche and Christopher Taylor, eds., *Inside the Bank of England: Memoirs of Christopher Dow, Chief Economist 1973–84* (Basingstoke: Palgrave Macmillan, 2013), 88.

53 'Lord Richardson of Duntisbourne Obituary', *Daily Telegraph,* 24 January 2010: telegraph.co.uk/news/obituaries/politics-obituaries/7066584/Lord-Richardson-of-Duntisbourne-KG.html

54 Fay, *Portrait of an Old Lady*, 12.

55 Dow, *Inside the Bank of England*, 126.

56 BoE, G1/567, 3 November 1978, Galpin: Management Style (draft).

57 BoE, G1/567, 28 February 1979, Croham: Directors and Management.

58 Dow, *Inside the Bank of England*, 124.

59 Capie, *The Bank of England*, 828.

60 Obituary of John Page, *Central Banking,* 20 May 2005: centralbanking.com/central-banking-journal/feature/2072346/obituary-john-page-1923–2005

61 Email of Sir Angus Deaton, 6 December 2019.

62 BoE, G1/567, 5 November 1979, G. Blunden: The Court.

63 BoE, G1/567, 8 January 1980, Galpin: Senior Management Structure.

64 John Fforde, 'Setting Monetary Objectives', *BEQB* vol. 23, Q2 (June 1983): 200. This was originally a paper presented at a Federal Reserve Bank of New York conference on monetary targeting in May 1982. See also Anthony Hotson, 'British Monetary Targets, 1976 to 1987: A View from the Fourth Floor of the Bank of England', LSE Financial Markets Group Paper Series, Special Paper 190, April 2010.

65 Hirsch, *The Pound Sterling*, 143.

66 BoE, 10A114/24, John C. Townend, November 1990, 'The Orientation of Monetary Policy and the Monetary Policy Decision-Making Process in the United Kingdom'.

67 Walter Bagehot, *Lombard Street: A Description of the Money Market* (New York: John Wiley, 1999, originally published in 1873), 300.

68 *The London Discount Market: A Guide to Its Role in the Economy and Its Contribution to Industry and Finance*, 3rd ed. (London: Gerrard and National, 1981), 8.

69 BoE, G18/2, 15 March 1944, Note: The Selection of Directors.

70 Peter J. Laugharne, 'The Treasury and Civil Service Select Committee during the Thatcher Administration', *Parliamentary History* vol. 26 (2007): 225–244.

71 BoE, 6A163/27, Minutes of Evidence Taken Before the TCSSC, 28 January 1985, 8.

72 Paul Tucker, *Unelected Power: The Quest for Legitimacy in Central Banking and the Regulatory State* (Princeton: Princeton University Press, 2018), 374. Also Cheryl Schonhardt-Bailey, 'Monetary Policy Oversight in Comparative Perspective: Britain and America during the Financial Crisis', *London School of Economics* no. 3 (2014).

73 BoE, G4/211, 12 April 1984: The Court.

74 Fay, *Portrait of an Old Lady*, 201.

75 Philip Geddes, *Inside the Bank of England* (London: Boxtree, 1987), 2.

76 Andrew G. Haldane, 'A Little More Conversation, a Little Less Action', speech given at Federal Reserve Bank of San Francisco Macroeconomics and Monetary Policy Conference, 31 March 2017.

77 BoE, ADM33/13, Memo: New Men for a New Age, no date [documentation prepared for R. S. Sayers in the early 1970s].

78 BoE, 7A148/3, 22 June 1987, Availability and Deployment of Economists.

79 BoE, 1A68/1, 2 October 1978, Couzens, The EMS: An Interim Assessment.

80 See Donald Brash, 'New Zealand's Remarkable Reforms', the Fifth IEA Annual Hayek Memorial Lecture, Institute of Economic Affairs Occasional Paper no. 100, 1996.

81 BoE, 12A110/17, 18 November 1998, Footman note.

Foreign Fetters

1 Richard Roberts, *When Britain Went Bust* (London: OMFIF, 2017), 10.
2 Capie, *The Bank of England,* 745.
3 Roberts, *When Britain Went Bust,* 40.
4 Douglas Wass, *Decline to Fall: The Making of British Macro-Economic Policy and the 1976 IMF Crisis* (Oxford: Oxford University Press, 2008), 336.
5 Edmund Dell, *A Hard Pounding: Politics and Economic Crisis 1974–76* (Oxford: Oxford University Press, 1991), 189.
6 BoE, 7A133/1, 25 October 1976, Richardson to Healey.
7 Roberts, *When Britain Went Bust,* 83.
8 BoE, 7A133/1, 26 November 1976, McMahon: Conversation with the Chancellor on Sunday night. Capie, *The Bank of England,* 754.
9 Peter Jenkins, *Mrs. Thatcher's Revolution: The Ending of the Socialist Era* (London: Jonathan Cape, 1987), 18.
10 Roberts, *When Britain Went Bust,* 12.
11 TNA, T 386/16, 16 July 1976, Wass to PPS: 'Monetary Targets'.
12 'Economic Policy and the IMF Credit', quoted in Roberts, *When Britain Went Bust,* 93.
13 Dell, *A Hard Pounding,* 230–231; Leo Pliatzky, *Getting and Spending: Public Expenditure, Employment and Inflation* (Oxford: Basil Blackwell, 1982), 150.
14 Wass, *Decline to Fall,* 272.
15 Ibid., 298.
16 Quoted in Wass, *Decline to Fall,* 247.
17 Capie, *The Bank of England,* 756.
18 Denis Healey, *The Time of My Life* (New York: Norton, 1990), 433.
19 Wass, *Decline to Fall,* 309.
20 This was also the title of a book by Alec Cairncross and Kathleen Burk, *'Goodbye, Great Britain': The 1976 IMF Crisis* (New Haven, CT: Yale University Press, 1992).
21 The supplementary special deposits scheme, *Bank of England Quarterly Bulletin* Q1 (1982): 74–85. See also Capie, *The Bank of England,* 521–523.
22 The corset could also be circumvented by a move into commercial bills.
23 Catherine R. Schenk, 'The Origins of the Eurodollar Market in London, 1955–1963', *Explorations in Economic History* vol. 35 (April 1998): 221–238.
24 BoE, 7A361/3, Bill Clowser, Exchange Control Enforcement, no date; *Private Eye* 15 October 1976 'In the City'.
25 Capie, *The Bank of England,* 766.
26 BoE, 7A88/1, 13 July 1977, McMahon: London as an International Financial Centre.
27 TNA PREM 19/437, 11 October 1979, Howe to Thatcher: Exchange Control.
28 BoE, EC5/647, 20 August 1979, Dawkins: The Future of Exchange Control.
29 BoE, 7A88/1, 13 July 1977, McMahon: London as an International Financial Centre.
30 Dow, *Memoirs,* 143.
31 M. S. Mendelsohn, 'British Life Exchange Controls for First Time since 1938', *The American Banker,* 24 October 1979.
32 BoE, 3A148/1, 31 October 1979, C. A. Stremes: Note.

33 Gordon T. Pepper and Michael J. Oliver, *Monetarism under Thatcher: Lessons for the Future* (London: Edward Elgar, 2001), 20.

34 BoE, 13A231/1, 17 May 1983, McMahon: Exchange Control.

The Performance of the UK Economy

1 Andrew Sentance, 'UK Macroeconomic Policy and Economic Performance', in Tony Buxton, Paul Chapman and Paul Temple, eds., *Britain's Economic Performance* (Abingdon: Routledge, 1988), 38.

2 BoE, 6A163/25, 21 March 1984, Leigh-Pemberton: Minutes of Evidence before TCSSC, 12.

3 J. C. R. [Christopher] Dow, *The Management of the British Economy* (Cambridge: Cambridge University Press, 1964) 497; also *Major Recessions: Britain and the World 1920–1995* (Oxford: Oxford University Press, 1998), 260. The point about Dow's consistency is made by Roger Middleton, 'Economic Policy and Management', in Roderick Floud, Jane Humphries and Paul Johnson, eds., *The Cambridge Economic History of Modern Britain, Volume 1: 1700–1870*, 2nd ed., (Cambridge: Cambridge University Press, 2014), 497.

4 Such increases in VAT are a hallmark of a centre-right approach to fiscal policy: see Vitor Gaspar, Sanjeev Gupta and Carlos Mulas-Granados, eds., *Fiscal Politics* (Washington, DC: IMF, 2017), 9.

5 Christine Ennew, Sir David Greenaway and Geoffrey Reed, 'Further Evidence on Effective Tariffs and Effective Protection in the UK', *Oxford Bulletin of Economics and Statistics* vol. 52, no. 1 (1990): 69–78; David S. Jacks, Christopher M. Meissner and Dennis Novy, 'Trade Costs 1870–2000', *American Economic Review: Papers and Proceedings* vol. 98, no. 2 (2008): 529–534.

6 See Nauro Campos and Fabrizio Coricelli, 'EU Membership or Thatcher's Structural Reforms: What Drove the Great British Reversal?' CEPR DP 11856 (2017); also Michael Gasiorek, Alasdair Smith and Anthony J. Venables, 'The Accession of the UK to the EC: A Welfare Analysis', *Journal of Common Market Studies* vol. 40, no. 3 (2002): 425–447; and Harald Badinger, Growth Effects of Economic Integration: Evidence from the EU Member States, *Review of World Economics / Weltwirtschaftliches Archiv* vol. 141, no. 1 (2005): 50–78.

7 Simon Lee, 'The British Model of Political Economy', in Matt Beech and Simon Lee, eds. *Ten Years of New Labour* (Basingstoke: Palgrave Macmillan, 2008), 17–34.

8 Paul R. Krugman, *The Age of Diminished Expectations: U.S. Economic Policy in the 1990s* (Cambridge, MA: MIT Press, 1994), 11.

9 Charles R. Bean and James Symons, 'Ten Years of Mrs. T.', NBER *Macroeconomics Annual* vol. 4, no. 1 (1989): 15.

10 Peter Riddell, *The Thatcher Government* (Oxford: M. Robertson, 1983), 78. See also Anthony Hotson, 'British Monetary Targets 1976 to 1987: A View from the Fourth Floor of the Bank of England', Financial Markets Group Special Papers 190, 2010.

11 Nicholas Crafts, 'The Economic Legacy of Mrs. Thatcher', *Vox*, 7 April 2013, available at: voxeu.org/article/economic-legacy-mrs-thatcher

12 Nicholas Crafts, 'Deindustrialisation and Economic Growth', *Economic Journal* vol. 106, no. 1 (January 1996): 172–183, quote from p. 178.

13 Stanley Fischer, 'Recent Developments in Macroeconomics', *Economic Journal* vol. 98, no. 391 (June 1988): 331.

14 See Sebastian Mallaby, *The Man Who Knew: The Life and Times of Alan Greenspan* (London: Bloomsbury, 2016), 335.

15 See Martin Fitzgerald, 'Better Data Brings Reward at the Bank of England', *MIT Sloan Management Record,* 26 May 2016.

16 See Nicholas Bloom, M. Ayhan Kose and Marco E. Terrones, 'Held Back by Uncertainty', *Finance and Development* vol. 50, no. 1 (2013): 38–41.

17 Abigail Haddow, Chris Hare, John Hooley and Tamarah Shakir, 'Macroeconomic Uncertainty: What Is It, How Can We Measure It and Why Does It Matter?', *BEQB* Q2 (2013): 100–109.

The Inexplicable in Pursuit of the Uncontrollable

1 15 May 1979, Queen's speech, as quoted in Joseph Whitaker, *Whitaker's Almanack 1980* (London: J. Whitaker & Sons, Ltd., 1979), 361.

2 House of Commons Parliamentary Papers Online: fc95d419f4478b3b6e5f-3f71d0fe2b653c4f00f32175760e96e7.r87.cf1.rackcdn.com

3 *Weekend World*, ITN, 9 November 1980, quoted in Edward Nelson, 'Reaffirming the Influence of Milton Friedman on U.K. Economic Policy', February 2017.

4 Nigel Lawson, *The View from No. 11: Memoirs of a Tory Radical* (New York: Bantam Press, 1992), 45.

5 William Keegan, *Mrs. Thatcher's Economic Experiment* (New York: Penguin, 1985), 103.

6 See Fred Hirsch and John H. Goldthorpe, eds., *The Political Economy of Inflation* (Cambridge, MA: Harvard University Press, 1978).

7 Eric Roll, *Independent and Accountable: A New Mandate for the Bank of England* (Washington, DC: CEPR, 1993), 8.

8 See Edward Nelson, 'What Does the UK's Monetary Policy and Inflation Experience Tell Us about the Transmission Mechanism?' CEPR Discussion Paper No. 3047, August 2001, 4–5.

9 Edward Nelson, 'An Overhaul of Doctrine: The Underpinning of UK Inflation Targeting', *Economic Journal* vol. 119, no. 538 (2009): 333–368.

10 Roy Harrod, 'Imperfect Competition, Aggregate Demand and Inflation', *Economic Journal* vol. 82, no. 325 (1972): 392–401.

11 Thomas Balogh, *Labour and Inflation* (London: Fabian Society, 1970), quoted in Edward Nelson, 'What Does the UK's Monetary Policy and Inflation Experience Tell Us about the Transmission Mechanism?' CEPR Discussion Paper No. 3047, November 2001, p. 21.

12 Conservative Party manifesto 1970, available at: conservativemanifesto.com/1970/1970-conservative-manifesto.shtml

13 Peter Clarke, *Hope and Glory: Britain 1900–1990* (London: Allen Lane, 1996), 347.

14 K. Holden, D. Peel and John L. Thompson, *Economics of Wage Controls* (Basingstoke: Palgrave Macmillan, 1987), 10–11.

15 Gordon Richardson, 'Reflections on the Conduct of Monetary Policy', Mais Lecture, *BEQB* (March 1978): 32 and 34. The speech was largely written by Charles

Goodhart, with some major contributions by Christopher Dow: see Capie, *Bank of England*, 686.

16 Dow, *Inside the Bank of England*, 96.

17 Ibid., 88.

18 Lord Richardson obituary in *Guardian:* theguardian.com/theguardian/2010/jan/24/ lord-richardson-of-duntisbourne-obituary

19 Interview with Sir Paul Tucker.

20 See Mervyn King, 'Monetary Policy Instruments: The UK Experience', *BEQB* Q3 (August 1994): 271.

21 As suggested by Anthony Hotson, 'British Monetary Targets 1976 to 1987', LSE Financial Markets Group Paper Series (April 2010): 13. For the multiple targets, see *BEQB* vol. 17, Q2 (June 1977): 151–152.

22 Anthony Hotson believes that DCE reflected the Bank's rather than the IMF's policy preferences, and thus was not really imposed on the UK.

23 Domestic Credit Expansion, *BEQB* vol. 9, Q3 (September 1969): 363–382; Capie, *Bank of England*, 452.

24 See Edmund Dell, *A Hard Pounding: Politics and Economic Crisis 1974–76* (Oxford: Oxford University Press, 1991), 273; Harold James, *International Monetary Cooperation Since Bretton Woods* (New York: Oxford University Press, 1996), 281; Richard Roberts, *When Britain Went Bust: The 1976 IMF Crisis* (London: OMFIF, 2016), 107.

25 8 May 1977, Declaration: Downing Street Summit Conference: g8.utoronto.ca/sum mit/1977london/communique.html

26 Speech of 17 January 1977, in *Bank of England Quarterly Bulletin* vol. 3 (1977): 48–50.

27 European Community Committee of Central Bank Governors, meeting 119, Basel, 14 March 1978.

28 Michael D. Bordo, 'The Contribution of a Monetary History of the United States: 1867 to 1960 to Monetary History', in Michael D. Bordo, ed., *Money, History and International Finance: Essays in Honor of Anna J. Schwartz* (Chicago: University of Chicago Press for the NBER, 1989), 51.

29 David Laidler and Michael Parkin, 'The Demand for Money in the United Kingdom 1956–1967: Preliminary Estimates', *The Manchester School* 38 (3 September 1970): 187–208.

30 See David Laidler, 'Monetarism: An Interpretation and an Assessment', *Economic Journal* vol. 91, no. 361 (March 1981): 1–28. Also Graham Hacche, 'Demand for Money', *BEQB* Q3 (1974): 284–305.

31 Christopher Dow, *Major Recessions: Britain and the World, 1920–1995* (Oxford: Oxford University Press, 1998).

32 BoE 2A128/4, McMahon to Posner, 16 September 1970, quoted in Capie, *Bank of England*, 468.

33 See the analysis by Capie, *Bank of England*, 100–137.

34 See Nicoletta Batini and Edward Nelson, 'The U.K.'s Rocky Road to Stability', FRB of St. Louis Working Paper No. 2005-020A, March 2005.

35 David Gowland, *Monetary Policy and Credit Control: The UK Experience* (London: Croome Helm, 1978), 40; John Fforde, 'The United Kingdom – Setting Monetary Objectives', in P. Meek, ed., *Central Bank Views on Monetary Targeting* (New York: Federal Reserve Bank of New York, 1983).

36 See Gordon Pepper, *Inside Thatcher's Monetarist Revolution* (London: Institute of Economic Affairs, 1998).

37 Tim Congdon, *Central Banking in a Free Society* (London: Institute of Economic Affairs, 2009).

38 Nicoletta Batini and Edward Nelson, 'The UK's Rocky Road to Stability', FRB of St Louis Working Paper No. 2005–020, 6.

39 Charles Goodhart, *The Central Bank and the Financial System* (Cambridge, MA: MIT Press, 1995), 238 (originally in 'Advising the Bank of England', *LSE Annual Review* [1992]: 14–17).

40 BoE, 2A128/1, 20 December 1968, Charles Goodhart, Mr. Pepper (of Greenwell's) Papers on Money Supply.

41 J. C. R. Dow and I. D. Saville, *A Critique of Monetary Policy: Theory and British Experience* (Oxford: Oxford University Press, 1990), 235.

42 William A. Allen, *Monetary Policy and Financial Repression in Britain, 1951–59* (Basingstoke: Palgrave Macmillan, 2014).

43 BoE, 2A128/1, 1 October 1968 AD Crockett, The Money Supply and Expenditure.

44 C. Goodhart, MDKW Foot, A. C. Hotson, 'Monetary Base Control', *BEQB* vol. 19, Q2 (June 1979): 154.

45 Michael Cockerell, *Live from Number 10: The Inside Story of Prime Ministers and Television* (London: Faber, 1988), 288; also telegraph.co.uk/obituaries/2016/08/23/sir-antony-jay-co-author-of-yes-minister – obituary

46 Mallaby, *Greenspan*, 179–180.

47 William Keegan, *Mrs. Thatcher's Economic Experiment* (New York: Penguin, 1985), 200.

48 Charles Moore, *Margaret Thatcher: From Grantham to the Falklands: The Authorized Biography* (New York: Knopf), 641.

49 Dow, *Memoirs*, 110–111.

50 Ibid., 134.

51 Moore, *Margaret Thatcher*, 462.

52 Ibid., 531.

53 House of Commons budget speech, 12 June 1979: margaretthatcher.org/document/109497

54 TNA, PREM19/177 f40, 19 March 1980; Monetary Policy: Treasury note to Lawson ('Monetary Control').

55 See 'Supplementary Special Deposits Scheme', *BEQB* Q1 (1982): 74–85. The SSDS was activated three times – from December 1973 to February 1975; from November 1976 to August 1977; and from June 1978 to June 1980.

56 'Economic Commentary', *BEQB* Q4 (December 1977): 433.

57 Milton Friedman, 'Response to Questionnaire on Monetary Policy', in *Treasury and Civil Service Committee, Memoranda on Monetary Policy* (London: HMSO, 1980), 57; see also Gordon T. Pepper and Michael Oliver, *Monetarism Under Thatcher: Lessons for the Future* (Cheltenham: Edward Elgar, 2001), 20.

58 BoE, 1A5/3, Panel of Academic Consultants, 18 April 1980.

59 Brian Griffiths, Roy A. Batchelor, E. Bendle, and Geoffrey E. Wood, 'Reforming Monetary Control in the United Kingdom', *The Banker* (April/May 1980): 75–80; this article also appeared as 'Monetary Control: A Critique of Cmnd 7958', in

Treasury and Civil Service Committee (House of Commons), Monetary Control: Third Report, Vol. 2: Appendices (London: HMSO, 1980), 35–39.

60 Keith Joseph, *Monetarism Is Not Enough* (London: Centre for Policy Studies, 1976), 17.

61 Statement by Paul A. Volcker, Chairman, Board of Governors of the Federal Reserve System, before the Joint Economic Committee of the U.S. Congress, 1 February 1980, *Federal Reserve Bulletin* (February 1980): 140.

62 BoE, 6A163/6, Charles Goodhart, 'Other Policies as Complements to Monetary Policy', 23 June 1980.

63 Alan Budd, 'Economic Viewpoint: Monetary Targets and a Financial Plan', *London Business School Economic Outlook* vol. 4, no. 2 (November 1979): 12.

64 See Nicholas H. Dimsdale, 'The Treasury and Civil Service Committee and the British Monetarist Experiment', in Mauro Baranzini, ed., *Advances in Economic Theory* (Basingstoke: Palgrave Macmillan, 1982), 189; also Alan Budd, Geoffrey Dicks and Giles Keating, 'Government Borrowing and Financial Markets', *National Institute Economic Review* vol. 113 (August 1985): 93, quoting HM Treasury, Memorandum to Treasury and Civil Service Committee, 'Background to the Government's Economic Policy', 1980.

65 Moore, *Margaret Thatcher*, 531; see on relationship to Walters, Forrest Capie and Mike Anson interview with Sir Nigel Wicks, 18 September 2008.

66 *Yes Prime Minister*, 'Official Secrets', broadcast 10 December 1987.

67 House of Commons, Treasury and Civil Service Committee, Session 1993–1994, 'The Role of the Bank of England, First Report', viii; House of Commons, Treasury and Civil Service Committee, Session 1987–1988, 'The 1988 Budget, Fourth Report', Q251, 400; House of Commons, Treasury and Civil Service Committee, Session 1987–1988, 'The Government's Economic Policy, First Report from the Committee', Q139, 197.

68 Dow, *Inside the Bank of England*, 101.

69 BoE, 7A133/5, 5 July 1983, McMahon: Papers for HMT; 1 December 1982, Exchange Rate Strategy.

70 Keegan, *Mrs. Thatcher's*, 154.

71 TNA, T450/173, 25 May 1982, Middleton to Wass.

72 Text from Lawson, *The View from No. 11*, 69.

73 Geoffrey Howe, 'The 364 Economists: Ten Years On', *Fiscal Studies* vol. 12, no. 4, (November 1991): 92–107; Lawson, *The View from No. 11*, 66; Moore, *Margaret Thatcher*, 505.

74 Moore, *Margaret Thatcher*, 505.

75 Lawson, *The View from No. 11*, 83.

76 BoE, 6A50/31, 24 October 1979, draft letter of Goodhart to Budd. See Duncan Needham, *UK Monetary Policy from Devaluation to Thatcher, 1967–82* (Basingstoke: Palgrave Macmillan, 2014), 164.

77 BoE, 7A148/1, Note of the Governor's telephone conversation with Lankester, 22 February 1980.

78 BoE, 7A133/2, 22 February 1980, Monetary Policy: Bank of England record of conversation (Chancellor of the Exchequer & Governor of the Bank of England).

79 Green Paper, Monetary Control, Cmnd 7858 (HMSO, March 1980).

80 For instance, Andrew Kilpatrick, 'The Performance of Broad Money', *Treasury Bulletin* vol. 2, no. 3 (December 1991): 3.

81 Margaret Thatcher, *The Downing Street Years* (New York: HarperCollins, 1993), 96.

82 TNA, PREM19/177 f162, 7 March 1980, Monetary Policy: Chancellor of the Exchequer minute to MT (draft Consultative Document on Monetary Control).

83 HM Treasury Archive, PO-CH-GH0045A f40, 4 March 1980, Monetary Policy: Biffen minute for Chancellor ('Medium Term Financial Strategy').

84 TNA, PREM19/177 f132, 7 March 1980, Monetary Policy: Chancellor of the Exchequer minute to Biffen ('Medium Term Financial Strategy').

85 BoE, 10A114/1, 24 January 1980, Ryrie to McMahon.

86 Introduced in *BEQB* September 1979. PSL2 measured the liquid sterling assets of the non-bank and non-building society private sector; it involved M1 plus private-sector time deposits with a maturity of up to two years, private-sector holdings of sterling certificates of deposit and private-sector holdings of monetary instruments (bank bills, Treasury bills, local authority deposits, certificates of tax deposit), plus private-sector holdings of building society deposits (excluding term shares and SAYE), plus National savings (excluding saving certificates, SAYE and other long-term deposits), minus building society holdings of money market instruments and bank deposits. See *BEQB* Q1 (1984): 79.

87 Graham Hacche, 'The Demand for Money in the United Kingdom: Experience since 1971', *BEQB*, September 1974; William A. Allen, 'Intermediation and Pure Liquidity Creation in Banking Systems', *Greek Economic Review* vol. 4, no. 2 (1981): 149–173.

88 BoE, 10A114/1, McMahon, 25 January 1980, 'Towards a Bank View on Monetary Policy'.

89 BoE, 13A223/2, Goodhart, 23 February 1981, 'Fiscal Policy and Intermediate Targets'.

'A Good Deal of Advice'

1 BoE, C55/126, 13 February 1980, Market diary.

2 BoE, 10A114/1, Note of a meeting in the Chancellor of the Exchequer's room, HM Treasury on Monday 3 March 1980, at 10:15 a.m.

3 BoE, C55/126, 3 April 1980, LDMA meeting.

4 TNA PREM19/178 f106, 3 July 1980, Monetary Policy: No. 10 record of conversation (MT-Chancellor of the Exchequer-Governor of the Bank of England).

5 'Bank of England Cuts Lending Rate', *New York Times,* 4 July 1980.

6 John Whitmore, 'Minimum Lending Rate Cut to 16 Per Cent', *The Times* (London), 4 July 1980, p. 1.

7 Peter Riddell, 'MLR Cut: Caution Is the Watchword', *Financial Times,* 5 July 1980, p. 14.

8 'Guarded Welcome for Cut in MLR', *The Times* (London), 4 July 1980, p. 21.

9 BoE, C55/126, 3 and 10 July 1980, markets meeting with LDMA.

10 BoE, 10A114/1, 21 August 1980, John Fforde: Money.

11 BoE, 7A149/3, 15 September 1980, Christopher Dow: Defence of the Bank's Position.

12 BoE, 10A114/1, 21 August 1980, John Fforde: Money.

13 Peter Riddell, 'Governor Lifts Veil on Intervention', *Financial Times,* 11 February 1980, p. 11.

14 BoE, 10A114/1, 25 February 1980, Note for the Record (Intervention) re: meeting on 19 February.

15 Geoffrey Howe, 28 July 1980, testimony, in *Treasury and Civil Service Committee, Monetary Policy, Volume II: Minutes of Evidence* (London: HMSO, 1981), 199.

16 Charles Goodhart, 7 July 1980, testimony, in *Treasury and Civil Service Committee, Monetary Policy, Volume II: Minutes of Evidence* (London: HMSO, 1981), 65.

17 *BEQB* vol. 21, no. 3 (September 1981): 383 (Statistical Annex).

18 *BEQB* vol. 23, no. 2 (June 1983): 172 (Box: Domestic Credit Expansion).

19 Fforde, 'Setting Monetary Objectives', 201–208.

20 See Ryland Thomas, 'Understanding Broad Money', *BEQB* Q3 (August 1996): 163–179. Also Ryland Thomas, 'The Demand for M4: A Sectoral Analysis, Part 1 – The Personal Sector', BoE Working Paper No. 61, 1997; and Ryland Thomas, 'The Demand for M4: A Sectoral Analysis, Part 2 – The Corporate Sector', BoE Working Paper No. 62, 1997.

21 BoE, 7A133/2, Note of a Meeting held at No. 11 Downing Street at 5:30 p.m. on Wednesday, 30 July 1980.

22 BoE, 10A114/1, 29 August 1980, Middleton, Monetary Policy (for Chancellor of the Exchequer).

23 TNA, PREM 19/179 f.247, 7 October 1980, Monetary Policy: Chancellor of the Exchequer minute to MT ('Money Supply, Interest Rates, the PSBR & the exchange rate').

24 BoE, 10A161/1, 8 October 1980, Middleton, Monetary Control.

25 BoE, C8/52, Foreign Exchange and Gold Markets: Dealers' Reports

26 BoE, 13A102/1, 24 October 1980, thirteenth meeting of Panel of Academic Consultants.

27 Monetary Base Control, *BEQB* Q2 (1979): 149–159. See also C. A. E. Goodhart, 'The Conduct of Monetary Policy', *Economic Journal* vol. 99, no. 396 (1989): 323; Duncan Needham, *UK Monetary Policy from Devaluation to Thatcher 1967–1982* (Basingstoke: Palgrave Macmillan, 2014), 144.

28 BoE, 7A174/5, Goodhart, 6 July 1979, Monetary Base.

29 BoE, 7A174/5, 6 July 1979, Middleton draft paper.

30 BoE, 7A174/5, 12 July 1979, John Fforde: Prime Minister's Monetary Seminar.

31 BoE, 7A174/5, 12 July 1979, Treasury paper, 'Monetary Objectives and Prospects'.

32 BoE, 7A133/2, 3 September 1980, Mike Pattison (private secretary, 10 Downing Street), to A. J. Wiggins (HM Treasury) on meeting of 3 September 1980, of Prime Minister with Chancellor and Governor.

33 BoE, 7A133/2, Note of a meeting held at No. 11 Downing Street at 9:30 a.m. on Wednesday, 3 September 1980.

34 BoE, 7A174/6, September 1980, draft letter to Prime Minister.

35 BoE, 4A68/5, 10 October 1980, Richardson to Margaret Thatcher.

36 See Geoffrey Howe, *Conflict of Loyalty* (London: Methuen, 1994), 186.

37 BoE, 7A133/2, 9 September 1980, Tim Lankester to A. J. Wiggins.

38 Keegan, *Mrs. Thatcher's Monetary Experiment,* 154.

39 BoE, 7A133/2, 18 September 1980, Tim Lankester to A. J. Wiggins (on meeting in 10 Downing Street with Prime Minister).

40 BoE, 7A133/2, 17 September 1980, A. J. Wiggins, note of a meeting held in the Chancellor of the Exchequer's room, HM Treasury, at 4:45 p.m. on Tuesday, 16 September 1980.

41 BoE, 7A133/2, 18 September 1980, Tim Lankester to A. J. Wiggins.

42 BoE, 7A133/2, 8 October 1980, Note for the Record: Chancellor's phone call with Governor.

43 BoE, 7A133/2, Note of a meeting held at No. 11 Downing Street on Saturday, 11 October 1980, at 10:45 a.m.

44 TNA, PREM 19/178 f. 53, 10 September 1980, Monetary Policy: Karl Brunner letter to PM (monetary control).

45 BoE, 7A174/6, Note of a seminar with foreign experts on Monday, 30 September 1980, Monetary Base Control.

46 BoE, 6A163/12, 11 November 1980, Select Committee: Dr. Dudler's appearance.

47 As quoted in Lindley H. Clark Jr., 'Battle of the Bank of England', *Wall Street Journal*, 7 April 1981, p. 35.

48 TNA, PREM 19/179 f.275, 30 September 1980, Monetary Policy: No. 10 record of conversation (MBC economists visit MT).

49 Margaret Thatcher interview with Brian Walden, *Weekend World*, London Weekend Television, 1 February 1981, Margaret Thatcher Complete Public Statements Archive, Thatcher Foundation, margaretthatcher.org/document/104210

50 BoE, 7A134/16, 29 September 1980, Monetary Policy: Treasury minute (Middleton to Chancellor of the Exchequer). MBC: Seminar with outside economists at Church House.

51 Dow, *Memoirs*, 169.

52 BoE, 7A174/6, 14 October 1980, No. 10 note on meeting of 13 October.

53 Dow, *Memoirs*, 170.

54 Harry Anderson with Anthony Collins, 'Maggie's Money Muddle', *Newsweek*, 24 November 1980, p. 93; also see Edward Nelson, 'Reaffirming the Influence of Milton Friedman on U.K. Economic Policy', Working Paper 2017–01, University of Sydney, School of Economics, revised February 2017.

55 BoE, 10A114/2, 2 October 1980, W. A. Allen memorandum.

56 BoE, 10A153/5, 28 November 1980, Dow: Monetary – and Economic – Policy.

57 It was published in 1981 as a working paper, 'The Appreciation of Sterling: Causes, Effects, Policies', by the Rochester Center for Research in Government Policy and Business.

58 Keegan, *Mrs. Thatcher's Economic Experiment*, 99.

59 Alan Walters, diary, 7 January 1981 Churchill College Cambridge; available at: margaretthatcher.org/document/137536

60 BoE, 7A174/7, 17 November 1980, PE Middleton: 'A 2% Fall in Interest Rates'.

61 BoE, 7A174/7, 20 November 1980, 10 Downing Street note (on Tuesday seminar meeting, 18 November 1980).

62 BoE, 7A133/3, 11 February 1981, note for the record (on meeting of Chancellor, Governor and Prime Minister).

63 BoE, 13A223/2, 16 February 1981, Goodhart: Monetary Targets and Conditionality.

64 BoE, 13A223/2, 12 February 1981, Fforde: Monetary Targets and Conditionality.

65 BoE, 13A223/2, 12 February 1981, McMahon: Monetary Targets and Conditionality.

66 See Robert Neild, 'The 1981 Statement by 364 Economists', in Duncan Needham and Anthony Hotson, eds., *Expansionary Fiscal Contraction: The Thatcher Government's 1981 Budget in Perspective* (Cambridge: Cambridge University Press, 2014): 1–9.

67 Kwasi Kwarteng, *Thatcher's Trial: Six Months that Defined a Leader* (London: Bloomsbury, 2015): 162.

68 BoE, 13A231/1 Governor's Office File: Secret and Personal Duplicate Memoranda, 13 April 1983, CWM: Economics Division.

69 BoE, 5A198/11, 11 March 1981, Modelling in the Bank.

70 William Keegan and Rupert Pennant-Rea, *Who Runs the Economy? Control and Influence in British Economic Policy* (London: Maurice Temple Smith, 1979), 54.

71 BoE, 13A102/2, Panel of Academic Consultants, 20 March 1981, 'The Usefulness of Macroeconomic Models'.

72 See Dow, *Inside the Bank of England*, 249.

73 BoE, 8A388/5, 12 February 1985, J. S. Flemming: The Organisation of the Economic Work of the Bank.

74 See particularly Needham and Hotson, eds., *Expansionary Fiscal Contraction*.

75 BoE, C55/127, 12 February 1981, LDMA meeting.

76 BoE, 7A174/7, 4 June 1981, Margaret Thatcher: Monetary Control.

77 Dow, *Memoirs*, 165.

78 Walters diary entry, 11 May 1981, Churchill College Cambridge; available at: margaretthatcher.org/document/137536

79 BoE, 8A388/1, 27 May 1981, Deputy Governor's Committee; 9 June 1981, Deputy Governor's Committee.

80 Lord Richardson of Duntisborne obituary, *Independent*, 8 February 2010: independent.co.uk/news/obituaries/lord-richardson-of-duntisbourne-governor-of-the-bank-of-england-during-the-troubled-times-of-the-1893352.html

81 TNA, T448/31, 6 July 1981, Wass, 'The Relationship between the Treasury and the Bank of England'.

82 TNA T448/31, M. T. Folgar, 28 August 1981, note.

83 For more details on the regular monetary operations, see Anthony C. Hotson, 'The Role of the Bank of England in the Money Market', *BEQB* vol. 22, Q1 (March 1982): 86–94.

84 There is a rich literature on this: see R. S. Sayers, *The Bank of England 1891–1944: Volume I* (Cambridge: Cambridge University Press, 1976), 275–277; recently Marc Flandreau and Stefano Ugolini, 'Where It All Began: Lending of Last Resort at the Bank of England during the Overend-Gurney Panic of 1866', in Michael D. Bordo and William Roberds, eds., *The Origins, History, and Future of the Federal Reserve: A Return to Jekyll Island* (Cambridge: Cambridge University Press, 2013), 113–161; Carolyn Sissoko, 'How to Stabilize the Banking System: Lessons from the Pre-1914 Money Market', *Financial History Review* vol. 23, no. 1 (April 2016): 1–20.

85 A point eloquently made by Carolyn Sissoko, in 'How to Stabilize the Banking System', 1–20.

86 Sayers, *The Bank of England*, 282.

87 Tony Coleby, 'The Bank's Operational Procedures for Meeting Monetary Objectives', *BEQB* vol. 23, no. 2 (1 June 1983): 209–215, quote from p. 213; see also Paul Tucker, 'Managing the Central Bank's Balance Sheet: Where Monetary Policy Meets Financial Stability', *BEQB* (Autumn 2004): 359–382.

88 Tucker, 'Managing the Central Bank's', 359.

89 BoE, 17A126/1, ALC (Tony Coleby), 5 January 1981: 'Primary Liquidity in the Context of Monetary Control'.

90 BoE, 17A126/1, 11 March 1981, Middleton to Fforde.

91 *The London Discount Market*, 9 and 11.

92 See 'The Bank of England's Operations in the Sterling Money Market', *BEQB* vol. 38, no. 3 (August 1988): 202.

93 BoE, C55/127, 23 April 1981, LDMA meeting.

94 BoE, Committee of Treasury, G8/92, 30 July 1981.

95 BoE, 7A174/7, 4 June 1981, Thatcher to Howe.

96 BoE, 10A161/1, 14 August 1981, 'Interest Rate Policy: The Next Few Weeks'.

97 BoE, 10A114/4, 19 May 1983, 'Briefing Labour: Domestic Financial Policy, Lomax (Treasury)'.

98 BoE, C55/127, 9 July 1981, LDMA meeting.

99 'The Role of the Bank of England in the Money Market', *BEQB* vol. 22, Q1 (March 1982): 94.

100 Tucker, 'Managing the Central Bank's Balance Sheet', 269.

101 'Operation of Monetary Policy', *BEQB* vol. 32, Q2 (June 1982): 195; also Nicoletta Batini and Edward Nelson, 'The UK's Rocky Road to Stability', *Trends in Inflation Research* (2006): 42.

102 BoE, 5A19/3, J. S. Rumins, 'Bankers' Balances', 22 May 1981.

103 BoE, 5A19/3, Committee of Treasury, 5 February 1981.

104 Dow, *Inside the Bank*, 181.

105 BoE, 5A19/5, McMahon to Governor, 25 August 1983.

106 BoE, 5A19/5, Lawson to Leigh-Pemberton, 3 October 1983: 'I welcome your agreement to the formula by which your payment in lieu of dividend would be one third of pre-tax profits.'

107 Walters diary entry, 3 June 1981, Churchill College Cambridge; available at: margaretthatcher.org/document/137536

108 BoE, 10A161/1, 14 August 1981, 'Interest Rate Policy: The Next Few Weeks'.

109 BoE, 7A148/2, 4 August 1982, conversation with Middleton; 5 August 1982, meeting with Sir Douglas Wass.

110 BoE, 10A161/1, 8 October 1981, 'Interest Rates over the Next Few Weeks'.

111 BoE, C55/127, 12 November 1981, LDMA meeting.

112 Walters diary, 19 December 1981, Churchill College archive, at: margaretthatcher.org/document/140745

113 BoE, 10A114/2, 7 July 1981, the Seminar with the PM (Goodhart).

114 BoE, 13A223/2, 18 December 1981, W. A. Allen, 'Monetary Targets for Ever?'

115 BoE, 10A161/1, Meeting in Mr Middleton's room on 5 June 1981.

116 'The Role of the Bank of England in the Money Market', *BEQB* vol. 22, Q1 (March 1982): 94.

117 BoE, 10A114/3, 2 October 1981, 'Monetary Prospects.'

118 BoE, 7A133/3, 14 September 1981, J. O. Kerr (Treasury) to T. Lankester (10 Downing Street).
119 BoE, 8A388/1, 22 September 1981, Deputy Governor's Committee.
120 BoE, 7A174/7, 7 July 1981, the seminar with the PM.
121 Dow, *Memoirs*, 178.
122 BoE, 7A174/7, 18 September 1981, Howe to Thatcher.
123 BoE, 7A174/7, 7 July 1981, the seminar with the PM, handwritten comments.
124 Dow, *Memoirs*, 186.
125 BoE, 7A174/7, 13 November 1981, Richardson to Howe.
126 For instance, BoE, 10A114/4, 7 January 1983, George, 'Monetary Tactics – the Next Phase'.
127 BoE, 17A126/3, J. S. Fforde, 'Monetary Policy: Autumn 1981', 10 September 1981.
128 BoE, 10A161/1, 13 October 1981, Ryrie meeting.
129 BoE, 8A388/1, 17 November 1981, DGC.
130 BoE, 10A114/4, 10 January 1983, George: Monetary Tactics.
131 BoE, 7A174/7, 4 February 1982, Richardson to Michael Scholar.
132 BoE, 7A133/4, 19 January 1982, Michael Scholar letter to John (Kerr).
133 BoE, 7A133/4, 19 January 1982, Michael Scholar letter to John (Kerr); with 'I do not recall this being put so explicitly' in Governor's handwriting.
134 BoE, 7A133/4, 14 January 1982, Burns, 'Policy Implications of the Winter Forecast'.
135 Steven Rattner, 'Britain's Monetarist Muddle', *New York Times,* 14 February 1982, p. 34.
136 BoE, 7A133/4, Note of a meeting held in the Chancellor of the Exchequer's room, HM Treasury on Thursday, 4 February 1982.
137 See Batini and Nelson, 'UK's Rocky Road', 52.
138 A. L. Coleby, 'Bills of Exchange: Current Issues in a Historical Perspective', *BEQB* vol. 22, Q3 (November 1982): 516.
139 William A. Allen, 'Government Debt Management and Monetary Policy in Britain Since 1919', BIS Working Paper No. 65.
140 BoE, 10A161/2, 13 May 1982, Middleton, 'Debt Sales and Monetary Policy.'
141 BoE, 10A114/4, 21 January 1983, 'Influencing Interest Rates'.
142 BoE, 7A148/2, 5 January 1983, discussion with Middleton.
143 BoE, 13A112/2, 10 November 1982, Plenderleith: AHC Meeting: Corporate Bond Issues.
144 BoE, 13A112/6, 16 April 1987, Short-Term Corporate Bonds: Scope for Liberalisation?
145 BoE, C55/128, LDMA meetings 14 October and 11 November 1982.
146 BoE, 10A153/5, 18 October 1982, George: Policy and the Economy.
147 BoE, 10A114/4, 18 February 1983, Richardson to Howe.
148 BoE, 10A114/4, 19 May 1983, 'Briefing Labour: Domestic Financial Policy', Lomax (Treasury).
149 BoE, 13A115/2, 28 April 1983, note.
150 BoE, 10A114/4, 19 May 1983, 'Briefing Labour: Domestic Financial Policy', Lomax (Treasury).
151 BoE, 10A114/4, 1 June 1983, discussion with Chancellor.

152 Walters diary entry, 8 January 1982, Churchill College Cambridge; available at: margaretthatcher.org/document/144182

153 Lowri Stafford, 'Respects paid to former Bank of England governor Lord Kingsdown, Robin Leigh-Pemberton, at Canterbury Cathedral', Kent Online (6 February 2014), available at kentonline.co.uk/canterbury/news/hundreds-pay-respects-to-lord-12410/

154 Peter Riddell, 'Bank Governor Not Treasury Choice', *Financial Times*, 4 January 1983, p. 1.

155 Alan Friedman, 'Keeping a Low Profile', in *Financial Times Banking Survey*, 26 September 1983.

156 Samuel Brittan, 'A Missed Opportunity – and Thus a Blunder', *Financial Times*, 6 January 1983, p. 11.

157 Hugo Young, 'Another Job for Her Boys', *The Sunday Times* (London), 2 January 1983, p. 9.

158 Peter Rodgers, 'Nat West Chief for Bank of England', *Guardian*, 24 December 1982, p. 1.

159 Kim Sengupta, 'I'm No Rabid Right-winger Says Bank's New Governor', *Daily Mail*, 3 January 1983, pp. 16–17.

160 BoE, 13A231/1, 17 June 1983, McMahon, Note for record.

161 Walters diary, 27 October 1982, Churchill College archives, at: margaretthatcher .org/document/144397

162 BoE, Committee of Treasury minutes, G8/93 and G8/95.

163 BoE, 13A231/1, 8 April 1983, McMahon, 'Administrative Arrangements for the Bank under the New Governor'.

164 BoE, 13A231/1, 6 May 1983, McMahon note [no title].

165 BoE, 8A388/3, 17 May 1984, Deputy Governor's Committee.

166 BoE, 6A41/49, 30 September 2008 Michael Foot, oral history interview with Forrest Capie and Michael Anson.

167 'Lucky enough to have a job like this'. (Interview with Alan Friedman), *Financial Times*, 9 September 1983, p. 21.

168 Alan Friedman, 'Keeping a Low Profile – Profile – Robin Leigh-Pemberton, Governor, Bank of England', *Financial Times Survey: UK Banking*, 26 September 1983, page II.

169 BoE, 10A114/4, 4 July 1983, George, 'Monetary Policy – The Next Few Weeks'.

170 BoE, 10A114/5, 3 October 1983, George, 'Monetary Strategy.'

171 BoE, 10A161/3, 15 November 1983, 'The Middleton Meeting'.

172 BoE, C55/129, 18 August 1983, LDMA markets meeting.

173 BoE, 10A114/5, 28 December 1983, Meeting with Treasury Officials on monetary targets in the medium-term financial strategy.

174 BoE, 13A115, Books, 25 November 1983.

175 BoE, C55/129, 1 September 1983, LDMA Markets meeting.

176 Bank of England, *The Development and Operation of Monetary Policy 1960–1983: A Selection of Material from the Quarterly Bulletin of the Bank of England* (Oxford: Oxford University Press, 1984); Charles Goodhart, *Monetary Theory and Practice: The UK Experience* (Basingstoke: Palgrave Macmillan, 1984).

177 BoE, 10A153/3, Goodhart, 13 January 1983, Economic Policy and the Exchange Rate; 4 July 1983, George: Monetary Policy.

178 BoE, 10A153/3, 12 July 1983, George: Monetary Policy: Your Meeting with the Chancellor, 13 July 1983.
179 M0 plus bank deposits, including interest-bearing deposits.
180 BoE, 7A133/6, 'Monetary Targets:' Note of a discussion in the Chancellor's Office at 2:45 p.m. on 13 January 1984.
181 BoE, 10A161/4, 18 December 1984.
182 BoE, 10A114/6, 20 July 1984, F. Cassell, 'Resisting a Rise in Interest Rates'.
183 BoE, 13A115/3, 3 October 1983, Books.
184 BoE, 10A114/6, 23 October 1984, Leigh-Pemberton to Lawson.
185 BoE, 13A115/6, 18 January 1985, Books.
186 BoE, 13A256/1, 28 January 1985, Turnbull, 'Interest Rates and the Exchange Rate' (note of meeting in No. 10 Downing Street).
187 BoE, 13A256/1, 20 February 1985, Note of a meeting held at 4:30 p.m., Tuesday, 19 February 1985, in Sir Peter Middleton's room, HM Treasury.
188 BoE, 13A256/1, 15 February 1985, Treasury Paper: 'The Monetary Targets in the MTFS'.
189 BoE, 10A114/7, 19 February 1985, meeting in Middleton's room.
190 BoE, G4/212, 21 March 1985.
191 Max Wilkinson, 'Money Supply Policies: UK – Why Interest Rates Will Stay High', 25 May 1985, *Financial Times,* p. 8.
192 BoE, 13A256/1, Leigh-Pemberton, Note of a meeting in HM Treasury on Tuesday 7 May 1985, at 10:30 a.m.
193 BoE, 13A256/1, 28 February 1985, informal meeting with Sir Peter Middleton.
194 TNA, T438/524, Notes of a meeting in Sir Peter Middleton's room, 7 May 1985.
195 BoE, 10A193/7, 20 June 1985, Monetary Control: The Bank of England's Views.
196 BoE, 10A193/7, 20 June 1985, Treasury paper: Monetary Control.
197 BoE, 10A193/7, 20 June 1985, Monetary Control: The Bank of England's Views.
198 BoE, 13A256/1, 13 June 1985, Leigh-Pemberton, Informal conversation between myself and the Chancellor with Mrs. Lomax: 11 June 1985.
199 BoE, 13A256/1, 12 June 1985, Chancellor's meetings with the Governor: Tuesday, 11 June and Wednesday, 12 June 1985.
200 BoE, 13A256/1, 12 June 1985, George, 'The Chancellor's Meeting with Alan Walters', 7 June 1985.
201 BoE, 10A114/8, Note of a meeting at No. 11 Downing Street on Monday, 7 June 1985, at 11:45 a.m.
202 BoE, 13A256/1, 6 June 1985, Turnbull to Lomax: Monetary Policy.
203 BoE, 13A256/1, 14 June 1985, 'Monetary Control – The Bank of England's View' (draft).
204 BoE, 13A256/2, 16 July 1985, Turnbull: Monetary Policy; see also Lawson, *View from No. 11,* 480.
205 See Walters memorandum for Andrew Turnbull, 24 June 1985, TNA, PREM 19/1457 f13.
206 TNA, T438/254, 16 July 1985, 10 Downing Street meeting: 'Monetary Policy'.
207 'The Instruments of Monetary Policy', *BEQB* vol. 27, Q3 (August 1987): 365; BoE, 6A163/32, 6 April 1989, A. L. Coleby, 'Background Briefing on Funding/Overfunding and Monetary Policy'.
208 BoE, 13A256/2, 21 July 1985, Monetary Policy in August.

209 BoE, 13A256/2, Lunch with the Chancellor: Tuesday, 3 September 1985.

210 Lawson, *The View from No. 11*, 459; Mansion House Speech, 17 October 1985.

211 BoE, 10A161/12, September 1991, Glenn Hogarth: Middleton Letters.

212 Graham Hacche, 'Review of Forrest Capie's History of the Bank of England', *Economica* vol. 80 (2013): 373.

213 Tim Congdon, 'Monetarism Lost, and Why It Must Be Regained', Centre for Policy Studies Policy Study No. 106, 1989, p. 21.

214 Philip Stephens, 'Alternative Policies: Keynes Is Still Waiting in the Wings', *Financial Times*, 17 September 1984, 'World Economy' section, p. 5; Peter Jenkins, *Mrs. Thatcher's Revolution: The Ending of the Socialist Era* (Cambridge, MA: Harvard University Press, 1988): 282–283; Samuel Brittan, 'Economic Viewpoint: Monetarism: Far from Dead', *Financial Times*, 24 October 1985, p. 25.

215 Forrest Capie, Charles Goodhart and Norberts Schnadt, *The Development of Central Banking: The Tercentenary Symposium of the Bank of England* (Cambridge: Cambridge University Press, 1994), 83–84.

216 Paul Volcker, 'The Triumph of Central Banking', the Per Jacobsson Lecture, 23 September 1990 (Washington, DC: International Monetary Fund, Per Jacobsson Foundation, 1990), 11.

The Long Shadow of the Deutschemark

1 Geddes, *Inside the Bank of England*, 73–74. Report from Select Committee on banks of issue: with the Minutes of evidence, Appendix and Index, London: House of Commons, Q1840, 39 (Evidence of 14 April 1840).

2 TNA, PREM 16.1615, John Hunt: Chancellor Schmidt, the Snake and Pooling Reserves, 6 April 1978.

3 TNA, PREM 16/1634, 22 June 1978, DWH: European Currency Arrangements.

4 HC Debates, 967, column 48, 15 May 1979; Matthew Smith, *Policy-making in the Treasury* (Basingstoke: Palgrave Macmillan, 2014), 68.

5 BoE, 8A388/1, 17 November 1981, Deputy Governor's Committee.

6 BoE, 13A231/1, 14 June 1983, conversation with Peter Middleton.

7 M. Smith, *Policy-making in the Treasury*, 90.

8 BoE, 8A388/2, 14 July 1983, Deputy Governor's Committee.

9 Lawson, *The View from No. 11*, 450.

10 BoE, 13A115/2, Nico Colchester: The 'FCO reconsidering the case for joining EMS'.

11 BoE, 8A388/4, 14 September 1984, Deputy Governor's Committee.

12 BoE, 8A388/4, 14 September 1984, note.

13 BoE, 10A114/7, 7 February 1985, EMS, George.

14 BoE, 13A231/2, 12 October 1984, meeting with Sir Peter Middleton.

15 BoE, 11A21/9, 15 January 1985, A. C. Hotson, Deputy Governor's Conversations with Sir Peter Middleton.

16 BoE, 10A161/5, 15 January 1985, handwritten notes of Bank-Treasury meeting.

17 Charles Moore, *Margaret Thatcher: The Authorized Biography, Volume 2: Everything She Wants* (New York: Penguin, 2015), 411–412; Thatcher, *Downing Street Years*, 695.

18 BoE, 13A256/2, 4 September 1985, note for the Record.

19 BoE, 13A256/2, 17 September 1985, meeting with the Chancellor.

20 Ibid.

21 William Keegan, *Mr. Lawson's Gamble* (London: Hodder and Stoughton, 1989), 173.

22 BoE, 13A256/1, 25 February 1985, lunch with Chancellor.

23 BoE, C8/64, 26 September 1985, 'Foreign Exchange and Gold Markets' report.

24 BoE, 11A21/10, 19 December 1985, intervention (GMG).

25 Moore, *Margaret Thatcher, Vol. 2*, 420.

26 BoE, 13A231/3, 23 October 1985, Note for Record: Lunch with Chancellor, Wednesday, 23 October.

27 BoE, 7A148/3, 17 January 1986, aide-memoire.

28 BoE, 11A21/11, 22 January 1986, intervention.

29 BoE, 11A21/11, 15 January 1986, intervention policy.

30 BoE, 11A21/11, 8 February 1986, G. M. Gill coordinated intervention.

31 BoE, 6A163/27, Minutes of evidence taken before the TCSSC, 28 January 1985, 9.

32 BoE, 7A148/3, 16 January 1986, conversation with Sir Peter Middleton.

33 BoE, 13A115/8, 14 May 1986, report on discussion with Middleton on 13 May.

34 BoE, 10A114/11, 8 April 1986, Lawson to Leigh-Pemberton.

35 BoE, 10A161/6, 5 November 1986, Cassell letter to Eddie George.

36 BoE, 10A114/11, 16 April 1986, Lawson speech at Lombard Association.

37 BoE, 10A114/11, 25 April 1986, Leigh-Pemberton to Lawson.

38 BoE, G4/213, Court of Directors, 29 May 1986.

39 BoE, 10A114/11, 19 May 1986, 'Your Meeting with the Chancellor this Morning'.

40 BoE, 10A114/13, 30 July 1986, meeting in Chancellor's room.

41 BoE, 10A114/13, 27 August 1986, A. L. Coleby, 'Your Meeting with the Chancellor, 28 August'.

42 BoE, 10A114/15, 10 October 1986, meeting in No. 11 Downing Street.

43 Christopher Smallwood and David Hughes, 'Lawson on Rack as Slide Goes On', *Sunday Times* (London), 19 October 1986, p. 1.

44 BoE, 7A148/3, 10 December 1986, Private Secretary, 10 Downing Street to Governor of the Bank of England: Interest Rates.

45 'Financial Change and Board Money', Robin Leigh-Pemberton, Governor of the Bank of England, the First Loughborough University Banking Centre Annual Lecture in Finance at Loughborough University Banking Centre, Wednesday, 22 October 1986, published in *BEQB* vol. 26, Q4 (November 1986): 499–507.

46 BoE, 10A114/17, 29 January 1987, meeting in Treasury: 'Monetary Policy and the 1987 MTFS'.

47 BoE, 10A114/17, David Peretz, 'Which Broad Money Measure?' 17 February 1987.

48 BoE, 13A256/4, 26 November 1986, meeting in Chancellor's room, HM Treasury.

49 BoE, 11A21/11, 23 February 1987, note for the Record (Leigh-Pemberton).

50 BoE, 11A21/11, 6 April 1987, note: Comparative Intervention.

51 Thatcher, *Downing Street Years*, 699.

52 BoE, 10A114/19, 5 May 1987, meeting held at No. 11 Downing Street.

53 BoE, 11A21/11, 8 April 1987, 'Understandings on Intervention'.

54 BoE, 11A21/11, 8 April 1987, meeting of G-5.

55 BoE, 10A161/7, 29 April 1987, meeting.

56 Ibid.

57 BoE, 13A256/5, 16 June 1987, George (dictated): 'Monetary Policy: Your Meeting with the Chancellor This Afternoon'.

58 BoE, 13A256/5, 26 June 1987, note of consultation with Chancellor at Lunch.

59 BoE, 13A256/5, 16 June 1987, George note.

60 IMF WEO April 2016 database.

61 'A Weapon for Mr. Lawson', *Financial Times*, 28 September 1987, p. 24.

62 BoE, 2A56/3, 30 April 1987, LDMA meeting.

63 BoE, 7A148/3, 26 June 1987, lunch with Chancellor.

64 BoE, 10A114/19, 24 July 1987, meeting in No. 11 Downing Street.

65 BoE, 2A56/3, 5 November 1987, LDMA meeting.

66 BoE, 10A114/20, 7 October 1987, Leigh-Pemberton to Lawson.

67 See Lawson, *View from No. 11*, 784.

68 BoE, 10A114/20, 14 October 1987, meeting in Chancellor's room.

69 Ibid.

70 Harold James, *International Monetary Cooperation since Bretton Woods* (New York: Oxford University Press, 1996), 454.

71 BoE, 11A21/11, 19 October 1987, Louvre Accord.

72 BoE, 7A148/4, 24 February 1988, A. C. S. Allan to Footman, lunch with Chancellor.

73 Lawson, *View from No. 11*, 735–738.

74 Keegan, *Mr. Lawson's Gamble*, 211.

75 BoE, C8/71, 28 September 1987, Foreign Exchange and Gold Markets.

76 BoE, C8/71, 26 October 1987, Foreign Exchange and Gold Markets.

77 BoE, 10A161/7, 27 July 1987, handwritten notes (Middleton speaking).

78 Gerald Holtham, Giles Keating and Peter Spencer, 'A Reformed EMS Is Right for Britain', *Financial Times*, 19 September 1987, p. 23.

79 BoE, 10A161/8, 25 February 1988, note.

80 BoE, 10A161/8, 1 March 1988, meeting at Treasury.

81 BoE, 13A256/6, 7 September 1987, meeting with PM in Dunphail.

82 Peter Riddell, 'Thatcher Stands Firm against Full EMS Role', *Financial Times*, 23 November 23, p. 1; Thatcher, *Downing Street Years*, 701.

83 BoE, 13A231/5, 29 December 1987, intervention.

84 Lawson, *View from No. 11*, 799.

85 Charles Moore, *Margaret Thatcher: The Authorized Biography, Volume Three: Herself Alone* (London: Allen Lane, 2019), 109.

86 BoE, 10A161/7, 2 December 1987 Middleton meeting.

87 BoE, 2A56/3, 10 December 1987, LDMA meeting.

88 BoE, 10A114/20, 18 December 1987, meeting in Chancellor's office.

89 BoE, 10A161/7, 2 November 1987, meeting.

90 BoE, 10A161/9, 11 January 1989, Treasury Bank of England meeting.

91 BoE, 11A21/11, 4 December 1987, meeting in No. 11 Downing Street.

92 BoE, 11A21/11, 7 December 1987, Note: 4 December telephone conversations.

93 BoE, 11A21/11, 9 December 1987, Note; also 9 December 1987, Pöhl to Leigh-Pemberton.

94 BoE, 11A21/11, 9 December 1987, intervention in DM.

95 BoE, 11A21/11, 9 December 1987, Chancellor to Governor.

96 BoE, 11A21/11, 10 December 1987, intervention.
97 BoE, 11A21/11, 10 December 1987, Governor to Chancellor.
98 BoE, 11A21/11, 14 December 1987, Loehnis note.
99 BoE, 11A21/12, 11 January 1988, intervention.
100 BoE, 11A21/12, 20 April 1988, Pöhl letter.
101 BoE, 11A21/11, 15 December 1987, 'Monetary Strategy' (George).
102 BoE, 11A21/11, 16 December 1987.
103 BoE, 10A114/21, 15 January 1988, meeting in Chancellor's office.
104 BoE, 2A56/4, 7 January 1988, LDMA meeting (Deputy Governor).
105 BoE, 11A21/12, 3 March 1988, Intervention Policy.
106 BoE, 11A21/12, 3 March 1988, New York Fed Protests over Our Recent Forex Behaviour.
107 Lawson, *View from No. 11*, 794.
108 BoE, 10A114/21, Minutes of meeting in No. 11 Downing Street at 3:30 p.m. on Friday, 4 March [1988].
109 Keegan, *Mr. Lawson's Gamble*, 224; Lawson, *View from No. 11*, 795.
110 Treasury and Civil Service Committee (House of Commons), *The Government's Economic Policy: Autumn Statement, First Report, Together with the Proceedings of the Committee, Minutes of Evidence and Appendices* (London: HMSO, 1987), 19; also Lawson, *View from No. 11*, 797.
111 BoE, 2A56/4, 10 March 1988, LDMA meeting.
112 BoE, 13A231/6, 19 April 1988, meeting with Sir Peter Middleton, 18 April.
113 BoE, 10A114/21, 23 March 1988, George: meeting with the PM, 25 March.
114 BoE, 10A114/21, 24 March 1988, Burns: Exchange Rate Policy Paper.
115 BoE, 2A56/4, 31 March 1988, LDMA meeting (Governor).
116 BoE, 10A114/21, 8 April 1988, meeting in Treasury.
117 BoE, C8/73, 13 May 1988, Foreign Exchange and Gold Markets.
118 BoE, 2A56/4, 19 May 1988, LDMA meeting (Governor).
119 'The Roman Chancellor', *Financial Times*, 11 March 1988, p. 18; also Keegan, *Mr. Lawson's Gamble*, 222.
120 BoE, 10A114/22, 16 June 1988, meeting in Chancellor's room.
121 BoE, 10A161/8, 6 June 1988, meeting.
122 BoE, 10A161/8, 28 June 1988, meeting.
123 Moore, *Thatcher: Herself Alone*, p. 141.
124 BoE, 2A56/4, 4 August 1988, LDMA meeting.
125 BoE, 2A56/4, 11 August 1988, LDMA meeting.
126 BoE, C8/74, 28 September 1988, Foreign Exchange and Gold Markets.
127 BoE, 2A56/4, 13 October 1988, LDMA meeting.
128 BoE, 2A56/4, 24 November 1988, LDMA meeting.
129 BoE, 10A161/8, 2 November 1988, meeting.
130 BoE, 2A56/4, 2 December 1988, LDMA meeting.
131 BoE, 7A148/4, 6 September 1988, meeting with Sir Peter Middleton, Tuesday, 6 September 1988.
132 BoE, 13A115/13, 3 November 1988, Books.
133 BoE, 10A161/9, 11 January 1989, meeting.
134 BoE, 10A161/9, 1 February 1989, meeting.
135 BoE, 2A56/5, 5 January 1989, LDMA meeting.

136 BoE, 2A56/5, 4 May 1989, LDMA meeting.

137 BoE, 10A161/9, 3 May 1989, Middleton meeting.

138 BoE, G4/216, Court, 26 January 1989.

139 BoE, 10A114/23, 9 February 1989, Leigh-Pemberton to Lawson.

140 BoE, 10A114/23, 12 October 1989, George to Michael Scholar.

141 BoE, 13A115/14, 23 May 1989, Books.

142 Philip Norman and Simon Holberton, 'Agreement to Differ Leaves EMS Time Bomb Ticking', *Financial Times*, 14 June 1989, p. 12.

143 BoE, 10A114/24, John C. Townend, 'The Orientation of Monetary Policy and the Monetary Policy Decision-making Process in the United Kingdom', November 1990.

144 Lord Kingsdown, obituary, *Daily Telegraph*, 25 November 2013: telegraph.co.uk /news/obituaries/10473025/Lord-Kingsdown-Obituary.html

145 BoE, 7A148/5, 27 September 1989, Note on meeting with Middleton, 26 September.

146 BoE, 2A56/5, 6 July 1989, LDMA meeting.

147 BoE, 7A107/34, Handwritten comment on JREF note of 6 December 1988, on Adam Smith speech.

148 Tim Congdon, *Reflections on Monetarism: Britain's Vain Search for a Successful Economic Strategy* (Cheltenham: Edward Elgar, 1992), 3.

149 Kydland and Prescott, 'Rules Rather Than Discretion', 473–490; Robert J. Barro and David B. Gordon. 'Rules, Discretion and Reputation in a Model of Monetary Policy', *Journal of Monetary Economics* vol. 12, no. 1 (July 1983): 101–121.

150 See Lars E. O. Svensson, 'Inflation Forecast Targeting: Implementing and Monitoring Inflation Targets', *European Economic Review* vol. 41 (1997): 1111–1146.

151 Charles Bean and Nigel Jenkinson, 'The Formulation of Monetary Policy at the Bank of England', *BEQB* vol. 41, no. 4 (2001): 434–441; Bennett T. McCallum and Edward Nelson, 'Targeting Versus Instrument Rules for Monetary Policy', *FRB St. Louis Review* vol. 87 (September/October 2005): 597–611.

152 Mervyn King, 'The Inflation Target Five Years On', lecture delivered at the London School of Economics, 29 October 1997.

153 John B. Taylor, 'Discretion Versus Policy Rules in Practice', *Carnegie-Rochester Conference Series on Public Policy* vol. 39 (1993): 195–214.

154 Edward Nelson and Kalin Nikolov, 'UK Inflation in the 1970s and 1980s: The Role of Output Gap Mismeasurement', BoE Working Paper 2001; on the problem of real-time versus ex post data, see Athanasios Orphanides and S. van Norden, 'The Reliability of Output Gap Estimates in Real Time', FEDS Paper 1999–38, Federal Reserve Board; and Athanasios Orphanides, et al., 'Errors in the Measurement of the Output Gap and the Design of Monetary Policy', *Journal of Economics and Business* vol. 52, no. 1 (2000): 117–141.

155 Ivor Owen, 'PM Stands By 3% Inflation Target', *Financial Times*, 17 April 1985, p. 15; Robin Leigh-Pemberton, 'Monetary Policy in the Second Half of the 1980s', *BEQB* vol. 30, Q2 (May 1990): 215.

156 See Michael D. Bordo, Ehsan U. Choudhri, Anna J. Schwartz, 'Money Stock Targeting, Base Drift and Price-Level Predictability: Lessons from the U.K. Experience', *Journal of Monetary Economics*, vol. 25/21 (March 1990): 253–272.

157 Bennett T. McCallum, 'Alternative Monetary Policy Rules: A Comparison with Historical Settings for the United States, the United Kingdom, and Japan', NBER Working Paper No. 7725, June 2000.

158 Michael D. Bordo and Pierre L. Siklos, 'Central Bank Credibility: An Historical and Quantitative Exploration', NBER Working Paper No. 20824, January 2015.

159 Thomas J. Sargent, 'Inflation: Causes and Effects', in Robert E. Hall, ed., *The Ends of Four Big Inflations* (Cambridge, MA: NBER Books, 1982), 41–98.

Hong Kong

1 Priscilla Chiu, 'Hong Kong's Experience in Operating the Currency Board System, 2001': imf.org/external/pubs/ft/seminar/2001/err/eng/chiu.pdf

2 BoE, 13A218/2, 31 January 1983, Hong Kong: January 1983.

3 Richard Roberts and David Kynaston, *The Lion Wakes: A Modern History of HSBC* (London: Profile Books, 2015), 71.

4 BoE, 13A218/1, 16 June 1981, CWM (McMahon): 'What Do We Have against HSBC'.

5 Roberts and Kynaston, *The Lion Wakes*, 83.

6 BoE, 13A218/2, 28 September 1983, J. B. Unwin: Hong Kong.

7 John Greenwood, *Hong Kong's Link to the US Dollar: Origins and Evolution* (Hong Kong: Hong Kong University Press, 2008), 145.

8 BoE, 13A218/2, 28 September 1983, D. G. Holland, Hong Kong: Call from Tony Latter.

9 Milton Friedman and Rose D. Friedman, *Two Lucky People: Memoirs* (Chicago: University of Chicago Press, 1998), 326.

10 Greenwood, *Hong Kong's Link*, 151.

11 BoE, 13A218/2, 30 September 1983, Goodhart: The Crisis in Hong Kong.

12 BoE, 13A218/2, 6 October 1983, David Peretz: The Hong Kong Dollar: First Report of the Peretz/Goodhart Visit.

13 BoE, 13A218/2, 6 October 1983, Charles Goodhart: Report on Proposed Exchange Rate Scheme.

14 BoE, 13A218/2, 10 November 1983, P. W. Allsopp: Hong Kong.

15 Ibid.

16 BoE, 13A218/2, 18 October 1983, Goodhart: Hong Kong.

17 BoE, 13A218/2, 15 December 1983, M. G. Hignett, Hong Kong: 'Exchange Arrangements'.

18 BoE, 13A218/2, 22 December 1983, J. G. Littler (Treasury): Hong Kong.

19 John Greenwood, '5 Misconceptions about the Government's Plan', *Asian Wall Street Journal*, 2 November 1983.

20 BoE, 13A218/3, 4 June 1984, Contingency Plan – Denham.

21 BoE, 13A218/3, 23 July 1984, C. D. Ellston: The Hong Dollar 'Problem', 6–16 July.

22 BoE, 13A218/3, Goodhart, 17 September 1984, Visit to Hong Kong, 1–6 September 1984.

23 BoE, 13A218/3, 18 June 1984, Hong Kong Financial Matters.

24 BoE, 13A218/4, 22 March 1985, Informal Conversation with Mr. Michael Sandberg.

25 BoE, 13A218/4, 31 May 1985, Foreign Office, A. C. Galsworthy: The Hong Kong and Shanghai Bank.

26 BoE, 13A218/4, A. R. Latter: Draft 20 September 1985, Hong Kong Monetary Policy and 1997.

27 BoE, 8A29/1, 16 October 1985, D. G. Holland: The Hong Kong and Shanghai Bank.

28 BoE, 8A29/1, 16 September 1985, K. F. Murphy: Note of a Meeting in HM Treasury, 12 September 1985.

29 BoE, 8A29/1, 1ay 1985, Sandberg's Call of May 17 W P C (Cooke) marginal comments.

30 BoE, 13A218/4, Len Appleyard (FCO), 23 September 1985, Mr. Sandberg.

31 BoE, 13A218/4, 30 October 1985, D. G. Holland, HSBC: Meeting with the Foreign Secretary and the Chancellor of the Exchequer.

32 BoE, 13A218/4, 8 November 1985, Appleyard (Foreign Office) to Charles Powell.

33 BoE, 13A218/5, 2 October 1986, note for Record, dictated by Governor.

34 BoE, 13A218/5, 10 October 1986, R. N. Culshaw (FCO) to John Footman (BoE).

35 BoE, 13A218/5, 17 November 1986, RLP (Leigh-Pemberton): note of conversation with William Purves.

36 BoE, 13A218/7, 11 November 1987, Footman, HSBC/Midland: Note for Record.

37 Tony Latter, 'Rules versus Discretion in Managing the Hong Kong Dollar 1983–2007', in Catherine R. Schenk, ed., *Hong Kong SAR's Monetary and Exchange Rate Challenges: Historical Perspectives* (Basingstoke: Palgrave Macmillan, 2009), 105.

38 Joseph Yam, 'The Origin and Evolution of Hong Kong's Currency Board II', in Schenk, *Hong Kong SAR's*, 153.

39 BoE, 13A218/9, 30 June 1989, cable.

40 BoE, 13A218/9, 9 June 1989, Brian Quinn: Midland/Hong Kong Bank.

41 BoE, 13A218/9, 29 June 1989, Brian Quinn: Midland/Hong Kong Bank.

42 See 'Hong Kong Monetary Authority, Monetary Operations under the Currency Board System: The Experience of Hong Kong', BIS Paper 73, 145.

43 BoE, 13A218/9, 21 August 1989, J. E. W. Kirby, Hong Kong and Shanghai Banking Corporation: Options for the Future.

44 BoE, 13A231/12, 19 July 1990, Note on 18 July meeting with Deputy Governor and Quinn.

45 Roberts and Kynaston, *The Lion Wakes*, 188.

Shaved Eyebrows

1 See Piet Clement, 'The Term "Macroprudential:" Origins and Evolution', *BIS Bulletin* (March 2010): 59–67.

2 See Carolyn Sissoko, 'How to Stabilize', 1–20.

3 Peter J. Cain and Anthony G. Hopkins, 'Gentlemanly Capitalism and British Expansion Overseas I. The Old Colonial System, 1688–1850', *Economic History Review* vol. 39, no. 4 (1986): 501–525; Cain and Hopkins, 'Gentlemanly Capitalism and British Expansion', 1–26. See also Philip Augar, *The Death of Gentlemanly Capitalism: The Rise and Fall of London's Investment Banks* (New York: Penguin, 2000).

4 See Rhiannon Sowerbutts, Marco Schneebalg and Florence Hubert, 'The Demise of Overend Gurney', *BEQB* vol. 56, Q2 (2016): 94–106; and R. H. Patterson, 'On Our Home Monetary Drains, and the Crisis of 1866', *Journal of the Statistical Society of London* vol. 33, no. 2 (June 1870): 216–242.

5 Forrest M. Capie, 'Can There Be an International Lender-of-Last-Resort?' *International Finance* vol. 1, no. 2 (1998): 311–325.

6 BoE, G4/63, 25 February 1841, tourt; G15/62, August 1935, committee on Advances and Discounts.

7 See Sayers, *The Bank of England*, 269; also the files complied by R. S. Sayers on this issue in BoE, ADM33/20.

8 See Allen, *Monetary Policy and Financial*; also, more generally, Carmen M. Reinhart, M. Belen Sbrancia, 'The Liquidation of Government Debt', NBER Working Paper No. 16893, March 2011.

9 BoE, 7A149/2, 20 January 1978, Secondary Banking: The Antecedents (Fforde).

10 See 'The Secondary Banking Crisis and the Bank of England's Support Operations', *BEQB* Q2 (April 1978): 230–239. On the secondary banking crisis in general see Margaret Reid, *Secondary Banking Crisis*; and Capie, *Bank of England*, pp. 524 ff.

11 TNA T450/173, 31 July 1978, Douglas Wass to Gordon Richardson.

12 BoE, 1A179/17, 6 March 1978, The Supervision of Deposit Taking Institutions.

13 BoE, 7A282/5, for details.

14 BoE, 7A147/1, Note: Banking Supervision, n.d. [1979].

15 Quoted in Augar, *Death of Gentlemanly Capitalism*, 5.

16 Nigel Lawson, budget speech, 18 March 1986, Hansard HC 94, column 177; available at: margaretthatcher.org/document/109503

17 BoE, 7A149/3, 15 April 1982: Note.

18 BoE, 7A149/3, 10 June 1982: Note for Record.

19 See BoE, 9A257/6, 23 March 1992, Big Four Clearing Banks: Liquidity Policy.

20 BoE, 3A143/1, 13 May 1980, P. H. Kent, EDC: Apocalypse Now.

21 BoE, 3A143/2, August 1980, P. H. Kent, Consequences of Debt Service Failure by a Major Borrowing Country.

22 BoE, 3A143/7, 22 July 1982, P. H. Kent, EDC: Apocalypse Now.

23 TNA, T437/248, 22 January 1982, Bank of England paper (John Ellis): Pilot Study on Country Risk Indicators.

24 IMF RD AN88/274, Box 5, Section 269, 22 November 1982, de Larosière London meeting notes.

25 BoE, 7A174/8, 24 August 1982, T. E. Allen note.

26 BoE, 7A174/8, 2 September 1982, ADL: The Prime Minister's Seminar on the International Banking Scene (Meeting on 1 September).

27 BoE, 7A174/8, Seminar on the International Banking Scene (Meeting on 1 September).

28 Sue Branford, 'Debt Attack by Governor', *The Times* (London), 23 November 1985, p. 25.

29 BoE, 7A282/7, 16 July 1984, International Debt Issues.

30 BoE, 7A133/6, 31 July 1984, conversation with Chancellor, Monday, 31 July.

31 BoE, C155/6, 8 January 1988, discussion.

32 'Boom in Britain: London Is Regaining a Key Financial Role', *Wall Street Journal*, 6 December 1983, 1.

33 BoE, 13A115/2, 17 May 1983, Books.

34 BoE, 7A148/3, 5 August 1987, briefing for the Deputy Governor.

35 David Kynaston, *City of London: The History* (London: Pimlico, 2011), 632.

36 See David Kynaston, *Till Time's Last Sand: A History of the Bank of England 1694–2013* (London: Bloomsbury, 2017), 593.

37 BoE, 15A91/9, Goodhart draft paper, April 1987, 'The Economics of "Big Bang"'.

38 See Christopher Bellringer and Ranald Michie, 'Big Bang in the City of London: An Intentional Revolution or an Accident?' *Financial History Review* vol. 21, no. 2 (2014): 111–138.

39 BoE, 13A115/3, 4 July 1983 and 30 November 1983, Books.

40 BoE, C55/128, 14 October 1982 and C55/129, 22 December 1983, LDMA markets meetings.

41 BoE, 15A91/3, 12 August 1983, Leigh-Pemberton to Lawson.

42 BoE, 13A231/2, 19 April 1984, Conversation with Mackworth-Young (Morgan Grenfell).

43 BoE, 7A148/3, 17 January 1986, Chancellor's lunch with the Governor.

44 BoE, 7A148/3, 29 January 1986, Supervisory Matters.

45 BoE, 13A231/4, 26 March 1986, John Bartlett, Note for Record: Ownership of Leading UK Banks.

46 BoE, 8A388/13, 20 April 1989, Deputy Governor's Committee.

47 BoE, 13A115/13, 20 October 1988, Books.

48 BoE, 7A320/8, Leigh-Pemberton speech at the President's Banquet, Northern Ireland Chamber of Commerce, 13 October 1987.

49 BoE, 15A91/5, 7 December 1983, Galpin: The Stock Exchange.

50 BoE, 10A191/9, 11 June 1981 and 2 November 1981, Thomson notes.

51 BoE, 10A191/11, 26 January 1983, Johnson Matthey Bankers Ltd.

52 BoE, 10A191/11, 28 October 1983 and 2 November 1983, Note: Johnson Matthey Bankers Ltd.

53 BoE, 10A191/12, 22 February 1984 handwritten note; January 1984, ADL note.

54 Chris Blackhurst, 'Arrest in Johnson Matthey Case', *The Independent*, 16 November 1997, p. 1.

55 BoE, 10A191/9, 9 August 1984, Thomson note.

56 BoE, 10A191/9, 24 August 1984, Thomson note.

57 BoE, 13A231/2, 26 September 1984, Johnson Matthey.

58 BoE, 7A148/2, 22 October 1982.

59 BoE, 13A231/2, 22 October 1984, conversation with Chancellor.

60 BoE, 10A191/18, 23 November 1984, Quinn: The Reasons for the Rescue of Johnson Matthey.

61 Rodney Galpin Obituary, *Daily Telegraph*, 13 November 2011.

62 Tyler Marshall, 'Shock Waves Rock Financial Community', *Los Angeles Times*, 22 September 1985, p. 2.

63 House of Commons debate, 8 November 1985.

64 Ibid.

65 House of Commons debate, 17 December 1984.

66 BoE, 10A191/16, 17 October 1984, Byatt for DG.

67 Rodney Galpin Obituary, *Daily Telegraph*, 13 November 2011.

68 BoE, 7A133/6, 27 November 1984, meeting at No.11 Downing Street.

69 BoE, 7A148/2, 27 November 1984, meeting.

70 BoE, 7A148/2, 22 July 1985, meeting with Chancellor; 1 August 1985, informal meeting with Chancellor.

71 TNA, PREM 19/1458 f176, 23 September 1985, Monetary Policy: No. 10 record of conversation (MT-Lawson).

72 BoE, 7A148/2, 3 September 1985, Handwritten note of conversation with Chancellor.

73 BoE, 14A132/1, 15 October 1985, A Banking Commission (on Treasury paper of 10 October).

74 BoE, 14A132/1, 15 October 1985, A Banking Commission?

75 BoE, 13A231/4, 23 January 1986, Galpin: Banking Supervision Division.

76 Cmnd9550, report, Committee to Consider the System of Banking Supervision.

77 'Finding the Truth about Barings', *Financial Times*, 7 March 1995, p. 19.

78 BoE, 8A388/10, 5 November 1987, Men Not for Jobs.

79 BoE, 13A115/13, 4 July 1988, Books.

80 BoE, 8A388/10, 20 August 1987, Note.

81 BoE, 7A149/5, 27 June 1989, BBS meeting.

82 BoE, 13A231/5, 6 January 1987, Deputy Governor's Committee minutes (Morgan Grenfell).

83 BoE, 7A149/5, 27 February 1989, Tucker: Board of Banking Supervision.

84 BoE, 13A231/18, 7 July 1992, Tucker: Central Banking and Bank Supervision.

85 Kynaston, *City of London*, 682.

86 David Brewerton, Sir Kenneth Berrill obituary, *The Guardian*: theguardian.com /politics/2009/jun/26/obituary-sir-kenneth-berrill

87 BoE, 7A107/34, JREF, 15 December 1988, draft for Adam Smith Institute speech.

88 BoE, 7A320/10, 20 January 1989, Adam Smith Institute luncheon remarks.

89 BoE, 9A97/8, 27 October 1987, Loehnis: BP Issue.

90 BoE, 9A97/8, 29 October 1987, Consultation under Clause 8 of the BP Final Price Offer Underwriting Agreement.

91 Kenneth Fleet, 'Lawson Decision Day on BP: City Pleads for Sell-off Delay as Share Prices Continue Plunge', *The Times* (London), 27 October 1987, p. 1.

92 BoE, 9A97/11, 27 October 1987, BP Assessment (note for Record).

93 BoE, 9A97/11, 29 October 1987, meeting at Rothschilds, 11:30–12:00; 29 October 1987, meeting at HM Treasury, 8:30 p.m.

94 Philip Stephens and John Hunt, 'Treasury Hits at Bank over BP', *Financial Times*, 2 November 1987, p. 1.

95 David Lascelles, 'Bankers at the Mansion House: Peace Breaks Out over BP Issue', *Financial Times*, 5 November 1987, p. 10.

96 'Rights Delay', *The Times* (London), 29 September 1987, p. 27.

97 'Slings and Blues Arrows', *Economist*, 20 February 1988, pp. 84–85.

98 BoE, 13A224/7, 21 February 1989, Blunden to Middleton.

99 BoE, 7A149/5, 23 March 1988, Companies Act Cases, Meeting on City Issues.

100 'If It Pleases Your "Honour"', *Economist*, 1 October 1988, pp. 118–119.

101 Peter Rodgers, 'DTI Says NatWest Executives and Phillips & Drew Deliberately Set Out to Evade Clear Legal Requirements', *The Guardian*, 21 July 1989.

102 John Mason, 'Damage-limitation Claim over Blue Arrow Is Denied', *Financial Times*, 29 June 1991, p. 4.

103 Steven Greenhouse, 'NatWest's Chairman Resigns', *New York Times*, 26 July 1989, p. D1.

104 Frank Kane, 'DTI's Investigation Clears NatWest of Dishonesty in the Blue Arrow Affair', *The Guardian*, 15 January 1993, p. 14.

105 BoE, 13A231/17, 27 March 1992, Tucker: National Westminster Bank and Blue Arrow.

106 'Everyone's a Loser: Blue Arrow', *Economist*, 22 February 1992, p. 95; 'NatWest and the Bank of England: An Apology', *Economist*, 22 January 1993, p. 86.

107 Kynaston, *City of London*, 713.

108 BoE, 7A149/6, 16 January 1990: FSA Regulation, 12 January 1990.

109 BoE, 13A231/8, 20 September 1989, Deputy Governors' Committee.

110 BoE, 13A231/12, Meeting with the Chancellor, Monday, 16 July 1990.

111 BoE, 13A231/12, 18 July 1990, Meeting with DG and Quinn (19 July 1990).

112 BoE, 8A388/12, Deputy Governor's Committee, 10 November 1988.

113 International Convergence of Capital Measurement and Capital Standards, Basel Committee, July 1988.

114 First Council Directive 77/780/EEC of 12 December 1977, on the coordination of the laws, regulations and administrative provisions relating to the taking up and pursuit of the business of credit institutions.

115 BoE, 8A388/10, 3 September 1987, Note: EC Liberalization.

116 BoE, 13A263/1, 8 July 1988, meeting of City Committee 7 July Mergers Policy – Foreign Takeovers.

117 BoE, 13A231/9, 11 December 1989, Discussion with Lamfalussy.

118 BoE, 8A388/12, 3 November 1988, Delors Committee.

119 BoE, 13A231/9, 18 October 1989, Note: Meeting of 16 October.

120 BoE, 13A115/15, 20 November 1989, Books.

121 BoE, 13A115/15, 13 September and 17 November 1989, Books. Also, Terry Dodsworth and Hugo Dixon, 'Ferranti Nears Agreement with Banks for Immediate Credit', *Financial Times*, 21 September 1989, p. 1.

122 BoE, 13A231/20, 20 December 1993, Norton Study on Banking Supervision: Meeting with Treasury.

Tunneling Deep

1 BoE, 6A339/7, 28 June 1983, David Walker speech to Open Dining Club, The British Industrial Problem.

2 See Andrew G Haldane, 'Productivity Puzzles', speech given at London School of Economics, 20 March 2017.

3 BoE, 7A149/1, 21 October 1977, J. C. R. Dow: The Impact of Policy on British Industry.

4 Churchill to Niemeyer, 22 February 1925, quoted in Donald E. Moggridge, *British Monetary Policy 1924–1931: The Norman Conquest of $4.86* (Cambridge: Cambridge University Press, 1972), 76.

5 Raymond Frost, 'The Macmillan Gap 1931–1953', *Oxford Economic Papers* vol. 6, no. 2 (1954): 181–201.

6 Paragraph 404 of Macmillan report.

7 BoE, 6A310/37, 17 August 1992, Pen Ken to Alan Wheatley (Chairman 3i).

8 BoE, 6A310/30, 2 March 1990, Clive Briault, 3i; 30 April 1990, National Westminster, Alternative Proposals for 3i.

9 BoE, 6A310/34, 19 July 1991, Jonathan Charkham, Sir John Cuckney.

10 '3i May Delay Float as Profits Plunge', *The Independent*, 20 December 1991, p. 25.

11 BoE, 6A310/38, 1 December 1992, D. W. Green, 3i.

12 BoE, 6A310/48, 13 July 1994, Note.

13 BoE, 6A310/42, 30 March 1994, Kenneth Clarke (Chancellor of Exchequer) to Governor; 8 April 1994, R. V. Darbyshire, Sale of 3i.

14 Richard Copey and Donald Clarke, *3i: Fifty Years Investing in Industry* (Oxford: Oxford University Press, 1995), 375.

15 BoE, 2A132/10, draft paper: Budgetary and Monetary Policy 1974–1975.

16 BoE, 6A135/1, 15 April 1975, draft press notice; Capie, *The Bank of England*, 803.

17 Margaret Reid, 'Equity Bank Will Not Fund Lame Ducks', *Financial Times*, 14 May 1976, p. 1.

18 'Business Diary: Lord and Master in Pursuit of Art', *The Times* (London), 4 April 1978, p. 19.

19 Margaret Reid, 'Seeing Industry through the Recession', *Banking World*, July 1983, pp. 10–12.

20 'Techniques for Assessing Corporate Financial Strength', *BEQB* Q2 (June 1982): 221–223.

21 BoE, EID9/61, 12 March 1981, meeting.

22 Margaret Reid, 'Seeing Industry', 12.

23 TNA T443/86, 18 November 1981, John Biffen to Leon Brittan: Laker Airways.

24 Walters diary entry, 5 February 1982, Churchill College Cambridge; available at: margaretthatcher.org/document/144208

25 TNA, T443/86, Meeting at No. 10 Downing Street, 8 February 1982, Laker Airways.

26 BoE, 9A388/1, 6 January 1981, Walker to McMahon.

27 BoE, 6A339/6, 5 October 1982, Roger Lomax, Special Situations – Possible Requests for New Share Capital.

28 BoE, 6A339/4, Dow to McMahon, 31 October 1980 and 1 November 1980.

29 BoE, 6A339/7, 3 January 1984, Jennings to Walker, CAG Case Statistics.

30 Pen Kent, 'The London Approach', *BEQB* Q1 (February 1993): 111.

31 BoE, 10A114/25, 22 February 1991, Leigh-Pemberton to Sir Anthony Durrant MP.

32 TNA, T460/110, 4 September 1984, M. A. Hall, Proof of Bank of England Shareholding; 4 September 1984, G. E. Grimston, Portals: 'Privatisation'.

33 BoE, 13A251/1, 24 June 1986, David Somerset, Portals.

34 BoE, G1/566. 'Governor's File: Sale of Bank's Shares in Portals and Possible Privatisation of the Printing Works'.

35 BoE, 13A129/2, Deputy Governor's committee, 7 November 1986.

36 BoE, 13A115/9, Books, 29 October 1986.

37 Obituary of Sir Alastair Morton, *Economist*, 9 September 2004.

38 Terry Gourvish, with Mike Anson, *The Official History of the Channel Tunnel* (Abingdon: Routledge, 2006), 297.

39 Ibid., 316.

40 BoE, 9A405/10, 5 January 1990, Leigh-Pemberton note of conversation with Morton.

41 Gourvish, *Channel Tunnel*, 318–319.

42 BoE, 7A320/13, Leigh-Pemberton, 25 October 1990, Speech at annual dinner of the Equipment Leasing Association.
43 Kent, 'The London Approach', 115.

Great Leap in the Dark

1 BoE, 8A249/1, 3 May 1988, Monetary Committee.
2 Lawson, *The View from No. 11*, 902–903.
3 BoE, 13A231/6, 22 July 1988, J. R. E. Footman: Delors Committee.
4 BoE, 13A231/6, 22 July 1988, Delors Committee.
5 BoE, 8A250/1, 4 July 1988, J. R. E. Footman: Delors Committee.
6 BoE, 8A249/2, 9 August 1988, Littler: Delors Committee.
7 Lawson, *The View from No. 11*, 908.
8 BoE, 7A148/4, 6 September 1988, lunch with Chancellor.
9 BoE, 8A249/2, 12 September 1988, J. A. A. Arrowsmith note: Whitehall access to Delors Committee papers; 8A250/1, 14 September 1988, Leigh-Pemberton to Lawson.
10 BoE, 13A224/7, 17 February 1989, Leigh-Pemberton to Thatcher.
11 BoE, 7A149/5, 8 September 1988, note.
12 The Bruges speech, 20 September 1988: margaretthatcher.org/document/107332
13 CoG, First meeting of Delors committee, 13 September 1988, transcript.
14 BoE, 13A115/13, 12 October 1988, Books.
15 BoE, 13A231/6, Note of a Conversation with Chancellor at Lunch, Monday, 24 October 1988.
16 BoE, 13A115/13, 9 November 1988, Books.
17 BoE, 13A231/6, 13 December 1988, meeting with Sir Peter Middleton on 12 December.
18 BoE, 7A148/4, 8 December 1988, Allan to Footman (on 7 December meeting of Governor and Chancellor).
19 BoE, 7A148/5, 16 January 1989.
20 BoE, 7A107/34, 30 January 1989, JREF, Delors.
21 Van den Berg, *Making of Statute*, 64.
22 Banque de France, Direction des changes, Compte-rendu de la session de 14 mars du Comité Delors, quoted in Olivier Feiertag, 'La conversion de la Banque de France à l'unification monétaire européenne: le tournant du comité Delors (1987–1992)' in Olivier Feiertag and Michel Margairaz, eds., *Les banques centrales à l'échelle du monde du 20e au 21 siècle/Central Banks at world's scale from the 20th to the 21st century* (Paris: Presses de Sciences Po, 2012).
23 BoE, 8A215/3, 20 March 1989, Arrowsmith note.
24 BoE, 7A148/5, 4 April 1989, note on meeting with Sir Peter Middleton (on 3 April).
25 Tape of Delors Committee, 11–12 April 1989, European Central Bank historical archive.
26 Delors Report: Committee for the Study of Economic and Monetary Union, *Report on Economic and Monetary Union in the European Community. Presented April 17, 1989, EU Commission – Working Document*, available as http://aei.pitt.edu/1007/1/monetary_delors.pdf

27 David Buchan, Philip Stephens and William Dawkins, 'EC Moves on Monetary Union', *Financial Times*, 28 June 1989, p. 1.

28 HADB, B330/24118, 12 November 1990, statement of Governor of Bank of England.

29 BoE, 7A148/5, 8 November 1989, Gieve to Tucker, Chancellor's bilateral with the Governor: Tuesday, 7 November.

30 BoE, 8A388/14, DGC, 1–2 November 1989.

31 BoE, 13A231/12, 13 June 1990, conversation with Barry Potter, 10 Downing Street.

32 Economic and Monetary Union Beyond Stage One: Possible Treaty Provisions and a Statute for a European Monetary Fund, 8 January 1991.

33 BoE, 8A222/1, 14 July 1989, S. D. H. Sargent, Alternative Models of Economic and Monetary Union. UK Treasury, *An Evolutionary Approach to European Monetary Union*, 1989; CoG 3.1/10–9, 10 June 1990, Leigh-Pemberton note.

34 Stephen Wall, *A Stranger in Europe: Britain and the EU from Thatcher to Blair* (Oxford: Oxford University Press, 2008),87; 98–99; 102–103.

35 BoE, 13A256/11, 3 July 1990, John Gieve to Charles Powell: Chancellor's meeting with the President of the Bundesbank.

36 BoE, 13A231/13, 9 November 1990, R.L.P.: Pöhl's meeting with the Prime Minister [meeting on 8 November].

The Spine Theory and Its Collapse

1 Thomas J. Sargent, *Rational Expectations and Inflation* (New York: Harper and Row, 1986), 121; see also Mervyn King, 'How Should Central Banks Reduce Inflation? – Conceptual Issues', *BEQB* Q4 (1996): 439.

2 Thatcher, *Downing Street Years,* 690.

3 Robin Leigh-Pemberton, *The Future of Monetary Agreements in Europe* (London: Institute of Economic Affairs, 1989), 22. The special lecture was given at the Queen Elizabeth II Conference Centre and also reprinted in *BEQB* vol. 29, Q3 (August 1989): 368–374.

4 BoE, 7A148/6, 12 June 1990, Leigh-Pemberton: Telephone conversation with Alan Greenspan. See also Wall, *A Stranger in Europe*, 92–93.

5 See Mallaby, *Greenspan*, 267–269.

6 BoE, 7A148/4, 8 September 1988, Handwritten comments of Leigh-Pemberton.

7 BoE, 13A256/11, 3 July 1990, John Gieve to Charles Powell: Chancellor's meeting with the President of the Bundesbank.

8 John Major, *John Major: The Autobiography* (New York: HarperCollins, 1999), 153–154; Smith, *Policy-making in the Treasury*, 102.

9 William Keegan, David Marsh and Richard Roberts, *Six Days in September: Black Wednesday, Brexit and the Making of Europe* (London: OMFIF Press, 2017), 60.

10 Moore, *Thatcher: Herself Alone*, p. 587.

11 BoE, 171618, 9 May 1986, Notice to the Banking Staff.

12 BoE, 7A149/5, 28 January 1987, Loehnis: Communication and Coordination Within the Bank.

13 Peter Norman, 'Bank Opposes Britain's Early Entry into the EMS', *Financial Times,* 12 May 1989, p. 1.

14 BoE, 7A149/5, 12 May 1989, Tucker note.

15　BoE, 7A149/6, 2 January 1990, UK participation in ERM.

16　BoE, 4A39/11, 17 September 1990, Crockett, Short-Term Economic Prospects.

17　BoE, 10A114/24, 19 April 1990; 18 April 1990, Meeting; The Course of Monetary Policy.

18　BoE, 7A149/6, 22 December 1989, UK Participation in the ERM.

19　BoE, 10A114/24, 5 November 1990, Informal Court Discussion, Thursday, 20 September 1990, The Monetary Debate Continued.

20　BoE, 13A256/11, 23 April 1990, note of a meeting on 20 April 1990, held in Sir Peter Middleton's room, HM Treasury.

21　Kenneth Dyson and Kevin Featherstone, *The Road to Maastricht: Negotiating Economic and Monetary Union* (New York: Oxford University Press, 1999), p. 555.

22　CoG, 8 October 1990, Monetary Committee Report to Ministers.

23　Stephens, *Politics and the Pound,* p. 168.

24　John Major, *John Major: The Autobiography* (London: HarperCollins, 1999), p. 314.

25　Margaret Thatcher party conference speech, 12 October 1990, available at: margar etthatcher.org/document/108217

26　BoE, 13A224/8, 4 October 1990, Leigh-Pemberton to Margaret Thatcher.

27　Keegan, Marsh, and Roberts, *Six Days in September,* 65.

28　BoE, 14A133/1, 23 October 1990, John Gieve to Paul Tucker, Governor's Meeting with the Chancellor on 22 October 1990.

29　BoE, 7A149/5, 20 April 1989, Footman: Note on the Markets Meeting.

30　BoE, 14A133/6, 26 February 1991, James Lingard and Ian Watt, KALE: Interim Report.

31　Peter Rodgers, 'Discount House in ERM Tip-off Row', *The Independent,* 11 October 1990, p. 30. Also Anthony Bevins, 'Gerrard & National Is Named over ERM Leak', *The Independent,* 16 January 1991, p. 22.

32　BoE, 14A133/1, 29 October 1990, David Walker to Governor.

33　BoE, 13A256/11, Minutes of a meeting held in Chancellor's Room HM Treasury at 11:15 a.m. on Monday, 12 November 1990.

34　BoE, 10A114/24, 3 December 1990, 30 November meeting with Chancellor, Monetary conditions and European and Monetary Union.

35　BoE, 13A256/11, 3 December 1990, Monetary condition and European and Monetary Union (meeting with the new Chancellor).

36　BoE, 7A149/7, Meeting at No. 11 Downing Street on Sunday, 22 December 1991.

37　BoE, 13A256/11, 12 December 1990, meeting in Treasury (note of 13 December).

38　Anatole Kaletsky, 'Treasury Ready for Interest Rate to Fall Sooner than Expected', *The Times* (London), 19 December 1990, p. 1.

39　BoE, 13A256/11, 19 December 1990, Tucker: Meeting with the Prime Minister, Thursday, 20 December 1990.

40　BoE, 10A114/24, 13 December 1990, minutes of a meeting held in Chancellor's room HM Treasury at 9:45 a.m. on Wednesday, 12 December.

41　Anatole Kaletsky, 'Treasury Ready for Interest Rate'; 13A256/11, Paul Tucker: 19 December 1990, Meeting with the Prime Minister: Thursday, 20 December 1990.

42 See Sebastian Mallaby, *More Money than God: Hedge Funds and the Making of a New Elite* (New York: Penguin, 2010), 151.

43 BoE, 13A256/12, Telephone conversation with President Pöhl: 24 January 1991.

44 BoE, 10A114/25, 21 February 1991, Paul Tucker: Telephone call from Andrew Turnbull.

45 BoE, 10A114/26, 26 April 1991, Leigh-Pemberton to Lamont.

46 CoG, Committee of Alternates, 13 May 1991.

47 BoE, 13A256/12, 25 April 1991, lunch with the Chancellor, 25 April 1991.

48 Michael Jones, David Smith, and David Hughes, 'Nightmare', *The Sunday Times* (London), 19 May 1991, 10.

49 BoE, 10A114/26, Governor's Lunch with the Chancellor, 17 June 1991.

50 BoE, 13A256/12, 19 September 1991, Governor and Sir Terry Burns Bilateral.

51 BoE, 10A114/26, 22 December 1991, meeting in Treasury.

52 BoE, 7A149/8, Leigh-Pemberton, Meeting of European G4, Paris, 7 January 1992.

53 BoE, 13A256/13, Minutes of Meeting in Chancellor's Room, HM Treasury, 25 February 1992.

54 BoE, 2A56/8, 9 January 1992, markets meeting.

55 BoE, 13A231/17, 8 April 1992, Economic Policy and Market Questions Concerning a Possible Labour Government.

56 See Edward Nelson, 'An Overhaul of Doctrine: The Underpinning of UK Inflation Targeting', *Economic Journal* vol. 119, no. 538 (June 2009): F333–F368.

57 BoE, 10A114/24, Markets Meeting, 30 April 1992.

58 Neil Bennett, 'Bank Cashes in on Gilt Market Surge', *The Times* (London), 11 April 1992, p. 41.

59 BoE, 9A376/2, 10 June 1992, Schlesinger Comments to the *Herald Tribune*.

60 CoG, Meeting 264, Basel, 10 March 1992.

61 CoG, Meeting 268, Basel, 14 July 1992.

62 Andrew Fisher and David Marsh, 'Germany "on Money Supply Tightrope": Dilemma for Bundesbank in Fixing Monetary Target', *Financial Times*, 13 July 1992, p. 1.

63 BoE, 8A316/35, 15 July 1992, MDKW Foot. EC Governors – Basel Meeting, 14 July 1992.

64 Hans Tietmeyer, Herausforderung Euro: Wie es zum Euro kam und was es für Deutschlands Zukunft bedeutet (Munich: Hanser, 2005), 178.

65 HADB Bundesbank ZBR 850, 16 July 1992.

66 Tietmeyer, *Herausforderung*, 178.

67 BoE, 9A376/2, 14 July 1992, FCO to Bonn embassy.

68 Federal Reserve Open Market Committee, 6 October 1992, transcript.

69 Quoted in UK Treasury, ERM Project Paper, 21 December 1993.

70 BoE, 2A56/8, 3 September 1992, markets meeting.

71 Tim Jackson and Stephen Castle, 'Pound Gets Help from Germans', *The Independent*, 6 September 1992, p. 1.

72 BoE, 9A391/19, 7 September 1992, Andres Kees to members of the Monetary Committee.

73 BoE, 8A316/36, 9 September 1992, EC Governors' Committee, 8 September 1992, Basel.

74 Committee of Governors' Meeting, 8 September 1992, Basel.

75 Mallaby, *More Money,* 156–157.
76 Fischer Black and Myron Scholes 'The Pricing of Options and Corporate Liabilities', *Journal of Political Economy* vol. 81, no. 3 (1973): 637–654.
77 BoE, 9A376/2, 10 September 1992, Handwritten note.
78 BoE, 1A50/3, 11 September 1992, Crockett: Conversation with Borges (Bank of Portugal).
79 Keegan, Marsh and Roberts, *Six Days in September,* 109.
80 Anatole Kaletsky, 'After the Lira, How Vulnerable Is Sterling', *The Times* (London), 15 September 1992, p. 1.
81 Gene G. Marcial, *Secrets of the Street: The Dark Side of Making Money* (New York: McGraw-Hill, 1995), 210.
82 Anatole Kaletsky, 'How Mr. Soros Made a Billion by Betting against the Pound', *The Times* (London), 26 October 1992, p. 38.
83 William Allen, Events surrounding departure from ERM, 20/9/92.
84 BoE, 14A99/2, 15 September 1992, meeting in Treasury (Chancellor's Room), 7:00 p.m.
85 Keegan, Marsh and Roberts, *Six Days in September,* 111.
86 Allen, Events.
87 BoE, 9A368/1, 18 September 1992, Sir Peter Petrie to Governor's Private Secretary.
88 Allen, Events.
89 Douglas Hurd, *Memoirs* (New York: Little, Brown, 2003), 468–469; see also Keegan, Marsh and Roberts, *Six Days in September,* 118.
90 BoE, 13A231/19, 24 September 1992, Market Conversations (on 16 September), C. A. J. C. Butler.
91 BoE, 13A231/19, 16 September 1992, Concertation with EC Governors (Tucker).
92 BoE, 9A351/2, 1 December 1992, Monetary Committee.
93 Peter Norman, 'The ERM and Maastricht – Bad Blood as a Relationship Hits Its Floor', *Financial Times,* 1 October 1992, p. 2.
94 BoE, 4A39/11 EEC-ERM, 30 September 1992, letter.
95 Peter Norman, 'Treasury Angered by Leaked Report of Bundesbank's Defence over Black Wednesday', *Financial Times,* 1 October 1992, p. 1.
96 BoE, 13A231/19, 1 October 1992, C. A. J. C. Butler, Note for Record: Conversation with Schlesinger.
97 Mervyn King, 'Monetary Policy in the UK', *Fiscal Studies* vol. 15, no. 3 (1994): 109 –128 (quote from p. 115).
98 BoE, 9A368/2, M. A. Hannam and N. J. Butterworth, 'The Cost of Intervention, 3 August 1992–1 April 1993', 21 July 1993.
99 Treasury paper, 6 August 1997, 'The Cost of Black Wednesday Reconsidered'. Available at: margaretthatcher.org/document/137077
100 The documents on the Treasury side were released in July 2018: see Ben Chapman, 'How John Major and Norman Lamont Hid the Cost of the Black Wednesday Disaster', *The Independent,* 23 July 2018, independent.co.uk/news/business/news/black-wednesday-john-major-norman-lamont-1992-bank-cost-a8460626.html
101 BoE, 13A231/20, 6 January 1993: Conversation between the Governor and Chancellor about Reserves Management (6 January, noon).
102 Alan Budd, 2004 Wincott Lecture on Black Wednesday, Institute of Economic Affairs, 2005, p. 15.

103 Stephen Wall, *A Stranger in Europe: Britain and the EU from Thatcher to Blair* (Oxford: Oxford University Press, 2008), 142.

104 Major, *John Major*, 341.

105 Michael D. Bordo and Pierre L. Siklos, 'Central Bank Credibility: An Historical and Quantitative Exploration', NBER Working Paper No. 20824, January 2015.

106 Paul Krugman, 'A Model of Balance of Payments Crises', *Journal of Money, Credit and Banking* vol. 11 (1979): 311–325.

107 Willem Buiter, Giancarlo Corsetti and Paolo Pesenti, Interpreting the ERM Crisis: Country-Specific and Systemic Issues, Princeton Studies in International Economics, International Economics Section, Department of Economics Princeton University, 1998; Maurice Obstfeld, 'The Logic of Currency Crises', *Cahiers Economiques et Monétaires* (1994): 189–213; Maurice Obstfeld, 'Models of Currency Crises with Self-fulfilling Features', *European Economic Review* vol. 40 (1996): 1037–1047; Olivier Jeanne, 'Currency Crises: A Perspective on Recent Theoretical Developments', Special Papers in International Economics, No. 20, International Finance Section, Princeton University, 2000.

108 Barry Eichengreen, 2000. 'The EMS Crisis in Retrospect', NBER Working Papers 8035.

'You Can't Be In and Out at the Same Time':

1 Smith, *Policy-making in the Treasury*, 127.

2 Commons debates Col. 865, 11 December 1991.

3 BoE, 15A38/1, 25 June 1998, Governor phone call with Duisenberg.

4 Huib Muller, 7 December 1988, Note for EC-Governors, Prudential Supervision of Banks in the European Community.

5 CoG, Meeting 243, 13 March 1990, Basel.

6 Charles Goodhart, *The Basel Committee on Banking Supervision: A History of the Early Years, 1974–1997* (Cambridge: Cambridge University Press, 2011), 551.

7 HADB, B330/018462, 26 January 1989, Wolfgang Kuntz to Pöhl; 20 February 1989, Tietmeyer to Pöhl; 23 February 1989, Pöhl to Kuntze; BdF, 1489200205/118, 5 May 1992, Commission bancaire: Note pour le Gouverneur.

8 HADB, B330/24112, 22 February 1990, Report on Monetary Policy Committee.

9 CoG, Meeting 243, 13 March 1990.

10 CoG, Committee of Alternates, 29 June 1990; see also van den Berg, *Making of Statute*, 67.

11 CoG, Committee of Alternates, 16 October 1990.

12 BoE, 14A86/30, 26 March 1998, Lender of Last Resort Post-EMU.

13 BoE, G4/220, 13 August 1992, Court.

14 BoE, 9A403/2, 9 April 1992, Note for the Record.

15 BoE, 4A2/97, 18 September 2002, Court paper: The Bank and the Euro.

16 BoE, 14A86/8, 1 March 1996, Monetary co-existence in Europe: CEPR/BNL Seminar: Rome: 26 February 1996.

17 BoE, 14A86/1, 1 August 1994, M. R. Lewis, Transition to EMU: Views of the Economic Secretary.

18 BoE, 14A86/5, 10 October 1995, W. Allen, EMU: Ins and Outs.

19 BoE, 16A121/19, December 1995, Peter Andrews, Clive Briault and David Ingram, Market Consequences of a Delay to EMU.

20 BoE, 14A86/2, 10 January 1995, John Shepherd (British Embassy Bonn): The German Approach to EMU.

21 BoE, 14A117/3, 22 January 1997, J. L. Carr: Bank Work on Creative Accounting.

22 BoE, 14A117/4, 9 October 1997, Sir Peter Petrie: EMU Convergence Criteria and the Bank.

23 Bank of England Annual Report 1999, p. 27.

24 BoE, 17A106/3, 8 September 1998, John Trundle: Tietmeyer's Attitude to TARGET Decisions.

25 BoE, 14A117/3, 6 June 1997, Mark Wharton: Market Surveillance Visit to Lehman Brothers, 21 May 1997.

26 BoE, 14A86/25, 22 October 1997, British Embassy Washington (Andrew Dawson) to Nigel Wicks, HM Treasury.

27 BoE, 16A118/16, 24 February 1997, King: Meeting with Soros Fund Management.

28 BoE, 14A86/24, 8 October 1997, George to Lord Kingsdown.

29 BoE, 16A118/16, 14 March 1997, WP3 Meeting, 1 March 1997.

30 26 June 2002, Mansion House speech: theguardian.com/politics/2002/jun/27/econ omy.uk

31 Select Committee on Education and Employment Minutes of Evidence, Thursday, 27 May 1999: publications.parliament.uk/pa/cm199899/cmselect/cmeduemp/547/ 9052704.htm

32 BoE, 16A118/25, 3 April 2003, King: Changing the Inflation Target.

Horses for Courses

1 Paul Volcker, 'The Triumph of Central Banking', the 1990 Per Jacobsson Lecture (Washington: International Monetary Fund, Per Jacobsson Foundation, 23 September 1990).

2 George A. Selgin, 'The Futility of Central Banking', *Cato Journal* vol. 30, no. 3 (Fall 2010): 465–473.

3 BoE, 13A115/15, 1 November 1989, Books.

4 House of Commons, Treasury and Civil Service Committee, Session 1993–1994, 'The Role of the Bank of England, First Report, Evidence', Q476, 88.

5 BoE, 7A149/6, 7 June 1990, Tucker note on Visit to Treasury.

6 Sarah Curtis, ed., *The Journals of Woodrow Wyatt, Volume Two* (London: Pan Books, 1999), 186.

7 Peter Wilson-Smith, 'Profile: A Central Banker Breaks Free', *The Independent*, 4 February 1990, p. 8.

8 BoE, 7A320/11, 14 February 1990, George Blunden, Julian Hodge Bank Annual Lecture: The Role of the Central Bank.

9 BoE, 13A231/10, Informal Court discussion, 22 February 1990.

10 BoE, 13A231/11, 18 April 1990, The Bank of England: Purposes, Responsibilities and Philosophy; see also G4/217, 14 June 1990, Court paper, George: The Bank of England: Purposes, Responsibilities and Philosophy.

11 BoE, 13A231/12, 12 July 1990, Independence/Accountability.

12 BoE, 16A32/2, 18 November 1993, George: The Pursuit of Financial Stability.

13 BoE, 13A231/17, 27 March 1992, Leigh-Pemberton to George.

14 BoE, 13A231/19, 17 September 1992, CB (for Deputy Governor): Policy.

15 BoE, 16A118/7, 17 September 1992 memo.

16 Edward Nelson, 'An Overhaul of Doctrine: The Underpinning of UK Inflation Targeting', *Economic Journal* vol. 119, no. 538 (June 2009): F363.

17 BoE, G4/219, Court, 19 March 1992.

18 Christopher Sims, 'Macroeconomics and Reality', *Econometrica* vol. 48, no. 1 (1980): 1–48.

19 BoE, 10A161/13, Meeting on the new monetary framework, held in Sir Terry Burns's room at 9:30 a.m., Friday, 2 October 1992.

20 BoE, 13A231/19, Conversation with Sir Terry Burns on 6 October 1992 (7 October 1992).

21 BoE, 10A114/27, 6 October 1992, Leigh-Pemberton to Lamont.

22 BoE, 10A114/27, 6 October 1992, Attachment: Price Stability.

23 BoE, 3A78/5, 8 October 1992, Lamont to TCSC.

24 BoE, 7A320/23, 8 October 1992, Speech given by the Rt. Hon. Robin Leigh-Pemberton Governor of the Bank of England at the CBI Eastern Region Annual Dinner on Thursday, 8 October 1992.

25 BoE, 13A231/19, 20 October 1992, P. M. W. Tucker, Note for Record: Conduct of Economic and Monetary Policy.

26 Norman Lamont, 'Chancellor's Mansion House Speech Oct. 29, 1992', *Treasury Bulletin* vol. 3, no. 3 (December 1992): 46–50.

27 BoE, 13A256/13, 27 October 1992, Treasury meeting.

28 Pennington, 'Secrecy Pays', *The Times* (London), 13 July 1994.

29 29 October 1992, Mansion House speech; available at: gov.uk/government/publica tions/chancellors-mansion-house-speeches-1985–1994

30 BoE, 13A231/20, 14 May 1993, Inflation Report.

31 BoE, 16A118/16, 3 February 1997, Tucker: UK Monetary Policy, explaining that one of the original objectives of the Inflation Report was 'providing a lever over Ministers'.

32 Bank of England Inflation Report, February 1993, p. 4.

33 Bank of England Inflation Report, May 1993, p. 4.

34 This point was made by Larry Summers, 'How Should Long-Term Monetary Policy be Determined?' *Journal of Money Credit and Banking* vol. 123 (1991), 625–631. King pushed back against this interpretation: see: 'Challenges for Monetary Policy: New and Old', in Federal Reserve Bank of Kansas City, New Challenges for Monetary Policy: A symposium sponsored by the Federal Reserve Bank of Kansas City Jackson Hole, Wyoming, 26–28 August 1999, 21–24. See also Ben S. Bernanke, *Inflation Targeting: Lessons from the International Experience*, Princeton: Princeton University Press, 1999.

35 Mervyn King, 'Changes in UL Monetary Policy: Rules and Discretion in Practice', *Journal of Monetary Economics* vol. 39 (1997): 96.

36 BoE, 16A118/11, 6 September 1993, Whither the ERM?

37 BoE, 16A118/11, 26 July 1993, 23 July meeting: Release of Official Statistics.

38 BoE, 16A118/10, 30 April 1993, Budd to King.

39 BoE, 10A143/1, 29 October 1992, Minutes of Meeting Held in Chancellor's Room HM Treasury at 3:30 pm Tuesday, 27 October 1992.

40 BoE, 10A143/1, 21 October 1992, Burns to George.
41 BoE, 4A16/1, 12 November 1992, Court.
42 Nicholas Wood and Janet Bush, 'Lamont's Surprise Cut Puts Rate at 15-Year Low', *The Times* (London), 27 January 1993, p. 1.
43 BoE, 7A148/9, 14 January 1993, Jeremy Heywood to John Trundle: Budget Strategy.
44 BoE, 7A148/9, 15 January 1993, Trundle: Lunch with the Chancellor: 13 January, Budget.
45 Andrew Grice and David Smith, 'Major Takes Charge of Economy', *Sunday Times* (London), 31 January 1993, p. 1.
46 BoE, 13A231/20, 2 February 1993, C. A. J. C. Butler, Conversation with Sarah Hogg.
47 Peter Marsh, 'Quiet Coup at the Linoleum Palace: Reforms Are Under Way at the Treasury, But Some Critics Believe They Do Not Go Far Enough', *Financial Times*, 13 January 1993, p. 17.
48 Will Hutton and Ruth Kelly, '"Wise Men" and CBI Demand Rate Cut', *The Guardian*, 22 January 1993, p. 16.
49 BoE, 13A183/5, J. R. E. Footman, 17 June 1993, Bank Independence.
50 publications.parliament.uk/pa/cm199293/cmhansrd/1993–06-09/Debate-1.html
51 BoE, 13A231/20, 10 February 1993, Draft letter to the Prime Minister.
52 BoE, 13A224/11, 22 April 1993, Governor to Prime Minister.
53 BoE, 13A231/20, 11 March 1993, Operational Autonomy (note on a meeting of March 10 with Deputy Governors and Directors).
54 BoE, 13A183/5, No. 10 Downing Street, Prime Minister's Meeting with the Governor and Deputy Governor of the Bank of England, 25 May 1993.
55 telegraph.co.uk/news/obituaries/finance-obituaries/9172100/Sir-George-Blunden.html
56 BoE, 7A148/5, 8 November 1989, Gieve to Tucker: Chancellor's Bilateral with the Governor: Tuesday, 7 November.
57 BoE, 7A148/6, 31 January 1990, Meeting with Chancellor, 26 January.
58 BoE, 7A148/6, 5 February 1990, Lunch with the Chancellor, 5 February.
59 Mervyn King, 'Prospects for Tax Reform in 1988', LSE Financial Markets Discussion Paper No. 10, 1987; William Keegan, *Mr. Lawson's Gamble*, 221.
60 BoE, 13A231/1, 19 August 1983, McMahon: Succession at Court.
61 Rachel Johnson, 'The Old Lady Wields Her New Broom: The Bank of England Is Forging Closer Relations with the City', *Financial Times*, 10 June 1991, p. 7.
62 BoE, 16A118/8, 14 December 1992, King, Comments for Court: Independence.
63 BoE, 13A183/3, 11 December 1992, draft: Independence for the Bank of England (Mervyn King).
64 BoE, 13A183/3, 16 December 1992, Andrew Crockett: Independence for the Bank of England.
65 BoE, 13A183/3, 21 December 1992, Note for Record: Independence for the Bank of England (on meeting of 18 December).
66 House of Commons, Treasury and Civil Service Committee, Session 1993–1994, The Role of the Bank of England, First Report, v, xxiii.
67 House of Commons, Treasury and Civil Service Committee, Session 1993–1994, The Role of the Bank of England, First Report, Evidence,

(Q465), 86. Also Observer – Sir Peter, QED, *Financial Times*, 2 November 1993, p. 23.

68 Ibid., xxviii.

69 Roll, *Independent and Accountable*, 5, 40.

70 Stanley Fischer, 'Modern Central Banking', in Forrest Capie et al., *The Future of Central Banking*, 262–308.

71 BoE, 13A183/5, J. R. E. Footman, 17 June 1993, Bank Independence. See also Major, *John Major*, 675.

72 BoE, 13A183/5, 9 November 1993, RPR, After the TCSC Report.

73 BoE, 8A388/18, 24 July 1991, Deputy Governor's Committee.

74 Ivan Fallon, 'Right Man for the Job, by George', *Sunday Times* (London), 24 January 1993, p. 2.

75 Janet Bush and Peter Riddell, 'Major Picks Eddie George to Head Bank of England', *The Times* (London), 23 January 1993, p. 1.

76 Rodney Hobson, 'Should the Old Lady Become Detached', *The Times* (London), 27 July 1994, p. 28.

77 'Observer – Old Lady's Flower Power', *Financial Times*, 27 January 1992, p. 19.

78 Robert Chote and Peter Rodgers, 'George Warns against "Political" Interest Rate Cuts', *The Independent*, 1 July 1993, p. 31; Peter Norman, 'New Bank Head Sees Potential for Lasting Recovery', *Financial Times*, 1 July 1993, pp. 1 and 24.

79 Peter Norman and Richard Lambert, 'A Steady Hand at the Helm', *Financial Times*, 1 July 1993, p. 23.

80 Ibid., 23

81 BoE, 9A226/1, Glenn Hoggarth, 21 October 1993, Ashridge Management College Meeting.

82 Norman and Lambert, 'A Steady Hand', p. 23.

83 BoE, 18A55/3, 24 July 1995, Governor's Bilateral with Mr. Quinn.

84 BoE, 1A50/3, 17 September 1992, Andrew Crockett: Policy.

85 BoE, 16A118/9, 8 January 1993, Contingency Planning for the ERM.

86 BoE, 9A226/1, 29 November 1993, The International Divisions.

87 BoE, 9A226/1, 11 November 1993, P. D. Mortimer-Lee, Ashridge.

88 BoE, 9A226/1, 1 December 1993, The New Bank (King).

89 BoE 9A226/1, 5 January 1994, Financial Stability Functions (Quinn).

90 BoE, 16A121/12, 16 September 1993, King to Currie.

91 BoE, 16A118/22, 15 December 2000, King: Introduction for Market Analysis induction course.

92 Peter Norman, 'On a Wing and a Prayer – Bank of England', *Financial Times*, 29 April 1994, p. 19.

93 BoE, 13A231/20, 7 October 1993, Staff Structure Pay and Morale.

94 BoE, 8A388/27, EXCO, 28 October 1994.

95 Rupert Pennant-Rea, *Gold Foil* (London: Bodley Head, 1978), pp. 9 and 214.

96 John Kampfner and Robert Peston, 'Clarke Sought to Stop Bank Departure', *Financial Times*, 23 March 1995, p. 11.

97 Michael Cassell and Gillian Tett, 'Bank Called to Act on Matter of the Heart: Allegations of an Affair Have Forced the Old Lady to Deal with a Problem Close to Home', *Financial Times*, 20 March 1995, p. 6.

98 'One Bonk and You're Out', *Newsweek,* 3 April 1995: europe.newsweek.com/one-bonk-and-youre-out-181768?rm=eu

99 'A Depressing Departure', *Financial Times,* 22 March 1995, p. 17.

100 BoE, 13A231/22, Trundle: Note for Record: Conversations with Terry Burns, Sir David Scholey, and the Chancellor, 20 March[1995].

101 The discontent was widely reported. See Larry Elliott, 'Old Lady's Personnel Chief Quits as Outsider Experiment Founders', *The Guardian,* 3 May 1996, 18.

102 BoE, 7A148/11, 2 October 1995, Lunch with the Governor, 28 September 1995.

103 BoE, 3A161/135, Mervyn King, 'How Should Central Banks Reduce Inflation? – Conceptual Issues', *BEQB* Q4 (1996), paper prepared for the symposium on 'Achieving Price Stability', sponsored by the Federal Reserve Bank of Kansas City, Jackson Hole, WY, 29–31 August 1996.

104 BoE, 13A231/19, 10 November 1992, Note for the Record.

105 House of Commons, Treasury and Civil Service Committee, Session 1993–1994, 'The Role of the Bank of England, First Report, Evidence', Q154, 30.

106 BoE, 18A55/2, Governor's Bilateral, 5 January 1994.

107 Norman and Lambert, 'A Steady Hand at the Helm', 23.

108 King, *End of Alchemy,* 170.

109 Tucker, *Unelected Power,* 419.

110 BoE, 16A118/9, 5 February 1993, Burns meeting on MTFS.

111 'Clarke Hints at Future Tax Cuts – Mansion House Speech', *Financial Times,* 15 June 1995.

112 The two years' time frame had been suggested by research by Milton Friedman in the early 1970s. It described well the lagged reaction to monetary expansion in the Heath period, and then became a rule of thumb for British policy making. See Nicoletta Batini and Edward Nelson, 'The Lag from Monetary Policy Actions to Inflation: Friedman Revisited', *International Finance* vol. 4, no. 3 (Winter 2001): 381–400.

113 Although King talked about the contribution of an inflation target to stabilizing real output: 26 September 1995, speech, 'Do Inflation Targets Work?'

114 BoE, 12A110/12, 20 November 1996, Court.

115 BoE, 15A39/9, 8 October 1996, Long Policy Planning Committee. M0 and M4 Monitoring Ranges: A Quick Review.

116 BoE, 2A56/10, 7 July 1994, LDMA meeting.

117 BoE, 252534, 3 March 1995, Plenderleith: The Treasury's Debt Management Review.

118 BoE, 252534, 3 November 1994, Chris Kelly (Deputy Secretary HM Treasury) to Plenderleith.

119 BoE, 287739, March 1995, HM Treasury Debt Management Review: Interim Report.

120 Figures from BoE, 287742.

121 'The Gilt-Edged Market: Developments in 1996', *BEQB* Q1 (February 1997): 63–74.

122 IMF WEO Database (October 2018).

123 BoE, 290666.

124 BoE, 252534, 17 February 1995, J. Cunliffe (Treasury) to Paul Tucker: Summary of Views of GEMMs.

125 BoE, 252534, 3 March 1995, Plenderleith: The Treasury's Debt Management Review.

126 BoE, 252534, 7 March 1995, Tucker: Debt Management Review.

127 BoE, 290659, 1 September 1995, Nigel Althaus to Paul Tucker.

128 BoE, 252534, 6 March 1995, King to Plenderleith: The Treasury's Debt Management Review.

129 Kenneth Garbade, 'The Evolution of Repo Contracting Conventions in the 1980s', *Economic Policy Review* vol. 12, no. 1 (2006): 27–42 (quotation from p. 36). See also Daniela Gabor, 'The (Impossible) Repo Trinity: The Political Economy of Repo Markets', *Review of International Political Economy* vol. 23, no. 6 (2016): 967–1000.

130 BoE, 252597, 19 February 1993, Tucker: Gilt Repos Paper.

131 BoE, 15A56/18, 3 March 1994, Philippa de Villoutreys, Telephone conversation with M. Trichet, 2 March 1994.

132 BoE, 15A56/18, 25 April 1994, Purchases of Gilts from the Market.

133 Janet Bush and Robert Miller, 'Gilts Auction Flops for the First Time', *The Times* (London), 28 September 1995, p. 25.

134 BoE, 14A86/5, 28 September 1995, Chancellor lunch with Governor.

135 BoE, 3A161/135, 11 October 1996, Tucker: Money Market Reform.

136 'Sterling Market Liquidity over the Y2K Period', *BEQB* Q4 (1999): 325–326.

137 BoE, 13A231/20, 3 June 1993, Trundle: Meeting with Chancellor, 2 June 1993.

138 BoE, 7A148/9, 21 June 1993, Jeremy Heywood to John Trundle: Chancellor's Bilateral with Governor, 17 June 1993.

139 Alan Blinder, 'Talking about Monetary Policy: The Virtues (and Vices?) of Central Bank Communication', BIS Working Papers No. 274, March 2009, 2.

140 William Poole and Robert H. Rasche, 'The Impact of Changes in FOMC Disclosure Practices on the Transparency of Monetary Policy: Are Markets and the FOMC Better "Synched?"' *Federal Reserve Bank of St. Louis Review* vol. 85, no. 1 (2003): 1–10.

141 Graham Bowley and Philip Coggan, 'Minutes Reveal Sharp Rift at the Top', *Financial Times,* 14 April 1994, p. 9.

142 Mark Duckenfield, *Business and the Euro: Business Groups and the Politics of EMU in Britain and Germany* (Basingstoke: Palgrave Macmillan, 2006), 130.

143 Martin Wolf, 'The Power of Politics: Inflation', *Financial Times,* 7 September 1996, p. 2.

144 See Mallaby, *The Man Who Knew,* 335.

145 BoE, 16A118/10, 30 April 1993: Budd to King.

146 BoE, 10A143/4, 6 September 1993, Robert Culpin (Treasury) to A. L. Coleby.

147 BoE, 10A143/4, 6 September 1993, Robert Culpin (Treasury) to A. L. Coleby, Monthly Monetary Minutes.

148 HM Treasury, Monthly Monetary Meeting: February 1994.

149 Anatole Kaletsky, 'Markets Need Not Panic But the Tories Might', *The Times* (London), 10 February 1994, p. 27.

150 BoE, 7A148/10, 11 February 1994, Telephone conversation with Sir Terence Burns: 10 February 1994.

151 Rachel Johnson and James Blitz, 'City Jitters Greet Clarke's Cut in Rates', *Financial Times,* 12 February 1994, p. 6.

152 Christopher Huhne, 'Harsh Reception for a Failing Double Act', *The Independent,* 20 February 1994, p. 8.

153 Robert Chote, 'George Continues Campaign to Wrest Control of Rates', *The Independent,* 2 February 1994, p. 28.

154 BoE, 10A143/6, 1 March 1994, Stephen Pickford (Treasury): Publishable Minutes of the February Monthly Meeting.

155 Treasury, Monthly Monetary Meeting, 2 March 1994.

156 Bowley and Coggan, 'Minutes Reveal Sharp Rift', p. 9.

157 BoE, 10A143/7, 28 July 1994, R. D. Clews, Governor/Chancellor: Preparing for September.

158 David Walton, 'Can the Chancellor Be Trusted on Inflation?' *The Times* (London), 24 January 1994, p. 38. Note: Walton worked for Goldman Sachs.

159 Inflation Report, February 1996, p. 46. Box: The Bank's inflation forecasting record.

160 Robert Chote, 'An Opening for the Governor', *The Independent,* 17 April 1994, p. 8.

161 Minutes of Monthly Monetary Meeting, 7 September 1994.

162 Janet Bush, 'Credibility Is the Name of the Game Two Years after Sterling's ERM Exit', *The Times* (London), 17 September 1994, p. 27.

163 Neil MacKinnon of Citibank, quoted in 'Markets Report – UK Rate Rise Lifts Sterling', *Financial Times,* 13 September 1994, p. 37.

164 BoE, 7A148/10, 23 November 1994, N. I. Macpherson to John Trundle, Lunch with the Governor: 22 November.

165 Minutes of Monthly Monetary Meeting, 7 December 1994.

166 Anatole Kaletsky, 'There Is Nothing to Fear but the Bank's Fear Itself', *The Times* (London), 3 November 1994, p. 29.

167 Monthly Monetary Meeting, 5 May 1995.

168 Robert Peston, Gillian Tett, and Motoko Rich, 'Bank Sees Threat to Inflation Target', *Financial Times,* 11 May 1995, p. 22.

169 Philip Coggan, 'Rise in Base Rates Widely Expected', *Financial Times,* 1 May 1995, p. 23.

170 Robert Chote, Philip Coggan, and Robert Peston, 'Pound Hit as Clarke Fails to Lift Rates: Suspicion of Rift between Chancellor and George – Decision Takes City by Surprise', *Financial Times,* 6 May 1995, p. 1.

171 'Can Clarke Be Caesar's Wife?' *Financial Times,* 6 May 1995, p. 8.

172 Robert Chote, 'Clarke Ignored Inflation Warning: Chancellor's May Meeting with Bank Governor', *Financial Times,* 22 June 1995, p. 9.

173 Monthly Monetary Meeting: 7 June 1995.

174 'Clarke Hints at Future Tax Cuts – Mansion House Speeches', *Financial Times,* 15 June 1995, p. 10.

175 Samuel Brittan, 'The Kremlinology of UK Policy', *Financial Times,* 27 July 1995, p. 16.

176 BoE, 7A148/11, 16 June 1995, Lunch with the Governor: 18 May 1995.

177 Peter Marsh, 'George to Revive Row about EMU', *Financial Times,* 6 May 1996, p. 6.

178 Minutes of Monthly Monetary Meeting: 7 March 1996.

179 Minutes of Monthly Monetary Meeting, 3 April 1996.

180 Minutes of Monthly Monetary Meeting, 8 May 1986

181 Minutes of Monthly Monetary Meeting, 5 June 1986.

182 BoE, 17A16/1, 23 February 1996, Davies: Meeting with Sir Terry Burns, HM Treasury, 22 February 1996.
183 Robert Chote and Gillian Tett, 'Rate Cut Aims to Boost Industry: Fears Over Strong Pound Prompt Surprise Quarter-Point Reduction', *Financial Times*, 7 June 1996, p. 1.
184 Minutes of Monthly Monetary Meeting: 5 June 1996.
185 BoE, 17A16/1, 21 September 1996, Davies: Meeting with Sir Terry Burns, HM Treasury, 20 September 1996.
186 BoE, 7A148/12, 17 July 1996, N. I. Macpherson to Andrew Bailey, Lunch with the Governor 16 July 1996.
187 BoE, 7A148/12, 18 December 1996, N. I. Macpherson to Andrew Bailey, Lunch with the Governor, 17 December.
188 BoE, 7A148/12, 28 January 1997, Lunch for the Chancellor, 23 January 1997.
189 Minutes of Monthly Monetary Meeting, 15 January 1997.
190 Samuel Brittan, 'Superpound and the Euro – Economic Viewpoint', *Financial Times*, 13 February 1997, p. 22.
191 BoE, 10A143/12, Q&A Monetary Policy Is Behind the Game [1997].
192 Minutes of Monthly Monetary Meeting, 5 February 1997.
193 Minutes of Monthly Monetary Meeting, 4 March 1997.
194 Minutes of Monthly Monetary Meeting, 10 April 1997.
195 Robert Chote, '"Canny Ken" Snubs Bank Pressure over Interest', *Financial Times*, 5April 1997, p. 9; 'The Ghost at the Banquet', *Financial Times*, 5 April 1997 p. 10.

Failure of Internal Communication

1 BoE, 2A164/5, 23 July 1996, The Bank's Review of Supervision.
2 Alan Greenspan, 'The Evolving Role of Regulators', speech at 32nd Annual Conference on Bank Structure and Competition, Chicago, 2 May 1996.
3 Andrew Freeman and Richard Donkin, 'Record City Takings Will Prove Difficult to Cash', *Financial Times*, 3 May 1990, p. 10; John Dennis, 'Britain's Biggest Robberies', *The Guardian*, 16 February 2002.
4 BoE, G4/219, 2 April 1992, Court.
5 Richard Donkin, 'Four European Central Banks Are Monitoring BCCI Dealings', *Financial Times*, 18 October 1988, p. 28.
6 BoE, 13A115/13, 18 October 1988, Books (Warland).
7 Donkin, 'Four Central Banks', p. 28.
8 BoE, 7A282/2, 15 May 1981, BCCI Summary.
9 'BCCI Scandal: Long Legal Wrangling over Collapsed Bank', *Guardian*, 17 May 2012: theguardian.com/business/2012/may/17/bcci-scandal-long-legal-wranglings
10 BoE, 7A282/2, 15 May 1981, BCCI Summary.
11 *Inquiry into the Supervision of the Bank of Credit and Commerce International (BCCI)* [Bingham report] (London: HMSO, 1992), 44.
12 BoE, 13A115/12 23 March 1988, Books.
13 BoE, 7A148/4, 24 October 1988, Conversation with Chancellor at lunch; 31 October 1988, A. C. S. Allan to John Footman (on 24 October 1988, lunch).
14 BoE, 810529, Luxembourg College, Meetings of 5 October 1990.

15 Bingham Report.

16 BoE, 13A256/13, 17 July 1991, Meeting in Chancellor's Room.

17 Ibid.

18 BoE, 13A231/18, 15 July 1992, David Mallett.

19 BoE, G4/218, 25 July 1991, Court.

20 William E. Schmidt, 'Bank of England Criticized on B.C.C.I.', *New York Times,* 23 October 1992, p. D2.

21 Peter Rodgers, 'Bank of England Criticised on BCCI', *The Independent,* 23 October 1992, p. 1.

22 BoE, G4/220, 3 September 1992, Court.

23 Peter Rodgers, 'Bank Denies Retirement of Barnes Is Linked with BCCI', *The Independent,* 10 February 1993, p. 22.

24 BoE, G4/220, 6 August 1992, Court.

25 BoE, 13A231/18, 20 July 1992, Tucker: Bingham Inquiry: Meeting with the Chancellor, 21 July 1992.

26 Dan Conaghan, *The Bank: Inside the Bank of England* (London: Biteback Publishing 2012) 113–117; also Michael Salib, A History of the Bank's Legal Directorate (2019, unpublished Bank of England paper)

27 BoE, 9A257/5, 24 January 1992, The Economic Background.

28 BoE, 9A257/4, 2 December 1991, The support measures taken in July/ August 1991.

29 BoE, 9A257/1, 14 July 1991, Wholesale Funding of Small Banks.

30 David Owen, 'B&C Rescue Attempts End in Failure', *Financial Times,* 4 June 1990, p. 1.

31 BoE, 9A257/6, 11 February 1992, John Gieve, Secondary Banks and Bank Rescues.

32 David Owen, 'Union Discount Warns of £ 6.5m Loss', *Financial Times,* 22 June 1991, p. 8.

33 BoE, G4/219, 6 February 1992, Court.

34 Peter Beaumont, '"House Catastrophe Brewing" as Losses Sour', *Observer,* 8 December 1991, p. 6.

35 BoE, 9A257/2, 22 July 1991, Creon Butler: Note for Record.

36 BoE, 9A257/5, 13 January 1992, Secondary Banks: Meeting in HM Treasury (Gieve, Treasury).

37 BoE, G4/218, 25 July 1991, Court.

38 BoE, G4/218, 8 August 1991, Court.

39 BoE, 9A257/9, 30 June 1993, G. S. Thomson: DGIV Enquiry on Bank of England Support Operation.

40 BoE, 13A256/13, Meeting in Chancellor's Room, 17 July 1991.

41 BoE, 9A257/6, 23 February 1992, Big four clearing banks: Liquidity policy.

42 BoE, 9A257/8, 30 March 1993, Support Facilities.

43 BoE, 9A257/9, 10 May 1993, Kenyan Asian Banks in the UK.

44 BoE, 9A257/6, Secondary Banks: Note of a meeting held at 4:15 p.m. on 20 March 1992, in HM Treasury.

45 BoE, 14A135/1, 3 January 1991, D. T. R. Carse, Midland Bank.

46 BoE, 14A135/1, 8 January 1991, B. Quinn, Midland Bank.

47 BoE, 14A135/1, 14 January 1991, Midland Bank (Report on meeting of 10 January).

48 BoE, 14A135/1, 15 January 1991, BBS meeting.

49 BoE, 13A231/12, 23 July 1990, Midland Bank (Tucker).

50 BoE, 13A231/12, 19 July 1990, Standard Chartered and Midland Bank.

51 BoE, 14A135/3, 18 February 1991, Conversation with Sir Kit McMahon, Monday, 18 February 1991.

52 BoE, 14A135/3, 22 February 1991, Handwritten Tucker note on meeting with Cazenoves.

53 BoE, 14A135/4, 1 March 1991, Tucker to Gieve: Enclosing draft letters of support.

54 BoE, 14A135/3, 22 February 1991, Telephone conversation with Willie Purves, 22 February 1991; 22 February 1991, Conversation with Sir David Scholey.

55 Melvyn Marckus and Nick Goodway, 'Midland Called to Account – The Woes of Midland Bank Culminated on Tuesday with the Departure of Sir Kit McMahon', *The Observer,* 10 March 1991, p. 31.

56 Obituary, for Sir John Quinton, *Daily Telegraph,* 1 May 2012: telegraph.co.uk /news/obituaries/finance-obituaries/9239493/Sir-John-Quinton.html

57 Abigail Hofman, 'The Middleton Way', *Daily Telegraph,* 27 June 2004, p. 56.

58 BoE, 13A231/20, 22 April 1993, J. M. Trundle, Barclays Bank.

59 BoE, 13A231/20, 27 April 1993, Discussion with John Kemp-Walsh (Barclays).

60 Sarah Whitebloom, 'Barclays Bows to Mounting Pressure and Seeks Outsider as Chief Executive', *The Guardian,* 25 March 1993, p. 16.

61 Peter Rodgers, 'Shareholders Tell Barclays Chief to Go', *The Independent,* 30 April 1993, p. 25.

62 BoE, 8A388/11, Deputy Governor's Committee, 23 June 1988.

63 BoE, 187652, 18 November 1988, Tucker: Payment and Settlement Systems Review.

64 BoE, 8A388/13, 30 March 1989, Payment and Settlement Systems.

65 BoE, 8A388/18, 13 November 1991, Netting and Cash Collateral.

66 BoE, G4/220, 23 July 1992, Court: Discussion of Kentfield and Allsopp paper on 'Interbank Credit Risk in Payments Systems'.

67 BoE, 8A388/20, Deputy Governor's Committee.

68 BoE, 12A110/9, 18 January 1995, Court.

69 BoE, 12A110/6, 3 March 1994, Foot in Court.

70 Helga Drummond, *The Dynamics of Organizational Collapse: The Case of Barings Bank* (Abingdon: Routledge, 2008), 103.

71 John Gapper, 'Bank "Not Told of Barings Move"', *Financial Times,* 6 April 1995, p. 1.

72 BoE, 16A110/1/1/27, 11 August 1994, SWOT: Baring Brothers & Co.

73 BoE, 16A110/1/1/27, 16 November 1994, visit of Andrew Tuckey and Peter Norris.

74 theguardian.com/theguardian/2013/nov/15/good-to-meet-you-howard-welwyn

75 Nick Leeson, *Rogue Trader* (London: Sphere, 1996), ch. 5.

76 BoE, 16A110/1/1/27, Walwyn, Barings: Japanese Stock Exchange Margin Exposures.

77 BoE, 16A110/1/1/27, 1 February 1995, Bank of England to Barings: Japanese Stock Exchanges: Margin Exposure.

78 BoE, 16A110/1/1/29, 28 February 1995, Foot: Note for Record.

79 BoE, 16A110/1/1/29, 28 February 1995, Telephone Conversation with Koh Beng Seng (MSA), 25 February.

80 Stephen Fay, *The Collapse of Barings* (London: Richard Cohen, 1996), 213.

81 BoE, 16A110/1/1/39, 6 April 1995, George to Alastair Ross Goobey.

82 Ibid.

83 Clive Wolman, 'Barings – A Bungled Affair?' *Mail on Sunday* (London), 19 March 1995, p. 4.

84 BoE, 16A110/1/1/29, 28 February 1995, Michael Foot: Note for Record; 13A231/22, 27 March 1995, Trundle: Note for Record, Meeting with Lord Airlie, 17 March.

85 'Banking on Boredom', *The Times* (London), 22 November 2016, p. 12.

86 BoE, 12A110/10, 12 July 1995, Court.

87 Robert Miller, 'Bank Supervisor Denies Barings Inquiry Charges', *The Times* (London), 21 July 1995, p. 21.

88 BoE, 2A164/3, July 1996, Arthur Andersen: Findings and Recommendations of the Review of Supervision and Surveillance; BoE, 13A166/1, 24 July 1996, The Bank's Review of Supervision.

89 BoE, 12A110/12, 17 July 1996, Court.

90 BoE, 12A110/12, 16 October 1996, Court.

91 BoE, 8A388/28, 18 February 1995, Executive Committee.

92 BoE, 2A164/5, 6 June 1996, Howard Davies memo for Polco: Arthur Andersen Review.

93 BoE, 18A55/3, 20 November 1995, Governors' Bilateral, 16 November 1995.

94 *Financial Stability Review*, Autumn 1996, p. 10.

95 The problems are set out well – and in respect of the Bank of England – in Gillian Tett's examination of *Silos*.

96 See Ranald Michie, *The London Stock Exchange: A History* (Cambridge: Oxford University Press, 1999), 608.

97 BoE, 15A106/2, The Case for TAURUS, 1 June 1988.

98 For instance, BoE, 15A106/14, June 22, 1990, Herschel Post (Shearson Lehman) to Pen Kent.

99 John Willcock, 'Rawlins Paid over £500,000 Despite Collapse of Taurus', *The Independent*, 19 June 1993, p. 19.

100 Norma Cohen, 'Bank Seeks Control over Share Settlement System', *Financial Times*, 16 February 1994, p. 24.

101 BoE, 7A148/10, note on 21 January 1994, Chancellor's lunch with Governor, 18 January 1994.

102 *Commercial and Financial Chronicle* vol. 16, no. 393 (4 January 1873): 7.

103 Pierre L. Siklos, *Central Banks into the Breach* (Oxford: Oxford University Press, 2017), 238–240.

104 BoE, 9A226/1, 5 January 1994, Quinn: Financial Stability Functions.

105 James H. Stock and Mark W. Watson, 'Has the Business Cycle Changed? Evidence and Explanations', FRB Kansas City symposium, Jackson Hole, WY, 28–30 August 2003, p. 40.

106 Andrew Haldane, et al., 'Financial Stability and Macroeconomic Models', *Bank of England Financial Stability Review* 16 (2004): 80–88; Geoffrey Wood, 'Review of Unelected Power: The Quest for Legitimacy in Central Banking and the Regulatory State by Paul Tucker', *Economic Affairs* vol. 38, no. 3 (2018): 456–457.

107 Wood, 'Review', 456.

108 Anna J. Schwartz, 'Why Financial Stability Depends on Price Stability', *Economic Affairs* vol. 4, no. 15 (Autumn 1995): 21–25 (quote from p. 21); Michael D. Bordo and David C. Wheelock, 'Price Stability and Financial Stability: The Historical Record', *Federal Reserve Bank of St. Louis Review* vol. 80,no. 5 (September/October 1998): 41–62 (concentrating on disruptions caused by disinflation).

109 BoE, 7A320/25, Eddie George, 'The Pursuit of Financial Stability', speech of 18 November 1993.

110 Claudio Borio and Philip Lowe, 'Asset Prices, Financial and Monetary Stability: Exploring the Nexus', BIS Working Papers 114, 2 July 2002.

111 James R. Barth, Gerard Caprio and Ross Levine, 'World Bank Surveys on Bank Regulation Database'; see James R. Barth, Gerard Caprio and Ross Levine, 'Bank Regulation and Supervision in 180 Countries from 1999 to 2011', NBER Working Paper No. 18733 (2013).

112 Luc Laeven and Fabian Valencia, 'Systemic Banking Crises: A New Database', IMF Working Paper WP/08/224.

113 Benton E. Gup, *Bank Failures in the Major Trading Countries of the World: Causes and Remedies* (Westport, CT: Greenwood Publishing Group, 1998), 25–26.

114 Patricia Jackson, 'Deposit Protection and Bank Failures in the United Kingdom', *Financial Stability Review* no. 1 (Autumn 1996): 38–43.

115 BoE, 15A61/10, 29 August 2000, Paul Richards to Alastair Clark email (6:37 a.m.), RE: Wise Men.

116 BoE, 13A112/10, 19 November 2001, C. M. Miller, Note for Record: Meeting with Mr. Bill Winters, Managing Director JP Morgan Securities Ltd., 16 November 2001.

117 William A. Allen and Geoffrey Wood, 'Defining and Achieving Financial Stability', *Journal of Financial Stability* vol. 2, no. 2 (2006): 152–172.

The New Bank

1 The manuscript is still in the Bank's archive.

2 William Keegan, *The Prudence of Gordon Brown* (Chichester: John Wiley, 2003), 155.

3 BoE, 12A110/4, 23 September 1993, Court.

4 BoE, 12A110/10, 30 September 1995, Court.

5 Ed Balls, 'Euro-Monetarism: Why Britain Was Ensnared and How It Should Escape', Fabian Society Discussion Pamphlet No. 14, 1992. Keegan, *Prudence*, 132.

6 Gordon Brown, 'Labour's Macroeconomic Framework', speech to Labour Finance and Industry Group, 17 May 1995; Keegan, *Prudence*, 164.

7 Keegan, *Prudence*, 157.

8 Tucker, *Unelected Power*, 412.

9 BoE, 16A26/1, 3 February 1997, Tucker: UK Monetary Framework Post-Labour.

10 BoE, 16A26/1, 11 February 1997, Andrew Bailey: The Governor's Meeting with Gordon Brown (6 February).

11 BoE, 8A388/36, 5 February 1997, GovCo.

12 Gordon Brown, *My Life, Our Times* (London: Bodley Head, 2017), 121.

13 BoE, 17A56/1, 25 February 1997, Howard Davies to Governor.

14 Robert Chote, 'Lamont's "Seven Wise Men" Fall Out as Professor Goes on the Attack', *The Independent,* 6 March 1993: independent.co.uk/news/uk/lamonts-seven-wise-men-fall-out-as-professor-goes-on-the-attack-robert-chote-argues-that-an-internal-1496279.html

15 Brown, *My Life,* 117.

16 BoE, 13A224/16, 3 March 1998, A. J. Bailey to Tom Scholar; lunch for the Chancellor: 25 February 1998.

17 David Smith, 'Independence Day', *The Sunday Times* (London), 11 May 1997, p. 3.

18 Diane Coyle and Nic Cicutti, 'At Last, Independence for the Bank', *The Independent,* 7 May 1997, p. 20.

19 BoE, 12A110/14, Court, 14 May 1997.

20 BoE, 16A129/1, 12 May 1997, Bailey: Meeting with Sir Terry Burns (9 May).

21 Email of James Steel, HM Treasury, 15 September 1998, in Correspondence and financial statistics relating to the sale of part of the UK gold reserves, Treasury FOI release 31 March 2010, available at: gov.uk/government/publications/the-sale-of-part-of-the-uk-gold-reserves-1999–2002

22 Christopher Adams, 'Britain – Digging for Central Bank Chief's Views on Gold Sale', *Financial Times,* 17 August 1999, p. 8.

23 Gillian O'Connor, 'Market Stunned as Gold Standard Loses Its Glister', *Financial Times,* 8 May 1999, p. 8.

24 Patrick Chalmers, 'Interview: Ex-BOE Forex Head Decries UK Gold Sale', Reuters, 13 May 1999.

25 BoE, 13A231/33, 8 February 2000, Gold Meeting.

26 Adrian Ash, 'The Outlook for Gold', *Daily Telegraph,* 19 December 2008: telegraph.co.uk/finance/personalfinance/investing/3849910/The-outlook-for-gold.html

27 Keegan, *Prudence,* 182.

28 Ibid., 183.

29 HM Treasury and Bank of England, Report of the Debt Management Review, July 1995.

30 House of Commons, Treasury and Civil Service Committee, Session 1993–1994, 'The Role of the Bank of England, First Report, Evidence', Q486, 89.

31 Andrew Rawnsley, *Servants of the People: The Inside Story of New Labour* (London: Penguin, 2001), 42.

32 BoE, 12A110/14, 20 May 1997, Court.

33 BoE, 7A148/12, 1 August 1997, PM's Bilateral with Governor.

34 BoE, 14A36/1, 18 August 1997, George to Alistair Darling.

35 BoE, 7A320/25, 18 November 1993, George: The Pursuit of Financial Stability.

36 BoE, 2A164/5, 23 July 1996, The Bank's Review of Supervision: Q&A Briefing.

37 FSA, 'A New Regulator for the New Millenium', January 2000; see also 'Competition in UK Banking: A Report to the Chancellor', 2000 (Cruickshank report).

38 Brown, *My Life,* 121.

39 Deloitte Touche, Securities and Banking Update, June 1997, p. 2.

40 BoE, 290524, 15 February 1999, Millennium Effects in Money Markets.

41 BoE, 270131, 6 January 1998, John Footman: Millennium Risk: Next Steps.

42 BoE, 297059, 6 July 1999, Plenderleith: Market Dislocations from Y2K.

43 BoE, 299754, Moody's Investor Service, 30 April 1998. Ryan O'Connell 'Heading toward Judgment Day', remarks at FRBNY conference 'Assessing 2000 Credit Risk'.

44 BoE, 4A2/55, 16 August 2000, Court.

45 Chris Giles, 'The Court of King Mervyn', *Financial Times*, 4 May 2012, p. 14.

46 BoE Annual Report 1999, p. 21.

47 BoE, 8A388/37, POLCO 22 May 1997.

48 BoE, 4A2/111, 17 September 2003, Court Paper, Governor (King): The Bank of England: The Next Five Years.

49 BoE, 4A2/63, 13 February 2001, Resources for Monetary Policy.

50 Financial Stability Review, December 2003, p. 75.

51 BoE, 16A32/24, 29 November 1999, Brierley to Governor.

52 BoE, 16A32/42, 10 May 2001, FSC meeting.

53 BoE, 16A32/42, 10 May 2001, FSC meeting.

54 BoE, 16A32/33, 4 September 2000, FSC meeting (Clark).

55 BoE, 16A32/44, 25 July 2001, FSC meeting.

56 BoE, 16A32/42, 10 May 2001, FSC meeting.

57 BoE, 16A32/11, 12 November 1998, Some Issues Arising from the 30 October Declaration of G-7 Finance Ministers and Central Bank Governors.

58 FSR, December 2003, p. 77.

59 BoE, 16A32/39, 5 March 2011, FSA meeting.

60 BoE, 13A224/16, 3 March 1998, A. J. Bailey to Tom Scholar, Lunch for the Chancellor: 25 February 1998.

61 BoE, 16A26/1, 20 January 1997, Schaling comments on Paul Tucker paper: UK Monetary Framework Post Labour.

62 Though even in 1989 DeAnne Julius had written a letter to the *Financial Times* criticizing the use of 'an analytical framework which takes insufficient account of Britain's linkages to the international economy in both goods and factor markets'. (13 January 1989, p. 13).

63 Marc Champion and Michael R. Sesit, 'Labour Can Thank Bank of England for Its Big Lead: Blair Gained by Giving Up Power over Interest Rates', *Wall Street Journal Europe*, 1 June 2001, p. 1.

64 BoE, 8A388/37, POLCO 22 May 1997.

65 Select Committee on Education and Employment Minutes of Evidence, Thursday, 27 May 1999: publications.parliament.uk/pa/cm199899/cmselect/cmeduemp/547/9052704.htm

66 See Tony Yates blog, longandvariable.wordpress.com/2014/03/01/dear-george-can-we-have-fed-style-transcripts-of-uk-monetary-policy-meetings-please/

67 Kevin Warsh, Transparency and the Bank of England's Monetary Policy Committee (Warsh review), December 2014, p. 9.

68 MPC minutes, 8–9 July 1998.

69 BoE, 16A118/18, 9 February 1998, King memo, MPC Day 2, 5 February 1998.

70 Martin Wolf, 'Brown's Blunders', *Financial Times*, 3 July 1998, p. 18.

71 Philip Stephens, 'Dissent into Chaos', *Financial Times*, 17 July 1998, p. 20.

72 MPC minutes, 6–7 August 1997.

73 MPC minutes, 9–10 June 1999.

74 MPC minutes, 9–10 February 2000.

75 Philip Turner, Macroprudential Policies, the Long-Term Interest rate and the Exchange Rate, BIS Working Papers No. 588, October 2016.

76 BoE, 16A118/21, 10 February 2000, King: MPC 10 February 2000.

77 news.bbc.co.uk/2/hi/business/197995.stm

78 news.bbc.co.uk/2/hi/business/285249.stm

79 news.bbc.co.uk/2/hi/business/287879.stm

80 Select Committee on Education and Employment Minutes of Evidence, Thursday, 27 May 1999: publications.parliament.uk/pa/cm199899/cmselect/cmeduemp/547/9052704.htm

81 MPC minutes, 4–5 November 1998.

82 David Smith, 'Bank's Leading Dove Spreads Her Wings', *Sunday Times* (London), 29 April 2001, p. 7.

83 Guy Dresser, 'Nine-Strong Group of Best (or Worst)', *Birmingham Post,* 24 July 1998, p. 13.

84 James O'Brien and Chris Gray, 'Bank Hawk Comes Clean', *Birmingham Post,* 13 November 1998, p. 1.

85 Gillian Tett, *The Silo Effect: The Peril of Expertise and the Promise of Breaking Down Barriers* (New York: Simon and Schuster, 2015).

86 Communication of Edward Nelson, 2017.

87 BoE, 13A231/32, 4 October 1999, Governor's Meeting with the External MPC Members, 28 September.

88 BoE, 12A110/19, 20 October 1999, Court.

89 BoE, 12A110/26, 15 November 2000, Court.

90 BoE, 12A110/19, 20 October 1999, Court.

91 BoE, 12A110/19, 17 November 1999, Court.

92 BoE, 13A224/17, 2 March 1999, Eddie George to Gordon Brown; 13A224/18, 17 January 2000, Eddie George to Gordon Brown.

93 House of Commons Treasury Committee, 'The Monetary Policy Committee of the Bank of England: Confirmation Hearings, as Our Seventh Report of Session 1999–2000' (HC 520), 24 May 2000.

94 BoE, 13A231/32, 4 October 1999, Governor's Meeting with the External MPC Members, 28 September.

95 Ben S. Bernanke, 'Deflation: Making Sure "It" Doesn't Happen Here', speech to National Economists Club, Washington, DC, 21 November 2002.

96 MPC minutes 9–10 January 2002.

97 R. E. Dundas, 'King's Dissent Fuels Bank's Four-Four Split', *The Herald* (London), 12 March 1998, p. 21.

98 House of Commons, research paper 01/59, 'The Monetary Policy Committee: Theory and Performance', 26 June 2001, pp. 12–13.

99 MPC minutes, 7–8 April 1999.

100 MPC minutes, 6–7 December 2000.

101 MPC minutes, 4–5 April 2001.

102 MPC minutes, 18 September 2001.

103 MPC minutes, 6–7 February 2002.

104 MPC minutes, 7–8 February 2001.

105 MPC minutes, 5–6 June 2001.

106 FSR, June 2001, p. 82.

107 Stephen G. Cecchetti, et al., *Asset Prices and Central Bank Policy: Geneva Reports on the World Economy 2* (Geneva: International Center for Monetary and Banking Studies, 2000), xix.

108 Cecchetti, *Asset Prices*, 119.

109 BBC, 'Bank Weighs Two-Speed Economy', 4 July 2001; bbc.co.uk/2/hi/business/1419906.stm

110 BoE, 16A118/23, 3 August 2001, King: MPC meeting, 2 August 2001.

111 King, *End of Alchemy*, 329–330; George speech, bankofengland.co.uk/publications/Documents/speeches/2002/speech156.pdf

112 BoE, 7A320/40, Mervyn King, 'Balancing the Economic See-Saw', speech delivered at the Plymouth Chamber of Commerce and Industry, 14 April 2000.

113 Speech given by Sir Edward George, at the Northwest Development Agency/Bank of England Dinner, Manchester, 15 October 2002, available at: bankofengland.co.uk/publications/Pages/speeches/default.aspx

114 MPC minutes, 6–7 February 2002.

115 MPC minutes, 9–10 October 2002.

116 BoE, 12A110/30, 15 January 2003.

117 BoE, 4A2/58, 18 October 2000, Don Kohn, Report on Monetary Analysis Processes and the Work of Monetary Analysis.

118 IMF, Executive Board discussion, 2 March 2001; the speaker was the Japanese Executive Director Kashiwagi.

119 House of Commons, 'The Monetary Policy Committee of the Bank of England: Ten Years On', 18 September 2007, p. 9.

120 Tucker, *Unelected Power*, 421.

121 House of Commons, 'Ten Years On', pp. 12–23, and Questions 8–9.

122 Notably, Stephen Cecchetti, Hans Genberg, John Lipsky and Sushil Wadhwani, *Asset Prices and Central Bank Policy* (Geneva: International Center for Monetary and Banking Studies, 2000).

123 For a magisterial overview, see Michael Bordo's Presidential Address at the Economic History Association, San Jose California, September 2017.

124 4A2/111, 17 September 2003, Court Paper, Governor (King): The Bank of England: The Next Five Years.

125 4A2/63, November 2000, Public Attitudes to Inflation.

126 House of Commons, 'Ten Years On', Question 7.

127 Claudio Borio, 'Monetary and Financial Stability: Here to Stay?' *Journal of Banking & Finance* vol. 30, no. 12 (December 2006): 3407–3414.

128 BIS, 75th Annual Report, 2005, p. 9.

129 Chris Giles, 'Bank of England Would Be Sorely Tested by Another Financial Crisis', *Financial Times,* 3 May 2017: ft.com/content/33bdb17a-2ff7-11e7-9555-23ef563ecf9a
See also Ed Balls and Anna Stansbury, 'Twenty Years On: Is There Still a Case for Bank of England Independence?' VoxEU, 1 May 2017: voxeu.org/article/twenty-years-there-still-case-bank-england-independence; Ed Balls, James Howat and Anna Stansbury, 'Central Bank Independence Revisited: After the Financial Crisis, What Should a Model Central Bank Look Like?' Harvard Kennedy School Mossavar-Rahmani Center for Business and Government Associate Working Paper No. 67, 2016.

130 House of Lords, Select Committee on Economic Affairs, UK Stationery Office, Banking Supervision and Regulation: 2nd Report of Session 2008–2009, vol. 2 (evidence of 20 January 2009): 9.

Epilogue

1 BoE, 18A55/1, 9 December 1993, Governor's Bilateral, 8 December 1993.
2 Øyvind Eitrheim, et al., *A Monetary History of Norway, 1816–2016, Studies in Macroeconomic History* (Cambridge: Cambridge University Press, 2017), 547–550.
3 IMF Country Report No. 05/80, UK: 2004 Article IV Consultation – Staff Report, March 2005.
4 Philip Webster, et al., 'Bank Chief's Broadside Splinters Brown Plan for Stimulus', *The Times* (London), 25 March 2009.
5 Brown, *My Life,* 353 and 385.
6 Henry Mance, 'Labour Considers Moving Bank of England to Birmingham', *Financial Times,* 10 December 2017.
7 There is a compilation of these and other remarks in: Sean Farrell, 'How Criticising Mark Carney Became the New Tory Sport', *The Guardian,* 21 October 2016: the guardian.com/business/2016/oct/21/criticising-mark-carney-tory-hobby-bank-england-governor
8 Theresa May's conference speech in full, *Daily Telegraph,* 5 October 2016: telegraph .co.uk/news/2016/10/05/theresa-mays-conference-speech-in-full/
9 Christopher Adolph, *Bankers, Bureaucrats, and Central Bank Politics: The Myth of Neutrality* (Cambridge: Cambridge University Press, 2013), 256–263.
10 Tucker, *Unelected Power,* 458.
11 theguardian.com/business/live/2017/sep/28/bank-of-england-independence-theresa-may-mark-carney-ed-balls-business-live
12 See for instance Lucrezia Reichlin, *La Banque centrale européenne et la crise de l'euro* (Paris: Fayard, 2019), 16.
13 Speech given by Mervyn King, Governor of the Bank of England, East Midlands Development Agency/Bank of England Dinner, Leicester, 14 October 2003.
14 Mervyn King, *The End of Alchemy: Money, Banking, and the Future of the Global Economy* (New York: W. W. Norton, 2016), 322.
15 Paul Tucker, 'Macro, Asset Price, and Financial System Uncertainties', Roy Bridge Lecture delivered by Mr Tucker, Executive Director Markets and Member of the Monetary Policy Committee of the Bank of England, at the BoE, London, 11 December 2006: bis.org/review/r070112f.pdf
16 Tett, *The Silo Effect,* 121–123.
17 Paul Volcker speech to Economic Club of New York, 8 April 2008: blogs .denverpost.com/lewis/files/2008/04/volckernyeconclubspeech04-08-2008.pdf
18 Frederic S. Mishkin and Eugene N. White, 'Unprecedented Actions: The Federal Reserve's Response to the Global Financial Crisis in Historical Perspective', Federal Reserve Bank of Dallas Globalization and Monetary Policy Institute Working Paper No. 209, 2014: dallasfed.org/assets/documents/institute/wpa pers/2014/0209.pdf
19 theguardian.com/business/live/2017/sep/28/bank-of-england-independence-theresa-may-mark-carney-ed-balls-business-live

20 Alan Blinder, 'Global Policy Perspectives: Central Bank Independence and Credibility during and after a Crisis', Proceedings – Economic Policy Symposium – Jackson Hole, Federal Reserve Bank of Kansas City, 2012, 485.

21 Kamal Ahmed, 'Adair Turner: Bankers "No Longer in Denial"', *Daily Telegraph,* 16 March 2013: telegraph.co.uk/finance/newsbysector/banksandfinance/9934819/Adair-Turner-Bankers-no-longer-in-denial.html

22 BoE, 18 March 2014, Strategic Plan: Background information. See https://webarchive.nationalarchives.gov.uk/20140804111146/http://www.bankofengland.co.uk/about/Pages/strategicplan/default.aspx

23 Caroline Binham, George Parker and Jim Brunsden, 'Bank of England, Treasury and FCA Act in Unison to Charm EU Banks', *Financial Times,* 21 December 2017.

Bibliography

Abramson, Daniel M. *Building the Bank of England: Money, Architecture, Society 1694–1942*. New Haven, CT: Yale University Press, 2005.

Adolph, Christopher. *Bankers, Bureaucrats, and Central Bank Politics: The Myth of Neutrality*. New York: Cambridge University Press, 2013.

Allen, Margaret. *The Times Guide to International Finance: How the World Money System Works*. London: Times Books, 1991.

Allen, William A. *Monetary Policy and Financial Repression in Britain, 1951–59*. Basingstoke: Palgrave Macmillan, 2014.

Allen, William A. and Geoffrey Wood. 'Defining and Achieving Financial Stability', *Journal of Financial Stability* vol. 2, no. 2 (2006): 152–172.

Augar, Philip. *The Death of Gentlemanly Capitalism: The Rise and Fall of London's Investment Banks*. New York: Penguin, 2000.

Bagehot, Walter. Edited by R. H. S. Crossman. *The English Constitution*. London: Collins/Fontana, 1963 [1867].

Bagehot, Walter. *Lombard Street: A Description of the Money Market*. New York: John Wiley, 1999 [1873].

Bank of England. *The Development and Operation of Monetary Policy 1960–1983: A Selection of Material from the Quarterly Bulletin of the Bank of England*. Oxford: Oxford University Press, 1984.

Barro, Robert J. and David B. Gordon. 'Rules, Discretion and Reputation in a Model of Monetary Policy', *Journal of Monetary Economics* vol. 12, no. 1 (July 1983): 102–121.

Batini, Nicoletta and Edward Nelson. 'The Lag from Monetary Policy Actions to Inflation: Friedman Revisited', *International Finance* vol. 4, no. 3 (Winter 2001): 381–400.

Batini, Nicoletta and Edward Nelson. 'The UK's Rocky Road to Stability' ed. Barbara T. Credan, *Trends in Inflation Research* (2006): 1–86.

Bean, Charles R. and James Symons. 'Ten Years of Mrs. T.', NBER *Macroeconomics Annual* vol. 4, no. 1 (1989): 13–72.

Bean, Charles R. and Nigel Jenkinson. 'The Formulation of Monetary Policy at the Bank of England', *Bank of England Quarterly Bulletin* vol. 41 (2001): 434–441.

Bernanke, Ben S. *Inflation Targeting: Lessons from the International Experience*. Princeton, NJ: Princeton University Press, 1999.

Black, Fischer and Myron Scholes. 'The Pricing of Options and Corporate Liabilities', *Journal of Political Economy* vol. 81, no. 3 (1973): 637–654.

Blinder, Alan S. 'Global Policy Perspectives: Central Bank Independence and Credibility during and after a Crisis', Proceedings – Economic Policy Symposium – Jackson Hole, Federal Reserve Bank of Kansas City, 2012, 483–491.

Bloom, Nicholas, M., Ayhan Kose and Marco E. Terrones. 'Held Back by Uncertainty', *Finance and Development* vol. 50, no. 1 (2013): 38–41.

Bordo, Michael D., Ehsan U. Choudhri and Anna J. Schwartz. 'Money Stock Targeting, Base Drift and Price-Level Predictability: Lessons from the U.K. Experience', *Journal of Monetary Economics* vol. 25, no. 21 (March 1990): 253–272.

Bordo, Michael D. and William Roberds, eds. *The Origins, History, and Future of the Federal Reserve: A Return to Jekyll Island.* Cambridge: Cambridge University Press, 2013.

Borio, Claudio. 'Monetary and Financial Stability: Here to Stay?' *Journal of Banking & Finance* vol. 30, no. 12 (December 2006): 3407–3414.

Boyle, Andrew. *Montagu Norman: A Biography.* London: Cassell, 1967.

Budd, Alan. 'Economic Viewpoint: Monetary Targets and a Financial Plan', *London Business School Economic Outlook* vol. 4, no. 2 (November 1979): 11–14.

Cain, Peter J. and Anthony G. Hopkins. 'Gentlemanly Capitalism and British Expansion Overseas I. The Old Colonial System, 1688–1850', *Economic History Review* vol. 39, no. 4 (1986): 501–525.

Cairncross, Alec and Kathleen Burk. *'Goodbye, Great Britain': The 1976 IMF Crisis.* New Haven, CT: Yale University Press, 1992.

Capie, Forrest M. *The Bank of England: 1950s to 1979.* New York: Cambridge University Press, 2010.

Capie, Forrest M. 'Can There Be an International Lender-of-Last-Resort?' *International Finance* vol. 1, no. 2 (1998): 311–325.

Capie, Forrest M., Stanley Fischer, Charles Goodhart, and Norbert Schnadt. *The Future of Central Banking – The Tercentenary Symposium of the Bank of England.* Cambridge: Cambridge University Press, 1994.

Cecchetti, Stephen, Hans Genberg, and John Lipsky. *Asset Prices and Central Bank Policy.* Geneva: International Center for Monetary and Banking Studies, 2000.

Clarke, Peter. *Hope and Glory: Britain 1900–1990* (Penguin History of Britain). London: Allen Lane, 1996.

Cockerell, Michael. *Live from Number 10: The Inside Story of Prime Ministers and Television.* London: Faber, 1988.

Coleby, A. L. 'The Bank's Operational Procedures for Meeting Monetary Objectives', *Bank of England Quarterly Bulletin* vol. 23, no. 2 (1 June 1983): 209–215.

Coleby, A. L. 'Bills of Exchange: Current Issues in a Historical Perspective', *Bank of England Quarterly Bulletin* vol. 22, no. 3 (November 1982): 514–518.

Conaghan, Dan. *The Bank: Inside the Bank of England.* London: Biteback Publishing, 2012.

Congdon, Tim. *Central Banking in a Free Society.* London: Institute of Economic Affairs, 2009.

Congdon, Tim. *Reflections on Monetarism: Britain's Vain Search for a Successful Economic Strategy.* Cheltenham: Edward Elgar, 1992.

Conti-Brown, Peter. *The Power and Independence of the Federal Reserve*. Princeton, NJ: Princeton University Press, 2016.

Copey, Richard and Donald Clarke. *3i: Fifty Years Investing in Industry*. Oxford: Oxford University Press, 1995.

Crafts, Nicholas. 'Deindustrialisation and Economic Growth', *Economic Journal* vol. 106, no. 1 (January 1996): 172–183.

Curtis, Sarah, ed. *The Journals of Woodrow Wyatt, Volume Two*. London: Pan Books, 1999.

Darling, Alastair. *Back from the Brink*. London: Atlantic Books, 2011.

Dell, Edmund. *A Hard Pounding: Politics and Economic Crisis 1974–76*. New York: Oxford University Press, 1991.

Dincer, N. and Barry Eichengreen. 'Central Bank Transparency and Independence: Updates', *New Measures' International Journal of Central Banking* vol. 38, no. 3 (2014): 189–253.

Dow, Christopher. Edited by Graham Hacche and Christopher Taylor. *Inside the Bank of England: Memoirs of Christopher Dow, Chief Economist 1973–84*. Basingstoke: Palgrave Macmillan, 2013.

Dow, Christopher. *Major Recessions: Britain and the World, 1920–1995*. Oxford: Oxford University Press, 1998.

Dow, Christopher. *The Management of the British Economy*. Cambridge: Cambridge University Press, 1964.

Dow, Christopher and I. D. Saville. *A Critique of Monetary Policy: Theory and British Experience*. Oxford: Oxford University Press, 1990.

Dresser, Guy. 'Nine-Strong Group of Best (Or Worst)', *Birmingham Post*, 24 July 1998.

Drummond, Helga. *The Dynamics of Organizational Collapse: The Case of Barings Bank*. Abingdon: Routledge, 2008.

Duckenfield, Mark. *Business and the Euro: Business Groups and the Politics of EMU in Britain and Germany*. Basingstoke: Palgrave Macmillan, 2006.

Eijffinger, Sylvester C. W. and Eric Schaling. 'Central Bank Independence in Twelve Industrial Countries', *Banca Nazionale del Lavoro Quarterly Review* vol. 184 (March 1993): 49–89.

Eijffinger, Sylvester C. W. and Jakob de Haan. 'The Political Economy of Central-Bank Independence', *Princeton Studies in International Economics* vol. 19. Princeton, NJ: International Economics Section, Department of Economics Princeton University, 1996.

Einzig, Paul. *Montagu Norman: A Study in Financial Statesmanship*. Abingdon: Routledge, 1932.

Eitrheim, Øyvind, et al. *A Monetary History of Norway, 1816–2016, Studies in Macroeconomic History*. Cambridge: Cambridge University Press, 2017.

Fay, Stephen. *The Collapse of Barings*. London: Richard Cohen, 1996.

Fay, Stephen. *Portrait of an Old Lady: Turmoil at the Bank of England*. Harmondsworth: Penguin, 1988.

Feiertag, Olivier and Michel Margairaz, eds. *Les banques centrales à l'échelle du monde du 20e au 21 siècle/Central Banks at World's Scale from the 20th to the 21st century*. Paris: Presses de Sciences Po, 2012.

Fitzgerald, Martin. 'Better Data Brings Reward at the Bank of England', *MIT Sloan Management Record*, 26 May 2016.

Fforde, John. *The Bank of England and Public Policy, 1941–1958.* Cambridge: Cambridge University Press, 1992.

Fforde, John. 'Setting Monetary Objectives,' *Bank of England Quarterly Bulletin* vol. 23, no. 2 (June 1983): 200–208.

Fischerand, Stanley and Norbert Schnadt. *The Future of Central Banking – The Tercentenary Symposium of the Bank of England.* Cambridge: Cambridge University Press, 1994.

Friedman, Alan. 'Keeping a Low Profile – Profile – Robin Leigh-Pemberton, Governor, Bank of England', *Financial Times Survey: UK Banking*, 26 September 1983.

Friedman, Milton and Rose D. Friedman. *Two Lucky People: Memoirs.* Chicago: University of Chicago Press, 1998.

Frost, Raymond. 'The Macmillan Gap 1931–1953', *Oxford Economic Papers* vol. 6, no. 2 (1954): 181–201.

Gabor, Daniela. 'The (Impossible) Repo Trinity: The Political Economy of Repo Markets', *Review of International Political Economy* vol. 23, no. 6 (2016): 967–1000.

Garbade, Kenneth. 'The Evolution of Repo Contracting Conventions in the 1980s', *Economic Policy Review* vol. 12, no. 1 (2006): 27–42.

Geddes, Philip. *Inside the Bank of England.* London: Boxtree, 1987.

Goodhart, Charles A. E. *The Basel Committee on Banking Supervision: A History of the Early Years, 1974–1997.* Cambridge: Cambridge University Press, 2011.

Goodhart, Charles A. E. 'The Conduct of Monetary Policy', *Economic Journal* vol. 99, no. 396 (1989): 293–346.

Goodhart, Charles A. E. *Monetary Theory and Practice: The UK Experience.* London: Macmillan, 1984.

Goodhart, Charles A. E., et al. 'Monetary Base Control', *Bank of England Quarterly Bulletin* vol. 19, no. 2 (June 1979): 202–218.

Gourvish, Terry and Mike Anson. *The Official History of the Channel Tunnel.* London: Routledge, 2006.

Gowland, David. *Monetary Policy and Credit Control: The UK Experience.* London: Croome Helm, 1978.

Greenwood, John. *Hong Kong's Link to the US Dollar: Origins and Evolution.* Hong Kong: Hong Kong University Press, 2008.

Gup, Benton E. *Bank Failures in the Major Trading Countries of the World: Causes and Remedies.* Westport, CT: Greenwood Publishing Group, 1998.

Hacche, Graham. 'Review of Forrest Capie's History of the Bank of England', *Economica* vol. 80 (2013): 372–378.

Haddow, Abigail, et al. 'Macroeconomic Uncertainty: What Is It, How Can We Measure It and Why Does It Matter?' *Bank of England Quarterly Bulletin* Q2 (2013): 100–109.

Haldane, Andrew G. 'Halfway Up the Stairs', *Central Banking Journal* (5 August 2014): 27–32.

Haldane, Andrew, et al., 'Financial Stability and Macroeconomic Models', *Bank of England Financial Stability Review* vol. 16 (2004): 80–88.

Hall, Robert E., ed. *The Ends of Four Big Inflations.* Cambridge, MA: NBER Books, 1982.

Hargrave, John. *Professor Skinner Alias Montagu Norman.* London: Wells Gardner, Darton, 1939.

Harrod, Roy. 'Imperfect Competition, Aggregate Demand and Inflation', *Economic Journal* vol. 82, no. 325 (1972): 392–401.

Healey, Denis. *The Time of My Life*. New York: W. W. Norton, 1990.

Hirsch, Fred. *The Pound Sterling: A Polemic*. London: Victor Gollancz, 1965.

Hirsch, Fred and John H. Goldthorpe, eds. *The Political Economy of Inflation*. Cambridge, MA: Harvard University Press, 1978.

Holden, K., et al. *Economics of Wage Controls*. Basingstoke: Palgrave Macmillan, 1987.

Holmes, Douglas. *Economy of Words: Communicative Imperatives in Central Banks*. Chicago: University of Chicago Press, 2014.

Howe, Geoffrey. 'The 364 Economists: Ten Years On', *Fiscal Studies* vol. 12, no. 4 (November 1991): 92–107.

Hotson, Anthony C. *Respectable Banking: The Search for Stability in London's Money and Credit Markets Since 1695*. Cambridge: Cambridge University Press, 2017.

Hotson, Anthony C. 'The Role of the Bank of England in the Money Market', *Bank of England Quarterly Bulletin* vol. 22, no. 1 (March 1982): 86–94.

Jackson, Patricia. 'Deposit Protection and Bank Failures in the United Kingdom', *Financial Stability Review* no. 1 (Autumn 1996): 38–43.

James, Harold. *International Monetary Cooperation since Bretton Woods*. Oxford: Oxford University Press, 1996.

Jenkins, Peter. *Mrs. Thatcher's Revolution: The Ending of the Socialist Era*. Cambridge, MA: Harvard University Press, 1988.

Jones, David M. *Understanding Central Banking: The New Era of Activism*. London: Routledge, 2014.

Keegan, William. *Mr. Lawson's Gamble*. London: Hodder and Stoughton, 1989.

Keegan, William. *Mrs. Thatcher's Economic Experiment*. New York: Penguin, 1985.

Keegan, William. *The Prudence of Gordon Brown*. Chichester: John Wiley, 2003.

Keegan, William, David Marsh, and Richard Roberts. *Six Days in September: Black Wednesday, Brexit and the Making of Europe*. London: OMFIF Press, 2017.

Keegan, William and Rupert Pennant-Rea. *Who Runs the Economy? Control and Influence in British Economic Policy*. London: Maurice Temple Smith, 1979.

Kent, Pen. 'The London Approach', *Bank of England Quarterly Bulletin* Q1 (February 1993): 110–115.

Kilpatrick, Andrew. 'The Performance of Broad Money', *Treasury Bulletin* vol. 2, no. 3 (December 1991).

King, Mervyn. 'Changes in UK Monetary Policy: Rules and Discretion in Practice', *Journal of Monetary Economics* vol. 39 (1997): 81–97.

King, Mervyn. 'Challenges for Monetary Policy: new and Old,' in Federal Reserve Bank of Kansas City, New Challenges for Monetary Policy: A symposium sponsored by the Federal Reserve Bank of Kansas City, Jackson Hole, Wyoming, 26–28 August 1999, 11–57.

King, Mervyn. *The End of Alchemy: Money, Banking, and the Future of the Global Economy*. New York: W. W. Norton, 2016.

King, Mervyn. 'How Should Central Banks Reduce Inflation? – Conceptual Issues', *Bank of England Quarterly Bulletin* Q4 (1996): 434–448.

King, Mervyn. 'Monetary Policy Instruments: The UK Experience', *Bank of England Quarterly Bulletin* Q3 (August 1994): 268–276.

King, Mervyn. 'Monetary Policy in the UK', *Fiscal Studies* vol. 15, no. 3 (1994): 109–128.

King, Mervyn. 'Monetary Policy: Rhyme or Reason?' *Bank of England Quarterly Bulletin* vol. 37, no. 1 (February 1997): 88–97.

Krugman, Paul R. *The Age of Diminished Expectations: U.S. Economic Policy in the 1990s*. Cambridge, MA: MIT Press, 1994.

Kwarteng, Kwasi. *Thatcher's Trial: Six Months That Defined a Leader*. London: Bloomsbury, 2015.

Kydland, Fynn and Edward Prescott. 'Rules Rather Than Discretion: The Inconsistency of Optimal Plans', *Journal of Political Economy* vol. 85 (1977): 473–492.

Kynaston, David. *City of London: The History*. London: Chatto & Windus, 2011.

Laidler, David. 'Monetarism: An Interpretation and an Assessment', *Economic Journal* vol. 91, no. 361 (March 1981): 1–28.

Laidler, David and Michael Parkin. 'The Demand for Money in the United Kingdom 1956–1967: Preliminary Estimates', *The Manchester School* vol. 38 (3 September 1970): 187–208.

Lamont, Norman. 'Chancellor's Mansion House Speech Oct. 29, 1992', *Treasury Bulletin* vol. 3, no. 3 (December 1992): 46–50.

Lastra, Rosa. *A History of the Bank's Legal Directorate*, 2019.

Laugharne, Peter J. 'The Treasury and Civil Service Select Committee during the Thatcher Administration', *Parliamentary History* vol. 26 (2007): 225–244.

Lawson, Nigel. *The View from No. 11: Memoirs of a Tory Radical*. New York: Bantam Press, 1992.

Lee, Simon, edited by Matt Beech and Simon Lee. *Ten Years of New Labour*. Basingstoke: Palgrave Macmillan, 2008.

Leeson, Nick. *Rogue Trader*. London: Sphere, 1996.

Leigh-Pemberton, Robin. *The Future of Monetary Agreements in Europe*. London: Institute of Economic Affairs, 1989.

Leigh-Pemberton, Robin. *The London Discount Market: A Guide to Its Role in the Economy and Its Contribution to Industry and Finance*, 3rd edition. London: Gerrard and National, 1981.

Leigh-Pemberton, Robin. 'Monetary Policy in the Second Half of the 1980s', *Bank of England Quarterly Bulletin* vol. 30, no. 2 (May 1990): 215–220.

Major, John. *John Major: The Autobiography*. New York: HarperCollins, 1999.

Mallaby, Sebastian. *The Man Who Knew: The Life and Times of Alan Greenspan*. London: Bloomsbury, 2016.

Mallaby, Sebastian. *More Money than God: Hedge Funds and the Making of a New Elite*. New York: Penguin, 2010.

Marcial, Gene G. *The Secrets of the Street: The Dark Side of Making Money*. New York: McGraw-Hill, 1995.

McCallum, Bennett T. and Edward Nelson. 'Targeting Versus Instrument Rules for Monetary Policy', *FRB St. Louis Review* vol. 87 (September/October 2005): 597–612.

Meek, P., ed. *Central Bank Views on Monetary Targeting*. New York: Federal Reserve Bank of New York, 1983.

Michie, Ranald C. *British Banking: Continuity and Change from 1694 to the Present*. Oxford: Oxford University Press, 2016.

Michie, Ranald. *The London Stock Exchange: A History*. Cambridge: Oxford University Press, 1999.

Middleton, Roger. *The Cambridge Economic History of Modern Britain, Volume 1: 1700–1870*, 2nd edition. Cambridge: Cambridge University Press, 2014.

Moore, Charles. *Margaret Thatcher: From Grantham to the Falklands: The Authorized Biography*. New York: Knopf, 2015.

Moore, Charles. *Margaret Thatcher: The Authorized Biography, Volume 2: Everything She Wants*. New York: Penguin, 2015.

Moore, Charles. *Margaret Thatcher: The Authorized Biography, Volume 3: Herself Alone*. London: Allen Lane, 2019.

Needham, Duncan and Anthony Hotson, eds. *Expansionary Fiscal Contraction: The Thatcher Government's 1981 Budget in Perspective*. Cambridge: Cambridge University Press, 2014.

Nelson, Edward. 'An Overhaul of Doctrine: The Underpinning of UK Inflation Targeting', *Economic Journal* vol. 119, no. 538 (June 2009): 333–368.

Orphanides, Athanasios, et al. 'Errors in the Measurement of the Output Gap and the Design of Monetary Policy', *Journal of Economics and Business* vol. 52, no. 1 (2000): 117–141.

Patterson, R. H. 'On Our Home Monetary Drains, and the Crisis of 1866', *Journal of the Statistical Society of London* vol. 33, no. 2 (June 1870): 216–242.

Pennant-Rea, Rupert. *Gold Foil*. London: Bodley Head, 1978.

Pepper, Gordon. *Inside Thatcher's Monetarist Revolution*. London: Institute of Economic Affairs, 1998.

Pepper, Gordon T. and Michael Oliver. *Monetarism under Thatcher: Lessons for the Future*. Cheltenham: Edward Elgar, 2001.

Pliatzky, Leo. *Getting and Spending: Public Expenditure, Employment and Inflation*. Oxford: Basil Blackwell, 1982.

Poole, William and Robert H. Rasche. 'The Impact of Changes in FOMC Disclosure Practices on the Transparency of Monetary Policy: Are Markets and the FOMC Better "Synched"?' *Federal Reserve Bank of St. Louis Review* vol. 85, no. 1 (2003): 1–10.

Rawnsley, Andrew. *Servants of the People: The Inside Story of New Labour*. London: Penguin, 2001.

Reichlin, Lucrezia. *La Banque centrale européenne et la crise de l'euro*. Paris: Fayard, 2019.

Roberts, Richard. *When Britain Went Bust: The 1976 IMF Crisis*. London: OMFIF Press, 2017.

Roberts, Richard and David Kynaston. *The Lion Wakes: A Modern History of HSBC*. London: Profile Books, 2015.

Roll, Eric. *Independent and Accountable: A New Mandate for the Bank of England*. Washington, DC: CEPR, 1993.

Sampson, Anthony. *The Moneylenders: Bankers in a Dangerous World*. London: Coronet, 1982.

Sargent, Thomas J. *Rational Expectations and Inflation*. New York: Harper and Row, 1986.

Sayers, R. S. *The Bank of England 1891–1944: Volume I*. Cambridge: Cambridge University Press, 1976.

Bank of England, 'The Secondary Banking Crisis and the Bank of England's Support Operations', *Bank of England Quarterly Bulletin* Q2 (April 1978): 230–239.

Schwartz, Anna J. 'Why Financial Stability Depends on Price Stability', *Economic Affairs* vol. 4, no. 15 (Autumn 1995): 21–25.

Selgin, George A. 'The Futility of Central Banking', *Cato Journal* vol. 30, no. 3 (Fall 2010): 465–473.

Sentance, Andrew. *Britain's Economic Performance*. London: Routledge, 1988.

Schenk, Catherine R., ed. *Hong Kong SAR's Monetary and Exchange Rate Challenges: Historical Perspectives*. Basingstoke: Palgrave Macmillan, 2009.

Siklos, Pierre L. *Central Banks into the Breach*. Oxford: Oxford University Press, 2017.

Sims, Christopher. 'Macroeconomics and Reality', *Econometrica* vol. 48, no. 1, (1980): 1–48.

Sissoko, Carolyn. 'How to Stabilize the Banking System: Lessons from the Pre-1914 Money Market', *Financial History Review* vol. 23, no. 1 (April 2016): 1–20.

Smith, Adam. Edited by Edwin Cannan. *An Inquiry into the Nature and Causes of the Wealth of Nations*. Chicago: University of Chicago Press, 1967 [1776].

Smith, Matthew. *Policy-making in the Treasury: Explaining Britain's Chosen Path on European Economic and Monetary Union*. Basingstoke: Palgrave Macmillan, 2014.

Sowerbutts, Rhiannon, Marco Schneebalg, and Florence Hubert. 'The Demise of Overend Gurney', *Bank of England Quarterly Bulletin* vol. 56, no. 2 (2016): 94–106.

Summers, Larry. 'How Should Long-Term Monetary Policy be Determined?' *Journal of Money Credit and Banking* vol. 123 (1991): 625–631.

Svensson, Lars E. O. 'Inflation Forecast Targeting: Implementing and Monitoring Inflation Targets', *European Economic Review* vol. 41 (1997): 1111–1146.

Taylor, A. J. P. *English History: 1914–1945*. Oxford: Oxford University Press, 1965.

Tett, Gillian. *The Silo Effect: The Peril of Expertise and the Promise of Breaking Down Barriers*. New York: Simon & Schuster, 2015.

Thatcher, Margaret. *The Downing Street Years*. New York: HarperCollins, 1993.

Tietmeyer, Hans. *Herausforderung Euro: Wie es zum Euro kam und was es für Deutschlands Zukunft bedeutet*. Munich: Hanser, 2005.

Treasury and Civil Service Committee (House of Commons). *The Government's Economic Policy: Autumn Statement, First Report, Together with the Proceedings of the Committee, Minutes of Evidence and Appendices*. London: HMSO, 1987.

Tucker, Paul. 'Managing the Central Bank's Balance Sheet: Where Monetary Policy Meets Financial Stability', *Bank of England Quarterly Bulletin* Q3 (Autumn 2004): 359–382.

Tucker, Paul. *Unelected Power: The Quest for Legitimacy in Central Banking and the Regulatory State*. Princeton, NJ: Princeton University Press, 2018.

Turner, Philip. Macroprudential Policies, the Long-Term Interest Rate and the Exchange Rate, BIS Working Papers No. 588, October 2016

van den Berg, Carel C. A. *Making of Statute of European System of Central Banks*. West Lafayette, IN: Purdue University Press, 2005.

Wall, Stephen. *A Stranger in Europe: Britain and the EU from Thatcher to Blair*. Oxford: Oxford University Press, 2008.

Warsh, Kevin. *Transparency and the Bank of England Monetary Policy Committee*. Stanford: Hoover Institution, 2014.

Wass, Douglas. *Decline to Fall: The Making of British Macro-Economic Policy and the 1976 IMF Crisis*. Oxford: Oxford University Press, 2008.

Wood, Geoffrey. 'Review of *Unelected Power: The Quest for Legitimacy in Central Banking and the Regulatory State* by Paul Tucker', *Economic Affairs* vol. 38, no. 3 (2018): 456–457.

Index

Lightning Source UK Ltd.
Milton Keynes UK
UKHW020657091220
374671UK00019B/567